THE ANNELE TRILOGY

The *Annele* Trilogy

A BOOK FOR YOUNG AND OLD

ANNA BRIGADERE

Translated by ILZE KĻAVIŅA MUELLER

YTTERLI PRESS

A translation of *Dievs, daba, darbs* (© 1926 Anna Brigadere), *Skarbos vējos*
(© 1930 Anna Brigadere), *Akmens sprostā* (© 1933 Anna Brigadere)
from the Latvian editions published by Apgāds "Grāmatu draugs" (1946), Tilta
Apgāds (1960), and Latvijas valsts izdevniecība (Riga, 1957).
Translation © 2014, by Ilze Kļaviņa Mueller.

Drawings in text published with permission of Džemma Skulme.
Cover drawing © 2014, by Linda Treija. For further information about
this artist: www.americanlatvianartists.org

ISBN 978-0-9893270-2-2
Published by Ytterli Press
2211 Buford Avenue, Saint Paul, Minnesota 55108

To contact the translator or order a copy: anneletrilogy1@gmail.com
Book is also available on amazon.com

Library of Congress Catalog Card Number applied for.
Printed in the United States of America.
All rights reserved.

Book design by Sylvia Ruud

CONTENTS

The Annele Trilogy: Introduction

Latvia, now part of the European Union, is a small country in northeastern Europe whose independence was renewed after the fall of the Soviet Union. The Latvia of today is urbanized, multiethnic, concentrated in the capital city of Rīga. But Latvia has been home to the Latvian people for at least 2000 years, and until World War I it was a rural country, in which Latvians were the subjects of German barons, Swedish or Polish kings, and Russian czars.

For Latvians, despite urbanization, home means the countryside, the farm, and farm life. Home is neither grand nor necessarily prosperous. Home is the fields, the woods, a little house, the family, the small scope of the immediate neighborhood. In *The Annele Trilogy*, a fictionalized memoir describing her childhood and adolescence, beloved Latvian author Anna Brigadere (1861–1933) shared with her readers rural and urban scenes with which they were familiar, and introduced these memories to the children of the 1930s as well. Today, four generations later, Latvian schoolchildren still read excerpts of the *Trilogy* as short stories, while adults are more likely to read the entire series of three novels.

Brigadere was born in the southern Latvian province of Zemgale in the 1860s. During Brigadere's childhood and adolescence, the Latvian economy was volatile, and small farmers' lives uncertain. The author's father was a laborer, not a landowner, and the family moved from farm to farm almost every year. Like most Latvian country girls of her time, she had only a few years of formal schooling at the local schools in her district. After her father's death, continuing school was impossible; she had to work for a living. From Jelgava, where the adolescent girl helped her dressmaker sister in order to support the family, Brigadere moved to the town of Ventspils, and later went to live with her brother, Jānis, in the capital city of Rīga.

It was an exciting period in Latvian history. Only recently freed from serfdom, Latvians now had access to higher education and some professions hitherto denied to them; they were buying land, making their own way. The power of the German gentry was diminishing, and a sense of self-suffiency and self-worth was growing among Latvian farmers. The Latvian National Awakening, a cultural and political movement that had its beginnings in this era, valued the Latvian heritage, language, and folklore as never before. Anna Brigadere's brother Jānis and his wife were actors in Rīga, and while living with them, she met many rising artists and writers. Later, Brigadere was to witness the first calls for an independent Latvia, and saw the birth of the Latvian state in 1918.

Until she was well established as a writer, she worked as a governess, moving as far away as Moscow and Yaroslavl in Russia; later she earned her living as a private tutor for wealthy merchant families, as a teacher, and as an editor.

Although Brigadere began writing in the 1890s, she did not become famous until 1903, when her fairytale play *Sprīdītis* (*Tom Thumb*) was first performed. The early decades of the 20th century brought political uprisings and war. The author was forced to spend several years during World War I as a refugee in Russia. She was a supporter of the Latvian independence movement, though she was not exceedingly political. Upon the proclamation of Latvia's independence in 1918, back in her native land, she produced poems that expressed her pride in the new nation.

In 1922, the Latvian state presented the author with a country home in the district of her birth. The home was later renamed after her iconic character Sprīdītis, and today is a museum dedicated to the famous writer and her works.

Her life work encompasses poetry, short stories and novels, plays, and memoir. The semiautobiographical *Annele Trilogy* was published near the end of her life. The three parts of the *Trilogy* appeared in 1926, 1930, and 1933 respectively, and recreate the period from 1865 to 1880. Brigadere speaks of a time well known to her readers, a quickly vanishing era. Her most enthusiastic fans would have been the children who grew up watching her plays, and who grew to adulthood reading her poems.

Paula Jēger-Freimane, in her essay on Brigadere in *History of Latvian Literature* (1936), refers to the *Trilogy* as Brigadere's "greatest achievement in literary prose." She speculates that though her readers clamored for a fourth installment of the stories, Brigadere would not have acquiesced. The writer felt most at home in her childhood, and continuing the story of Annele as an adult would have been too difficult. Even the third book, *In a Stone Cage*, was written more slowly and was released just months before Brigadere's death. Thus Annele remains forever young, forever radiant and optimistic, and, though touched by hardship, never succumbs to it.

The first part of the *Trilogy – God, Nature, Work –* begins when the protagonist, Annele, is four years old. The setting is Tērvete, a picturesque region in the middle of Latvia, in the province of Zemgale. The second part, *Harsh Winds*, includes the moving story of Annele's father's death in 1874, when the protagonist is 13 and the family comes upon even harder times. In the last part, *In a Stone Cage*, Annele and her mother join Annele's sister in Jelgava, the provincial capital of Kurzeme. The story ends as Annele, now 16, after years of working as a seamstress for her sister, envisions a chance to further her education at last.

Brigadere came from a poor, landless family, but portrays her family life as one filled with the glow of love, hope, and cooperation. Her character Annele is hopeful despite the hardship of her life. This hopefulness made the *Trilogy* widely popular in its time, and it has been in print since its first publication.

The fictional Annele is the youngest of three siblings. Her brother is already living away from home, and her older sister Līziņa is sent to the city to learn a trade early in the first book. Annele is a favorite of her father, whom she adores. She and her mother have a more antagonistic relationship: her mother finds it difficult to understand her highly imaginative, precocious, sensitive little girl. Of course, Annele is no angel, and Brigadere is a didactic writer; after each conflict, Annele is sure to learn her lesson – or not – by the end of the chapter. A truthful child with a pronounced sense of justice, she is sometimes teased by older kids, and is reprimanded and punished by grown-ups. What makes her unique is her worldview, one of wonder and gratitude, easily overwhelmed by new sights and sounds. Annele is deeply part of her world; it encompasses her, surrounds her, lights her soul.

Through the eyes of a keenly observant child, the three novels present the social history of the late 19th century in Latvia: the migration of poorer Latvians from the country to the city in search of better-paid work, some to be Germanized as they join the urban middle class; at the same time, there is the rise of a young educated generation who are proud to be Latvian. The girl Annele watches a stratified society: Germans versus Latvians; prosperous Latvian farmers versus poor rural workers like Annele's own parents; outsiders belonging to other ethnicities, such as Jews and Gypsies; and stirrings of liberation from the economic dominance of German landowners. Again and again, she sees the strangling effect of poverty on young creative people, graphically embodied in the figure of her talented older sister, whose tragedy she portrays in the third novel.

The Annele Trilogy has been compared to the popular American *Little House* books about the American frontier written by Laura Ingalls Wilder. Indeed, the main characters, Laura and Annele, live in the same period and have similar backgrounds. Wilder was born in 1867, just six years after Brigadere. Both girls love their fathers, both fathers are restless wanderers. Farm life for the two families is hard, and their economic situation is difficult. Both Laura and Annele find beauty in blue skies, grasshoppers, and flowers; both have mothers who would prefer them to be more ladylike. As young adults, both girls take on jobs – sewing and teaching – to help their families. The *Little House* books, like the story of Annele, continue to be a relevant connection to a bygone era. But Brigadere's books are far more complex than Wilder's. Brigadere describes, in great depth, how her young protagonist grows up from child to young adult, evolving an ever more mature personal concept of God and religion, developing close ties to the natural world, and learning a work ethic that stands her in good stead even as a humble seamstress. Nourished by inextinguishable stubbornness, joy, and humor, she survives circumstances that could easily deaden a young person's soul. Yes, joy and humor – for hers is not a tale of woe.

Brigadere never had children of her own, yet she found a strong connection to young people through her writing. She writes of choices and consequences, moral dilemmas and bursts of beauty. Though in *The Annele Trilogy* she sees the world through a child's eyes, her works are not childishly simple. God, nature, and work define her protagonist, and, she hopes, define her readers as well.

—Elisa Freimane and Ilze Kļaviņa Mueller

Translator's Introduction

Like many Latvians, my mother was a great reader and a great buyer of books. When I was little, our library, a small room off our dining room in Tukums, Latvia, had all the Latvian classics as well as translations of world literature into Latvian. I grew up with Tom Sawyer and Huckleberry Finn, Winnie the Pooh, the Twins series of Lucy Fitch Perkins, *Gulliver's Travels*, Hector Malot's *Nobody's Girl* and *Nobody's Boy*, and Marie Hamsun's series about the children of Langerud, not to mention Selma Lagerlöf's Nils Holgersson.

The books I remember most, however, were *Baltā grāmata* (*The White Book*) – the childhood memories of Jānis Jaunsudrabiņš – and Anna Brigadere's semiautobiographical *Dievs, daba, darbs* (*God, Nature, Work*). Little Jancis and Annele were so alive they seemed more real than my own schoolmates. Though I myself was a small-town girl born in the mid-1930s, I felt at home in the late-19th-century rural world in which they had grown up. Thus my life seamlessly extends back into Annele's 1860s and '70s and Jancis' 1880s. I know what country people wore, what they ate, how they celebrated their holidays, what they thought about, and I see their lives through the eyes of these extraordinary child observers. For a large part of my life I have been a city dweller, but oddly, deep down, because of these books, I identify as a country person.

In the 1980s, a fairly recent arrival in Minnesota, I began translating Latvian literature into English. The host of a now defunct children's program at Minneapolis's listener-sponsored FM station KFAI invited me to read some of my translations on the air. I became a frequent visitor to the program, reading chapters from *The White Book* and, later, excerpts from Brigadere's famous *Trilogy*. I felt excited and happy to share the work of these beloved Latvian writers with listeners in the Twin Cities.

Eventually I decided to translate the entire *Trilogy*. At first this seemed a daunting task. I lacked a dictionary that encompassed the vocabulary for the almost vanished, distant rural culture in which Annele grew up. Help arrived when I inherited the six-volume *Dictionary of the Latvian Language* by Karl Mühlenbach and Jānis Endzelīns. Another aid to my work was my new computer, then in its infancy but far preferable to my old typewriter and all those bottles of Wite-Out correction fluid.

It is difficult to render Brigadere's style in English. I did not always do it justice. For instance, Latvian often omits the verb *to be*, or the subjects of other verbs. To leave these out in English foreignizes the translation, but including them makes the translation much wordier. It was often not possible to translate certain expressions correctly and at the same time keep them elegantly laconic. Hardest of all to translate were the folksongs quoted in the text, for which I gave only the meaning without attempting to reproduce the rhythm. *Traduttore traditore*, as the saying goes. The translator is a traitor.

I chose to keep the names of Latvian characters in their original (and nominative) form, and use the names of Germans and other foreigners in the form they would have in their own language. While Latvian geographical names are used throughout (Tērvete, Rīga, Jelgava, etc.), I decided to translate into English the names of farms (Spring Farm, Chisel Farm, etc.), since these were names invented by the author.

To help readers with pronunciation, I've included a list at the end of the book of the rough English phonetic equivalents of Latvian vowels and consonants. I've kept footnotes to a bare minimum. What is a *pastala*, what does *klēts* mean? I hope readers will figure this out for themselves. The *Annele Trilogy* takes them to another time and place, and they must fend for themselves. I am certain they will.

I want to express my thanks to all the people who have encouraged me to translate and publish the *Annele Trilogy*: Elizabeth Thurber and Everett Forte; my late brother-in-law Tālis Gulbis, who bequeathed me his dictionary; the local Latvian academic group who heard my presentation of the work in progress; the members of my writing group who looked at the chapters as they were translated one by one; and all the friends and relations who read the translation of the *Trilogy* once it was printed at Kinko's. Without their support I would have abandoned the task before it was finished.

—Ilze Kļaviņa Mueller

PART I

GOD, NATURE, WORK

Farm Workers

Ludis the cowherd rushed in and out, leaving the door wide open like a gate. No one reprimanded him. No one guarded the warmth anymore as they had in winter. The wind blew in through the door and windows. All the corners of the house were empty. They were being dusted and swept by a woman who was leaving, so that later there would be no grumbling by the new arrivals about left-behind dirt and cobwebs.

Ludis was the older cowherd this summer, hired right at the neighboring farm. He knew Bumblebee Farm like the palm of his hand, for he ran over for a visit just about every other day. There was nothing more to explore here. Yet he had come bright and early to see with his own eyes who was leaving Bumblebee Farm and who would be arriving this St. George's Day.

Every time he rushed into the room, he'd come over to Annele.

"What do your father and mother do?"

"They're farmhands."

"Where are they going?"

"To the other end of the world."

"Where's the other end of the world?"

"Beyond the sun, beyond the moon, hundreds and thousands of miles away," Annele recited, nodding her head and trying with all her might to pronounce the difficult "r" sound in "hundreds."

Ludis laughed a hearty, loud laugh, abruptly turned on his heels and ran off, but he was back again soon – to ask Annele what her father and mother did and where the other end of the world was.

This was already the third time.

Annele pressed her lips together tighter than tight and pulled her neck in. No more.

Although Ludis was one of the people who enjoyed Annele's confidence, there were grounds for suspicion here. Why did he ask her so many times, and why did he laugh like that?

"Now tell me, girl, tell me – where are you going? To the other end of the world? Where is the other end of the world?" Ludis cross-questioned her, trying to extract from Annele the wisdom he himself had partly coached her to repeat.

Annele remained silent.

"All right, all right, don't tell me, but then you won't find out what farmhands are," Ludis said to spite her. "Well, tell me – what are farmhands?"

After vainly waiting for an answer, Ludis got mad.

"Your father and mother, of course, silly! You don't know, see! Silly, you're silly, what can I do with a silly like you!" Ludis cuffed the child, and off he went.

Annele stayed put, wrapped up like bundle, alone with her mother's spinning chair on which they had placed her. Early in the morning, they had wrapped her in shawls. Later, a few more that someone had forgotten to pack in the trunk had been added to the bundle; now she was as long as she was round, and she couldn't budge from the spot.

When she tilted her head sideways a bit, she could see the big people running across the yard excitedly: her mother, sister and brother. Sister's scarf had slid back from her flushed face, Brother's new *pastalas* had become muddy, after a tearful struggle yesterday for the right to wear them for the first time today. But Mother didn't notice. She had no time to scold. Just now, she led out Pearl and tied her to the fence. Pearl pulled, pranced, and bellowed. There were answering bellows from all the stables. This was goodbye.

A flock of sheep with trembling little white lambs ran across the yard, and after it chased Sister and Brother, waving long switches. Mother untied Pearl and hurriedly dragged her in the same direction. Two wagons loaded with household belongings drove out wobbling down the rutted dirt road and disappeared from sight.

Annele's eyes grew dark. What was this? Wasn't anyone coming back for her? Would no one call her? She had been forgotten. What would she do now in this empty corner where Mother's high bed had stood with its beautiful plaid blanket and white pillows, and which was bare, dark, and unlovable now!

Was this the great, long-awaited, much-talked-about St. George's Day? She'd have to stay alone, all by herself.

Tears began to overwhelm her, stung her eyes like fiery little needles. With all her might, Annele was resisting dark, blind fear. She couldn't cry, not for the world. If she did, Ludis would make fun of her again. But she knew she could not bear it any more, not if no one came.

Ludis was whistling outside and shouting something. Another voice shouted a reply. It was Annele's father.

Father! He was still here. He loaded the last wagon of belongings and then went back to check the old familiar places to see if anything had been forgotten. Ludis faithfully dogged his footsteps. Now all was well. Father would come, Father would come!

And Father did come, took Annele, while Ludis took Mother's last chair. Now the room was completely bare. Ludis's cot and little trunk still stood in the middle of the yard. The farmer's wife was waiting for the new farmhands to arrive, and would then assign each of them their place.

Father lifted Annele high above his head and set her on top of the wagon. It took the girl's breath away a bit, but this was joy, not fear. What was there to be afraid of on Father's wagon? For he was Annele's "mighty fortress."

From sitting so long all the shawls had slipped off her. Father climbed up on the wagon and tied them as well as he could. Annele laughed and shook her head, and all the shawls fell off again. Then Father sternly wagged his finger at her and tied them tighter. Now she no longer dared to do it. It was clear that Father was in no mood for play.

When the wagon began to move, Ludis grabbed hold of the rope that tied down the load on the wagon and, bracing himself with his feet, let himself be pulled along for a while as his coattails dragged in the mud, to Annele's great amusement, for his tongue, like a little red flame, flickered now on one, now on the other side of the narrow yellow box. Then Father noticed him and swung his whip.

"Shame on you, you little imp!"

Ludis jumped off right where he happened to be, in a big mud puddle, and remained there, looking after the wagon. Then, as though suddenly remembering, he yelled:

"Annele, what do your father and mother do?"

But in response he got a sharp gust of wind in his mouth, and nearly choked.

The clouds directly overhead cracked, dissolved, and vanished as water will when there is a wind. There was a gleam of bright blue sky and a glittering sun.

When you looked back at the bend in the road, Bumblebee Farm began to crumble. Suddenly the threshing barn disappeared, then the *klēts*, the house, the garden. A little while longer, the well sweep stood there outstretched like an index finger, then it too was hidden from sight as they approached a thicket. Bumblebee Farm, and Ludis along with it, seemed to have vanished from the face of the earth.

But then another farm, whose name Annele had so often heard mentioned when she still lived at Bumblebee Farm, emerged in the distance.

"There's Edgeditch Farm," Father pointed with the handle of his whip. Edgeditch Farm was a sulky old farmstead. The house leaned toward the road like a feeble old woman with her chin pulled into a grimace. But in the other direction, the buildings of Wolf Farm shone in the sunlight, dazzling white and stately, like milk churns. In the courtyard of Wolf Farm, there were empty and loaded wagons, brightly colored headscarves flashed in the sun, cattle were lowing. Then this, too, was all behind them and had disappeared.

For a while the road led along marshy scrub where peewits darted low over cotton grass and stumps, and brown water gleamed in the deep roadside ditches; then out into the open, where a field of rye unrolled green up to the rim of the woods and, from the blue sky, larks endlessly scattered their trills like strings of silver beads; then there was a crossroad, where roads unwound as if from a ball of yarn in all four directions, and along each one of them, weaving back and forth as though in a vast polonaise, farm workers were driving their wagons amid a jingling of harness bells. Annele's father's wagonload crossed the highway, but continued in its previous direction.

Suddenly the road broke off. On the edge of a deep ravine, the wagons stopped and then slowly began to sink into the ravine. It took Annele's breath away. She had never seen such a bottomless deep. And what was that running below there, at a

breakneck pace, foaming and thundering! So infinitely large and powerful compared to the tiny human speck of dust on the wagon!

"Dad, Dad, what's that roaring down there?" the girl asked her father, pointing
in awestruck wonder.

"That's the Tērvete River, child. These are still the spring floods, and that's why
it's so big."

"Tērvete," thought Annele and remained alone with her sense of wonder, for
she was none the wiser for her father's explanation. "Tērvete, Tērvete, that's the
Tērvete," she repeated over and over again. How it runs, how it rushes and foams!
And she had the feeling that the same lovely, lovely sonorous song murmured and
sang and roared in her breast as well!

Below, the wagons crossed a bridge. The water, tossing up foam, spun black and
awesomely deep, and ran so fast neither wind nor clouds could catch up with it.

The bottom of the ravine was sheltered from the wind, and it was as warm there
as in a little pot. Mother with Pearl, Brother and Sister with the sheep were already
ahead of them. There was soft, green grass along the river where they could let the
animals graze and have a rest.

Rest was what they all needed. The men stopped the horses and slipped
nosebags over their heads. Annele was lifted off the top of the wagon. Mother took a
bundle from one of the wagons. In it was half a loaf of bread with a hole cut in the
middle. The hole had been filled with freshly churned butter and covered with a lid
of crust. Mother cut slices of bread and spread them with butter for all of them. They
all sat down in the grass like Gypsies. Only the big children did not respond to the
call to come eat. They had run off toward the thundering Tērvete, one to get osier
whistles, the other to pick flowers, which were already in bloom here in colorful profusion.

Annele was not allowed to go anywhere, and she could not walk anyway. As
soon as she took a step, she would become entangled in the shawls and tumble
down, while the others laughed heartily.

But what need had she to go anywhere! Her sister ran back bringing flowers, all
of them for Annele; her brother came with osier whistles, and they too were all for
Annele.

The leftover bread was crumbled for the little lambs, while Pearl got the crusts.
The men had time to have a smoke, and then they resumed their journey. Up the
steep road out of the ravine, each wagon was led separately, and each was accompanied by Father pushing and holding on, for here and there the spring floods after a
long harsh winter had gouged out ruts the size of ditches.

When Father, sweaty and flushed, came down for the last wagon, they all rose to
their feet. Away from the lovely valley. The lambs were carried uphill like babies so
they would not get too tired.

When they reached the top of the hill, a sharp, biting wind grabbed them and
gave them a good shake. Here was a new world. It opened before them like a book,
infinitely distant and vast, or shrank till it was narrow and small; now its reflection
was imposing and resplendent, causing the white houses, pale green birch groves,
the faraway hills to stand out as though on the crest of a wave, now the landscape

darkened under a huge floating cloud that passed across the sun as menacing as a monster. All these inexhaustible images, which unendingly succeeded each other, entered Annele's eyes and remained there. This continued for such a long time that finally her head grew heavy and sad with the weight of them and began to nod like an ear of wheat. Forests, fields, meadows, clouds came toppling down on her and tried to crush her. She cried out.

"Annele, hold on! Open your eyes wide!"

Annele opened her eyes as wide as she could, and saw Father's smiling, bright face.

"Where's Mother?"

"She's far ahead by now."

"Isn't this the other end of the world yet?"

"We'll be there soon."

Suddenly the wind stopped as if someone had struck it across the mouth. Before them, like a shimmering, wavy fabric with a green hem, stretched a birch grove. Into this they drove. Fringed shadows swayed across the road, sticky catkin-hung branches with tiny crumpled leaves caressed Annele's cheeks. Cuckoo, cuckoo, cuckoo! The cry of the cuckoo resounded far and near.

"Father, what's that calling?"

"That's the big bell of the forest."

"The big bell of the forest?" wondered Annele.

"And there are the little bells," Father pointed to the winged flock twittering and warbling in the branches.

Aha! Now Annele understood. Yes, that's the kind of bells they were. They really did make the forest ring. More richly and with many more voices than even the loud, swift Tērvete. The deeper in the forest, the lovelier they sounded. Now she again had her eyes and ears full, to watch and to listen.

The road ran out into the light. On the right, the forest receded, making a circle around a wide forest meadow, while on the left it grew alongside the road like a living, shiny wall. At the place where both suddenly ended was the forester's farmstead, Chisel Farm. The rest of Annele's people were ahead of them waiting there.

The wagons stopped in the courtyard. They were home. The big step from St. George's Day to St. George's Day had been taken, and now the small day-to-day tasks could begin.

Two tall young women with yellow braids wearing pink jackets with wide puffed sleeves came up to Annele, chatted loudly, and laughed and tried every way they could to make friends with her, promising her wonderful things.

"Just look, Annele, look, these are your cousins," urged Mother. But Annele tucked her head into her sleeve like a little bird into down, and no longer felt like seeing anything. Her eyes were full of all she had looked at, and heavy as flowers from morning dew. Their lids dropped shut.

My Finger Hurts

Spring grew toward summer, and the bigger it grew, the bigger the chores grew. People never went anywhere except at a run.

Mother's responsibilities were endless. But Annele felt safe only when she was clinging to her mother's skirts. For on this unfamiliar farm who could trust these strange corners, the faces of strangers that sometimes ducked down from grown-up heights to this little human creature, laughing, mockingly threatening or cajoling her? Yes, there was as yet no way of knowing if they were friends or enemies.

Mother grew tired of her tenacious companion, and would often send her away, telling her to play by herself. But Annele had no idea yet how to undertake life on her own.

One morning Annele was squatting by the fire, where Mother was hurriedly preparing breakfast. Next to her, on a black hook, a large kettle was boiling, sending up clouds of steam. The flames crackled merrily, sending up streak after streak of red beads of soot that sheathed the kettle's fat bottom in rapidly moving chains. Annele was awfully tempted to stick out her finger and touch these beads. But every time she stretched it out, her mother shouted a stern warning: "Hey, careful, that burns!" – and she would drop her finger again.

But if she always listened to her mother, then how would she find out what "burning" was? She'd touch the beads!

And Annele touches them.

Oh, the pain! That fiery sting through every bone, every vein in her body! Now Annele knows what it is: it burns, burns, burns! She also knows it's her own fault. She mustn't raise her voice; what now? She tries to pull her voice inward as much as she can. But inside there's nowhere for it to go! Her voice gets stuck in her throat, and once it breaks loose, it comes with such a mighty rush that Mother's ears are deafened and the ladle tumbles out of her hands.

The finger has jumped up straight like a little rabbit. Her mother grabs it, takes a look: there's no blood, no cut. Crying about a trifle like that! Annele gets a poke in the ribs for scaring Mother needlessly and for being disobedient.

Her mother had hit her! That smarted far, far worse than her burned finger. But she couldn't say where. Deep, deep inside. Annele pressed her hand to her breast and, wailing piteously, curled up like a bit of birch bark.

It burns, burns, burns! But she didn't know where it was burning.

Mother doesn't care. She grabs the dishes, ready to run outside again.

Not if Annele can help it. She'd force her to acknowledge the great wrong the nasty kettle has done to her. Mother should at least give the kettle a good scolding. And then kiss and make the terrible burning pain all better.

And so – wherever Mother turns, Annele is underfoot; Mother pushes away one hand, Annele catches hold with both and, drawing in her feet, hangs from Mother's skirts like an apple from a branch; told to be quiet, she squeals like a stuck pig; when Mother, bucket on one side and Annele on the other, tries to hurry out the door at a run, they both get stuck. Annele gets another poke in the ribs and barely manages to grab the doorpost and thus to stay on her feet. But Mother walks away, promising to come back with a birch rod.

Annele, flattened against the doorpost, clutches it, and waters it with bitter tears. In the doorway she is in everybody's way, but she won't budge. Everyone who passes by gives her a push: "My goodness, aren't you ashamed of yourself? A big girl like you bawling like a heifer!"

How could Annele help being ashamed? She is so ashamed she can't even look up. But what is she to do if she can't budge the heavy weight of pain and stubbornness that is in her bones?

Here comes the big cousin who was the first to meet them on St. George's Day, the one with the pink puffed sleeves. She's a real tease. As soon as she catches sight of Annele, she immediately recites:

> "Look, folks, look:
> The buck ran off,
> And left his horns!
> Search for them, find them:
> Where can they be?
> Look, look: on Annele's forehead
> Growing sharp as nails!"

And she points at Annele's forehead with her finger.

Annele, deathly afraid, stops in the middle of a sob and quickly touches her forehead with that same hurting finger.

Oh dear! Suppose there really are horns growing from her forehead!

No, it's as smooth as smooth, no matter how hard she rubs.

But the big girl stands there shaking with laughter.

Annele now sees that she's been tricked, and tears fill her eyes again.

Does that big girl have to laugh at someone else's troubles? Oh, no place feels good anymore. Wherever she looks, everything is breaking and falling apart. She can't see anything clearly anymore; only, as in a fog, Mother scurrying about somewhere, probably looking for a birch rod; but if she brings that, it's all over. No, there's no other choice: Annele must run away, out into the world, away, away from all these people.

Her feet carry Annele to where she's never been before, far, far away. Beyond the *klētis*, beyond the garden, what does she care now! Now she's even on the other side of the threshing barn. The new rye field floats past like a green river. Let it float. Annele must run away.

But suddenly she finds herself in front of a big, big hole, big enough to fall into up to your neck. No room to take another step. Annele has to stand still.

But what could that be, shining there – deep, deep down in that hole? She must go and take a look.

Annele lies down on her tummy and slides down together with a sticky clay pillow, as if on ice.

And what is down there? There is brown water, an overturned barrel in the middle of it, and a big green frog on the very top of the barrel. Glistening in the sun, it croaks:

"Good morning, Annele!"

Annele isn't quite sure yet whether she knows the frog or not.

She thinks she does. She squats down on her clay pillow and sucks in the words: "My finger hurts."

"Green grass, green grass," the frog chants through one puffed-out nostril.

Annele tilts her head sideways. – Where?

Yes, so there is. The hole is edged with a fold of soft velvety turf. It would feel good to touch it, but Annele can't help heaving a big sigh:

"It hurts so bad!"

"White birches, white birches," the frog chants through the other nostril.

Annele throws back her head all the way.

Yes, there he stands, a birch man, with one foot nearly in the hole, and behind him lots and lots of other men like him.

But that first birch man is so deeply rooted in the abyss of the sky that she can see no end to him, however long she looks. She can't leave it at that, she must go and find out where he ends.

The edge of the hole won't let her up again, though. Wherever she puts her foot, little clay pillows bounce off and go summersaulting down merrily, taking Annele back down with them.

"I can't," Annele tearfully complains to the frog.

"Green grass, green grass," the frog coaches her.

Well now, if she uses the green grass, she can do it, it works.

The green grass gives her a tuft here for one hand to hold on to, a tuft there for her other hand, another for both, and in no time at all Annele is out of the hole.

"Birch man, birch man, is there an end to you?" Annele now goes searching as she runs around the birch in a circle. There is no end, not ever.

"You're much, much bigger than the threshing barn at Chisel Farm!" she marvels.

"The barn at Chisel Farm! Pooh! I could stick it in my breast pocket!" boasts the birch man.

"How warm your breast is."

Annele presses her little cheek to the white silk bark. Warm! She strokes it gently, caresses, kisses it.

The supple, twining branches caress Annele, too, like a faintly scented wave.

"Long, long hair," Annele says admiringly, measuring the slender tress against her own little white frizzy mousetails that form rings of curls around her yellow head scarf.

"Mine isn't as long as yours."

"It will be, it will be! It will grow, you'll see!" the birch reassures her.

"Where is your voice?" Annele searches, throwing back her head.

"Look for it, look for it!"

Where else would it be but in that green interlaced tangle, that deep blue abyss? There it sits at the very top flapping its wings.

"Hoo!" Whooping wildly, Annele up and tries again to throw her stubby little arms all the way around the birch.

She can't.

"So fat, so fat!"

"All fat, all good," chants the birch tree's voice at the very top.

Yes, they're all good. There they stand. Lots and lots of them. Annele is going to go and count them: "One, two, five; one, two, five!"

But as soon as she counts those, others appear: as soon as she has counted them, there are still more. "One, two, five; one, two, five!"

Annele walks slowly, she goes at a run: white, nothing but white. All of them the same, each one like all the others: "One, two, five!"

But when she has counted many of them, the birch men start to hide. One by one they disappear, and up comes a long, long row of others, kind of low and squat, cloaked down to the ground in thick green overcoats. There they stand shoulder to shoulder, leaving no gap for her to pass through.

Annele feels unsure, but why should that stop her? As soon as she gets closer to those squatting green fellows, the ground begins to sway; one more step and her foot sinks into what feels like a cushion. Her little *pastala* fills up like a trough, oooh! An icy chill runs through her bones.

Annele puts her other foot next to the first, and it, too, fills with water. Now there are two little troughs. Making brown bubbles, a little stream oozes over the laces of her *pastalas*, up to her ankles. Deeper, deeper.

Oh dear! What's this? Annele can no longer move. Annele is stuck. This is something nasty. Those squatting green men aren't nice. "Clack, clack!" goes something in the thicket.

Oh dear! Annele looks back. All the birch men are now in back of her. What can they do? They, too, are stuck. But they're all good.

"Birch men, birch men, help me!"

"Throw your arms! Pull up your feet!"

Now that's something Annele can do.

She throws up her hands, flings herself backwards, swings, balances herself, pulls up first one foot, then the other, sinks in again; but then, quickly, quickly, no longer allows the little troughs to fill up and, as soon as her feet reach firm ground, is off straight for where the trunks of the birches gleam white, fear at her heels, past them all, past them all, making for the gold of the open space beckoning and shimmering in the distance.

Annele runs out into the sunlight. Here is the meadow, here, along the edge of the forest, goes the same road she arrived by on St. George's Day. Then it was black, now it's green as green, scattered all over with little yellow stars. In places, their light has already gone out. There, little bristly white-headed "towheads" stand in clusters. No sooner does the wind knock against their heads than the little bristles drop and fly away, floating off on the breeze.

If the wind can do it, so can Annele. She fills her lungs with air and blows such a wind at the "towheads" that a whole slew of them suddenly take fright and scatter in less than no time. But Annele, blowing like a bellows, pursues them everywhere, round and round across the meadow until finally the "towheads" have all escaped and hidden, who knows where, and there are no more left for her to chase.

Now that this job has been successfully accomplished, Annele can stretch her legs. After all, she's walked half across the world.

The grass is thick as could be, the blades of grass stand tall, and all around little reddish or greenish buttons sway on slender stems. What could be inside those buttons?

The little buttons are hard. My, how hard! Annele squeezes with all her might. Finally she crushes them alright.

Annele, Annele!

A smarting, burning pain slaps her fingers. That's what you get for being naughty! The big blister on her burn has popped.

"Oh, how it hurts, my finger hurts!" Annele shakes her head, wails, looking this way and that.

There's no one. Nothing.

Annele keeps looking, suddenly scared.

Oh dear, oh dear, what's this?

Where is home? Oh, where is home?

Thick grass, spikes, slim stalks full of buds. But home is gone. Home is lost, vanished from the face of the earth.

"Come here, come here!" Annele calls and waits, and doesn't know who it is she wants to come. The grief in her breast tightens, stinging and heavy, rises into her throat like a cloud, and now there is a cloudburst of tears as well.

Where, oh where is home?

Crying, the girl gets to her feet and runs off searching for home, but runs deeper and deeper into the meadow. She is so small she cannot see across the meadow, where behind a gently sloping rise, on the other side of the new rye field, squats the roof of the threshing barn of Chisel Farm.

In the middle of the meadow, there's a clump of bright red catchflies in bloom. As soon as Annele gets in among them, they twine themselves around her feet with their sticky stalks in a wild tangle, and Annele winds up flat on the ground. Startled by the fall, a big green grasshopper jumps straight into Annele's lap and is surprised.

Annele suddenly stops crying. Her fear vanishes abruptly. The grasshopper! – He's an old friend and acquaintance.

"Chirr, chirr, chirr! Blue sky! Blue sky!" chirrs the grasshopper, raising first one, then the other antenna.

Annele's sobs abate, like a thunderstorm passing.

Blue, blue sky. Good.

The grasshopper raises first one antenna, then the other, and goggles at her.

"Chirr – chirr – chirr! Sun, sun, sun!"

One leap, and he rebounds off Annele's forehead and into the meadow.

The sun is hot as an oven. Annele's stretched-out feet are steaming, her *pastalas* are beginning to curl up and shrink. After long persistent efforts, rubbing one foot against the other, she succeeds in pulling the *pastalas* off her feet, but how is she to untie the swelled-up laces? – It's fine! It's fine as it is.

Everything ought to be fine. Her bed is as soft as a pillow, her arms, her legs glow bright, bright, but somewhere things are not as they should be, somewhere something is dark.

Her finger feels dark.

No, not just her finger – left in her chest somewhere is the sting of a tiny bit of darkness, and the sun circles it, knocks against it with a little hammer as though calling out to it: rat-tat-tat! But Annele can't tell what it is. For a long, long time Annele looks into the sky and thinks. Her head grows heavy.

"Hushaby, lullaby!" the wind whispers among the blades of grass.

"Chirr-chirr-chirr! Sun, sun, sun!" the grass, the flowers, the spikes of buds, swaying with a thousand voices, caress Annele's cheeks.

"Lullaby!" laughs the wind and disappears into thin air.

Yes, the wind has vanished, but who's that coming now?

Look, it's a woman thrusting her head toward Annele; a big, tall woman – she almost looks like Grandmother, but it isn't Grandmother; with one hand she covers up the sun, with the other she pulls a long, long shawl, comes straight at Annele, is almost on top of her: "Give me that finger!" shouts the woman. And Annele is forced to obey. But as soon as the woman takes her finger, she takes Annele as well, presses her eyes shut with a corner of her big shawl and off she goes as fast as the wind. Annele feels: she is no longer being held at all, now she will be dropped altogether, and once she starts to fall, she'll fall right through the earth, and when the earth is no longer there, there won't be anywhere for her to fall on. Oh, the grief, the terrible grief of it! "Hold me, hold me!" somebody screams in Annele's throat, screams, but

cannot get the scream out. Since she can't get the scream out, Annele makes a great effort – she'll do it, she'll open her eyes!

And what does Annele see as soon as her eyes are open? Not a sign of the big woman. But there *is* someone running across the meadow, somebody calling:

"Annele, Annele!"

It is Mother, Annele's own dear little mommy. Now all her troubles are over!

But perhaps Mommy has birch rods in her hand? Annele can't be sure. Better put up her protective shield.

"My finger hurts!" Annele's wails greet her mother from afar.

Mother arrives as quick as the wind.

"It won't hurt any more, it won't! I'll bandage it, I'll cuddle my darling, my little one, my dear darling little one – –"

And Mother picks up and carries Annele off in her arms, kisses and caresses her, keeps kissing and caressing her, and never mentions birch rods, or a naughty child, or wet feet, or anything.

And the sun searches and no longer finds a single bit of darkness in Annele.

Images

Nobody knows how it happened, but Annele can now read whole words. Whether it's a book or an old newspaper, the label of a discarded bottle or a yellowed strip of paper pasted on a storm window, Annele puts together letter after letter, pronounces them together, and the result is a word. The wonder of it! And as soon as there is a word, an image appears at the very same moment. Miraculously, something appears that isn't there at all. She spells w-i-n-t-e-r-winter, and at once sees white fields, gardens full of snowdrifts and children outside with their sleds, just the way it was at Bumblebee Farm; whereas when she reads f-l-o-w-e-r-s-flowers, it's the magnificent meadow at Chisel Farm she sees, yellow and red with buttercups and sheep sorrel; she spells s-u-n-sun, and there it is at once, flashing white sparks, high above the linden tree by the well, plunging the end of the house in the flames of its red light. As soon as she spells a word, a new miracle appears. This is the lovely new game Annele has learned, and she'll never grow tired of it.

But sometimes Annele has a hard time. She spells a word, but it remains silent no matter how much she turns and twists it. If she asks Mother, Mother will tell her if she has time, but if she doesn't, Annele gets short shrift: "You don't need to know that. If you want to know everything, you'll soon grow old."

Old! That's the least of her troubles. All right then, she'll grow old! And what does that mean: old, and how can she grow old? That won't be for thousands and thousands of years, when she's learned all the words and knows how to do every kind of work.

But how long can she walk around like this – heavy with ignorance like an ear of wheat wet with rain? If Mother won't tell her, she'll go to that same big cousin who sits in front of the *klēts* mending flour sacks and whistling like a farmhand.

Annele squats down close to the cousin, props her elbows on her knees and watches for a while as the needle runs flashing in and out of the weft threads.

"Should I say it or not?" ponders Annele. She is on somewhat uneasy terms with this cousin. There are times when she'd like to believe her, but at other times the cousin is so full of mischief that Annele can't understand why the grown-ups don't scold her and put her in her place just as they do Annele when she is being naughty. That's why she hesitates for a while.

But then the word has already escaped her lips like a bird, never to be recaptured.

"What's a-rise?"

The mending needle stops, the whistling breaks off, the gray-blue eyes flash suddenly.

"A-rise? What does arise mean?"

"Yes."

"You want to know that?"

"Ye-es."

"Can you stand up?"

"Ye-es."

"Well then, stand up, then you'll arise."

Annele thinks for a while and shakes her head.

"It doesn't work."

"What doesn't work?"

"There are other words with it. M-y s-o-u-l."

"Soul!" the cousin bursts out laughing. "You little grasshopper you, where'd you get those words?"

"Yes, s-o-u-l, what kind of a word is that? Tell me!"

"Oh, so I'm supposed to tell a clown like you! Why don't you tell me first where you got that word!"

"It's in the book."

"What book?"

"The big one."

"The big book? How do you know?"

"'Cause I saw it."

"Show me the book!" her cousin commands curtly and quickly.

Annele trots off into the house straight as a pointer to get the book. The book is no longer on the little dresser where it always used to be kept. It has moved up to a shelf attached to the posts of her parents' bed. Annele has to make a stepladder and climb up to get it down. First the chair, a little footstool on top of that, then the bed. The surface of the bed yields treacherously like corn snow in spring; not till Annele rolls both of the white pillows up into a ball and puts them one on top of the other does she get firm ground under her feet. Now it looks as though she can reach the sharp-edged corner of the book, which protrudes over the edge of the shelf, but she can't get hold of it. For a while Annele labors, boring with her fingertips, willing the book to come with every ounce of mental energy, impatient, cheeks burning – and success is as sudden as an avalanche: the book comes tumbling past the tip of Annele's nose down on the white pillows and then to the floor, taking all the pillows and a terrified Annele with it. But nothing bad has happened to it or to Annele.

Book in hand, Annele is out of the house like greased lightning. Without her cousin's help, she finds the place and, guiding her finger through furrows of letters, reads:

"A-rise, o-h m-y s-o-u-l."

Laughing loudly, her cousin snatches the book from Annele and, waving it mischievously, shouts to announce the news to the whole world:

"Hey, everybody, listen, come over here! That spook knows how to read!"

Annele's heart quakes. She only hopes this shouting bodes well for her.

And just as she suspected, it bodes her no good at all.

The cousin startles Annele's mother and old Amaļa, who have been picking greens in the nearby garden, out of their wits.

"What's this about the girl?" Amaļa asks sternly, straightening up.

"She's spelling out of the book. Come and listen!"

"Don't laugh, you crazy girl, is God's word something to laugh at?" Old Amaļa at once leaves her work, comes out of the garden and furiously snatches the book from the cousin, examining it from all sides to see whether it has been in sinful hands or not. Indeed it has. Amaļa, who is the grandmother of the laborer's wife, Big Blicene, has seen everything in this world, but never has she seen a child as small as Annele brazen enough to go and fool around with the Holy Scripture, from which the blast of the Spirit blows so powerfully it can bring to the ground even a mossy hollyhock like Amaļa, let alone a little creeper like Annele.

"What is the world coming to? Of all the insane ways to raise a child!" Amaļa places the book on the stone porch of the *klēts* and shakes her finger sternly at Annele's mother.

Mother, too, comes out of the garden, for isn't Annele her child? She defends herself. She neither forced Annele to read, she says, nor gave her the book.

"You think somebody taught her? She's been babbling like that all on her own whenever she finds anything that's in print. What's so sinful about that?"

"Oh, so you don't think it's a sin! It'll addle her wits, then you'll know why it's a sin. There are others like her, too smart for their own good, flying in the face of God. A little whippersnapper like her and already able to read print – why, if you let her, she'll be jabbering away, and read handwriting, too. I'm telling you, you'll live to see the day!" And, realizing that Annele has picked up the book again in the meantime, Amaļa interrupts her flow of speech with a stern command:

"Take that book away from her! Take it away at once! Hide it!"

Annele holds the book as though it were clenched in her teeth. "It's mine! Mine!"

"There, you see! Didn't I tell you? You see the kind of child you're raising? What she needs is a good hiding!" Amaļa mutters as she runs into the garden full of great fury and starts picking leaves snorting angrily. For all she cares, she announces, they can raise Annele to be a sinner. There's no way *she* wants to get a heart attack or even die all on account of someone else's child. But God's punishment is sure to come, she says, never you fear.

Mother can't just curtly send Amaļa about her business, for Amaļa's wrath is a holy wrath, and has been roused in the defense of the Scripture. If Annele needs to be punished, she must be punished, the law is clear. But what isn't clear to Mother is whether Annele's being able to read is an offence or not.

She decides to question Annele to find out.

"Who gave you permission to take the book?"

That's a completely unanswerable question.

"How could you take the book?"

How obstinately and strangely these grown-ups persist in asking questions! How can Annele tell her that?

Annele is angry. She does not beg. She sheds no tears. She stands there stubborn as a billy goat.

"What kind of a life can you look forward to with a child like that, Mother?" Amaļa cries aloud from the garden as though from a pulpit.

Annele gets cuffed on the ribs, and the cuff propels her into the house.

And here a pretty how-do-you-do greets their eyes! There, thrown aside carelessly in the dust, are Mother's white pillows and her blanket, a tenfold demonstration of her guilt.

With another cuff, Annele is sent to stand in the corner. What good does it do her now that she can watch from under lowered eyelids where Mother hides the book in a new place? She no longer needs it. Let it lie there for a hundred years! What does Annele care! Why did she have anything to do with that cousin? Why did she have to want to know so badly? And why did all her fervent wanting always end like this?

No, Annele decides – she'll never ask anyone, not ever again. She'd rather think for herself.

She'll think and think till she figures it out.

She can start this vast and long process of figuring things out right here in the corner.

What is really at the bottom of this business with the book? They threaten to give her a hiding for being able to read whole words, but last winter, at Bumblebee Farm, they spanked Gedene's son Kristapelis for *not* being able to. He couldn't do it, just plain couldn't do it.

As soon as Annele begins thinking about Kristapelis, all the bitterness that was stuck in her throat vanishes, and she feels like laughing. How funny Kristapelis was! Every morning, even the beginning of a reading lesson would start with a scolding. As soon as Gedene would sit down at her spinning wheel and open the book with the pointer left inside it, Kristapelis would no longer be there. Where was Kristapelis? She ran all over the place asking people. Nobody knew. Kristapelis could crawl into places where even a mouse would not have found him. But Gedene found him. Gedene would soon herd him back inside, scolding and brandishing the switch in back of him. Kristapelis would come in with long, stiff legs, his shoulders pulled up so high that his jersey rode up above the belt of his pants. After sitting down, he would keep dawdling and scratching for a long, long time while Gedene pushed back her spinning wheel into its proper position. His mother would have to put the pointer and book in his hand, he couldn't do it himself. When his mother would shout at him, he would begin "spelling" the catechism, drawling dolefully and stabbing at each word with the pointer: "I-ay-emm-I am, tee-aich-ee-the-I am the, ell-oe-arr-dee-lo-arr-dee."

"Lord, Lord," Gedene cuffed him.

"Lord, Lord," Kristapelis repeated in exactly the same tone of voice.

"Are you going to parrot me, you rascal? Does it say 'Lord' twice, huh? It just says it once. Say: Lord."

"Say Lord," Kristapelis repeated in a whining voice.

"I'll teach you to say 'say Lord'," Kristapelis got another cuff on his back. "You think you're going to blaspheme against the word of God, you naughty boy?" And raising a rageful voice, Ģedene prompted Kristapelis, bellowing, "I am the Lord. Say it after me."

"I-I a-am the Lord," Kristapelis whistled through his sobs, and big drops went running down the tip of his nose.

That's how the two of them struggled every day.

Kristapelis floated through the catechism until it was as soggy as a sauna broom. Then Ģedene would furiously snatch it from him, and Kristapelis's nose immediately stopped dripping. While his mother exchanged the catechism for the big hymnal, he would squint sideways in Annele's direction; no matter where she was, he would hunch his back, spread his mouth to his ears with both thumbs, waggle his fingers dreadfully, and make the most awful face he knew. Annele, however, was no longer a baby that could be frightened so easily. She would just laugh and move closer to Kristapelis, which she never did while he was spelling his way through the catechism. She liked the hymnal, and she didn't like the catechism. Kristapelis had already worked his way through the hymnal, he was merely going over it again, and to Annele, too, it felt like home, for since the first snowfall Kristapelis had been reading from it day after day.

Annele, too, learned by heart all the hymns that Kristapelis read. When the reader made a mistake in a difficult word, Annele, hanging around nearby, helped him to guess it, and this easily slid by Ģedene's attention, lulled by the gentle hum of the spinning wheel as it was. Kristapelis rewarded Annele for this. When he managed to get hold of the book outside of his reading time, he showed Annele all its secrets, quite smart and boastful now. Those stern gees and kays, that stuck-up aich, those softies, the enns and the ells, those furious eshes and chahs and all the rest of their brothers and sisters. Oh, this was a different sort of spelling lesson for Kristapelis than the one with his mother. And, once Annele knew each individual letter, it was mere child's play for her to put them together into words.

When Annele in her corner had had a nice visit at Bumblebee Farm, had read through all the hymns and was just sledding—whee!—down the field at Bumblebee Farm along with the other kids, her mother came in. She said Annele could go if she would be good. Why shouldn't Annele be good? She promises at once, just so as to set free her feet and run away like the wind. But Mother takes her by the hand, and the two of them go to the *klēts*.

"Mother, Mother, you're going to the trunk, you're going to show me the shawls!" Annele jumps from one foot to the other.

Yes, Mother walks over to the green trunk ornamented with red roosters. When the heavy lid falls back behind the trunk, Annele claps her hands. She no longer has to rise on tiptoe or stretch her neck, she can look into the trunk's deep secret standing on her own feet.

"Mother, our trunk has gotten smaller," she exclaims in surprise.

"No, you've grown tall," Mother says.

"Tall?" Annele puts her hand on her head. "How do I grow, I wonder?"

And she has to think about it the time it takes Mother to shake out and air all the silk shawls; now, Mother lifts up the heavy lid from behind the trunk. Together with the lid, a whole series of strange little men and women leap up, crowded together on the inside of the lid.

"Mother, what are those? What farm are they from?"

"They're not from a farm. They're ladies and lords."

"Ladies and lords!" Annele exclaims in rapture, catching the lid with both hands, not letting it close. Her mother has to give her time to look at them.

So that's what lords and ladies are like! One is wearing long stockings, above his knees, and shoes with gold buckles, his trousers are short, and around his hips they're stuffed like balloons; a little short green cloak hangs from his shoulders, and a long white feather sways on his hat. On one side he has a sword, on the other a dagger. He stands there with his mustache proudly twirled, one hand on his hip, the other on the hilt of his sword, looking straight at Annele: "Well, what do you think of me?" – "Don Ju-an," Annele reads the words written below. Another, dressed in a different array of colors, differently built, stands further over to the side. Arms outstretched, he has unrolled a long, long scroll, and is pointing to something. "Le-po-rel-lo," Annele reads below. And then come the ladies, so stately and magnificent they dazzle your eyes. "Donna Anna" has folded her hands as though in prayer, "Don-na El-vi-ra" clutches her breast with both hands. And there are many more queer and lovely figures to see, but Mother has gotten tired of it and that's enough. Before Annele has time to open her mouth and plead with her, Mother slams the lid shut, and all the don juans and donnas fall back into the green trunk as though into a grave.

In vain though. Who can bury them now that they've appeared from the innards of the trunk. Wherever Annele goes, they're there by her side. She goes to her big Pinecone Castle at the edge of the forest, where Annele has all sorts of fine arrangements – gardens, barns, houses, big herds of cattle – and they're always in the middle of everything. "What farm are you from?" Annele asks them boldly. "We're from the big farms out in the world," they answer in thin little voices. And they're not stuck-up at all. The ladies and lords do everything Annele tells them to. Donna Anna and Donna Elvira hitch up their silk skirts and go off to milk the cows, while Leporello goes to spread out the grain to dry, and Don Juan rides off to watch the horses for the night. Just look at his white feather flashing by past the sauna willows! – But when Annele prepares a feast, it's a sight to be seen! Then Pinecone Castle is the gathering place not only for the guests from the green trunk, but Mother's and Father's relatives, plus their relatives as well; the place is crawling with children, and there are such huge crowds of lords and ladies that there's no more room for them in Pinecone Castle, and they have to be pushed out the windows. But they don't mind. There's an endless meadow right there where all the seedpods are princes while the grasses and flowers are beautiful princesses; here no matter how high-born and fine a gentleman is, no matter how elegant a lady, they can play all kinds of games and sports to their heart's delight.

This goes on all summer, but when winter approaches with its great frosts and blizzards, Annele together with all her characters moves into some quiet corner of the house, and she has all she needs, for she spreads the golden web of her fantasy and captures the whole world in it.

But then comes a dark morning, and Annele as she wakes up has the feeling that someone has stuck her eyelids together with wax and fettered her arms and legs to the bed. When she forces her eyes open, she sees that a black fog has settled in all the corners and – look – from it rise Don Juan with his long feather, Leporello, Donna Elvira, and many others, a motley crowd. Intermingling like the shadows of drifting clouds, they are drawn out long as threads with broad, bloated faces, turn into horrible monsters, thrust themselves upon her, pressing her eyes closed, lie down on her very eyelids, pile up on her chest blowing a sweltering hot blast and choking her breath. "Mother, Mother!" Annele barely has a chance to exclaim, and as from a grave she hears her mother's voice and sees her hands stretching toward her as though out of a fog, and then loses consciousness.

For a long time, Annele is in the power of the apparitions, who want to lure her through dark, distant labyrinths to their shadow kingdom, and only after long weeks of being lost does memory lead her by a fine white silk thread back into the light.

And by then, the blackbirds have started whistling, it's St. George's Day again, and the family is on its way to a new home.

Birch Hills

With the same enthusiasm and restlessness, the same secret joyous sense of expectation as the year before, Annele has been swaying in this day's happenings like a waterweed in a rushing stream. The wagons stand in the middle of the yard. They are being loaded. Cows are lowing, sheep bleat, and the wind blusters, shaking Chisel Farm, which stands in its corner of the woods facing straight north. No matter how hard the wind shakes, it cannot shake the farm out of its place. Here's where the wind found it squatting, and here it will leave it, while Annele will fly off like the missel thrush: one moment whistling in the pear tree, and the next – look! – up and away across the treetops and into the woods!

She wishes it would happen sooner! But this morning with all its adventures is as long and colorful as a whole week. How many times already has Annele gotten in the grown-ups' way and been poked in the side for it, how many times has she cried and cried and then cheered up again, how many times has she been scolded and later been given a hug, until at last the moment arrives when everything has been loaded into the wagons and those who are leaving tearfully say goodbye to those who are staying. Annele isn't crying. "Aren't you sad that we have to part?" they ask her. She doesn't know the meaning of the word: part.

On the very top of Father's wagonload a table has been tied, legs pointing toward the clouds. That's Annele's place. She sits there as if under a canopy whose roof is made of the blue silk of the sky, decorated with white cloud roses. Sticky, budding branches caress her cheeks just as they did last year, and the cuckoo calls, "Cuckoo! Where are you off to?"

"To another place, to another place!"

"Cuckoo! Where are you off to? What kind of place?"

"Toward the sun, toward the sun!"

The forest with its wind is left behind singing. Annele, too, rides along humming an endless song. It's a long ride. Then the wheels begin to roll along with a wobble, and it seems to her as though the wagon is about to turn a summersault. She gets scared. What will happen to her then? Her father's head surfaces from below.

"Now, now, hold on, lass! We're just driving down the hill. I'm right here."

"Do we have far to go?"

"We're almost there."

Then down the hill, then through a sunny valley, across bridges, then up a hill and straight into the yard of Spring Farm.

But in the yard, a tiny little stooped old woman stands waiting for the newcomers. She is the mother of Annele's father, whom no one ever calls anything but Mother Avots. Her first words are, "Is the little girl sitting there on top your Annele?"

"That's right," answers Father, lifting Annele from the wagon.

And once Granny takes Annele's hand, she won't let go of it anymore.

"Come, let's go inside, maybe there's something left over for you in that cupboard of mine."

And as she and Granny walk inside, suddenly three more little mushrooms appear, like steps in a ladder going down. These are Lulīte, Tincīte, and Julcīte, Granny's little granddaughters just like Annele, from the neighboring farm. They've come to watch St. George's Day at Spring Farm.

Granny takes a little white object from the cupboard, like a little stick of chalk. She places a knife on it, and with a light hammer blow splits off a little piece for each child, putting the little stick back in the cupboard. Julcīte is the only one to toss hers into her mouth at once and bite down on it, crunching it between her teeth with enjoyment. Annele does not know what to do with hers and hides it in the palm of her hand, but Lulīte whispers, "If you take a bite of that with birch sap, it's delicious."

As soon as Granny sends the girls out to play, Lulīte immediately urges, "Let's go to Big Father!"

"To Big Father," repeats Tincīte.

"Yeth, yeth! Big Fahwer," lisps Julcīte.

All three of them want to hold hands with Annele. But Annele only has two. Lulīte holds on tight to one, while the two little ones fight for the other hand, jostling each other aside.

"Why do you tease the child?" Lulīte chases away Tincīte, and Julcīte now has the upper hand and proudly walks beside Annele.

"Why d'you teathe the chide?" Julcīte scolds.

"Well, where is Big Father?" asks Annele.

"On the birch hill," Lulīte answers, pointing it out from afar: "Look, that's Big Father over there!"

"Dat'th Big Fahwer over dere!" Julcīte shakes her little rosy finger the same way.

Big Father is a big, big birch tree at the very top of the hill.

"Hear it running?" Lulīte listens attentively. "No other birch has such delicious sap."

"Deyishious thap," Julcīte smacks her lips.

Annele climbs full of amazement. She's never climbed such a big hill. Spring Farm and all its rooftops are left below their feet, while the hill keeps getting higher and higher.

Big Father's little spring of sap flows at a steady murmuring trickle. A barefoot boy in linen shorts, his hair like a bundle of flax, is hopping around it.

"Come over here! I've got something to show you," yells the boy.

When the girls come close, he dips out handfuls of birch sap and splashes it in their eyes.

Lulīte stamps her foot. Sternly she scolds, "Will you get away from here, you nasty boy!"

"I'm not going, so there," the boy teases. "I'll show that new girl where the pinecones grow."

"So where do they grow? On a pine tree!" Lulīte retorts, curious.

"No, they don't!" the boy snaps back. "Look!" And from his palm with a snap of his fingers he flicks a fat pine cone right at the tip of Annele's nose. "Well? Hurts, huh?" he asks with gusto, as though sucking on a sugar cube.

It hurts like the dickens, but there's no way Annele is going to let the boy see that.

"Too bad it's not winter, then I'd show that new girl where Rīga is!" the boy gloats boastfully, rolling his eyes.

"So where is Rīga?" Lulīte again wants to know.

"Ha! Here's what you do, see? You chill a knife blade on the ice till it's all white and then—blam!—touch somebody's tongue with it. And right away they'll see Rīga!"

"Just don't listen to him," Lulīte instructs them, as though to protect Annele and, acting very self-assured, invites the girls to help themselves to the birch sap, letting each in turn taste the delicious liquid, and battling the boy all the while — he'd love to snap his fingers at the back of the children's heads, suddenly yell in their ears or do some other naughty thing. But when Lulīte herself bends down to drink sap from the container, the boy creeps up behind the girls' backs and lies down full length at their feet, and when they all turn around at once, they suddenly fall all in a heap. What a fright they get, how they scream and how angry they are, and how the boy now laughs with glee!

But for this Lulīte gives him a good piece of her mind. Annele has no idea where Lulīte gets all these unheard-of swear words. And whatever Lulīte says, Julcīte lisps. The boy, however, is not a bit afraid of the scolding girls. He hops from one foot to the other teasing them.

Suddenly, the neighing of horses and barking of dogs is heard from below. The boy streaks down the hill quick as an arrow.

"Don't you be scared of him," Lulīte reassures Annele. "He's an awful boy, but he's going to leave soon. His mother is going to come and get him, and send him away to be a herdboy. What else can you do with a rascal like him?"

"A yascal like him," echoes Julcīte.

Now that the boy is gone, they could play on the birch hill undisturbed. There's wild ginger blooming here, the first cowslips are beginning to open, there are quite a few good nuts under last year's leaves, and they could sample the sap in the buckets from the other birch trees, but a long-drawn-out yoo-hoo suddenly reaches their ears from an unknown part of the birch hill. Lulīte straightens up and strains her ears to discover where the long yoo-hoo comes from.

"It's Mother. She's calling us home." Lulīte looks across to the neighboring farm, whose courtyard is in full view. A woman stands in the yard, shouting and scolding: "Oh you big girl, where have you dragged those children off to? Over to the hills at Spring Farm! Just you wait, you'll catch it when you get home."

"Mother's calling. Let's go, let's go!"

"Mother's calling, Mother's calling!"

"Cawyin', cawyin'! Yet'th go, yet'th go!"

All three little girls tumble down the hill holding hands, with not another glance at Annele. And, appearing again from God knows where, the boy jumps out of the bushes, yells after them: "Look, look, there runs a pot with two little handles!"

When, after reaching the *klētis* of Spring Farm, Annele turns off in the direction of the yard, a big black shaggy dog runs out to meet her, plants himself across her path and stops in his tracks.

"Doggy, doggy, let me pass!"

"No, no, no!" wide-jaws shouts back.

What now? Annele can't go a single step forward, nor the dog a single step back.

"Citron, Citron, aren't you ashamed of yourself?" calls a young woman from the yard, drops her yoke and buckets and runs to Annele's rescue. She gives the big shaggy creature a good scolding: "What are you doing barking at children? Don't you see she's come to live here? Come on, calm down now! Give her your paw, there's a good dog!"

The dog stops barking.

"Now pet him," she tells Annele.

Hesitantly the girl puts her hand on the shaggy one's head. Citron flattens his ears, pushes his nose into her hand. And what's she got in her hand? Granny's sugar cube. Citron gulps it down before you can say "knife."

"There, now you're friends. Citron won't bark at you any more."

Yes, after swallowing the sugar, Citron licks the girl's palm and now wags his tail nonstop.

The young woman goes back to her buckets. She is tall, ruddy-complexioned, with bushy blond hair.

The sun is just setting. Līziņa comes, calls Annele. She must go to bed this minute. Līziņa is going to show her to her sleeping place.

At the new sleeping place, there is a fresh straw mattress, a clean white sheet. Līziņa puts the girl to bed, she's in a great hurry. Outside, from somewhere far away, there is a peal of sound!

"Listen, what a long, long bell!"

"That's not a bell, those are maids singing. They're welcoming in the spring. We're going soon, too. They say the sound from the hills of Spring Farm is so powerful! Just wait till we start singing, and our voices answer theirs!"

"Take me with you! I want to go too!"

"We can't, we can't! You're still little. The frogs will make you deaf with their croaking. Just us big people. Mother's coming too. Her voice carries a long way. The other married women will be there, too. And the maids, Luze and Karlīne."

"Is Karlīne the one with the blond hair?"

"Yes."

"She's pretty."

"Lie down now, lie down and listen! We'll be singing any minute now."

And Līziņa is gone. Now Annele should by rights be sad that she wasn't allowed

to go along, but a motley procession of images come and stand in front of the sadness. She has to let them all pass before her eyes. There is Chisel Farm. The woods in
spring. The blue sky. The white clouds. Granny. Lulīte, Tincīte, Julcīte. The boy in
the linen shorts. Citron. Karlīne. The birch hill. –

Suddenly a wave of sounds ripples upward from that very same birch hill and
washes all the images away. It dies away in the distance slowly, slowly, intertwining
with other faint sounds wandering this way from somewhere out there. Hardly has it
faded away when another leaps up as if from the eddying deep. The singing is clear,
high-pitched, long drawn-out. No more emptiness anywhere. The fields, the farm,
Annele's heart, all are full. Delicious, delicious sounds! More delicious than the
sweetest birch sap. Gently they unbind her, rock and lift her, carry her somewhere
up high. –

The sound goes on and on!

"So this is Spring Farm," thinks Annele.

The Cursing Woman

The birch sap is still running.

On the hill by the big birch trees, the containers of sap overflow every morning. In some the sap is so sweet that it sticks to your lips like honey. Father often climbs the hill to check if the birches aren't being damaged: when it has given enough, the birch is sealed up. The spigot is removed, and a plug is driven into the hole. No tribute is taken from the young birches. They are free to let their strength stream into their branches and leaves. To glitter and be fragrant.

Annele sits in the yard on the velvety green lawn filled with wonder. How high the arc of the sky curves here! So deep and blue! You can see no end to it on either side. Surely the center of the universe must be here, at Spring Farm!

And how many miraculous things there are here! You never notice how easily the day passes. Not until evening does it grow heavy like a basket filled with beautiful bright-colored flowers. Now would be a good time to start making a garland out of the flowers that have been picked, but Annele's eyes close in sleep. Her arms hugging the basket, the picker has fallen asleep. But tomorrow there will be a new basket and new flowers.

There are many, many birds at Spring Farm, for the rich city of the Forest is just outside the gate. And people walk with light steps here. They have to run uphill and downhill. They all talk to Annele. The girl is so mortified she doesn't know which way to look. Those who don't talk, laugh, and those who don't laugh, smile; whenever they walk past, they look at Annele.

Except for Kaminskene—she doesn't smile.

Over by the garden fence sits the same boy she met yesterday, the one with the yellow mop of hair, scaring the sparrows, yelling and throwing rocks. Annele would love to know his name. But how is she supposed to find out?

Noise comes from below, from the farmhands' *klētis*. It's women quarreling. "Tee-hee," exclaims the boy with the yellow mop of hair, "listen to Kaminskene – she's on the rampage again!"

Who did he say that to? He was looking at the sparrows, not at Annele. But Annele's eyes opened wide.

"Kaminskene is on the rampage? Oh dear! Wonder how she does that?"

It might be possible to talk to this boy. He no longer seems nearly as awful as yesterday.

"Me mom says Kaminskene always makes the fur fly."

Annele ventures to give the speaker a sidelong look. Makes the fur fly? She ought to tell the boy that Kaminskene isn't wearing a fur coat, but a sheepskin jacket. But who would say a thing like that?

"Me mom says Kaminskene is always green with envy."

Green with envy? How does she manage to look like that?

Oh dear! And there she comes in person – there's Kaminskene.

Annele sits still as though frozen.

Up the slope along the path a woman comes running, swinging a cooking pot by the handle. She is tall, skinny, hunched forward a little. A wide, gathered skirt flaps around her legs. She has a short, dirty sheepskin jacket on, with a wide fleecy hem at the bottom. She wears a big scarf with a paisley pattern, wound around her head Turkish style. Big black eyes dart in all directions, burning fiercely. All living creatures give her a wide berth. Chickens flee squawking, flapping their wings, ducklings roll out of her way cheeping.

Before her, the light parts like the waters of the Red Sea before the children of Israel. She seems to leave a black furrow in her wake.

She throws open the back door. Behind it, shut in the kitchen, whining, waiting impatiently, stands Citron. As soon as the door opens, he squeezes out past her with a rush. A whack with the pot at one flank, then at the other and, howling, skidding, looking back in terror, Citron makes his escape across the courtyard.

Annele and the boy by the fence sit motionless each in their spot looking at each other. Annele's eyes are filled with fear.

"Tee-hee, now she's going to start cursing," says the boy.

"Cursing?" wonders Annele. She doesn't know that word.

"Me mom says: whenever she's mad, it's out into the kitchen. And down on her knees. And then it's ashes on her head, cursing away!"

"How does she curse?" Annele asks the boy.

"She just – curses! Me mom says, whatever she curses turns black."

"Whatever she curses?" Annele wonders. "Does she curse living things? People?"

"People, dogs, cats. Whatever comes along! That's what me mom says."

Kaminskene threw open the door of the summer kitchen and hissed past the children like a gale, in the direction of the farmhands' *klēts*. The boy jumped up from where he sat by the fence, made his hands into a trumpet behind her back and trumpeted, "Ta-da! Ta-da! There goes the witch! Tantara! There goes the witch!" – then took off in the same direction as Citron.

Annele was on her feet, too. She wanted to do something, she had to do something. She was burning with curiosity to hear Kaminskene curse.

Annele knew how things usually go. For a long time, there's fear and uncertainty about beginning something, and then all of a sudden you pluck up courage and do it.

She plucked up courage and ran into the kitchen quick as a flash before Kaminskene returned. She huddled in the very darkest corner and waited.

The kitchen walls glistened with black specks of soot, and rose high, high up. They rose into the chimney up to the blue sky. Kettles were hanging from black

hooks over the hearths. The hearths were dark. Only in one corner, under a tripod, was there a banked fire with Kaminskene's little pot above it. Until your eyes got used to it, everything was dark, for the light entered only through the chimney.

Kaminskene ran inside and slammed the door so hard that the little flame suddenly fluttered sideways in terror. She bolted the door. Annele's heart froze. For a while the woman busied herself with the pot. She sprinkled, stirred, banked up the fire. On the feebly lit wall, her shadow spookily accompanied her every movement, as though mimicking her.

Then she put the lid on the little pot, blew her nose, and wiped her eyes for a long time. She sat down by the hearth, put her arms around her knees and began rocking them. She rocked, rocked for a while, slowly began to sob, then louder and louder, and suddenly began to mutter.

"This is it, now she's cursing!" Annele thought, trembling.

Kaminskene "cursed":

"Shatter my enemies, o Lord, shatter my enemies! Topple them from their thrones, from their proud seats, from their lofty chairs. Destroy them, rend them apart, place them as a footstool beneath my feet. May the sun no longer shine upon them by day, nor the moon by night. Let their tongues cleave to their jaws, let them dry up and wither like grass that is mowed down!

"Let them cease to be!

"Spit them from your holy mouth, and let them cease to be!

"Shatter my enemies, shatter my enemies, O Lord! Let the sun grow dark, let the stars be extinguished like candles, shatter, shatter them! – "

Annele is no longer listening. She presses her ears shut with her fists and flattens her face against the sooty wall. She clenches her teeth to keep from bursting into sobs.

"Oh dear, oh dear! What shall I do now? Now I'm done for. This is the end of everything! The sun is black, the stars have gone out. Oh dear, oh dear! Now I'm in the grave! No one can save me now. Kaminskene has put a curse on me."

Though her ears are stopped up, yet now Annele can hear that Kaminskene's voice has changed. She plucks up courage and looks back. Kaminskene is on her feet, gesturing over the hearth and scolding, "Stop, you miserable, nasty thing you! Stop it, will you? Now it'll be all over everything! Now it'll all go up in steam! You crazy thing! Damn! It's gone and boiled over!"

Kaminskene's little pot has spilled its whole contents. The fire, doused, sputters, the chimney is full of white steam. Kaminskene snatches the pot off the fire, throws it down in the embers, and she herself tears outside to the *klēts*, leaving the door wide open.

Right behind her, Annele flies out like a bird that's been held by its wings. She flies out into the hot mid-morning light.

The sun! The sun is alive!

Annele races across the yard as fast as her feet will carry her. "Annele, where are you running to, lass? Listen to me! Come here! Wouldn't you like some bread?" her grandmother calls from the *klēts*. Annele obeys. Grandmother is the loveliest wonder of Spring Farm. During these two days, she and Annele have gotten to know each other so well it's as if they had spent a whole lifetime together. One minute she sends Annele one place, the next she asks her to do something else. Grandmother has a lot of jobs to give a person. She talks to Annele as though to a grown-up. She pats her on the head. Says a kind word. And when she opens her withered hand, there's always some marvelous surprise in it.

Grandmother is holding a big slice of bread spread with a thick layer of freshly churned butter.

"Want some, lass?"

Annele's eyes shine: How could she not want bread and butter? It's a rare treat. There was no butter to be had last winter at the other farm. Mother did have Brownie, but Brownie didn't give any milk in winter. When Annele asked why this was so, the grown-ups laughed and said she should wait until the seven lean years were over. Then the milk would flow again.

And now they were over, those seven lean years. Anybody could see that.

Annele holds the bread and butter up to the sun for a while to let it get good and warm; then carefully pushes back the layer of butter with her teeth and bites off the first tasty mouthful. The same with the next one. She wants the little butter dam to grow. She wants all the buttery goodness to be saved up for the end, for the last bites!

But Citron, too, has already smelled the scent of bread. Here he comes, wagging his tail, with big leaps. He's coming to renew the friendship they began yesterday.

"Hey, how're your flanks? Has Kaminskene's blow stopped hurting?" Annele asks.

Oh, that! The sun healed it a long time ago. Citron wants some bread and butter. He fawns before Annele, calling, "Food, food!" loudly and boldly.

Annele breaks off a little piece of her slice and throws it into the bottomless pit of Citron's gullet. It's a mere drop in the bucket for Citron.

"Food, food, food!" he calls again.

"All right, here's some more!" Annele throws in another mouthful.

Citron is up on his hind legs, pawing at Annele's clothes and hands: "Food, food, food!"

Annele has a feeling that she shouldn't give him any more, not another bite. She wavers. – Citron barely knows her. And yet isn't it bad manners for him to keep insisting and to ask her like this? He ought to be ashamed of himself.

"Food, food!" Citron calls, waving his tail in affirmation.

It's obvious that he knows no shame. She decides to toss a third mouthful into that bottomless pit.

But after the third mouthful, Citron has his paws on her chest like a shot. His black eyes, burning greedily, dart from side to side like the eyes in Kaminskene's head. He himself is black and shaggy.

Citron wants it all.

"Food!" he barks right by Annele's ear, hurling his front paws way above Annele's head.

This isn't right.

Suddenly Annele feels scared.

"Here, here!"

She tosses the whole slice into his gullet. There goes the buttery dam, the lovely last mouthfuls.

Now there's peace and quiet! Citron gratefully snorts and is once more a polite dog. He trots in a happy circle around Annele, waves his tail amiably a bit. But it no longer pays for him to stay by Annele.

Annele is on the verge of crying for her piece of bread and butter, but after rubbing her eyes she sees a place where she's never been before. There's a juniper bush near the birch hills, and one tree is looking her way with a hundred rosy eyes. Why not run and take a look?

It's the wild crabapple tree, which will bloom tomorrow.

Annele lies under the crabapple tree and thinks. She thinks about Kaminskene.

What kind of a person is Kaminskene?

The way she cursed!

Where did she come from?

On Saint George's Day, Annele drove into Spring Farm through one gate, and Kaminskene came in through the other. Full of fury.

And who were they, those "enemies" of hers? – And why did she curse them? And what is she doing now?

Is she squatting by the hearth again, pouring ashes on her head? And muttering those terrible words?

And will that great danger really overwhelm her enemies? – –

A big column of smoke rises from the chimney of Spring Farm. Oh dear! Look, look! There's Kaminskene herself!

Did you see that? She rises upward, spreads to giant size, stays there as though marveling at the great light, at the blue sky. Slowly topples to one side, floats across the thatched roof of the stable. The glistening moss on the roof takes fright and turns black. Kaminskene bends in the direction of the farmhands' *klēts*, but a breeze shoots out from under the willow tree and whirls her around in a circle twice. She rolls over on her side like an emaciated tramp: any minute now she'll start to curse! But the wind is already tearing at her ragged skirts. The tatters that come off are gone for good; the rest the wind rolls into a ball, tosses it, rocks it. For a little while the wind rocks it – rocks it, and suddenly – there's nothing left! Where has she gone, with all her cursing? Swept into the light like a coal into a soft snowdrift.

There's nothing left.

Nothing but the glorious, mighty blue vault of the sky! And she hasn't put a curse on the sun, or the stars, or the human race.

It was all for nothing! All those curses gone up in smoke!

May Sunday

It's a bright blue Sunday morning in May! Father and Mother are going to walk to Chisel Farm and take Annele with them. Annele skips for joy. To Chisel Farm! Although it's barely a few weeks since she came to Spring Farm from there, it seems to her that Chisel Farm is already far, far away and that when they walk there they'll have to walk back a distance, beyond time and beyond eternity.

"Don't wear yourself out running around so much, and don't get tired for nothing. We have a long way to walk. What if Father has to carry you later?" warns Mother when Annele skips up and down the shoulders of the road, now to get a pussytoe, now a bird's eye primrose, now a cowslip.

How could the walk wear Annele out? Even if the road were a hundred miles long, she'd run all the way. All she wants is to be left alone, not to be called back constantly. How can she get tired when she has her hands full of work? Walking down the road is not all she has to do – there's all kinds of business to attend to along the way as well.

Annele has already picked many little bunches of flowers and placed them in the roadside ditch: they must wait till she comes back. Then she'll fix up some meadows right here. This is a good place. And by the meadows there'll be a forest. Now, a forest is something she can make right away. And she struggles with a small young birch tree, trying to break its supple branches but unable to break them off.

Her father stops walking and rebukes her:

"Oh, baby, what do you think you're doing? You've been picking all those little flowers and throwing them down as soon as they wilt. And now you won't leave the little birch tree alone. Do you think he can grow back as fast as you break him? How will he feel standing among the others with broken-off branches, like a little cripple without hands? Remember that he's a child of God too, just like you. A living creature, who feels pain just like you."

Annele is startled. Flushed, with guilty eyes, she looks at her father: "The birch tree feels pain? The flowers feel pain? Just like me?" – she asks in surprise.

"Of course," Father continues gravely. "Don't break them! Never damage the trees for fun. Let them grow, let them be glad in God's sunshine."

For a good while Annele walks along deep in thought. A bright flower beckons over there, a succulent green branch over here, but she admonishes herself: "God's creature. A child of God like you. It feels pain. Don't break it!"

But what is she to do now? Father and Mother are walking along so very slowly.

They talk and talk. Annele runs ahead to measure off a big stretch of road, measures it off running back, and they're still at it, still talking. What could they possibly be talking about at such great length?

Now they turn off the road altogether. In a sunny spot by a beautiful birch tree with dense foliage they sit down in the grass. Father has thrown down his cap, Mother's head scarf has slid off her head. There they sit, their backs against the birch tree.

Annele, too, drops in the grass. She is as quiet as could be. It's nice here. Let's pretend this is Chisel Farm. All right! She can play here all day long.

"Why doesn't anybody talk anymore?" she wonders. She watches her parents. Her mother is looking somewhere into the distance. When Annele lets her eyes follow her mother's, they are whirled far away, high up, into the deep blue sky.

Then her eyes return back again. They seek out her father and mother. Oh, how she loves to look at them! Every child should have a father and mother like hers! And they're so very very different from the way they were yesterday and the day before. Father has eyes like the sky, and Mother has cheeks and a mouth like – well, like what? Annele can't find any flowers that are like her mother, none to compare her with. She likes looking at them both the same way she likes looking at flowers, at birch trees, at the blue sky. And why is that? Why is today like nothing that has ever been before? Annele thinks about it. She figures it out. It's because today is Sunday. The forest, the flowers, the blue sky are Sunday, Father and Mother are Sunday. Their hands are Sunday. There is no work in their hands. There is no hurry in their feet. There are no words in their mouths that say, "Come on, child, move, you're in the way. I don't have time."

Mother's hands are quite still, clasped together. Her eyes have not returned from the depths of the sky yet. Her lips are moving. She is speaking to someone. Not with Father, not with Annele. Then whom is she speaking to? Now she's using words. Her words flow, undulating gently like the waves in the slow stream they crossed this morning:

> "The Lord is my shepherd, I shall not want,
> He makes me lie down in green pastures,
> He leads me beside still waters."

The Lord? Annele flings herself back on her elbows and again allows her eyes to sweep back down the distant path of the sky. Where is he? Does Mother see him? – No, no. It's not like that. One doesn't see him with ordinary eyes. One can see him, but with another kind of eyes, eyes that make it possible to see many, many wonderful things. And he is behind all things. A severe thunderstorm or a soft breeze; the hot sun or the sweet shadow. A rye field under the morning wind, or the forest where the cuckoo repeats its plaintive call. He is there, and there, and there, and if you wish he is in the very center of your heart. Closer than Father, closer than Mother. There is nothing, nothing you can hide from him, nothing you can tell him! He comes and plucks all your thoughts himself, like flowers from a meadow. He is the Lord; no, he is really a dear heavenly father; no, he is he! He is much, much more than all his names, no one word can say who he is.

Mother says: The Lord is a shepherd. A shepherd? Yes, when Annele uses her other eyes, then he is a shepherd. His cloak is like flecks of foam, and its hem is made of blue sky. He is big, oh so big. The tips of his golden wings glide across the forest. Wherever they pass, the meadow and the sunny clearing begin to bloom with thousands of flowers. But he is looking, searching. What is he searching for? Well, if he is a shepherd, then of course he's looking for those that are in his care.

> "He refreshes my soul,
> He leads me in the paths of righteousness
> for his name's sake."

Soul? Annele pricks up her ears. What's a soul? Where is this soul? That's the word that was still unfamiliar to her. "A-rise, oh-my-soul," was what it said in the hymnbook that Annele read at Chisel Farm. Her cousin laughed when she read it aloud, but wouldn't tell her what a soul was. A soul – a soul – ! Is it the soul that can see him? Yes, oh yes, that must be it. It is the soul that has those invisible eyes that are nevertheless able to see – see the most marvelous things, and it is the soul that has those inaudible voices that tell you so much, more than all the grown-ups know or are willing to tell you. Yes, yes, it exists! Annele's got one too – a soul! She herself lies in the grass while her soul speeds away to the furthest fields of heaven; she herself closes her eyes, while her soul sees, sees... It longs to see everything. Its hunger can't be satisfied with bread, nor its thirst quenched with water. It keeps wanting something. Sometimes it is sunlight, or flowers, or the songs of birds, or the speed of a bird's wings. Today it wants tomorrow, tomorrow it'll want the day after tomorrow, and on and on. Sometimes it's so full of sadness that it needs to be refreshed. That's when the great shepherd comes and refreshes it. Then there's peace. And then it's Sunday. The blue sky is Sunday, the forest, the meadows, the flowers, the birds, Father, Mother – all is Sunday then.

> "Even though I walk through the valley of the shadow of death,
> I fear no evil. Your rod and your staff comfort me."

The valley of the shadow of death! No, no, no, not there!

Annele doesn't want to hear that, doesn't want to see that. What's that to her? But she *must* see it. The soul wants it. Even the valley of the shadow of death. The soul opens its invisible eyes and looks. It not only looks, it has already entered there. The earth opens like the covers of a book, fathomless walls plummet downward. Deeper, deeper! Down to where there is nothing but black caverns and piles of rocks. Frost and darkness. Ravines rise steeply. The soul no longer sees the greenery of the earth or the brightness of the blue sky. It rushes from one end to the other. It roams about lost, cannot find the way. What will save it from such great darkness, from this abyss?

Your rod and your staff. Suddenly there is a flash of light, like lightning. The golden staff of the great shepherd reaches down. From the very roof of heaven, it reaches down to the depths of the valley of death. And the soul soars upward with it as though up a golden staircase, back to the greenery or earth, the blue of the sky.

> "You prepare a table before me in the presence
> of my enemies, you anoint my head with oil,
> my cup overflows."

Out of the valley of death! Out, out! The earth is the earth again. The earth is a green hall with the sky as its roof. Snowy white tables. Everybody is seated around them. Father, Mother, her brother and sister, dear old Granny and the other people of Spring Farm. They all have golden goblets in their hands. God's servants, dressed in white, girded with golden belts, walk around pouring sweet, sweet birch sap into the goblets. Oh, how delicious the birch sap tastes! There's none like it even on the hills of Spring Farm. Even big grandfather birch has none like it.

> "Goodness and mercy shall follow me
> all the days of my life, and I shall dwell
> in the house of the Lord for ever."

How could it be otherwise! They're going to dwell in the house of the Lord! This is where it is, this is the house of the Lord. This is where they are going to dwell. Tall green trees, thick shrubs, a sunlit field all in bloom rocked by gentle breezes. This is where we'll stay.

Annele presses her cheek to the ground. It is damp as though with sweet tears. It smells like honey. Dear, dear earth!

"Let's go now, child!"

Mother has risen to her feet, shakes out her scarf, ties it around her head.

"Well, did you rest your feet?" asks Father. "You're not thirsty, are you?"

Yes. Annele is terribly thirsty. Birch sap from a golden goblet would make her unutterably happy, but she knows: you can't see the birch sap with your visible eyes, it's not running any more, for Pentecost is drawing near, but there's nothing else to drink here in the woods. She'll have to be patient until they reach Chisel Farm.

Father takes one of her hands, Mother the other one. Dapples of sunlight appear, disappear and mingle in the silken net of shadows over the road. Annele pulls in her feet and, swinging from the hands of both her parents, flies over the dapples, and her heart leaps joyfully when her parents give her leave to do this. That's because it's Sunday. And because the cuckoo is singing in the forest, and round marsh marigolds and bird's eye primroses are in bloom.

Voices

Today Annele has run up and down every little path and played everyplace around the farm, but there's still a long stretch of day left and she doesn't know what to do with herself.

Well, since she doesn't know what to do with herself, Annele decides to lie down on the sunny lawn by the garden and to listen to the voices. Then she'll know what to do all right.

Voices? What voices?

Oh, there are many of them. Each one is different. They advise her, warn her, tell stories, chatter. But there are two in particular that always argue with each other. If one wants something, the other doesn't; if one is bold, the other is timid.

The demanding voice is like one of Pharaoh's lean cows. It can swallow the sun, the stars, the earth, and still not be satisfied. Until finally it swallows the reluctant voice as well, and then it has the upper hand. The upper hand? Why? – Because then Annele's hands and feet will obey it.

Annele decides to listen to what it wants today – that demanding voice. – And here's what it wants: today it needs the forest, the big, frightening forest of Spring Farm. And here's how it nags at her:

"Hey, Annele, when are you finally going to that forest? Here it is, right under your nose, within reach of your hand. So green, so glorious."

Meanwhile the reluctant voice warns her, as if wagging its finger at her.

"Don't go, Annele! How can a little kid go into such a terrible forest? In there, terror lurks behind every juniper bush. If you go inside, the terror will grow bigger, and then just wait and see what happens."

On and on they argue.

The demanding voice retorts: "The woods at Chisel Farm were big, too. How come you weren't scared there?"

The reluctant voice answers back: "The woods at Chisel Farm were full of light and you could see through them. The birches in those woods stood far apart, stout, like married men on a Sunday morning, turned toward each other. What was there to be scared of?"

The demanding voice: "And what's there to be scared of here? You're not a baby anymore, you're a big girl. Shame on you for being scared! Don't you know there are people, like old Anyus, who go into the forest at one end and come out again at the other, and nothing happens to them? How long are you going to wait, huh? You'll have to go into those woods some time, you know!"

Yes, I certainly will, thinks Annele, jumping to her feet recklessly. And immediately her hands obey, her feet obey, and she's off to the forest along with her bold voice.

"Forward, forward!" it calls to her now in that devil-may-care way it has, laughing ahead of Annele, now from a wooded hill, now from the highest sun-rocked treetop.

But Annele can't follow that madcap right away.

She has to investigate those bright green, soft pillows into which her feet sink – sink without being engulfed.

And what about the wooded hill itself, radiant with white starflowers? And those junipers squatting here, with that greenish shimmering light behind them? And what are these clumps of berry bushes with their clusters of red berries?

And the pines themselves, in cloaks as blue as the sky?

Annele walks from one to the other until she is friends with them all. Until she knows what all of them are: trees, shrubs, flowers, berry bushes, silence, and sun, until she knows what they are asking:

"Well, Annele? Aren't you scared?"

"I'm not scared," Annele boldly tells them straight to their faces and continues her climb.

Annele is at the top of the hill. Yet over there, as though across a deep lake, is a hilltop just like this one. Then another, and a third. But behind them is a wall of thick forest.

"Watch out, Annele! Something's about to happen," the fearful voice suddenly calls out to her from the furthest corner of her heart.

And it peals right in her ears:

"There's somebody coming! There's somebody coming!"

And then, growing quite faint, it goes off and hides.

Yes, somebody certainly *is* coming!

A shadow flits past behind the wingspread of a large hazel bush, a noise snaps off.

There's somebody standing behind the hazel bush.

Whichever hazel window Annele looks through – right or left or up or down – there's always a head before her eyes.

What is this mysterious something?

There's a stinging and sparkling in her eye sockets. She just hopes the tears won't come and fog her eyes, for what will she do then?

"You're not scared, are you? You're not!" the bold voice responds from somewhere nearby.

Annele shakes off the numbness, takes a step forward. All right, come out, whoever you are!

A "woof!" drops into the hazel bush like a fat fir cone. It sounds a bit like the bark of big Citron at Spring Farm. But this isn't Citron. When Citron starts barking, his woofs drop one after another like peas, while this one is quiet again, so quiet that

Annele can hear his strange breathing on the other side of the hazel leaves. The two of them stand there and breathe like this for quite a while.

"Woof!" There it goes again, numbing Annele to the tips of her toes. And this woof is fiercer, seeming to ask:

"Who are you? What are you standing there for? What do you want?"

Why does he ask those questions? What's he frightening her for? Who is this, standing there like that?

As soon as Annele takes a step sideways, the creature does, too. And now he is face to face with her – turned sideways, his little front paws pulled in. Skinny-legged, skinny-waisted, little black ears fiercely pricked. Two glimmering eyes burn at Annele, and behind his bared teeth something rumbles like a mill: Rrrrrowr!

"It's a wild animal!" thinks Annele, and her heart begins to tremble. What a wonderful, beautiful, extraordinary wild animal!

"Rrrrrowr! Rrrrrowr! You stupid girl! Run for your life!" the wild animal growls behind bared teeth. No, Annele has no intention of running away. After all, what can he do to her? – And slowly, slowly, as a sign of peace, she raises her hand.

But the forest creature recoils. A hurried "woof!" drops from his red mouth, then the bushy tail laps suddenly like a wave over his head. One leap – and he's vanished in the green gully.

And at that same instant the fearful voice jumps out of the cage of Annele's breast and cascades over her head like a surge of icy water.

"Run, Annele!"

What a good thing it is that her *pastalas* slide down the hill like the runners of a sled, that the road to the church is on the other side of the gully and its thick hazel bushes, and that the fields begin just beyond that! As soon as Annele runs out in the open field, her two quarreling voices are there too.

"See what happened?" teases the reluctant voice. "What if the big animal had grabbed you?"

"Well, what do you think that big wild animal could do to me?" the bold voice cheerfully rejoins. "Why, that big animal was just as scared as me. Scared of Annele. – That's why he ran off so fast."

"Funny!" thinks Annele. "Then why all this fear?" The animal had been afraid of her, and she of the animal. There they had stood, facing each other, while between them was what felt like a river. No way to cross to the other side, no way to touch and feel how long was the hair in the wild creature's beautiful fur, how velvety soft were his little black ears. And so he had left. They had seen each other, yes, but without getting to know each other. Fear and fierceness had come and stood between them. "Rrrrrowr!" – growled the wild animal. "Don't you come into my world!"

Still, it's a good thing that she's been to the forest. She's done something important. Now she knows that she can indeed walk inside and come out again, and that nothing bad will happen.

The forest has been conquered. The forest is her friend. And after so successful a venture, Annele has still more daring things in mind.

More tempting than the forest is the big hill at whose foot the farm lies. Annele hasn't had the courage to go near it yet.

Not because it's so steep she couldn't climb it. She could run up that hill in no time at all, in one go, but the fearful voice has always warned her not to go up there.

Because if she goes up to the very top, it tells her, she'll see things that will instantly make her heart stop. So? Even if her heart stops, she's simply got to climb the hill today. The demanding voice eggs Annele on.

Wonder what you can see from up there?

The sea maybe?

Definitely the sea! The sea is the mightiest thing Annele can imagine. Everybody talks about it, but not one person has seen it. Not even old Anyus, and she knows everything. She says she'll die without having seen the sea. Anyus merely knows the same thing as everybody else: the sea, she says, has neither beginning nor end.

How can there be something that has neither beginning nor end? That's the greatest of all miracles. And what if you can see it from the hill?

Her mind is made up! – Annele climbs the hill.

Spring Farm sinks below her feet with all its buildings and orchards, the rooftops stretch out flat. You could walk on them like walking in the yard and not feel at all scared of how terribly steep they are, the way you do when you look at them from below. Meanwhile the buildings of the neighboring farm are flattened against the ground, like a flock of crows with their wings spread out. New farms seem to grow out of the ground here, there, and everywhere: trees emerge with their tops first, and houses with chimneys and roofs. Distant herds of cattle appear to be motionless in their green pastures, like Annele's little fir-cone cows, while farms lie along the hillsides like diminutive toys in a little net of paths. So many unknown new places that she's never seen before!

Annele walks up to the very top of the hill until she can't climb any higher. A large cloud, sifting silver, has covered the sun, and along the distant borders of the shadows it casts, fields, hills, forests, farms keep rising in an endless panorama. Beyond all this, though, there is blue, blue without beginning or end.

"The sea, the sea!" But after looking more closely, the girl shakes her head. No, that can't be the sea. The blue arc expands, expands, throwing off the waves of shadows with lightning speed. The cloud cover floats away, growing gray, fading. Already, Hilltop Farm and Dale Farm again gleam in the sunlight so brightly that Annele can make out each building, each tree. There is an apple tree and a pear tree, a linden tree and a birch. A girl is running along the paths and collecting the wash from the fences. – The wide water meadow, too, begins to glow and displays people raking hay, white shirts flashing bright. – The tall pine forest begins to gleam with its rose-red, hundred-branched candlesticks. The highway runs out of the shadows, rolls shimmering down Cīpe Hill and, after climbing the next hill, shoots far off into the distance through fields of rye. Travelers in wagons and on foot move along it like black beetles, raising clouds of sand behind them.

The highway! Where is its beginning, its end? The smaller roads run from farm to farm, some veer aside, others run inside the courtyard of a farm and end there, but the big highway has no home anywhere to run to. The grown-ups say that if you follow the highway you can go to every part of the world and then come back to the place you started from. Wonder if that's really true? – thinks Annele.

They say the highway comes from the world and goes into the world.

Where is the world, though?

And suddenly it seems to the girl that a multitude of sonorous voices ring out in answer from the meadow, from the river, from the forest, from the highway as it rolls away into the distance: "Here it is, Annele, don't you see? Here it is, here is the world!"

Annele folds her hands and listens in silence.

The big wide world! There it is – where the highway goes, where the voices ring out.

Well then, ring out, ring out, all you voices!

Midsummer Day

The maids were running about hurriedly doing last-minute chores, just breezing along. They heated the oven, baked flat cakes, scrubbed the floors, tables, and benches, washed the windows.

Annele had been giving them a hand whenever she got a chance, working with the same fervor.

But now all the chores seemed to be done. Karlīne finished the last one. Resting her feet, Annele pulled them up under her on the scrubbed bench and asked Karlīne: "Midsummer Day? What *is* Midsummer Day?"

"What, you don't know yet? Are you ever a stupid girl!" Karlīne made fun of her.

"So what!" Annele retorted defiantly.

"Then get off the bench!" Karlīne tried to chase her away.

Annele wouldn't go. Karlīne gave her a good shake. She still wouldn't go. For that she now got a smarting pain in her shoulder: "All right then, don't obey! See what happens!"

The house was suddenly flooded with the smell of freshly baked flatcakes.

At break that afternoon, everybody got a tasty, fragrant flatcake with meat.

Now the day's chores were done. Līziņa and Karlīne put on clean jackets, tied their company scarves around their heads. Over her arm, each had a little basket with a ball of yarn and a knife. Annele knew: they would go down to the Tērvete River to get oak branches. But Karlīne was mad today. She wouldn't let her come, that was certain.

The girl ran outside. Stood by the kitchen garden. Waited with avid eyes. Would they really pass her by? Surely they'd call her?

Karlīne definitely wasn't going to. She hurried off at a furious pace. Līziņa followed behind. But by the big linden tree near the stable she looked back.

"Well, girl, why are you standing there dawdling? Come on! Quick, quick, so we can catch up with Karlīne."

Annele didn't need to be told twice. Oh, how well the two of them could run! Already they had almost caught up with Karlīne. If only she had waited a little bit. But she didn't.

She didn't look back till she reached the edge of the woods. She got pretty mad.

"Well, Līziņa, if you're going to drag that runt along, then goodbye, I'm not going to wait for you any longer."

She ran off down the path in a cloud of dust.

Annele choked down her sobs:

"A runt, she said I'm a runt!"

Her eyes misted over. She couldn't walk.

"Oh, go on with you, what makes you think Karlīne was calling you a runt? She meant that jackdaw, look, up in the pine tree!"

"But a jackdaw doesn't drag along, he flies."

"Then she must have meant a little beetle. See, here's one on the ground, with golden wings."

"A beetle flies, too."

"Then so will we! Let's show that Karlīne what we can do," said Līziņa cheerfully.

And so they ran through the woods out into an unfamiliar field. There was not a sign of Karlīne. Let her run! They walked on by themselves, looking for a short cut. They waded through a field of thick rye, along a narrow boundary ridge. Līziņa's head, with the sunlight on it, rose above the rye, while the ears of rye glided by above Annele's head.

The boundary ridge ended in a field of clover. There were two deer grazing in the field. They raised their heads and watched motionless to see what the approaching people would do. Would they need to run away, or was it all right to stay? When Līziņa and Annele turned off in the direction of the Tērvete bluffs, the deer began grazing peacefully again.

The bluffs were high and steep, magnificently overgrown with all kinds of deciduous trees. The most beautiful, however, were the oaks, which rose row by row where the bluffs were steepest. Oaks, oaks! Oh, how tall, how stately! Annele had never seen such trees.

Though the branches of the oak trees seemed to hang down quite close to the ground, it was hard to get near them, for the ground sloped abruptly. In vain Līziņa made a grab for the branches, leaping now from one side, now from the other. Suddenly she lost her footing. With a merry shout, she slid down the slope as if someone were dragging her, taking Annele with her in her fall. Though the sisters held on to bushes and weeds and blackberry canes, they didn't regain their balance until the very bottom, where a great flowering meadow spread before them in all its splendor. There gleamed the Tērvete River, meandering through the valley. It was closed in by the high thickly wooded bluffs. Above them grew the big pine forest. Birds twittered on the banks, wild turtledoves cooed, and a plaintive little jugging voice called louder than all the others.

"A marsh nightingale – listen! It's too bad the real one isn't singing anymore. Then you'd really be amazed!"

Annele was amazed even so. What trees there were here, what a meadow, and what majestic winding riverbanks! The birds were different, the flowers were quite different than at Spring Farm. Creeping forget-me-nots grew close together, as though woven into a cloak decorated with bright yellow and blue specks, daisies shone like huge stars, strange flowers with stalks that had golden blossoms rose high above Annele's head, and Līziņa gave them such a proud name: royal scepter!

"There are no flowers like this at Spring Farm."

"At Spring Farm, the winds roam across the hills, but here the bluff stands in the way of the great winds and protects the flowers. And if the bluff provides shelter, the sun its warmth, and the river its moisture, how could the flowers keep from blooming here in all their beauty?"

The girls climbed the bluff again, taking the path in a place where the slope was less steep. Here there was a whole thicket of young oak trees whose branches were easier to cope with; here they could take a generous tithe of the trees' dense foliage. Having gathered bunches of oak twigs from among the lower branches, Līziņa sat down on the slope of the bluff and was soon hard at work making garlands, while Annele went further up the bluff to look at the unfamiliar landscape: how different the hills, the banks, the low-lying meadows were here; and then more hills, unfamiliar farms, birch groves, forests. From two chimneys deep in fields of rye, lovely blue columns of smoke were rising straight into the air. Meanwhile over the fields in the slanting rays of the sun, the air, grown warm, rippled and trembled in tiny little waves.

"What are those chimneys over there?" asked Annele in a whisper, as though afraid to disturb the sunlit silence.

"That's Edgefield Farm. They're close relatives of ours. We'll go visit them one of these days."

The girl stood for a long, long time. Dear world! Lovely, quiet world!

She was abruptly startled when the first song shot up from the hill across the river valley:

"Jāņi, Jāņi, what is Jāņi, līgo, līgo!
Who'll be the first to celebrate it in song? līgo, līgo!
Who'll be the first to celebrate it in song? līgo, līgo!
First shepherds, then plowmen, līgo, līgo!"

Immediately, there was an answering voice from the other hill:

"First shepherds, then plowmen, līgo, līgo!
Last of all the young girls, līgo, līgo!
And then the old grandmother, līgo, līgo!
Picking the herbs of Jāņi, līgo, līgo!"

And now the singing was coming from nearby, from far off, from this side of the river, from the other. The shepherds and cowherds were singing, all of them.

"Just listen! This is the beginning of Jāņi! The shepherds and cowherds start off the celebration with their songs, you see."

At that very moment, someone began singing lustily in the ravine not far from the sisters.

"O Jānīti, son of god, līgo, līgo!
What have you brought with you in your wagon, līgo, līgo!
Beaded finery for the young women, līgo, līgo!
Marten fur caps for the young men, līgo, līgo!"

"Hear that singing? That's Karlīne! Can't be anybody else. That's her voice all right – booming like a black grouse's. Yoohoo, Karlīne, yoohoo! We're over here."

There was an answering shout from Karlīne. She came out of the trees right near them. "Yoohoo! Think I didn't hear you? I wasn't far from you, I just didn't let on I was here, because I wanted to finish my garlands before you. And that's why mine are a lot prettier! Look! Got any like these?"

Karlīne gave a shake to the garlands that were strung on her arm. Then from among them she took one she had kept hidden, and tossed it on Annele's head.

"That's for you, for calling you a runt!" she said, laughing heartily.

The garland was made of strawberry stalks and leaves, thick as could be, full of juicy red berries.

How nice Karlīne was.

"Wait just a little bit, then I'll be finished too, and we can go together," said Līziņa.

"I'm not waiting another minute. There's still the gate to be decorated, the cattle to bring in, and I've got to give the men their supper. If Ingus doesn't have his supper on the table on time, he'll raise the roof. Tonight of all nights, when there are the lamps to get ready!"

The rye stirred as Karlīne hurried off along the boundary ridge. You could hear her singing even at a distance:

"Dieviņš walked through a field of rye, līgo, līgo!
With a gray cloak, līgo, līgo!
Walk slowly, walk gently, Dieviņš, līgo, līgo!
Don't harm its flowering, līgo, līgo!"

Now Līziņa, too, was finished with her garlands. One for Granny made out of nothing but oak leaves, one for Father of red clover alternating with white, Mother's out of blue cornflowers, one for Uncle Ansis made with daisies. Now they could go home.

On the opposite bank, the pine trees were beginning to glow red. In the greenish red sky, over the dark forest, a bright white crescent moon began to gleam. A cloud of fine white fog concealed one of the osiers by the river.

Līgo, līgo, līgo! – echoed incessantly in the air from hill to hill, far and near.

The birch groves and fields of grain stood hushed as if holding their breath, as if listening joyfully to the lovely sound of human voices.

Three Tailors

For a long time now, little Jurītis's mother Zete had been complaining that her husband needed new linen pants for the hay harvest, but there wasn't a single tailor in sight. When there had been no need for a tailor, she said, one of those bums would no sooner leave than another would be coming in the door, for there were plenty of them around, that's for sure, with the Jewish town of Žagare practically next door, but now there was not one to be seen.

One day, as she was again grumbling like this – speak of the devil! – Joske and little Joskele came in the door. Joske was a rather highly thought-of tailor, still quite young, but he passed Joskele off as his son. He did this as a joke, for the little Jewish boy was only his apprentice. As a joke, too, he called him Joskele, his own name, although the boy's real name was completely different. So everyone else also called him that, and people used to say that maybe big Joske would teach little Joskele all kinds of tricks and foolishness, but the one thing he'd never teach him was the tailor's trade.

As soon as Joske came into the house, little Joskele disappeared like a needle in a haystack. Out of big Joske's sight he became feverishly active. Having gathered kids his own age around him with surreptitious nods and calls, he bedazzled their eyes and ears with all sorts of tricks he had picked up at various farms the way a fur coat picks up bits of straw. His pockets were full of colorful bits of cloth, colored glass, horseshoe nails, empty spools, and large quantities of pieces of chalk of all sizes. The chalk made the boy's pockets dusty, like little sacks of flour. In addition, he also had a good handful of greasy trumps, deuces, treys, and fivers. He handled the chalk and the trumps like some great magician. With his eyes blindfolded, he would guess which trump was in another person's hand, while no one was ever able to guess the one he had himself. He could quickly turn a glass filled with water upside down without spilling a single drop, and he would draw mysterious curves and forked figures with one stroke, without taking his hand away, but just let anybody try to do the same! They couldn't. He would make chalk marks on the table and count each accent with his eyes shut:

/   /   /   /

How many marks do you think I'll make?

/   /   /   /

I'll make fifteen in a row.

/   /   /   /
If you doubt me, take a look,
/   /   /   /
Fifteen marks is all it took!

And when *he* did it, there'd be no more than fifteen, while there was just no way the others could get rid of that sixteenth mark, no matter how hard they tried. Because of all these skills, Joskelis was very popular with the kids at all the farms. He was in no hurry, for big Joske would stay for the noon meal whichever farm he stopped at. Big Joske, just like Little Joske, never got tired of gossiping, and other people never got tired of him either. He acted as a matchmaker between the young maidservants and the male farmhands, at the same time offering himself as a bridegroom, proudly showing off, throwing back his bushy head and raising his chin, which jutted forward with its neatly trimmed wedge-shaped little beard like a billy goat's. He could tell you all the news, he knew by heart every new ballad about all sorts of well-known personalities, he would dance on the clay floor or even on the table when he was really crazy; at times he could so enrage the maids that they would chase him with ladles and broomsticks, but what do you know? – soon he would make peace with them again, and then he was their favorite, more so than other Jews.

It seemed that Joske had come just in time to sew Zangus a pair of pants, and you would have thought he would start work right away, but no! He sat and gossiped, and it didn't even occur to him to think how close it was getting to the hay season, and that Zangus would have nothing to wear. He haggled with Zete: he might sew them, and then again he might not. If Zete paid him half a ruble, he might sew them.

What, pay him half a ruble? Not Zete! Such an exorbitant sum! She'd have to be off her head to do a thing like that. No, no, nothing doing. She was still in her right mind.

It doesn't cost more than twenty kopecks to sew a pair of linen pants, hay season or not.

So what if it costs twenty kopecks! Joske doesn't need those twenty kopecks. He doesn't need Zete's half ruble, either. Even if she were to give it to him. He is a tailor who works for farmers and single farm hands, not married farm hands. He is accustomed to work sitting down, on the single men's big table, but who's going to let him sew Zangus's pants on the big table? For Zangus is a married man. No, he'd rather not sew the pants at all. Or is he supposed to crawl into Zete's corner of the house to sew them? No, that would bring him disgrace. Why, even the dogs would laugh.

And Joske himself laughs heartily.

Zete doesn't laugh at all, she's mad. She's really and truly mad, and now she mercilessly lays into Joske: she doesn't need Joske at all, she says, him and his goatee. Why, last night on her way home old Anyus saw Slow Jaņķelis trudging down the highway. No doubt he's spent the night at the neighbors', and he is bound to come to Spring Farm today. Where else would he be going, after all?

Fine. So let Slow Jaņķelis come and sew stuff for fifteen kopecks if he likes. It's no skin off Joske's back. "He'll sew fifteen kopecks' worth for you, and he'll eat fifty kopecks' worth of your food," Joske says gleefully, making Zete even more furious.

And Jaŋkelis does arrive. As the sun's heat becomes more oppressive toward noon, sure enough, there he comes, up from the valley along the narrow little path from the neighboring farm, climbing slowly as if he had to measure each step he takes in the world with his ell. But he isn't measuring steps. He whirls his ell, which hangs from a string, around him, whizzing like the wheel of a windmill, thus fighting off Citron, who jumps about him barking fiercely, but runs from the whizzing object for fear that it will hurt his nose. In back of Jaŋkelis, facing the other way, comes his *ingele*, teasing the dog with a stick.

Slow Jaŋkelis hasn't been at Spring Farm since before Easter. Usually he had arranged things so that he would get to celebrate Shabbes here. But once, on a Friday night, as he was warming himself by the kitchen fire, Granny had asked him to throw a piece of firewood on the fire once in a while to warm up the water for starting the batter for bread. Jaŋkelis hadn't answered a word, but when Granny had come back into the kitchen after doing her chores, she saw: the fire had completely gone out, while Jaŋkelis sat on the stack of firewood black and blue with cold. "Oh you lazy Jew, is this how you keep the fire going?" Granny had exclaimed angrily, but Jaŋkelis had answered, "Oy, how can I break the commandments on my Shabbes just for the sake of your measly fire?" – "But you want to eat my bread, and it's got to be baked first," Granny had scolded, and ever since then she had forbidden Jaŋkelis to come observe his Shabbes at Spring Farm. This was quite a long time ago, however, and Jaŋkelis thinks that that time is forgotten and that nobody will hold it against him anymore.

When Slow Jaŋkelis came into the house and heard there was work waiting for him here, he immediately gave a startled jump and turned back toward the door. Sew? No! He wasn't going to sew. He was going to Springupi Farm. This was his constant excuse when he didn't feel like working. And he never felt like working. Springupi was a farm far beyond the forest. Nobody could know what unending labors awaited him there, but no doubt there was nothing of the kind there, for he would hurry away from Springupi Farm the same way if the people there threatened

to give him something to do, saying that he had to go to some other farm immediately. He never did a stroke of work anywhere, but if he was unavoidably forced to take on a job, he would leave it half done and flee hell-bent for leather.

When Slow Jaŋķelis heard that Joske, too, had been offered the sewing job but hadn't accepted it, he calmed down. Now he could safely stay. If Joske wouldn't sew the pants for Zangus, then neither would he – not for fifteen, nor twenty, nor even for fifty kopecks. Why should he? He'd go to another farm where there were piles of work. But for the time being he won't go anywhere, for it is close to noon and the sun is unbearably hot. If Joske is staying, then he will too. He stretches out at full length on the single men's bench, nestles his head in his hand and listens as Joske tells him a funny story, rolling Yiddish words around in his mouth and making his goatee bob up and down. Jaŋķelis, sprawling lazily, laughs and laughs at all this, while his narrow eyes, shedding tears, almost sink into his chubby cheeks. But Zete, walking in and out, angrily looks at the tailors, thinking, "Well! Those lazy bums are just asking for it!" But what can she do? She is only a farmhand's wife and the ruler over her own corner. Nothing more.

And then, on top of everything, Zangus comes back from the mill at the hour of noon, while after him, elegantly waving his ell, runs yet another Jewish tailor whom Zangus has met on the road and has immediately invited and hired to sew him a pair of pants. This is the third well-known master of the needle, nicknamed Speedy Jaŋkelis.

Speedy Jaŋkelis, like Slow Jaŋkelis, did not have a good reputation as a worker. Although he did not avoid work, but practically tore it out of people's hands wherever he found any, those who knew him well did not like to give him jobs to do. But Zangus did not know him, and Zete was glad that now the two Jews who were there before him could no longer pester her with their haggling. Now there would be someone who would cut the ground from under them and do the job, which is why she at once brought Speedy the cloth. Speedy, without even casting a glance at his compatriots, grabbed the table, pulled it out into the middle of the room, tossed the bale of cloth on it and – slash, slash! – hacked into it with his big scissors. He had promised he would sew Zangus a pair of pants over the noon break, for the mowers were to leave that very day to go help out a distant neighbor.

Now, of course, he had to hurry. But the two other tailors fooled around and kept making fun of Zete. Slow Jaŋkelis said Speedy would certainly sew the pants over the noon break, but they'd last just until Zangus drove out of the yard, while Joske even claimed that was too long a time, they'd last until Zangus finished harnessing the horse. He was ready to lay a wager on this. If he lost, he'd give one sewing needle and one darner out of his collection of needles to Zete, while if Zete lost she should give him some trifle, like a calfskin, a lambskin, and a few handfuls of pig bristles. Thus he fibbed and importuned Zete, insisting on shaking hands to confirm the wager, and although she was evasive, slapped his fingers, and would not hear of such a wager, he insisted: the bet was on now, and now he had to wait for Speedy to finish the pants in order to see who would win. What was he to do in the meantime, though? He and Slow Jaŋkelis decided to crawl into the hay barn and have a quick nap, because there was no sense in tramping off to another farm right in the noonday heat, either.

Everybody went off to their midday rest. Only the flies buzzed, and Speedy sewed, pouncing on the work like a hawk. The hand with the needle flashed so fast that a breeze streamed around Speedy as though around the sails of a windmill. He didn't even give himself a moment of rest to have a bite to eat. When his little son had finished cooking their food and brought in the little pan, Speedy snatched a few bites and rushed back to work again. When Joske and Slow Jaŋkelis came in a couple of hours later stretching and yawning, Speedy was already working on the pants buttons. But they stationed themselves each on one side of him and glared like wolves as Speedy rapidly stitched each button to the cloth.

As soon as this had been done, the crafty tailors both simultaneously, each from a different direction, quickly stuck their ells in the pants and raised them aloft suddenly as though on pikes. Speedy kicked, threatened, yelled, fought them off, his restless eyes darting from one to the other, but there was nothing he could do. "Zete, Zete, Zete!" shouted Joske.

Zete came running.

"What's going on here?"

"I just wanted to prove to you that I won my bet," Joske said and, seizing one leg of the pants, tossed the other to Slow Jaŋķelis. They both pulled hard on each end, like stretching a rope. Rrrrip! – went the seams.

"Oy, gevalt!" Speedy grabbed his head in his hands.

Zete didn't know what to think.

"Crazy Jews, are you out of your mind?"

But Joske just kept pulling on the pants, gleefully shouting, "They're ripping, they're ripping, they're ripping!"

"Crazy Jews, crazy Jews, if you don't let go you're going to catch it!" Zete, furious now and at a loss for words, threatened, grabbing hold of the newly finished pants with her strong hands as well.

"I'll show you! Let go, will you?"

But nobody let go. And since all of them were pulling at the same time as hard as they could, the pants had to tear.

And tear they did. Right across the seams, with a great noise, the new fabric ripped apart.

When that happened, all three threw down the pants on the table.

"Now you've done it!" gasped Zete. She was so angry she couldn't say another word.

"There, you see that I won my bet, but I'll make you a present of it, I don't want anything from you," Joske boasted like the rogue he was, secretly looking around for his bundle, for once Zete in her fury had had time to think things over and started calling for her husband Zangus, the laugh would be on the tailors. Slow Jaŋķelis also knew this and he, too, tied his bundle on his back as fast as he was able.

"Jews, Jews – why do you yell: Jews! If it weren't for the Jews, then where would you get a good laugh?" Joske put his head up close to Zete's and laughed in her face. Then he disappeared out the door.

Zete snatched Speedy Jaŋķelis's ell and tore off in pursuit of him, but she was already too late.

The ripped-up pants made a vest and pants for little Jurītis, and Speedy cut a new pair of pants for Zangus. But while he sewed them, Zete sat by his side and kept a sharp eye on him to make sure he would sew the seams so they'd last.

The Sower

"Come along, Annele, we're going to see Father."

"Where is Father?"

"In the field by the highway, on the other side of the hill."

There's nothing Annele would like better. She is eager to go, hills or no hills, no matter how far away.

Her mother cannot give her a hand to hold – her hands are full of bundles. Annele hangs on to her mother's skirts and lets herself be pulled up the hill.

The top of the hill curves inward like a trough. The blue sky arches over the trough's shallow rim, tucked around by woods. All the stems of the overblown flowers, the dry grasses, the rye stubble, even the trees and the bushes in the woods are spun full of light, silvery threads. Many of them have nothing to cling to. The gossamer threads stream, floating in the air, stick to their clothes, their hair as they walk. There is still white dew on the ground at the edge of the woods.

A shadow sweeps by overhead with a rustling noise. Something that sounds like a call: "Goodbye, Annele!" Annele throws back her head and looks up at the sky. A black triangle, undulating slightly, glides away into the blue distance.

"What are those, Mother?"

"Migrant birds. They're fleeing from the winter."

"Where are they fleeing to?"

"To the warm countries."

"To the warm countries? How warm? As warm as Midsummer?"

"Maybe. I've heard say they have no snow or frost there."

"No snow or frost! So there's always anemones and bird's eye primroses in bloom there, and the cuckoo sings all the time?"

"I can't tell you, I've never been there. But those who have tell wonderful stories."

"Wonderful stories? Why don't we go to the warm countries, Mother?"

"We have no money. Those who have no money have no way to go to the warm countries."

"Do the birds have money, then?"

"Get along with you, little silly!"

"All right, all right. But how do the birds know the way? Do they have money under their wings?"

Mother doesn't reply.

"What's money like? And where does it come from? Can we never ever get any?"

"Don't ask so many questions, there's a good girl! Why don't you look where Father is?"

By now they've crossed over the hill. Here, a level field stretches toward the sun. The field is quite black, freshly harrowed. A person wearing a white shirt and white trousers is walking down the field.

"Is that man over there Father, then?"

"Don't you recognize him?"

"What made him grow so short? He's the same size as me!"

"That's because we're at the top of the hill, while Father is down below. From the top of a hill everything looks smaller. But the person who's standing at the top looks bigger."

"Why is that?"

"How can I tell you all those things?"

Annele stands there in great amazement. How oddly Father walks! With his feet lifted high, light, as though they were strung on a string. When he lifts one foot, his hand slides into a big basket that hangs around his neck; when he lifts the other foot, the hand, quick as lightning, throws a bit of gray mist. The mist at once sinks into the ground. Not once does the foot step down faster or the hand slow down its throw. And so it goes, on and on. What is he throwing? It could be tiny birds the size of specks of dust. One-and! – he grabs from the basket. Two-and – he scatters into the field. One-and! Two-and! One-and! Two-and! – counts Annele. And her own feet, too, seem to rise and fall like Father's feet. When Father has reached the end of his

walk, he wheels around as nimbly as a hoop on its round rim and lightly, lightly walks back along the same path again. One-and! Two-and! One-and! Two-and!

"Come along, lass, what are you looking at?"

"Why does Father dance like that?"

Annele bursts out laughing.

"He isn't dancing, child, he's sowing new bread. Don't laugh, that's holy work."

Annele falls silent.

"Holy work? That's holy work?"

Now they've climbed down the hill to Father.

At the edge of the field on the boundary ridge, Mother spreads a white linen towel, takes out a spoon and bread, puts down a jug of gruel with clotted milk. But Father won't come and eat until all the seed in his basket has been sown. Then he comes over to them smiling, walking at his accustomed pace.

"Well, have you come to give me a hand? What do you think, little one, can you take over for me? Here's the basket!"

And just for fun he makes as if to hang the basket around the girl's neck. Holding it by its straps, he lets it slide lightly over her shoulders. To Annele it feels like a millstone. By no stretch of her imagination can she see how she would reach the other rim of it with her little hand.

"Ow, ow, ow, how heavy it is!"

"And that's when the basket is empty. But when Father fills it to the brim and carries it all day long until the big fields are sown, then there'd really be a reason for yelling that it's heavy."

Yes, Annele realizes that. She certainly couldn't dance up and down the field along with Father with the basket hanging from her shoulders. That is work she could never do.

Father wipes his forehead and his face, lets his eyes wander over the blue field of the sky and calmly begins to eat. Gossamer threads flutter gleaming around him.

Another call high above them. The rustle of white wings.

All three of them throw their heads back. They watch for a long time, until the moving, living triangle sinks out of sight behind the sun, beyond the horizon.

"Migrant birds."

"Wild geese. I've heard them calling all morning. Going to be an early winter."

"Then will the sun turn cold?" asks Annele.

"That's right."

"There's no way we can get to see the warm countries, the way the birds do," says Mother in a mournful sort of voice.

"That's all right. Our warm country will come back like a migrant bird, you'll see. We'll put our scythes to work right here, in this black field, next year. The ears of wheat will swish and rustle like a forest. We'll take them and tie them into sheaves. There'll be new bread. That'll be a sight to see. Right, lass?" asks Father, looking straight at Annele.

"Yes," Annele answers, laughing as she looks into his eyes.

As long as Father works in the fields of Spring Farm, the warm country is right here.

The Logger

For about two weeks running, the room where the farmhands lived had been full of loggers who were here to cut sleepers. They would come back from the big woods at dark with muddy feet, their beards white with hoarfrost, and flood the room with dampness and discomfort. The big room hummed like a beehive when, in their rough voices, the loggers told of their adventures.

But now they were gone. The room had been swept and fumigated with junipers. Only one of the crew, who was sick, had remained behind. He lay on a bunk in the corner. As soon as he got well he would be leaving. Against his long hair and his bushy beard trimmed in the shape of a semicircle, his face – rosy, with a whiter, shiny forehead – stood out as a recumbent half-moon stands out against rain clouds. He did not wear bandannas like the others, but a quilted collar made of black lasting, a short jacket of gray cloth, and nankeen breeches whose knees were shiny where the breeches ended in tall jackboots, as though they had fed on half a pound of grease a day. He did not talk much, but when he did, he always knew better and told everybody what to do or, for the most part, admonished them. He himself never flaunted his adventures and his knowledge, but it seemed that everybody believed in his superiority and his better judgment.

Apparently the bearded man was not aware that his companions had gone away and left him there alone. He lay in a heavy sleep, only occasionally uttering a deep moan. The people of the farm went over to him from time to time, and in a loud voice, as though he needed to be called back from somewhere, asked him how he was doing, offered him milk gruel, pease dumplings, cabbage, potato and herring, and whatever other delicacies each of them had, but the sick man never responded; only Karlīne, the maid, complained she could hardly keep the big yellow earthenware pitcher filled with water.

The clay floor had been swept, the loggers had left, and Līziņa had a book about Rose of Pine Hill! Tonight they'd have a fine time reading aloud.

The maids brought their spinning wheels out into the middle of the room, Līziņa sat down under the lamp, while Annele squatted down on the floor, snuggling up close to her so that Mother would not notice her, or else she would be sent to bed.

One spinning wheel after another grew silent. Only the maids were still spinning and Līziņa was still reading. There was still a lot left to hear about Rose of Pine Hill when Granny came out and urged them to go to sleep.

The maids did not want to sleep yet. Never mind, never mind – after all, you can't bake bread from sleep. One of them had to finish her spindle, the other to cast off her mitten. Jobs that couldn't be put off till tomorrow.

"You'll just waste my kerosene. Look, the can is almost empty," Grandmother pointed at the lamp.

"Can" was Grandmother's name for a lamp; it was a general term she used for all sorts of newfangled inventions.

"What do we need the lamp for," exclaimed Luze, the herd girl, "can't we burn some kindling?"

"Kindling, indeed. Do you even know how to make kindling?" said Grandmother in a mournful sort of voice.

Luze jumped to her feet.

"I've got a whole armful of kindling in the kitchen. All shiny with resin like silk ribbons and sticky as honey. It crackles like anything when it burns. Just let me have the holder!"

"Do I have a holder?!"

"Yes, you do, hidden under your bed. I saw it myself. The handle's been taken off, but the holder is under the bed."

The maids laughed, for they knew where Granny kept the holder.

"Aren't you a cheeky one! Well, all right, take it, I don't mind! Just don't stay awake till cockcrow!" Granny warned them.

Now the maids pressed closer around the torch, and the spinning wheels whirred peacefully as an accompaniment to Līziņa's sonorous voice. As though on silent butterfly wings, their thoughts flew away with Rose of Pine Hill, loved and suffered with her. Annele did not take her eyes off Līziņa's face: Rose of Pine Hill must have looked exactly like that. Līziņa read, herself enraptured. Her face shone, her expression changed from moment to moment, her finely chiseled nostrils trembled, the circlet of golden-brown curls that glistened around her forehead slowly rose and fell from the heat of the flaming kindling. Once in a while she raised her long black lashes and her eyes met Annele's. Then they understood each other, they were far away in another world altogether, just the two of them. Neither Zete nor Karlīne nor Luze could follow them there. Only the two of them were there with Rose of Pine Hill; and when Rose was once more restored to honor and good fortune, she accompanied them out through her castle gate, and there stood her coach, a glass coach with snow-white horses, and she invited Annele and Līziņa to get in. And so they drove off. The coach turned into a little white cloud. The little white cloud rose – rose with a swaying motion; Annele slipped, fell, and tightly grabbed Līziņa's hands in her terror.

"Līziņa!"

The maids burst into loud laughter. Līziņa was just closing the book.

"And you said you were going to stay awake! Get up now! Let's go beddy-bye."

"No, no, no! I'm not sleepy at all! – Are the maids going to bed already, too?"

The maids were preparing for something mysterious. On tiptoe they carried the spinning wheels off into the corners. Again on tiptoe they hurried back. They whispered to each other softly, softly. What on earth were they going to do?

They pulled the piece of kindling wood from its holder, stepped on the fire to put it out, carried the kindling holder into the corner.

In the broad ribbon of light that the moon, standing right in the window, unrolled into the room, the floor was left covered with silver when the kindling went out.

The branching, snow-covered apple tree in front of the window was full of moonbeams; the faint blue light of the moon, strewn with snow spangles, sparkled like diamonds, and the sky over the dark pinewoods was filled with shining stars.

The maids and Līziņa took up their places in a square, a little distance apart from each other, and began to dance. In the moonlight first one head, then another, then a third flashed into view, disappeared in the darkness; reappeared once more, so fast that Annele's eyes grew dizzy. Then all four took hands, whirled around so fast that the wind whistled past their ears. They let go, held on to each other, their arms stretched out full length, again pulled together in a tangle, spun around in pairs. Līziņa called and gave commands. Her long braids twisted and spun, now at one end of the room, now at the other: she glided along almost imperceptibly, as though her feet were not touching the floor. Finally, exhausted from dancing and laughing, the maids dropped on the bed and called, as they tried to catch their breath:

"I can't go on, I simply can't."

"I can't either!"

"Stop, Līziņa, stop!"

The maids gasped for breath and laughed. Līziņa remained by the window standing in the light. She was not laughing, her breath could not be heard, all one saw was her breast rising and falling. Her face was as enraptured as before when she was reading, her lips were half open, her nostrils trembled, her eyes, large, silent, and shining, gazed as though they could see no one. Then her figure once more began to glide in the dark – in the light, in the dark – in the light, with admirable speed, ethereal as a swirl of mist. The maids nudged each other, fell silent, watched. And it seemed to Annele as though together with Līziņa and the mild light of the moon a flood of mysterious dancers had entered the room, as though a throng of little white shoes poured over the windowsill and the room were filled with airy, winged, snow-white shining figures. It was as though little clouds of snow were whirling around Līziņa. The forked branches of the apple trees in the orchard, the glittering thatched roofs – everything was teeming with them.

If only Luze hadn't come in with kindling in her hand! Swish, and the white ribbon of moonbeams that sparkled and teemed as if alive, stretched out silent and cold. The shining little white shoes melted away, vanished, or stuck to the frost flowers on the windowpane like soft white bits of down!

Luze was holding something else as well – a green earthenware pot with handles. She held it up high for them to see, smiling a greedy, mysterious smile.

"Guess what I have!"

"Something to eat? Oh, how I want some! Let's have it! What have you got there?"

"*Pigarica*! It's sweet and sour like wine. There's honey in it! Come over here! I'll let you all have some."

They all crowded around Luze and, sharing a spoon, ate the delicious midnight meal licking their lips – rye bread crumbled into sweetened water.

Suddenly the bearded man in the corner gave a strange sort of groan. Karlīne went over to him, listened.

The sick man was waving his hands around restlessly.

"Would you like a drink of water?" asked Karlīne.

No answer.

They all waited. It was obvious that the sick man was oblivious of them.

"He doesn't seem to want a drink. Maybe it'll pass by itself. – It's high time for us to go to bed, though!" urged Karlīne.

Suddenly the sick man uttered another drawn-out, weak, wheezing groan.

"Lordy! What's that? That's not a good sign!" Zete was startled.

"We've got to wake up the others! – Look how he's twitching!"

"And how he wheezes – and wheezes – . You're right. I just hope – do you suppose he's dying?"

"Oh dear, don't even mention it, don't say it, I'm scared! Luze, light the kindling! We have to wake Grandmother."

But Granny was already slowly opening the door.

"Oh you shameless creatures you," she scolded, "a person lets them have a bit of freedom and they stay up half the night and raise a hullabaloo. Off to bed with you!"

"How can we? – Look at the bearded man. – Twitching... moaning..."

"And he slept so quietly all night, too," said Luze, as though reproaching the sick man for disturbing them.

Granny went up to the sick man, looked in his face.

"Go wake up your father," she told Līziņa.

"What is it, what is it?" asked the maids.

"He's dying!"

"Good Lord! Dying!"

"That's just what I thought, that it wasn't a good sign. Dying."

"Shall we wake up the whole household?"

"Wake them up, of course! How can we let a person pass away like this? It's a holy hour."

"I wouldn't go in that kitchen again if you killed me," whispered Luze, trembling.

The maids woke up the household.

"Get up, get up! The man's dying!"

"What is it? Who's dying?"

"The stranger's dying. Get up!"

"God have mercy on us sinners! Dying? Who'd have thought it? Why, just yesterday – – And now – dying! –"

Everybody gathered around the dying man.

They went and got their hymnbooks.

"Are we going to start singing already?"

"No, let him pass over into God's peace first. He's hardly conscious now in any case. Let God himself speak with his soul. – All we can do is humbly bend our knees before God – " Granny said softly.

"Wonder if there isn't some way we could still help him?" somebody hazarded a question.

"Yes, but how? Just try fighting with that strong a power! If death comes, it comes."

For a little while, everyone fell silent. And then there were whispered remarks.

"It won't be long now."

"Maybe till cockcrow."

"Not at all! He's going to pass away any minute!"

"And nobody knows where on earth he's from, from what end of the world he came here."

"It's as though he came out of the forest and is now going back to the forest again."

"Isn't that the way with all of us?"

"I'm sure someone will probably come look for him when the district advertises that he's dead."

"What does he care if anybody comes to look for him or not."

"It's terrible to die like that in a strange place – no kinfolk near or anything."

"Why? The sand in our churchyard is no worse than anywhere else, is it? And it's not as though we won't show him our last respects."

"Shush now, shush!" Grandmother interrupted the speakers. "Let's say the Our Father."

They all slowly folded their hands and went down on their knees.

Then, slowly, they began to sing the hymn for the dying. – –

Annele lay next to Līziņa, in Grandmother's little room. The moon, which had come around the corner of the house, began spreading its white sheets in the little window. But Annele wasn't sleepy: her heart felt all trembly – she couldn't tell whether from horror or from grief. Stealthily she lifted her head to see whether Līziņa was asleep. No. Her eyes were wide open; it seemed to the girl that big tears were rolling down her cheeks onto the pillow. "Līziņa!" the girl whispered. And pressed close to her big sister. And that's how the two of them fell asleep, in each other's arms.

Granny

Granny spoke little and did not like to listen to long speeches, especially if they were about work. On such occasions she might curtly say, "Talking doesn't help, it's doing that helps," – and, while the maids were still arguing which of them should go to the spring to fetch water, she'd already taken the yoke and the buckets and was going down the hill at a run with tiny steps, like a little partridge. But it was hard to climb back up the hill, and even harder to get over the threshold with full buckets. Then she would sometimes sigh heavily: "Oh strength, strength, I wonder what happened to you?"

Annele did a lot of thinking about the strength Granny said she had lost. And as sometimes happens, she once involuntarily said her thoughts out loud: "Strength, Granny's strength, what happened to you?" Old Anyus overheard her and answered:

"Yes, what did happen to Granny's strength? She used it all up right here, moving those big mountains."

"Moving mountains? Where?" Annele asked in surprise.

"Right here at Spring Farm."

"Were there big mountains? Bigger than the hills we've got today?"

"Well, what do you think!"

"And what happened to them?"

"Look, there goes one of them now," pointed Anyus, raising her cane.

But the one that was going past was Annele's father. Now she was puzzled. But Anyus went on.

"And your granny had six just like your father. And two daughters. And a couple more, but they're buried in the graveyard now. And then there were cattle and fields, miles and miles to run. And grain to thresh, and no time to sleep. And then the people who came in from outside: Gypsies, Jews, beggars, not to mention those who came seeking help from all over, to see her about their illnesses and troubles. You tell me if all of that wasn't just as big a job as moving mountains. Why, a king in his palace couldn't have done more than your granny has done in this world. She'd have walked five times around the earth by now if anyone had measured her steps."

Now of course Annele understood what sort of mountains Granny had had to move.

Granny stands on the threshold between two ages and holds the keys to both. Whatever she says, whatever she does, it always turns out differently than when other people do it. And whatever she does, whatever she says, is eagerly received by a little somebody who follows her at a run and observes everything especially closely – Annele, the little daughter of Granny's son.

From the threshold of the farmhouse at Spring Farm, many little paths radiated like branches from their root. But there were three in particular along which the distance Granny had walked, had anyone counted her steps throughout her lifetime, would have measured five times around the earth, as Anyus said. One such path went down to the spring. For a long, long succession of years, Granny had walked along it carrying buckets of water up the hill. In summer, during work hours, when the maids were busy out in the fields, she had to single-handedly look after a large household of children and farm workers, and the cattle as well. Many other women who carried yokes of water buckets had come and gone, while she always remained the same, the one who refreshed and tended everyone, cared for and thought of them all.

The second path went straight across the field into the woods and then steeply up the hill to the road that led toward the church. How many countless times Granny had walked along it! Church was the only distant place she went to, it was her chance to visit, it was town, it was the place to meet distant relatives and acquaintances. And no matter how weary and feeble she was, church was a place one was always supposed to walk to. To wear out a horse on a Sunday was tantamount to a sin. They hadn't ever done it in her young days, and in her old age she adhered strictly to the way things had been then, and refused to alter these praiseworthy traditions.

The third path, which by Annele's time had become overgrown, led to the summer kitchen. The place where it had been was still marked by two remaining stones. Around them grew the young apple trees Uncle Ansis had planted, for this is where he had laid out a new orchard. When Granny was a young farm wife, the squire had had a clay hut – but without a hearth then – hastily put up as living quarters to replace the farmhouse that had burned down. The summer kitchen had been a similar hut daubed with clay, set up with a chimney and iron hooks as the place for a fire and for cooking food. It was to this drafty hut that the young farm wife's daily chores had brought her for more than ten years, winter and summer, from morning till night.

On winter mornings particularly, getting up at cockcrow, she had been the first to go there, wondering anxiously whether the winds and the frost had not found and extinguished the sparks so carefully covered and preserved deep under the ashes of the hearth. It was bad when the fire had to be started with the help of a tinderbox and flint, for in those days matches were hardly known. But if some good spirit had preserved the sparks and, revived by warm breath, they burst into flame crackling at the end of a dry piece of kindling or in brown juniper twigs, and the light swept the spooky shadows clean off the black walls of the hut, then this meant a joyful start to the entire coming day, its work, and its cares.

To lock the *klētis*, to make sure that the dogs have been fed, to cover the embers in the hearth as she has been accustomed to do since her youth – those are Granny's last chores of the day even now. Covering the fire especially is a job she will entrust to no one else. When the gleaming coals have been knocked off and the logs that are still burning have been completely extinguished, Granny puts them together in one place, buries the glowing coals and sparks deep in the ashes, pulls around them first the warm layer of ashes that is immediately next to them, then the layer that is further away, and finally the one furthest away, the one that is already completely cold. When the little pile has been raked into a pyramid, and not a single spark remains visible from the outside anymore, Granny makes the sign of the cross over it, softly reciting something as she does so. It could be: God the father, God the son, God the holy ghost! It could be: Mother of Fire, Mother of Fire, keep, protect, preserve, do not let the holy spark of this hearth go out!

Although Granny herself left home rarely, there was no lack of all kinds of company at Spring Farm. Actually, many of them could probably not be called company. They would drive or walk to Spring Farm only on one single occasion, never to be seen again. They came to Granny for help in all sorts of troubles and diseases that afflicted cattle or sometimes themselves. Women would bring their children, even Jewish women from Žagare or more distant places. The children looked emaciated, with disproportionately large, oddly shaped heads, and people said Granny could make such heads well-proportioned and healthy again. Of one Jewish woman there was the following story: Granny had stroked and examined the child's every limb just as she did with the other little patients, had then weighed the child, and thereupon given the child's mother a bottle of medicine and a bundle of roots, instructing her how to use them and how the child should be cared for and washed in a decoction of the roots every day. But the mother had either forgotten the other instructions or had been too lazy to look after the child, or else had thought that the weighing was the most important thing of all, and so she had kept weighing the child morning and night on the scales, but the child had kept getting thinner and thinner. After a while she had returned to Spring Farm in tears: "I weighed and weighed my *ingele*, but those scales are no help at all!"

The woman's words were often quoted at Spring Farm when somebody expected results from some action that had been incorrectly understood.

It was usually around noon that she saw those who sought her help, and had a long quiet consultation with them. Granny would always ask questions, while the patient or the person sent by the patient answered. Those who had arrived earlier and were not in too much of a hurry had to wait till noon, when the house was quiet and Granny herself had more time to spare. But even when she did she couldn't stay still. After she had drawn one chalk circle after another with a cross in the center of each, mostly on a piece of gray or blue paper used for wrapping sugar, she would carry the paper with her, silently whispering mysterious words as she walked to the *klēts* or the cellar doing her chores, continuing her mysterious whispering a predetermined number of times, and lightly brushing the paper and the crosses on it with the fingertips of her right hand. At such times even Citron, when he happened to run across her path, crept softly to one side, as though not daring to fawn on her and wag his tail. And Annele's only rights on such occasions were to watch stealthily, without asking questions.

In the attic, behind the rafters, hung bundles of many dried flowers and roots whose healing powers were known only to Granny. Some of these flowers had to be

picked at sunrise, others at the noon hour, others late in the evening. There were roots that had been dug in early spring, others in fall; some were dried only in the gentle shade, others in the sun, a third type in a roaring hot oven.

The medicinal plants were largely gathered by Granny herself, particularly those that grew in the neighborhood that was familiar to her, plants whose location she had known year-in, year-out, but many were also brought to her by old women who had come from far off and exchanged the herbs for a little sack of flour or groats. Also, an old Gypsy woman, herself very knowledgeable about medicinal plants, came occasionally with a rare, unusual plant, dug up root and all in some thicket. Granny would carefully inspect it: rubbing the roots, tasting the juice of the leaves, learning to distinguish the flowers, and if she was satisfied with what had been brought, the Gypsy woman had no reason to complain of the payment.

Before the big jobs of the summer, Spring Farm had its "dyeing days." Then all the fences were covered with skeins of wool in many colors. Granny had jar after jar filled with concoctions and extracts made from different-colored flowers, barks, and roots. She could dye yarn a beautiful indigo blue as no other farm woman could. She had practiced the art of dyeing to an even greater degree in her younger days. There was a story that once Grandfather had forgotten to bring back from town the necessary copper sulfate or some other chemical ingredient that had to be added to the dye so that the colors would brighten and remain faster. The story went that Granny reproached him for this just at the moment when Grandfather was sitting down, taking off his *pastalas* after coming home from the field. The reproach had nettled him so much that he had leapt to his feet at once with one foot still shod and the other bare, jumped into a manure wagon that stood in the yarn still harnessed, rushed to town and been back with the required purchase as people were getting up from their midday nap. Afterwards he had given all married men the following advice: that it was better to stay out of your wife's sight if she got the urge to start dyeing.

There are times when Annele is put to sleep in Granny's little bedroom. And sometimes when she wakes up in the middle of the night, by the dim light of the little window, she sees Granny sitting there, her big knitting needles jingling faintly like the tiny bells of gnomes. Granny is knitting a long stocking, gray like evening twilight itself. But her lips are whispering. She is reciting something. The rhythmical lines of the words flow like a brook murmuring underground. Then she folds her

knitting, clasps her hands, and her murmuring now becomes even deeper, more sincere, more imploring, as though her dearest friend were standing before her and in the darkness of the night they were discussing something that other people and the world must not hear.

Often on clear nights Granny gets up, goes over to the window and looks at the stars for a long time. Her footsteps are soft as a breeze. At such times Annele has the feeling that Granny has gone very far away and that she shouldn't call her then, for she is not alone. Who these are that surround Granny, Annele doesn't know. They are good spirits, though. The people of Spring Farm can sleep peacefully.

One clear winter day, as Annele is running around outside, she sees Granny by the garden fence looking westward. What's there to look at, the girl wants to know.

But it's as though Granny doesn't even feel the girl's presence. The wind hisses and shakes her clothes, and on her cheeks there are tears that haven't had time to dry.

And what is so empty and bare over there, toward the west? What's missing?

Oh dear! Oh dear! Annele is suddenly startled. Why, the big birch hill over there is gone! Or rather: the hill is still there, but there's not a single birch tree, or any other kind of tree on it anymore. Everything has been shaved as if with a razor. The mighty trunks of the birches in their white shirts lie in big stacks.

"Where's the birch hill, Granny? Where are the birches?"

"See for yourself, child!"

"Who did it, Granny?"

"Never mind," answers Granny, seemingly reluctantly.

"But why did you let them?"

"What can I do anymore? When your children are grown, they follow their own counsel and no longer accept their parents' advice. He could have waited until my eyes close, but he says this way is better. Maybe it *is* better, but next summer we won't see the beauty of it any more."

Annele realizes that it is Uncle Ansis who had the birches cut down, and asks no more questions.

Summer will come, and the beauty of the birches will be gone. Gone will be the buckets of sweet sap, gone the wonderful flowers that grew on the shady hill, the sun-warmed path between the birches and the field where the wheat rose over Annele's head.

So they both stand by the garden fence and grieve for the lovely birch hill.

The Mummers Are Coming!

Christmas comes riding
In a carved sleigh!
　　—Latvian folksong

Yes, now it is here, that infinitely long-awaited Christmas! It is already caroling and exulting in Annele's heart!

The chores of Saturday before Christmas are done. As evening draws close, the maids throw the front door wide open. A gray, chilly flood of air pours into every corner washing away the smells of freshly baked flatcakes and stew. Then the maids light bundles of fresh juniper twigs and quickly make the rounds of every corner of the house. Running outside again, they return with big armfuls of fir branches, secretly decorated in the evenings with long, elaborately scalloped white, red, blue, yellow paper ribbons. They tack them across the ceiling so that not one sooty board is visible anymore, and then sweep the clay floor. Now it's Christmas.

One by one, people return from the sauna, light and flushed rosy pink. Wearing white linen shirts, they sit down at the immaculately scrubbed table, on which there are a basket of flatcakes and a huge bowl full of meat. And in every corner on a clean chair or a little table the size of your fist it's the same: flatcakes and meat. The holiday feast! The first intimation of holidays envelops them all like gently tremulous waves. There is no loud conversation. Just quiet talk and smiles. The ceiling lamp, almost concealed among green branches, softly shimmers like a glowworm daydreaming in a flowery meadow.

And then? – Then there's nothing more. Everyone goes to bed betimes, for this morning they all rose before cockcrow. Here is their chance to really sleep off the heaviness of workaday toil for a change. There's nowhere to hurry to next morning.

One corner of the house after another falls silent. The maids clear away the dishes and disappear. Granny is the last to come in, and she puts out the lamp. At once, the cricket in the corner by the stove begins to chirp.

But can this really be all there is? Oh no! After all, it's Christmas Eve! The very holiest of all holidays! Annele's heart beats. Questioning and waiting. Sleep is unthinkable. Let it rock all the others, like a peaceful lake lapping on the shore. How can she sleep when there in the window is Christmas night, dusky blue, wrapping the entire world in its huge starry mantle! It takes Annele's thoughts and carries them over the starlit tops of the pinewoods into that great mystery which may be witnessed by no human eye or ear, when at the stroke of midnight beasts, birds, trees, and rocks awake and join in a thousand-voiced song of praise. Annele's thoughts soar far above the earth! And when they return home again, filling her heart with bliss like a nectar-laden bee on a June morning, the house is no longer the workaday house, it is an enchanted palace with a floor that shimmers like silver, with translucent green jeweled windows, with glittering gray pearl walls and ceilings, fragrant as a young grove in spring.

On Christmas morning the floor in the farmhands' and the farmer's living quarters is strewn with snow-white sand and chopped pine needles. And then the holiday hours begin rolling by, light and filled to overflowing. She can hardly take in all that each of them has to offer. But the more of them are gone, the shorter they shrink. Yet her heart simply can't stop waiting and asking: can this really be all there is? Surely there's something completely unprecedented in store, isn't there?

Meanwhile the second day of Christmas is already here.

And on the second day of Christmas, as dusk begins to fall, someone suddenly throws open the door.

"The mummers are coming!"

There, you see! That must be it – the unprecedented event!

What's happened to the caller, whose voice no one recognizes? Where is the rest of the household? All the young folks are gone. Something mysterious is approaching.

The mummers are coming! Mummers! What's that? What will they be like? Terrible or kindly, fearful or merry? Wouldn't it be smarter to run and hide? But oh how she'd love to see them! And how can you run and hide when they're already here? Listen to them! Listen to them drawing close!

The mummers come from all directions. The roofs rattle, the walls shake, branches swish past the windows, dreadful voices whisk back and forth, cry out on all sides. There is the sound of heavy footsteps.

The door bursts open. The darkness of the entryway is filled with a motley group of figures. They mill around, stir, whisper to each other, snort. And then suddenly, eddying like stormy winds, they come tumbling inside, inscrutable: women or men with monstrous faces, teeth bared in a fixed grin, eyes hollow. They shout and sing in disguised voices:

"We come, we come, from faraway lands!"

"Where are those lands of yours?" inquire the members of the household, shouting no less loudly.

"Beyond thrice nine mountains, beyond thrice nine forests, beyond thrice nine seas!"

"What are your seas like?" That's the members of the household again.

"Deep as tubs and salty as brine."

"What are the forests like?"

"Thick and big as scrubbing brushes."

"What are the mountains like?"

"High as a rooster's perch." And so the people of the farm keep asking and asking, for they want to know what the land of the mummers looks like, what people eat there, what they drink, what kind of work they do. The mummers reply that in their country they eat locusts' wings, drink air gruel, and the only work there is, is beating the wind.

Old Anyus, who is sitting on her bunk by the door, asks the most questions. None of the mummers can keep up with her questions, while she parries all theirs in such a way that the mummers almost split their sides laughing. The mummers form a half-circle around Anyus, for no one person alone is capable of answering her.

As they all press close to old Anyus, one suddenly leaps into the center, hopping about like a grasshopper. His long black tailcoat is buckled around his fat paunch, and he wears a tall paper hat with fluttering green and red ribbons. His mask has terribly swollen cheeks and a turned-up nose. "Your Grace, may I have the honor of this dance?" he bows and twirls around on one foot so that Anyus can get a good look at him from all sides. "Your Lordship, I thank you," Anyus responds and gets up off her little stool, stick in hand and pipe in the corner of her mouth.

Anyus is a fine lady.

"Where are the musicians?" calls Anyus, thumping her stick on the floor. And at the lady's command, three come leaping in through the door: one scraping away on his fiddle, the second drumming on a pot, and the third blowing on some combs.

"Let's have some steam here!" Anyus the fine lady shouts again, and the music and dancing start with a bang. The stick on one side, the mummer lord on the other, and Anyus in the middle.

Anyus twists and turns this way and that, flings her legs about outlandishly, spins around in a circle and shuffles across the room, while the mummers imitate her every gesture. Everyone laughs and applauds, the mummers join hands with the members of the household, and dance a round dance with them so wildly that their rags shake: they threaten not to let the lord and lady out again. But Anyus is nimbler than all of them: suddenly her stick thrusts itself into the crazy wheeling circle; turning somersaults the wheel of dancers collapses amid such hubbub that for a long time they can no longer find their own hands and feet. Meanwhile Anyus is already sitting back on her bunk puffing her little tobacco pipe, warding off her attackers, who have now recovered from the hubbub, as though butter wouldn't melt in her mouth: "Get away with you, do! You ought to be ashamed of yourselves! Can't even give an old woman a moment's peace." But her eyes are flashing and her lips laugh. Honestly, if this is old Anyus, she's wearing just the same sort of mask as the mummers, except that this is one of the really nice ones.

But wait – what's going on over there?

Terrible screams are heard behind her, in the middle of the room. Shrieking, everybody runs from Anyus, even the mummers themselves hide in the corners. An animal trainer is in the center of the floor – with a frightful beast that must surely be a bear.

"Stoi! Smirno! Kuda! Smirno!" shouts the trainer in his own language, and the beast understands everything: it dances on one leg, on three legs, turns around in a circle, growls, tosses a hoop, turns a somersault. When everybody has laughed their fill, the trainer takes the bear's leash from his neck and shouts a command: "Go after the maids!" So clever an animal doesn't need to be told twice. Paws raised, he throws himself upon the group of maids, but before he knows it he's been swung around in a circle and flung to the ground, and blows fall on him like hailstones from all directions. "That'll teach you to go after the maids! That'll teach you!" How long can a poor bear put up with it! He first lets out a long howl and when that is no use, begins to beseech them in a queerly human voice: "Oy, gevalt! Gevalt! Don't hit me! It's me! Joskele!" And from under the fur escapes the red-haired, curlyheaded tailor's boy, tailor Joske's apprentice – the wag, always the first to try all sorts of tricks. He's come over from Žagare late last night, where he had no peace while the holidays were being celebrated in Kurzeme. Acting out of character, Joskele escapes, bearskin and all, into the entryway, where new surprises are being prepared.

While the mummers' dance resumes again with shouting and songs, while the fiddler scrapes his fiddle, and old Anyus claps her hands keeping time, a nimble hand turns off the lamp, and in the general fright and silence the door slowly, slowly opens. Across the threshold, with inaudible footsteps, comes a white figure. Its clothes trail on the ground, its pointed head knocks against the ceiling. Its cheeks are white as chalk, its eyes like deep hollows. Between its rows of teeth, it blows red flames of pitch and sulfur like a dragon.

"Death! Go away, you scoundrel! Why do you come and scare the children?" shouts echo from all directions. But hell's fire turns out to be perfidious. When Death takes a deeper breath, it suddenly chokes. "Confound it, my tongue got burned!" exclaims Death in quite a recognizable human voice and, spluttering and spitting out all the pitch and sulfur, rushes out the door accompanied by general laughter. Only the white paper head is left hanging from a fir branch on the ceiling.

When the lamp is relit, they notice that the large table where the farmhands usually eat has been quietly set with all kinds of delicacies. There is headcheese and meat, there are piles of flatcakes and hot sausages. Grandmother invites the visitors to help themselves.

The disguises and masks fall away. And now you can see that these are all the good and familiar people from the neighborhood.

This marks the beginning of merry conversation as they relive the night's events. While things are still fresh in their minds, they each discuss how successfully they played their parts and how well they were able to conceal their identity. Joskele, too, comes creeping back and receives a flatcake and a chunk of sausage, for everyone knows he is far from strict about keeping kosher and has wolfed down many a slice of ham, just as long as his master doesn't find out about it – though Joskele isn't too scared of him either.

When the mummers have been regaled, they get dressed and take off, for they still have to put in an appearance at other farms. Those who have shown that they can behave like good mummers are all taken along. Including Joskele.

They leave expressing their thanks, laughing, banging their drums, and singing. Snatches of their talk and laughter can long be heard across the snowy plain.

The major fun is over, but you can stay up a while longer. You can play foxtails, spindles, shoemakers, and dollar, dollar. Now that many of the young folks have run off with the mummers, all the grown-ups come in a drove to play with the little kids, including old Anyus, with her stick – the biggest joker and buffoon of them all.

Then that, too, must come to an end, and finally those sad, unpleasant words are uttered: "Time to turn in now."

The great wave has ebbed, Christmas is over, and it seems as though it has torn away a piece of Annele's heart, that's how sorry she is to see it go – so very sorry.

Old Anyus is already snoring. In the twilight of the crystal-green window, her breast rises and falls, her chin, covered with white down, trembles slightly and looks so inexorably hard and stern.

Christmas is hurrying away with seven-league boots.

The Paupers' Banquet

But after the holidays came the days of post-holiday celebration. One such was the fourth day of Christmas, for that was paupers' day at Spring Farm. A big kettle full of meat was bubbling in the kitchen. Granny brought a basket of holiday rolls and placed them on the table in two small piles.

Then the guests Granny had invited for the interim between the holidays began to arrive.

The first to come was Vilītis. He had a long way to walk, and he had set out early in the morning. Vilītis was neither young nor old. His eyes were pale blue, and he was all shriveled, as though he didn't have the right to straighten up. When he came begging, he never said his prayers, just sat down and waited. When the maids asked him jokingly, "Vilītis, where's your girlfriend?" his pale eyes began darting about in terror like partridge chicks frightened by a hawk, and he uttered incomprehensible words. When Granny saw that, the maids would get a scolding. The story was that Vilītis had been a handsome tall figure of a young man, the proud heir to a farm. He had fallen in love with a farmhand's daughter, but his parents had forbidden him to marry her. Then one day the young woman had vanished. So Vilītis had begun to brood and had set off in search of her. He had walked around looking for her day and night, always just around his farm, for he no longer knew any other roads. Since that time, though he had recovered somewhat, he had never regained his full sanity. He no longer did any work, either. The other heirs had gradually stripped him of everything he owned, and had broken off contact with him, so that all he had left was a beggar's staff.

When he comes visiting, Vilītis dresses just as he does every day – he wears his gray coat belted with an old strap, except that he doesn't have his little sack around his neck. Shyly and diffidently he takes a seat at the table wherever he is invited to sit, and waits.

Now old Karlīne, too, comes across the yard, looking about her, fearful that Citron might attack her. But Citron, the bitterest enemy of all such visiting strangers, has been locked up today by Granny's orders and is tearing around the shed like a roaring lion.

As always, old Karlīne sings her one and only song about her son who was exiled to Siberia, about her great troubles, and her life as a beggar woman. Although everybody has heard the song before, yet they always like to hear it again. When the song is over, Karlīne is given a seat at the table next to Vilītis, and the people of the household treat her like company.

    Uninvited, old Zurausis or Zurauŝķis, as everyone calls him to tease him, comes driving into the courtyard. This is a fierce and persistent beggar. He is never satisfied with what he is given, but always demands more, and demands it like the lord of the manor. He has a weak little nag harnessed with knotted reins and hitched to a clap-trap cart. He himself sits on straw, without a bolster. Not that he hasn't got one. It's so he'll look more like a beggar. In a loud voice he yells for someone to come and help him out of the cart, for he is lame in both legs. After he limps inside, he immediately sits down uninvited at the table between Vilītis and old Karlīne. But he is not agreeable as befits a guest. With strong words of derision, he begins by belittling both Vilītis and Karlīne, who shrink back without a word and seemingly frightened each into their own corner, taking up as little room as possible. Though of small stature himself, Zurausis sits between the other two like some wealthy landowner, for he is dressed decently and well. He has a healthy, strong wife who takes care not only of Zurausis himself, but of four children as well. That's the kind of man he is. He insists on his rights as a horse-owning beggar, and is good at lamenting and complaining piteously. Driving far afield, even into other districts, he demands a richer bounty than the beggars who run around on foot carrying a niggardly sack. And he's certainly not doing badly. He's already started sending his children to school, and that's more than you can say for a lot of farmers. It isn't a good idea to make fun of Zurausis, as people sometimes will with other beggars, for you might get stung. He's like a bundle of nettles, that's how sharp and wicked his tongue is. That's why even

today he is trying to show how much better he is than Vilītis and old Karlīne, calling them simpletons or worse.

With loud good-days the church beggars come in together: Skriemeltiņš and his wife, Pupalaksts, Žiglene, big Knābene and a couple of others. The Skriemeltiņš couple takes care of the graves of Granny's relatives. The wife, Skriemeltene herself, weeds gardens in summer and runs all kinds of minor errands. Skriemeltene inherited Granny's family graves from her goddaughter Anlīze, a once prominent church beggar whom she had helped out, taking turns with her husband, during the last years of Anlīze's life. It was at Anlīze's behest that the Skriemeltiņš couple had recently managed to join the church beggars. Their position was still somewhat precarious, however, but Skriemeltene in particular was trying to consolidate it, either by obeying without contradiction whenever she as the youngest was given the harder share of the work when there were joint chores to be done, or by obliging and being obsequious toward the head beggarwomen, especially big Knābene. When Granny invited her to come over during the holiday interim, she had immediately exclaimed: "What about Knābene? You haven't asked her? Tut-tut, how could you? That's not right. You must ask Knābene!" And when given permission to invite Knābene, Skriemeltene wanted Pupalaksts, Žiglene, and several others to be invited as well, for she could thus all at once gain greater brilliance and even advantages in their eyes by later pointing out how it was thanks to her that they had all been invited to Spring Farm that day.

Hardly anyone knew Knābene's real name. She was called Knābene because she had a large curved nose like a bird's beak. It was not often a person would come across a nose like that. Big black eyes glittered above her nose, and her chin was covered with a growth of hair an adolescent boy would have been proud of. You could see at a glance that she was the most powerful of the church beggars. It was said that she did not make way even for the sacristan, let alone the bell ringer or other ordinary folks. She knew how to please the minister though, better than anyone else. When she managed to kiss the hem of his coat, it was done on behalf of all of them, and with a wave of her hand she would force the other beggars, who also sometimes tried to follow suit, to fall back. When the minister would bless a grave, Knābene alone had won the right to hold the shovel filled with dirt on the minister's right-hand side. When the minister led the confirmands around the church, Knābene was the first to strew flowers on the path, and only then were the other women allowed to do likewise. This was true on other important occasions, too. Toward everyone who had direct dealings with the minister, such as wedding, baptism, and funeral guests, Knābene also behaved respectfully and submissively, but God forbid if some uninvited person arrogantly dared to look into a decorated grave before the ceremony without her permission, or to cross a path strewn with flowers and white sand in readiness for those who were being honored that Sunday, especially if these were prominent parishioners. Then Knābene lashed out at them with her sharp tongue and her no less sharp looks, or menaced them with her cane, though only little feet fled from the latter, leaping away like grasshoppers. Yet she kept people in awe of her as far as her power reached.

When Knābene came into the house at Spring Farm, she looked closely at the faces around the table: who were these people that had arrived ahead of her? She didn't have much to say about Vilītis and old Karlīne. Let them sit. They were just poor wretches and simpletons. She had no quarrel with them. As for Zurausis, she at once firmly took him to task. This was a man with whom she was accustomed to engage in violent verbal skirmishes. The louder and the more impertinent Zurausis was, the more Knābene outdid him. Finally she brought Zurausis to his knees. His tongue, though sharp, was lacking in ready wit. Furiously he dismissed her with a wave of his hand, saying: "There's no way I can outtalk your mouth!"

Knābene laughed with great relish, for she had gotten the upper hand over Zurausis, and along with her so had all the others. Vilītis and Karlīne smiled, too.

"There, you see," said Knābene, "I have a mouth, I have hands, I have a knack for doing things, but what have you got? Go on, tell me – what have you got? All you've got is that impudent mouth of yours."

Zurausis had rallied once more and was about to strike back when the door opened and in came old Bungatiņš with his wooden leg.

"Greetings to those who provide us with bread, greetings to those who eat it, may the Lord give you joy," he said courteously, delighted to see so many acquaintances and unexpected guests gathered together. After shaking hands with everybody, he sat down next to Zurausis, took off his cap, smoothed back his hair, cleared his throat, and recited: "How lovely is thy dwelling place, O Lord, how lovely is thy dwelling place." He recited this entire psalm of David while the beggar women, folding their hands, acted as if they were reciting it along with him, though they did not know by heart the text he was reciting. Zurausis, on the other hand, was still fiercely rolling his eyes in one direction and the other, but dared not interrupt.

During the recital of the psalm, the maid Karlīne had already entered with a large steaming bowl of pork and barley stew. She was followed by Grandmother, carrying earthenware plates and spoons. Karlīne set down the bowl and said to Bungatiņš: "Well, Bungatiņš, if you had been here just a moment ago and heard how lovely this dwelling place was, you'd really have been amazed," – and she glanced in the direction of Zurausis and Knābene. But the latter either felt rebuked by the scriptures Bungatiņš had quoted, or touched by the bowl of delicious pork snout stew, so they didn't say another word.

"Come, come, lass," Bungatiņš said with a wave of his hand, "the human heart and mind is wicked from childhood, but God's will makes it good and kind. You just trust in him!"

"Go ahead, help yourselves!" urged Grandmother.

"But you come too, mistress of Spring Farm! Come join the paupers and receive their blessing! For blessed are they who take care of the poor, the Lord shall save them during evil days," Bungatiņš was still speaking solemnly.

Knābene stirred impatiently, pulling her woolen shawl closer about her shoulders. "Whoa there! Is he going to recite the whole Bible? Who does he think he is, a Bible scholar?"

Suddenly Zurausis, too, agreed with her. "Don't think you're the only one who's smart," he scolded Bungatiņš. The two important personages didn't like it that Bungatiņš surpassed them in his knowledge of the scriptures.

But Bungatiņš merely smiled: "Why be angry, dear children? Everything that is in God's world is good."

Since Granny had not repeated her invitation, nobody touched the bowl. They were all waiting.

But when she came in again with a corked bottle full of clear brown liquid settled over a thick sediment of roots and buds at the bottom of the bottle, and a little glass the size of a thimble in her other hand, the guests looked up with eager eyes.

Grandmother poured a glass and handed it to Bungatiņš.

"Here's to your good heart," he nodded at her and tossed it down like a berry.

"All right then, here's to our aching bones," said Zurausis, receiving the glass with pleasure.

"Strong but good," Knābene praised after drinking hers.

"Well then, here's to your very good health," said Pupalaksts.

"Confound it, where do you get such strong stuff?" wondered Skriemeltiņš. And so each of them said their say, but Vilītis and Karlīne said nothing. They only shuddered as soon as they touched it to their lips, and gave back the glass unempted.

"Come, help yourselves," Grandmother invited them again, turning directly to Knābene.

"Hear, hear!" answered Knābene and began at once. Now all the others also hurriedly filled their plates. They ate and extolled the food, expressing their appreciation of it and singing its praises, so that Karlīne soon had to go and fetch another bowlful. When they had all eaten their fill, they all looked merry and cheerful, not at all as they had looked when they came begging. Even Zurausis sat there as though he had been pressed smooth by a tailor's flatiron, trying to make the others laugh by telling jokes, though he didn't meet with much success. Everybody preferred to listen to Bungatiņš, for no one else could say things so beautifully. Zurausis got mad. "Some prophet! One minute he uses the name of God, and the next he's blabbering nonsense!" he jeered at the one-legged man.

"Everything that comes into God's sweet world is good," Bungatiņš answered gaily. "There's a time to quote the words of the prophet, and a time to sing silly songs. Right now, here we are, eating our share of the feast at the table of Spring Farm, living in clover, as they say, while last year was a year of famine, when many a one of us had to tighten his belt; that, mistress of Spring Farm, was the year the beggars fell into your house like snow at Shrovetide. Because of course it was widely known that the fields of grain on the hills of Spring Farm had rippled like the wheat in the land of Goshen. Isn't that true, now?"

"True enough," agreed Granny, "why, that was when the threshold stones never had a chance to cool during the day. Especially those Lithuanian folks were coming in droves, for they were harder pressed by hunger than folks hereabouts. It was worst in the spring, right after St. George's Day. We asked the children to count all the comings and goings each day. They put down a piece of kindling for each beggar, and then added them up at night. One day it turned out to be close to forty. Look, that very girl there was the one that put down the pieces of kindling. She's not so good at counting yet, you see."

And Granny points at Annele, who is huddling in a corner so that, unnoticed, she can get a good look at what's happening at table.

Everyone turns to look at the girl.

"Would that be your son's daughter?" inquires Knābene, taking a good look at the girl.

"That's right," answers Granny, while Bungatiņš makes a friendly gesture of invitation, slapping his wooden leg.

"Come 'ere, little grasshopper, I'll give you a gallop on my little wooden horse."

Immediately Knābene is ready to make fun of him.

"A fine gallop you'll give her, I'll bet. Better hold on tight yourself, or you might fall on the floor."

"Don't say that," it is Bungatiņš's turn to brag now. "You're welcome to tackle me yourself with all four limbs, and I will not only hold my own but even cut you down like an ear of wheat there on the floor without budging from the spot myself."

"Will you listen to that bragging!" Skriemeltene gets in her pennyworth.

"I'd like to see that!" Knābene draws back proudly on her bench.

"Well then, come here if you want to see," Bungatiņš challenges her directly, getting up and taking his stand in the middle of the room.

"Hey, and suppose I do come?" Knābene stirs menacingly.

"Why boast like a skunk?" Bungatiņš holds out his arm. "This arm is made of iron, it's still more than a match for any female."

"And this one's not made of clay, either," Knābene retorts, quickly rising to her feet and throwing down her big shawl.

"That's right, you show him," the other women urge Knābene on.

"I want to show you what happens to people who talk big, you jackdaw, you," Knābene proudly takes up a position in the center of the room.

"Here's my arm," shouts Bungatiņš, rising to his feet. "Budge it if you can."

"I'll toss you on the floor with my little finger!" yells Knābene.

"You won't make me budge an inch!"

"I'll show you where the cockroaches live," Knābene gets more heated.

"I want you to know I've fought against Turkish generals!"

And now Knābene advances against Bungatiņš first from the right, then the left, using now one arm, now both, but she can't budge Bungatiņš. Everyone is laughing, shouting, applauding. The women are backing Knābene; the men tend to be on Bungatiņš's side, and both sides encourage their own champion with exclamations, laughter, praise, meanwhile cruelly making fun of and taunting the opponent. This is especially true of the Skriemeltiņš couple. The more fiercely Knābene attacked, the more Bungatiņš resisted, red as a lobster, boasting mercilessly: "There's nothing you can do to a man who's walked all across the land of the Turks."

In the midst of this great hubbub, the door opened and in came the farmhand Ingus. As though he couldn't believe his eyes, he stopped at the door; then turned as if to leave again; opened his mouth and closed it again as if he felt any word uttered here was superfluous, yet finally did utter it, and so loudly that the beggars got scared.

"Well! What's going on here, I'd like to know? Has Spring Farm really turned into a poorhouse?"

Knābene used the interruption to leave her opponent unvanquished without loss of face: why should she mess around with a beggar like him, she exclaimed. But Bungatiņš in the excitement of victory turned to Ingus: "Don't you get mad, son," he said, "this is no shiftless good-for-nothing you're looking at. When I was your age, I was strong as an oak. Why, I could even have handled five fellows all by myself, no problem. But where is the glory of this world now? I left it in the Turkish wars, don't you see. The same thing could happen to you one day."

He held out his hand to Ingus, but Ingus pushed it away: "Go to blazes, you old beggar!" That's how mad he was. Coming to the table, he threw down his cap and asked with a frown: "Isn't there going to be any dinner today?"

"In a minute, in a minute," Karlīne obsequiously cleared a corner of the table.

Muttering their thanks and wishing their hosts all the best, the paupers left one after another.

But as Ingus was eating heartily all by himself, leaning over the bowl of pork and barley grits, Granny came up to him and softly said, "You know, son, you can't act like that toward the poor beggars. You haven't reached out and touched the end of your own life yet! God alone knows what fate has decreed for each of us. Well, am I right?"

And Ingus, his mouth full of pork and grits, grunted a seemingly embarrassed response: "Guess you're right."

After all, how could he contradict her? Granny was not only the mistress of Spring Farm, but the mother of Spring Farm as well.

Driķītis

Naughty, naughty girl! That's what everyone calls Annele today. But she can't understand why she's a naughty girl. If she's naughty, why then, the wind is much naughtier, the way he shakes the fence pickets and makes them crack, almost breaking off the still half-bare trees and branches. And Annele simply wants to run around a bit for the wind to toss. She wants it to wheel her around in circles and then, when she can no longer keep up with it, she wants to shout her ringing voice into the wind for it to carry over the treetops, up to the very clouds scudding on high. But when this same harsh wind finally blows her into the house, her cheeks red, her hands frozen, the grown-ups sternly admonish her: "Naughty girl, stay inside, will you!"

All right. She'll stay inside. There's certainly plenty of leisure and lots of space everywhere today. On this inclement, cool spring Sunday, the folks of Spring Farm have gone visiting. Annele's parents, too. And that's why she can now fill all the empty corners and rooms with her playing. That's why she can now fulfill all sorts of desires that fizz like brewer's yeast against the bung of a barrel. But, worse luck, such reckless desires cross other people's desires, and that means trouble. Immediately tyrants and commanders appear in Annele's path. One tells her to be quiet, another scolds her, a third threatens to thrash her or even make her stand in the corner. But there's no way Annele's going to obey them. What right do they have to tell her to be quiet? After all, they're not her parents! They're all strangers, recent arrivals! Why don't they mind their own business?

But when Annele doesn't obey anyone, no one feels obliged to defend her anymore. When no one defends her, she becomes obstinate. The more obstinate she is, the more the grown-ups tease her until she has no choice but to resort to all her resources for self-defense: her fists, her nails, and shrieks so loud that the grown-ups' ears ring.

And in the midst of all this hubbub one of the grown-ups says, pointing at the door of the farmer's living quarters: "Just you wait, you'll see what happens to you when *he* comes out of the chamber."

Annele glances at the door slightly alarmed, but incredulous.

Out of the chamber? Why should anyone come out of there? Why, there's no one in there.

And still she has an uneasy feeling, for suddenly they've all grown silent and watch the door expectantly.

The door creaks, and "he" really and truly does come out of the chamber. A tall stranger comes across the threshold. Sternly he asks:

"What was all that noise?"

"The girl's been naughty," they tell him. And accusingly they look at Annele so that she wishes the earth would open under her feet.

The tall man goes straight to Annele, who stands in her corner alone. He comes up close and shakes a long, extended forefinger under her nose.

"Just you wait! I heard everything. I'm going to tell your mother everything."

And then, raising his other hand whose finger is also extended and has a pipe hanging from it as long as Anyus's stick, the stranger turns and goes back into the chamber.

Annele stands frozen.

Who is this man? Nobody like him has ever been seen at Spring Farm.

He had a sort of long, gray coat down to his heels, belted with a red silk cord with big tassels; his beard was combed out in both directions away from his chin like a broom; his whiskers so long the ends could have been wrapped around his ears; his hair parted from his forehead to the nape of his neck, the like of which she had never seen on any other man's head.

Now that the stranger has finished scolding Annele, the grown-ups are friends with her again and tell her that the stranger's name is Driķītis. Driķītis arrived late last night from abroad, where he served for many long years as a chamber valet with a high-ranking family. Now he is old and has been discharged and sent back to the parish to eat the bread of charity.

"Chamber valet, chamber valet!" speculates Annele. Why did he have to appear, why did he have to come to the chamber at Spring Farm of all places when all this time it had been getting along fine without a valet of its own?

A heavy sullenness veils the girl's cheerful mood as a cloud veils the April sun. No good would come from that tall man, from his menacing long finger.

She proves to be right. That afternoon, when from the sunny birch hill she catches sight of her mother returning from her visit and disappearing inside the house, and when she herself races down the hill with stormy haste to go to her, what does she see? The tall man is already standing next to Mother telling her how her little girl has been naughty, really naughty. Nobody, he says, was able to control her, she wouldn't obey anyone.

Annele hears this, and her heart sinks. Her arms drop to her sides. What will Mother say? Fearfully her eyes seek her mother's.

They don't look like eyes that have had their first sight of Annele after so many hours away visiting. They've grown dark and stern.

"What have you been doing? What must I hear? Such a disgrace! A complaint from a stranger, who's met you for the first time! Own up!"

Annele stands stock-still. What should she own up to? What has she done? They can kill her if they like, she doesn't know.

"Apologize!" the tall man prompts her.

What's she supposed to apologize for? – And though her heart impels her, urges her toward her mother, it's impossible, completely impossible with this man standing there, and waiting, and watching. So Annele keeps silent, teeth clenched, like biting down on a rock.

"Look at the nerve of her! What's to become of a girl like her? She won't do you any credit, I'll tell you that. But so it goes: common people don't know how to educate their children. Take a look at how the gentry educate theirs. You have instant obedience – forward march! – at a word. And on the spot. They're certainly not allowed to show the kind of brazenness this chit of a girl shows you. No, no, no! She's got to be disciplined, disciplined, I tell you! Things simply can't go on like this."

And the tall man immediately begins to discipline Annele.

"Well, can't you beg your mother's pardon? Is it so hard for you to kiss her hand? To say: I won't do it again? Is that so hard, huh?"

Yes, it certainly seems to be hard, even impossible. And no matter how zealously he and Mother set about disciplining Annele, it's no use, no use at all. Annele's arms and legs are stiff and disobedient, her heart is frozen and disobedient. Her heart demands: Why doesn't that man go away, why doesn't he disappear from the world altogether, then all will be well, then she'll obey at once.

"There, you see, what can you do with a stubborn girl like her," the tall man says with a sigh at the end of their long efforts.

Annele is pushed. Annele is shoved, but she remains speechless and stiff.

"Well, if that's the way she's going to be, if she insists on being headstrong and doing whatever she feels like, then this is no place for me anymore. Then I'll just go back where I came from."

Having said this, Mother picks up the new shoes she's just taken off and puts them on again.

"Then I'll go away again if I'm not wanted here," Mother repeats, tying on her headscarf and picking up her shawl.

A hot wave of blood rushes to Annele's face.

What's this? What's Mother doing? Why is she getting dressed? Is she going to leave again? Really leave? No, no, surely she won't do that. She'll laugh a bit, and everything's going to be all right!

But she doesn't laugh at all. It does take a long time for her to put on the scarf and shawl, but finally that, too, is done.

"Well then, goodbye," says Mother, going toward the door.

"Mother, Mother," shouts Annele's heart. She herself cries out loud. And she doesn't know how it happened, but suddenly she's by the door, barring her mother's way, enveloped by her shawl, by her arms.

"See, that's the way to discipline them," says the tall man with satisfaction, disappearing in the chamber.

Annele cuddles up to her mother, close, so close.

And now everything could be all right again, but it isn't.

She doesn't even have to own up or apologize, as is usually demanded in such cases at the threat of dire punishment. This time Mother herself says, "I know, I know, you'll never do it again," – and she strokes tear-soaked strands of hair back from Annele's forehead.

And you'd think it would be all right, but it's not all right. It's blocked off by something dark. What exactly was this thing with Mother? Annele keeps thinking agonizing thoughts.

Did Mother really intend to do as she threatened, and leave Annele forever? And *could* she have done such a thing? Or was it just a joke, and was Mother trying to trick her, saying she would go; would she not have gone anywhere even if Annele hadn't hurried to bar her way? – But was Mother capable of playing such a trick on Annele?

These are agonizing thoughts and deep, lonely worries that make the rest of the day strange and sad.

Meanwhile, Driķītis continues to live at Spring Farm and eat his bread of charity, which Annele has had a chance to investigate quite thoroughly. The bread of charity is a chop with scrambled eggs, alternating with rice porridge, flatbread, or "caterpillar" noodles made of finely ground flour, and tea. Whereas the rest of the household has wheat dumplings on Sundays, grits cooked with pork fat on Mondays, lamb's quarters on Tuesdays, milk porridge on Wednesdays, dumplings again on Thursdays, pease porridge on Fridays, porridge on Saturdays – Driķītis always gets his own food and nothing else. The bread of charity is boring, thinks Annele.

When Annele's mother or Granny fry the eggs, they're pale yellow like beeswax, but when Karlīne has made the scrambled eggs, they're black, and Driķītis throws down his plate on the table and scolds so fiercely that the tops of his whiskers twitch. Driķītis won't let the maids get away with any kind of slovenliness. If they haven't brought in clean water, he scolds, if a towel hasn't been hung up, he scolds, if his room isn't swept on time, he scolds. And when Driķītis scolds, the maids run like greased lightning. He knows what's proper, he's been with the gentry.

Driķītis himself is also agile as quicksilver. When the weather is nice, he's out in the garden. With big shears, a saw, or a spade. He trims the unnecessary branches from the trees, widens the paths, and surfaces them with yellow gravel. At such times he takes off the coat with the tasseled cord and works away in a white shirt and a colorful velvet vest. He has a lot of such colorful velvet and silk vests, he's given Annele's father one also. There are days when Driķītis sings and warbles, that's when he's generous, too, especially toward the maids, quickly slipping them something or other wrapped in green and red paper, and then they fall all over themselves with haste. But as for Annele, there's nothing Driķītis can offer her to wheedle himself into her good graces, though he's tried several times. Ever since that first encounter, Annele has fled from him as soon as she catches sight of him from afar, and hasn't set foot in the places ruled by Driķītis, such as the garden or the chamber.

But she certainly does spend a lot of time thinking about Driķītis. How come things are like this? How come the nice people, the people she loves, like Līziņa, aren't home – how come Līziņa spends weeks on end at her godmother's at Hook Farm where she is learning needlework, while a good-for-nothing like Driķītis hangs around at Spring Farm? Wouldn't it be far better for somebody like him to go to Hook Farm to learn needlework? And Annele can't figure out the ways of the world, and why it is that often things happen that she doesn't like, for she is still an ignorant little girl.

When the weather is rainy, Driķītis stays inside wearing his long coat. In his hand is a fly swatter, wide as a bird's webbed foot on a brightly polished handle. With eyes like the robber chief's in the picture on Karlīne's wall, he lies in wait for the swarms of flies on the table, the windowpanes, walls, and ceiling. Aha! Eins-zwei-drei! And – smack – the swatter strikes, and flies drop dead by the dozens. When all the flies inside have been killed, Driķītis goes outside and with his swatter picks them off the walls and windows there as well, making the whole house so clean that people who come to Spring Farm are amazed: What kind of farm is this where there are no flies? Why, it's like the drawing room at a lord's mansion.

In Driķītis's eyes, even Anyus is just like any other no-account woman, and as for Kaminskene, she doesn't count at all. On Sunday afternoons or at night, when the household gathers inside the house, you should hear Driķītis hold forth. He wants all eyes, all ears fixed on his lips. Anyus, of course, resists as hard as she can, but how can she hold out? Her gentry are small fry compared to Driķītis's gentry!

When Anyus comes driving up with the twenty horses, fifty dogs, and thirty estates of her gentry, Driķītis immediately counters with the fifty horses, five hundred dogs, and a hundred estates and mansions of his former employers, who have property in all four corners of the earth. Anyus's master is a count – an equerry to the emperor himself, and as good as the little finger on the emperor's hand, while Driķītis's master is a prince, the emperor's chamberlain, and as good as his right hand. When Anyus used to talk about her gentry, she'd always do it in such a submissive voice: "His gracious lordship, her gracious ladyship" – while Driķītis used to call his master and mistress simply: "the old man" and "the mistress," but referred to their children even more simply as Michael, Leon, Sonya, and Masha. And they in turn just called him Jean. "Listen, Jean, do thus and so for us!" And there wasn't a single thing that Driķītis-Jean wasn't capable of doing, he says. That's the sort of man he was.

When Anyus has vainly tried and tried to get a word in edgewise as Driķītis holds forth, hoping for a chance to open her mouth, she merely spits and says: "You conceited devil, you." And leaves. She no longer wants to listen to this fellow filling the world with his bragging.

When Driķītis has sufficiently amazed the household with his stories, he disappears in the chamber, and when he comes out again, he is no longer Driķītis but a total stranger. His hair is different, and his beard is different, and he's wearing a long, black, elegantly buttoned coat, and has a shiny top hat on his head and a thin cane with a shiny knob in his hand. Now he makes the rounds bowing to them all, flinging his hands this way and that, looking at everybody through a piece of glass screwed up to one of his eyes and speaking with everybody in an incomprehensible language, but after he has given everybody a good laugh, he takes off his false hair and is suddenly Driķītis again. Yes, that's how he used to go about, he says – looking like himself by day, but disguising himself like that by night as he accompanied Michael or Leon through towns where there are deep rivers instead of streets, and through towns where the streets are steep as the ridges of roofs while the sea roars deep underfoot, and through towns whose streets are so narrow you can reach from one building to another, and only at the very top is there a glimpse of the blue sky like a bright thin thread. That's where he walked with Leon or Michael, through buildings, under stone vaults, on floors polished smooth as glass in halls as brightly lit as hell itself.

"So what were you looking for, bumming around there like that?" asks Ingus, who seems pretty infuriated by Driķītis's stories.

"Why, Satan's children, of course," answers Driķītis with a laugh.

Annele, listening from afar, feels her heart tremble at such audacity, but Driķītis has performed even greater feats.

Another time, he says, he goes with Sonya or Masha to a secret rendez-vous with those selfsame "children of Satan," or else carries letters from them to others, back and forth; then, he says, he sometimes has to climb rope ladders up white buildings, to windows and balconies that hang from the walls like dovecotes. And to him it's child's play.

And another time he has to watch to make sure that strangers don't discover the place where his master's children are spending time with Satan's children. And that the prince himself doesn't discover them, which would be even more terrible. Then he signals, clattering like a stork with his throat and tongue, calling like a cuckoo, or else clacking like a windmill, whatever he's asked to do. One time, the old prince himself comes pursuing their trail in the snow, but once he gets there, sees nothing but imprints of Jean rolling in the fresh snow, now on his back with his arms spread wide, now face down with his nose and forehead making hollows in the snow, now on his side with those long whiskers like a tomcat. And no more tracks or anything, so that the Prince just spits, shrugs in disgust, and leaves.

Thus Driķītis with his long stories completely silenced Anyus, and she walked around furious, refusing to be appeased. But gradually she slowly floated to the top again, for, since she hung around at the estate, she found something new to tell people every day, while Driķītis had nothing but things that had happened long ago. And who knows if that was the real reason, but there had been more than one rumor that Driķītis no longer enjoyed being at Spring Farm.

And one day a horse stood harnessed in the yard and a maid carried out Driķītis's boxes and bags, strapped with leather straps and studded with shiny studs. And then out came Driķītis himself, wearing a long black topcoat and a gray broad-brimmed hat, like a gentleman. He drove away. The others said he was fed up with constantly eating chops and scrambled eggs, he was going somewhere where the cooking was more elegant. Anyus said he'd told enough lies here and was off to blow the rest of the world full of his stuff and nonsense.

Annele was now again able to race through all the places where Driķītis had once held sway. Everything was the way it had been before. In the chamber, the same single bed, the table by the window, the clock ticking in the corner, the floor swept clean, as though awaiting the red slippers of Driķītis: only not a sign of all the things that Driķītis had at various times carried out of the chamber as if from a mysterious treasure trove. She wondered if it was these wondrous things she missed, or was it Driķītis himself? Something was missing, and there was something Annele suddenly felt sad about.

The Lord's Supper

Spring Farm is spotlessly clean. Each window gets at least two buckets of water. Water and sand have also not been spared scouring the tables and the chamber floors, which are drying, white as chalk. Luze and Karlīne are scurrying like ants. One more hardworking than the other, one more obliging than the other. It's a race to see which of them can do more, and do it faster. They do not grumble or scold, neither each other nor anyone else. Nobody's making them, nobody's telling them what to do, they're self-propelled, like spinning tops. They're wonderful, those maids!

What can it all mean? Is it some sort of feast day tomorrow? Easter? No, Easter, they say, will be close to St. George's Day. And it isn't St. George's Day yet. The gooseberry bushes still have only tiny, tiny green buds. Once everything is green, and not until then, it will be St. George's Day.

The more Annele wants to know what's happening tomorrow, the more the maids refuse to tell her.

When everything is spick and span but evening is still a long way off, the maids are thick as thieves in between the remaining chores. All you hear is "Sister dear!" and "Sister dear!"

Although this is Luze's first year as a maidservant, she's much wealthier than Karlīne. Her trunk is full of things, while Karlīne doesn't have a trunk at all: everything she owns is kept in a sort of brown army footlocker. Luze has a mother who takes good care of her, and decent, hardworking relatives, while Karlīne is an orphan.

Karlīne wants to know which scarf Luze is going to wear tomorrow. And Luze hasn't the slightest idea which of her five silk kerchiefs would be most appropriate for tomorrow.

If she wears the rainbow-colored one, then maybe it would have been better to wear the brown one, and if she wears the brown one, then maybe the yellow one would have been better! No, better wear the white one. Even though it's Lent, it still looks best on Luze.

When Karlīne hears that, she laments:

"Oh, sister dear, if you wear your white silk, I'll have to walk way behind you. How can I go slinking up to you like a Gypsy from the backwoods if you come with your white silk? I'd be so humiliated – I'd sink through the floor."

No, no! Karlīne mustn't be humiliated! Luze won't even hear of it. After all, she's got plenty of scarves. Karlīne can pick out whichever one she likes. She can have the white silk one and welcome, Luze will give it with all her heart.

"Oh sister dear, I'd never have dreamed you were so kind!"

Karlīne loudly kisses Luze on both cheeks, and both of them run off to the *klēts* to pick out scarves for tomorrow.

Joyous as a bird, Annele flies off to her mother.

"Mother, you know what, Mother, you know what? Luze and Karlīne are sisters now."

Mother makes no reply. She is rearranging and folding the Sunday clothes and reciting something softly. It takes such a long, long time. Annele sees that she won't get an answer just now and that she'll be wasting her time. She must go and see what the rest of the household are doing.

In every corner and in each of the farmhands' *klētis*, something different is happening, and yet it has something in common with all the rest. People are at work sweeping, cleaning, putting things in order not just indoors but outdoors as well. Kaminskene is up on a footstool with a long broom cleaning out last year's cobwebs and bird droppings even from the space under the rafters. And no one is surprised. Only Anyus is grumbling, but it might not have anything to do with Kaminskene. She says the biggest pile of manure needs the longest pitchfork! True, Kaminskene is the tallest woman at Spring Farm, but Anyus is certainly not so short either. Still, it's a good thing Kaminskene didn't hear Anyus talking like that.

While Kaminskene is busy in her *klēts*, Anyus is in the middle of the yard, bedding and all. Her pillows and blankets are flung about on the fence posts. Anyus flails at them with the laundry paddle so hard that the dust flies thick as autumn fog. The dust makes Anyus herself sneeze constantly, so that there's no way her little tobacco pipe can stay in the corner of her mouth.

As Ingus walks past Anyus, his tongue at once begins to itch.

"Well, well, so Anyus is out threshing now! I bet those old rags haven't had such a beating since the world began!"

"There's bound to be a fight now," thinks Annele anxiously.

But there isn't. Anyus just makes a face and says:

"A child speaks like a child."

"Oh, won't Ingus be wild that she said that! He'll make mincemeat out of Anyus now!" thinks Annele.

But he doesn't. Ingus, too, just stares for a while, makes a face and goes inside.

"Where are the maids?" shouts Ingus. The farmer has told the farmhands to call it a day so that everyone can get to the sauna and to bed in good time. Well, what about it? Has the water been heated, have the towels and shirts been made ready?

"They are, everything's ready!" Karlīne, her sleeves rolled up, wearing a white linen apron, runs out in the kitchen and fills the buckets with water from the steaming kettle; then back to Ingus, who stands waiting in the middle of the room, legs wide apart.

"Here, and be off with you!"

She throws a fine white shirt, mangled so it's nice and soft, over his shoulder.

Ingus doesn't say a word. So what if she throws it over his shoulder! He just stands there for a little while with a pleased smile on his face, then tears outside like the wind, and look, there he is running across the yard with his steaming bucket, water sloshing at every step. After him, slowly, go the rest of the men as well. Last of all goes Jurītis's grandfather, tottering with tiny steps as he carries his little bucket of water.

The maids are back at work again. Everywhere on the beds, white sheets have been spread on which flat circles of dough, rolled thin, lightly covered with flour, have been set out to dry. When they are sufficiently dry, they are placed on the clean table, divided into strips, which are stacked on top of each other and then, with a sharp knife, using a chopping motion, are cut into "caterpillar" noodles. The faster the knife falls and rises, the finer the noodles, the quicker and the more dexterous the maid. Tick-tick, tick-tick, tick-tick-tick! It goes faster than a young rooster pecking grain.

Annele's mother comes and gives the maids permission to go and feed the animals, or they might be too late. She says she will finish whatever is still left to do here.

Now it's Annele's turn. She can't control herself any longer, no matter how often her question has been rejected today. Surely Mother will tell her something.

"Will it be Easter tomorrow?"

Of course Annele knows full well that it won't be Easter tomorrow, but she doesn't know how else to ask the question.

"No, child," Mother answers lovingly, "tomorrow we're going to the Lord's Supper."

"To the Lord's Supper!" the exclamation catches in Annele's throat. And only a moment later she recollects herself enough to take advantage of Mother's willingness to answer questions.

"Where?"

"In church!"

Annele flushes to the roots of her hair.

"Are you taking me, too?"

"Get away with you, you little silly!" Mother answers with a smile.

Annele knows. When she's told she's a little silly, it's useless to ask any more questions and to beg, for nothing will come of it.

Tick-tick! Tick-tick-tick-tick-tick! – clicks Mother's knife, and the work dwindles and draws to a close under her hands much faster than could have been done by two maids, but then God forbid anyone should come and pester her with questions!

Annele is thinking.

The Lord's Supper. Oh, the wonder of it! So that's why they're all getting ready and dressing up, and why they're so loving and kind, beaming like suns. Look at the things grown-ups are able to do! They'll boldly walk into church, to that holy place on the other side of the white railings, where on a crimson cloth there are gold vessels covered with gold-fringed towels. Candles gleam on both sides, while in the middle stands the Savior, looking, waiting for the grown-up people with his arms outspread. Yes, that's the Lord's table! Annele saw it when Mother took her inside last summer to show her the church.

Annele makes the rounds of the garden. The brownish, tiny buds seem to have become fatter today. Annele caresses some of the branches, touches one, then another. "Do you know what's happening tomorrow?" she asks. And they respond as if they could communicate with Annele: "We know, we know!"

Citron is sitting in front of the door. He's having a good day, too, for no one has driven him away with a gruff "Scram!"

"Do you know what's happening tomorrow?" Annele hugs Citron's shaggy head.

"Yea-oo!" Citron howls in response, half-yawning, contorting his jaws, and fawningly brushing Annele's shoulder with his nose.

"I know, I know! I know everything!"

But now the sauna-goers are coming back, and he has to run and greet them with loud barking. Why do they hurry so strangely, almost at a trot, turning their ruddy faces this way and that, their feet red and bare!

It's lovely, quiet, and tender tonight. There is no laughter, but a sense of holy and great expectation.

After the men get home from the sauna, the women and children go in turn, and then the whole household is clean to the last little seam.

A heavy, sweet peace shimmers blue from the woods and from the reddish-brown meadows, which have barely shed their blanket of snow.

Sunday morning arrives even quieter, even less ordinary. It feels as though everybody were walking on tiptoe, and even avoiding talking to each other. The hearths are cold, for no breakfast will be cooked this morning. After prayers have been said, long, long prayers including all the articles of faith, during which everybody still sits there wearing their usual clothes, the people of the household disappear in their own corners and *klētis* and get dressed for church. Then they gather in the big room once more, waiting for something silently. Granny comes in, and now begins the strangest part of that whole morning. They all first kiss Granny's hand, then kiss each other: women kiss women, husbands their wives; the young kiss the hands of all the older folks, even Anyus's and Kaminskene's hands. Not a word is spoken all the while. The women are wiping their tears, even sobbing. Kaminskene is crying so hard she has to take a deep sobbing breath several times. Like all the other old women, she is wearing a colorful silk scarf over her flounced bonnet, and over this is yet another – black silk, pulled lengthwise across her forehead. Her head looks as wide as a bushel basket. Clothes are rustling all around Annele, there is the trampling of heavy Sunday footwear. Then everyone goes out the door again quietly, one by one or in couples. Karlīne goes with Luze, while Ingus walks on the other side of her. And Karlīne is wearing Luze's white scarf, for of course they're as loving as sisters.

Now there is freedom! All the grown-ups are gone! She can do what she likes, go wherever she likes. The boys take to their heels after grabbing their morning bread, before auntie from the neighbors, who has come to make the midday meal and watch the house, has a chance to tell them to take a book and be good and behave decently while the service is going on. Them and good? Will they hurry off to read their Sunday books? Not likely! Bet they'll come back around noon with their feet wet, whole armfuls of pussy willows, and their pockets stuffed with new-made osier whistles.

But what is Annele to do?

Auntie goes out to make herself useful outdoors, to take a look at the barns and the *klētis*. It's too early yet to make the noon meal. For Sunday dinner, Granny has already set out a colander full of noodles and a bowlful of cut-up meat, for today's festive meal is to be shared by the whole household.

Annele is alone in the house. The house has never felt like this before. She can play with her toys, talk in different voices, sing Sunday hymns and silly songs to her heart's content. There's no one to say, What's with that girl? No one to make her keep out of the way or be quiet. When Annele runs out of songs, she hears another speaker murmuring somewhere. The big clock in the chamber throbs incessantly like a trusty watchman: I'm here, I'm here! But the walls, drowsily silent, seem to be saying: We don't care. It's all the same to us.

When she hears the clock, Annele's eyes light up: we're alive, the two of us. Now we can talk! And she hurries at once to this other live creature.

But the heart of the clock throbs deep, deep inside. Untouchable, inaccessible, regardless of whether there's anyone home or not.

Can it really be that there's no way to get to it? Annele crawls behind the box, scratches at the walls with her fingernail, bores into the keyhole: in vain! Nothing moves, nothing opens! If she climbs on the chair, all she can do is run her hand over the round face of this throbbing creature. It's smooth and cold. Around its edges, circled by painted moons, stand the hours, which Annele already knows how to count. Three times she accompanies her finger around past them, asking each one, Is that you? And the clock answers each question with a tick-tock! It has nothing else to say, and so all conversation with it is soon exhausted.

In the farmer's living quarters, the white sand and chopped green fir twigs scattered on the floor are still fresh and untouched. For a while there's work for Annele to do here. She does her best to trample every last nook and cranny as smooth as the floor of the servants' quarters. After a good deal of effort she almost succeeds. But then all of a sudden it occurs to her that she must hurry and go to the Lord's Supper. The grown-ups must be in church by now.

She must get dressed, quickly, quickly. And Annele now collects articles of clothing from various *klētis*. Grandmother's big shawl, Mother's jacket, a towel, a colorful garter somebody dropped – good things, every one of them. The shawl goes around her, the towel over it, and Mother's jacket with the garter tied round it turns into a cheerful sort of coat, like something a logger might wear. As soon as she has changed and said her prayers, she has to start saying goodbye. Annele kisses first Grandmother (the big clock), then Father and Mother (the two big tables), and then the people of the household in all the corners, where there are slews of them. Then, importantly, she walks outside.

Once she's outside, she's got to look for the road.

It's right under her feet. But where's Annele's church going to be? She searches for a long time and can't find one anywhere.

One gooseberry bush, sheltered from the wind, is already green. Almost green! Wonder how that happened? How could one bush wake up when the others all about it are still asleep?

Could it be because it's not a bush at all, but a church? Yes, this is the church right here! All she has to do is fix it up and decorate it. – Annele now sets out chairs, hangs chandeliers, marks off railings, puts down a white stone table. And in the very middle the Savior is going to stand with his arms outstretched. Why, there he is! His shining blue eyes are looking directly at her.

"Annele, you have not adorned the Lord's table properly yet."

"What else do we need?"

"Well, can't you see?"

Yes, Annele does see. There's no golden altar cloth. Where is she going to find a golden cloth for the Lord's table?

Where can she find a golden cloth? Annele is sad.

"Here, Annele."

The sun suddenly surfaces from a deep crevice in the clouds, the sun throws a golden cloth over Annele's arms, unrolls it over the shadows, over Annele's arms, over her church, over the yard, tosses it into the fields, wraps it around the distant hilltops, spreads it over the even more distant blue forests. Oh, look! How infinitely vast the Lord's table is now! Covered all over with the big golden cloth! It rolls gleaming from one horizon to the other. And what a church it is! Now Annele has a different kind of church with blue sky walls. She can go to the big Lord's table! Annele can be a guest at it everywhere she turns. Now she wants to be wherever she sees its golden shimmer over the vanished shadows. And because the heavy church-going clothes are in her way, she pulls them off one by one and races away with the sun so that her fair hair flutters like loose tow.

What happened to the time? The lovely morning! The time has passed like sand falling through her fingers. They're coming! – loudly exclaims Citron, who's been sitting on his haunches behind the hill on the road to church all this time waiting for Karlīne, the person who feeds him.

They're on their way! Citron trumpets loudly, leaping and tearing in circles around the first couple to return from church. It's Ingus and Karlīne. "Food, I want food, girl! Is the whey soup done? Have the sand pies finished baking?" yells Ingus in a funny loud voice when he catches sight of Annele. And hurries past, his cap pushed back on his head. "Here, girl, a present for you!" Karlīne tosses a little bunch of the first hepaticas into Annele's lap, but they're all squashed and crumpled. She hurries past, too. The white scarf has dropped on her shoulders. She is so quick, merry, and flushed. While Luze, who follows a short distance behind her, is just the opposite. Luze is not in a good mood. "She's sorry she gave Karlīne the white scarf," Annele can't help thinking, and she starts feeling quite sad. For she can see: No, Luze and Karlīne are no longer sisters.

But now Annele suddenly remembers her own sins, heavy as boulders. Where are the clothes? She flushes red as a beet. If Mother comes home and sees all the mischief, there'll be a bad scolding. Quick, she must hurry and get rid of every trace. She must find all the clothes, hide them so Mother won't scold.

That's how it always is with those grown-ups. As soon as they appear on the scene, all the wonderful magic is gone.

That afternoon, the big people are the same as always, and no one regrets the lovely communion morning as much as little Annele.

Looking for Land

On Sunday afternoons, men from the surrounding farms often come to visit Spring Farm. They don't play cards, for they are not carefree, as bachelors are. They don't go and make the rounds of the fields of Spring Farm, for they have no horses and fields of their own; they are hired hands on farms that belong to others, just as Annele's father is a hired man at Spring Farm. They come to visit Father in order to talk.

Annele likes to watch what the men are like and how they talk. Ģelžu Miķelis is a shrimp of a man wearing checkered pants and a light gray jacket with long tails that he calls his courting jacket. As he comes into the room, some smart aleck usually greets him with, "Well, Miķelis, writhe and thine, the larkths are thinging." Whereupon Miķelis responds, "Lithen, you rathcalth, be grateful to God that your tongueth are nimble." And beyond this, he doesn't hold it against them. He's used to being made fun of, ever since he was a young man, for not being able to pronounce certain sounds, and for waking the other hired hands one morning with the words, "Writhe and thine, the larkth are thinging." Miķelis is not a big talker, but he makes up for it by listening with his eyes, his ears, and his mouth wide open. And every time, no matter who finishes speaking, he agrees: "Yeah, right. That'th what I thay, too." And his pale blue eyes shine and his rosy cheeks glisten, that's how much he enjoys each speaker.

Rudmetu Vilis, on the other hand, is hot and fierce as a crackling juniper branch. No matter who says something, he immediately counters it with a remark of his own, always threatening god knows whom. He walks around perspiring in thick knitted sweaters, with his red beard sticking out, occasionally raking his fingers through his thick, curly hair. Don't anybody get in his way at times like that!

The men talk of distant foreign lands, of wars and peace treaties, of princes and kings, of masters and servants. But more than anything else they talk about land. As springs flow into a brook and brooks into a river, so all their discussions finally flow together into one subject, and that is land. In the center of all the discussions is Annele's father. When he speaks, the other men listen attentively and even Rudmetu Vilis doesn't interrupt. Father mostly stands in the middle of the room and the others are grouped around him. The more fervent and younger men remain standing, the older and cooler ones sit.

Many is the time Annele has heard them talk about land until she finally understands that the men need land, and that land is something that one should look for in

whatever way possible. The bachelors don't set much store by land. Ingus says, "What do I care about your land? Me, I'm single – just myself to worry about."

But then Father answers: "Once you have a wife and children, you'll have the same worries as us."

"There's no justice in the world, none at all," Rudmetu Vilis angrily speaks up. "If there were any justice, we'd each have our own piece of land. Whereas now – another fellow's got some and I don't. Why don't I have any?"

"Yeah, right. That'th what I thay, too," Miķelis immediately chimes in.

"There must be justice in the world. All we have to do is look for it," reasons Zangus, Jurītis's father.

But Rudmetu Vilis cuts in:

"We've got to look for it with clubs in our hands. What gives the country estates their splendor? What gives the gentry their splendor? The sweat of our brow, wouldn't you say? You think the poor will be given justice if they don't look for it themselves? And what I keep saying is, you need a big stick."

Rudmetu Vilis flickers like a glowing stick of kindling waved about in the dark, while Annele's father calmly says:

"Will a bud blossom if you tear it open by force, before its time? Can you force a field to give you a harvest of rye on St. George's Day? To every thing there is a season. I'm simply telling you: one day justice will come and there'll be land."

"Yeah, right. That'th what I thay, too," Miķelis agrees eagerly. And Rudmetu Vilis, too, sniffs and keeps his peace.

That's how they talk. Always, they calm down at Annele's father's words, but start all over again another Sunday. Until Annele knows with certainty: to look for land is to look for justice.

And one morning she wakes up with one fervent desire: today the most pressing of all her pressing tasks is – to find land and to work it.

But she's walked all over the place outside: nowhere can she find the kind of land she needs. No wonder the men haven't found it either. It's difficult business. She'll have to walk a long, long way. Make a thorough search. But first she has to get properly equipped.

And Annele goes into the house, where there's this and that she can use in Mother's mending basket. There's enough for an apron, a shawl, something to wrap around her head. But she immediately swerves from her direct path out the door when she glances toward the window. By the window the maid Karlīne is winding gray linen thread. On the windowsill are the big horn-rimmed glasses of Jurītis's grandfather. When Grandfather can't see or find something, he always hooks the glasses on his nose and immediately he can see. Now Annele, too, knows: as soon as she puts on the glasses, she'll see some land. Sure thing.

But what will Karlīne say? – Well, let's find out!

Annele softly creeps to the window.

"Can I take those?" she lifts her finger slightly, pointing at the glasses.

"Are they fighting back?" Karlīne responds with another question. "Why don't you see if you can take them?"

Does that mean she can't? Annele wonders and hesitates, then stretches out her hand, firmly resolved. "I'm going to take them."

"If you can take them, then go ahead!"

And Annele not only takes them, but puts the glasses on the very tip of her nose, and Karlīne not only doesn't say anything, but even helps Annele wrap the tapes of the handles around both ears. Only she laughs so hard that Annele, too, can't help laughing.

Yes – once she goes out in the yard with the glasses, she doesn't have to search too long – she's found land!

And it's located in such a lovely secret spot that no one except Annele has any idea where it is.

You simply crawl on your stomach under a high board fence, and then you can work in the sweat of your brow.

The land Annele has had the good luck to find is round, arched like a loaf of bread, and surrounded by a forest of thick, tall leaves. It's got puny little red-dish-brown plants growing on it with a couple of tiny leaves each.

Annele doesn't need those. She picks them out one by one and puts them among the tall leaves.

Then she goes to work cultivating the land. She plows it, harrows it, makes furrows, and sensibly provides for everyone who has no land. She plants potatoes for Jurītis's father, sows barley for Ģelžu Miķelis, rye for Rudmetu Vilis – since he's so good at mowing the fields. But for her own father she prepares the largest piece of land of all to sow wheat in. And thus, cultivating the ground and making the rounds of the fields in between times to see if there's any green showing and, where none can be seen, sowing fresh seed, she has to drop all her wraps; and even the glasses, once they have found the land and thus fulfilled their purpose, have slid down goodness knows where and vanished from her consciousness.

Who knows what all Annele could have grown if, right when her lovely work was at its peak, she hadn't been startled by a horrible scream, like a roll of thunder from above. When she looked up, the fringe of Kaminskene's gray scarf shook just above Annele's head, hanging over the board fence, and below the fringe darted Kaminskene's fierce black eyes. And this is what she yelled:

"My bed, my bed! Will you look, everybody, will you look what's been done to my bed? What kind of people will spoil their child like that? And I ask you, is this a child? This is a wild animal! What's to become of a child like that? She won't make way for God nor man... But I won't put up with it! I want to be reimbursed for this! I want to be paid down to the last penny – –"

Annele sees that it's high time to leave her fields and make a run for it. And she runs, her heart beating loudly, through weeds and nettles. But where can she run to? The world contracts, curls up, until at last there's nothing left but one chastising hand. It's the hand of Annele's mother. Close, close, oh, much too close! And this day's great, lovely work ends and comes to grief in deep and long sobbing.

All afternoon Annele is sad, sad. She'd rather go to the pines at the edge of the woods, the forget-me-nots in the ditch down in the marsh, than be with people. Forget-me-nots and pines are allowed to bloom and grow, they may do what they like, but Annele had to swear solemnly never to behave as she had today. And, so that she would not forget her promise, she got a spanking.

The spanking doesn't matter. It passed easily, she was careful to pull her muscles in successfully at the spot where she was punished. But what hurt horribly was the demarcation line between two periods of her life and two ways of looking at things.

With what sweet joy Annele had gone out to look for land and justice, and now it turned out that justice and land both belonged to that fierce Kaminskene.

Long after the sobs had abated, Karlīne, happening to go past, shook her finger at Annele.

"Hey, better watch out! If I hadn't put away the old man's glasses, you would have gotten quite a different kind of hiding."

Annele couldn't answer a single word. Was this Karlīne talking like that, Karlīne who that morning had been such a friend and ally, had herself helped put on the glasses and laughed so heartily and nicely?

Gypsies

On waking up this morning Annele's first thoughts are: the Gypsies. Is she going to see them this morning or not, and if she does, what will they look like?

Yesterday Jancis the herdboy was saying that four wagons had arrived on Gypsy Hill in the morning and four more had come after noon. The females had gone begging toward Zaḷenieki. The males with the horses, he said, were lolling about on the field. Toward evening the manor had come to have a look at the Gypsies. The countess had put down naked Gypsy babies on a piece of paper. The news gave Annele a lot to think about.

Gypsy Hill. Annele knows it well. It's a small arid hill by the low-lying meadow at the edge of the woods, so thickly overgrown with young bushy pines that it faces the wind like a wall. But the sun as it circles the sky seems to spend all its time on Gypsy Hill. Morning, noon, or evening, there's always sun on Gypsy Hill.

But "females" and "males"! Wonder what they were like. Did they hop on both feet like sparrows? And did they have wings? Females and males! That was really funny!

Another thing: the manor had come to have a look and the countess had put down the Gypsy children on a piece of paper?

Could the manor house really sit on a wagon and come over, and were Gypsy children light as feathers that they could be put down on a piece of paper?

She'd better ask Mother about all these things. And since a visitor who's come to see Grandmother has just given Annele a freshly baked wheaten flatcake, something rare and unprecedented in spring, and Annele would have to wait an impossibly long time holding it in her hands uneaten till evening, when Mother will come home, she has twice the reason and is twice as pleased to run to Mother out on the field where she's gone with the maids to spread manure.

Both Mother and the maids are delighted about the flatcake, but they refuse to take a single bite, wanting Annele to have it all herself.

Now would be a good time for Annele to ask about the Gypsies, the thing that is burning on the tip of her tongue, but how can she ask about those males and females and the manor house driving to Gypsy Hill when she can see Karlīne's mocking eyes on her? Immediately she bites her tongue: no, it's probably not a good idea. Karlīne will laugh and then Annele will be embarrassed. She'd better figure out by herself what this business with the females is all about. Maybe she's seen some before.

And she pulls at her mother's skirt and asks her softly:

"Mother, have I ever seen any Gypsies?"

"Gypsies?" wonders her mother. "No, I don't think so. They never came to Chisel Farm, and at Bumblebee Farm you were too little to notice. No, I don't think you've ever seen any."

Karlīne has overheard what they are saying and merrily calls out, shaking her pitchfork: "Oh, so you're eager to see those distinguished guests, are you? Have patience! Tomorrow if not sooner, they'll be upon us like a swarm of locusts. Just tell Grandmother to mix up a batch of bread and cook a cauldron full of porridge. Feeding them is like filling a bottomless pit."

"A bottomless pit?" This business of the Gypsies is getting more and more puzzling.

And so this morning Annele walks around thinking about the Gypsies, although her desire to get to know them is no longer as fervent as it was yesterday.

Now the thing that is dearest to her heart is the flatcake that, saved from yesterday and caressed by her hands, has become as brown and smooth as a toy carved out of wood and should now be ready for eating.

If she keeps it any longer it might get moldy or dry, as Annele has seen happen to many a tidbit glimpsed in her grandmother's or mother's cupboard, shriveled away because it wasn't fed to the children in time. That's why she decides to eat the flatcake first and then to wait and see about the Gypsies.

But where should she eat it? In the house? No way. The place where she'll eat the flatcake as her morning snack must be as delicious and pleasing to her eyes as the flatcake itself is to her mouth.

Just as Annele runs outside with her decision, Citron, barking loudly, comes tearing up from the lower road, hurling the news at her:

"Woof, woof, strangers!" He rushes to the threshold of the house, then back again fast as the wind to delay the uninvited visitors with all his might. But he doesn't succeed. Waving big sticks and cursing, three big women are just now coming up from the ravine, their coal-black hair disheveled, with great big tattered shawls, shiny buckets tied in front of their chests, a child on one arm and another child or two by the other hand. Women? No, not women, females! A sting goes through Annele right to her toes, and she hurries to the *klēts* at a run. "Gypsies, Grandmother, Gypsies!" she shouts through the open door of the *klēts*, where Grandmother is busy by the bins. She comes outside at once and, quickly locking the door of the *klēts*, urges Annele to run after the Gypsy women who are just disappearing into the house, fighting off Citron all the while.

"Run, girl, run, you've got quicker feet, watch out that they don't pull a blanket off the beds or stuff a towel or shirt in their pockets."

"So that's what Gypsies are like!" thinks Annele, running into the main house, her heart aflutter.

In the meantime, all three women have sat down, one on the bench by the table, two like honest-to-goodness company on old Anyus's bed, and they're talking to each other in a loud, incomprehensible language.

The children were whining and fighting, but as if that wasn't enough, the women unwrapped the little kids from their shawls and let them loose all naked on the clay floor, where they crawled about like brown beetles. Their blazing dark eyes were all looking at Annele, boring into her, sharp as awls. The women were laughing among themselves.

"Oh, oh, how lovely! Golden hair, diamond eyes, rosy cheeks: a real little countess," one said to another and, as Annele looked about startled and wondered where this little countess was, she suddenly felt something grab her: two naked little Gypsies were stuck to her skirt like burs and were fighting for her uneaten flatcake, which was still in her hand completely forgotten.

"Let him have it, dearest, sweetest little countess, let the poor Gypsy baby have it. God will repay you a hundredfold," said the Gypsy woman.

Now Annele realized that she herself was the dear, sweet little countess who was supposed to give away her flatcake, and she also saw that she would no longer be able to save it.

Get away, get away!

She tried to chase them, call out, shake off the little beetles, but then the third and bigger Gypsy boy ran up to her from behind, came down with his fist like a hammer on the girl's forearm, and knocked the longed-for present out of her hands. It rolled across the floor like a hoop and after it, screaming, rushed all three little Gypsies. Dropping her hands to her sides, Annele watched mournfully.

The two little ones both grabbed the flatcake at the same time. But as soon as they had managed to tear off a chunk apiece, the big boy, after punching both of them hard, snatched the roll from their clutches, fled into the other corner, where the flatcake was devoured before you could say knife.

Now the little ones began sounding their trumpets again. Meanwhile the old Gypsy women laughed heartily, clapped their hands, and shouted encouragement to the naughty children.

Annele is struck dumb. She regrets the flatcake, and she's afraid of the insolent women. She is like a chick among young ravens who are, moreover, being encouraged by the old raven mothers to tear for all they're worth. It's an unfamiliar, incomprehensible world that offends her, makes her angry and resentful, but she clenches her teeth and remains silent.

Here comes Granny. At once all the Gypsy women in one voice begin clamoring for porridge, milk, and bread.

"Go out in the yard, there's porridge and bread for you there," answers Granny curtly. Chattering in loud voices, the covetous guests now rush outside and cluster around a big bowl of porridge on the lawn. In the meantime, other Gypsy women come into the yard and also fall to and begin eating the porridge without waiting for an invitation. Hastily and voraciously, they all but toss the food into their mouths, without interrupting their chatter in their rapid, choppy language as they eat. Soon the bowl of porridge is dry, but that means that the "poor little Gypsy babies with their bare tummies" haven't had their share yet, for the big Gypsy women have eaten their fill first. Grandmother has to bring out one more bowl of porridge. But that's not enough. Now all of them at once start begging the "lady with the diamond head," the "dear snow-white hand," the "great mistress of Spring Farm sitting in her farmhouse as grand as a lady in her mansion" – the chattering guests insist that she should give them milk, butter, flour, groats, meat, shirts for their bare-bellied little ones, skirts and shawls for the women themselves, and pillows and blankets for their beds. For all this they promise that God will repay her a hundred and a thousandfold. But Granny says: that's enough now. That's all. They can leave now. But the Gypsy women don't leave. Granny goes on with her chores, from the house to the well, from the well to the barn, but the Gypsy women follow her everywhere, and their mouths are going like mills.

When they get no answer at all, they get even nastier, thinking that the farm is empty of people. Just as excessively as they praised Granny, they now begin to curse and abuse her. Annele's heart begins to shake with fear, that's how abusive they are. She's never heard anyone say such nasty Gypsy words, especially to her dear, kind grandmother, who is respected by everyone, loved by everyone: Jews, beggars, and strangers. The quieter Granny becomes, the louder the Gypsy women shout, and when she now turns in the direction of the *klēts*, the women rush after her, waving their arms in the air and shooting sparks from their black eyes. All that Annele can think about is that the Gypsy women are trying to hurt her grandmother, and she throws herself in front of them.

"Oh dear! Granny, oh dear! Who will save us? Who'll save us now?"

Suddenly the window tinkled and swung open at the same moment. Through the window jumped Uncle Ansis; wearing nothing but a shirt, barefoot, his hair tousled, he had just this minute gotten out of bed. He had a long white whip in his hand. His big blue eyes flashed with anger, and the tips of his beard fluttered with agitation.

"I'll show you!" he cried. "You think you can come here and insult my mother! You better watch out!"

And the whip whistled through the air.

The Gypsy women's mouths instantly dropped open. They were petrified. Not one of them had imagined there was a man in the house, let alone the farmer himself. Then, uttering loud screams, they rushed to the children and, clutching them in their arms, ran for their lives. But after them raced Citron, barking pitilessly and snapping at their heels, followed by Uncle Ansis and his long whip.

Annele was terribly frightened by this hullabaloo no less than by her uncle's rage, and she ran behind a tree as though she, too, was to blame. The same hiding place sheltered one of the Gypsy women who had come later. As soon as she saw that the coast was clear, she ran to the bowl of porridge, quickly poured its contents into her tin bucket, darted her eyes this way and that, and tore off in the opposite direction.

Uncle came back from chasing the Gypsies, grumpy and out of breath.

"See that? That's what you get for your kind heart," he said to Granny. "I hope those curse words have taught you that you can't fill such foul mouths!"

"The curse words aren't going to stick to me, surely," answered Granny.

"You think Spring Farm is really like an inexhaustible fountain that can feed the whole world?"

"God's blessings, son, are an inexhaustible fountain," said Granny in the same calm tone.

"What can I say! There's no sense arguing with you," Uncle threw up his hands and walked into the house.

But when Granny went to get the porridge bowl, she saw that the Gypsy woman had poured out its contents, spoons and all.

"What a mean thing to do!" she exclaimed, shocked, shaking her head.

Evidently, she did regret losing the spoons.

"Oh Gypsies, Gypsies!" Annele too shook her head with amazement, "what a strange lot they are!"

The Women Who Went to America

On Saint George's Day, old Pērkons had arrived at Spring Farm with his bed, a brown wooden wardrobe, a little table and chair, and a large number of different tools: spokeshaves, shafts, chisels, axes, old scythes, and other tools.

Later, from various directions, Pērkons's three daughters came to stay with him: Trīne, Luze, and Čiepiņa, each with a spinning wheel and a green hope chest rosemåled with roosters and flowers.

Pērkons and his daughters lived not in the main house, but in an empty *klēts* reserved for the unmarried farmhands, for they had not come to live at the farm for long. None of them had hired themselves out to work as farm workers. They gathered at Spring Farm like migrating swallows on a telegraph wire. They were indeed migrating swallows, for they were getting ready to fly to America.

The most fervent in her desire to go to America was Čiepiņa, who had spent her first year as a maidservant at the other end of the parish. That part of the parish had been infected by a sort of America-going plague, and there were suddenly people at every farm eager to leave. There had been so much discussion and talk, and Čiepiņa had been so tempted by all the good things and marvels that awaited the people of Kurzeme beyond far distant seas that toward the end of winter, early one morning while it was still pitch dark, she had come running to Kūļi estate, where her father and her middle sister Luze lived and, strong-willed as she was, had insisted they must at once dissolve their whole household here, where it was impossible ever to make a decent living, and go to America to look for the good life where you could have it easy as picking flowers by the roadside if you only knew how.

Čiepiņa talked a mile a minute, and before her father and sister had managed to figure out what it was all about and what this America was, she'd already gone off to Bigwoods Farm to talk to her eldest sister Trīne. Trīne was a big woman, heavyset and hard to budge. What America? Where was this America? For a long time she had no idea what Čiepiņa was blathering about, and once she did, she refused. No, absolutely not. But how long could she hold out? Once Čiepiņa got an idea in her head, it would have been completely futile to resist. From the time she was little she had had a will of her own, a bullheadedness that neither her father or mother or sisters could resist. And now her mother was dead and Čiepiņa was the youngest, the family's darling, still a mere child. They couldn't let her go off alone with strangers, could they? And if the eldest and youngest sister both left, then what was Luze to do, like a tooth pulled out from the middle? And if the children left, what would become of the father, like an old tree with its branches gone? If they were to go, they'd all go together. That was God's commandment. And so they had decided to go.

Every morning, Pērkons left with an axe, a saw, or some other object, intending either to sell it, leave it as a keepsake for some relative, or to consult with people wiser than he: what if he were to take this thing along on the trip? for it was better to be on the safe side, and what was safer than having one's own belongings with you? But none of the advice seemed good enough to Pērkons, for that night, sure as fate, he was back again with that same implement. Then a new discussion would begin on the same subject with his daughters, with the rest of the household – but even here Pērkons easily rejected all their good advice. Yes, it was easy to give things away, but who would you get them from later, who would you ask? And thus he and his things stayed together. Time was passing, but he could not bear to part from his possessions.

One time he came back in a temper, fit to be tied. He called together his daughters and asked them sternly whether they had ever considered where they were going to put their hope chests. Was he supposed to drag those around as well? Did each of them think, maybe, that she could sail into America on her trunk the way you sit on a hay wagon, legs dangling? "Think again, my lovelies! No such thing! They've got strict authorities, not the way we do here. You'll be able to take whatever you've got on and as big a bundle of your possessions as you can lift on your shoulders, no more." That was the news Pērkons brought home. And this was his last word. No hope chests!

"What? Not one? Not a single one of the three hope chests?" three mouths exclaimed as one.

Well, maybe – if they begged and begged – maybe one. But three? – not a chance.

"Are they ever stupid," Trīne said incredulously, "how come they don't let us take all our hope chests with us?"

Pērkons planted himself right in front of Trīne and said, in a deep, important-sounding voice:

"Oh, you want to know why they don't let you take them? Do you have any idea where this America really is?"

"Well, so where is it?" asked Trīne.

Then Pērkons raised his arm in the air and, extending his index finger, plunged it straight toward the ground at the spot where he was standing and said in a voice that made objections superfluous:

"America, you understand, is down there."

All three sisters looked at each other shocked.

"Yeah, don't look at me like that! Right through the earth, on the other side – that's where they say your America is."

Trīne collapsed on the threshold of the *klēts*, but Čiepiņa tossed her head and said with conviction:

"Stuff and nonsense! That's just a fairytale. Why, there are people that have gone there and have sent back letters. Surely they didn't crawl through the earth."

Well, maybe one didn't exactly have to crawl through the earth, Pērkons couldn't really say, maybe one could go around one corner, but it all involved great hardships, and that's why the girls should put the three hope chests out of their mind.

Then Trīne, Luze, and Čiepiņa ran each to her own hope chest, clambered on top of it and said they would not be parted from their hope chests, come hell or high water. Trīne had inherited hers from her mother, Luze from her grandmother, and Čiepiņa from her godmother, who had died a spinster and bequeathed it to her crammed full to the brim with her dowry – Čiepiņa would not give up a single piece of it.

And then all three began to weep bitterly.

At this point Pērkons realized that the news he had brought home today was worthless, and that he must make fresh inquiries on the next day. Meanwhile his daughters began to reconcile themselves to the thought that they would have to part with the hope chests.

The sisters had been going over their things to some extent every day, but on the day after the great weeping they went through everything thoroughly. The entire contents of the chests had to be aired. Trīne reserved the section of the fence from the *klēts* to the main house, Luze took the section toward the sauna, while Čiepiņa piled her possessions on the fence of the apple orchard so as not to get them mixed up with those of her sisters, for some of the things all of them owned were identical, except that hers, since she was the youngest, were not as worn and brighter in color.

Little Annele was always hanging around Pērkons's daughters. There was such a lot to see that her eyes were dazzled. Čiepiņa was the one she got along with especially well. When Čiepiņa covered the fence with her brightly colored wool blankets and shawls, and spread the others to air on the bushes and grass, she did not mind, in this sunny sheltered spot, if Annele went to "church" or "visiting" with some particularly nice shawl. Čiepiņa dressed up too to go with her. Not stuck up at all. And when the two of them, holding hands, began whirling around in a dance as they went visiting, flashing bright ribbons and shiny silk scarves in the wind and mingling them all in a jumble, they looked like great big irises or peonies that have left the flower bed in front of the window and have started dancing.

When the sisters had carried their possessions back into the *klēts* and put them each in her own pile, they sat down and put their heads together: what should they do if it turned out that they wouldn't be allowed to ride into America with their hope chests? Would they have to bundle everything up? And if so, would they be able to carry the bundles? They decided to put it to the test at once. And they leapt up like squirrels each from her own pile of belongings.

Each spread one of the bigger blankets in her own corner of the *klēts* and heaped it as high as it would go. At the bottom, pieces of homespun, linen cloth, sheets, pillows; at the top, all the lighter and finer stuff. Half of it hadn't even been put on the pile when the bundle was already so big that you had to sweat like a pig to tie the corners together. With great effort they managed to do it. Now Trīne called Luze to help her be the first to lift the burden on her shoulders. Once that had been done, and the burden had leaped on her back with a sudden "ups-a-daisy," Trīne did totter around rather strangely in a semicircle, yet managed to stay on her feet and walk out the door in a fairly straight line. Both her sisters watched curiously as Trīne went tripping with her burden at a half-run first to the house, then to the barn, then turned right and vanished downhill in the direction of the church, and did not reappear until quite a while later, holding the corners of the blanket together with one hand, waving the other merrily, and circling her arm in the air to signal that the experiment had been a success, that the bundle felt comfortable on her shoulders, and that there was no longer any need to rack their brains over it.

Of course, Trīne had a pretty easy time of it, for she was twice as big as either of her younger sisters: they would have been incapable of lifting a burden such as Trīne's, let alone carrying it. And leaving aside the question of the bundle – what should they do with the things that didn't fit in the bundle? Their father had said they could also take whatever they wore on their back. They must find out how much they could put on. The remainder of their things consisted almost entirely of skirts and shawls.

Čiepiņa counted a dozen skirts, and now she must put them all on. She began: at the very bottom, her grandmother's rose-colored skirt, more than a hundred years old and with tiny pleats at the waistline, like an accordion. Then over that one, layer after layer, she put on skirts with zigzag patterns and skirts spangled with stars, striped ones, dotted ones, plaid ones, until the ones that were underneath had slid down to her hips and dragged on the ground, while the ones on top, with waistbands just below her breasts, barely reached her knees. And as she grew petals from bottom to top like a dahlia, she burst into peals of laughter. Everybody must watch the fun. She ran into the middle of the yard like a lady with a crinoline, twirled around, and, clapping her hands, shouted: "Over here, everybody!"

People did gather – Karlīne from the house, Zete from the garden, old

Kaminskene from her *klēts* exclaiming with surprise from afar: my, how those Pērkons girls carried on, and what silly pranks they played, with all that time on their hands!

And as though in defiance of Kaminskene, Trīne and Luze also pranced into the middle of the yard wrapped in shawls, in brightly colored bedspreads, as if on their way to a masquerade. They began to fool around, played tag, got tangled up with each other, stumbled on purpose, collapsed in a heap, rolled bodily down the little hill in the yard, and almost died laughing when they finally flopped on their bundles inside their *klēts*. What else could you expect of people with time to burn!

The women of Spring Farm came into the *klēts* to find out what the hullabaloo was all about, and when they saw all that wealth on the floor, they threw up their hands dumbstruck. Of course everyone had said that Pērkons's late wife had been a hard worker and a great one for saving, but still it was really amazing that she had prepared such dowries for her daughters, for she had been a mere laborer's wife. Karlīne, herself an orphan, said in a plaintive voice that if she had gotten even a tenth as many things from her mother, you could promise her the moon, but she would never go gadding about any Americas and squandering her possessions about the world. Kaminskene grimly looked first in one corner, then in another, spat and walked out. Her *klēts* was just next door, and she had company, old Graudene from Blackcurrant Farm.

The Pērkons girls put back their stuff, and no longer felt like laughing. They concluded that the idea of wearing so many clothes and tying them into bundles was probably just a lot of foolishness, and if so, the whole thing wasn't worth it. For the time being, though, there was nothing they could do but wait for their father. They sat each on her hope chest feeling downcast.

It was no longer any fun for Annele in the Pērkonses' *klēts* either. All the clothes had been looked at, and it was the sisters' turn to be silent. Annele was just about to dash out the door when Čiepiņa exclaimed, "Shush!" – and became still and straight as a pole, her neck stretched as long as a crane's, her ear cocked in the direction of Kaminskene's *klēts*. The sisters followed suit. "Can you hear what those witches are brewing in there?" yelled Čiepiņa. Now, there was no need to yell, for her sisters were not deaf. Kaminskene wasn't deaf, either, and her ears were just on the other side of the wall.

"Listen to that, everybody, I guess we must be the witches," Kaminskene's voice shouted in reply just as loudly from the other *klēts*.

"Like hens. First they lay an egg, then they cackle," Luze said calmly but scathingly.

"Gossips! Scandalmongers!" continued Čiepiņa even more loudly.

"Show-offs! Vagrants! America-goers!" came the response from the other *klēts*.

My, how that word infuriated Čiepiņa. She pushed up her sleeves and with a leap she was in the doorway.

"Oh, is that right? America-goers, eh? We're the America-goers and you're the goodies, huh? Just you wait!"

Annele rushed out the door so quickly you'd have thought the *klēts* was collapsing over her head. Now you could no longer understand a single word. In the doorway of one *klēts* stood Čiepiņa and her sisters, in the other stood Kaminskene, with Graudene some distance behind her. They all kept shouting and flinging words like rocks at each other. Swearwords came pouring out of Čiepiņa. If Annele hadn't just seen Čiepiņa's skirt and dotted red scarf swishing through the air, she'd never have believed this was the very same Čiepiņa with whom she had spent such a nice morning – that's how terrifying she looked now. The way the other sisters looked would also have made a person scared to go near them, to say nothing of Kaminskene – *she* was always terrifying, but now she was black with rage.

Kaminskene didn't even have time to spit, something she always did when she was furious. From all the shouting her voice had cracked and when she raised it she barely managed a wheeze. In the meantime Čiepiņa and her sisters gained the upper hand. Kaminskene just kept opening and shutting her mouth and waving her clenched hands wildly in the air; when she regained her voice a bit, she began to shout and call out to people, telling them to come, to come and save her from the ravening beasts. Were they going to let this terrible Leviathan from hell devour her alive, she demanded. Now what did she mean by that Leviathan from hell? That wasn't Čiepiṇa, was it?

And yet, no matter how much Kaminskene called for help, no one came to save her, although there were plenty of people all around. Not only were Karlīne and the other married and single women standing at a distance, but the men, too, were just coming home for the noon break, and stopped to watch. To Annele's great surprise they all looked as if Pērkons's daughters and Kaminskene were putting on a show for laughs, judging from the way everyone's white teeth were grinning in their wide open mouths. And Ingus the farmhand even said, "Let 'em have it! You show 'em! That's the way! Make those rags shake!" Show whom? Nobody really knew, but Čiepiṇa's fists began sparring in an ominous sort of way. "Oh Lord, Lord!" Kaminskene exclaimed and fled from the *klēts*. And, as though a stopper had popped out of the door, Graudene rushed out immediately behind her, and vanished quick as a flash behind the buildings. Kaminskene ran into her kitchen garden. There she was safe. No one had ever dared to set foot there. Now she regained her power and the thundering force of her voice. Now the Pērkons girls were in trouble. Kaminskene threatened them with God's punishment and with the slough of hell. She said she'd go to the minister. To the squire. To all the high courts. To the "synot" and to the "supertendant." They'd see what happens when God's elect are blasphemed against. They'd see the angels leading her forth by her right hand, as Lot had been led out of Sodom and Gomorrah.

Annele's granny came along with a pail full of milk. She put it down in the middle of the yard, for she could no longer manage to carry it to the house in one go, and calmly said, "Will you stop already! Aren't you ashamed to use such language? Can't you see the neighbors standing there laughing at you?" Then she picked up her pail again and walked into the house.

Everybody looked over at the neighboring farm. Sure enough, women and children were lined up in the yard there observing what was going on at Spring Farm. This finally stopped all the angry tongues, and the wars were over.

The wars were over, but the day was now bleak and empty: Annele didn't like being anywhere. What had happened to this day? Fierce, bulging eyes had come between her and the day. The Čiepiṇa who had danced in the garden this morning with her shimmering scarves was nowhere to be found.

The Pērkons girls did not laugh, nor talk with anyone, and no one talked with them either. They walked around in a huff, while Kaminskene hissed. Annele hated even looking in the direction of the women's *klēts*. With timid footsteps she tripped after Granny.

"Say, what's the matter with you, lass? What are you down in the dumps about?" she finally asked after looking into Annele's sad little face.

"Why did they, why did they act like that?" Annele asked.

"Act like what?"

"Uh, swear at each other that nasty way?"

Her grandmother thought for a while and understood.

"It happens sometimes. What can you do! Such is human nature."

And that was all the explanation she gave.

"It happens sometimes. – But why does it have to happen like that?" Annele pondered. What was it, this human nature that was so wicked?

In the evening, Pērkons returned, spent some time in the *klēts*, had a talk with the old mistress of Spring Farm, and left again.

Karlīne knew what was up. She told Zete, who was scraping potatoes in front of the entrance: "Looks like they're leaving tomorrow. I hear the farmer's mother said that if they want to stay on, it would have to be with honor, but that they must never kick up such a row in her house again. And then it seems the old geezer immediately flew into a rage and ran off to look for a horse."

"Let 'em go. Who's stopping them?" Zete replied with indifference.

The following day, three wagons left Spring Farm with a green hope chest and two people sitting in each. The road went past the farm in a curve, first through the woods, then back alongside the field. In the field on a rock sat Annele, her feet drawn up close to her.

When the road approached the farm, all those who sat in the wagons turned in the direction of Spring Farm. And Annele could distinctly hear Čiepiņa say, "Isn't that that little girl hunkering on the rock over there?"

"That's right," replied Luze.

Then Čiepiņa pulled off her headscarf and waved.

Annele didn't even bat an eyelash. She didn't know what to do. Besides, she didn't have a scarf to wave back with. And in her heart there was a sort of sad and uneasy ache. Because of Čiepiņa, who else.

Suppose the people in America found out what a sorehead she was and didn't even let her come in their gate? Then Čiepiņa would have to travel across the whole world and back again with her green hope chest.

The Seam

Today will be a busy day! Last night, half asleep, Annele heard Father say that the chores need to be speeded up, for summer is coming to a close.

After quickly pulling on her smock, which she doesn't have time to button all the way down the back, the girl runs outside. Wonder what's more urgent just now? To go and do the chores, or to run and find out where and what is this close that summer is coming to.

First she must have a look at the orchard. The big white "candy" apple tree is exactly in the middle of the orchard. This morning it's dropped one of those huge apples, with an uneven angular split down the middle, full of sweet juice. Annele's eyes fill with delight. Having quickly tasted the morning's first gift, she runs on through the white dew. All the apple trees have worked mighty hard tonight! Yellow, red, white, jostling each other, bending the branches, their cheeks puffed out, the apples hang heavily from every bough, waiting to catch her eye. Too bad they're not within arm's reach! It will be a long time until she is as tall as that. In the meantime, her hands have to be satisfied with those that are hidden in the grass. God knows there's a whole slew of those, too! Annele bites into one: bitter; bites into another: sour; but at last, judiciously, she gathers a lapful nonetheless. Only her eyes are still greedy. By the fence there's a row of plum trees. For several days now, Annele has been eyeing the little amber pendants turning golden in the top branches. What good is that, though? Just an exchange of sweet, greedy glances, nothing more. The plum trees aren't ready to surrender their gifts yet, for not one plum has dropped to the ground.

In the meantime Annele has forgotten that she must go look for the close of summer. Through the trees she sees that something is happening by the threshing barn. Off she goes. That's where the urgent chores must be. And sure enough, the white stack of rye into which the whole lower field had gone has caved in from the top, and next to it there is now a pile of soft yellow straw. Father is rolling the straw into bales and tying the bales with rope.

Annele stands still, amazed, not knowing what to say. Father catches sight of her. His blue eyes are shining.

"You see, lass," he says merrily, "we finished threshing the new bread. Karlīne baked a batch with the last of the flour yesterday. Tomorrow we're going to the mill."

The new bread has been threshed. A job like that done without Annele! How could that be? How could she have slept through it?

The bale of straw bounces in the air, and Father has vanished. Look, the bale goes off barefoot, swaying and staggering with tiny, quick steps over to the barns, up the ladder, then rolls through the trapdoor. After a short time, Father comes out covered with dust, brushing straw from his neck and hair, slides down the ladder on his white linen pants, and here he is again. "Come, Annele, to work, hurry, hurry!"

How could Annele even think of anything else! It's time to really get busy! The pile of straw is endless, unformed material. You can pick up swaths of straw, twist it into wisps, tie it into sheaves. Look what armfuls Annele puts into her bale! She's always under his arms or by his feet. "What a helper, what a great helper I've got!" Father praises Annele.

When the bale is ready, Annele holds on to the rope with her hand. "Is that easier?"

"Yes, how could it not be easier!" And off they run, she and Father.

Annele can't follow him up the ladder. "That's all right, let me!" Father says, and Annele immediately complies. But what is she to do while Father is inside the trapdoor? Why not see if she can do what the big boys do?

Annele hangs from the rungs, swings, makes a sudden spurt of effort, and quick as a flash her own feet swish through her arms and over her head. She's done it! Joy suddenly rushes into the girl's breast up to her throat, and she shouts aloud. She was never able to do this, and now suddenly she can! A somersault through the rungs of the ladder, like Jancis the herdboy! Yes. Now she is big and bold like the boys. "I've got the knack of it!" she says in the same tone as her grandmother. And here goes – one somersault after another. Every one of them turns out well, and not a single one goes wrong now. She can have fun with this new pastime till nightfall even, maybe.

But suddenly her heart twists and the world crumples. There's a roaring in her ears, a darkness in her eyes, and nothing seems like fun any more. Annele gets scared. Could this be a punishment for acting like the boys?

No, perhaps it's only trouble come upon her. Now she must wait for time to pass. Then it'll go away. Grandmother says: All troubles pass with time.

Annele sits blinking her eyes. And meanwhile time has passed. And the trouble is gone as well. The darkness falls away, the end of the *klēts* emerges in sunlight, and now the whole yard is bright once more. Dear sun! At this Annele remembers that she must go see how far Karlīne has come with her bread-baking.

Annele arrives just in time. The bread trough lies stretched across the kitchen threshold like a drunkard, the white covering has been taken off, the sourdough has risen to the rim like a creek in flood. With a long poker Karlīne rakes all the coals into the front of the baking oven, throws on more wood, which flares up brightly, inspects the corners of the oven carefully to see if she's missed any coals, splashes a little water on the flame from a big wooden dipper and then grabs the long bread peel, places it on the bench in front of the oven, and sprinkles its tongue with flour till it's white as snow. Karlīne's skirt is gathered up under her girdle, a red kerchief is tied tightly on the nape of her neck so as to keep the corners out of the way, she herself glows like a coal, and her hands move at lightning speed. Annele dares not go closer; reverently, as though asking for silent assent, she squats on the threshold, which Karlīne doesn't object to. Let her squat.

Karlīne now wets her arms – her sleeves are rolled up – and plunges them up to her elbows in the dough, which at once separates, like a sponge, bubbly and sinewy. Karlīne tosses the split-off ball of dough from hand to hand for a while, stroking it, throws it on the bread peel, squeezes it flat, pats it into shape: taking off here, adding there, one end round, the other pointed, again wets her hands, caresses and smoothes it until the loaf looks as though it had been shaved with a plane, traces a cross on top with her index finger, and thrusts it across the glowing coals into the oven.

Annele's eyes yearn, her hands yearn. Oh, what work, what lovely work! She could certainly manage that! With her sleeves rolled up, her arms now in the pail, now in the trough, now on the bread peel: sprinkling flour, patting, squeezing, stroking, making the sign of the cross – she'd do it to a T! If only Karlīne would give her permission one single time, just to make one little loaf.

But Karlīne is stern. Don't you come near. If you dare come even half a foot closer, she'll yell at once: get out from under my feet!

Just now Ingus the farmhand comes in the front door, and right at that moment Karlīne's hands suddenly tremble and a lump of dough rolls to the ground. True, it's only a bit of leftover dough that Karlīne was going to put in a gap at the end of a loaf, but now she doesn't even notice what happened to it. She simply smoothes and smoothes until the gap fills up just the same, and the lump on the ground is left to go completely to waste.

Why let it go to waste? What's on the ground is for the dog. What's on the ground is for a child. While Karlīne, protecting her eyes from the glare, examines and counts how many loaves are already in the oven, Annele snatches the lump of dough and disappears unnoticed.

In the orchard by the berry bushes there is a place where you can be sure the grown-ups won't get under your feet. That's where the chores begin. There, Annele fetches wood, fetches water, fires the oven, kneads the dough in a clay trough, swaying her shoulders the way Karlīne does, forms loaves, and puts them in the oven to bake.

Now her greedy hands are more or less

satisfied, and Annele goes on her way.

By the house door, Jurītis's grandfather has driven a hook into the wall. He is spinning string. But on a little bench beside him is an armload of wood, sawed into elongated little blocks. Jurītis's grandfather does only two jobs: he either spins string or carves wooden spoons.

Annele has no particular desire to spin string. Of course, she can watch for a while how the bundles of string, wound on hooks, are twirled by the hands, bob, mingle-mangle as they twist, but there's no long pleasure in it, because you can immediately see what the end result will be. It's different with spoons. When the old man takes the spokeshave and begins to carve, pressing the elongated block of wood to his chest, there's no way of knowing the outcome: a ladle, a fat spoon for the men, or a slim one, looking as if it was made of a thin sheet of paper – for the women and children. When the block of wood has been measured for size, Grandpa makes a mark, and you can already see the spoon that's to come. Now all he needs to do is whittle away everything that's grown around it. Then as if by itself the handle appears, and the little bowl of the spoon, like a tiny loaf of bread split lengthwise. Then along comes the gouge and makes a hollow. Shavings fly in all directions, so white and fragile you can rub them into flour between your fingers. Now the spoon is done. Grandpa adds a few finishing touches, shaping and polishing it so smooth and fine that you can caress it like velvet and stroke your cheeks with it.

Carving wooden spoons would be an easy occupation for Annele, but Jurītis's grandfather turns her down: "Get out of here! This is no job for girls!"

For a while Annele sits by Grandpa, who is as silent as a fish. "Aren't you carving any spoons this morning?" she finally ventures to ask.

"I will, I will," grunts Grandpa and keeps on making his string.

"That'll be the day," thinks Annele sadly, and when she catches sight of Mother out of the corner of her eye, she suddenly remembers she has not been given her morning bread.

When the bread is eaten, Annele clings to her mother like a bur, following her everywhere she goes and whining.

"Why are you giving me such a hard time, girl, what are you sniveling about? What is it you want?" her mother asks in such a way that Annele can't pout or evade her. She has to give a direct answer.

"I want a job."

"Oh, you want a job," says Mother and thinks for a while. "All right, I guess you're big enough, I'll give you a job." She takes Annele by the hand and takes her to the *klēts*.

What can it be? Annele pricks up her ears. What job is she going to give me in the *klēts*? And the promise itself sounds as harsh as a threat. But what is she to do? After all, she walked into the trap herself.

Mother takes a piece of linen cloth from a trunk, cuts off a strip and calls Annele over to her. Tells her to sit next to her. Right beside her.

"Now watch how you do this!"

In the middle of the strip of cloth, Mother pulls out one warp thread, then a second next to it and a third, so that a broad gap is created, like a rack. Now Mother threads a needle with a long thread and shows Annele how she must sew a seam along the furrow of this rack. Annele watches wide-eyed. If only she could remember even a tiny bit of what Mother is saying! In one ear, out the other. What kind of a job is this, who ever heard or saw anything like it, and what use is it to anyone?

"Here, work on this and when you're finished, come and show me."

This last part Annele heard unmistakably. She takes the cloth with unwilling fingers and goes off to work. But she can't find a suitable place anywhere. On the threshold of the *klēts* would be fine, but tow drops on her head from the rafters, it's never done that before. At the end of the *klēts* there's such a wind that it tears the thread from your hands, how is a person to sew? When she goes into the *klēts*, it's completely dark inside; she runs down to the spring, on the big boulder, but it feels so hard she can't possibly sit there. And yet some of the work gets done at every one of her stops. The cloth is crisscrossed with the long thread – back and forth, up and down, so that the work looks like a snowy field full of rabbit tracks.

As Annele sits there working, the scorching hot delicious smell of bread suddenly comes flooding in her direction. Oh, of course! It's time to run and see what Annele's big bread oven is doing!

Karlīne is already taking hers out, carries it steaming into the house, where the brown loaves are lined up in rows crisp as pinecones. Let's hope Annele's bread isn't burnt!

Everything has worked out fine. The loaves are still where she put them. Annele taps each one with her finger on top, underneath: done!

What is she to do with so much bread? Now she must go and visit Chisel Farm, where Mother's sister is staying with little Milda and Einītis. Mother brings them part of every batch, they can always use some. It's a good thing Annele now has such a nice tablecloth, the one she just finished sewing, she can make it into a good-sized bundle, because in addition to the bread the relatives must also have something to put on it. Annele runs to her cellar, takes plenty of butter and meat, and ties these into the bundle together with the bread so tight that soupy stuff starts to ooze out. Now she can go calling.

It's a long way to go, and she has lots of complicated business to discuss with Einītis and Mildiņa, and then there's the long walk back. On one crossroad, Annele runs smack into her mother.

"Well, how's your work going? Is it done? Show me!"

Annele's knees buckle.

Her work? Oh yes, how *is* it going? – She promises to bring it at once.

But how can she bring it when it's lying in the clay bread trough, bundled around the bread and butter and meat? And it's all stuck together and she has to wring it out, like a dishrag. Annele does the best she can. She rinses it, wrings it out, smooths it with her hand till it's smooth as her sister Līziņa's church-going dress after ironing, and hangs it on an apple branch to dry. Then she hangs about on the other side of the farm, over by the hazel grove, even as far as the woods, just so she doesn't have to cross her mother's path. But then it's time to eat: they're shouting, calling the working folk to table, and Annele too. She has to go, there's no help for it, she has to go and show her work.

Mother picks up Annele's work, looks at it – wonder what's taking her such a long time?

"Oh, so that's the kind of work you do? Shame! Shame on you!"

And she says this quite slowly, takes hold of Annele's ear and counts the stitches and after every stitch tells Annele that she is an untidy, careless, inattentive, and totally useless girl; that her sewing looks like something dug up by a pig, not like work, and that it's a wonder how a big girl like her has so little sense. And when Mother lets go of Annele's ear, she tosses the work to her and says, "Rip it out and do it over!"

Annele sits in front of her little bowl of porridge crying her eyes out. A bit of food has lodged in her throat and won't let her swallow a drop, or a crumb of bread. After everyone has finished eating, Annele's bowl, too, is cleared away, to her great relief: if she doesn't want to eat, let her content herself with her "quick temper."

Annele sits by the fence reciting like a litany: "Rip it out and do it over, rip it out and do it over!" But what does that mean: rip out? She pulls at one corner, pulls at another, it all seems inaccessible, impenetrable, unconquerable. If she rips everything out, then how can she do it over again?

Yes, it's quite plain now! Annele can carry straw, can bake bread, can carve spoons if only grandfather would let her, but she can't sew a seam. – And anyway, can she carry straw, really and truly? If she were to crawl under Father's bale with nothing but her own strength, wonder which way the bale would roll? And even if Karlīne were to let her, could she really lift a big lump of dough from the bread trough and pick up the long bread peel? No way, no way! Her eyes can, that's true, but her hands cannot. Her hands cannot, try as they may. That was clear just now.

Annele's heart shrinks within her. She herself becomes as small as a tiny titmouse on a flower stalk and over her, like a lid, spreads a heavy, oppressive dejection.

Somebody is running through the garden, calling Annele, looking for her. It is Līziņa. She's here. She has a big handful of yellow plums that she has shaken from the very top of the tree with her strong young arms.

"What is it, lass, are you crying? What are you crying about?"

"Rip it out and do it over," Annele sobs, picking up her work.

"Aha!" Līziņa understands. She sits down next to the girl on the lawn, ready to teach her at once.

"Well, what do you do when you've been running in the wrong direction? You go back, right? All right now, your thread has also been running in the wrong direction. Let's take it back. Where's the first step? Look, here it is! It answers right away."

Līziņa tugs at the thread; wherever you see it pulling at the cloth, there is the first step. Once you pull the thread out, there's an empty place, and now you look for the next one. Annele's tears abate. The third and the fourth she can do by herself. "Let me have it, let me have it!" she calls impatiently, wiping her eyes with the palms of her hands. And so it goes, lickety-split, until the whole "field" has been cleared of tracks.

"Now we can start making the seam," Līziņa says importantly, putting her arm round the girl's shoulders.

"Look, right now there's a picket fence running down the middle, but it can easily come tumbling down if we don't weave it tighter. There! The needle will help us, and now let's take – three pickets back and three forward!"

Yes – that's something Annele understands at once. It's just as easy as baking bread. And her hands long to do it: give it to me, give it to me!

Līziņa now lets the girl have the work again, clapping her hands and reciting: "Jump, jump, little rabbit! Three pickets back, three pickets forward, on you go, on you go!"

But for all her laughter Līziņa is strict. The stitches must lie next to each other as round as grains. Not one must be bigger, or looser. The seam turns out as pretty as a braid, and before it even occurs to Annele to be bored, she's reached the last stitch.

"Hurrah!" shouts Līziņa, slips her hands under Annele's arms and twirls her around so fast that Annele's feet swish through the air. "Go on, run and show Mother!"

Annele runs. The lid of oppressive weight has cracked wide open. The seam has been conquered!

Bread and Honey

This Sunday, Annele has been promised a special treat: a visit to Edgefield Farm. Ever since church-going time, she's been running in and out, banging the door, once even running smack into Karline.

"Whoa! Where are *you* off to, like a locust on the wing?"

"To Edgefield Farm, let go!"

"Oh, so you're off to that land of Canaan, where milk and honey flows."

"How did you know?" Annele wonders, for Mother, too, just remarked, "It's right at the peak of the honey harvest at Edgefield Farm now. The gooseberries, too, are getting ripe."

Gooseberries are gooseberries. Annele's known them all summer. Green and hard little buttons. Are they ever sour! The grown-ups say that if you wait long enough they'll turn soft and sweet some day, but that day will surely never come at Spring Farm, for the simple reason that there aren't any left, not even on one single bush. There used to be some, but now they're gone.

What is honey, though? No matter which of her senses Annele asks, not one of them knows a thing about it. It's just that she's often heard grown-ups, when they wanted to describe something nice, say with relish, "Sweet as honey! Delicious as honey!"

"What's honey like, really?" Annele asked her mother on their way to Edgefield Farm. "Is it like morning glories, or like wood hyacinths?"

"Oh, get along with you, you little silly! Morning glories and wood hyacinths! Are those edible, huh? Why, they're flowers. Hmm – how can I describe it? I guess you'll see for yourself," answered Mother.

That's the way it always was. Grown-ups could never give you an answer to important questions. It was always: "You'll see for yourself."

When they came out of the woods, Edgefield Farm not only came into sight, but soon became audible as well. As though calling them even from afar, a wild racket greeted the visitors' ears. Every corner rang with the sound of barking.

"My, so many dogs!" Annele became frightened.

"Don't you worry! The dogs won't even see us!" her mother soothed her, turned off the road, along a path that crossed an unplowed field, made straight for the orchard, at the back of which there was a small gate, made in the fence as if on the sly. They entered the orchard and were safe. It is true that one of the dogs had run out to meet them, toward the fallow field, but when he saw that they had vanished, he sniffed out their tracks as far as the orchard, still barking, then gave a long howl and ran away. The visitors clearly had an eminent right to be here, which it would have been futile to fight against.

In the orchard, big apple trees stood in a row, and there was a row of gooseberry bushes with golden berries. Annele ran her eyes joyfully across all this, a look of getting acquainted; large clumps of tansy exuded their fragrance, hollyhocks, delphiniums, tiger lilies were in bloom, while right by the windows of the house there was a separate little fenced flower garden with small round beds; here grew uncommon flowers among which Annele knew only the calendulas and marigolds; Mother called the others by unfamiliar names: asters, stock, snapdragons. The space between the little beds and under the eaves had been swept clean and strewn with yellow sand.

When they opened the little gate, a woman's face suddenly appeared in the narrow little window of the house. A moment later, there was the sound of the door being unbolted and of friendly words of welcome:

"What company, what dear, long-awaited company! Come in, come right in! There's no dog in here just now."

Annele loved being welcomed like this, and she nearly forgot to kiss the hand of the mistress of Edgefield Farm as Mother had admonished her to do, so engrossed was she in examining their hostess from head to toe to see what she looked like: tall, scrawny, a little hunched forward, with a sizable nose, large deep blue eyes, her dark hair parted straight, smoothed over her ears; she wore a short cotton print jacket and striped Sunday apron, and her voice was so sweet no one at Spring Farm could speak like that.

"Is this your youngest?" she asked Mother, and answered herself, responding to Mother's questions at the same time. "Yes, of course. Of course! And company for my Ancīte, too, at last. Let me tell you, it was a long wait. My goodness, is she going to be happy when she gets back! No, no, my daughter isn't home just now. She went with her papa to make the rounds of the fields, and then she'll run down to the river, too. To the river, to the river! That's what she hankers for, but I just daren't let her go with the maids or the herd girl. Seeing as how her papa is free today, I can't begrudge her the pleasure. But it's been quite a while since they left, they should be home soon. Come on in, into the big room, and rest your feet."

As soon as they had crossed the threshold of the room, while the room itself was still a dim mist before Annele's eyes, a yellowish gray shaggy ball of fur dropped down from somewhere and rolled to the visitors' feet with a fierce "Woof, woof, woof!" Shoved aside by the mistress's "Down, boy!" it bounced back, spun round and round into the other corner, but once there – "Woof, woof, woof, woof!" – again rushed at the newcomers. This unexpected attack left Annele speechless: at Edgefield Farm, dogs came from every corner.

"Down, Bijou, down, fort, fort! Wirst du wohl! Fort!" the mistress called without interruption and scolded the little rascal in German, but was unable to control him until she grabbed his shaggy head in the palm of her hand. But even from the palm, he still growled fiercely, baring his teeth and flashing his little glittering black eyes at the guests.

"Don't be scared, don't be scared! All he does is bark. He won't bite, you know."

"He's just an itty bitty thing, don't you see, like a little lap dog," said Mother.

"That's just what he is. We got him from the baroness when her Lady had pups. My Ancīte was dying to have one like him, and so we did it to please the child."

"I guess that's why he can understand only German," said Mother.

"Well, of course, an itty bitty high-class little thing like him," his mistress very indulgently looked at the growling ball of fur.

This is how Annele discovered that the Laukmales' girl, whose namesake she was, was called not Annele, but Ancīte, and that she had her own dog, a lapdog no less! What a genteel, high-class thing to have!

"Sit down, stay for a while, I'll be right back," said Laukmaliene and, reprimanding her pooch with a "Ruhig, Bijou, now!" she left the room.

Annele could now examine the room undisturbed. It looked much smaller than the big room at Spring Farm, but there was three times as much furniture in it. Beds piled high with big pillows, a shiny yellow wardrobe, a big table, chairs, and against one wall something that looked like a bench or a bed with a back and arm rests, covered with black leather.

"What a funny bed!" Annele whispered, raising her finger to point, in response to which the shaggy ball of fur again jumped out of that same "bed" with his "woof, woof, woof"!

"That isn't a bed, it's called a zofa, it's something genteel that the gentry have."

"Zofa, zofa – well, what does Laukmaliene do with this zofa?"

"Don't say 'Laukmaliene.' She's Momma Laukmale. But you must call her Tante and call Papa Onkel. You know: he's Father's brother."

Yes, Annele knows.

"Momma, Papa, Tante, Onkel," she repeated and thought it would be good if they didn't have to be called one thing or another, because little people are ashamed to call big people by name, and anyway Annele often felt conversations with grown-ups were quite unnecessary.

Momma Laukmale came in and immediately resumed talking about Bijou: "So as I was saying. Her ladyship would have refused to give away one of Lady's pups to anyone else, but when Papa asked her for one to give to his daughter, she graciously agreed." And she had a lot more to tell about the puppy and its tricks. While talking she did not sit down with her guests – not at all, she busied herself about the room, going in and out several times on her errands, but always resuming the conversation upon entering at the same place where it had broken off.

Finally she came in from the other direction and invited them: "Come, come and sample some honey, so that the time until the afternoon meal will pass more quickly and you don't start feeling hungry."

She led the guests into a small pantry containing all kinds of crocks, baskets filled with eggs, household utensils hung from the walls and ceiling, and, on a small table, a deep trough with a strainer over it. But in the little window, on the panes, wasps buzzed and droned by the dozens and, as soon as the strainer was removed, began to circle around their heads, dropped on the trough in swarms. In the trough there was a thick amber-yellow liquid that oozed from a big pile of honeycomb bars like sap from a tree.

"Oh, what a lovely smell!" Mother exclaimed with delight.

"Fresh from the hives today, which is when you can really smell it. Well, sister-in-law, help yourself," Momma Laukmale urged Mother in a friendly voice, handing her a piece of bread.

She spread a second slice with a thick layer of transparent yellow honey and handed it to Annele, cordially saying:

"Here, child, eat and enjoy!"

"Don't get the floor dirty, don't get your clothes dirty!" Mother immediately added her warning, for the honey began to move outward from the center of the slice in all directions, like a living thing.

"You know what, child, you'd better go in the orchard. The gooseberries are ripe there, there may be a cherry or two left over and all sorts of berries. It's the best place for children at this time of year," Momma Laukmale, in order to get rid of the girl, opened the door and pushed her outside into the orchard.

Annele stood there not knowing exactly how to start on her slice of bread. The honey was running down her fingers. She bent the slice of bread inward, enclosing the sticky stream in a sort of little trough, but the stream busily found each little pore in the bread and pushed its way out with uncontrollable force. She had to put both hands underneath and hold the piece of bread as level as water.

"Here, child, eat!" she urged herself using Momma Laukmale's words, but she would not, could not obey. Go ahead, eat! First, though, she needed to know what it was really like, this honey. She must taste it all by itself. Then she would no doubt manage to eat it. And, taking care to aim for the center of the slice, Annele carefully stuck the pointed tip of her tongue into it.

Sticky, sweet, stinging, itchy!

Delicious?

No, not at all! She couldn't help shuddering.

Annele tasted it again.

Delicious?

No, no! Not the second time, either, and especially not the third time.

Each time, a sort of sweetly stinging itchy feeling ran across her tongue, her gums, her throat, ran numbing down to her toes, shook the girl.

No, no, no! She found the bread and honey unacceptable.

But what would Mother say? After all, this was the greatest delicacy in the world! And it was only so she would get some honey that she had been taken along on the visit. She decided to try again.

Reluctantly she nibbled at the edges of the piece of bread. She rolled and shifted a bit of bread around in her mouth for a long time, but couldn't swallow it. Impossible: she could not eat the bread and honey.

But where on earth should she put it? Where?

For a long time the girl considered what to do.

She could take it back, give it to Momma Laukmale, say, "Tante, I don't want it." That's exactly what she would say.

But how would she do that? Would it be all that simple? After all, people held honey in high esteem. Here was so great and rare a delicacy that everybody hankered for it, smacking their lips, and now this silly little girl visiting in a strange house goes and announces she doesn't want any. What would Momma Laukmale say then, after giving her the bread so cordially and generously? How would she look at her then? And Annele's own mother, who had brought her along on the visit, reminding her again and again to behave herself, and who would now see that Annele had refused such a rare treat – what would she say? And even if she said nothing, she'd just look at her with a look that Annele hated and would rather never see, seeming to say: What a trial that girl is. Not like other children at all. Doesn't even want any bread and honey. Who ever heard of such a thing? No, no, Annele can't give back the bread. Make such kind faces angry or even just questioning and reprimanding? No, she'd sooner – sooner hide the bread somewhere under the bushes, in the grass.

Annele now looked for such a spot, walked down the long row of berry bushes, full of juicy, tempting berries; under the bushes the grass was not long enough to hide the bread in, and even when it was, Annele was reluctant to hide the unwanted gift there, for – how easily Momma Laukmale could discover it there herself, even after Annele had already left, and what would she think of Annele then? What kind of a girl could be so ill behaved as to throw down God's gift, and what kind of a mother could have raised such a no-good girl? And even if nobody found the bread she had thrown away, she herself would always know, and would always be ashamed of what she had done.

By now the girl has reached the wattle fence at the edge of the orchard. It isn't high – the posts in the interstices of wattle are even lower, with round, flat tops like little tables. "Put your bread here," her common sense suddenly tells her. Yes, you couldn't find a better place, – Annele is delighted, jumps on a rail and puts down the bread as though on a tray. The birds can eat it. Somebody with a sweet tooth, running by the orchard, can have it. She hasn't shown disrespect for the bread, nor thrown it away.

Once that is done and her hands are free, the girl carefully wipes them on some grass and leaves so as to get rid of the stickiness and sweetness. She is in a hurry, for in the distance a girl is running toward her, calling her, looking for her. It's Ancīte. They shake hands and are immediately deep in conversation and great friends.

The house is empty. Momma Laukmale has taken Mother to see the calves and beef cattle.

Ancīte is a great talker, and she's also dying to show the visitor all her things: her dolls and toys. Let her see them and be amazed. But her guest doesn't know how to admire and praise things out loud, and her little hostess feels she ought to show her something that would strike her dumb with amazement.

"Hey, have you seen Bidžus yet?" she asks emphatically, thinking that now at least she'll be able to show her something extraordinary.

"That shaggy little dog? I thought his name was Bijou."

"Momma calls him Bijou, but I say: Bidžus. Because Bidžus is as shaggy as Didžus the Gypsy. And I can make him look like a Gypsy, wait, I'll show you."

Ancīte now pulls the furiously growling little dog off his warm spot on the sofa, ties back his mane on both sides like a beard, sticks a piece of kindling wood in one of his paws for a whip and now leads him up and down the room, making him dance on his hind legs and drilling him, and the more the pooch barks and kicks, the louder she laughs and teases him in all sorts of ways. But all this time, Bidžus, who bares his teeth and all but threatens to devour the girls, struggles and fights – not against Ancīte, the true culprit, but against the guest, as though correctly surmising that Annele is actually the true cause of all this disturbance.

"All right, that was Didžus, but now here's Didžus's wife," Ancīte called boisterously, let go of the little dog for the time being, climbed on one of the high beds, where there was a pile of neatly folded church-going shawls belonging to Momma Laukmale that the latter had left there when she came home from the service and had not yet had a chance to take back to the *klēts*. From the pile, the girl pulled a long, brightly colored silk scarf, the kind only Momma Laukmale had and that she wore to church or on festive occasions, to the envy of all the other farmers' wives. Scarf in hand, Ancīte approached Bidžus, who had already managed to roll up on his warm spot on the couch again and who blinked his eyes, watching distrustfully for what would come next, and giving an occasional warning groan as if to say, "No more tricks, all right? There's bound to be trouble."

But why should Ancīte listen to him? Let him snarl and growl; let him bark or even get ready to sink his teeth into Ancīte's mischief-loving hands. Ancīte is big while Bidžus is little, he gets smacked on the nose if he doesn't go along with what Ancīte wants, and so, although he whines pitifully, he gives in and allows her to tie the scarf like Didžus's wife's: first around his head, then crosswise over his chest with a big knot in the back and long ends like a tail. Holding on to the ends, Ancīte again gets ready to make her Bidžus dance a Gypsy dance, when the door opens and across a man's big feet a white calico cat leaps lithely into the room. It's like oil on a fire! Hissing, gnashing of teeth – Bidžus against the tomcat, the tomcat up on a chair, from the chair onto the bed, from the bed onto the wardrobe. Bidžus after him, wild, howling, whining, barking, rolling like a ball, silk scarf and all, with Ancīte still clutching the scarf.

Then Bidžus gets an unexpected kick and flees under the bed howling, while

Ancīte tumbles head over heels to the big feet of the hefty man who has just entered
the room. It's Papa Laukmalis himself. His face smooth and calm, his eyes piercing,
he watches the hubbub but does not say a single word. Calmly he picks up the soiled
and torn silk fabric, puts it on the bed, calmly raises his finger looking around for
that naughty girl. But she's on her feet quick as lightning. She's already grabbed her
visitor's hand: "Outside, outside, let's go outside!" And before Papa can turn
around, the room is empty. Leave him there by himself to give Bidžus and Muris a
good scolding for their great mischief.

In the yard, a new surprise awaited Annele. There stood a woman with a dirty
piece of bread in her hand, waiting for Momma Laukmale, who together with
Annele's mother was coming from the barns, where they had looked at the calves
and the other young animals. When both had come closer, the woman said:

"Look what kind of a household you have, ma'am! See what happens when you
do things out of the goodness of your heart? What kind of a wicked person could be
so spoiled that they'd throw whole slices of bread and honey to the dogs?"

"What dogs?" demanded Momma Laukmale sternly.

"Why, Turis here," the woman pointed to a black dog who stood, tail between
his legs and nose to the ground, as though profoundly aware of his guilt.

"Let me see," Momma said, coming closer, and at once, without even taking a
good look, began scolding the dog: "Oh you rascal! Why, that's the bread I just gave
to my visitor's child. He's snatched it out of the girl's hands. Isn't that so?" she
turned to Annele and then, as was her habit, answered her own question: "Of course,
of course – after all, he's a stray Gypsy dog, he grabs things shamelessly, just like a
Gypsy, you know what they say: like master, like servant. But don't you worry,
sweetie, come, we'll get you another piece of bread."

And not another word.

She took Annele by the hand. Annele was feeling so ashamed and guilty she
could barely breathe. "Wicked" was what the woman had said, sternly and fiercely.
This wicked person was Annele.

In a sweet voice, Momma Laukmale called her own daughter: Would she like
some bread and honey, maybe?

"Not me!" Ancīte answered boldly and remained outside.

"Oh, how I wish I could also say it like that! Then I'd be scot-free!" a happy
thought flashed through Annele's head, but her tongue remained silent. She was a
visitor, was guilty, must not contradict. Terrified, she watched as Momma Laukmale
in the goodness of her heart cut off an even larger second slice. What should she do
with it now? She could no longer hide it away somewhere, because Ancīte was with
her. There was no other way out: she'd have to eat it as a punishment for her former
bad behavior.

"Go ahead, eat it, the honey's running down your fingers, can't you see?" urged
Ancīte sulkily. She seemed to be annoyed about something. Maybe the bread and
honey.

"I can't," stammered Annele.

"Why can't you?"

"I don't want it."

"Then you're just as sick of honey as I am. Let me have the bread!"

"What are you going to do with it?"

"I'll give it to Turis! Here, Turi, boy!" she ran, calling the dog, who ran alongside her, avidly looking at her hands. She raced out of people's sight, deep into the orchard.

"Oh, Ancīte, if we give it to Turis again, then we'll be wicked. That's what the woman said."

"So what. You can't listen to all these women blathering," Ancīte tossed her head, her manner as superior as Momma Laukmale's own.

"But it isn't Turis's fault at all. That was my bread. I put it on the fence. I'm the one that was wicked," confessed Annele.

Ancīte, however, attached no special importance to this.

"Oh, so that was your bread? Momma gave it to you, but you didn't want it! Well, if Turis took that one, he'll have to take care of this one as well!"

Then she broke the bread into tiny little pieces and offered it to Turis. But Turis sniffed at the bread, shook his head bashfully and tried to sneak away.

"Turi!" Ancīte stamped her foot threateningly. "Get a move on!"

Turis wouldn't take it.

"So! Even a Gypsy dog is sick of eating honey. And here Momma wants us to eat it."

"But just you wait, Turi, you better think again!" Ancīte threatened, "if you don't take it, I'll give it to Bidžus, I'll give it to the other dogs. Here, Bidžu, here, Remi, here, Pluska! Get the bread!" the girl called, looking somewhere into the distance and summoning imaginary dogs.

The dog's honor was at stake. What? Give the share he had been promised to another dog? He couldn't. No, no! If there was food to be swallowed, he'd rather swallow it himself. Greed flared up in his greenish eyes. However, Ancīte would not give it to him right away, but teased the dog for quite a while until he himself, jumping and barking, reclaimed bite after bite, menacing the neighborhood with loud barks: "Mine, mine! Just you try to take what's mine!"

When the bread had been safely stowed away in the dog's stomach, the visit to Edgefield Farm became quite nice. The grown-ups were now in the house, which is why the girls preferred to roam around outside. Ancīte took her guest around to see all the lofts and attics, all the corners under the eaves where she had her favorite places to play, she talked about the chores she and the more noteworthy people at Edgefield Farm did; the girls looked through every skylight from which you had the best and the furthest view of the orchards and meadows; they were able to enter every door, for Ancīte locked and unlocked them as though she were the mistress herself. Annele was discovering a new world, she liked to listen to her cousin's stories, for Ancīte had different, funny words and expressions, she had words that were Edgefield words and were never heard at Spring Farm. Thus, imperceptibly, the shadows lengthened, and their lovely games and talk were unpleasantly interrupted by Mother's voice: "Come, child, the sun is already down by the woods, we must hurry home."

Oh dear, oh dear! Here it was again – this business of having to hurry home!

Not just yet, though – first they must pick berries for a present to take home, and then they must eat the afternoon meal. Momma Laukmale was calling them inside.

"Now Ancīte is going to catch it when Momma sees the torn silk scarf," Annele thought, worried for her new friend.

But although Momma Laukmale must have seen at a glance – as she had – what had happened to the scarf, for Papa had simply thrown it down on the bed as he had picked it up, she didn't seem to care. She shook the lovely fabric, folded it neatly and hastily carried it to the *klēts* with the rest of the scarves. That Ancīte would not get a scolding or any other kind of reprimand was clear.

Momma Laukmale accompanied her guests as far as the gate, but Ancīte ran with them for quite a distance, along the boundary, past the rye field, picking cornflowers and corn cockles and adding them to Annele's nosegay.

"Why don't you go back, child, here comes the forest," said Annele's mother.

"So what! I'm not scared. I can run through the whole forest," bragged Ancīte, but then suddenly she took a closer look at the forest, stopped walking, shook hands quickly and then raced back, without looking around once. As though the visitors had never existed.

Meanwhile Annele could not stop speaking of Ancīte this, Ancīte that. She was so full of the place they had visited and of this day's experiences that she spoke of nothing else. When Mother's answers were somewhat scanty, Annele walked all over Edgefield Farm in her imagination. One thought, however, suddenly burst out aloud:

"Why don't I have what Ancīte has?"

"What is it you don't have?"

"We-e-ll, all sorts of things," answered the girl.

"Ancīte has a lot of freedom, and you can't have that," Mother said as though reprimanding her.

"Can't have that, can't have that!" echoed the girl, and she felt as if something heavy was towering behind this "can't have that." But there was no time to think about that now. The forest came toward her with evening breezes and sweet, sweet smells. When they walked past a spring-fed meadow where huge clumps of mugworts with their clusters of flower heads on tall, fragile stems shimmered white, spreading their penetrating fragrance far and wide, Annele stood still, filled her lungs with air like a bellows.

"Mother, look, look!"

"What is it?"

"Look how much freedom I have. Lots and lots of freedom! Just like Ancīte." And she pounded her chest with both fists.

"Where? What freedom?"

"Such a sweet, sweet smell!" whispered the girl, breathing in rapturously, as if she wanted to drink in the whole forest.

"Funny child!" smiled Mother, shaking her head. "What kind of freedom is that?"

Anyus

If Kaminskene is a woman of consequence at Spring Farm, then Anyus is even more important. And much, much older. No doubt about it. So old that no one can count her years. Annele has asked around. But no one really knows. All they say is that Anyus has been living at this farm for an eternity. What's an eternity, though? Wonder where it starts and where it ends? You'd have to walk a long way to find out. But Annele's legs are still short.

Maybe Anyus is as old as the earth or as the dust on the highway to church when it hasn't rained for a while. For she is as gray as dust. Gray is the color of her full gathered skirt; gray: her short sheepskin jacket; gray: her headscarf tied like a turban; gray: the large eyes in her crumpled, wrinkled face. And her bed, right by the door, is the grayest of all the beds.

However, you should see this bed of hers when there's a holiday coming up. Take a look and eat your heart out. Then there are cambric sheets brought from the *klēts*, and big pillows with embroidered ends, and blankets: a blue and yellow and black one at Christmas, a green and red one at Easter, a gold and purple one at Whitsuntide, while on Midsummer Day there's a hundred-year-old one with tiny daisies that will dazzle your eyes. Come one, come all, and marvel: see what treasures Anyus has! Bet they'll be part of her daughter's dowry! But if anyone says that, Anyus fiercely retorts: "What, am I lying in my coffin that you're giving away my things? Are you envious of my place in the world, huh? Are you scared I'll die and take your grave from you?" And so on. Because of this sort of language people say that Anyus may well be rich, but that she guards her possessions like a dragon.

Anyus has three other things that no other woman has. Those are: a walking stick, a pipe, and a basket. The walking stick is made of peeled white juniper wood with a big crook at the end, so long that it reaches up to its owner's armpit; the pipe is a little brown smoke-stained clay pipe and always hangs out of the corner of Anyus's mouth unless she happens to be holding forth on an important subject or scolding; if the talk is trivial, Anyus will not take it out from between her teeth; and the basket is fine wickerwork, with a striped cover and handle; the basket is high-class, and Anyus says it was once carried by genteel hands.

It is only when she has these three things that Anyus is the way she should be. It's impossible to imagine that there could be another tall old woman who would dare to call herself Anyus. If there were such a woman and she encountered the real Anyus in the woods or fields, what a fight they'd have with their long sticks until one of

them turned into a mound of ashes, while the other would walk away upright, righteous, and wise as Solomon. And that one would be the real Anyus of Spring Farm.

The one word that Anyus mentions incessantly is "manor." Here's what Anyus's manor is like: One garden after another, one courtyard after another, one building after another. The lord of the manor has one, the manager has one, the coachmen, footmen, and other servants have theirs. And the dogs have theirs. Now, if the dogs' house is like a palace compared to any farmhouse, even one with a tiled roof, can you imagine what the houses for the people are like at the manor? You don't have twenty people living together in one house there, the way you do at Spring Farm, – no, one person has twenty rooms. No one has yet counted the squire's rooms, but you can imagine how many there must be when even the manager has a separate room for everything he does: one for eating, one for drinking, one each for sleeping, smoking his pipe, and playing cards. And talk of servants – it's so thick with servants you couldn't swing a cat! There are the upper servants and the lower servants. The upper ones are all for the squire, while the lower ones are for the upper servants. The footmen have servants to help them, and the housekeepers have maidservants to help them. When the squire orders the coachman to drive, the coachman in turn orders the lower servants, and they all run and take their places. One currycombs the horses, another harnesses them, a third washes the carriage, a fourth the footboards, a fifth ties the coachman's belt, and all the sixth does is hand him the reins and the whip. But when the squire himself comes out with her ladyship, the servants are so thick that even Anyus often gets to see them only through a kind of fog, for when it comes to looking at their lordships, she is merely a "common person." She's lucky if she occasionally catches sight of the footman who carries the train of her ladyship's blue silk gown through three rooms. Her ladyship's silk gown flows like water, but she hardly shows herself to the domestics. When she does, though, she is gracious. That's what the lady of the manor is like.

At night, when the chimneys begin to smoke, Anyus's basket, which has sat on her bed tightly covered, reveals its secret. With a generous hand, Anyus vanishes now into one corner of the house, now another. Here she stealthily gives away a "bulyan" (bouillon) bone, there an "orinch" (orange) peel, there a cockerel's head and feet. Then shaggy black Citron comes tearing along, sniffing and barking. And in the kitchen from Anyus's cooking pot comes a high-class smell that makes the household servants' nostrils flare and tells everybody: roast meat.

Only Annele avoids the manor house treats whenever she can. Ever since the time when, with tears in her eyes, she was forced to swallow one such terrible "orinch" peel, she has known: what is useful to the people at the manor is unfit for the consumption of people at home.

There is one other person at Spring Farm who hates the manor's "gifts." It's Ingus the farmhand. As soon as he comes in the door, he sniffs the air with his head flung back, and turns up his nose: "Stinks like the manor!" And in anger he tosses his cap any which where. And if Anyus is around, there's sure to be an argument. For these two powerful members of the Spring Farm household are always on the verge of colliding.

"Stinks like the manor! Well, I declare! Stop shooting off your big mouth, will you? What harm has the manor ever done to you? If it weren't for the manor running things, do you think there'd be anything for your fool stomach? Tell me that!"

That was Anyus. But Ingus comes right back at her.

"What? When has the manor ever given me anything? I give to the manor. If it weren't for my healthy limbs, you'd see what would become of your manor. Oho! It's not the manor that feeds me, I'm the one that's feeding the manor."

Ingus goes on talking and grumbling in this vein for a long time as he eats his gruel, takes off his *pastalas,* and tosses them away haphazardly: "The manor, always the manor! What good is your manor to me?"

For such rebellious talk, Anyus threatens him with disaster and God's punishment.

Evening is when Anyus comes into her own. Then she sits on her bed, resting her feet on a footstool, her walking stick beside her, puffs smoke, and talks louder than anyone else and more smartly than anyone else. First, manor business: whether their lordships are at home or have left on a trip; where they went; on what sort of business; which carriage they took; how many dogs, how many huntsmen went with them; how many words were graciously said about whom; what kind of dresses the young countesses were wearing, and what her ladyship wore – Anyus has the most detailed information on all these topics. If their lordships are not home, talk about the manor is quickly exhausted. Then she launches into parish events, for Anyus is well informed about all outside affairs. And what she says about anything, goes. What can Annele's mother have to say to her? A young wife's place is to listen and gather the good sense and knowledge that come welling out of Anyus as from a fountain of wisdom. And what do the maids know, with their "piddly little lives"? If they dare to "shoot off their mouths," Anyus will outtalk them a hundred to one.

When anyone annoys Anyus accidentally or on purpose, her eyes light up like coals and she shakes her long stick in the air. She is especially harsh toward the maids. They don't know how to bake good bread, or scrub the tables and benches clean, or get the shirts really white. They have neither properly sewn skirts, nor the kind of embroidered aprons and patterned mittens and stockings that would be a credit to the young women. Nor do they have any virtue, and what little they do have they can't protect as they ought to.

It's a good thing there's one young woman in the world who saves the parish's honor. And this is none other than Anyus's own flesh and blood, her daughter Trīne.

Trīne has never been seen at Spring Farm. She lives at the other end of the parish, where she fills the entire parish with her splendor. Once she gets the dowry her mother has collected for her, she'll be the most eligible young woman in the parish. In the meantime, she lives and amasses her own fame and honor, and protects her maidenly reputation as Anyus once did during the long years she was single.

Well, and is there anything Anyus's daughter lacks? Not a thing! She has high-heeled shoes and tulle jackets and striped skirts, she has veils like any fine lady. Every day she walks around dressed to the nines.

When Anyus begins praising her Trīne, the married women and the maids in their corners start whispering to each other and feeling envious. Let them! You show me another like her! So clever at everything, so hardworking. And no ogling the boys! Just let one of them so much as try to touch her with one finger, then see them run.

Oh that daughter, that famous daughter of Anyus's! How Annele wishes she could get to see her just once!

And then the day when she gets to see her actually arrives.

It's a lovely spring Sunday, and Anyus is sitting on her bed lost in a brown study with her walking stick and her pipe, when suddenly the door bursts open and in runs a stocky, pudgy young woman with purple cheeks, and bends over Anyus's hands to kiss them.

Anyus is startled. She pulls away her hand and also pulls her pipe out of her mouth. She does not say good day, but immediately confronts her:

"Trīne! What business have you come on?"

She asks her sternly, looking at her with grim eyes.

Meanwhile the stranger falls at her feet and bursts into loud sobs and bitter tears.

Anyus jumps to her feet and clutches her walking stick.

"Trīne, you're up to no good," she exclaims, as though cautioning her, and when her daughter will not stop, she grabs her by the arm, whispering: "Don't be such a fool! You don't want everybody to hear. Come with me to the *klēts*."

When they disappear out the door, Annele sees that one of Trīne's *pastalas* is down at the heel and slipping off her foot.

Annele sees all this and is stunned.

Was this Anyus's Trīne? The daughter who went around covered with praise and honor? Could this be her – her cheeks purple, her eyes red with weeping? With a tattered skirt and her *pastalas* down at the heels? No, no, no, Annele couldn't believe it.

Why, Trīne walked around as lovely as a princess, with embroidered aprons and skirts, and a veil that fluttered in the breeze like wings.

But she was forced to believe it all the same.

When Annele had raced down every path on the farm, she suddenly encountered Anyus and the strange young woman, barely managing to step out of their way. Anyus looked like a thundercloud. Her long legs were shaking, and so was her white walking stick as it struck the road. Trīne was still sobbing quietly. A long corner of her woolen shawl swept the dust.

Trīne must have done something really bad that her mother should scold her like this. And it was clear now: if there was a paragon of young womanhood, it was no longer Anyus's Trīne. Had Trīne ever been a paragon as Anyus claimed, Annele wondered. It was something that needed to be pondered at length.

Blue Marvels

Every morning, old Anyus leaves the farm alert and erect with her long walking stick, her handbasket, and a pipe in the corner of her mouth. She walks away like a gray shadow through the green freshness of the forest towards the manor, where in addition to other important business she has to pluck a couple of chickens for his lordship's table. And anyone who knows that the gentry eat nothing but chicken and white bread can easily guess what position Anyus holds at the manor. Toward evening she comes home, heavy with the day's work, heavy with the manor house delicacies stowed away in her basket, and heavy with news.

This autumn particularly, when great things were about to happen at the manor, everyone listened to Anyus's pronouncements as if they were gospel truth. Mind you, Anyus doesn't hide anything. Everyone is free to come and listen. Let them spread the news all over the parish. Here's the story:

The young squire is bringing his new wife to show her his father's estate. The old squire and his lady are coming with their young lordships. They're already on their way. They're coming from distant lands, traveling day and night; they're traveling by water and by land, they're traveling with iron horses and fiery carriages.

The whole parish has been notified to come and welcome them.

Outriders and huntsmen have already arrived posthaste from other estates with ten riding horses and twenty hounds.

All the ladders have been brought from dozens of farms so as to build a triumphal arch and decorate the lintels up to the roof ridges.

All the parish women have already been notified they must go into the woods to collect evergreen vines and bring them to the manor.

Goodness knows how many beef oxen and other cattle have been driven to the estate, and twelve barrels of beer have been rolled out of the brewery. Farmers will be given a meal in front of the manor house, below the veranda, a portion apiece, while the servants will only get something to drink, down by the brewery; they, on the other hand, can drink all they want.

Twenty trumpeters have already arrived and been quartered in the barn out in the fields. Two housekeepers have come to the manor, and five lady's maids.

A fireworks expert has arrived with all haste, and he's going to set off fire-spitting dragons, hissing snakes, and stars big as millwheels, and in blown-glass lanterns you'll see blue, green, and red lights that burn like flames but never go out.

There are many many more things that even Anyus's wise tongue can neither utter nor tell. In a word: there'll be blue marvels to see at the manor.

"Blue marvels!" thinks Annele. Wonder what they'll be like? Maybe really huge, as though the sky had opened up? Or maybe like in a dream, when you're carried up high on wings, so high it takes your breath away and you have to shut your eyes in terror so you don't have to look anymore. Yes indeed. "I don't suppose I'll ever get to see those blue marvels!" Everybody is getting ready as though for a wedding, but no one even mentions Annele.

The great day finally arrives. As early as mid-afternoon, everybody is given time off to prepare and get dressed. Anyus, too, comes home in wild haste to throw on her churchgoing clothes. And catches sight of Annele, still drab and gray, hanging around watching now one, now another with sad, expectant eyes.

"What about that girl? Why isn't she ready?" Anyus sternly asks the household members.

No one has thought of the girl. It's no place for a child, they reply.

At this, Anyus gets mad and glares at them furiously.

What do they mean, no place for a child? When even the halt and the lame and old billy goats with one foot in the grave are going! – This is aimed at little Jurītis's grandfather, who is just tripping off in the direction of the manor, at a half run, with tiny little steps, not caring a straw that he might be that billy goat. Yes, and since even the lame and the halt are going, then why not a child that will get to see marvels to re-member as long as she lives? Such things only happen once in a lifetime, and it would be a shame and a sin for a person to let them pass by without seeing them. She must go, she most certainly must, there are no two ways about it. Anyus herself would be glad to take the child along, but she has to be where the gentry are. Everybody can imagine how busy she is today, when the whole manor, the whole parish, is on the go.

When Anyus has resolved to do something, she does it. – She not only talks Annele's mother into letting the girl go to the manor, but also manages to grab hold of one of the household people who has not already run off. This is Luze, who has been delayed doing household chores. It is Luze's first year as a maidservant at Spring Farm, and she has to do as she is told.

While people were normally accustomed to obey Anyus's decrees, this was even more the case today; as someone who worked at the manor she had had a hand in decisions and choices involving all the great marvels. So Luze, although grudgingly, promised to look after the girl.

Annele was now scrubbed, washed, and dressed at breakneck speed, but her braids were merely given a cursory brushing, for Luze refused to wait till "that thicket was cleaned up one more time." Luze stood by the door all ready to go, did not lift a finger to get Annele dressed, and never cracked a smile. You could tell she wasn't pleased. She wanted to be repeatedly mollified and thanked for standing and waiting for Annele while everyone else had vanished into thin air.

It was not the hand of her mother or her sister Līziņa that pulled Annele at a half-gallop over roots and branches to catch up with the others. Though both of them were running as fast as they could, Luze kept prodding Annele constantly:

"Get a move on, don't drag your feet!" This cut Annele to the quick. First of all, she never dragged her feet, she was flying along; secondly, Luze's meanness hurt her deeply. If this was Luze's way of being nice, it would have been better not to do it at all.

Rushing along in such a hurry, Annele did not have a chance to linger in the forest thinking lovely thoughts at this unaccustomed time of day, as shadows lengthened and a mysterious darkness waited ahead on the road like a cloud. The initial pounding of her heart had hardly abated when they were already through the forest. They didn't catch up with the others until they reached the manor, for the others had trotted along no less quickly.

Through every gate, people streamed into the manor, then bridled like horses that have suddenly been reined back after racing hard. What now?

In front of the manor house there was a huge circular bed full of flowers and trees, surrounded by graveled walks. You were not supposed to set foot off the walks. That's what the men at the entrance with green badges on their caps said.

People thronged around the bed in a circle, craning their necks as they looked for the blue marvels. Those who were Annele's size butted against women's full skirts and the tails of men's jackets, and could see nothing.

"Listen! When are you finally going to start?" people called out to the guards.

"The 'lumination will start any minute now!" they shouted back.

"The 'lumination, the 'lumination! Now it will be as bright as day!" people exclaimed delightedly. The men with the green badges on their caps ran around among the shrubbery and lit thin little candles in little colored paper balloons. In the black thicket of shadows blue and green and red little points of light began to glitter. The trees and bushes began to gleam, a dawning glow that never finished dawning. The crowd of people surged back and forth in this glow like a current that is dammed in places and free to flow in others. But when nothing else appeared, they immediately began to grumble.

"Where's the fireworks expert? Where are the dragons and snakes?" people asked.

"In a minute, in a minute!" promised the men with the green badges.

And there they came.

Sh-sh-sh! One monster shot up from the very darkest corner of the park, above people's heads.

A dragon, a dragon! A snake!

"Watch out! It spits fire!" warned the guards.

People fled, screaming and ducking low to the ground.

Crack-crack-crack! it exploded in mid-air. A few little colored flakes rained over the crowd.

"Wait a while! That was just the beginning!"

People waited, their wide-open mouths raised skyward.

But nothing else came.

They waited for a long time.

What was wrong? "Why do they make promises and then not show anything?" they kept asking the guards, who rushed about perspiring.

The fireworks weren't going off, they said. The expert had said that they could not tolerate this kind of sky, the guards finally explained dejectedly.

People looked up. Fiddle-faddle! The sky was the same as always.

But Annele didn't think so. The sky was a bluish gray, oddly low and close. Funny-looking!

So where were those blue marvels? Maybe by the veranda of the mansion, where the lights were brighter? Every once in a while loud bursts of song came from that direction. But the guards would not let people get close: they said only the gentry, the German gentlefolks, and the officials were there.

Also, Annele could not budge from the side of Luze, who kept her close to her as though they were tied together. If anyone asked Luze to stroll about or to take a look around, she fiercely retorted: "How can I, when I've got that pesky girl! I'm tied to her like a Russian to his cartful of onions."

She would then get the reply: "You're right, it's no place for a small child in such a crowd!"

Oh, how guilty and sinful Annele felt when she heard that. She wished the earth would open beneath her feet.

Somewhere, trumpets began to sound.

"Here comes the entertainment!" people rejoiced.

And the entertainment came. Down from the veranda ran a person: neither a child nor a grown-up; came like a whirlwind, twirling down the paths in the direction of the crowd of people. She skipped along in thin little high-heeled shoes, as though on little posts. Over her shoulders she had a black silk cloak, and on her head, tied under her chin, she wore a little red silk kerchief whose corners stuck out in the back of her head like little horns. She dragged now one young fellow, now another, from the crowd.

"Tanzen, tanzen!"

When the fellows did not want to go with the German girl, she stuck out her tongue at them.

She was a pretty cocky young woman.

Now, quick as a flash, she ran up to a young man and jabbed his chest with three fingers. From the sudden push, the man fell over the wire enclosure into the flowers, while she dashed away laughing and whistling.

That crazy miss! people called her, but they were laughing.

They looked at no one but her. Now she was gone, now back again. Like a swallow. The red crest twirled through the crowd. Laughter flowed in her wake like a loud wave. Every neck craned after her.

"Weg, weg! Tanzen!"

Even from afar you could hear her coming back this way.

She emerged from the crowd, one hand elegantly curved, raised above her head, while with the other – oh goodness! – with the other she held on to Jurītis's grandfather, making him dance, going trallala, trallala. And Jurītis's grandfather was bowing and twirling and flinging about his legs just like her, and singing in a hoarse voice. His cap had fallen off, his vest was open, you could see his bare chest, with long white hairs on it. Where on earth had she dug him up?

Oh, how terrible!

Annele was frightened and hid her eyes.

"What's wrong with Jurītis's grandfather?" she asked fearfully.

"Not a thing! He's drunk as a skunk," everybody laughed. Annele didn't feel like laughing. She was sorry for Grandfather.

The young lady from the manor twirled the old man around her a couple of times and then let go of him. And so he stumbled, remained lying on the ground, panted for air, and coughed. What did she care! Her eyes darted in Annele's direction.

"Oh dear! I hope she doesn't see me!" worried Annele, hiding behind Luze as much as possible.

But she had already been seen. The young lady came straight for her quick as the wind, took her by the hand and pulled her forward.

"Du, Gör, komm mit, Gör!"

And now Luze at once let go of Annele and directed her: "Go on, go!" Everybody else did the same: "Go on, go!"

No one held Annele back, no one rescued her.

Of course she herself struggled with all her might to get away from the young lady, but her strength was far too paltry; in the end she was forced to dance along with the red-crested girl just as Jurītis's grandfather had danced with her.

She was dragged into the brightest lights and to an empty table in front of the mansion. The table was laden with plates, glasses, and scraps of food. The stranger thrust a glass full of brown liquid against Annele's lips: "Trink!"

Annele took a small mouthful. Bitter as tobacco, but she had to swallow it. What else could she do with it? The young lady watched and waited until the liquid climbed over the back of Annele's throat, like climbing over a hill. Annele shuddered as though with fever. Then she shut her lips and held them shut with her hand: no more!

Meanwhile the young lady kept twittering around the table.

She grabbed a link of sausage here, a piece of meat there, some bread over there, put it all on a plate in front of Annele: "Iss!"

Then she was off like a shot, across the veranda into the mansion.

Annele stood stiff as a post, her hands at her sides: she would not eat even if they killed her, she would not! She knew all about the "gifts" of the manor now.

But neither did she go away. She needed to find out something: what was going on here? Were these dreams, or ghosts? Were these the blue marvels that had been promised?

People were swarming through the shadows of the park; from the brewery below came bellowing, trumpets blared, the windows of the mansion were ablaze with light; from there, too, came laughter and music. But the sky! When Annele looked at the sky, she began to feel really scared. The sky was like the bottom of a blue-gray kettle turned upside-down. No, this was no longer the world she had grown to love more and more every morning. Here at the manor the world was completely different.

Annele moved her fingers. They were still flexible. Her blood flowed in spite of everything. She quickly turned away from the table. But as soon as she did she ran straight into the German woman in the black cloak, who held out a handful of red cake to Annele.

"Da! Kuchen! Iss!"

"No!" Annele opened her mouth in protest. But before she had time to close it, it was crammed full of cake, spongy as puffballs, sweet and sticky as glue.

No use. This is something Annele would not swallow.

"No-o," she shouts and opens her mouth even wider, opens it as far as she can and spits it all out, scraping, wiping, rubbing, shaking her lips and cheeks, till the last crumb is gone.

Get rid of it! Rid of it all! Every bit! So there's not even the tiniest particle left.

Spit it out! Spit it all out! Not just the sticky sweetness, but also the loud-mouthed trumpets, the blue-black sky, the littered table, the red-crested girl, manor, cake, and all!

Annele needs nothing, nothing from this manor. That's how obstinate she is.

Two fierce black eyes sting Annele's eyes. And a hand grabs her like a vise and squeezes and shakes her so hard that all the lights of the mansion dance around Annele.

Let her shake Annele! But the red cake is on the ground and is spoiled. She's not going to eat it!

"Du, Gör! Stockdummes Bauerngör, du! Bauerngör, du!" the German girl scolds furiously and pushes, shakes and pushes Annele. Hurls her so she'll stumble.

But Annele doesn't stumble. She resists with all her might, tears herself out of the German girl's hands, and is free. Free! Regaining the suppleness of her legs, she slips into the darkness like a bat.

"Gör. Stock. Bauer. Dummes. Gör. Stock. Bauer. Dummes." Annele runs and repeats, swallowing her sobs.

She doesn't understand what sort of words these are. But there is no kind meaning in them. Just as little kind meaning as in Luze's "pesky girl."

The lights have gone out. The park, forest, and sky are wrapped in deep darkness. But Annele just keeps walking. Somewhere, anywhere – –

Then someone takes her by the arm. An unfamiliar voice calls:

"Here, Luze, over here! Here's that girl of yours!"

Both the maids from Spring Farm come hurrying over. It's time to go home. People are starting to disperse.

Luze is just as mad at Annele as she has been all night. She scolds Annele, shakes her.

"Where have you been traipsing around? Can't find you anywhere! Are you going to spend your whole life wandering around in the bushes? Tomorrow's another day."

"It's nobody's fault but your own. Why did you make her go with that German woman? Come on, take the child piggyback and let's go," says Karlīne.

No way is Luze going to do that. For no amount of money is she going to carry that "little bag of chaff."

Annele doesn't want to hear what else Luze has to say, she feels that Karlīne is now her protector.

She tears herself loose and clings to the young woman tight, tight.

Karlīne, too, is no longer talking. She lifts Annele up in her strong arms and hugs her close to her.

Luze and Karlīne are really mad at each other. It seems that Luze wanted to dance, but Karlīne didn't, and when Karlīne didn't want to dance, then Luze couldn't either, and so they are angry. But Annele benefits by this.

Annele presses her head into the soft nest of Karlīne's hair and walks with Karlīne's feet. But the darkness presses against her with sweet heaviness and smothers all thought. There is nothing but the booming sound of departing footsteps, and she has a feeling that all these footsteps are dissatisfied with the blue marvels that were shown at the manor.

Oh yes, blue marvels! How lovely you were before anyone had seen you yet!

Father's Helper

"When is it going to be fall? When is it going to be fall?" With this question, Annele has been tormenting her mother ever since she told Annele, "Come fall you'll have to be Father's helper. You're certainly big enough now."

Countless times, Annele in turn has told each pine at the edge of the woods, each shrub in the orchard: "Come fall, I'm going to be Father's helper. I'm certainly big enough now."

"Good, good, Annele," the pines answer, quiet and wise as mothers.

And then fall finally arrives, late fall, when there's not a leaf left in the orchard and all the field work has been done, so that the indoor work can begin.

The morning after Martinmas dawns dark, but the little bell that is Annele's heart rings out merrily upon waking: "You know, today is your day at last. Now you'll be Father's helper."

Is Father going to start work today, though?

Yes, when Annele gets up, the crossbeams have been set up in the middle of the room with the big warping reel, and gusts blow from it in all directions. Father is winding the warp for the first length of fabric.

This is a job Annele cannot help with. She must be careful to get out from underfoot. Not till the warp has been wound is she allowed to sit on the base of the warping reel, and Father spins her around till her hair flutters and she gasps for breath. But when Father says, "That's enough," she has to be content. The crossbeams must be moved outside.

While Father winds the warp onto the warp beam and puts the heddles in place, Annele could roam around for a while, but fearing that someone else will be asked to help, she doesn't go very far, and as soon as Father calls, she's there like a flash. Father lifts her into the loom, onto the castle over the harnesses, puts a bundle of warp in one of her hands and instructs her how to separate thread after thread from the bundle and place it over Father's hook, while Father draws the thread of warp through the eye of each heddle. Initially Annele's work doesn't go well at all, and Father has to wait quite a while, but soon she gets the knack of it, so that her thread is at the gate of the heddle on time, and once she really gets the knack of it, she does even better than Father, so they begin to compete with each other, as though part of the same pattern.

But the threads are all gray. Annele thinks: how lovely it would be if there were blue, red, or yellow threads among them. For then after roaming about a bit her eyes would know where to stop and direct her hand to go: from blue to blue, from red to red. Well, she'll just have to be satisfied with nothing but gray.

Annele decides to pretend that the gray threads are all highways. Bumpy and smooth, full of hills and valleys. And it's lovely going down these roads. Annele rides down each one from the big Warp Beam Hill, and goes sliding through the Heddle Gate. Wheee! So it goes for a while, and she isn't the least bit tired. But wherever there are so many tiny little roads, you also need a crossroad! Annele decides to make one out of the fat bundle of threads in her left hand. But as soon as she does, Father looks up:

"Don't daydream, Annele! Work isn't sleep!" his voice reprimands her sternly.

Annele is startled. She looks into Father's eyes. Though loving and warm, they are serious: "Work is not a joke, lass," he says.

All right, Annele will remember. She'll endure it, she'll think that the warp threads are not highways but merely threads.

And when Annele has passed to Father as many bundles as she has fingers, the work will already be far, far along, and she can take a rest.

But they go through as many bundles as Annele has fingers, and go through as many again, and still there's just no end to it.

Annele has the feeling that time is no longer moving forward. Time has gone to sleep like a bear, it seems to have lodged itself in Annele's left side and gnaws at it so agonizingly that she thinks she can't stand it any more; now it reaches for Annele's right shoulder and squeezes and numbs her whole arm so badly that the thread has already slipped from her fingers twice. If only Annele could hold out just a tiny bit longer so her eyes wouldn't get blurry, for there is a sting of tears deep in the sockets of her eyes.

But by now Father, too, has noticed what ails Annele.

"Just look what a nice bridge the two of us have made together. The work goes so fast when there's such a great helper!" Father says, smiling and cheering up Annele.

Yes indeed – if Father himself says it's a bridge, it really is a nice bridge! Annele takes a look: thread after thread lying side by side evenly in the heddles like logs, none higher or lower than the others.

"We can't leave it half-done, now can we? Have to finish it, that's all. What do you think, Annele?"

"Of course we have to!" Annele agrees.

"All right then, pull yourself together, lass!"

And Annele sits up straight as a candle, the heavy bear rolls off her side, time starts to revolve again, and before she knows it, the last thread is on the hook and the whole bridge is completely finished.

As soon as Annele is allowed to move about again, she drops from the castle of the loom like a bird from a branch. She flings her arms about and is surprised: they're supple, even more supple, it seems, than they were before, although just a while ago she had thought she could never ever move them again. Her feet too seem to be carefree, she feels she could almost fling them above her head.

But flinging one's feet about like that is only allowed outdoors, and when

Annele has run outside in the teeth of the wind, she races down the hill and then up-hill again all the way to the forest; she feels those really aren't her feet anymore, but that she has grown wings in Father's loom. It's never been this easy.

All day long today she can run around outdoors, her nose blue with cold. No-body tells her not to.

Only at night, when she collides with old Anyus as she races into the house, Anyus isn't mad at all, but merely says, taking her pipe out of her mouth: "Go ahead, gad about all you can, they'll tie your gadfly down tomorrow."

What is she talking about? Annele is Father's helper now. Not everybody can do that!

On the second day, Annele again gets up with the same festive joy. Today the important work will start for real at last! The place where she is to work is in Granny's room, whose door to the big room is always open. The spooling wheel and the reel with a skein of thread stretched on it have already been placed there. Father is there, seated at the wheel, and he calls her to him to teach her how she is to work.

At the same time as Annele, Karlīne runs into the room. Let me wind the spools, she says. Why does that girl always meddle where there's grown-ups' work to be done? Old people and children should sit by the fireside. And she goes and thrusts herself in front of Father and tries to take away Annele's work.

But Annele is no longer a little girl that can be easily intimidated. By now she knows Karlīne and her tricks.

"Just go, back to your own work," she tells her with the seriousness of a working person. There's no way she will give her lovely work to Karlīne. Oh no! Then she dips her hand into the little basket and pleasurably rustles the pale yellow reed spools, of which there is a whole slew. But Father immediately warns her: "Be careful with those little spools, you might crush one. They're not for play but for work."

As if Annele didn't know that! Why, that's what she learned yesterday – tools are things that deserve respect. And yet there can be a big difference between spools and spools!

"Come and look – here's what I want you to do," calls Father. He picks up one of the spools, wraps the end of the thread around it and then puts it on the pointed holder of the spooling wheel, telling her at the same time that she must never push the little spool too deep on the holder, to keep it from cracking, for a cracked spool can no longer roll inside the shuttle. Then, guiding the thread with the fingers of one hand, turning the wheel with the other, Father fills the spool, giving instructions as he goes: "Look, here's how you wind around the thread at the start, your little fin-ger's breadth from the end, then let it run evenly to the other end, where you again leave just as wide an edge as at the first end; then let the layer flow shorter and sloping, like climbing a little hill. Don't hold it too tightly, or the thread will break, or too softly, or the thread will get pulled in; when you've climbed the top of the hill this way, and the spool is as full as a little loaf, then it'll be fine."

Why does Father give so many explanations and instructions, when Annele's willing fingers are just bursting to be allowed to start? After all, she's watched the work countless times and knows it's as easy as picking up a feather.

But as soon as the girl impetuously makes for the disk and starts to turn it, the

wheel suddenly falters, the disk jumps back, and the wheel stops. In the meantime the fingers with the thread have slipped off the spool. When Annele pushes a little harder, the spool breaks. Oh dear! Annele blushes all over and stealthily looks at Father, who stands by watching how she will get on. What will Father say now?

"Don't worry, it's all right!" Father reassures her, "nothing is as hard as the beginning. Start over again." And he himself untangles the thread and winds it back on the reel.

Annele starts over, but doesn't do any better. Her hands are awkward and heavy. Not for the world do they each want to do their separate jobs – both try to do exactly the same thing. But of course it doesn't even occur to Annele to think that it is her hands that are so clumsy. No, only the wheel is bad, and the thread is completely useless.

Father allows her to fill several spools in this manner, but Annele can't help seeing that they are no good for anything. Her eyes burn with shame and impatience. Angrily she shoves the spooling wheel.

"Slow down, lass, slow down, let the work teach you. Once you have mastered it, then you can teach it. Let me have a go now."

And Father sits down at the wheel himself and winds a basketful of spools. And in Father's hands it seems to be a different wheel and a different thread: both run as if they had been greased.

"Why don't they run smoothly for me?" wails Annele.

"Because you want to do it to please yourself and not the work," says Father. "Take yourself in hand and learn."

All right, thinks Annele, come what may, they will run smoothly for me now, too. And Annele takes herself in hand. Intently she watches to see that the disk doesn't turn faster than her hand is capable of turning it, that the other hand is not impatient and guides the thread evenly so that it doesn't run where it's not wanted, and when she makes this kind of effort, the little spool under her fingers imperceptibly turns out so well that she can show it to Father. Now, when Father calls: Annele, have you got it? Annele can fearlessly answer: Got it!

"You've certainly got the knack of it. Just keep on working," says Father.

After she has been spooling tirelessly for a while, Granny comes in.

"How's the work going? Are you sure it's not biting into your bones?" she asks with a smile.

"No, not my bones, but my hand," answers the girl, sucking in her breath. Across her palm, from the index finger, runs a little red path, gnawed out by the bits of woody waste in the flax thread.

"Learn to hold the thread in such a way that it doesn't bite – you won't know how to do the work until you learn that."

Good – Annele learns.

So it goes day after day now.

It's been a long time since Annele had to be taught the job. A long time since the buildup of excitement created by wanting work and not getting to do it was relieved: the craving of her hands, of her eyes, the craving to know was satisfied. But still she had to sit at the wheel, while the world was full of all kinds of new, untried tasks. If only someone would come and call her away!

Just now the sun suddenly appears, creeps into the living room of Spring Farm with its long, pale rays, and Annele has the feeling that it has come to her alone, saying: "Well, Annele, aren't you ever going to come outdoors anymore?"

"I will, I will, I'll come this minute!" Annele jumps up and follows the sun's call at once.

November has been hard at work during the night. Across all the frozen clods of dirt there are glass footbridges, and glistening bridges across puddles and wagon tracks. The ice has drunk the little puddles dry: when you race across, the shards explode in all directions, as though you were driving a coach and six; the big puddles, though, are deep as ditches. When Annele steers her coach and six across them, the arches break, and with a splash Annele is up to her ankles in water, *pastalas* and all. The water stings like nettles. And still the job has to be done. The bridges must be demolished. Then her mind will be at peace. Then Annele can hurry away to the edge of the woods, where life was always unfailingly lovely in summer. Now, however, the edge of the woods is like a house whose doors and windows have been smashed. The birches and hazel bushes let in the wind as if through an open gate, and the wind rules in the woods like a ravening wolf. Annele stands behind a juniper bush and watches what tricks the wind is up to. How it rolls in great gusts up from the open water meadow, whipping up great billows over her head, how it snatches an armful of rustling leaves, drives them in eddies into the tops of the pines, which shudder and crack, how it then drops to the ground somewhere in the thicket, gives a sudden snort, panting and hissing; then with a leap is out in the open again, a winged monster, hurtling between earth and sky. Fall! Late, deep fall! The face of nature is unkind and harsh, even though the sun sometimes rocks here and there in the tips of the branches.

Who cares if it is unkind? Annele stands and stands. She never gets tired of listening to the wind's mighty song, and standing there she could go numb like the stalk of pale, withered grass trembling ceaselessly at her feet, if she was not suddenly roused by a voice tossed into the wind: "Annele, Annele! Just you wait! Are you going to catch it now!"

"Whoa!" Annele gives a start, "they won't let me run where I want to anymore. I'm tied down. They've tied your gadfly down." She makes herself despondent with Anyus's words.

Father himself is already seated at the wheel. But his scolding doesn't amount to much.

"First do the work, then you can run about as free as a bird!" he says. But Annele knows full well that Father's silence is harsher than his scolding.

"Sure, do the work," she thinks, her spirit obstinate, "as if the work would ever get done!"

And, still obstinate and unwilling, she sits down in her accustomed place. She is as furious as the forest when the autumn wind hurts it. The wheel won't turn, the thread won't run. If only the wind would rush in and carry off the wheel and the reel! Twice Father tosses the spools back to her to do over again. And the second time he looks at her quite gravely: "You're getting careless, child."

This gnaws at Annele. The day is long, and she is chained to her work. Why is that? The day is long, and her troubles are even longer. She complains about them to herself, for she has no one else to complain to. They're all her enemies, her jailers, while she is the poor condemned prisoner.

All right, so be it.

All the stories about innocently condemned prisoners she has heard awaken and come to lament with her. She feels that these stories have now come true in her own life. She is sitting in a deep dungeon, the wheel is the door of her prison, the reel is her chain. She has been condemned although she is innocent. As Samson had to grind grain for the Philistines, so she has to wind spools so that linen cloth may be woven, piece after piece, hundreds of miles long. She has to work from morning until deep into the night, like those slaves who are chained to their galleys and must row forever, day after day, year after year. What's the use of anger and obstinacy? The poor condemned prisoners can only weep. And Annele weeps. She seems to have a lot of tears, for her head feels like a bucket. Streams flow from her eyes and nose. She has enough to weep not only for her own sad fate, but for unhappy Samson, the chained galley slaves, and all the other innocent sufferers as well.

Still, for all her troubles and obstinacy, the work goes well, and when Father leaves the room for a while, Annele gets all her spools full. Then she crawls behind the loom to be all by herself, in her favorite spot, intending to savor her troubles to the full there.

When Father comes in, though, they no longer seem distressing enough for her to need to indulge in them any longer, off by herself. She can't help watching Father. How he deftly lifts out the seat, sits down inside the loom, and how at once the beater begins to bang, the harnesses to rise and fall, the treadles to move up and down. The shuttle is thrown elegantly from the right to the left, from the left to the right hand. It's all a to and fro, flashing before her eyes. When the spool is empty, Father quickly exchanges it for a new one, and the work continues without interruption, without a pause, for a long time. But sometimes Father suddenly stops. Both hands then come to rest on the fabric, as though forgotten; he turns towards the window, but not to look at anything – Annele knows – but because his thoughts wish it. Something strange and wonderful is reflected in Father's face. The reflection remains like a smile around his lips and eyes, and does not vanish even when the banging of the beater resumes. How dear and beautiful Father's face is at such times! Where is he now? What thoughts is he thinking? Definitely not about chains and prison and dark dungeons, like Annele just a moment ago, for then he would surely look angry and gloomy. No, Father's thoughts are like birds with golden wing tips, they fly high, high, through holy places, across the plains of heaven, and the loom follows the flight of his thoughts, treadles and all.

But if Father at his loom soars across the plains of heaven, then why can't Annele do it at her wheel? Oh, what burning shame fills her at the thought of this hapless day! How small and insignificant is her little piece of work compared to Father's work. How many years already, winter and summer, from sunrise to sunset, has he worked and worked, without ever being angry or ill-tempered on account of his work! How lightly, like toys, his hands and feet move, how his eyes shine, and his mouth is so smiling and kind, as if it wanted to say something loving to Annele.

If only he'd say it!

Slowly, as though pushing herself, Annele moves close to Father. When he stops work to change spools, she snuggles up to him, timid and bashful. Father puts his broad, warm hand on her head: "Well, lass, where's your snoot? Why, that snoot of yours is all red." And they both look at each other laughing with warm, shining eyes. Annele suddenly feels so light, as though a bundle of rain-soaked grasses had rolled off her shoulders.

Soon, Annele came to realize that it is not enough to know how to do a job; you have to learn it so well that it flies from your hands joyfully and deftly. That's when it is accompanied by joyful thoughts. When she was able to fill the spools twice, even three times as fast as Father could use them up, there would be a break, a sweet and precious moment earned by hard work. Of course, sometimes it whizzed by so fast that before she could fill it, it was already over; but sometimes she was able to accomplish incredible things during this break. Also, the grown-ups no longer scolded her as often now, so that she could sometimes permit herself special privileges. For example, on dark and cold winter days, when her feet had grown numb with cold at the wheel, she was allowed to climb up on the brick oven bench that skirted the cookstove, and no one told her not to. She could hunker there, her feet drawn up under her knees, and take in the whole room at a glance, see what everybody looked like as they worked. Karlīne sat close to the farmer's living quarters, her golden hair fluttering in the breeze from her spinning wheel; as she spun, she would hum a song or talk brightly and merrily, so that everyone else had plenty to laugh about. Luze was usually closer to tears than to laughter; when it came to songs she only liked either "Where the maids bleach their linen I wended my way," or "Young Anthony was a delicate lad," or others that were even sadder. – His bottom bare, little Jurītis crawled all over the clay floor. He belonged in the big corner by the stove, but he paid little attention to this, he just crawled across the large room where the farm servants lived, wherever he had a mind to go. Right behind the big stove lived his grandmother. She was blind. As soon as she stirred out of her corner, groping her way with a little cane, Jurītis at once, no matter where he happened to be, came toddling over quickly with unsteady little steps to lead her out by the hand as though he were a big, grown-up man, looking about the whole room, challenging everybody: See what I can do? And everyone praised him for being a big strong man. And when Ingus the farmhand came in from outside, dashing and imperious as a young lord, it wasn't long before he was at war with the maids, who were joined by their helpful allies, the married women. Annele could barely get her fill of looking at all this before she heard a call from Father's loom, and had to run back to work once more.

Little Jurītis, Karlīne, Ingus, the gray tomcat, purring broad and warm on the tiles of the stove, shaggy Citron, who snuck in under the beds from the cold outdoors – each creature and each thing had its place in Annele's attention. And day by day everything she saw grew and increased in breadth, expanding the range of Annele's consciousness as well.

Evening Tales

At the end of November winter came on thick with frost, interrupting the indoor work. The men got ready to go to the forest. News came that there was a lot of snow in Lithuania as well, and the weather promised to remain freezing for quite a while. Messages were sent to the surrounding farms. There, too, bags of provisions were packed, and sleds were prepared. The forests in which the count allowed the people of the parish to cut wood were about ten miles away, boggy, marshy, and accessible only during the winter. That was why people from several farms would drive there together, for they had to stay for weeks while the wood was being gotten ready, so that they could return with full loads.

Annele's father, being in charge of the work, was the first to get up. The loom now remained empty. The fabric was covered with a clean towel to keep it from getting dusty. The spooling wheel was put away in the corner, the reel was folded up; areas that were normally filled with implements were now free and spacious as though it was Sunday. And still it didn't feel right.

The day passed, long and boring. Although you could race outside whenever you felt like it, yet you did not have the same pleasure as when such a short run had been stinted and saved up by speeding up the work. Also, the deep snow did not permit long jaunts. It was better by far to creep into a quiet little corner and to look with your invisible eyes how things were going in the big pine forest of Ģirkanči. And that's what Annele did. As soon as she closed her eyes, there it was, with bears and wolves, with unending roads, with green pine bough shelters in the middle of the woods, and big campfires around which the men sat at night and told stories, there it was with its dark, dark night, and thickets so dense not even a needle could pierce them, with lots and lots of workmen felling trees, sawing, splitting, so that the whole forest thundered. But when Annele's father began to speak, the big forest rang like a bell. Annele could clearly hear her father speaking and the big firs and pines rustling gently, the birches answering all at once. Passing on Father's voice, the tall trees carried it through the pine forest of Ģirkanči, across the highways and fields to Annele's window.

Toward evening, Simkus, the Jewish pedlar, drove up to the house, planning to ask for a night's shelter. But when he heard the men were not at home, he became alarmed and nervous. "Oy, if I knew you have no men here, I not have come here," Simkus lamented. For if thieves realized there were no strong people at home and attacked on just such a night, then who would save him and his pack? For a long time

Simkus sat on the long bench at the table snorting loud as a bellows through his large nostrils, and in a Yiddish that nobody understood held a consultation with himself as if he were talking with another Jew: should he go on to another farm or stay here? But where should he go, when all the farms had the same problem? Finally he decided to stay at Spring Farm after all – he had already been given permission to stay the night – so he unharnessed the horse, lugged his pack into the house moaning and groaning, placed it in the corner under the farmhands' bench, then collected old sacks, bundles of tow, and various other kinds of spinning waste, and threw them on top of it. Now the thieves would not know this was where Simkus's pack was.

When the lamp had been lit and Karlīne eagerly asked Simkus to show her some scarves and calicoes, he answered in a quiet, subdued voice, looking around him fearfully: "How I can show you? If God helps us survive the night till morning, then I show you!"

Having murmured his prayers and calmed down somewhat, Simkus sat at the corner of the table, peeling potatoes to go with his herring tail. The others, too, were about to eat supper when Citron, who had already been running in circles around the house for a while growling uneasily, began to bark suddenly and fiercely as though he were about to pounce on somebody. It had to be a stranger, and he was coming right toward the house, for Citron was already ripping into him at the very door. Any moment now he would open the door and come inside. Simkus dropped his knife with fear, he jumped to his feet, spread his arms, pale and trembling: "They coming, they coming, good people! I'm a dead man!" And not knowing which way to run, he made for Anyus's corner. Old Anyus, however, pushed him away from her bed and shouted back just as loudly: "Will you keep quiet, Simkus, and let the person come inside! What kind of robbers are you expecting, huh? Who's going to come and rob you? Maybe it's a perfectly honest person."

And it proved to be just as Anyus said.

The door opened, and with a merry, friendly good evening in came old Bungatiņš with his wooden leg. All those who had been waiting in terror for some horrible stranger responded to his good evening cheerfully, while Simkus even grew so bold that he clapped Bungatiņš on the shoulder condescendingly and said, "Well, Bungatine, you old beggar, why you run around in the dark of the night scaring folks?"

On a night like this, everyone greeted Bungatiņš as a welcome visitor, knowing that now there would be great storytelling and listening to stories, for this late visitor was not only someone who could recite the Bible and prayers by heart, but also knew many merry songs, could tell funny and scary stories, and was good at capping other people's wisecracks.

Who knew better than Bungatiņš the land of the Turks, the great Turkish war in which, moreover, he had lost his leg, and the famous retreat of the Russians before the Turkish army? Nobody could improve on Bungatiņš's retreat, he was so good at it. And besides, who else could tell more plausible tales about the lives of prominent parish figures, and about the goings-on among the gentry at the manor? Bungatiņš portrayed everyone as though he had seen them with his own eyes and as though he had been present at all the events. He claimed he had talked to the terrible Ūgrāfs as if he was a brother, and to the infamous German overseer who every spring drove the women serfs into the icy Tērvete River to wash the manor's huge piles of linen cloth while she herself sat in the sun on the manor hill – to this overseer he had said: "Come, my dear madam, go and see for yourself what it's like to dance in the icy water!" Yes, that's exactly what he had told her. "You don't want to believe it? – You don't have to."

Impatiently Annele hovers about Bungatiņš. You can't tell if he's ever going to start telling his stories or not – he eats so slowly, one mouthful at a time, cutting each piece off with his knife and tossing it into his mouth, talking all the while at great length about any topic brought up by some member of the household.

It looks like he's going to have to be begged and coaxed a lot. If only somebody would do it, for time is a-wasting! Annele, of course, can't do that. Let one of the grown-ups. Finally Karlīne, too, grows impatient.

"Hey, how about one of your stories?"

"What can I tell you? I don't know any stories."

"Are you serious? Not know any stories! Come on, tell us!"

"What do you want to hear about?"

"Anything you like. Just as long as it's a story."

"You knew Pela, too, didn't you?" asks Anyus.

"I certainly did! As well as I know my own thumb."

"Is that the man whose scalp Ūgrāfs tore off his head, hair and all?" asks Karlīne.

"The very same."

"Then why not tell us about him?"

Good. Pela it is.

And Bungatiņš begins.

"It happened like this: One time this Ūgrāfs is driving down the road, racing four horses, like he was the high lord of the manor himself. But as he drives along, there just happens to be a column of hay wagons, laborers from his own estate, at the bend of the road in the woods, where the embankments are steep and you can't get out of the way, neither to the right nor the left. And at the head of the column is Pela.

Ūgrāfs immediately glowers: "Make way, you blackguard!" That's how he yells at Pela, and the whole forest reverberates. But how can Pela make way when on both sides of the road it's as steep as a wall? The poor man, scared out of his wits, pulls his horse this way and that while Ūgrāfs just keeps thundering at him. And so Pela decides to drive right along the embankment. But when he drives along the embankment, his back wheel goes into the ravine, the wagon turns over and the road is blocked. As soon as the wagon turns over, Ūgrāfs gets out of his carriage. He calls the laborers together. The laborers all come, shaking. What are they going to be told to do? Pela must be flogged. As soon as Ūgrāfs says Pela must be flogged, Pela runs into the woods. He pulls up a good-sized pine tree as tall as two men, roots and all, and whirls it round and round about his head: "Come any closer and you're a goner!" Of course, Ūgrāfs rants and raves, threatens and cajoles, but no one will touch a man who looks as if he's going to smash the head of anyone who comes close – no one. So when Ūgrāfs can do nothing to Pela, he gets into his coach, and it's off to the manor. He wants the other laborers to come and chase Pela. All right. All the laborers go. But by the time they arrive, Pela is already in the woods like a jackrabbit! They search, they yell – and go home empty-handed. Pela's gone. Pela stays in the forest. But how long can you do that? When night comes, Pela sneaks back to his farm, hungry and dead on his feet. He comes home and sees that Ūgrāfs has had Pela's wife taken away to the manor. Now, Pela's wife is young and beautiful, they just had their wedding that same year. When Pela sees that his wife is gone, he rushes to the manor without even saying a prayer first. There they tell him that Ūgrāfs had the wife taken to his kitchen. Pela goes into Ūgrāfs's kitchen right on the spot, like Daniel into the lions' den. Yes, his wife, poor dear, is sitting in the kitchen crying. Pela grabs his wife, pushes her out the door telling her to run home, and has hardly had time to cross the threshold when Ūgrāfs's paw descends on his shoulder. Now between the two of them begins a wrestling match to the death, you might say. Strong though Ūgrāfs is, and big as a bear, Pela is stronger. No one knows if Ūgrāfs never called for help at all, or maybe everybody pretended to be deaf to save their own skins, but one thing is sure – no third person was present. Finally, though, Pela grows exhausted after the past day's great fear and torment, and is just thinking: "My time has come," when all of a sudden he catches sight of the open kitchen window. Gathering all his strength, he pushes Ūgrāfs down on the ground, jumps up on the windowsill and is almost across the sill when Ūgrāfs is up like a cat and manages to grab him by the hair. So Pela is caught there, hanging like Absolom between heaven and earth, but he tugs and tugs until he tugs himself loose. But his scalp with all his hair is left in Ūgrāfs's hands. They say Pela ran home covered with blood, took his wife and disappeared that same night, vanished into thin air as you might say. Ūgrāfs didn't try to track him down, either. They say Pela didn't reappear in the parish until Ūgrāfs was no longer among the living."

"Wonder if that's all true," Karlīne shrugs her shoulders skeptically when Bungatiņš finishes his story about Pela.

"Go and ask him, I bet he's still among the living somewhere," says Bungatiņš.

"Of course it's true!" Anyus hastens to add. "Those times aren't too far distant for people to forget what Ūgrāfs was like. He was certainly capable of pulling a person's scalp over their eyes. May God preserve us all from such as him! You tell them, Bungatiņš."

And Bungatiņš goes on:

"Yes, he was terrible, was Ūgrāfs. Fiercer than a wild beast. That's the way he was himself, and that's what his overseers and underlings were like. Tears and laments awaited him and accompanied him whether he came or went. Flogging was his morning prayer, flogging was his evensong. Flogging, flogging for the least little fault, or even for no fault at all. People walked around weighed down by sorrows and laments. And in the homesteads you never heard any happy songs, or even loud talking, as we're talking right now. May God protect us! Everybody used to make the sign of the cross whenever Ūgrāfs's name was even mentioned.

"And then his hour of judgment arrived.

"The Polish insurrection began, and people were beginning to tell of all sorts of unbelievable things. The Polish people themselves, it was said, were putting the landowners on trial and driving them out of their estates. The landed gentry of Kurzeme, too, all vanished and left in a hurry: some abroad, some to Petersburg to their safe fortresses. But Ūgrāfs in our count's mansion lived as he had always lived, and tortured and flogged the people just as he always had.

"But late one dark autumn night, when a storm was raging and the rain was coming down in buckets, six men on prancing swift horses rode right up to the gentlefolks' entrance, knocked at the door with hammer blows as you might say and shouted for admittance. Everyone was already asleep, and Ūgrāfs, as soon as he leapt up and heard the blows against the great door, realized at once that there was trouble afoot. And so he was suddenly seized by great fear about all the sins he had committed. This fear was the torment of his heart, of course. So then he ran through the rooms calling for the servants. But what could the servants do at this late date? They all came running, to be sure, but they were all shivering and shaking with fear. Ūgrāfs himself, ferocious and terrible strong man that he was, felt his knees shaking, but what could he do? When nobody would go open the door, he finally went himself. In came men terrible in appearance, with masks on. "Where is Ūgrāfs?" they shouted, though they had already recognized him, and immediately told the servants to be off. When they were alone with Ūgrāfs, they locked the doors and now they sat in judgment over Ūgrāfs.

"After that, they left and vanished into thin air, as you might say. After this night Ūgrāfs did live on for a while, no longer doing anyone any harm and avoiding people, but then he up and died. Later, people had all kinds of theories, of course, but no one ever found out who the men that tried him had been."

"Thank God that we no longer live in such times," Karlīne gives a sigh of relief and asks Bungatiņš to tell a more cheerful story.

However, once the storytelling has veered in the direction of tales of horror, there's no end in sight. One person knows of robbers who live deep, deep in the forest in lonely cabins and go out casing farms where there are few men just now, another knows of ghosts that wait at the crossroads, near cemeteries, or in other mysterious places, a third tells of the dreadful spirits of the dead who, after living a wicked life, cannot find peace, but come into houses during the long nights of autumn and, when they find a person alone, wreak such havoc that the person can only escape by running up into the attic. But even there, the spirits follow him, and the person barely manages to pull the ladder up behind him. And even that hardly bothers the spirits at all. They start climbing the walls after the person. The person struggles against them, either by making the sign of the cross, reciting the Lord's prayer in his fear, or by pushing the white spooks back, ladder and all; but then more and more spirits start to appear. There are as many of them as the night is black, and the person sees that he is powerless against them now. The person breaks out in a sweat with terror, the house is roaring with spirits, the trees outside hiss and bend. The spirits have already reached the attic, they are already reaching out shadowy hands to grab the person. But then a rooster suddenly crows, suddenly there is a rattling noise down the wall, like dried peas being scattered, the storm abates, the noise abates, something like a white mist swirls past the person's eyes and everything is back to the way it was. No matter how great a danger a person is in from spirits or ghosts, Annele knows for certain: nothing will happen to him. At the right moment, the rooster will suddenly crow, and he will be saved. And sometimes she so wishes the rooster wouldn't interfere in the mutual affairs of humans and ghosts so soon and would let them settle things by themselves, so she could see how everything would turn out. But no: a real storyteller like Bungatiņš always has a rooster on hand. As soon as the story had reached the part when your hair began to stand on end, suddenly here came "Then the rooster crowed", and all the ghosts were gone, and the story was over too. But at the end of this story, another narrator took the first one's place after eagerly awaiting his turn, and began: "But you haven't heard anything yet. Why, in the old days, when I worked for the manor..."

Those days were long gone, when Bungatiņš, old Anyus and Jurītis's grandmother "worked for the manor," when they had covered long distances in the dark of night to go threshing at the manor, leaving well before cockcrow; and then, as they walked past dangerous places, the call of the roosters from some nearby farm had scattered the terrifying ghostly shadows at the right moment. And in the threshing barns of the manors, among the great multitude of the workers, there was scarcely one who had never seen such shadows.

Annele hung spellbound on the words of these wonderful old-time storytellers. She couldn't hear or see enough of them. The numberless wrinkles in their withered faces were like the marks of bygone days, each of which had its own unique story. But who could tell them all? The storytellers themselves were like inexhaustible granaries full of countless hiding places. But many of these had become blocked with time and would no longer open. Often when the storytellers asked each other in reference to some story or distant event: "Do you still remember that time?" a sad answer would come after a moment's reflection: "No, no, I don't remember anymore!" And so that story remained untold.

When enough stories have been told, Granny comes out of her room.

"I think it's time to stop spinning yarns," she says. "Run outside, Karlīne dear, and see where the Seven Sisters are. The clock has stopped, and now I have to wind it again."

When it comes to looking for the Seven Sisters, all those who have young legs run outside. – Who'll be the first to discover them? Who else but Annele, she has the keenest eyes. She is the first to catch sight of the little cluster of seven tiny stars among the great multitude of stars. They seem almost to be hiding, fleeing far, far beyond all the bright proud glittering constellations of the sky. Annele knows what time it is when the Seven Sisters are at a man's height, when they are above the roof or at the top of the linden tree; she knows when it's time for the children to go to bed, or for the maids, and when the grown-ups must get up to thresh grain or do other difficult and time-consuming jobs. She can also find the Big Dipper and the Little Dipper, but Granny does not consider them to be as reliable for telling time as the Seven Sisters.

The sky is thick with stars. They are dazzlingly large and shiny. And they seem so close, so loving and dear that Annele's eyes burn looking at them. They seem like trusty sentinels, all looking after Spring Farm. Oh, how lovely it is to stand beneath the stars!

Annele is allowed to sleep with Mother, in the wide bed. It is a cheerful time, for when the two of them are alone, bedtime brings with it a lot of muttering and telling of stories about the people in the Bible. Among them Annele has her friends and her enemies. She thinks Abraham and Sarah are cruel, chasing away Hagar and Ishmael just so their own boy will get more money and property. Cunning and dishonest – that's Jacob, who, covered with kidskins, tricks simple Esau and robs him of his birthright. Annele is not at all fond of the God of Abraham and Isaac, who teaches them to do what is not good, and who hates and destroys the children of other people just so Abraham's children can have lots of space.

The God of Joseph, on the other hand, is full of light and goodness. He punishes the deceitful brothers in such a way that when Joseph reaches a position of great honor he is able to feed them during the famine. The God of Moses is mighty, in his thornbush that burns and is never consumed, and in the pillar of fire by the Red Sea and on Mount Sinai, where he shows Moses the Promised Land.

There are many, many such wonderful tales that have no end and that Annele wants to hear over and over again, till Mother says:

"You sleep now, all right? I'm sleepy too."

"Tell the one about Enģele. Just that one story about Enģele!"

"Which story would you like?"

"The sheep story."

"Well, all right," Mother answers, and Annele now listens, listens for the promised story. But she hears no more.

Instead of the story, there is only the regular hiss of deep breathing. Nothing else.

Mother has fallen asleep.

Annele dares not wake her, and she can tell the story of Enģele to herself.

Enģele was Mother's nurse back when Mother was even younger than Annele. She's been dead and buried for lo these many years, but Annele knows her as well as she knows old Anyus or Bungatiņš, and she always enjoys hearing about Enģele. She knows what sort of songs Enģele used to sing on different occasions, what kind of stories she used to tell and what kind of proverbs she quoted. By all accounts Enģele was a short little woman, always cheerful and kind to children. She'd lost her husband and children in the big epidemic, had then come to Mother's parents at Foresters Farm as a children's nurse, and had loved Annele's mother particularly like her own child. Thus Annele's mother never said: My mother did such and such, it was always: Eņģele did such and such, Eņģele taught me such and such. And anything Eņģele told or sang or taught her that was wise, Mother teaches and passes on to Annele.

The story of Eņģele and the sheep is from the days when Eņģele had just been confirmed and had started working for the manor.

And the story goes like this:

It's a dark, dark fall day. The wind is so sharp you can only escape from it in the forest. For about a week now, there's been soaking rain. Today is Eņģele's sheepherding day at the manor. She's driven the estate's sheep out to pasture, a huge flock of them. The sheep are white, black, fawn, gray. Every few minutes Eņģele counts them, for she is afraid they'll disappear into some juniper bush and be lost. Her little black dog Taksītis has sneaked away from the farm to be with her. He'd be good at herding sheep, for Eņģele has trained him with the sheep at home, but she dares not set him on the manor sheep for fear that someone will hear and tell the overseer. When Taksītis has no work, he keeps snuggling up to Eņģele, shivering with cold; she holds him close, and now the two of them are both warm. They'd love to crawl into a juniper bush to have shelter from the chilly rain at least, but Eņģele dares not do even that for fear of falling asleep. She can hardly keep her eyes open. Sleep thrusts itself upon her like a nightmare, and her shoulders are heavy, as though all the ghosts of autumn had come to sit on them in throngs. It was midnight when she left home to go threshing at the manor, and she has not had even a moment to nap before taking the sheep out to pasture again. Eņģele holds out as long as she can, but at last her legs sink to the ground. She thinks, "I'll just lean against a pine tree for a minute, for a single moment. Looks like there's a little dry spot over there, right at the foot of the tree. I'll close my eyes a bit. Just enough to stave off sleep."

But as soon as she leans against the pine, she is immediately overwhelmed by her hunger for sleep, and she is no longer aware what is going on. Taksītis growls, Taksītis barks, Taksītis pulls at her clothes. Eņģele is like a stone at the bottom of a river. Then Taksītis, too, pushes his head even deeper into her bosom, and the two of them now roll like a warm ball of yarn through a thick fog of sleep.

Eņģele struggles against sleep, against dreams, as if they were her enemies – she knows: she must climb steep, high mountains, like climbing on a roof; she must force her way through thickets that tear her clothes; she must wade through deep rivers up to her eyes in water, but with no place to climb up on, no way to wade out: her feet stumble and get entangled, something is pressing down on her chest; she must, she must shout! But what's that she's shouting? Sixty, seventy, ninety, a hundred! A hundred, a hundred, a hundred!

And suddenly her eyes are open. Where are the sheep? – There's not a hundred, nor sixty, nor even a single one! Not even a tail, nor one little fleece!

Eņģele leaps to her feet quick as a flash. Every trace of sleep is gone. She looks this way, then the other: nothing but rain, rain and a gray misty forest, bare hazel bushes. Not a bird, nor any other living soul. Where is she to go? Whom can she ask? "Go get them!" she tells Taksītis. He runs back and forth a bit, sniffs at the tracks, just snorts a bit, wags his tail as though he, too, was asking for directions, and crawls back into the warmth of her arms. It can't be helped. She picks up the little dog and goes toward the edge of the forest to begin her search in the field of new rye.

Not a trace, not a sign at the edge of the forest. Eṇģele runs back into the forest again. From the forest to another field, from there back to the forest once more. In vain! She's lost all feeling in her legs, in her other limbs, all she can think of is: they're manor sheep! If she goes home without them, she's as good as dead.

What on earth will she do if she shows up at the manor without the sheep? Her life is worth less than a pebble thrown down at the roadside, than a stick broken off a stump, or dry grass in autumn. If she does not find the sheep, she cannot show her face at the manor, she'll roam the woods till the end of time, until she collapses unconscious.

Evening comes and then, swiftly, night. A night so deep you can't see your hand in front of your face. But Eṇģele just walks and walks, without a road or a path; downhill, uphill, sometimes no longer fully conscious of anything, merely groping her way with her feet and hands. If it weren't for Taksītis whimpering under her arm once in a while, she would no longer know she is in the world of the living.

And so she hardly knows anymore how long she has been walking when suddenly her feet no longer find a path at all. Wherever she puts her feet, she walks into what seems like a wall, and stumbles. Eṇģele gropes about with her hands and touches crosses. Now she realizes she has wandered into a graveyard. When she looks up, she is able to see as in a fog, high above her head, the slim outlines of something dense: it's a church tower.

Groping her way with the help of the crosses, Eṇģele makes her way toward the church. Sodden branches strike at her hands and face, drenching her with drops of dew. But at each stroke Eṇģele trembles with fear, for it seems to her that the branches are stirred by invisible hands.

The bell tower with its open entrance is like a horribly gaping black maw. But what is she to do? Eṇģele enters it on tiptoe, striving to be quieter than night itself, and sinks into a corner, on one of those low wooden benches placed along the wall on each side on which the parish's beggars sit on Sundays during services. She recites the Lord's Prayer, makes the sign of the cross and thinks: Now may God's will be done, I simply can't go on. At least I have a roof over my head. When day breaks, I'll see what I must do and where to go from here. – And at once, heavy as lead, sleep overwhelms her.

How long has she been dozing like this? Eṇģele doesn't know, but suddenly she is wide-awake again as Taksītis gives a start and begins to growl. He sniffs, snorts a bit, and again begins to growl. Listen! Now she can hear it too. She hears the sound of distant footsteps. Cold shudders go up and down her spine. It feels as though her wet clothes were rattling against her flesh. Spirits! – the chill bursts chattering through her teeth. The season of ghosts, a dark night, the witching hour! The dead are coming into the church. All the old stories say that this is what happens.

The dog gives a short bark, but Eṇģele muffles it. She presses the little dog close to her, pets him, holds his mouth closed. As though to please Eņģele, or because he's frightened too, the little dog suddenly whimpers, then stops, whimpers, and stops again. The footsteps become louder and louder. Now they are close. They come from the right, from the left, so many that the walls reverberate. Eņģele thinks that any moment now the great church doors are going to burst open, the candles will begin to glow, the organ will start to peal, but any living person who sees all of this is doomed to turn into a heap of ashes on the spot. So as not to turn into a heap of ashes, Eņģele shrinks deep into her little corner, pulls her cloak over her head to keep from seeing or hearing, and surrenders: come what may. I shall not, shall not watch.

Clop, clop, clop! The first footsteps are at the entrance now, on the hard brick floor. Clop, clop, clop! they are followed by others, and others again; so many that Eņģele thinks: they're coming not by tens but by hundreds and thousands. And that's as it should be. Through the ages, no small number of spirits have gathered in the graveyard, after all. But they go no further. The church door does not open to admit them. They simply crowd into the bell tower, and Eņģele has the feeling that the air stands erect with their fullness. Murmuring and hissing in strange voices, they press around Eņģele like a wall; wet and warm they press around her, so warm that it seems to Eņģele that by now the air is beginning to steam with their warmth. What kind of spirits are these, steamy and warm? Eņģele wonders and sticks her hand outside the cloak a bit to see what is actually there, but without uncovering her head. She just wants to touch them a bit. Whatever happens will happen. – But as she reaches out, she catches hold of long, wetly warm, soft wool right by her knees. And now she slides her other hand over the wool across a broad back to a head, to curving horns: Why, of course! It's old Crooked Horns, the manor's expensive big ram! And at the same time as Taksītis, escaping from Eņģele's lap, leaps down among the sheep barking excitedly, Eņģele too cries out and, with tears of joy, falls on her knees on the brick floor: giving thanks to God, and wishing she could gather all the sheep to her heart in her great, great happiness! No one has ever lain on the bell tower's cold floor as happy as Eņģele feels tonight.

With all her heart, Annele feels Eņģele deserves this happiness after such great grief. Now she can sleep her fill. Pressed to the cold church wall, she can sleep the sleep of the blessed. The sheep too, exhausted from roaming and straying, lie down to sleep, warming the air with their breath. Let the rain come pouring down, let it flow gurgling down the pipes from the church roof, let the souls of the dead and the spirits roam around all they please, tonight they cannot enter the church, for the sheep lie in front of it in droves.

"Where is Eņģele now?" wonders Annele. Is she roaming around as a spirit, and would Annele be afraid of her if she came in at this moment? No, she wouldn't be afraid, she answers her own thoughts. Eņģele is so good and kind – how could she hurt a child?

Does she know anything about me, though, the way I do about her? Maybe she's already come in, maybe she's standing by the bed? – No, no, that isn't Eņģele, it's someone else. – When everyone is asleep and only Annele is alone with her heart, then she can hear; then the one who knows everything, from whom nothing is hidden, is present – the one whose starry cloak enfolds the whole world tonight. Is it

God? asks Annele, and after a moment's reflection answers her own question: Yes, indeed, it is God. None other. And when she thinks these thoughts, she can hear the breath in her throat and she feels as if the one who knows everything had come so very, very close to her. Her little heart feels like a captured little bird in his palm, and it's as though a voice softly, softly asked her: Is that you, Annele? And just as softly she replies: Yes, it's me. And she cannot say any more. No: not Almighty, nor The Eternal (words her uncle reads from books of sermons on Sunday mornings) – Annele does not need words like that. – What can she say to the one who knows everything? For he himself has come with the glowing light that fills Annele's heart like the brightest summer sun. No evil can befall anyone, for God is in the house at Spring Farm. He looks lovingly at all those who are asleep, setting just as much store by little Jurītis as by old Anyus, by Bungatiņš as by Simkus. Simkus is not a whit better because he is a child of Israel. Not at all. He is not only the God of the children of Israel, but the God of all people, and as he appeared to Moses in the fiery garments of the thornbush, so he manifests himself to all people in the brightness of the stars that blaze in the sky.

For just a short moment time seems to have stopped: her whole heart is aglow with infinite light. He is there. But the moment passes, and now it feels as though the one who was just here slowly moves away from the bed and leaves the house, accompanied by a kind of gradually fading light. Though she still feels perfectly safe and good, the glowing warmth she had been feeling in her heart just now is no longer there. The bed is all about her, her limbs become light, she feels so close to herself. She snuggles into the curve of her mother's body, as far away as she can from the icily glistening wall, for the bed is wide. "Tock, tock!" she hears a throbbing in her breast. "Tick, tick!" a slower echo responds somewhere. It's the big clock in Uncle Ansis's room. It's all alone, for Uncle Ansis is not at home. "Tick, tick! There's still my story to think about," says the big clock.

"All right, all right," says Annele, but she no longer feels like thinking.

Swaying slightly, the soft tick-tick spins off somewhere into the distance and vanishes. Lullaby, lullaby! Sleep, sleep, sleep! But now suddenly there's a muttering from Simkus's corner again. What's going on? Far away by the door, Simkus sits outlined against the window with his beard jutting out. He gropes for the pitcher of water that is usually on the table. But the pitcher must be empty. Simkus stands up shakily and walks groaning across the room toward where Jurītis's mother sleeps. Now he has managed to find a jug with something to drink: glug, glug! Simkus drinks. But suddenly a dreadful scream shatters the silence of the house: "Oy, people, people! Save me, save me! I'm dying!" shouts Simkus.

White figures in all the beds: "What is it? What is it?" Drowsy voices. Exclamations. Someone comes running with a torch. It's Karlīne. Simkus collapses on the floor. He wails. He moans, "Save me, people, save me!" Karlīne, rosy with sleep, sticks a broad resinous piece of kindling in Simkus's face: "Why are you screaming, scaring folks? What's the matter with you? Have you suddenly gone crazy?"

"Why are you screaming? What's wrong?" everybody wants to know.

Moaning, Simkus complains:

"People, good people! I eat that salt herring last night. And that herring burn like fire in my stomach. And I go to put out that fire. And I find a jug in that corner. And I drink from that jug. And when I drink from that jug, I drink poison. It burn me like the fire of hell. Save me, good people. In that jug was poison."

"What jug was it you drank from?" asks Zete. "Was it mine?"

"From that yellow jug."

"Oh Lordy me! That crazy Jew has gone and drunk the brine from the meat. There was brine in that jug. What did he have to go in that corner for? There was a cover on the jug!"

"Meat brine! What meat? Pork?" wails Simkus.

"Sure it was from pork. What other meat would I have?" answers Zete, looking into the jug: "The rascal! He should have known better than to grab it!"

"Meat brine! Brine from pork!" shouts Simkus, waving both his arms about. "Oy, gevalt! I break the commandments! I take poison! I break the commandments!"

"Karlīne dear, go into my room and bring him a cup of milk," Granny quietly tells Karlīne and then reassures Simkus: "Shush now, shush, Simkus, it's not going to kill you. It'll be all right, you'll see. We won't tell that you broke your commandments."

Karlīne goes back laughing to the kitchen with her torch.

But that's all Annele remembers seeing. Then she wraps both arms around her shoulders. Her arms are full of sleep, clouds and clouds of it.

The Little White Coffin

One day after Christmas a stranger came to Spring Farm. She said good day, sat down on the bench at the big table, but did not strike up a conversation. Granny, walking through the room, stopped near the stranger, who seemed to be waiting for her.

"Don't I know you? You're from Pinewood Farm, aren't you?"

"That's right," said the stranger.

"Well, how are things at your house? Is everyone well?"

"They are now," said the stranger, lifted a corner of her kerchief and wiped her eyes.

"How so? Was anyone sick with influenza or some other illness?" asked Granny intently, as though she had a foreboding that something was wrong.

"Yes indeed. But have no fear. He was, but he's well again." And in a monotonous voice the stranger suddenly recited, "The master and mistress send their regards and invite you to come to a funeral on Saturday night."

"A funeral! Oh dear! What happened? Who died at your house?"

The stranger again hid her face in the kerchief as though quite unable to speak, then suddenly sobbed aloud and exclaimed between sobs:

"Jānītis is dead!"

"Jānītis? What? That nice strong boy? What did he die of?"

"It was like he was strangled to death. Just yesterday he was all right. Sure, he was sick, but he could talk and everything. And then during the night – God only knows what came over him, you never saw anything like it – he started tossing so dreadfully, croaking – something was choking the poor lad, and there was nothing we could do, of course everyone came running, but even if we'd have carried him in our arms, what can you do when you're up against death? And so he passed over. Now his father is weeping, his mother is weeping, the whole household is weeping."

"Jānītis is dead, Jānītis is dead!"

Annele feels herself sinking with a kind of sudden heaviness, deep, terribly deep, and far away, barely audible, voices echo reverberating inside some dark bell: "Jānītis is dead."

And just as nearby objects emerge from thick fog when it is blown away by a breeze, so at these words she suddenly remembers, and realizes who Jānītis is.

Jānītis is the son of the Aizpriedes of Pinewood Farm. When Annele was very, very small, just a little half-pint, she too lived at Pinewood Farm. Dimly she remembers a lot of children running around – and one of them was Jānītis. She wanted to play with him, but he chased her away, grabbed toys out of her hands, and when his mother intervened, there would sometimes be a lot of tears. On the other hand, he would often give her a really nice toy that he had made himself. Annele would not let it out of her hands, not even at night. That's how nice the toys were that Jānītis knew how to make out of pine bark, wood shavings, and little blocks of wood. He was allowed to take all sorts of tools that belonged to his father, and to work with them like a grown-up. Also his father liked to send him on errands, or have him carry messages, and then Jānītis would walk with his head proudly raised, like the farmer himself.

One time Annele saw Jānītis running across the yard to the house. She hunkered down behind the door. She wanted to give Jānītis a scare, the way Jānītis sometimes scared her. When he threw open the door, she jumped up suddenly. Jānītis had the big heavy key of the *klēts* in his hand, and whether out of fright, mischief, or surprise, the key fell on Annele's head. The blow caused her to collapse on the floor and lose consciousness.

When she woke up, she was in her mother's lap, and Jānītis was also there with his mother. Jānītis was screaming and sobbing so hard that his chest rose and fell like a bellows. His mother, though, scolded angrily, threatened, and brandished a bundle of switches around his head. Annele thought she was going to hit Jānītis, and screamed at the top of her lungs: "No, no, no! Don't hit! Don't hit!"

Each of the mothers took her own child. Annele was put to bed, but she still kept yelling: "No, no, no! Don't hit!"

A little while later Jānītis's mother brought her boy to Annele.

"Beg your little sister's pardon," she said.

Jānītis stood there and wouldn't apologize.

Annele stretched her little hand toward him. "Don't hit, Jānīti!" she said plaintively.

All Jānītis could do, though, was to start sobbing once more, and nobody could figure him out.

After that, when everything was all right again, Jānītis rarely chased Annele out from underfoot. She always got the nicest toys, and he would even show her how to play with them; when Annele ran after his nimble feet and had trouble catching up with him, he would wait for her, take her by the hand, and walk more slowly, adjusting his pace to the girl's little steps.

Thus they became accustomed to being together.

"Jānīti, Jānīti!" Annele would call in the morning as soon as she woke up. And Jānītis was there, was there in the morning, at night, all day long.

But all that was a long, long time ago. A summer had passed, then another, and this had taken place before those two summers. But now it no longer seemed like two faraway summers ago at all, it seemed like yesterday or today: Jānītis sitting on the floor, feet outstretched, carving little toys, roaming far afield with Annele, coming in the door with the big key, right here. And now he was gone.

No, it was impossible that Jānītis should disappear, like the strange logger whose dead body had been taken away from Spring Farm, who would never come back again. No – why, Jānītis was here, he belonged to Pinewood Farm, he was close kin, everyone, everyone knew him. How could he vanish?

But no matter how much she refused to believe it, when the stranger spoke mournfully and the whole household joined her in mourning, she had to believe it.

Annele no longer felt like doing anything. She looked at the walls, accusing: "Jānītis is dead!"

"Yes, he certainly is," the walls seemed to echo apathetically.

She looked out the window and sighed: "Jānītis is dead."

"That's right," came the answer.

She crept into her little corner, closed her eyes, and heard only the big clock.

"Jānītis is dead," she whispered to it.

"I know, I know, but there's nothing to be done," ticked the big clock and went on climbing its long climb like a tireless wanderer.

"Jānītis is dead," she awoke in the mornings and immediately told the next day, and the day turned bleak and sad.

When Saturday came, Mother told Granny, "I think I'll take the little one along, too. So she can have a last look at Jānītis."

Granny, after thinking it over for a while, answered, "Yes, do that, dear. It might be something she'll remember her whole life."

As evening approached, Annele rode with her father and mother through the darkening forest to Pinewood Farm. The woods rustled gloomily, and the pines looked tall and sad. They all knew that tonight was Jānītis's funeral.

At Pinewood Farm, lights shone in all the windows. In the yard, farmhands stood with hurricane lanterns to receive the horses of arriving guests and take them to be fed and watered. At the door, Aizpriedis himself welcomed the guests, showed them to a dressing room and invited them inside.

The mistress of Pinewood Farm, Aizpriedene, was Annele's father's sister and her real godmother. She stroked Annele's hair: "Good, good, you came along to take one more look at your dear little brother. Many's the time you used to play together. He was one of those children that liked to spend time with the younger ones."

The words were choked by sobs.

"There, there," Annele's mother comforted her. "We must submit to God's will. It's not as though he had taken your last child. You still have God's blessings, you know."

"But the little one is gone, the little one is gone, he was the one I loved most," Godmother says, wiping her tears. And then, in her usual voice, she invites the guests in. "In one room, the tables have already been set, don't wait till you're asked, just go inside yourselves and give some to the child, too; she must be hungry after coming all that way."

Holding Mother's hand, Annele walks into the main room of the farmhouse. Among little spruce trees and burning candles, a little white coffin stands in the middle, with people all around like a wall. The two of them stay closer to the door, waiting for people to leave. The room has the sweet smell of resin, a Christmas smell. Everything – ceiling and walls – is decorated as though for a big holiday, densely branched spruces stand in the corners. On both sides there are long tables around which people are sitting all in a row, with books in their hands. Mother pulls Annele closer to the little coffin, and bowing their heads they say the Lord's Prayer. A hymn begins, and the women from the tables press closer. Annele sees that Godmother is once more at the head end, weeping, weeping bitterly. She weeps while the hymn is sung. The other women, too, keep wiping their eyes.

When the hymn is over, Godmother walks among the guests and in a soft, kind voice invites them into the farmers' end of the house. She herself takes Annele by the hand and brings her inside. In the room a table stands along the wall, set with steaming bowls, piles of white bread between them. Fat candles burn at intervals, stuck into bottles. Around the table people are crowded close together. Annele stands, lips tightly closed, and won't let herself be persuaded to taste any of God's bountiful gifts.

"What's this? Isn't the child having anything to eat?" Aizpriedene asks solicitously after making the round of the table, again stopping by the two of them.

"No, not a thing. Guess her heart is aching for Jānītis," replies Mother, looking at the girl.

"I wish they'd leave me alone," Annele sadly thinks and looks at the ceiling, as if trying to escape the others' eyes.

Just as in the main room, the ceiling here, too, is beautifully decorated with evergreen branches, long garlands of traveler's-joy, colorful paper fringes light as snow flakes, and fleecy strings from which swing little blue, green, red, and yellow paper birds.

"You like that?" asks Godmother, following the girl's gaze, "You know, the maids worked night after night making all those decorations."

"They're certainly something – decorations fit for a wedding," responds the mistress of Wolf Farm, another of Annele's godmothers, who is sitting just on the other side, wrapped in black silk shawls.

"It really is less like a funeral and more like a wedding. All the relatives invited, just about the whole parish here," says another relative.

"Well, this *is* his wedding. All the wedding he'll ever have. He'll not live to see another," Aizpriedene says softly, mournfully.

The farmer is also speaking, standing in back of the guests, urging them to eat and offering them special delicacies.

"How could I begrudge or deny him anything? He was like my right hand. Obeyed me at a word. You'd send him somewhere, and if he could, he'd do it like a grown person."

And again the mistress of Wolf Farm speaks up: "Yes, I came to visit last fall. He's right there, reaching for the horses' reins. It was too funny! Said he'd drive them to the barn to feed them and tend to them. And that's just what he did. Jumps into the buggy standing up and drives off like a grown-up. A farmhand couldn't have done it better."

"That was child's play for him! Even goodness knows how many years ago, when he was barely as tall as that table, he had no more fear of a horse than of a lamb. And when it came to putting a wagon away, he was the first to volunteer. Never overturned a single wagon," his father spoke again quietly in a sorrowful voice.

"Yes, he'd have been a hard worker if he'd grown up."

"And did he have any book learning?" asked another woman relative.

"Did he ever! He could read print and writing both, it was a joy to hear. Whatever he picked up from the big kids he would learn by heart, easy as pie. Just recently he'd been looking forward to school, 'cause he was close to eleven years old. But now God has taken him to be his own."

"Our older children were that fond of him, too, he was the apple of their eye," Jānītis's father spoke up again, "his big brother carried him around in his arms the whole night of his dying, and would have been glad to carry him both day and night and never grown tired of it if only he could have carried him back into life."

"Tell me one person that didn't love or accept him. He rang like a little bell from morning till night. Made everybody laugh, made everybody happy. Take the maids, crying their eyes out now. Whatever is it going to be like when he's taken to the graveyard? It will be empty, empty everywhere at our place," said Aizpriedene, slowly shaking her head back and forth.

"Yes indeed, he was a joy to behold for you parents. Where else would you find another child so smart and so good-looking, too? Why, he was as pretty as a picture. Rosy as an apple, yellow curly hair, big blue eyes. To lose one like him is enough to break a mother's heart."

Thus, one after the other, the father, mother, and relatives mourned Jānītis.

In the house the singing never stopped. They sang sorrowfully, plaintively, drawing out the notes. About this world and eternity. About death and life.

A young woman lifted up Annele so that she could look into the coffin. Now she saw Jānītis. How unfamiliar, how strange he looked! As though he had suddenly grown taller, he lay there in a long white shirt, with a green myrtle twig in his fingers. Like somebody who was fast asleep. His yellow hair glistened in the candlelight like a little golden wreath. It was Jānītis, and then again it wasn't. So dear and familiar, and so strange and unfamiliar, like someone from a distant country.

"Jānīti, Jānīti, where are you?" a small woebegone and uncomprehending heart asked deep in her breast. And it was as if the cord that had choked it so long had broken, and an eddying stream of sobs and tears poured over it.

Annele could no longer hold back her sobs, so violent that it seemed her heart would break.

"Why is that child crying so?" the women exclaimed in surprise, "can a child like that know anything yet, do you think?"

"I shouldn't have brought her. Maybe she's sleepy, too. Who can tell with a child?" worried Mother.

Annele was carried to the kitchen end of the house, where there was a bed that had not yet been carried outside, and she was put to bed there. When she woke up, it was already broad daylight. In the courtyard, harnessed horses were neighing and pawing the ground. A big wagon with a pair of horses was waiting right in front of the entrance. The horses and wagon were decorated with green garlands, little red, yellow, and white paper roses; patterned mittens hung from the shafts of the wagon, fringed tassels fluttered from the horses' backs and manes.

Mother came to wake Annele. She was followed by the young woman who had carried Annele to bed the night before. Both were dressed for the road.

"Well, what are you going to do with this big crybaby? Are you going to bring her along to the graveyard?" asked the young woman sounding as though they were off to see some great entertainment.

"No, I'm not. Let her stay here. There are plenty of others her age here just now," replied Mother, turning to an older woman who stood nearby holding the hands of two children about Annele's size.

"Will you look after my daughter, too?"

"I'll look after her, don't worry, you go right ahead. I'll make sure she has something to eat and that she behaves herself. The mistress of Wolf Farm brought me her children to watch, don't you know. I'll watch yours at the same time. There might be a couple more."

"And meanwhile I'll go to the graveyard with you instead of the little lass. But you won't catch me crying for Jānītis like this girl," said the cheerful young woman and laughed.

Annele did not like the way she talked. How could she laugh and talk so loudly when Jānītis was dead? She didn't feel like staying with the strange children, either, and she pressed closer to leave with her mother. She wanted to see Jānītis one more time.

In the big room there were even more people than yesterday, for many had arrived in the morning to swell the number of guests. There were also quite a few children among the crowd. People stood and sang. Aizpriedene, her eyes red with weeping, a black silk kerchief tied around her head, carried in a pile of white towels and patterned mittens. The family gathered around the coffin to say goodbye, but Mother didn't let Annele go near any more.

"You saw him yesterday. Remember Jānītis as he was then." She took Annele over to the window. "You stand here and watch."

As all the mourners sang, four young men carried the little coffin outside and lifted it into the decorated wagon. Then two sat on each side. Jānītis's big brother took the reins and put his other arm over the coffin, for the road was uneven. Then the first wagon began to move. Now the mourners, too, went and sat in their wagons, a long, long line of them. By the time all of them started moving, the first wagon had disappeared from sight. But at a curve in the road, it came meandering out again and reappeared at the head of the line. The little coffin looked a lot smaller now. The line of wagons moved further into the distance. Not far from the forest the little coffin was now visible only as a white stripe. Now even that was a thin, thin sliver. It was swallowed by the green forest and disappeared.

When the Pussy Willows Bloom

Palm Sunday. Father has the last piece of fabric on his loom. Today it will be finished, and no new one will be started. The spring chores are crying to be done.

The gooseberries have tiny greenish buttons as big as the head of a pin.

Palm Sunday! One more week and Lent will be over. Let it go! It's no longer wanted.

True, there's still a long Holy Week to come. But that's fine. It's right on the doorstep of Easter.

Annele has already finished reading all the stories of the Passion. Well, she can read them one more time. Then, her conscience clear as after a job well done, she can run outside, in the sun.

Annele takes the New Testament off the shelf and finds a place by the window. But as she reads, her heart trembles a little, as though she had a guilty conscience: the stories no longer seem half as sad as when there was still snow and ice and those severe spring blizzards. It really is true. The world really did grow numb with pain when the sun went out over Mount Golgotha and Christ exclaimed, "My God, my God, why hast thou forsaken me?" And yet: they already knew that three days later there would be the resurrection. Resurrection as the sun rose!

The stories of the Passion were illuminated by the sun of Easter!

Except for one. That story remained in her soul like a gloomy shadow and burrowed its way inside with deep sorrow.

It was the story in which Peter denies Christ.

It's one of those dark, dark nights. A crowd of people and soldiers take Christ to high priest Caiaphas. All the disciples have fled. Peter alone follows at a distance. Peter has promised to go with Christ, even if he is led to prison or death. The servants of Caiaphas have lit a fire in the middle of the courtyard and have gathered around it to keep warm. Peter, too, sits down among them, and in the reflection of the fire's red blaze, a maidservant recognizes him and says, "You were one of the people with Jesus of Galilee." – "I really don't know what you're talking about," Peter is surprised, as if this was all completely new to him. And he decides he'd better get up and move further away from the fire so as not to be so conspicuous. In vain, though. Here, too, a soldier recognizes him and says, "This man was also with Jesus of Nazareth." And again Peter denies this, "I don't know the man at all." Then others come and say the same thing: "It's obvious just from your way of speaking that you are one of those people from Galilee." Quite furious now, Peter begins to curse and swear: "I am not one of those people, I don't know the man and don't know what you are talking about." But at that moment the cock crows and Christ, who is being led past by soldiers, turns and looks at Peter. Now Peter remembers the Lord's words, "Before the cock crows twice you will deny me three times." He leaves the house of Caiaphas and weeps bitterly.

When the story reaches this point, it seems to be carved in stone. Nothing else happens, there are no more changes.

It seems as though Christ stands there, fixed for all eternity. His gaze is like a river that can never stop flowing and streaming past, and this gaze seeks out Peter.

"Do you know me, Peter?" asks Christ's gaze.

And Peter, his heart quaking, with bitter tears and forever and ever can answer only:

"Yes, Lord, I know you."

This morning this story, too, wants to be read and thought about faster, as though the book was in a great hurry to get back on the shelf.

It's easy to put away the holy book when outside the sun is smiling, and white clouds bloom like flowers. She won't pick it up again today. Maybe not tomorrow either. For other books will arrive, after a long journey. They're coming with her sister Līziņa from the distant farm where Līziņa spent all winter being taught by her talented godmother. Today she is coming home to spend all Easter, and she's planning to bring as many books as she can get, for her godfather has a great deal of them, and is happy to share them.

Annele's only job now is to wait for her sister. She runs far into the field in the direction from which her sister will come, hunkers down on the big rock and tucks her feet under her. The rock is hot as a stove on one side, but stings like ice on the other. The north wind hurls itself around the rock hissing and roaring. "It's too early for you to dawdle here on the rock," it yells. "Ha! So what?" answers the girl obstinately and holds on as tight as she can. She pulls off her little head scarf and spreads it before the wind like a sail. Tat-tat-tat; tat-tat-tat! the little scarf flutters against her cheeks and her ears, knocking her braids off the top of her head. What does she care? She ties together the ends of her braids, dangles in them with both knees and rocks back and forth in the sun for a while. It feels good and warm. And she's not going inside, so there!

"Oho! So you won't go, eh? I can't wait to see this!" the wind suddenly cries out again somewhere deep in the hollow, and here it comes! Whirling a black cloud, it flings the sun under a shadow and tumbles the girl head over heels off the rock. An icy chill stabs through her limbs. Now she really does have to flee. She has no choice. And she runs headlong all the way to the house, whose wide eaves welcome her like a lap.

But when she looks back, she sees Līziņa running straight across the field. She's already caught sight of Annele. With one hand she waves her little handbasket, as if promising something good, while with her other hand she signals warningly that her little sister should not run out in the icy wind.

At the sight of her sister, Annele starts with surprise, joy, and something like fear. She's been waiting, waiting for such a long time – to no avail, and now all of a sudden – Līziņa's here! Annele would like to fly to meet her sister like a bird, but there's something she cannot overcome. A sort of awestruck timidity. No, better run inside and hide. She does, with a beating heart, listening as her sister approaches.

Līziņa's voice is already in the entryway, on the other side of the door. Good day, good day! As though a little bell had come into the room. All heads turn in her direction, all eyes smile. She shakes hands with everyone, looks around. Doesn't see Annele.

"Where's the little one? I could have sworn she was outside. Where did she go? Ah, there you are!"

And Līziņa has to drag her little sister out of the corner. There's no hiding from her sharp eyes.

"Such a silly girl! What did you hide for, huh? You scared of me? Have you forgotten me in one short week?"

Annele can't say. No matter how eagerly awaited her sister's return is, it feels utterly new, surprising, sudden once it comes. What will she be like? Let's hope she hasn't become too dignified and smart. Let's hope she's brought back no foreign ways from foreign parts. Long days have elapsed in the meantime. And Annele has no idea what her big sister has been doing all the while.

But Līziņa simply takes hold of her. Pulls her close, embracing her with both arms.

"Why, you've grown taller while I've been away from home."

"It's a whole winter's growth, you know. But you couldn't see it until now, with the coming of the spring sun," replies Father and looks at the two of them with a smile.

The girls now go into Granny's room and close the door. There is Līziņa's basket with its secret. Wonder what could be inside?

Inside are a whole lot of good and lovely things. Little dried-up cakes with a sharp taste, like a puff of spring wind, and carefully wrapped little parcels full of colorful bits of fabric, pieces of yarn, garter ends. They've been saved over the long week for the little one from her big sister's work. And as they scatter from her fingers, many-colored, each one different and unique, they fill the room with an odd sort of abundance, for attached to each is its own personage, its own story. Here is Līziņa's whole workweek. The red one, for example, is Sape from Marigold Farm. She's got a jacket like that, recently completed at Godmother's house. And Annele immediately gets to hear what Sape is like. Sape is short, fat, and loud like thunder. She can carry a hundred-pound sack. That makes the hired hands mad. She gets mad at them in turn. If anyone so much as touches her, she smacks them so hard that there's a bruise. She never walks, she runs. With her short gray skirt and red jacket she rushes around outside like a red mushroom that the wind has snatched up in the woods and driven outside on the field.

And here's a little piece of dark green homespun. That's what the churchgoing dress of Līnīte of Hook Farm is like. Līnīte is the Āķises' oldest daughter. She is tall, skinny, quite stooped, but speaks in a whisper, gently, at the front of her lips, like a little girl who must be cajoled. This mannerism is a legacy from her childhood, when she was much indulged: for a long time, she was her parents' only child. She keeps

house at Hook Farm for her unmarried brother, and although she has many odd
habits, everyone likes her and is glad to do her bidding, for there is not one person on
the farm to whom she hasn't given some tidbit on the quiet, to whom she hasn't said
something nice, or whom she hasn't caressed affectionately.

A blue and green and red and yellow woven garter can tell what Druvmalis, the
Āķises' neighbor, is like. Getting on in years already, but unmarried. Comes over to
Hook Farm every day, twice or more some days. Only the Āķises' youngest daughter
Līzīte, who is Annele's sister Līziņa's godmother, knows how to weave the kind of
garters he needs. While she is weaving them, Druvmalis likes to sit next to her and
watch. When the garter is finished, he can try it on for size right away. He wears
knickerbockers that reach down to his knees, and long, bright indigo blue stockings,
wrapped crosswise very beautifully across the shins with this type of garter. That's
why he needs the garters. Always new ones, always beautiful. But once he's got
enough of that item, he still enjoys sitting in Līzīte's room, engaged in inexhaustible
conversation. Aunt Līzīte, however, outtalks him every time, no matter how good he
is at conversation. Then he is finally forced to keep silent. Still, he doesn't leave. He
takes Godmother's scissors and starts cutting out all kinds of paper animals, birds,
human figures, and objects. He knows how to cut out human figures in such a way
that each person can recognize himself, though they look very funny. This is how he
amuses some people, while he sometimes annoys others mercilessly, but gets a kick
out of it in either case. Līziņa has brought along a whole slew of figures cut out by
Druvmalis, and here you can see what the man himself is like, and the kind of work
he does.

"Don't you have any books?" the girl can no longer refrain from asking.

"All right, have a feel, go ahead," Līziņa now opens the basket all the way and
tells the girl to stick her hand in all the way to the bottom.

Ah, there they lie – smooth, with colorful covers, dear silent books!

"What are they called?"

"Amanda and Florida."

Annele's eyes grow wide.

"Amanda and Florida? Are they from faraway lands? From Africa and Australia?"

Līziņa bursts out laughing.

"Why do you think they're from Australia?"

"No, I didn't mean the books, but those – those Floridas," Annele blushes. She
knows she has said something that isn't right, and now she is embarrassed.

"One of the books *is* from faraway, distant lands. From India. We'll read that
one first. But not now. Tonight. Right now let's go and get some pussy willows,"
Līziņa makes a quick decision.

Annele now no longer needs to look after herself. Her big sister does it. Having
obtained Mother's permission to take the little one to the water meadows by the
Skujene River, she gets her dressed and brings her something to eat. Then off they
run, into the wind, which no longer seems sharp and cold at all. Annele's mouth
runs like a windmill. Now she can ask countless questions. Here at last is someone

who never makes fun of her, dismisses her, or leaves important questions unanswered. Hook Farm for one! Most of their talk is about that.

Hook Farm is big and splendid, it's Granny's family farm. From Hook Farm, at the age of sixteen, she was brought to Spring Farm as a bride. That's why it's no wonder that she has seen her brother, now referred to as old Āķis, about as often as any stranger. Hook Farm is away from the big highway, in the opposite direction from the church, and access by road is difficult in spring and fall, which is why Granny has been to visit her father's farm only a few times in her long life. The Āķis family came to visit Spring Farm about once a year, on their way to church. They had fine horses, a fine buggy. They had such a lordly bearing that Annele would rather not go near them.

And it was these relatives that Līziņa now frequented. So there were naturally plenty of questions as to what each of them looked like.

Old Āķis was a dignified man. He was a man of our times, said Līziņa. A man of our times must be like him, Annele thought. He smoked a long pipe and was able to talk German not only with the Jews but with the pastor, the sexton, and any of the gentry. Having given the farm to his oldest son, who farmed it together with his sister Līnīte, he spent his days as follows: he'd make the rounds of the fields alone, read books, or come and talk to Aunt Līzīte. Then they would all speak German, and during working hours Līziņa, too, was expected to learn the foreign language, her godmother strictly insisted on that.

Beside the two above-mentioned sisters and brother, Father Āķis had another daughter – the middle one – and the very youngest, a son. They all lived unmarried and on their father's farm so lovingly and harmoniously that none of them could bear to part from the rest, nor would the others have allowed it. The most beautiful of the lot, and the smartest, was Līzīte. She still had many suitors, and Druvmalis for one would have given his eyeteeth to marry her any day she named, but she did not want to part either from her father, or her sisters and brothers, or the beloved farm. Why, what would become of Hook Farm if she left! She was the farm's beauty and glory. She gave good counsel, kept everything in order, beautified every nook and cranny.

Līziņa has the most tales to tell about this godmother, and Annele listens full of admiration.

"If she is so kind, then I'm sure she never scolds you," the girl says enthusiastically.

"Why not? She's constantly scolding me. Her big bright eyes see everything a person does wrong."

"But then you have to cry, right?"

"Not at all. She knows how to scold you in such a way that you feel like laughing. You see, she never scolds you with anger, just with laughter."

"Then she scolds just like our father, right?" Annele exclaims joyfully.

"Yes, you hit the nail on the head, that's exactly right," answers her sister.

They walk for a while. Līziņa, her head turned in the direction of the road to Hook Farm, pensively looks into the distance.

"That's a road I'll never walk again," she says with a sigh.

"Why won't you?"

"After Easter I'm being sent to Jelgava to be an apprentice, hadn't you heard?"

"Oh dear!" the girl claps her hands with shock and suddenly stops walking. "To Jelgava! That's even further than Hook Farm, isn't it? Oh dear, oh dear!"

"It's still a long time away. Why, Easter is a week from now, and it's after that, even! And in summer you'll come and visit me, then you'll get to see Jelgava, won't that be nice?"

Yes, Annele, too, has a feeling that it's a very, very long time away, Līziņa leaving for Jelgava.

They've reached the water meadows along the Skujene. And, to keep Annele from replying or getting even more anxious, her big sister picks her up by the armpits and, hopping from one mound of dry ground to another like a little wagtail, carries her across the marshy place to the river bank, which is already completely dry.

The river runs black, huge, eddying, curving around the bend. Why, just look at it! Slow in summer, barely in motion, now it races like a restive stallion, whipping up foam. The osiers by the bank are half in the water. There is such a volume of water that it pulls the flexible lower branches into it and makes the little gray pussy willow heads at the top quiver. Here and there, caught in the osiers, there's an ice floe or two. Moving helplessly like a fish in a creel, the ice floe waits for someone to set it free. But no more ice floes are coming downstream along the banks. Those that are left, carried out of streams and lakes, have been pulled into the middle of the current and shoot along like arrows.

Annele is sorry for those that have been tossed on the bank, which must sadly watch their brothers being carried downstream. "We ought to set them free," the girl begs.

"Yes, that's an idea," agrees Līziņa. And they set to work. In the bushes they collect a dry alder branch here, an abandoned stake or broken-off rail there, carry them to the bank, and now begin to nudge what's left of the winter. It's no easy matter to get some of the piled-up ice, packed together layer upon layer, out of the osier trap. You've got to hop nimbly from mound to mound, and sometimes the mound vanishes in the brown water, and your foot with it, – but when you get the knack of it, your efforts are quickly crowned with success. How good your ice fellow feels then, as he whirls around himself like a dancer a couple of times after escaping from his pen, finally rushing into the current at lightning speed! The girls see every one of them off with loud exclamations of joy: free, free, free! until it has vanished from sight, now rising, now sinking, racing downstream.

When the river bank has been put in order as far as they can reach, the girls stop, their cheeks flushed, but feeling very satisfied, and search the bare water meadow to see whether bird's eye primroses, dandelions, or cowslips have already begun to come up, but there's not a sign of them yet; only here and there in the osier thickets, around mounds of higher ground, the odd marsh marigold leaf is already up, though there's not a single flower. But what's that gleaming so golden right in the middle of the shrubs, on the sunny side of three young pine trees? Is it pussy willows in bloom?

The pussy willows are in bloom! A whole bush of pussy willows. How wonderfully full it stands there in its yellow finery, lighting up the lustreless little gray heads of all the others. The first tribute to spring must be taken from this bush, there's nothing else for it. But how to get to it? How else but with much skill and good will, swaying on hummocks, picking your way carefully, forced at times to step in the chilly water.

When the girls climb the slope of the water meadow with their armfuls of pussy willows, they remain standing up there for a long time as the wind shakes them, sings, and whistles around them. Līziņa exclaims:

"Look, look, how lovely! How fast the waves flow! Oh river, river! How big, how wide it is now! Oh the foaming black floods of spring!"

The lovely, bountiful day is over. When the sun, close to the horizon, glows red through the little window of their room, comes the nicest moment of all, just as after a delicious meal there is still the most delicious morsel for dessert: the books! The two sisters sit down in the deep recess of the window, on the white windowsill, and Līziņa reads the wonderful legend about the Indian prince.

"It happened far, far away, in the distant land of India. And there was a king, powerful and rich, who ruled over vast lands. The king had many children, but they all died one after another in a big epidemic, and only one was left, the youngest son. And the king decided that this son must never see either old age, or sickness, or death, and he had a mighty palace built, white as snow, with sky blue, gilded towers. Like twelve rings, twelve gardens enclosed the palace with gates that faced each other and shone like suns with all kinds of precious ornaments. These gardens were like the gardens of paradise, with trees whose tops reached the clouds, with flowers as big as human heads, with marvelous birds and butterflies whose wings gleamed in all the colors of the rainbow. Every day, the prince would ride out on a white elephant with golden stirrups, sitting in a little golden cage. He was allowed to ride through all the gates, into the furthest gardens, but not through the twelfth gate. Eternal joy reigned in the palace: laughter and dancing from morning till night. Twelve footmen served the prince day and night, and twelve playfellows were always near him. These were young men chosen for their great beauty and health from all the countries ruled over by the great king. No one was allowed to approach the prince except with smiles on his face. Not one malicious, ill-tempered, or harsh word was heard in the palace, nor was a face contorted with pain ever seen there. The prince had not the slightest idea that there is also poverty, sickness, or even death in the world.

"One day, however, the prince's favorite playfellow suddenly became ill. He was removed from the palace without delay, and died that same day. But to the prince they lied that he had gone out for a walk in the twelfth garden and had perhaps lost his way there.

"Unable to sleep or do anything, the prince waited day and night for his play-fellow to return. But they brought him a whole group of other young men instead, more charming and handsome than the one who was lost. He was told he could choose a new companion. But the prince rejected them all. He wished for no other to replace his dear companion. The longer he waited in vain for the lost friend, the more fervent grew his longing for him, the sharper his pain. He no longer wanted to

hear either dances, or songs, or laughter, nor did he smile himself. Without companions, he roamed through the gardens. The king left him alone, hoping that his
sorrow would soon cease. But that was not so. The prince merely became silent and
no longer talked to anyone. And one night, when all the footmen and courtiers were
asleep, the prince rose from his bed all alone, walked past all the guards, through all
the gardens, and at dawn reached the twelfth gate. The sleepy guards dared not resist
the prince's command when he suddenly appeared before them and ordered them
to open the heavy padlocks and bolts and to let him through the gate.

"Now the prince walked and walked. Behind him disappeared the palace with
the twelve towers, twelve gardens, and twelve gates, but he no longer thought of
going back, only forward. The sun was burning terribly, he was tormented by thirst
and hunger. By the roadside there were abandoned villages, wretched, half-dilapi-
dated huts, but not a single human being – great plagues and starvation had ravaged
the land and its people. Late, toward evening, he caught sight of an old man sitting
by the side of the road dressed in rags and covered with sores. The prince, who had
never in his life seen poverty, old age, or sickness, stopped in front of the old man,
doubting and wondering whether this was a human being or only a creature that re-
sembled a human being. But the old man said: 'Greetings, O prince! I have been
waiting for you since dawn. You are now at a crossroads. Behind you are wealth, fortune, joy, honor, and glory. Turn around, and in a short while you will be back in
your father's palace, and it will be as though you had only lost your way for a moment – you will have forgotten it by tomorrow. You will have forgotten your playfellow, too, as though you had never seen him. You will no longer be tormented by
pain and grief for him, and you will live as heretofore, in uninterrupted peace and
happiness.' Thus spoke the leprous old man by the roadside. But the prince no
longer wanted to go back, only forward. What was the good of riches, joy, fortune,
and glory when they could not give him back his dear playfellow, and when no one
in the palace could tell him where his companion had gone. 'Good, – if you want to
come with me, you will learn to understand, and know where your playfellow has
gone,' said the beggar. 'Except that you will then no longer be a prince, but like myself, who am the poorest beggar in your father's kingdom. Where we are going, we
will meet with poverty, suffering, and the misery and evil of the whole world; if you
are willing to accept all this, then come!'

"Come what may, I must know all this, thought the king's son, and he went with
the old beggar. Then came darkness and a terrible thunderstorm. They entered a
deep forest. The rain poured down, thunder roared, and lightnings flashed so often
it seemed as if the forest was all aflame, but they just walked and walked. All around
them, ravenous beasts were howling – –" Is Līziņa really reading this out of the book
or telling it in her own words? It's not easy to tell, for by now it is no longer possible
to see the rows of letters. The sun has set, and the light in the little window is fading
fast, for with the coming of spring the time of lighting lamps at night has ended. At
the place in the story where the "ravenous beasts" appear, Līziņa claps the book shut
and jumps down from the windowsill.

"That's enough now! Grandmother's coming. Quick, quick, to bed!"

Granny sleeps in her own bed, with the girls in the other one, by the opposite wall. Annele is not at all happy that the story was interrupted so suddenly, but what can she do? When Granny is asleep, you can't go on asking a lot of questions and whispering. But her thoughts refuse to leave the prince just at this moment, as he sets out on such a perilous journey. It is true that she herself cannot help him in any way, but she must have a talk about it with God. And she does.

"Dear God, heavenly father! Don't you see that the prince isn't bad just because he left the palace? You mustn't blame him for that. He loves his playfellow and doesn't want another in his place, that's good. But oh how full of grief he will be when he finds out that a person who has died can never, never be found again! And when he finds out all about diseases, suffering, poverty, and death, he will have even more grief. But you can help him endure. The old beggar covered with sores is your good spirit, and he will surely guide the prince through all the evil." – But suppose he is an evil spirit? – Another thought suddenly intrudes itself into Annele's mind, but she immediately reassures herself: "If he is an evil spirit, you will give the prince enough strength to realize in time how evil he is, so he can come to know about everything and overcome everything. And you will guide him through the storm and the thick forest and protect him against ravenous beasts. No, you will never abandon the prince, although he will have a very, very hard time – –"

"Listen, girl, aren't you ever going to be done with your Lord's Prayer tonight?" asks Līziņa in a whisper.

"I'm not saying the Lord's Prayer."

"What are you doing then?"

"I'm just – just – saying things."

"Who are you saying them to?"

Annele would rather not answer at all. But her heart is like a morning sky without clouds, and she is incapable of hiding anything from her sister, so she breathes barely audibly:

"To God."

Līziņa doesn't respond, but it seems to Annele that she gives a sort of moan under the blanket, as though she were swallowing a little giggle. Annele raises her head and listens.

The fading glow in the window is sliced through by the red streak of sunset. The pussy willows smell sweet in the pitcher, in the corner of the little room.

Līziņa is already breathing deeply. As for the little giggle, Annele must have heard wrong.

The pussy willows smell sweet, sweet!

Day by day now, the pussy willows bloomed more and more gloriously. Whoever came in from outside, across the river, would bring a branch or two, either sticking it behind the rafters or putting it in a big crock; mountains of sweet fragrance rolled from them. And already it seemed like Easter every day. For were these really workdays, these days between Palm Sunday and Maundy Thursday? Why, they were all holy and light, except that they were not supposed to be noisy. And that's what made them especially nice. So that the sun and the wind had all the time they needed to weave the glorious gown of Easter in this still stillness. Maundy Thursday, when the maids planted myrtles and other potted plants so they would

grow well, Good Friday, so hushed that not a single loud word was allowed, passed in constant suppressed restlessness, while Saturday passed in constant laughter, however the grown-ups might scold or whatever else they might do. And when she woke up on Easter morning – well, here it was at last! By the bed, on the chair, lay her new dress and a dotted white headscarf. Līziņa brushed and braided first her own, then her little sister's long braids, put on the new dress, and thus dressed up they went out into the main house. It was high time. Everybody is already seated. Uncle is by the table with the big book of sermons and hymns, the one with the metal clasps. He has already practiced the hymns, he says the number and immediately begins, "Christ our Lord has risen." Yes, now Easter is here indeed!

Annele is singing from Līziņa's book, and when she gets lost every now and then, Līziņa shows her the right place again. She knows all the tunes, and it is so easy to sing along with Līziņa. But then the girl wants to hear for herself what everybody sounds like together, and for a while she listens. The best singers are Father, Mother, and Uncle too, but when Līziņa's voice twines through all the others, Annele no longer listens to the words at all – the sounds alone sparkle and glisten like the candles in the big chandeliers at church. The rest of the household are not particularly

good singers, they tend to growl, have a hard time staying in tune, for they do not know the new melodies. Karlīne could sing, but Uncle has given her strict injunctions not to give free rein to her voice, because according to him it goes off on its own and blares like a trumpet.

The hymn is followed by a long prayer. How can anyone recite it all! So that the grown-ups will get done sooner, Annele allows her eyes to roam around a bit. The house and the household are a sight to see this morning. The clay floor has been strewn with white sand and chopped fir twigs, the rafters decorated with pussy willows, fir branches, and colored paper fringes, the beds covered with new striped blankets and white pillows, the men are wearing snow-white shirts, the maids have head scarves they haven't worn before and new calico jackets. And Annele's new dress, secretly sewn by Līziņa, is not half bad either. She can't wait to show it to the blackbirds that are whistling so loudly in the pear tree outside the window. The ray of sunlight that has come to lie wide across Annele's lap also keeps beckoning to Annele to come outside. But Uncle has barely begun his sermon.

However, even the longest sermon has its "amen." Then comes another hymn, then "Lord God," as befits a high holy day, and then – yes, now Easter finally begins for real!

In addition to other Easter joys, there's going to be something special today: Līziņa is expecting a guest.

And, if the truth be told, they're all expecting her along with Līziņa. Around noon, Karlīne comes running inside.

"Līziņa, come on, go and meet her! Here she comes, will you look at that! Your guest, with high-heeled boots, a real Fräulein if I ever saw one."

Līziņa runs outside to meet her guest, but those inside, married women and maids both, all run to the windows.

"Why, it's Alma from Gladden Farm. I lived there one year as a herd girl," says Luze. "She's grown mighty tall. Like a reed. It's a wonder her mother let her come. Why, she used to be that careful of her, wouldn't let the slightest breeze touch her."

"Damn, she's pretty!" Karlīne remarks.

"Yes, her face is different, but she's almost as pretty as our Līžele," Zete, too, hurries to have her say, and has no time for more, because Līziņa and her company are coming into the room.

Alma is as tall and slim as Līziņa, she's wearing a gray skirt and a fashionably cut jacket of the same fabric, a white scarf on her head.

It's immediately apparent that she is the daughter of a patrician family. She says hello boldly, shaking hands with everyone. In her other hand a beautiful bunch of pussy willows shines like gold.

"Well? Are the pussy willows at your house as big as these?" asks Alma, showing off her pussy willows.

"No, we certainly don't have any this big and beautiful."

"That's because pussy willows like these only grow in the water meadows of Gladden Farm," Luze says obsequiously.

"Then that must be why your farm is called Gladden Farm, if everything is so beautiful there. Isn't that right?" asks Karlīne.

"What, Gladden Farm? Why, there's nothing special about it. They do say, though, that you've got a much finer place here, which is why I came to see for myself," answers Alma, as is the habit of guests, to please the people they are visiting.

Līziņa leads her deeper inside, into the big room at the farmer's end.

Meanwhile, from the darker room next door, through the open door, Annele can see what the new visitor is like. At first she seemed unfamiliar and somehow unappealing, but now that Annele looks more closely, she is indeed beautiful. Gladden Farm must be the only place where you can find young women like her, for Annele has never seen anyone resembling her. Annele had thought that all young women had wide blue eyes, fair hair, and cheeks rosy as mountain cranberries, but Alma was different. Her eyes and hair were black, her face delicate, pale, almost transparent, while her lips were red as cherries.

"Do take off your jacket," Līziņa invited her guest courteously.

Alma didn't want to. She hesitated. She wasn't staying long, she said, her mother was expecting her home, she'd sit down for a while just as she had come. But Līziņa insisted, and then the guest finally took off her jacket and scarf. Now, this was a totally different Alma! A lovely white cardigan came into view, gold earrings dangled from her ears, and a gold brooch was pinned to her cardigan. Līziņa noticed and admired it all, but Alma, with a shrug of her shoulders, remarked that there was nothing special about it, that she dressed like this every Sunday. Līziņa now hastened to put on the table the holiday loaf, honey, butter, and other good things, she coaxed and urged, but for a long time the guest would touch nothing, until finally, after being begged and implored, she took the handle of a knife between the tips of two fingers and after dangling it for a while began cutting the bread in tiny pieces, putting a tiny dollop of honey on each before she put it into her mouth. When she was served some tea, she again played with the spoon, her hand elegantly splayed, before she allowed the spoon to slide into the glass of tea. She did everything so strangely, in a way Annele had never seen before. I wonder why? – thought Annele. Is it to show she comes from a well-bred family? Or so people will look at her fingers? Alma's fingers were white and delicate.

The young women now began a long conversation, and there was nothing for her to listen to any more. Alma had also been in training with Līziņa's godmother at Hook Farm, which was where she and Līziņa had met. That was why the two of them had a lot to talk about.

On Birch Hill by the swing, people from the neighboring farm had gathered,

both big and little. The little ones hunkered waiting their turn, their noses blue, wrapped in shawls like bales of cloth. Each held in one hand an egg boiled in onionskins and placed in an ant heap to make it speckled. This had to be given to the person who pushed the swing. The hardest-working swing pushers were next summer's cowherds from both farms, constantly teasing the little ones and demanding their egg, though in the end they did not take it from them, but pushed everyone's swing for free.

After a while, Alma and Līziņa came outside, too, but only watched the swing from afar. Alma apparently was reluctant to come closer. Then Līziņa gave the guest a tour of the most beautiful spots of Spring Farm, and once they had been to them all, Annele saw them at the edge of the woods, across from the swing, by the great linden tree, which with its roots had raised a whole mound.

"Yoohoo! Annele, come here!" called Līziņa over to where the birch trees stood green.

Annele was startled. What? Was Līziņa calling *her*? She did not move.

"Come on now, girl! You heard me call."

Yes, there was no longer any doubt about it. She was calling. And when her sister called, Annele must go. But it was hard. The two big girls stood looking in her direction. She had to walk right up to them.

"And this is the one who reads all those books?" asked Alma.

"Yes, this is our little girl. Go on, shake hands," Līziņa pushed the girl closer.

Annele curtsied, not taking her eyes from the stranger's face, which was now so close. How the eyes changed, now dark, now laughing and merry, how the hair curled around the forehead, how the lips grimaced. And why was she watching Annele like this, and what did she want of her?

"You're pretty good at praying, too, I hear?"

Good at praying? Annele didn't understand. She compressed her lips and firmly shook her head.

"Well yes, don't you pray to God, say your prayers?"

"Do people pray to God when they say their prayers?"

"Well, aren't you something!" exclaimed Alma in amazement. "Oh, so you don't pray to God when you say your prayers?"

The girl shook her head.

When Līziņa saw that Annele risked losing the good reputation she had built up for her with Alma, she flew to her aid.

"She makes up her own prayers, you see, and she doesn't call them prayers. Right, Annele? Prayers are just prayers, but you ask for God's help all on your own, don't you?"

"Yes," Annele answered, squirming her shoulders as though something heavy was pressing down on them. She did not like such cross-questioning.

"Well, tell us one of your prayers. Alma would like to hear it, too."

No answer.

"Have you forgotten them all? No, you haven't, have you? Come on, tell us one."

And suddenly something occurred to her. Affectionately she bent down to her little sister.

"You know, the way you prayed about that prince the other night. You remember, don't you? Come on, tell us that one."

Annele would really like to please her sister. But why is she asking for this? Is it possible to say such words out loud? How Annele wishes she'd stop asking!

But she won't stop. She continues more softly, as though rebuking her.

"If you're so stubborn, Alma will think you're a naughty girl."

It seems Annele doesn't care what Alma thinks. She can't get her mouth to open.

"Look at you. You don't even obey me. You could say it to make me happy, couldn't you? If you don't, I'll have to think that you're not my dear little sister any more."

Annele can't bear it any longer. When her sister speaks like this, her resistence is broken. Come what may, she's got to say it now. The words climb over a hill as it were, heavy and cold. But are these her words? They are uttered in what seems the voice of a stranger – lifeless, trembling, pale. She's ashamed of them. She wishes the ground would swallow her up. How she wishes they were over at last.

Suddenly there is an interruption – a choking sound, laughter against lips pressed tightly together. Annele looks at the stranger. She is holding her cheeks with both hands, as though she could not hold back the laughter that now pours out loud and uncontrollable. She has no intention of stopping. She bends sideways, twisting her whole body, laughs and laughs as heartily as if she had never heard anything as laughable as what this little girl just said.

Annele is struck dumb. A hot wave washes over her from head to foot. Then she turns about face and rushes off as fast as her legs will carry her.

"Annele, girl, wait! Come back here!"

She doesn't listen.

Now she knows she shouldn't have obeyed, she shouldn't have given in. No matter how much her sister wanted it. For a voice inside, in her breast, had kept calling: No, no, no, don't say it, Annele! She should have obeyed it.

Now it was too late. She couldn't recapture the words that had been said. And Alma's laughter – that would now ring in her ears morning, noon, and night.

What she had done was a sin. Yes, now she knew what a sin is – when you say out loud, for everyone to laugh at, what had been said to God alone.

And Līziņa! That was the bitterest blow of all! Why had she wanted this? Why had she forced Annele? Wasn't it merely to give Alma something to laugh about? If that's what her sister was like, then Annele no longer had a sister.

So Annele kept running, with bitterness and anger, with sorrow and defiance. She didn't go to back to the swing, for joy felt repugnant. She crept alone along the rust-brown ditch, down to the little brook, where there were lots of pussy willows. Some were in full bloom, while others had already finished blooming, scattering what looked like golden sand on the ground. But even the pussy willows no longer gave her pleasure. Easter itself seemed to have finished blooming.

Walking up the forest path on her way home, Annele suddenly caught sight of her big sister coming toward her not far away. She had seen Alma off and was now returning. Full of joy, her sister spread out her arms and waited for the little girl to come flying into them as always.

But she waited in vain. Annele, as though frightened, immediately jumped off the path and ran in the opposite direction as fast as she could.

However, her sister's strides were twice as long. In no time at all she was in front of Annele, clasped her around the waist, pressed her close, forced her to look into her eyes. Her eyes were warm, questioning, and affectionate.

"Girl, girl, you little sorehead, now you're mad at me, aren't you? I shouldn't have done that. But how was I to know it would turn out like this!"

"That Alma" – Annele released the stored-up sobs. The more her anger toward her sister dissolved, the more she wanted to turn it against the despised stranger.

"Alma isn't wicked, but she didn't know either. It's all my fault. How could I be so bossy? But now everything's going to be all right again, won't it? It's going to be all right."

Annele stopped sobbing. They walked holding hands, close together, and Easter again seemed to be Easter.

But something painful still hurt and would not go away. It was the lesson that there are things one can't tell even one's dearest sister. Just to God alone.

Herding the Pigs

"Get up, get up!" someone calls close to Annele's head and pulls away her blanket. "Get up! The sun is high in the sky. What kind of a herd girl are you, still in the sack!"

The caller runs outside.

Annele gropes for the blanket, pulls it up to her chin and dreams:

The night is still long, long... as long as the distance to Lowland Farm, longer even; as long as the way to Pētermuiža, longer even ... she can sleep for hours – hours, hours, – and dream so sweetly.

The door rattles sharply.

"Annele, Annele, oh my, oh my! Suppose Mother should come with a switch!"

It's Annele's granny. She comes closer, pulls the blanket down as far as Annele's legs and tucks it around them. But she won't let her sleep. "Take a big stick and chase that sleep away, go on! Can't bake bread out of sleep, you know! Run and wash your eyes in the spring, and your sleep will vanish like a cloud."

Annele sits up in bed like a little rabbit, but her eyelids are glued together. – "I'd give all the riches in the world if only I was allowed to sleep," whispering half in a dream, she makes a promise to someone who is just as imaginary as "all the riches in the world."

Grandmother comes back inside, sees Annele sitting up and praises her:

"That's right, lass. That's good. Here's a chunk of bread for your morning snack. Nobody's going to bring you breakfast today, you know. It's a busy time."

Annele's eyelids are still glued shut. Her eyes are wrapped in the blanket.

"Grandmother, is it sunny or rainy today?"

"My, my, lass, don't you have eyes? Shame on you, shame! You're still fighting that sleep!"

The big room with its thick old stone walls is damp and chilly like a cellar. Annele quickly removes her hands with the blanket from her eyes and looks: Yes, it's sunny! The big apple tree, which spreads across the whole window, is full of splashes of sunlight like golden birds. Annele's sleep vanishes "like a cloud."

The front entryway is full to the ceiling with sunlight. There is the sun, which has just climbed the stable roof.

Mother has just brought the animals outside. She's waiting beyond the gate, calling Annele.

"What's keeping that girl? Hurry, will you! My fingers are burning, I'm in that big a hurry to get to work. – Well, have you got everything? The bag? A switch? Did you put in the food? Then take the herd to the ravine. It's a good place to herd in the mornings. And I'll know where to find you to call you home. Well, off you go, off you go!"

Mother says the last words with affection, but Annele is already gone, following as best she can after her herd, which tumbles headlong toward the ravine, grunting and squealing.

If anyone asks Annele, "How long have you been herding?" she knits her brow in two deep furrows, thinks for a while, and says:

"Oh dear, it's been a long, long time. Since St. George's Day."

But now Midsummer Day is almost here.

Annele was present when her fate as a herd girl was decided. The terms of Father's wages specify that he must herd every third day.

"What shall we do now? We can't pay a herder, can we?" worries Mother.

"Yes, but we'll have to. What else can we do?" answers Father quickly.

"I was thinking – the girl can go..." and Mother looks fixedly at Annele.

"The little one?" Father wonders and puts his hand on Annele's head.

"What do you mean, little? She's seven already."

"Not until fall."

"So what? Her legs are long like a nine-year-old's, her mind is grown-up too, I'd be surprised if she can't do the job!"

"I'm sure she can do it!" Father just chuckles. "Let her learn – it won't be long now till she has to go out as the main herder, and every day, too."

And thus it happened that Annele would now have two easy days while the third was hard, two lovely days, while the third was often the loveliest of them all.

In the ravine, Annele "keeps her herd in check." She runs in a circle around the animals, rounds them up, and "teaches them a lesson." The lesson consists in flicking the switch through the air; Annele recognizes no harsher punishment. The herd is already deep in the succulent roots of the fallow land.

On one side of the ravine is a big pine forest, thick as a wall with undergrowth right up to the edge of the field, on the other – birch hills, covered with a new growth of slender trees.

In the long shadow of the woods, the grass is still full of white dew. Annele runs over, and wades through the dewy grass, leaving an embroidery of wide black seams. – All the dew collects in her *pastalas*. But her mind is not at ease. She runs as far as the birch hills. The tips of the trees droop into the blue lake of the sky; only here and there, where a bird alights on it, a branch suddenly begins to sway; otherwise not a leaf trembles.

How Annele's feet itch with an urge to run – run someplace else. She's already missed so much, what a shame she wasn't awake earlier; the morning has brought something never yet seen heretofore – never has there been a day as wonderful as today; she ought to run, get ahead of the sun so it doesn't secretly perform its miracles before Annele can be there herself and watch it all. Cuckoo! comes a call from the forest. Annele bounds across the ravine, through the wall of leaves, like an arrow. – Cuckoo, cuckoo! – there's a call far away on the other side: cuckoo! – nearby again.

Annele flattens herself against a hazel bush. Quiet as a mouse. Just above her head
there's an outpouring: cuckoo, cuckoo, and cuckoo, on and on.

Annele sees through the branches that the cuckooing bird's head wobbles at
each call, like a knife whose handle has come unglued.

"Cuck, that's enough, cuck!" she shouts and laughs.

– Cuck –, the cuckoo hurriedly exclaims and breaks off in mid-call from fright,
only dropping the second half in a distant part of the woods: – koo!

Annele is no longer listening to it. Her ears are dizzy with all the voices that
twitter, trill, whistle, warble, make the forest ring. She, too, decides to add her voice
to the others.

"Yoohoo!" she tries calling slowly. Her voice drops to the ground in the green
hazelwort nearby. Annele draws it out longer, sends it to the treetops: "Yooo-hooo!"
The birds outshout her. Annele now fills her lungs, raises her voice high and sends a
long call above all the birds and treetops, far, far away, until her chest caves in and
cleaves to her back: "Yoo...hoo!" she ends exuberantly. The tops of the notes, slender
like silver pointers, glide away out of earshot! All the birds are amazed: hell's bells!

Annele remembers her herd with a start, crashes her way through the undergrowth toward the edge of the field. She counts them again, pointing her finger at
each one. They're all there! Of course the black-and-white sow, thief that she is, is
close to the forest already: but when the long switch reprimands her, she turns back,
kicking her legs and grunting angrily, then pushes her snout into the sow thistles of
the fallow field.

The fallow field is ablaze with color. Field chamomile, daisies, wild pansies have
all gathered here; just now the morning glories and poppies are beginning to stir; the
sun comes over to them: get up! get up! and pulls the blanket off each one, like
Annele's mother this morning.

The flowers are blooming, the forest shouts in exultation, the trees sparkle in
the shimmering sky, Annele's heart is like a container filled to the top that has been
stoppered: she'd like to run into the forest, where all the paths are full of sunlight, to
the new growth forest beyond the birch hills where – who knows? – strawberries may
already be turning red, to the meadow, where yesterday she saw forget-me-nots in
the marsh drainage ditch – she'd like to, yes! but she can't! she mustn't! Duty
shackles her feet.

Suddenly Annele's forehead flushes, lightnings flash in her eyes. With big
strides she runs to her herder's bag, tossed down in the shade at the edge of the
woods. She feels the bag: thick! Now she knows. Last night as she was falling asleep
she heard her sister Līziṇa say something. In the bag is Līziṇa's new book!

Annele caresses and holds the bag tight: "So dear, so kind, so dear, so kind!" It is
Līziṇa who is "so dear, so kind." Annele didn't dare to ask her for the book, but
Līziṇa noticed the longing in her eyes, and gave it to her of her own accord.

The book is Līziṇa's confirmation present, small, with a black cover and
gilt-edged pages that are stuck together, "newfangled," says Grandmother. At the very
beginning is a picture of the Savior. Annele folds her hands and looks at it for a long
time. She looks, and feels a burning flood rise in her eyes, to her throat, her fingertips.

The book is like an old acquaintance in a new guise. Short prayers, excerpts from Bible stories and hymns. Many, many hymns! Annele knows all the tunes. With parts and without – as is the fashion now. When during prayers everyone sings the lower part, she and Līziņa "hold" the tune and sing loud and high, raising their voices above everyone else's. No one can sing like Annele and Līziņa, they "fill every corner with their singing," as Grandmother says.

Annele turns over the pages and searches. All the hymns are beautiful, but there is no single one that is the most beautiful of all – a hymn that would express everything in the woods and sky today, out there and inside her heart.

And here it is. There is none more beautiful than this one:

> O that I had a thousand tongues,
> A thousand mouths to sing thy praise,
> I'd be the first, the very first
> To sing thy glories, God!

Annele's voice begins with a slight quaver, growing in exultation, soars over the ravine into the green hill, beyond the treetops into the blue sky. Annele herself vibrates like a harp, filled to her fingertips with "a thousand voices" – the gray pines and the flowers of the fallow land and the sparkling expanse of the sky listen to her song, her eyes are filled with hot tears, she dares neither move nor look back, she knows: God is standing behind her, looking over her shoulder into the book with the gilt-edged pages.

⌒≈

Midday. Annele races across the yard.

"Go take a nap, Annele! Why, we couldn't get you up this morning; you'll be perishing with sleep by tonight!"

Quick as a flash, Annele veers aside behind a pile of brushwood, hands behind her back, and in her hands is a little clay jug. She stands, burns in the sun, and waits.

The "big" kids come running outside, each from a different direction, gather in a clump, whisper together, gallop off toward the woods. Annele after them. The leader looks back: faster, faster! he commands. Nothing doing! Annele's long legs are right at their heels.

Near the woods, the whole clump turns suddenly as one, facing Annele menacingly. Annele too stands, feet riveted to the ground, without blinking an eye. The leader yells:

"Will you go home, huh? You know where we're going?"

"Berry-picking!"

"Unhunh! No, we're not!"

"So why d'you have those mugs hidden away under your shirts?"

"But you're not allowed to come, so there! D'you even know where it is we're going?"

"Yeah! D'you even know what kind of a place it is, huh?"

How could Annele not know? For a long, long time now, Annele has been yearning for Irši game preserve, where at night not a living soul dares go past for fear of being consumed by crackling blue and red flames that dart about there; and at midday, if you walk there alone, ghostly white women appear behind every bush.

Irši game preserve is a forbidden secret, a wonderful place – the forester spares no one who is caught there. At Irši game preserve, a person can suddenly disappear right in front of your eyes, and nobody knows what happened to them. At Irši game preserve, you might suddenly hear the singing of wonderful voices, but go and try looking for the singers, and you'll see where you end up! At Irši game preserve there are birds with feathers so shiny that your eyes are dazzled looking at them, and at Irši game preserve there are strawberries as big as the tip of your thumb.

"Don't you dare tag along after us! We're going to run away and hide, and when the witch with the green eyes catches sight of you, your head will freeze on your shoulders."

"A bird of ill omen will put a spell on you, you won't even have a chance to cross yourself before your neck gets twisted around."

"Suddenly someone will call your name, you'll look back and turn into a pillar of salt, like Lot's wife."

"The forester's going to come, we'll have run away, but he'll grab you and throw you in a pit like Joseph."

"Yeah, in a murderers' pit!"

"At Irši game preserve there's murderers' pits all over the place."

Annele doesn't blink an eye or say a word. However, there is every indication that she's determined to go with them, regardless of whether Irši game preserve is chock-full of danger or not.

They are forced to calm down and come to terms.

"Let her come along if she wants to that much. Better that she should come than for somebody in the house to hear the racket; then the fun will be over."

"Let her come! But don't blame me if anything happens."

"What could happen to her? A big girl. Why, she's already a herder."

A girl grabs Annele by the hand, and with that the fight is over.

The whole group now races downhill – uphill, downhill – uphill; in the hollows the girls hold hands, and as they pass the thickets all eyes are aghast, wide open: there's nothing there! There is just the forest floor in the deepest thickets, like a lake scattered with tiny diamond eggs that rock on the black shadows.

Suddenly, as though sliced off, the pinewoods end in a vast, fiery hot, fragrant brightness. Irši game preserve!

It is a large rectangular space full of second-growth trees. Small young pine trees, just about half-grown, stand singly or in clusters, emerging from thick succulent branches close to the ground, rise slender like countless little church towers to the crosses at their tops. Sunlight pours in streams among all the crosses. Bees, dragonflies, locusts, hornets, gadflies thrash around like bathers in a sauna through the white heat. For in the dense shadows flowers are spread like embroidered shawls. Meanwhile in the high grassy pillows there is a profusion of – strawberries!

They all fall upon the nearest spot.

"I was first!"

"No, me! Don't come here! Away, get away! Those are my berries. Go find your own!" And one spreads his arms across the berries and chases away the others. Meanwhile another calls, "Come on, over here! Here you can grab them by the handfuls! Come here! Let that greedyguts eat his all by himself!" And again they all fall upon the second cluster.

That's not the way to do it. More get squashed and trampled here than picked. The big boy decides they must each pick on their own. Just don't stray too far and call to each other real softly, with a short "Oo!" so the forester won't hear.

Their eyes have already gotten used to the wonders. None of them yell any more when, right by their spot, there, and there, and there! they see more strawberries, and much finer ones; they've realized that at Irši game preserve there are more berries than you can shake a stick at, and that they can't be picked in a single day. These are the very first, the season's harbingers, for there are none to be seen in the woods yet.

Annele's little jug is full. She's heaped the very plumpest and reddest berries on top. Annele squeezes into the shadow of a little pine and stretches her legs out in front of her. Now she can catch her breath, rub away the shirt that is stuck to her back. She rolls to one side, then the other, turns on her stomach; as far as her hand can reach, all the berries wind up in her mouth. But right at her fingertips there are clusters of fringed downy wild pinks and wonderfully fragrant wild violets. As soon as Annele gets up, she's going to pick them.

But when Annele tries to get up, she turns heavy as lead. And the pinks start to grow and grow almost to the very clouds and come straight at Annele. – Oh wonder of wonders! There are no more pinks, nor anything, only a tall gray man with green eyes. Annele tries to move, but she can't. She is riveted to the ground. And the green eyes jump out of the man's head, bump into Annele's forehead – bang! – and vanish. And after that, two more: bang! they hit Annele's forehead and vanish. And so do the next two. Now Annele can no longer stand it, but tries to cry out. But she's hardly had time to open her mouth when the gray man himself shouts fit to burst her eardrums: "The forester, run!"

Annele is flabbergasted. How did her head get under the green branches of the pine next to the very trunk? No time to think. All around her there's rustling, branches move; the others jumping up from their spots, flashing by, whispering as they run: "Get going, get going, quick, quick, quick!"

Annele grabs her jug and runs after them. Far ahead in front of her, branches move as people run by, she is the very last. Fear, needle-sharp, goes through her to the tips of her hair. All the stories of witches, ghosts, mad dogs, snakes run with her, tread on her heels. Faster, faster, her heart urges, her feet hardly touch the ground. With a leap she jumps out of Irši game preserve, stumbles into the pinewoods, where the other children are already standing waiting for her. They stand in silence, only their panic-stricken eyes call and summon Annele forth from the terrible game preserve. Not until Annele rejoins the others does she, too, dare to look back.

"Who was that?" someone asks aloud, and they all suddenly feel as though they've been released from a nightmare.

"The forester!"

"Did you see him?"

"No, not me!"

"Who did, then?"

Everyone is silent. Nobody saw him.

"But I did hear a rustling. As soon as I bent down to the berries – big as fists they were – there's this rustle! I thought – must be a snake! But I heard somebody coming, whistling through his teeth; coming and disappearing, coming and disappearing!"

"And I just saw everybody running, and the branches shaking, and I thought: a mad dog, what else? And so I took off, too."

Look at them all, laughing and chattering! Each had been scared of his own fear, but now they all want to be big heroes and laugh at the others' fear.

Right after the noon break, Annele is back in the ravine again. But now herding is no longer as easy as it was this morning. Only after a long, relentless battle does Annele manage to control the herd, which is struggling to get back to the cool sties. Not till the bristly rebels, huffing and puffing, dig themselves in and lie down on the ground, does Annele realize she has kept the upper hand.

It seems as though everything were trying to crawl into the ground. Flower petals droop, the treetops have shrunk, the forest is silent, even the sun is dull and lazy, propped up by long white spikes. It almost seems as if it was still where it was at noon, except that it burns even hotter. Could it be that it's really standing still? The idea startles Annele. Maybe somewhere God's people is fighting its enemies, as Joshua did once in the valley of Gibeon when he commanded: Stand thou still, O sun, in Gibeon, and thou, O moon, in the valley of Aijalon?

Placing one foot in front of the other, Annele quickly measures the shadow. Aha! it's longer than it was at Irši game preserve! So the sun *is* moving, though very slowly, as one might expect in such great heat.

Annele drags herself over to the edge of the field, into the shadow of a hawthorn tree, and drops to the ground. The sultry heat is in her arms and legs, and sadness is in her heart. What happened to that clear morning of exultation? Where did her joy go? Now everybody's having a hard time, so how can you skip or laugh any more?

Annele flattens herself against the ground and thinks. Thinks long thoughts.

Why did they have to run to the game preserve on the sly? Why weren't they allowed to pick berries there? Because they trampled the grass? – But no one mowed the grass in there, and the young pine trees were so tall that the children were dwarfed by them. Why did the forester ill-treat the people and the children who went inside the preserve? Because they picked the berries? But there was such a lot of berries that the whole parish couldn't have picked them all. – Because the count had forbidden it, people said. But the count himself didn't pick berries there. What did he care about Irši game preserve! He had so many forests he couldn't have visited every one of them in one day; as far as the eye could see, wherever there was a pinewood or a birch grove, it all belonged to the count; old Mikus, when he was still alive, used to say that if he had a single pine every year, he'd have enough firewood, but the count had millions and millions of pines. What did he have so many forests for?

What does a count do every day, she wonders. The grown-ups sometimes say that all he does is eat and sleep. But that can't be so. How can any person stand that?

But maybe the count isn't a real person?

No, surely he is! And surely it's just as Ingus the farmhand said: the count spends all day counting money. That must be it! Because everybody brings the count money, of course. Look at Grandmother when there's not enough flour or candles or sugar: "We can't, we can't buy any," she says, "What'll we bring the count when fall comes?" The same with the uncles. When you go visit them and they come back with Father after walking around the fields – their foreheads furrowed: it doesn't matter how hard it is to make ends meet at the farm, they say, just so's there's something to bring the count. True, Father doesn't bring the count anything, but he goes and works all year so Godfather will have something to bring the count.

No, surely the count doesn't spend all day counting money! He may be a count, but surely nobody could stand that! Sometimes, maybe, he goes for a ride. Here's how: he puts on white piqué trousers, a little red cap on his head, and off he goes! Like the one who rode into the yard the other week with the crazy countess. Whee, how the two of them came riding like storm winds out of the woods up the hill! The countess has one horse by its mane, and is riding another. It stamps restlessly and rears, but the countess stays glued to its back. Everybody runs to the doors and windows, while Godfather goes out in the yard to meet them. Godfather scurries over to kiss the countess's hand. – Funny, him kissing a young person's hand! The countess makes her horse prance and wags the coxcomb of feathers on her head, she talks "funny talk," the way Janka the herdboy does sometimes when he's clowning around: "My goot farmer, vy you drife avay dose Chypsies from your pasture? Vere can dey go, dose Chypsies?" That morning Godfather ran the Gypsies off his land on Gypsy Hill; the Gypsies had grazed their animals in his meadow; they're no end of trouble for people: stealing, grazing the fields, going around panhandling every day. But the crazy countess, they say, gets the Gypsy kids to plant black radishes and then paints pictures of them. Godfather scratches his head, at a loss for words, while the countess, wagging her coxcomb and making her horses pirouette, goes, "Tank you, my goot man, tank you," and gallops away again like the wind. The redcap after her.

She's certainly funny, that countess! It's obvious that she is female, but then again in a way she's not. Wonder if the countess is even a real person?

There are certainly a lot of things in the world that aren't the way they should be. Take Godfather, for example – he never works like other people. The same goes for all the children of farmers. They don't go herding, they can run outside in winter because they're never given work to do, they can go to school even before their regular winter of schooling arrives. Farmers' children are allowed to do a whole lot of stuff that is a "sin" for Annele.

Wonder what the mansion is like where the count and countess live? Old Anyus says: silk chairs, golden walls, china dishes, and varnished floors. Gee! How it must all sparkle!

Annele was near the mansion the night they showed the blue marvels, but did she get inside? Not by a long shot.

But never mind about the mansion! A person could go to the mansion. Old Anyus went daily, and so did Godfather – everyone who brought the count money went to the mansion. – But the count is away from home for long periods of time. When he's collected all the money, he goes to foreign countries where the sun never sets. Foreign countries! That's something else!

That's where the birds of passage fly to in fall.

That's where none, none of our people can go, and where the count can travel, 'cause he's got money to burn.

But it is possible to go there. So what if only the count can go? It's possible to go to all the foreign countries. – But what exists where nobody can travel? What is beyond all the many forests, beyond the sky, beyond the place where the sun rises and where it sets again? There must be something there that no human ear has heard and no human eye has seen!

Can you go there when you die? Is that where old Mika the pensioner is now, the one who died last winter after living at Spring Farm for a short, short while? Not his body of course, his body was put in a coffin and taken to the cemetery, but what happened to his aliveness and his voice? Every day, as far back as she can remember, he walked, and talked, and scolded, and all of a sudden he wasn't there any more! No matter how long she waited to hear the sound of Mika's voice among the others, it was in vain! She could hear them all, but she never heard Mika's voice again; no matter how long she looked at the door, as though any moment, any moment now it would open and Mika would come in, it was in vain! The place where he ought to have been was empty now.

Anyus said Mika was in heaven now. But you couldn't believe everything Anyus said. How many times, while Mika was still alive, she had said he would end up in hell because he used such terrible swearwords. And the things she had said about the amazing things at the mansion weren't true, either.

Mika certainly did swear like a trooper. He would kick dogs that happened to be underfoot; but Mother said Mika had been "broken by hard work." And he never said a bad word to any of the children, or teach them to do bad things.

No, Mika would certainly not go to hell. And even if God wanted him to, the Savior wouldn't allow it. The Savior would take Mika by the hand and implore God until he forgave all of Mika's sins.

And what about God? – How would he profit if Mika went to hell? Why should God care about Mika's sins? God has eyes like morning stars and garments that shine like the sun, it's no great hardship for him to wash away Mika's sins with hyssop till they become white as the driven snow. For God is almighty and ever present, isn't he?

Is he really present at all times and everywhere, though? He was this morning. This morning, when God looked into Annele's book, her heart expanded like the world and burned like the thornbush in Moses' desert, but now she has shrunk to the size of a tiny insect that wishes the earth would swallow it up. God stands at a distance and no longer draws her to him.

Why does God no longer draw her heart to him? – It must be because her heart has become sinful.

Annele breathes a heavy sigh.

Sinful, that's it. For man is conceived and born in sin. Where can you escape sin?

She shouldn't have gone to Irši game preserve. She should have taken a nap when she was told to. – That was disobedience.

But was it always possible to obey? You might as well leave the world then, 'cause you could hardly live if you did. There were many times when it was a sin to skip and laugh; on Sundays it was a sin to read any book except God's word, while on workdays it was a sin to read any book at all, because you had to work then; oftentimes you couldn't even figure out what was a sin and what wasn't. Of course, old Anyus says you shouldn't brood too much, for the imagination of a man's heart is evil from his youth, and that is why a person should always purify himself.

Wicked, wicked. Annele feels it. Tears sting her eyes, and her heart is so heavy she can no longer bear it, and she recites out loud as tears drop on her folded hands: "Create a pure heart within me, O God, and renew a constant spirit. Do not turn your countenance from me and do not take your holy spirit from me."

Now everything is all right. Such lightness fills her heart. Her thoughts wander every which way, then settle down. Annele pulls her knees up to her chest and half closes her eyes; even through the little chink between her eyelids, she can see what her herd is up to.

And so Annele sits.

Time stretches long, long and slow as a worm.

Suddenly, beyond the forest, there is a surge of hollow rumbling that reverberates through the forest, rolls, and fades across the hills and fallow field.

Annele's eyes widen. A storm? – She waits for a while.

"No, it was probably nothing! I must have been asleep." Still, it seems as though the hills, the trees, the flowers are withdrawing within themselves, waiting. Silence. Annele bows her head on her knees.

Again – an even more violent surge of rumbling. At its very center, the forest gives itself a shake, fierce and threatening as a wild beast awakening.

Annele jumps to her feet, runs away from the forest a little distance and throws back her head. Yes – a thunderstorm! It's already here!

The entire section of sky behind the forest has filled with black cloud mountains with faint gray edges. The sun is about to sink into them, with all its spikes of light glowing white-hot.

Lightning. Annele counts how far away the thunderstorm is, but she gets mixed up; her heart, beating right in her throat, is what mixes her up. She can't even count up to six before the rumbling surges again, its tremor rising almost to the very zenith.

There is a roaring in the clouds! The forest stands transfixed in a lurid light, the leaves seemingly stuck together, not a blade of grass stirs, the roaring echoes hollowly in the silent forest and seems to be racing this way with giant strides; rusty white piles of clouds, like whipped foam, come boiling up over the gray ones.

"It's coming! It's here! It's overhead now!" shouts Annele, but without budging.

Howling, eddying round and round, the whirlwind hurls itself into the forest. With a cracking noise, treetops fall in wide swaths; before there's time to make the sign of the cross, the whole forest is already under the crushing power of the gale. But the roaring clouds overhead are drowning out the noise of the whirlwind.

And now, clattering loudly, an eruption from the clouds sweeps through the forest like pebbles suddenly scattered over a giant tin plate!

"Hail, hail!" Annele whispers, her hands clenched, running as though perplexed in the direction of the pigs, but there's no sign of them.

"Home, got to get home!"

But you can no longer see anything. Everything is submerged in the foaming torrents. Enormous grains, even chunks, of hail beat down on Annele's back, her shoulders, her neck; she tries to cover and protect her head with her hands, runs haphazardly homeward – when suddenly glittering lightnings flash before her eyes, and she is knocked to the ground...

Annele recovers from the thunderclap. Her teeth are chattering, her limbs are stiff; she stretches one leg, then the other: she is able to move them.

"It will pass, it will, I'll live through it! It won't kill me, it won't!" she reassures herself, gets to her feet again and goes on running.

Out of the gushing downpour, somebody quickly comes toward her, dressed only in shirt and trousers, his head bare. It's Annele's father.

Without a word he lifts Annele on his shoulders and with big, long steps, like rowing with oars, carries her across the raging waters.

When Father and Annele enter the house, they flood everything. Rivulets of water run wherever they stand. In comes Grandmother, a big, rough shawl over her head – the pigs were all over the gardens, she says, she had trouble getting them into the sty.

Annele's cheeks flush hot. "There! What good did it do?" she thinks dejectedly: "I didn't do my job!"

Annele lies in bed, dressed in dry clothes, but her eyes are red. Why are her eyes red, Mother wants to know.

"Did the hail hit you pretty hard?"

"It did."

"Does it hurt so badly?"

"No!"

"Well then, why are you crying?"

Annele doesn't answer.

"Did you get terribly scared?"

"I did."

"Is that why you're crying?"

"No, why should I cry about that?"

"Well then, tell me, what *are* you crying about?" Mother insists sternly.

Then Annele gasps between sobs: "I – didn't – do – my – job, I – didn't – do – my – job!"

Mother takes Annele's head in the palm of one hand, shakes it laughing.

"Get on with you, you silly girl, you! Here she is beaten black and blue: I didn't do my job! Even a grown-up couldn't have done that job!"

The room is as quiet and cool as it was this morning. Not even a mouse rustles. Annele, from the head of the bed, looks at the sun, which is now in the window on the other side of the room, and almost down to the ground. Just now, strip by strip, first the big pear tree grew red, then the new clover field began to burn... now it's gone out. The sun sinks to the ground almost precipitously – now only half of it shows – now a rim – now just a tiny rim – now all that's left are two long, long golden horns...

Two long golden horns are left hanging in Annele's eyelids.

Jelgava

Hardly had Līziņa left to go and be an apprentice in Jelgava than Annele began thinking and wondering endlessly: let's see if Father and Mother will go and visit Līziņa, and will they take me too or not? They had certainly promised, as a reward for the days of herding, but she couldn't be too sure that they'd keep the promise. How often such a promise made by grown-ups somehow seemed to be forgotten and then remained unremembered forever. The safest were promises that were kept on the spot. But those were few and far between.

Of course there was reason for hope – food would have to be taken to Līziņa at infrequent intervals. Now and then Father and Mother spoke of going to Jelgava, looking at Annele with a sort of grin as they did so.

Maybe, maybe!

Her hopes began to assume the appearance of reality when Simkus the kerchief peddler drove up to the farm, rousing the whole household as usual. When, running back and forth, he wheezed his "Come buy, come buy, come buy my lurvely kerchiefs, calicoes, aprons, ticking!" the maids and married women came from all the corners, *klētis,* and gardens, for it was the beginning of summer, and there was great need for light summer jackets and kerchiefs. Simkus spread out his wares, tossed and turned kerchiefs and bolts of cloth from side to side, praising and extolling them, but not allowing the hands of strangers to touch them. Annele's mother, too, stood by, watched and appraised, evidently eager to buy something.

"Vell, vat you vant? Who you vant it for?" Simkus asked her curtly.

"I want it for that girl there. Have to take her to see Jelgava, so she's got to have a new dress," Mother said, half turned to Simkus, half to the other women.

Shivers of joy ran through Annele, down to her toes. So they really *were* taking her to Jelgava! And they'd even buy her a new dress! Oh Mother, Mother, how good she was! Annele couldn't have imagined such happiness even in her dreams. No, she hadn't had the slightest idea that she'd get a dress.

It was also sweet to hear that the other women agreed with Mother's reasoning. Of course, of course – after all, you couldn't let a child stew in a homespun skirt in weather this hot. In town – so everyone said – it was hotter than in the country. In town you had to dress differently. There needed to be clothes suitable for each place.

In the meantime, having rummaged through his merchandise, riffling through it with his fingers as though through the pages of a book, Simkus pulled out a bolt of cloth and tossed it on top with a grand gesture.

"Vell, here it iss!"

And he began to praise it.

Here, he said, was merchandise that was a stroke above everything else. You could find nothing better for that little gal, not in Žagare, nor in Dobele.

Oh, you hateful Simkus! Annele made a face. He must have pulled that one out just to tease her. Why, such cloth was fit only for old Anyus, or Kaminskene when she again got a craving to lie in the ashes and curse.

The cloth was a dark rusty color, like the tarnished bottom of a pot, with tiny black and brownish flecks, she hated even looking at it! But Simkus just kept turning it this way and that, and spreading it now against the light, now the shadow, holding it up against his own body, then against Annele's, who pulled away from it sullenly and hid, as though trying to disappear from sight.

He dared them to find anything better. Cloth like this, the girl could wear herding, on the farm, to the fair, to church; she'd wear it in good health – ten years on one side, and ten years turned outside in, why, she'd never be able to wear it out to her dying day provided she took good care of it. And in addition to all these great advantages he'd let them have it for a song, because this was all he had left, these few yards, just enough for a kitten like this kid.

In panic the girl saw that her mother was not only listening to Simkus as he cast his spell, but also examined the cloth herself, stretching and rubbing it and apparently finding it acceptable. The other women, too, unanimously agreed that the

cloth was just fine for a child like this: for it would neither fade, nor get dusty, nor show stains. Only Karlīne, as soon as she approached, shrugged and said in a loud voice: "What, a cloth like that for a child? Why, it would make a good shroud for a corpse." At this, Simkus got awfully mad at her, glowering and rolling his eyes, and berated her: a maidservant like her should stop blathering such nonsense, all the rich farmers' wives had found the cloth suitable for their children and bought it, so how could she say it wasn't good enough for 'vun dumb laborer's kid'?

And, wheezing fiercely, he tossed back his merchandise as though he didn't care: take it or leave it.

With all her might, Annele tried to persuade her mother not to buy this ugly dress length – either by pulling on her clothes, or pointing to where glints of pink, green, yellow, and red shone forth among Simkus's merchandise. Just look, there were lovely things galore in there! But it was all in vain. The yellow one was too light, the pink one too flimsy, the red one too expensive. No, no, this particular cloth was good, this one alone was good. And Mother bought it.

"Too bad, girl, such is your fate!" laughed Karlīne.

Terribly dejected, Annele crept away. Why couldn't her fate have been the light pink, the green, the yellow, or the red – why this dirty pot bottom? She couldn't understand. It was a drop of wormwood in the sweet cup of the realization of her hopes.

The Sunday when the trip to Jelgava had been planned was coming closer and closer. Annele worried and wondered if there was anything special she could bring as a present for Līziņa. And she hit upon the very best idea. A little jug of sweet strawberries, a bunch of the first wood hyacinths. All of Saturday afternoon was spent looking for these rare treasures.

On Sunday morning they had to leave before sunrise. Still quite drugged with sleep, the girl was dressed and seated in the buggy, where she continued to snooze. In the dreadful hollow of the Black Tavern, she finally woke up, for the first ray of the sun sharply stung her eyes.

Aha! So this was the infamous hollow of the highwaymen!

She shot lightning glances toward one side of the road, then the other, to see if any of the highwaymen about whom there were so many legends would come creeping out of the thicket, but only the birds were twittering and singing; somewhere deep below murmured a tiny brook. The highwaymen must be awfully sleepy, too, on such a nice Sunday morning, and they were letting the buggy and its occupants sneak past them unnoticed. When they drove up to the top of the hill, the forest ended. Open, level fields, proud red-roofed farms, big manor houses with stately gates and green quickset hedges trimmed smooth as walls. Above the thick crowns of trees, flags were fluttering. Splendid, splendid! This is how they entered Annele's consciousness. And to think these were only manor houses, and this wasn't even town yet! Wonder what town would look like? Annele remembered the hymn, "Jerusalem, a lofty city." Was Jelgava like Jerusalem? And was Jerusalem like Jelgava?

When they came to level fields and yet more fields, she dropped off to sleep again.

The buggy rumbled: dar-dar-dar; dar-dar-dar!

Annele was going to Jerusalem. Steep as a wall rose the lofty city. And they had to drive up there. The road became thin as a thread. How would they be able to keep their balance on a road like that? On one side or on the other they would be forced to crash into the abyss. But where was this abyss? Something was banging terribly. Somewhere there was the sound of hammering: clang-clang-clang-clang-clang! Now they were in Jerusalem. The people of Jerusalem ran out angrily: What is that terrible banging? Who is this waking us from sleep so painfully?

"Here, look at the Svēte River!" Annele heard her mother's voice, and her wide eyes were filled with the ford of the river they had just crossed. Father turned the horse into the shadow, under the trees, and hung a little bag of oats around the horse's neck. "Come, get down and stretch your legs," he invited them affectionately.

Taking her first step on the ground, the girl stumbled over something long. What was it? She glanced down at herself.

"Be careful! Lift your new dress so you won't step on it and tear it," Mother scolded.

Oh dear yes! Annele was wearing the new dress! It was long, down to the ground, with a big hem, and at every step it rolled underfoot, hobbling her. The sleeves reached down to the tips of her fingernails.

"It *is* a bit long," said Mother, scrutinizing Annele's outfit. "Like anything that's been made without being fitted. She didn't bring it till late last night. Of course I did tell the seamstress to add a bit extra so there'd be room to grow, but it's turned out even more on the generous side. Well, in three, four years it will fit you just right," she reassured herself, pulled the girl's skirt higher all around and told her to be sure and hold it tight and not let it drag on the ground.

Looking at her hands, Annele was shocked to see that the heads of the wood hyacinths were drooping. What would she bring Līziņa now?

"They'll recover, they'll recover," her mother comforted her, "let's put them in the Svēte."

She took the flowers and stuck them among the pebbles along the bank.

"Why, the Svēte is quite shallow," the girl was amazed, for she had imagined it to be a fabulously wide, magnificent stream.

"It isn't at all. We turned off the road and crossed over at the ford, because Father wanted to water and feed the horse. But over where the road is, where they've built the bridge now, it's so deep that in the old days both cattle and people often got drowned there."

Rippling, made shimmery by the sunlight, tiny waves wound their way through little pebbles, and small fry darted about as Annele skipped across them.

"Svēte, Svēte, why do they call you Svēte (holy)?" she asked the river.

"Well, am I not holy?" asked the shimmering, rippling water, the dew-drenched, magnificent banks. "Don't you feel holy and happy when you see me?"

"Yes, I do," Annele thought after watching the banks for a long time, "but the Tērvete River is like that, too. And so is the Skujene."

"Well, my dear, don't you recognize me? I am that same Skujene, that same

Tērvete. Still your old acquaintance, but in a new home!" the Svēte retorted as if in jest and hurried on its murmuring course.

"Could that be true?" Annele speculated. She never did figure it out, for Mother was calling her. The flowers had drunk their fill, the horse had been fed, Father urged them to continue the journey.

After driving for a short time, Father raised the handle of his whip and pointed into the distance. "Look, we're nearly in Jelgava."

Numbing sparks shot through Annele's breast. Jelgava! Where was it, this Jelgava? She looked up. There was nothing there. She looked lower down. From the gray mist emerged unfamiliar roofs and towers, but they did not shimmer in the least. How could this be Jelgava if it wasn't built in a lofty place and if it didn't shimmer? No, Jelgava must not be like Jerusalem at all.

They began driving on a paved road. The buggy rumbled the way it had crossing the ford of the Svēte River. On both sides stood gray houses with little gray dusty gardens.

"What are those houses?"

"The houses of Jelgava."

"But what are they called?"

"The houses of Jelgava."

"Who is that man walking toward us?"

"A Jelgava man."

"And those others over there?"

"The people of Jelgava."

"Why don't they say good morning?"

"They don't know us. In Jelgava, you only say good morning to people you know. Who could ever say good morning to so many people?"

"But there's not a lot of us."

"There are lots of them."

"But where is Jelgava itself?"

"What Jelgava is it you want? This is it, don't you see?"

Annele shook her head. It seemed to her that this was not Jelgava.

"It's early yet. The gentry are all asleep. Wait till the gentry get up. Then all the streets will be full. And don't ask so many questions. Look for yourself!"

How could Annele not look! So much that was unfamiliar forced itself upon her eyes, ears, nostrils, every pore in her body. Now the houses stood close together; rarely, there would be a tree between them or, even more rarely, a garden with a high fence; nobody could see inside; many windows were still shuttered, others were wide open, with snow-white curtains. Through one window a bird loudly warbled, through another someone stuck a head in a nightcap, scrutinized the street in one direction, then the other, looked fiercely at the travelers and shook a hand at them, while they slowly and loudly rat-tat-tatted down the silent cobblestoned pavement, like knocking one stone against another; then the head withdrew inside. Dogs ran toward them, noses raised, as though sniffing the rising sun, but none of them barked. Then suddenly out of the row of houses leaped a golden pretzel on a long pole; on the other side of the street, on a similar pole, swung an imposing boot, most likely dropped by the fellow with the seven-league boots in the fairytale. Then another golden pretzel. In between there were all sorts of pictures: in one a man with a white apron and blue trousers had leaned back another man in a chair, had lathered his beard, and was shaving the lather off his cheek; in another a tailor was taking one gentleman's measurements, while other gentlemen who wore shiny black top hats, green and red tailcoats, white waistcoats, and white gloves, and brandished thin canes, stood around the man who was taking the measurements and looked on as though they were witnessing some great marvel. In yet another picture, a terrible heavyset red-faced man with a white apron, one arm raised for a blow, was about to split open the head of a big steer. The steer waited, kicking up all fours, his horns raised, while another steer next to him was already dead, and blood came streaming from his throat.

"Oh ugh! Mother!" Annele exclaimed in horror and clutched her mother's hand, hiding her face. She didn't want to look anymore.

"Such awful men!"

"No need to be scared," her mother reassured her. "They're only signboards so the townspeople will know where to get meat, or bread, or have clothes or boots made, or get a shave. You don't have to be afraid of those!"

Now they drove into a large rectangular yard paved with cobblestones. A man with a blue apron, broom in hand, came up to them. He looked kind and familiar. Father handed the horse over to him, and he promised to feed it, water it, and take care of it in every way, telling them not to worry and just go about their business.

Mother took some bundles from the buggy. From one she took fresh flatbread, and gave a piece each to Father, Annele, and the Jelgava man as well. He immediately began to eat with relish, breaking off tiny pieces, complimenting them how soft and tasty the bread was, and saying it was a long time since he'd had any like it.

They ate right there, sitting amicably on the buggy. Only Annele was somehow not very hungry. She didn't like the taste of Jelgava, which kept coming into her mouth with the food. "Maybe the child is thirsty," remarked the Jelgava man, hurrying off to bring a jug of water. They all drank with thanks. The water tasted good, and the Jelgava man was nice and helpful – he even saw them to the gate and recommended the shortest way to Līziņa's house.

Loaded down with bundles, all three of them now went in search of Līziņa. Annele was still holding her gathered skirt in one hand, while in the other she carried her gifts from the forest, which she refused to let go of. Suddenly, high above them, magnificent sounds rang out, pulling Annele's head back in awe and wonder. There stood a huge building, the tip of whose tower she could not see. Dong – dong! the sounds thundered, sang, rent the air, which seemed to reel with intoxication, shaking like an aspen in the wind.

"Is that a church?" the girl asked bewildered.

"Saint Anne's. That's right," Mother explained.

"My, how big, how big!"

"Yes, you could put three the size of ours into this one."

Yes indeed – you could see right away what a Jelgava church was like!

Annele walked in silence. She was preoccupied. Next to the little church back home she had to place the great church of St. Anne with all its towers and bells.

Green Street! That sounded nice! True, it was just as gray as the other streets, but on it was the house that Līziņa lived in. When our friends had found the house after counting the numbers, Father inspected every wall from top to bottom; he crossed over to the other side of the street, and studied and observed it just as long, as though counting the windows and doors. That must be the way one had to look at houses in Jelgava, thought Annele. Not until he had inspected it thoroughly did Father cross back to the other side, open the door boldly, and now slowly, one after the other, they climbed the creaking wooden stairs. At the top of the stairs there were three doors in different directions. They did not look at them, but climbed one flight higher. Here there was only one door. Father now put down the bundles, took out a handkerchief, wiped his forehead and face, smoothed his hair, straightened his coat on all sides and then, with one finger, slowly knocked. No one came to open. In a whisper Mother said he should knock louder. When the second knock, too, produced no results, Mother went to the door boldly determined, and knocked on the door with her fist. Yes – at once, somewhere inside, the sound of running footsteps could be heard, the door quickly opened, and in the doorway stood Līziņa. She uttered a cry, clapped her hands, hugged Mother, kissed Father's hand, picked up Annele, laid Annele's cheek close to her own. Yes, here was Jelgava at last!

"What a pleasure! What an unexpected pleasure! And you brought the little one too! Well, come in, come in!" Līziņa urged them, took all of Father's bundles as though they were goodness knows how hard to carry; taking one under her arm, another in her hands, she quickly hurried through two rather dark rooms crammed with all kinds of objects, and took them into a brighter room. Here there was a stove, a big white table, all kinds of dishes on the shelves. At the table sat a grayish-haired lady with a black dress and a little black bonnet who was drinking something out of a white cup. Līziņa said a few words in German, the lady got up, said hello to Father and Mother, patted Annele's head and told her she should grow up to be just as hardworking and clever as her big sister. She patted Līziņa on the back, as though showing her off to Father and Mother: "Gutes Kind, gutes Kind. Vun goot child."

Mother unwrapped her present: a bottle of sweet cream and a little bowl of butter. The lady accepted them courteously, said thank you and asked in her funny way of talking which sometimes sounded clear, while at other times it sounded like jabbering: "You haff hat your coffee, nicht wahr?"

"We certainly have," Mother hastened to reply, "we already had some at the inn."

"Funny," thought Annele, "cold water that you drink at an inn is called coffee in Jelgava."

Līziņa would not let her guests linger downstairs, and urged them to come up to her place.

One more little door, up a short, narrow staircase, and there they were at the top of the house, under the very roof, which was now practically steaming from the rays of the sun. There, swept clean and tidy, was Līziņa's corner, and her clothes, hung from a crossbeam and wrapped in a white sheet. Instead of a table she had an old crate covered with a towel. On it, in a tin can, was a little bunch of wildflowers.

Now Annele, too, remembered her strawberries and wood hyacinths. Oh dear, what a shaking they had had, and how wilted the flowers were! Shamefacedly she handed them to her sister. But Līziņa beamed like the sun, and lovingly kissed Annele for the nice presents. Strawberries, she said, were an unprecedented treat for her, and she knew how to revive the flowers in such a way that she could enjoy them for at least another week.

Still talking, she went deeper into the attic, brought out an old chair as well as a couple of small logs of firewood for the guests to sit on.

Mother anxiously peered farther into the attic:

"Surely you don't sleep here at night?"

"No, at night I sleep at Madame's place. She's scared down there all by herself."

"That's what I thought." Mother calmed down. "This place is fit only for rats!"

"It's not that bad," laughed Līziņa, "the rats may be smart, but I'm smart, too – I can hide my things so well that they can't get at them, even if they break their teeth."

Her shining eyes showed that Līziņa enjoyed fighting this war against the rats.

Now Mother wanted to know how Līziņa got along with Madame. Madame was the same woman who had once taught Līziņa's godmother from Hook Farm. It was the latter who had recommended Madame to Līziņa as a good person and as someone who was skilled at her work.

Līziņa said that they managed to get along well. Of course Madame was some-times funny – she gave a laugh and broke off – yes, but they managed to get along. There was an awful lot of work, though. Among Madame's customers, there were a few stuck-up baronesses and countesses, and sometimes the work had to be rushed so fast that they had to go far into the night, or even work on Sunday. It was espe-cially inconvenient that at night she could not leave and be free like the other ap-prentices, who did not live with Madame. But every cloud has a silver lining. She was learning twice as fast, she said, and twice as much as the others. Thus she not only got to do all the special and fine work, but Madame would also send her to the homes of important clients for fittings, relying completely on her suggestions and taste. Once she had been to a place, the customers themselves would beg Madame to let that golden-brown girl do the fitting, and said they were completely satisfied with her.

"And you're not at all afraid to assume such a responsibility?" worried Mother, "suppose you ruin something one of these days? Why, you're still a mere child."

"So far, I've always been lucky. Thank God! I dream up something for each lady that looks good only on her, and none of the others can imitate her. They like that. And I get something out of it too. I can run about outside more often, see other houses and other people and – even make a bit of money."

So saying, she clapped her hands, as though to announce some special surprise, ran to her little trunk and, taking a bright-colored little cloth bag, jingled it: there was the clink of small silver coins.

"Look, girl – want some? I'll buy you the whole of Jelgava for this today," she told Annele boastfully.

Mother laughed. Father, too, smiled, saying: "Well, I'll be! And here I tried to save money so I could bring you a few pennies!"

"I don't need them. Save them for your son! Yes, Father, Mother: you must definitely let the boy get some higher schooling. I shall keep pestering you about it day and night. And the same goes for this little one," Līziņa said, completely serious now.

"Of course, child – it's not that we're against it," Father replied just as seriously, "but surely you know our financial circumstances? An education in Jelgava! How is a poor laborer to manage a thing like that?"

"Don't worry – we'll think of something!" Līziņa raised her head confidently. "But now let's go. What are we doing dillydallying around indoors on a day as nice as this? – C'm'ere, girl!"

She grabbed Annele under the arms and lifted her to the little skylight. Oh the roofs, the roofs, a forest of red roofs! In between, an occasional tree or even several, and a high tower here and there. But in the distance, an imposing white building encircled by a thick cluster of trees like green clouds. A big, big river curved around these like a blue ribbon.

"You're not getting dizzy, are you?"

"No."

"Like it?"

"Oh yes!"

"There's the palace."

"And that wide, blue one?"

"The Lielupe River!"

"It sure is lovely!"

"We're going there now. To the palace and the palace gardens. Wait just a moment."

Līziņa disappeared behind her curtain of clothes. A short time later she emerged wearing a pretty white dress edged with green, and a little green hat. They all exchanged glances of surprise. Because Līziņa was so beautiful, like a fine lady.

"Child, child, how did you manage to make yourself such an expensive and beautiful dress?"

"It's the cheapest fabric I could get, Mummy dear. The expense is all in my fingers. I embroidered it myself, I sewed it myself. I trimmed the hat myself, too."

Father looked, shook his head, sighed.

"It certainly is a shame, daughter – why, you could have done with some of that higher schooling yourself, don't you think?"

"Let's not talk about me!" interrupted Līziņa.

Madame was still sitting at the table reading. "Wart!" she called to Līziņa. She turned her this way and that. Inspected her from head to foot. "Hübsch, sehr hübsch! Vell, vat you say? Isn't your daughter like a little Fräulein? – But what's this, Lieschen? Ohne Sonnenschirm? Vait!"

Madame disappeared in the darkness of her apartment and soon returned with a little white flounced parasol.

"Dis iss from ven I vass a bride," she said. "But I don't mind if she haff it. Sie ist gar zu hübsch, dat Mädel of yours. She is much too pretty."

The street was already dizzy with sunshine. The cobblestone pavement, the houses on both sides of the street were sweltering hot. Many people hurried this way and that. They all seemed to be splendidly dressed. The ladies wore white, blue, red, their skirts round as wheels, light as clouds, little hats perched on hair that was piled high. Above their heads, parasols swayed like many-hued flowers. Gentlemen mingled among the crowd in colorful silk and velvet waistcoats, shiny top hats, or white boaters.

"You can let go of your skirt now," Mother quietly nudged Annele, afraid of speaking loudly, like someone who has entered a church.

The girl immediately obeyed, but the more she tried to walk, the more entangled she got: it was hard to keep up with the grown-ups, for of course she couldn't simply watch her feet, there was also Jelgava to take in with her eyes, her ears, even her mouth.

On the sidewalk several older girls in short pink dresses stood talking, and with them a boy in short pants, looking as if he was itching for a fight. The family had to make a detour around them, for of course they would not get out of the way. At the sight of Annele, the smaller of the girls nudged the other: "Sieh mal, das Gör!"

"Echtes Bauerngör!" the boy put in his pennyworth. And all three burst out laughing.

Annele froze. There was that word again – the one that had once given her such a fright.

"They're calling me a *gör* again, listen to them!" Annele complained to Līziņa in agitation.

"What's that? Who called you that?" asked Līziņa quickly and looked at the German children. Following the mocking glances of the strange girls, she scrutinized Annele from head to foot.

"Yes, but look at the way you're dressed! Mother, Mother, how could you dress the child like that! Why, she'll never grow into that dress, not if she wears it for five years. No wonder people are laughing. No, she can't go like this. Wait here while we go and fix her dress."

No sooner said than done: Līziņa took the girl with her and went back into the house. And while under her fingers the wretched dress magically assumed a different shape as she pinned, measured, and sewed, Annele sat in silence, and tears poured down her cheeks. Why had they called her by the same name as that German woman had, the day Annele went to the manor to see the manor's marvels? What kind of name was this? Why did it hurt so much? And why was she the only one that was called this name? Was she so bad, stupid, ugly? Why, why? She felt deeply hurt and humiliated.

"Why are you crying?" Līziņa asked her quickly, having noticed only now that Annele was sobbing. But she received no answer.

"Are you crying because of that German girl? Really, that's all we need! To cry on account of a person like that! Where's it going to get you if you go listening to everybody who says something to you on the street? If your heart is pure, you don't have to be scared of anybody!"

"A pure heart – that's all well and good – but – but – she – she called me a *gör*."

"So let her! Why d'you listen to her? Jelgava girls are loudmouths."

"But is that a bad name?" Annele persisted.

"What's so bad about it? Why, she's a *gör* herself. Like a cuckoo, she was calling her own name. – But now we must go. Now no one will make fun of you any more."

Annele closely watched everyone who came toward them, and indeed no one paid attention to her anymore. Big and small, old and young, those who did look in their direction looked not at Annele, but at Līziņa. Thank God!

They crossed a deep, dark river, entered a beautiful park with gravelled paths and big flowering shrubs, and then came that second vast, mightily flowing river. Yes, here was the Lielupe River at last! Then the white palace, as if made for horses to gallop around it, adorned with rows of windows like strings of pearls! They went past it time after time, looked their fill and admired it, and finally sat down on a bench by the Lielupe and talked about the great size and splendor of Jelgava. Now if it were possible to get into the emperor's rooms and halls, of which there were twenty or more in the palace, then they'd really have something to marvel at! But ordinary people were rarely admitted to those. Līziņa, too, had never been inside.

"Still, what good is all this?" Līziņa concluded her account of Jelgava, "it isn't the country, you know. And when you've been sitting inside those dark walls all day long, you want the country so much, you want the country the way a thirsty man wants water." And all the smiles had faded from her face.

"What can you do, daughter? You've got to go where the work tells you to go.

The work doesn't ask you if you feel good or bad, if you like it or dislike it. None of us has it easy, you know." And Father placed his hand on Līziņa's hand and looked at her lovingly. Then she began to smile again.

"But I'll tell you again, Father, and I won't stop telling you: you've got to let the boy get a higher education. He should have an easier life than me. I'll be earning money, too, and I'll help out as much as I can. After that, though, all of us combined are going to send the little one to school."

"Whoa, whoa there, daughter, I know you've got a man's courage," Father grasped Līziņa's hand warmly and firmly, while Annele clung to him on the other side like a bur. Thus the four of them sat and talked while the sun had long since passed noon. Now Father began to remind them it was time to leave. They had to set out betimes so they could get home by daylight, for tomorrow the haymaking would begin. Now Līziņa belatedly remembered all the things she had wanted to buy for Annele, everything she had planned to do. But there was nothing Annele saw that struck her fancy now. She was full of Jelgava, and wanted nothing else. Her feet were heavy, tired with walking on cobblestones, sore. Her shoes, borrowed from her Edgefield cousin for the trip to Jelgava, were too wide and too short. She walked with a limp.

Mother became impatient.

"What a nuisance that girl is! I'll certainly think twice before I take her any-where again. Such a slowpoke! Come on, pull yourself together!" After scolding her, she gave her a good shaking. The child was close to tears.

"Easy now, easy, it'll be all right, you'll see," comforted Līziņa, sat the girl down on the grass, took off her shoes, shook out her stockings, smoothed out the wrinkles in them, and when she now put on the shoes – there, Annele was able to walk again. It wasn't bad at all.

They had time to make the round of the market where, as could be expected on a Sunday, the pickings were pretty slim; they bought pilchards and flounders from the fishwives and pretzels from the women who were selling rolls, and then went straight to the inn while Līziņa ran home to change, for she wanted to see her com-pany off and go with them for quite a stretch.

The man at the inn was still walking around keeping an eye on the big yard, but was no longer as friendly with Annele and her family as he had been that morning. There was a buggy there, with two fine horses; it was green and shiny, with a leather seat, and he seemed to have eyes for nothing else now.

After Līziņa came and they had all refreshed themselves with the delicacies they had bought at the market and the good water of the yard man, it was time to leave. Through town they drove at a walking pace, for since the girls were sitting in front on the running board, their tongues had to be protected so they would not bite them off when the wheels banged against the bumpy cobblestone pavement; besides, they all wanted to prolong the short moments of farewell as much as possible. When the houses began to recede from the road and gave way to trees and open spaces, Mother anxiously said, "I'm sure it's time for you to go back!"

"No, no, not for a long time yet!" exclaimed Līziņa, and began talking more quickly about all sorts of profound matters that she had forgotten about and must now hurriedly bring up.

"Now you *must* go back, though. It worries me that you've come with us this far," Mother again spoke up a while later.

"I've had all this time to sit. I'll run back like a bird. There's no need to worry!"

"But still… It does worry me."

"Well, all right. Just to those trees there. And no further. But Father must drive more slowly."

No matter how slowly he drove, they finally did reach the trees. Then Father stopped the buggy. The last moment. Time to part.

Father said, "Get off now, child. We'll have to hurry now, too."

Līziņa got out, said goodbye to everybody once, twice, a third time, then the buggy began to move. She remained where she was.

For a long time Annele, who sat facing in Līziņa's direction, could still see her as she stood and waved first her hand, then her handkerchief, quickly began walking toward Jelgava, looked back again, waved. The white handkerchief fluttered. And so it continued until she became smaller and smaller, finally turning into just a dot, barely visible on the straight highway, and then disappeared from sight as suddenly as if she had never existed.

Meanwhile the travelers were welcomed by the fragrance of birch groves, wheat fields, fields of clover in their first bloom.

Stinging grief ached in Annele's heart. Why did Līziņa have to go back to that dusty, stony town? "You've got to go where the work tells you to go," Father had said. Was work a master so powerful that you couldn't resist? Would it take Annele into its power some day as well? She needed to think these thoughts through, but she couldn't. The closer to evening, the sweeter the fragrance of the fields. A pleasant weariness pressed her eyes shut. By the time they drove into the perilous Black Woods, Annele was fast asleep, and when she woke up she was sleeping in her own sleeping place, and morning shimmered outside. Her first run was into the garden, to the field, to the woods. Was everything still there, were the flowers still as bright and the birds as loud? Nothing had happened to them during her long absence, had it? No, everything was still in its proper place. And as wonderfully iridescent, fragrant, and sonorous as never before.

The Harsh Woman

And again it was winter.

For more than a week, the men were away logging. Then they came home with big loads of wood. White with hoarfrost, like hanks of wool, their sleds creaking. But they did not manage a second trip. The thaw came suddenly. The next morning, a wall of white fog surrounded the farm, so thick you could have cut it with a knife. Soon the eaves began to drip. The snow turned gray. A couple of days later it had turned into black mud that was impossible to wade through. The air was again heavy and damp, as in late fall.

People walked around as though they had lost their joy. Some complained of a heaviness in their bones. The men said that along the way, in a few of the farms, they had found almost all the inhabitants in bed, burning as though on fire. The great scourge! guessed the folks at home dejectedly. "Yes, the great scourge," said old Anyus when she returned from the manor. There, they were always the first to hear about all the latest happenings. The epidemic had already struck on many farms.

"Yes, this is a Harsh Woman," said old Anyus, thoughtfully puffing on her pipe, "she's going to take quite a few from our midst. I'm sure she won't pass us by without doing harm."

The great scourge! The Harsh Woman! It was the first time Annele had heard these expressions. What were they? What did they want? Why did they come? Why were they allowed into the farm? Couldn't anyone fight them? Not Father, nor Mother, nor Granny, nor anyone?

Apparently not. They came from somewhere out there. Like a thunderstorm that one couldn't escape – one simply had to wait patiently and endure it until it passed.

Thus Annele, too, waited daily for the Harsh Woman to come. No matter what she was like, Annele wanted to see her. But this waiting was somehow terribly eerie. Like at night, when after sunset shadows gather, and you don't know what the morning will bring.

All night the eaves dripped, but in the morning came snow mixed with rain. A stranger was walking up from the hollow, coming toward the farm, his chest hunched against the storm, warding off Citron with the handle of his whip as the dog flung himself at him, splashing around in the puddles. The stranger came into the house and after saying good day looked straight at Annele's father. Father likewise looked directly at the stranger, then approached.

"What business brings you here?"

"I was sent to you. The master was in Jelgava yesterday. Your girl has come down with the great scourge. You're to go and bring her home."

Annele grabbed Father's hand tight, she was shaking so. So she had come: the Harsh Woman! But Father was still standing there looking at the stranger. He had no more questions to ask him, nothing further to say to the stranger, but he still kept looking, speechlessly.

Suddenly Annele's hand dropped out of Father's palm. That's how quickly he turned, called Ingus, called Mother, hurried off to get dressed. Mother brought one article of clothing after another, also without uttering a word, merely wiping her eyes now and then. Ingus came in. Should the horses be harnessed? Yes, and hurry, hurry. The sleigh or the wagon? "How's the road?" he asked the strange farmhand. It was still frozen and smooth underneath. They could safely go by sleigh, said the stranger. After all, it was still winter.

Just as hastily as Father got dressed, Ingus harnessed the horses. The stranger stood next to Ingus in the middle of the yard a while longer, telling him a few things or giving him advice, then slowly, picking his way between puddles, crossed the yard and disappeared in the hollow.

Mother brought out pillows and a fur coat, put them away in the sleigh so they wouldn't get wet from the rain. She had no idea what else to bring so that Līziņa would be comfortable on the way home. And just like Mother, all the members of the household, when they found out Līziņa was sick, felt sorry for her and each in turn tried to show their affection for her. The young maidservant, Luze, even came running with her new white silk kerchief, which she was especially fond of. Now she didn't begrudge it: she said to tie it – so soft and caressing and warm – around Līziņa's head during the ride home. But Mother had already thought of everything, and she had no use for Luze's kerchief.

When Father left, Annele thought time had stopped. She didn't know what to do with herself. For a while she dogged Mother's footsteps: perhaps she could ask her a question about Līziņa, about the Harsh Woman, about everything that gnawed at her so painfully, but whenever Mother walked around deep in her own thoughts, she was taciturn and capable of curtly refusing to answer every question, which was more bitter than if she had remained silent. Annele knew this.

Time hung from her shoulders like a woolen throw soaked with rain. Sorrow was not like joy, which broke forth, impossible to control, which wanted to laugh and shout; sorrow forced you to go off in silence, where no one could see it. That is what Annele did. She crept behind the loom, by Father's window. Here there was a little corner that always welcomed everything that must be kept deeply hidden. The heaviness was outside as well, where the snow showed black, thawing beneath gray, storm-driven clouds. Thoughts of the Harsh Woman who had gained a hold over Līziņa did not leave Annele for a single moment, choked her breath, and made every bite of food at the midday meal unpalatable and bitter.

Around noon the rain stopped, but toward evening it started raining again. When darkness fell, the cattle had been fed, and the whole household was back indoors, suddenly something unusual alarmed their minds. A scarlet gleam appeared in the window. It couldn't have come from the sunset, for the sun had set long ago. Those who ran to the window on one side saw the whole sky red; those who ran to the one on the opposite side saw the same thing. Everybody looked at each other. Fearfully, they asked each other: What is it? What does it mean? Was there a fire somewhere in the neighborhood? Was there a fire on their own farm? They hurried outside, but there was not the trace of a fire.

The sky glowed grayish red all over, as though great flames were breaking through thick gray fog. The scarlet glow was brighter toward the top and thicker, darker toward the horizon, every object near and far showed dark outlines, as though from a candlestick held high but giving only dim light. The treetops of a nearby forest that grew on the slope of a hill were outlined with a jagged scarlet line; the trees in the orchard next to the house, the stable, the *klētis*, a cluster of people in the yard stood out as shadowy shapes. It was strange that they all looked the same, heads thrown back, while they themselves seemed to have shrunk forward, as though carrying some burden on their backs. They spoke softly, as if in terror of something. Old Anyus's mouth no longer had that cocksure certainty about everything, Karlīne the maid had lost her loudness, and Ingus the farmhand his obstinate pride.

"What *is* that?" Annele softly asked her mother, keeping close by her side.

"Who knows, child! The forces of nature! Who can understand them?" answered Mother.

"God's doing, it's all God's doing," Anyus said, as though reproving her. "He's showing us that we should fear him."

Nobody contradicted her, not even Ingus. Evidently no one knew what else to say.

The rain fell as though sifted through a fine sieve. In the red glow one could clearly see how the tiny drops fell from a great height, alternating and crossing, and vanished in the ground somewhere close by. Meanwhile in the distance the neighboring farms, hills, and birch groves glittered, spookily unfamiliar. This was no longer the world they knew, so eerily frightening, but also strangely beautiful. Thus for quite a while they stood motionless even though it was raining.

Then, as suddenly as it had turned scarlet, the sky began to fade. The horizon at first turned black, then quickly slid into impenetrable darkness; the darkness also engulfed the farm, the woods; thick clouds appeared at the zenith.

"This is a portent of great wars and bloodshed," said Anyus as though to frighten them, once everyone was back in the house. "You and your old wives' tales," Ingus immediately snarled back, but they didn't get into a bigger argument, for everybody was quite depressed by this day's sad news and fearful portents, and went to bed early; only Annele's mother got ready for what looked like a night's vigil. Annele hoped she too would be allowed to wait up for Līziņa, but Mother curtly told her to go to bed. With the weather and the road as bad as this, Father might not even be able to return tonight, and even if he did return, Annele must not get underfoot, she said. Annele obeyed, determined not to sleep a wink. This day's events seemed so enormous that it did not seem easy to lay them to rest under her eyelids. Especially the natural phenomenon they had just seen, so incomprehensible and eerily beautiful, stood indelibly before her eyes. How the sky had spread itself over everything like a flaming cloak, and how the things of earth had gleamed in the roundness of the sky, so unfamiliar and tiny, unable to find a hiding place! And people had been hunched over and timidly quiet, as though they, too, could no longer find refuge with each other from that great incomprehensible event. "The forces of nature," Mother had said; "God's doing," said old Anyus. Annele thought about it for a long time; she felt the red sky was somehow connected to the Harsh Woman. And what were "forces of nature"? Were they God's obedient servants? Yes, that must be it.

Līziņa had been brought home during the night and lay in Uncle Ansis's room. Mother went in to her, out again, softly opening and shutting the door, but she never took Annele inside, though Annele hadn't budged from the sickroom door. Mother seemed not to see the entreaty in Annele's eyes, or feel the touch of her hand. But worse was yet to come. One time when Mother came out she took the girl by the hand, took her aside and strictly, under threat of severe punishment, admonished her not to set foot in Līziņa's room. The girl became so frightened that she suddenly began to cry bitterly. Why wasn't she allowed inside? What was the matter with Līziņa? Didn't she want to see Annele any more?

But who was there to tell her? She tried to read from Mother's face, from the faces of the other members of the household what they knew about Līziņa. She was always around when they talked about Līziņa. But the news was bad. Līziņa was not aware of the world at all. She was in a delirium. She didn't recognize anyone. "Bad, bad," Anyus shook her old head, "if she doesn't break into a sweat, you can start making a coffin." When Anyus said these words, Mother burst out crying. Only Granny comforted Mother: "It's too soon to say, daughter. If it's God's will, she'll pull through. But we are powerless to do anything against his will."

Impatiently Annele waited for dusk. That was when for a while everybody would be doing the chores outdoors. Mother, too, finally went outside, though she had lingered in the house for a long time today. As soon as her mother left, the girl glided into the sickroom like a little thief, with beating heart.

The room where the patient lay had two windows, and was cool and quiet. The only furniture it contained was a table and a bench, a big clock, and a bed. High white pillows gleamed in the dusk. In the shadow of the pillows lay Līziņa. Līziņa's thick braids had come undone, her curly hair half covered her face, which was red as though from a great fire. She breathed rapidly, restlessly, murmured something, occasionally gave a laugh – Annele dared not go closer, but remained near the clock, her hands folded. "Now she'll see me, call my name," she thought. But no one called her.

"Līziņa, look, it's me. Can't you see me? Come on, talk to me!" whispered the girl.

No one looked at her. The patient's face was quite strange. She took no notice of Annele at all. She herself seemed to have something urgent to do, some place she needed to go, something invisible to struggle against. But she was completely powerless. She tossed from side to side as though she were tied down, but could not get free.

For a long time Annele looked at her sister as though at something alien and incomprehensible. After hoping in vain that she would be recognized and called by name, after waiting in vain for an answer, the girl was seized by an eerie feeling and, as noiselessly as she had come, she glided out of the sickroom.

She hid in her little corner and thought, thought endlessly. Now she knew how deeply Līziņa was in the Harsh Woman's power. But how could she be saved? No one could do it. No one knew how. Only God could do it. She must pray to God. Did she know how to, though?

It is true that every night she told God the joys and sorrows of her day and prayed that he would protect all those who lived and breathed at Spring Farm, but up till now they had all been well and happy – though what about sorrow as great as what had befallen them now? How would she know how to put it in a prayer? There weren't any words that could express everything she needed to say to God. – So the girl grieved and looked toward God's help like someone full of longing looking on from afar.

But then suddenly, like a little bird on a branch, her joyful, sure voice leapt up in her breast. "Oh you silly girl, does God really need such words?" – "Of course he doesn't," she replied just as surely and confidently. After all, he himself knows and understands everything. No matter how it turns out, it will be all right. And immediately she prayed, "God, God, heavenly father! Do make Līziņa better again. Do help her, please! 'Cause I don't know any other way to ask you. Dear, dear heavenly father! 'Cause you know everything. Please help!"

She suddenly felt so light. Slowly, her tears began to flow. Let them flow. Her limbs became wearily and pleasantly relaxed. She felt as though she were being carried lightly down a stream with high banks until she reached a mighty, shining gate. Beyond the gate was great strength, great power and help. All she had to do was open the gate and grasp God's hand. And there it was. Now there was no more need for words at all. "Help, help Līziņa!" said every heartbeat. And now God could hear it all, and everything was all right.

But the days came and went, and the patient's condition did not improve. Annele hoped and doubted, hoped and doubted. Annele's father and mother, too, complained of fever and weariness in their bones, but they had no time to lie down; they said they were sure they would overcome the sickness even if they stayed on their feet. That weekend Annele's big brother came home with a huge medicine bottle filled with a brown liquid. He had gotten it from the manor doctor, a German, who also took care of the schoolchildren. Today the children had come in droves, and they had all been given the same medicine with instructions to go home at once, get into bed, and drink the medicine "six time per day vun shpoonful." The brown liquid, which had a sweetish aftertaste, was familiar to all the patients; it was said that the doctor never prescribed any other medicine. But if you got the brown medicine, it was said, then the disease was not fatal; the doctor prescribed no medicine at all for fatal illnesses.

Brother's health really did improve soon, and Father and Mother began to feel better too, only Līziņa didn't. Whenever Mother came out of the sickroom in the mornings and people asked, "How is she?" she sadly shook her head: "Still the same." And there were no further questions to ask.

To Annele, all these days seemed to be heavily overcast. She didn't feel like running outside, skipping, laughing, even talking. When she crept off into her little corner, it felt as though she were crawling into a dark cave where even God could not keep his eye on her. She was a little girl, she didn't know how to pray to God properly, nor how to tell another person her troubles. Since the time when she had crept in to see her sick sister at dusk, there had been no other opportunity, though she waited for one every day. Father did the outside chores so that Mother would not have to leave the patient for any length of time.

But one day Father hastily called Mother to the barn. A calf had just been born. Throwing a shawl around her shoulders, Mother immediately followed him, and that same instant, quick as a flash, Annele was at the sickroom door. She did not know how to open it quietly. The door creaked, and from her sister's bed two dark blue eyes opened wide.

Annele stood stock-still. She was so happy she couldn't move a finger. Līziņa! Līziņa had woken up from her long, long sleep.

The patient looked at her for a long time without moving, as though not quite able to understand where she was. Motionless hands, pale as wax, lay on the blanket. A smile like a tiny spark flew up from her eyes, her lips whispered as though in surprise, "Girl! Little one?" Then the eyes moved on: over the big clock, across the ceiling, the floor, then turned toward the window and came back to Annele.

"Little one! How did you get here? Hey, come over here! Come on!"

Annele ran over to her, dropped on her knees by the bed, but could not say a single word. A big lump in her throat blocked the way.

Līziņa whispered something. It was hard to understand her. She tried to raise her hand in order to caress Annele, but it dropped on the blanket like something lifeless. But the smile, like a little spark, remained in her eyes, which looked, looked at Annele until at last they filled with big tears.

Mother came in. What had happened here? She was unable to grasp it, or to scold Annele for being here. All she could see was Līziņa.

"Darling, darling daughter! Now you'll be all right. Now you're over the worst!" And she hurried out to call Grandmother.

Grandmother, also hurrying, came in; filled with joy, she felt Līziņa's forehead and hands. "She's over it, she's over it! Glory and praise be to God!"

The patient yawned a deep, long yawn.

"That's all a good sign," Grandmother said with satisfaction.

They promised the patient something to eat.

"I feel more like sleeping. I'm so terribly sleepy," she scarcely breathed the words. "Strange. I must have slept such a long time, but I'm still sleepy."

"You're going to have something to eat and then you'll sleep. You can have some weak, weak broth, that shouldn't be too hard on you," Grandmother said, and as she left the room she took Annele by the hand and led her outside.

"You mustn't run in and out of your sister's room just now. Not at all."

Annele skipped through the house as though she had been given new legs. She even caressed little Jurītis, though he repaid her by scratching her and trying to tear her eyes out; Annele would have liked to caress every little thing – that's how good everything seemed. She ran out into the kitchen. There by the fire were Karlīne and old Kaminskene, who had always been so terribly forbidding. But Annele wasn't afraid of anybody now. She wrapped her arms around Karlīne's waist and laughed. She turned Karlīne around in a circle and laughed. She had a crazy urge to laugh and laugh.

Karlīne barely kept her feet. "Hey, what's gotten into you, girl? What's happened now? Why, you've been gone from the face of the earth all these many days! Are you out and about again? Must have been grieving for your sister, huh, while you were moping about like that?"

"Well, what do you think?" said Kaminskene, "I've also been watching that lass all this time. Walking around pale as death. Why, she's got the mind of a grown-up."

"But now they're saying there won't be any need to make a coffin for her sister, and so she's frisking around like a colt," laughed Karlīne.

But Annele was already outside, galloping around with Citron, who barked and flung his shaggy paws and big head first at one side of her, then at the other, until he finally rolled her into a snowdrift by pouncing at her legs, for which Annele paid him back by tricking him in all sorts of ways as she zigzagged back and forth and wore him out for no good reason. Citron certainly didn't mind, but the more wildly they played, the wilder he became in his demand for more. Yes, she and Citron had a lovely time! Although the entire household was so affectionate and kind today, even the forbidding Kaminskene, yet Annele had the feeling that Citron alone truly knew what it meant that her big sister Līziņa was now getting better.

But this fun ended suddenly. Citron could now jump, thrash his tail about, bark as loudly as he liked, look challengingly into Annele's eyes – she no longer saw or heard anything. She walked in silence, her eyes wholly engulfed in some great brightness, her lips whispering something. If Citron had understood, he might have heard something like this: "Dear heavenly father; dear, dear, dear heavenly father, thank you now! Thank you now, 'cause Līziņa is better!"

Laughing Medicine

One Sunday, as the harvest was already getting under way, Mother sent Annele to Black Earth Farm to borrow a fine strainer. They had talked about this for some time now, but today Mother explicitly told her: "Run and get the strainer, will you? Today, maybe, Melnzemene will have time to give it to you. You can visit for a little while, too, just not too long. Make sure you don't overstay your welcome. Don't wait till you're sent home."

An occasion when Annele went visiting all by herself occurred very rarely. And the place she visited was always Black Earth Farm. Of course it was right next door, within arm's reach. You ran down the path past the spring, then along the wide ditch in which forget-me-nots bloomed all summer – then across a small lush meadow, and then the dogs of Black Earth Farm would begin to bark.

Annele walked hesitantly, picking flowers as she went. As always, she did not go visiting with assurance. And so she first imagined what she would say, what she would do once she arrived at Black Earth Farm. Would she have to say good day, or would it be better not to say anything? If she said good day loud and clear like the grown-ups, people would think, looking at her: what sort of a visitor is this, with such a loud mouth? But what if she said nothing, just stood there and waited till somebody spoke to her? That, of course, would be much easier to do, she had seen other children do this, but it certainly looked stupid. It looked just as if such children had neither a tongue in their mouth nor enough sense to say what they had come for. No, Annele could not do this. No matter how hard it was, she'd have to say good day and clearly say what needed to be said. Only it mustn't come out loud, or else all heads would turn at once and stare straight at her, so that sometimes she didn't know which way to look.

This time all such worries were superfluous. Lulīte had already caught sight of her and ran out into the meadow happy and excited. With Lulīte, there was no need of a greeting, no need to talk. She didn't let her guest get a word in edgewise, but chattered merrily herself.

"Mother and Father are away visiting. They took Kristapelis with them. Let them. All he does is fight when he's home. I'm supposed to watch the little kids, but I can do whatever I want to. We can all do whatever we want to. There's a nursemaid, but what can the nursemaid do to me? She can sit inside and feed that silly baby. I'm not going to obey the nursemaid, no sirree. The little kids can obey her. And the little kids won't obey her either."

She led Annele across the yard, past Krancis, who was tied to the barn door. He struggled and barked, rattling his chain, just about ready to kill the new arrival. Lulīte called Krancis all kinds of names, scolded him, shamed him like a grown woman, but he paid not the slightest attention to the scolding. Not until the girls ran into the house did Krancis fling another couple of angry barks after them and then crawl back into his kennel. He had done his duty.

The little kids were Tincīte, Julcīte, Mincīte. They immediately surrounded Annele, each making her own complaint, and expecting a fair verdict from Annele. Tincīte was waving a little brown clay cow in the air, out of reach of the little ones.

"They want my little cow! My cow!"

"That's *my* little cow. Father brought it for me. I want her to give it back. Tell her to give it back, Annele."

"No way. She's lying. That's my little cow. Father brought it for *me*. Tell her to give it back, Annele."

"My little cow, my little cow! Fawer bwought it for me, Fawer bwought it for me," Mincīte yelled, throwing all the other toys with which her hands were filled down on the ground just to get the little cow, and fought for it, pulling on Tincīte's clothes and scratching.

"It's not hers. I want her to leave me alone," exclaimed Tincīte.

"It is so too mine. I want her to give it back!"

"My little cow! Fawer bwought it," Mincīte trumpeted the same tune over and over.

"Give the little cow back to the child," Lulīte commanded curtly.

"Back to the chile, back to the chile," Mincīte was persistent now, knowing that by putting her foot down like this she would win in the end as she usually did.

Tincīte would not hand over the little cow.

"Give back the little cow," Lulīte reinforced her command by stamping her foot.

"Ha, none of your business!"

Tincīte would not obey.

"You're going to be sorry!" threatened Lulīte and rushed to take the little cow back by force.

Tincīte stumbled over to Annele and pushed the little toy into her hand.

"Here! You take care of it and don't give it to anyone."

"Who does the little cow belong to?" Annele asked timidly, weighing the little cow in her hand.

"I don't care who it belongs to, give it to Mincīte. Then we'll have peace."

"How can I, when Tincīte gave it to me to take care of for her!"

"Oh, so you're going to be some kind of investigator? You don't know what our kids are like. Give the cow to me!" Lulīte quickly decided the matter and was just about to take the little cow out of Annele's hands in order to give it to Mincīte, when Tincīte managed to get to Annele first, snatched the little cow from her and hurled it at the wall as hard as she could. There was a sharp tinkling noise: chink, chink! The little cow was in fragments.

Tincīte's effrontery was followed by indescribable noise. Lulīte yelled, and

Tincīte yelled and fled. The two little ones screamed, without tears to be sure, but still at the top of their lungs. A woman threw open the door to the next room, but only spread her hands helplessly, as though the whole hullabaloo had rendered her speechless; she immediately hurried back into the next room, where she could be heard calming the baby with a fierce "hushaby, hushaby," while the baby squalled breathlessly as the cradle pole sharply creaked and sawed up and down. That was the nurse pacifying Little Mouse, Lulīte's even younger little sister.

After a while, when the racket would not stop, the nurse again appeared in the doorway. Only now did she catch sight of Annele.

"Aha," she said, "just as I thought – there's got to be somebody instigating all this noise. No, no, don't tell me! Our children alone surely wouldn't be making such a row if it weren't for that girl from Spring Farm." And again she slammed the door.

Annele was dumbfounded. How could this be? Here she had quietly stood in a corner trying to keep Lulīte and Tincīte from pushing her down while they fought with each other and chased each other, but she, Annele, was taken for the sole culprit.

"I'm going home," she turned toward the door.

"No you're not," Lulīte immediately stopped chasing Tincīte and ran to intercept Annele. "Why did you come then?"

"I came for a strainer."

"Well then, how can you go home if you came for the strainer? You've got to wait till Mother comes home, then you'll get it."

"It'll take a long time. I'd rather go home."

"No, you don't, no, you don't! Girls, don't let her," Lulīte ordered the flock of her little sisters, and suddenly Annele was hemmed in on all sides. Tincīte held her one hand, Julcīte the other, while Mincīte, clinging to her skirt, prattled non-stop: "Don't let 'er, girls, don't let 'er!" And now all of them were in the best of harmony and agreement.

Next door, Little Mouse had started her squalling again. "Hushaby, hushaby!" the nurse's voice could be heard, furious, and in between times she loudly scolded the girls, threatening them with all kinds of punishment.

"Let's go outside! Let's go to the hayloft!" called Lulīte.

Yes, no sooner said than done. They were off as if on wings.

They ran to the barn where, as the nice weather continued, the second hay harvest was in the process of being brought in. The men had just started stacking the last layer, and the layers rose step by step up to the very rafters. It was an easy matter for the girls to climb the stack of hay to a rafter. The bigger girls found it plain sailing, while the little ones had to be pushed and pulled until all of them sat up at the top like swallows on a rail. Then they began jumping into the hay, the loveliest of summer pastimes, which Annele, too, found so fascinating that she had long forgotten her resolve to go home at once. They jumped singly or all at the same time. The bigger girls looked for the scariest, deepest places, while the littler ones dared to drop into the hay only a few feet below, which is why they stuck to the space under the rafters, where the stack already reached almost all the way to the rafter. The children continued the game tirelessly until the whole stack had begun to slope like grass after a hailstorm. Here they could give free rein to recklessness, laughter, and boisterousness, here none of the grown-ups could hear, no one told them to stop.

Some time later, though, they heard the nurse outside. She was walking across the yard, looking for the children, scolding them for disappearing, and once more threatening them with all kinds of nasty things.

When they heard the nurse, the laughter and racket in the barn immediately came to a stop.

"I'm going home," Annele was the first to make up her mind. She did not like the nurse's eyes.

"You're not going anywhere. I know where the keys are," Lulīte told Annele mysteriously in a whisper.

Annele didn't quite understand.

"So what if you do?"

Lulīte took her firmly by the hand: "You're not going home, though." And she boldly led her out to face the nurse.

"Oh, you wicked girls, wait till I tell your mother, then you'll catch it," scolded the nurse, though no longer as sternly as she had in the house, perhaps because she wasn't quite sure what she would tell their mother – after all, except for hayseeds in the children's clothes and hair, she couldn't tell what other mischief they had been up to.

"Go to Little Mouse, there's a dear, while I make us some lunch," the nurse said to Lulīte.

"What are you going to make?"

"Whatever is there. I'll warm up some porridge."

"No, no, not porridge. Mother said you should make us some wheat flour dumplings."

"That's the first I've heard of it!" the nurse was surprised. "When did she say that? Did she say it to you?"

"Mother said! Wheaten dumplings!"

"Wheaten dumplings! Yes, yes! Mother said! Wheaten dumplings! Yes, yes!" shouted Julcīte, Tincīte, Mincīte, all at the same time.

"What am I supposed to make the dumplings with? Where's the flour?"

"In the *klēts*."

"Where are the keys?"

"I know."

"Well, if you know, then bring me some flour and I'll make some. It's all the same to me. I do what I'm told," retorted the nurse and went into the kitchen.

"Come with me and you'll see."

Without letting go of Annele's hand, Lulīte led her into her parents' room. Here she pulled a chair up to the wardrobe, placed a footstool on the chair and, having climbed both and standing on tiptoe, found the keys. There was one huge big key for the *klēts* and one little one. She took down both. The little one she hid in the bed under the pillow, while with the big one, which she proudly waved in her hand, she went to unlock the *klēts*.

Annele was surprised that Lulīte did all this.

"Did your mother show you where she keeps the keys?"

"No, I saw it myself."

"But are you allowed to take them?"

"Well, the flour is in the *klēts*."

"But did your mother give you permission to take the flour?"

"What are we supposed to eat then? Are the little kids supposed to die of hunger?"

"The nurse was going to warm up some porridge, wasn't she?"

"Right, porridge! You go and eat porridge while my folks feast on pancakes at the other house."

"But if your mother didn't give you permission, you can't take anything."

"What do you mean, she didn't give me permission? If Mother was home, she'd make wheaten dumplings, too. One time she said: on Sunday we'll have wheaten dumplings. And today is Sunday."

Annele was at a loss for words.

"Come, help me unlock the *klēts*," Lulīte called, having put the key in the padlock but unable to turn it.

Annele could not turn the key either.

Both of them struggled hard, but try as they might, it was no good. Lulīte ran and called the nurse.

The nurse unlocked the door, but would not go inside herself. Behind Lulīte, all the little girls burst into the *klēts*, grabbing whatever they could in this mysterious place that was always kept locked – Julcīte, a stale crust from a basket, Mincīte, even some chicken feed from a cutting board, for which Tincīte, who was able to make finer distinctions as to what was good and what was not, made fun of them and shamed them. As soon as Lulīte went to the sack with her little flour basket, Julcīte and Mincīte came too, crowing happily: "Wheaten dumplings! Wheaten dumplings!" Mincīte slapped both hands into the sack so that flour dust flew about in all directions, and grabbing a handful of flour, threw it in Julcīte's eyes. Julcīte had more of the same at hand to throw back, and it cost her no more than a: take that! But Mincīte took it as a great insult, with such a yell that it took her own breath away and blasted the others' ears. Even Lulīte was so startled that she immediately dropped the flour basket, cuffed Julcīte for teasing the child and Tincīte for even coming to the *klēts*, and pushed the two of them outside, but brushed the flour from Mincīte's eyes, dusted her face, dusted her clothes off and calmed her down: "You wait, you wait, big girls! When Mother comes home I'll tell her what they did to the child, and they'll get a good hiding."

"A good hidin'," Mincīte, still sobbing, threatened the imagined offenders.

Thus Lulīte always defended her youngest sister, regardless of whether she was innocent or guilty. Now it was Mincīte, just as formerly it had been Julcīte – and the result was that Lulīte was always on the side which had the most power: her mother's power, the nursemaid's, or Mincīte's own.

Not long after the nurse got the flour, she brought in a steaming bowl of white porridge chock-full of big hard dumplings. The folks at Black Earth Farm could afford to eat wheaten dumplings. Their wheat land was renowned, and Melnzemis, following Uncle Ansis's advice, had begun utilizing the productivity of his fields more effectively, milling the wheat and selling it as flour, which is why Lulīte was not satisfied with the delicious dumplings alone, for they had had them time and time again, but insisted that the nurse should give them a sauce to go with the dumplings. The nurse wouldn't hear of a sauce. Then Lulīte went to the *klēts* to get butter. The nurse had to go, too, to unlock the door. She did unlock the door, but again she would not go inside.

Lulīte brought some butter, put a good-sized lump in one plate for herself and Annele and in a second one for all three of the little girls together. She put the dumplings on top of the butter, slippery and hot, and let the butter flow and melt, yellow as beeswax. In the meantime the nurse whittled a long white stick for each of them out of kindling wood, which the little ones tore out of her hands, fighting and pushing each other away, the sooner the better – that's how much they wanted the dumplings.

The nurse leaned on the table with her elbows. Annele could feel her looking at her. Yes, when she looked up she met those other deep, piercing brown eyes, which seemed to say: "Really, why does that girl from Spring Farm come here to eat our children's dumplings?"

The piece of dumpling stuck in her throat, and she would have been unable to swallow it if the nurse hadn't left the room. She left without a word.

The little girls soon began to make a racket, to scuffle, to push each other. Mincīte was the naughtiest. Though she was the youngest, she pushed the two older sisters away from the plate, threw the dumplings on the table, threw them back in the bowl or wherever she could. Meanwhile Julcīte and Tincīte could cry and complain to Lulīte all they wanted to, only Mincīte got justice. It was only when Lulīte herself had a dumpling thrown by Mincīte fall in her lap that she lost patience and turned menacingly toward Mincīte.

Mincīte dropped the spoon and fled, but Lulīte, chasing Mincīte, threatened:

"Now you're going to catch it, just wait! Now you must be sick, go to bed, and get some medicine."

Mincīte fled into a corner and began to whine loudly, peeking between her fingers to see if Lulīte would really be powerful enough to carry out her threats, and what sort of medicine it was that she was being told to take.

"You must have some medicine at once, at once!" Lulīte reinforced her threat, for even Mincīte could not be allowed to undermine Lulīte's authority. "See, the medicine is in Father's cabinet, I'm going to take the key now and pour you some from the big bottle. And you'll have to drink it."

Lulīte took out the key she had stuck under the pillow just a while ago. It was the key to the cabinet. This was a key Lulīte was able to use without the nurse's help.

Mincīte was no longer whining now. Hands behind her back and her backside to the wall, she eagerly watched what would come forth from Father's cabinet.

Lulīte climbed on the chair and lifted out a big bottle, its middle girdled by red paper. In the same place she found a small glass with a stem. "Come on, here's your medicine!"

"What kind of medicine is it?" asked Annele, studying the bottle. She was quite familiar with various of her grandmother's medicine bottles, but there were none that had a red neck-band like this one.

"It's a medicine that Father drinks when company comes. Father drinks, and the company drink too. They drink the whole bottle."

"But are you allowed to take it like this without your father's permission?"

"Why d'you always go 'permission, permission'? Why shouldn't I have permission when Mother isn't home?" Lulīte retorted stubbornly, so that Annele would not think she didn't know what she was doing.

She filled the glass halfway.

"Touch your tongue to it," she invited Annele. Annele shook her head.

Then Lulīte did so herself, tasting it.

"It's sweet, but it stings. Try it!"

Now Annele, too, dipped the tip of her tongue in.

"Bitter medicine," she wiped the sticky bitterness from her mouth.

"'T isn't bitter at all," Lulīte insisted.

"Sweet? Give me some, too," demanded Tincīte.

"Me too, me too," called Julcīte.

But here came Mincīte tumbling out of her corner. What? The others wanted to drink the medicine that she had been promised herself? She felt cheated. No, no! She wasn't going to stand for it.

"My medthin, my medthin!" she yelled, forcing her way to the table with her fists. And before it even occurred to Lulīte to stop her, she grabbed the little glass and poured it into her mouth.

"Look what a brave little girl she is! You can't do that, any of you," praised Lulīte.

Mincīte liked this very much. She clapped her mouth shut and slammed the glass down on the table.

"More!"

Annele was still the most timid one of them all.

"Don't let her have any more! Not all medicines are good."

"Why, what could be wrong with this medicine? Let her drink," Lulīte poured the glass full to the top, for she always liked to do whatever others were opposed to.

"Let 'er dwink!" Mincīte babbled after her.

"Down the hatch," Lulīte said as she had heard the men say, and raised the glass to Mincīte's lips.

Mincīte gulped a whole mouthful, choked, gasped for breath, but couldn't breathe.

Lulīte pounded her back, protesting in amazement: "What happened now? What on earth happened?"

Finally Mincīte got her breath back with an earsplitting yell, but then curled up like a branch bowed by the storm: "Bitter, bitter!"

"It'll pass, it'll pass!" Lulīte soothed her. Now she, too, was frightened.

"I told you not all medicines are good," Annele was very frightened.

"Oh, what do you know about it?" Lulīte retorted peevishly, for she refused to admit it was her fault. "The bitterness will pass, you'll see, and it'll be all right."

Still, she did put the bottle back in the cabinet, and then returned the key to its former place.

The bitterness did indeed seem to have passed: Mincīte no longer cried at all, but started laughing. She laughed with tears still on her pudgy cheeks, just laughed and walked, bumping into the other girls, staggered, tumbled down on the ground, rolled about, it was impossible to get her to her feet, she seemed so flabby and just laughed and laughed. If anybody came close to her, she snorted in their faces, that's how naughty Mincīte was, she mimicked them, slobbered, uttered completely incomprehensible words, and just laughed. At first the girls laughed with her, but Mincīte was so hard to understand and so odd that even Lulīte became thoughtful: Something had happened to the child, she said.

"It must be from that medicine, I don't care what you say," said Annele.

Lulīte no longer protested.

"Yes, that must be it. And you know what? I think that was laughing medicine. My father, too – when he drinks some with his guests, he laughs and laughs and talks such a lot, much more than at other times. And his guests, too, laugh and laugh, but later, when the laughing has passed, they're like different people again. You'll see, Mincīte will get over the laughing, too."

Mincīte really did get over her laughing fit, but then the snoring came over her. The child suddenly paid no attention to anything, then fell into a sleep, snored, became delirious, tossed and turned, and was flushed as though from a fire.

"Oh dear, something's wrong, something's wrong!" Lulīte wailed and ran to get the nurse.

"What's the matter with the child? How did she suddenly get such a fever? Are you sure you didn't feed her too many dumplings?" the nursemaid asked, and Annele felt as though her furious glittering eyes were searching for her as the sole culprit. Then the nurse picked up Mincīte, put her over her arm with her head down and stuck her fat finger deep into the child's mouth. This immediately had the desired effect, and Mincīte threw up all the laughing medicine.

"What did you give that child? What did she drink? Why, she reeks of brandy!"

"I just gave her some medicine," tearfully murmured Lulīte.

"What medicine? That's brandy, don't you see? Oh you crazy, crazy girls!"

"Is brandy so terrible?" asked Annele, frightened.

"Oh really! You don't think it's terrible enough? I s'pose you think it's like milk and honey, huh? – Oh you crazy, crazy girls! If I hadn't run in here, that poor little life would just about have expired," said the nurse, as the children became more and more bewildered.

Mincīte was seemingly half unconscious, and cried that her head was hurting. The nurse put a wet towel on her forehead, and the child did become calmer, but then once more sank into what seemed to be a comatose sleep.

Lulīte and Annele did not stir from the sick girl's bedside.

"What will Mother say now?" wailed Lulīte. "I hope she doesn't come back until Mincīte gets better."

But the buggy was just driving into the yard.

Tincīte and Julcīte were the first to run outside and greet their mother: Mincīte,

they said, had been given laughing medicine. Mincīte had then gone crazy and was now lying in bed with a fever.

Melnzemene ran inside still wearing her Sunday best. What happened? What happened? She asked the nurse to tell the story.

The nurse acted completely calm.

Nothing, nothing. They'd been playing, the way children will. Well, maybe they had played a little rough, or bolted something down too fast; she hadn't been there, she hadn't seen a thing, it would be a sin for her to say anything; but even if the child had eaten something bad, she'd thrown up all of it, thank God, she was sleeping, and if she was sleeping, she'd be better soon.

Indeed! But whose fault had it been? Who was to blame? Melnzemene demanded sternly, looking about for a switch.

"It's hard to say who was at fault. How can you find the culprit? After all, the children of Black Earth Farm are good children, they're never up to any tricks, that's for sure; look at Lulīte, you could leave the youngest one in her care and she'd rock it and sing it to sleep better than any grown-up. But of course when you have mischief-makers from other farms showing up here, they'll talk even the best of children into being naughty. And it's certainly pretty obvious that such mischief-makers have been at work here with their wiles! Have you ever known the children of Black Earth Farm to do such things all on their own? No, never. Which just goes to show!"

Melnzemene looked around searchingly, and her eyes lighted directly on Annele. She didn't even see Lulīte. All the time she was talking with her mistress, the nurse had stationed herself in such a way that Lulīte was able to slip away unnoticed behind her back. Annele was left as the sole culprit.

Yes, she was taken for that by both the nurse and her mistress, she could see that clearly now. She blushed to the roots of her hair. Her feet and hands went numb as though someone had thrown an alien burden on her shoulders.

"Well? See what's become of Mincīte?" Melnzemene pointed at the sleeping child as though her words implied the most crushing accusation.

"She comes here and hangs about all day," the nurse said to her mistress, ignoring Annele as though she was not there at all.

"Isn't your mother expecting you at home?" asked Melnzemene directly.

At this question, Annele jerked her hands and feet out of their numbness, turned around suddenly and was out the door quick as a flash.

Krancis got to see only her heels.

She ran across the little meadow, jumped over the boundary ditch, flopped down on the ground at the edge of the ditch.

"They think it was my fault, they think it was my fault," she complained to the edge of the ditch.

"Your fault, your fault, your fault!" the brown eyes of the nurse seemed to say.

"No, no! It was Lulīte's fault. Who took the keys from their hiding place? – that wasn't allowed; who went to the *klēts* and told the nurse to make dumplings? – that wasn't allowed; who took the laughing medicine out of the cabinet and gave it to the child? – that wasn't allowed. It was Lulīte's fault."

But who went along with it? Who enjoyed eating dumplings with butter, the same as the others? Who touched her tongue to the laughing medicine, just like the others? And besides, who laughed at Mincîte when she was whirling around like someone half alive? Again, who allowed it all to happen? Who didn't run home long ago even though she realized that the nurse didn't want her there? She had just stayed on and on although she should have left long ago. Oh shame on her, shame! It was her fault, her fault!

This was not the nurse at Black Earth Farm reproaching her, this was another voice which could not be warded off, deep in Annele's breast.

"It was Lulīte's fault!"

She could say it all she wanted to, but that second voice kept repeating, "It was Lulīte's fault, but it was also your fault. Lulīte stayed at Black Earth Farm, while you're going to Spring Farm. You haven't brought the strainer Mother sent you to get, you didn't come right back as you should have done. You stayed at Black Earth Farm and shared in all the mischief."

The shadows were long, her heart was heavy, there were sobs in her throat. Her fault, her fault!

She had gone to get the strainer but had brought back shame, such enormous black shame that she had to wash it with bitter tears for a long time to come.

At the Parting of the Ways

Before Annele lived at Spring Farm, she had not known about time. Ahead of her were nothing but rosy mists from which single incidents and moments, like gilded steeples, would emerge, unfold, disperse in a magic glow, and again sink into the mists. But once she came to Spring Farm, time tied its thread to the last signpost and now simply unrolled days and nights, summers and winters, weeks and months, months and years from its big ball of yarn. Sometimes time with all its gifts flew as though with the wings of a bird, sometimes it lay in your bones heavy and motionless like the great scourge. Yet whatever time took, it never gave back, and whatever it gave away, never returned.

Thus at one time Līziņa had hurried home every Saturday from the direction of Hook Farm. Now she lived in Jelgava. But often when Saturday came, Annele, leaning out the window as in former times, would look into the distance and wait. She wanted Līziņa to come so that time, which had taken her sister away to a different place, would no longer be between them. She wanted the threads of time to be snapped so that they could be thrown away. And when time ceased to exist, Līziņa could come. The girl prayed fervently, intently, whispering with folded hands: "Līziņa, come! Līziņa, come!" She closed her eyes and thought: "When I next open them, the path will no longer be empty and black. Līziņa will come, the way she once used to."

But in vain. Līziņa could be seen only with invisible eyes. Then she came quick as the wind, smiling, swinging her little basket as she had once. And then she was already in the house. Everything became bright and warm. Father smiled, and Mother, and the whole household. And then the two of them were running outside – in winter Līziņa would be carrying her across the snowdrifts, in summer they'd be in the woods, among the birds' loud voices, the flowers. And they'd talk, they'd talk, the two of them. Her heart became light. It came unraveled, like a tangled little ball of yarn.

At other times, however, when Annele's power of imagination flagged, she preferred not go to the window at all. She no longer loved that place. She knew – no matter how much she looked, the path would remain empty, empty. Līziņa would never again come from that direction. That time was past.

It seemed to Annele that there were two different kinds of time: white and black. Once, time had always been white, and only rarely had had little black specks; this was when she was scolded or got smacked for doing something that the adults called naughty. Well, they could call it whatever they wanted to, it was no great misfortune. She'd stand in the corner for a while, for there was nothing else one could do against a superior force, she'd kiss the pain, disperse the bitterness of the tears, put her weight on one foot, then the other, and time was again white and lustrous like the dear white sun itself. But now that was no longer so. Sometimes the black specks of time would spread across moments, minutes, across hours. And sometimes Annele was tormented by a persistent thought that kept returning, that asked the same question whenever this or that incident or event occurred: Yes, but I wonder if things are really the way they seem, or completely different? She did suspect that things and events aren't only the way they appear to the eyes, but can also be viewed or perceived differently, in a way they never appear to the eyes. Similarly it sometimes seemed to her that people talk differently than they ought to talk, and that they sometimes laugh when there is nothing at all to laugh at. At such times, with a face full of laughter, they could say words to each other that would move the other person to tears of rage, of irritation, of pain. The married women in particular would do this to each other when suddenly, out of a clear blue sky, they began to scold each other and use bad words. Annele couldn't understand why people reviled and teased each other seemingly for their own pleasure. What kind of pleasure was this that did not come from what people liked? She so liked the sun, and flowers, birds, the woods, Līziņa, Granny, Father, and all the other people dear to her, but to take pleasure in bearing grudges and being abusive? – this was something Annele could not understand. This must be some kind of perverse pleasure. A pleasure that led to no good.

Work was now like daily bread for Annele, just as it was for the grown-ups. In summer – this was already the second one – she had to work as a herd girl every third day, and when fall came she was again given her old job of winding spools. Besides those, there were jobs both in summer and winter that had to be done by children, like weeding, gathering grass, picking leaves, knitting, sewing, pulling apart fleece and carding wool. It wasn't the work that bothered her. For each new task was begun with fervent good intentions – what she didn't like, however, was the tedious way you had to sit around doing the task, on and on, when in your thoughts you had already finished it a hundred times, and it was over and done with. Your thoughts could not reconcile themselves to the slow pace of the hands, and sometimes the thoughts forgot the hands, escaping far, far away into the wide open spaces of new worlds. Then there'd be a sharp tap on her shoulder. "Where are your thoughts, girl? Is that a way to work?" True, her thoughts did return to her hands in a flash, corrected the mistakes the hands had made, but they were hurt by the tap, they became sad, so sad. The thoughts had a lot of work to do, they had to create new worlds, had to fill them with all sorts of creatures, they came and went, they took their own freedom. How could Annele help it if they sometimes led her along a different path than the one she had been sent on, or made her hands toss something away, or caused her to forget what was so terribly important to the grown-ups? During that time it frequently happened that she felt a palpable reminder in her own body: you mustn't think, you mustn't dream. If such a reminder came from her mother, it often hurt her deeply. How could Mother do this? How could she punish her for something Annele didn't feel was her fault? At moments like this her mother seemed to have distanced herself from Annele, to have become more of a stranger. She apparently did not know about Annele's thoughts. No, apparently she knew nothing. For often, when Annele sometimes quite unwittingly let some question or remark escape her train of thought, at which the grown-ups sometimes laughed heartily or shrugged their shoulders, she was scolded or even slapped for it by her mother: Next time, don't talk so foolishly, her mother would say. This intimidated the child very much. Not only did she begin carefully to hide her thoughts and games from the grown-ups, but she also began to feel she was being treated unjustly, and by the very people who were closest to her. When she was punished, she would think: grown-ups punish you because they have the power to punish, regardless of whether the punishment is deserved or not, and that is why I must submit. She never cried, bargained, or begged to be let off. This is why Annele was said to be obstinate. People said that other children always cried and begged, while she didn't. Often the other married women would harp at Annele's mother that Annele wouldn't give her much joy in life, she would always be headstrong, for she was not at all like other children. This encouraged Mother to be even stricter about making sure that Annele's small tree of life should not produce unnecessary shoots, branch out unbecomingly, and grow even more obstinate. There really was something in Annele that battled against the world of the grown-ups, but she herself felt she had no obstinacy at all, she herself was sad that she was not like other children – she was a little creature that waited eagerly for the least little sign of kindness, or a smile in response to hers, ready to fly into her mother's embrace, to her mother's heart.

But as for cuddling your child, observing her, entering into her world, what working person had time to do that? That was only for rich people, for the gentry in their stately mansions, in a world of unlimited leisure.

Līziṇa's dear brightness was badly missed at Spring Farm, but merry Karlīne, too, had become silent and unsmiling. And once, going into Granny's room, Annele saw Karlīne standing there, eyes red with weeping.

She had never seen the cheerful and pretty young woman cry.

"Why does Karlīne have to cry?" asked the girl anxiously.

Granny did not answer her at once. First she closed the big hymnbook, a book only she owned, with a lovely elongated little picture at the beginning of each hymn, where the first letter of the hymn was ornamented with curlicues and tendrils, and the other letters, too, were so big you could feel them with your hands. She put the book back on the shelf, and only then said:

"Karlīne and Ingus are getting ready to go to the pastor."

Why did Karlīne have to go to the pastor with Ingus of all people? Annele did not understand, but she was no longer surprised that one had to cry on such an occasion, for everybody who said they were going to the pastor usually cried.

Still, Annele was sorry for Karlīne for some reason. She thought sadly of the time when Karlīne used to laugh and be loud, though she had often teased Annele.

There was a lot to be sad about. There was a lot that hurt.

This was the black time that often forced its way in among the rosy white time.

"Why is the girl like that?" the adults often asked.

"Is something hurting you?" Mother would ask.

How could Annele tell her what was hurting her?

"You're growing. That's when you get aches and pains here and there. In one limb or another. They're all growing pains."

At Spring Farm, things were no longer as they had been before. Something was about to change. And Annele had a vague foreboding that it had to do with all of them and Uncle Ansis as well.

Uncle Ansis was the master of Spring Farm, and Granny's youngest son. Each older son, once he was past the age when he could be drafted, had left the farm in favor of a younger one, for whoever was the farmer did not have to go into the Russian army in those days. And in order to save a brother from being drafted, each son would do his utmost, indeed, a good deal more than if the brother had to be saved from illness or even death. Thus at Spring Farm, as Granny's sons succeeded each other one by one, the youngest of them had finally become the farmer.

Annele's relationship to Uncle Ansis had not been very friendly right from the start. At their first meeting, when she had just arrived from Chisel Farm, Uncle, on catching sight of her, had opened his arms, exclaiming as if in surprise: "Aha, my little girlfriend has just arrived! Well now, come here, come here!" and had tried to grab hold of her and kiss her, while Annele had screamed, scratched, struck at him, and once she managed to get away had sought refuge under the bed, not knowing where else to go. After waiting for everything to be quiet again, she had finally dared to crawl out from under the bed, but suddenly Uncle had attacked her again from some hiding place, had lifted her up in his big, strong arms and kissed her, ignoring the girl's screams and resistance. When he let her go, she cried and wailed about it for close to an hour, while her mother, not knowing the reason for her wails but thinking it was mere obstinacy, had sent her even more deeply into the silence of the corner to think things over for a while. Since that time, Annele had avoided Uncle as much as possible, though she rather enjoyed observing what he did, what he talked about.

Uncle was often away from home. And when he was at home, he was rarely alone, for then guests would come and stay with him. Often he brought them with him. He said they were university students. They were all young and spirited. They'd sometimes stay for days. They would drink and sing. Foreign songs in German, occasionally in Latvian. They themselves also conversed in different languages. Granny would then make tea, one kettle after another, and fry chops. But you could tell that she did not like these guests – often she could be heard to say the word "windbags." That was all she said, but that one word alone was not good. She would see to it that the guests' horses were unharnessed and fed. If that wasn't done, they would neigh and paw the ground, impatient for their drivers. But often the drivers would leave as though they were in a great hurry. Then the horses had to be harnessed posthaste, and they would fly away quick as the wind, and Uncle with them.

Uncle would bring home all kinds of new implements, containers, and dishes for use in the household. Granny locked them in the cabinet and never touched them. She did not need any of these "cans."

Often, in talking about Uncle Ansis, Granny used to say: "These are new times, a new world, I can't understand it anymore, but what can I do? Let him do as he likes."

She petted and fed Ansis's favorite carriage horse more than the others, muttering, "Poor dear horse, he drives you too hard, much too hard."

Uncle was always in a hurry, arrived everywhere at the last moment, when the others were tired of waiting and out of their minds with anxiety about him. He was always full of new ideas and projects. On the south side of the house, Uncle began to plant a new orchard, and he intended to enlarge it year by year.

The other brothers shrugged. "Can it be done without laying out a lot of money? And what's the good of such an orchard? ... Will it feed you?"

"Not just yet, of course. But it may bring me a lot of profit some day," retorted Uncle and continued planting.

He bought up the grain of other farmers and took it to the mill together with his own, had it milled into flour and transported it to town. This is why the other farmers called him a huckster.

A huckster, was he? Uncle didn't care.

He spent most of his time in towns, in pubs, and also in law courts, for he was big on suing people. When he bought the inheritance rights to the farm, he had gotten into an argument with the count himself because of some injustice that had been done in this case, and he certainly didn't try to avoid a lawsuit with the count, merely laughing when others told him he would break his neck in this lawsuit.

Uncle was often invited to festive occasions, especially to funerals as an orator, and people said in his praise that no preacher could speak as beautifully as Avots, the master of Spring Farm. During Sunday prayers, when a kind of sleepiness settled over the room while he was reading the sermon, Uncle would raise his eyes from the book and begin to speak off the cuff, in his own words. Then all of a sudden all faces would turn toward him, all eyes would open wide. People would listen almost breathlessly, with tears in their eyes. His words flowed easily, like a stream, and they were something everyone could understand, familiar, much more familiar than the pastor's sermons, for Uncle knew what caused each of them pain and what made them happy.

But when Annele saw Granny standing in the yard sometimes toward evening, studying the distant horizon for a long time, where the big highway was visible, or quietly getting up at night and standing at the window like a shadow, she knew that Granny was waiting for Uncle Ansis, and that none of her children caused her as much worry as this broad-shouldered tall young man.

Once, towards spring, Uncle called Annele to him.

"Come here, lass! You know what's going to happen now? Come on, guess, guess! You can't? Then I'll tell you. Your sister's coming home at Easter. Well? Now you can thank me, can't you?"

Annele clapped her hands. She flushed with great joy and happiness, but she still owed him a thank-you. Besides, Uncle did not seem to expect it.

Palm Sunday came, warm as warm. At one end of the servants' *klēts*, on a narrow little wooden bench, sat Father, Mother, and Granny. They were deep in conversation and looked sad. What were the grown-ups talking about? Annele looked at them anxiously. Mother beckoned to her quietly, and when she came over questioningly, Mother took her on her lap, pressing her close. Annele was speechless with happy amazement. When had such a thing happened before? She was allowed to be present and listen.

"Isn't there any other way? Is this your final decision?" asked Granny, as though unable to grasp something inconceivable.

"That really is my final decision, Mother. Laukmalis and I closed the deal this morning. We have to go on St. George's Day," said Father.

"I'm sure Laukmalis will do well out of the deal. I don't begrudge him, for he is my child just like the others, but what will happen to Spring Farm when your eyes are no longer here to watch what happens?"

"Listen to you talking, Mother! What do you think will happen to Spring Farm? What's there to worry about? Why, the master of Spring Farm is no cripple, he's a healthy man. And a smart man, too."

"He never was and never will be the kind of man who follows the plow. You know that, surely."

"He will if he has to."

"No, no, son! Ansis had too easy a time of it growing up. While you were here, everything was coming along so well, it was a joy to see. All that drudgery and toil – no stranger can do that. But that's the way you need to work if you want to live at Spring Farm and make a living here. Those hills don't produce a thing if you don't give them all you've got."

"All right, all right, Mother. But a person can only work the way I've been working here if no one interferes. Ansis never did. This fall, though, he's planning to get married. What will it be like when a stranger gets involved – who can tell? I do know I don't want to cause anyone bitterness or trouble, neither myself nor other people."

"Never mind the stranger – this is still your father's farm, you know."

"Which I left with a white beggar's cane in my hand."

"True, child, true," Granny sighed. "If things had gone the way I wanted, it wouldn't have happened, but I couldn't do anything. Do you think it hasn't preyed on my mind?"

"And those who were able to, who should have done something, didn't do a thing. My brothers had made me a word-of-mouth promise to help get a farm, a place of my own, because each of them had taken his full share of our father's inheritance, while I hadn't. I wasn't given any property, I was given a promise: when the need arises, you'll get something. And when the need did arise, when the first place came along that I could have taken, who were the first people to talk me out of it? My brothers, that's who. One place was no good, and the next one was no good either, and the same with the ones after that. That's when I realized they would talk me out of every place, for fear that they'd have to lend me a helping hand, to do in all fairness what they should be in duty bound to do before God. Then I suppressed my longing for a piece of land of my own and let my plans be. Even if they had wanted to help me, there would never have been agreement among them about this. And I didn't want to stir up hatred among my brothers on my account."

"Your sense of justice is all the wealth you've got."

"Yes, I find it hard to bear injustice, or lack of freedom for that matter. It would be too difficult for me to work under somebody else. That's why I thought I'd go to Laukmalis, to work on the new farm he's building. The work will be hard. It will mean breaking new ground, because there's nothing there but bare fallow land, but am I the first ever to do such a thing, or the last? At least there I'll have the freedom to work as I deem it right, with nobody coming to me with some senseless instruction that I'd be ashamed to carry out. Yes – I still don't know what it's going to be like. I've never lived under the same roof with Laukmalis. He is just. Perhaps he'll turn out to be the best of my brothers. And another thing: we'll keep more animals there, sell a couple of pounds of butter now and then, so the boy can have his education. Yes, well, there's no point in talking about this anymore. It's been decided, and that's the way it has to be."

"And maybe it's all for the best. May God's will be done."

Granny rose and was unable to get to her feet.

"My legs are heavy," she smiled, "they've gone to sleep while I was sitting down. That's spring for you, the pain goes right through my bones."

Father helped her up and walked with her up the hill.

Mother hadn't said a single word the whole time, she just wiped her eyes now and then. She still said nothing.

Annele had never heard a conversation like the one between Father and Granny. She looked uncertainly from one to the other. What did it mean? What had already happened? What else was going to happen?

"Is Father leaving Spring Farm?" she asked dismayed when she and Mother were alone.

"Not just Father, we're all leaving."

"Leaving Spring Farm?"

"Yes."

"Leaving Spring Farm? For good?" Annele couldn't believe her ears.

"Yes, child, yes. Very soon, on St. George's Day."

"No, no!" Annele shook her head. "You're joking, aren't you? You're trying to trick me, I know it."

"You heard what Father was saying the whole time, didn't you? Was he joking?"

"But how can we leave Spring Farm?"

"Did you think we could live here the rest of our lives? It's not our home, you know. We don't have a home anywhere. You're ready to hear that. You're old enough, I guess. We're leaving on St. George's Day."

Yes, that was the way it was. It was all true. Father never joked, and Mother had not been tricking the child. Annele heard it all as though from far, far away, but she couldn't understand any of it. Never, never, never could she have imagined that one day they would have to leave Spring Farm.

Father had returned and sat down on the bench.

"Now you, too, will have to start working harder," he told Annele. "Herding every day."

"How can she be a full-time herder," Mother felt sorry for her, caressing the girl,

"she's barely eight. And then think of that big flock of sheep the Laukmalises are planning to bring over to graze through the summer! How can such little legs do so much running?"

"It's not that terrible. You mustn't scare her with work that has not yet had a chance to show how hard or how easy it is. The pasture is big, miles and miles of it – for the time being there are no fields to protect. And our child isn't spoiled. Little by little, she's been getting used to working. And what do you think, lass? Think you could be a full-time herder?" Father looked at Annele with a smile, but with something like sadness behind his smile.

The girl didn't quite know how to respond. It had all come so unexpectedly, as though it had been decided and agreed upon long ago, so that there was nothing Annele could change anymore, and there was nowhere to escape to from what was coming. It was the first time she had been given a chance to look at approaching events, and she saw the work ahead not as a game but as a difficult obligation. To her, it all seemed more like a dream than like reality.

"Yes, what can we do? Do you think I'm going to leave Spring Farm with a light heart? This is where my cradle stood, this is where I spent my childhood. And it's because I love all this that I've worked like a slave all these years. Do you think I enjoy tearing down my nest every spring on St. George's Day? But such is life!"

"Life? Life? What is that, life?" Annele raised her head as though startled. Father and Mother seemed not to understand her questioning eyes, however, but continued their conversation.

"There, you see," said Mother, "perhaps if you had obeyed your brothers back then, you wouldn't have to move from place to place anymore, you'd have your own home and your own farm. While they were single, time and time again, didn't your brothers take you from farm to farm where there were daughters who would inherit the land, so you could pick a place to marry into? But you didn't want to. You married a poor girl, and that's why things are the way they are."

"My brothers wanted me to live as they wish, not the way I want to live myself. And I preferred to live in poverty with you rather than in great wealth with a wife I didn't love. You were decent, beautiful, a hard worker – what more did I need?"

"And I didn't feel like that about you yet in those days," said Mother with a sort of faraway quiet smile.

"Is this something the child ought to hear?" Father apprehensively turned in Annele's direction, as though wanting to send her away.

"This is nothing bad, is it?" Mother replied with a question of her own, pulling the child closer to her as she spoke. "I think that what we're talking about is something the child can hear, too. Yes, at the time I was sweet on someone else, and I kept waiting for you to turn away from me and go and marry into some farm. That's why I kept putting off giving you an answer. At River Estate, where we were all in service at the time, there was a young fellow, maybe you remember – "

"Jirģēns?" Father exclaimed in amazement.

"That's the one. He was better-looking than you, and up to all sorts of tricks."

"I know, I know. Flighty!"

"You think a young person cares about that? I liked him. But my parents kept warning me. Forget about Jirģēns, that adventurer! They said nobody even knew who his people were. Here today, gone tomorrow. Whereas young Avots – everybody said he was a decent person – with a husband like that I'd never go hungry. And so – I'm not sure what the reason was – my parents' advice, your unshakable confidence, Jirģēns's flightiness – my mind began to change, had already changed before I knew it myself. And so, one spring day, later than now – the chokecherries were already in bloom – I'm at my parents' one Sunday at Foresters' Farm, and in the hollows I hear the forest resound, I can hear somebody coming along singing. Your voice sounded lovely, so lovely! And then all at once it was as if scales fell from my eyes: how decent, how good was this person singing there like that. And I knew there was none better anywhere. So right then and there I made up my mind: I would marry you."

Annele began to sob. All these words, heard for the first time, were like a burden too heavy for her that she wanted somehow to relieve.

Mother fell silent, as though frightened: maybe it really hadn't been a good idea to talk about all this in the presence of the child.

Father took the girl in his lap.

"Why are you crying, child? We're all still together. Alive. In good health. Life is ahead of us. God will help us, you'll see, I know everything's going to be all right." And looking at her radiantly he kissed the child.

After that Mother, too, kissed her, clasping her head affectionately in her hands.

These were like unprecedented and unheard-of miracles.

From the doorway of the house, Granny was hallooing for Father. He ran up the hill, obedient as a child. But Mother did not get up from the bench yet. She seemed to be far away somewhere with her thoughts.

"What were you both doing at River Estate?" asked the girl.

"Oh, River Estate? Father was the foreman there, while I worked as a chambermaid. Like him, I had to leave home quite young, because my parents only had that paltry forester's job, and there were a lot of us kids. The service at River Estate was my first and last job. The gentry were decent people, not like other Germans, and there wasn't a chore that was too hard for me. So I really couldn't complain. They would rather not have let the two of us go, though they didn't mind us getting married. But Father thought Pinewoods Farm would be easier for me than if I stayed at the manor. It wasn't bad at Pinewoods Farm, either. When you're young you can get along anywhere. But it's bitter hard to roam from one place to another when you've hardly had time to get used to a place. It was hard to leave Pinewoods Farm, where the first years of my marriage were spent and my children were born, and it's going to be even harder to leave this place."

"And why did Father leave Pinewoods Farm?"

"You see, it's like this: Father can't bear to hold a grudge against any person. He got along fine with the farmer of Pinewoods Farm, the husband of your father's sister. In addition to his wages it had been agreed that Father would also farm a piece of land, which he would take care of and cultivate himself. And when? At night, at noon, by going without sleep. On this piece of land of Father's, the grain always turned out especially fine. Well, and then another man began to covet it. The farmer's own brother came to Pinewoods Farm. He thought Father had been given the best piece of land and that this piece of land should by rights go to him, being a closer relative. He kept on and on about it to the farmer until he brought him round. But Father could not bear the injustice of having the land that he had cultivated in the sweat of his brow undeservedly assigned to someone else. So he left.

"And almost the same thing happened with Kamenis at Bumblebee Farm. Here, his contract said he would get to sow a hundredweight of wheat in the best land, but Kamenis tricked him and gave him some of the worst land for sowing the wheat, so that that summer we harvested nothing but bromegrass. Father could never forget his brother's deception, and he wouldn't stay another year, although Kamenis, when he saw what a fine worker Father was, talked to him from morning till night, trying to persuade him to stay, and promised him heaven knows what. But Father didn't believe him anymore."

Seeing Father coming down the hill, Mother fell silent.

With this, the day's conversation was over.

Annele left walking slowly, carrying her burden of thoughts. It felt as though in this one hour she had released and become aware of all the growing she had done unknowingly over these four years she had spent at Spring Farm. She perceived her parents' conversation not only as the retelling of what had happened or was still happening, but also as the connection between what was happening and herself, the world around her. And she felt she was connected to something unknowably deep. Although it hurt that they had to leave Spring Farm, although the course of her parents' life, the injustices and suffering inflicted on her father were bitter, yet she felt somehow free to breathe a sigh of relief, looking forward to something vast and distant as it were; somewhere there was an unknown force that promised help in overcoming everything, come what might.

⌐⫝⁓

Almost all those who had worked at the farm up to now were planning to go their separate ways. Uncle no longer wanted to keep on any married farmhands, and had hired only single men and maids. Karlīne and Ingus had been jointly hired at a farm in another district. Old Anyus was no longer being given work at the manor, and so she was going away to live with her daughter.

Uncle Ansis kept his word. During Easter week he brought back Līziņa with him from Jelgava. She could stay as late as St. George's Day, and she was planning to help the family move to the new farm.

Līziņa had grown taller, and Annele had the feeling that she had become more beautiful, but also more unfamiliar. Karlīne gazed at her for a long time, herself kind of sad.

"Look how pale, how pale that city has made our Sleeping Beauty," she said.

"Just wait, in a week I'll be as rosy-faced as in the old days. Now it's time to start running through the fields and woods again. I'm certainly not going to spend one more hour than necessary sitting indoors."

She and Annele got to run through the woods and water meadows many, many more times. But their conversations were no longer the same as in the old days. Often, gazing into the distance, Līziņa was self-absorbed, as though lost in thought somewhere, and her little sister was afraid to disturb her. She, too, had her own conversations with the hills, the trees.

"Annele, Annele, they say you want to leave us?" each of them asked, as though surprised and reproachful.

"No, no, no," Annele cried out.

"You'll go away and leave us."

"Even if I go away, I'll never forget you, never, never, not one dear tree, not one hill."

⌐⫝⁓

Easter arrived. A swing had been hung on the hill, between two mighty birch trees. It was Ingus's strong arms that had helped hang it there. He wanted people at Spring Farm to go on remembering him, he said. The neighbors' children and young folks came to swing. They were all thrilled how lightly and how high the swing rose.

On the second day of Easter, even the people from the manor came over. One handsome slender young man, who wore shiny high boots and a red cap, no sooner came up to Līziņa than he stuck to her like a bur.

Annele scowled at him with all the rage she could muster, but he was so thick-skinned he didn't have the decency to move on, and even when he did move away for a little while, he was back like a shot a short while later. But Annele just as loyally stuck close to Līziņa. When the handsome young man noticed this, he looked in the girl's eyes with a friendly, winning smile.

"Come on, girl, let's be friends!"

But he could read the answer clearly in Annele's eyes: "We're not going to be friends, so go away!"

But Līziņa looked at the two of them, gave a laugh, and shook her head. Then she ran off and jumped into the swing. At once, two of next summer's herd boys pulled on the rope.

"How high do you want to go?"

"As high as you've got the strength to swing me."

They were trying to show her now. Like a shuttle the swing flew higher and higher at each push. Just under the crossbeam, then level with it, then above it flashed Līziņa's golden head with its thick braids.

"Oh, how far I can see! Blue hills, blue forests, red houses! None of you can see this far," she cried exultantly. But she didn't waste another look on the handsome young fellow from the estate.

There were two more important events after Easter.

During Easter week, Ingus and Karlīne went to the pastor again, and this time Father and Uncle Ansis went with them.

Meanwhile at home Granny made "caterpillar" noodle soup and roasted meat for Ingus and Karlīne's celebration. When they returned, everyone was invited to the meal.

But they did not sit down at once. Solemnly Uncle Ansis folded his hands and spoke to Ingus and Karlīne, who stood there just as solemnly and somehow bashfully, about their new life, about joys and sorrows, about harmony and love. Karlīne sobbed into her sleeve the whole time. After the speech, everybody said the Our Father out loud. That's when Annele realized that Ingus and Karlīne were now man and wife. She supposed it was probably a good thing, but this was no longer the Karlīne she knew.

Just after Easter, Annele's brother was confirmed. When she saw him, tall and stately, in his homespun suit with his white neckerchief, Annele was almost shocked and recoiled in awe. Should she now respect and honor her brother like a grown-up? Could she now no longer permit herself to be naughty or even disobedient toward him? She'd have to give that a good deal of thought. All afternoon, after church, he did not leave Līziņa's side, talked to her alone about what was to happen now, what they would do, and Annele was not allowed to stay nearby and listen.

The last days seemed to plunge headlong into an abyss, so swift, so swift. Now there were only five days till St. George's Day, then only three, and then came their last evening at Spring Farm.

They were all quiet. Supper was cleared away untouched.

The morning of St. George's Day dawned. She had often imagined it, thought about it, but her heart still didn't believe it, still would not accept it.

"I'll run to the woods one more time, to the big birch tree, to the little spring," thought Annele.

"Don't you disappear on us, lass, we're leaving right away, you need to help us drive the cattle," Mother told her firmly, thus unloosing the girl's thoughts from everything that had been, and attaching them to her new task.

This St. George's Day, no one lifted Annele on top of the wagon. She had to run along the road on her side and carefully watch that the cattle did not stray into the fields where new grain was sprouting.

Every time she looked back, Spring Farm receded further and further into the distance. Further and further receded its hilly pinewoods fragrant with resin, its hollows with their springs, its budding apple orchards.

PART II

HARSH WINDS

The New Farm

The sky was new again and the earth was new. Making the air vibrate and pouring their trills tirelessly down on the earth, larks emerged from the endless azure one by one like tiny, barely perceptible, trembling specks, only to sink back, barely glimpsed, into the lake of the sky, scattering songs like uninterrupted strings of beads on both sides of the road. Flowers, the same ones Annele had always loved, yet ever new, looked up from the edges of ditches and meadows, and were left behind to make way for others and yet again others. The sun and the winds played on the walls of unfamiliar farmhouses, and plucked at ramshackle roofs that in their destitution still looked so dear and familiar, and washed clean somehow.

Annele was now walking along the road that could be seen from the hill at Spring Farm. It led into the world. But when their procession had reached the crossroads, the wagons with their belongings, the first of which was driven by Father, turned into an unexpected direction, away from that bright road for which Annele's senses yearned and which seemed to grow uphill somewhere in the distance.

The cattle ran ahead of the wagons. By the first little bridge that joined the country lane to the highway, Mother stopped and shouted into the wind:

"Is this where we turn off?"

"Further on, further on!" Father shouted his reply.

Now they went on for a good long while. Not until the third bridge did Father point and wave for them to turn right.

The wagons sank into a muddy country road, and moved forward only slowly. The drovers had to give all their attention to the little herd of animals, to keep them from doing even the least damage to the fields of other farmers. But although she was constantly being reminded to keep in mind her duties, Annele managed to observe everything that was noteworthy this St. George's Day journey.

The farms along the road were beautiful and splendid. Here was the one with the gleaming red roofs that could be glimpsed on the horizon from the hill at Spring Farm. The buildings were spick and span, the fences in good repair, the orchards big. This, too, would be a good place to settle and live in if there was really no way to stay at Spring Farm. Here there were doors and gates that seemed to beckon and call: in the orchards there were lovely, mysterious nooks and crannies that you could enter like a forest. And once you got really close to this kind of farm, a silvery brook would suddenly come running out of a clump of alder bushes and bubble under the bridge.

Any one of these could have been their new home where it would be pleasant to

settle down, but the procession of wagons hurried past every one of them. Nor did Annele ask anyone if it was a long way to their destination – after all, once they got there, she'd see for herself, but in the meantime she could pick out the loveliest places along the sides of the road for her eyes and her thoughts to alight on and visit for a while, as birds do on the masts of ships on their way south.

It was pretty late in the afternoon when they left all the farms behind them, and the road, too, suddenly broke off like the string of a fiddle. A wide-open space stretched before them – neither meadow, nor field, nor clearing, bounded by the blue stripe of a forest. Fawn-colored, puny blades of grass were barely poking out of the ground.

"You can let the animals roam free. There's nothing to watch here, you see," said Father.

Mother stopped walking, folded her hands, and silently shook her head.

"Oh, so this is the barrens?" That was all she said.

The wagons now drove straight across country. They drove wobbling over mounds of grass and across marshland where here and there you could see wheel tracks. This must be a new road in the making.

But where were they going?

Right in the middle of the barrens, and in its lowest part, a little building with a white thatched roof gleamed in the light of the setting sun. It was this little building that the wagons were moving toward.

"What's that shack over there?" Annele asked.

"That's New Farm, I guess."

Annele was stunned. Two contradictory feelings suddenly lodged in her throat.

Laughter was the first to leap up, about this funny little house, standing there so helplessly in the vast barrens like the witch's house on chicken feet in the fairy tale, calling itself "New Farm," but the laughter was at once strangled by a kind of stinging bitterness: yes, here it was, this thing that her heart did not want to accept; here it was, and it was inescapable. And something heavy, unlovable, and as yet incomprehensible seemed to hover over the new place like a menacing cloud.

At that moment a huge, swirling column of smoke shot up out of the forest and flew like a bird along a black trail, pulling behind it a long row of some kind of strange little houses.

"Look, more little shacks! And they're running!" the girl exclaimed with great surprise. And immediately blushed when she saw the others laughing heartily at her words.

"Don't be so silly," the grown-ups informed her, "the thing that's running is a railroad train: the locomotive's in front, and those things that you thought were shacks are railroad cars. People sit inside the cars the way you would in a room, and travel long distances."

Annele's eyes grew wide. A railroad train, a locomotive, cars! Now here was something people at Spring Farm knew nothing about.

The closer they got, the more their new home seemed to grow. It rose up out of its low-lying site.

"Why is it in such a low spot, though?" asked the girl.

"So as to be closer to the water, silly," they informed her again.

Behind the straw-thatched little house, there was the foundation of some other building. It was a barnyard, growing up with brown clay walls. Next to one wall, fairly large temporary pens had been constructed to hold the cattle.

Twenty or so yards away rippled a large body of water. Although her feet felt heavy, Annele hurried to explore it.

Such wide water! Could this be a lake? She had never seen a lake. That would be something new. All around the water, the ground was full of hummocks of grass, bumpy as a cobblestoned road. Water spurted from the hummocks, they sank under her feet. From every hummock, a crested bird flew up, darted above the girl, darted back, circled in loops around her head and forehead, touching her hair and piteously, frantically screaming: peewit, peewit, peewit! Away, away, away!

As though telling each other the news, shooting back and forth through the air, or running to and fro across the hummocks and screaming ceaselessly, the peewits aroused the whole area adjacent to the lake. Wherever the girl put her foot, she heard the rush of their wings like a swarm of mosquitoes. The birds were afraid for their nests, of which there were huge numbers here among the hummocks. In vain she clasped her hands and assured them: "Dear birds, dear peewits, I don't mean you any harm! I'm not going to hurt you!" The peewits wouldn't listen. The peewits considered her an enemy, an intruder who had no business in their domain, and they kept screaming nonstop: peewit, peewit! Away, away!

Annele was well aware what this "away!" meant. She knew that the peewits, clever birds that they were, would always run in a different direction and entice a person away from their nests, lead them far into the barrens. "I'm sure they'll realize

I can't be enticed away, that I do them no harm, that they must get accustomed to me," she thought and went on walking, but the peewits accompanied her, screaming even more loudly and piteously.

The surface of the little lake, under the evening sky, glittered like glass. In reality the little lake was only a good-sized pond. The whole barrens formed a depression like a shallow trough, and this was the deepest place.

Smoke was coming from the narrow chimney of the new house. The tall blue column rose straight in the air. "Come on over!" it invited Annele.

Where else? From now on that was the only place she would have to run to. Every day, every hour, for this was her home now.

The new house was small indeed. It was as though those who built it had been afraid to make too deep a gash in the large sheet of the barrens. The rough-hewn log walls, their chinks stuffed with moss, exuded the smell of resin. The little four-pane window let in as much light as it was able to. All of this looked as though it had been put there and furnished in the twinkling of an eye. At the little table sat two men from Edgefield Farm who had helped bring the household furnishings. One of them was Ģelžu Miķelis. He was living at Edgefield Farm now. Mother had fried chops and scrambled eggs for the men. This was the food typically served on St. George's Day. They ate unhurriedly, though the road back was none too short. "We'll get back, don't you worry. Home ith not a rabbit. It'th not going to run away," said Miķelis, always smiling and talkative, but also eager to listen to the talk of others.

"Well, Krišjān," he said. "Now you've got land, and you've got a cabin. Though it's not your own, there's plenty of backbreaking work here to last you the rest of your life. Did I say the rest of your life? Why, a man could spend five lifetimes slaving here. This here wilderness stretches for miles, don't you know!"

Father was preoccupied, and did not feel like talking. He smoothed back his hair, muttered something, didn't want to answer Miķelis. So their talk was nipped in the bud, as it were. Annele felt that this time Miķelis had tackled the conversation from the wrong end. No one kept the ball rolling. The men said their goodbyes.

The distant forest was beginning to get crimson in the light of the setting sun. Miķelis, as he got into the wagon, cocked one ear and listened for a long time to the sounds of the barrens.

"It may be a wilderness, but it's got its own armies," he said. "No sooner has one lot gone to sleep than another one gets up! Listen to that hullabaloo!"

In the vicinity of the little lake, where only recently the startled peewits had darted back and forth, frogs were now croaking. A countless regiment of frogs. And, a bit further away, there was another one. And another beyond that one. As far as the ears could hear, millions of frogs made the air over the barrens reverberate.

But at Spring Farm there had once been a St. George's Day when the married and single women welcomed spring into the world with their songs. When had that happened? Where? It felt as though a hundred years had passed since the time Annele drove into Spring Farm on St. George's Day from the direction of Chisel Farm. There, she had been met by nightingales – here it was peewits and frogs.

Her thoughts flew to Spring Farm and ran down every little path, looked at each bud in the garden that would open tomorrow. And, half asleep, she tried to deceive herself: it can't be, it just can't be; when I wake up tomorrow, I'll be back at Spring Farm. It was a sweet deception. Lulled by this deception, she fell asleep.

The sun hadn't been up long when Mother wakened her. They must let the cattle out to graze, for no fodder had been brought from their former home.

"Yes, I guess this is the beginning," thought Annele as she hurriedly got dressed. Her feet and hands were indeed quick and obedient, but her heart was still incredulous. Had the time that her father had talked about before Easter at Spring Farm really arrived? Could it really be that a chink would not appear in this inescapable situation through which she could sneak out into freedom? Her heart refused to believe it.

Mother was already waiting outside in the cool of the morning.

"Well, got everything?"

Annele didn't have a thing. What did a herder need?

Her mother's impatient hand led her back into the house.

"Can't you see where I put your things? Take the wrap!" She picked up a heavy blanket from the chair. It was not exactly a blanket, but a kind of skirt made of rough homespun, gathered with a string. Only she had never seen Mother wearing one like it. No doubt it had been specially made for her to cover herself with while watching the herd.

What was she supposed to do with it? Put it on over her head like Kaminskene and old Anyus when they walked about in rainy weather at Spring Farm, covered with their rough gathered skirts?

"I don't want it! I don't need a wrap like that, I'm not an old woman!" Annele pushed the blanket away with both hands.

But Mother with all her strength pulled the blanket over Annele's heavy braids.

"Don't talk nonsense: 'not an old woman' indeed! I bet you don't know that there's not a ravine nor a tree to hide behind from the wind, from the rain; you'll be grateful one of these days that you have a wrap like that. The days are so long you could get all kinds of weather. It isn't summer yet, when you can take the herd back to the farm at noon. We'll be lucky if the animals find enough all day long to fill their stomachs. The barrens, as far as the eye can see, are still bare as the palm of your hand. Here's a switch for you. Here's the little basket."

"What's in the basket?"

"A knitting I've started for you, and a chunk of bread for your snack. I'll bring you your lunch if you drive the herd closer to the farm. And now go, and good luck to you. At first the animals will be restless, looking for lusher grass. Don't you doze off yourself, take a look around where the grazing is better. I'm sure you'll see."

"All right, all right," answered Annele, "but how far can I take the herd?"

"How far? I don't know either! – How far can she take the herd?" Mother passed the question on to Father, who was trimming the bark from a fat log by the barnyard. He was in his shirtsleeves. His gleaming axe shone in the sun. Now he straightened up and pointed:

"Toward the south you can go as far as the wide ditch – you can't miss it, – toward the north as far as another ditch just like the first; toward the east you mustn't let the herd stray across the dirt road you'll see there, and toward the west no further than the straggly pines and bushes that are the forerunners of the big forest. Those are your boundaries. Between the bushes and the forest there's a meadow. The animals will be bursting to go there, but make sure you keep an eye on them, that's somebody else's property."

"And the forest?"

"The forest belongs to somebody else, too. Don't go in there whatever you do!"

"Good," Annele says, but doesn't budge. The axe leaps up joyously and falls again glittering in the sun, dark in the shadow. Big chips of wood spurt from the log, rich with resin. Now he could look up, maybe say something to Annele, but no, he doesn't look at her again.

"Girl, are you asleep or what? The animals are miles away!"

"Coming, coming this minute!"

With big leaps Annele races after her herd. She fetches up at the big ditch that Father mentioned. It is deep, wide, freshly dug. Who dug it? Are there any other people living on the barrens?

No, there's not a trace of human beings anywhere. On the other side of the ditch there are scattered bushes, grassy hummocks, marshy water left over from the spring floods. Beyond

the boundary road are the fields of Fork Farm. A boy was herding sheep there. Further in the distance, you could see Fork Farm, a fine farmstead in a clump of trees. They had passed it yesterday.

The boy came up close to the road with the sheep. Annele remained on her side. They both stood there stiff as pokers and looked at each other. The boy was quite a bit bigger than Annele, and had flaxen hair. When they had had their fill of looking, the boy took an osier whistle from his pocket and played on it. His playing didn't amount to much. But Annele had no whistle, and she could only go on looking.

The boy was done playing his whistle. Next he took a knife and played with it, too, opened it at an angle, made it somersault through the air, caught it again by the blade. After that he made a big show of all the stuff you can do with rocks. Two or three at a time, he made them skip from hand to hand at a dazzling speed. After each of these tricks, he looked at Annele boastfully, as if to challenge her: here's what I can do, but what can you do?

That was all fine and good. But why didn't the boy say something? Couldn't he talk? It didn't occur to her that she hadn't said a word either.

No, the boy certainly wasn't dumb. Suddenly he yelled a really bad word, grabbed a long whip with a knotted cord that was lying on the ground, brandished it horrifyingly, and hit Annele's big white ewe across the legs. The ewe had crossed the road, no doubt with friendly intentions, for she and the sheep of Fork Farm had been calling to each other.

"Got no eyes in your head? I'll teach you to trespass on other people's property!" And even from across the road, the boy cracked his long whip.

The white ewe fled panic-stricken to seek refuge among the other sheep, and the whole terrified flock went charging away across the barrens.

Annele went hot all over. So that's what the boy was like. No, there was no way she could get along with him!

⚭

A strange call trembled in the air. Great shadows flew past overhead. Mighty birds with gray silken wings, linked in a sort of big hook, slid downward, alighted in the marshy shrubbery beyond the ditch.

What kind of birds were they?

As soon as she approached them, she was met by a warning call: don't come!

The flock of birds took wing and alighted in a different place.

This happened several times. All morning the girl longed to get closer to the birds. In vain! The warner and caller was more watchful than she. It was always the same bird. While the others were busily searching the marshy waters with their long beaks, it was the only one that just stood there, head raised, watching for the uninvited intruder. The girl tried every way she could to approach it behind its back, but it was no use. This was a watcher that would not let anyone trick it. A real corporal.

Mother came with lunch.

"Mother, Mother, such big, big birds!"

"Where's your wrap?" Mother asked in turn.

Annele grabbed for her head: the wrap was gone. She turned around: it wasn't there either.

"Just as I thought – that blanket will warm the barrens a lot more than it will warm you," Mother said, but with something like a smile. And urged her as she put a little warm yellow clay bowl in the girl's hands: "Well, go ahead and eat!"

"Yes, Mother, but what are those big, big gray birds?"

"Those are cranes! Marsh birds. You see, the whole barrens are a veritable kingdom of birds."

"Cranes? But they don't let me get close."

"I can well believe it. Cranes are very smart and shy birds. They post sentinels. The sentinels will stand there like soldiers. That's so no human beings can come near them."

"But suppose it's a person that won't do them any harm?"

"Go ask the cranes who does them harm. Birds have their own wisdom and their own way of knowing."

"But I want to know their wisdom too!"

"Then you'll have to make them stand still and wait for you, the way Miķelis the fool did."

"What did he do?"

"He sprinkled salt on the sparrows' tails, and then he could catch them. Maybe it'll work for cranes, too."

If Mother is going to talk like that, then Annele can, too. She looks at Mother sideways and says:

"I bet it was our own Ģelžu Miķelis that did this."

Mother makes no reply. She lightly presses together two fingers and snaps them right under Annele's nose. It doesn't hurt, but it is a warning:

"Is that a way to talk about grown-up people?"

Toward evening, a big flock of sheep driven by two women comes down the little hill by Fork Farm. These can't be the sheep of Fork Farm, for they cross the boundary road and run over the barrens. One of the women places herself in front of the sheep while the other goes to New Farm. Soon she emerges again with Annele's mother, and now all three women turn the flock and drive it toward the forest, right up to Annele's herd.

Now she realizes that the big flock is the sheep of Edgefield Farm, which have been brought to be grazed on the barrens. The ones Father mentioned way back at Spring Farm.

The sheep flow around Annele like water. Little mouths, big mouths murmur, bleat, baa. Pearl's and Magpie's long surprised moos seem to ask: "Hey, what's the meaning of this? Who are these?" Meanwhile Annele's own little flock of sheep, fearful and agitated, flees off to one side. A tall young woman with rather pale cheeks comes over to Annele and says:

"Hello, little herd girl! Look what we brought you. Momma Laukmale sends you a present and asks me to give you her regards and to tell you that if you do a good job herding you'll get a pair of shoes in fall as sure as fate."

"Will you listen to that!" Mother tries to cheer her.

But Annele seems neither to hear nor to see. She doesn't lift a finger to receive Momma Laukmale's present. The woman puts it in her arms.

So this is what life is like! Annele had been told that the sheep of Edgefield Farm would be brought over for her to herd, and here they were, sure enough. There was no escaping them.

Such were Annele's thoughts.

Want

Annele had often heard her mother say, "No matter how hard life has been for us, we've never had to live in want, we've always had bread to eat, and we've been able to reach out a helping hand to others who are in need. What more could anybody want out of life?"

Wandering across the barrens with her herd, Annele remembers everything the grown-ups have said. And she turns it over in her mind.

Bread? Yes, she's never lacked for bread. Every morning there's a chunk of bread in the basket for her with a little hollow carved in the middle for the butter, though it's never deep enough to last till she's finished the whole piece. But if she knows how to divide it up, and eats half of the bread dry, then she can have quite a sumptuous meal with the second half. The bread Mother bakes, even without butter, is as delicious as wine and honey. Bread is not the problem, they've never had to do without it and they still don't have to, but is bread everything? That's something she's not so sure about.

Spring Farm, Spring Farm! Yes, there they had everything. But they don't at New Farm. At New Farm there's want.

At Spring Farm the spring arrived with such abundance you couldn't have welcomed it even with ten arms. New birches, pussy willows, marsh marigolds, a golden expanse of dandelions! And the delicious sour grass, and delicate wood sorrel, which the children ate hungrily in spring! Not to mention birch sap. Even the king himself had no drink as good as that. At Spring Farm every day grew with the sun, every day offered something unprecedented: apple, cherry, strawberry blossoms promised a wonderful summer, a rich fall.

On the barrens there was not a sign of all this. When you stood on a hummock, you could see, in the distance around other farmsteads, the mist of blossoming orchards as they came into flower, then shed their blossoms, while on the barrens slow shoots poked up above the mossy ground; shamefaced, the pitiful little flowers of scarcity would appear – thistles and burdocks. The herd was hell-bent to get to the alder bushes, where in the shade the grass grew thicker. There were even a blooming strawberry plant or two, but the sharp teeth of the sheep cut them off like scissors. It would be a vain hope to expect they would ever have berries. If that wasn't want, what was?

Spring dragged on late and cool. From various points of the compass, great winds raced across the barrens. One morning the sun rose from a dazzling white blanket, as though it were winter. The snow was soft and tender as powdered sugar, and by breakfast time it flowed away in tiny rivulets. Only then, warmer days began to come. And then Pentecost was at the door.

Pentecost! This was a word that dawned in Annele's heart like a ray of morning light. Pentecost was the magic key to the wonderful storehouses of summer, it was the beginning of the fulfillment of countless wishes and of the long dreams of winter.

Yes, that's what Pentecost at Spring Farm had been like! But what would it be like here on the barrens? Well, she'd soon know!

When, on the Saturday before Pentecost, Annele drove the herd home at noon, she looked around quickly and made sure there was dough rising in the little trough. That meant there would be flatcakes after all. "But – yes – but – aren't we going to have any birch boughs?" she asked her mother, blushing suddenly.

"Birch boughs?" her mother asked in surprise. "No, child, where would we get birch boughs around here?"

"Well, it's not as though there were no birches here at all."

"So you think Father will go get birches on someone else's property? On the sly maybe, so as not to get caught?" Mother spoke sternly, but when she saw that Annele was ashamed enough as it was, she finished on a gentler note: "No, no, child, you mustn't expect that."

Annele crept away, shaking her head mournfully: "No, no, child, you mustn't expect that."

But the child she said that to was obstinately hopeful. The child tossed her head with a devil-may-care expression.

Impossible – how could there be a Pentecost without birch boughs? Who ever heard of such a thing? Annele was sure they would make their appearance somehow. After all, the birch boughs at Spring Farm had also appeared mysteriously. The farmhands never talked about them beforehand, but merely went off somewhere and later – lo and behold – the house, the rooms were filled with rustling as fragrant armfuls came inside like the vast forest itself.

It was lovely waiting for Pentecost. All afternoon Annele looked for the tiny flowers of the barrens to make garlands for the cows. There were few she was happy with. For Pearl, she made one out of rose-red pussytoes. They were downy and delicate like sunset clouds. But Pearl tossed her horns until at last she pulled apart the garland and one end dangled to the ground. With her wide, pink tongue, she licked it into her mouth, and that was the end of that. Pearl was so good at chewing that even a rock could not survive her teeth intact.

Early on, Annele began looking in the direction of the house: perhaps Mother would soon be calling her home? Nothing doing though! Toward sunset Mother herself came to meet her: she said Annele should let the animals graze somewhere where the grass was richer. Of course. Annele remembered now. On the night before Pentecost and on Midsummer Eve the cows were allowed to go in places that were hard to graze, where the protected grass grew thick. But where would they find a place like that?

It appeared that Mother knew better. She drove the animals toward the slough. It was a lush and succulently green spot, with a wide ditch, where the water had been drained away. A week ago Father had dug this ditch. Now he was leveling the dirt and making a dam.

He looked at the girl with a friendly smile. Annele smiled too. She was always happy to be near Father.

"There won't be a whole lot of herding for you this time," said Father, "but wait till a field of clover starts rippling here a few years down the line – then you'll see how the cows love it."

"Will there be clover growing here some day?" Annele asked, wide-eyed with amazement.

"Yes indeed, lass, and will it ever grow! Not only clover, but rye and barley and oats and wheat as well. The wheat will grow tall as a wall. Look at this soil. This is a veritable gold mine!"

Father grabbed a handful of the rich soil, tossed it in his palm like grain when you estimate its weight. The girl did not know anything about it, but looked at Father trustingly. How good it was that Father was happy!

Mother looked away.

"Sure it is, sure! But is it going to be your field?"

Annele took a quick look at Father. What would he say?

Apparently he was at a loss for an immediate answer. But the smile did not leave his lips. And after a while he said:

"So what if it isn't mine! Why should that make me feel any less pleased?" Then he went on digging. Now Mother, too, smiled and shrugged:

"You'll never change!"

Annele's eyes began to

burn. No matter what Father said, she loved to hear it. Father was so dear, so dear.

Annele was quite, quite sure that when she came into the house that night she would see birch boughs. There weren't any, though. There was a little bowl of clabbered milk, and a flatcake, but it just didn't feel right, eating a Pentecost flatcake in a house that hadn't been ornamented for the holiday. Even though the milk had had cream added to it, it was the same as always. But everyone knew that what people really ate at Pentecost was *pūtelis*. There was none of that either.

Her spoon in the bowl of milk, Annele forgot herself and began to dream. Look, there she was, lying in the yard at Spring Farm, and next to her a big white sheet had been spread with a thick layer of *pūtelis* ingredients to dry in the sun: boiled peas, cracked wheat and barley, and other grains. These had to be protected from the birds. It was work that Annele enjoyed. But she herself was surely the biggest bird of all. With a ringing and scrunching sound, the *pūtelis* grains rolled about in her mouth. Were they ever delicious!

Even more delicious, though, once they had been ground in a coarse mill and poured into a mixture of clabbered milk and cream specially prepared for the *pūtelis*. There was no other food that tasted so much like spring! You could have eaten it even on your deathbed!

"Aren't we going to have any *pūtelis* for Pentecost?" Annele had recently asked Mother.

"Don't ask, greedyguts! Where would we get a delicacy like that?" Mother had answered. And that was all.

Hmmm. If *pūtelis* was a delicacy, it was no use dreaming. There were no delicacies here on the barrens.

"Come on, what is it, are you woolgathering again? Aren't you hungry?" Annele heard Mother's voice.

"I *am* eating," Annele began to stir her milk.

Darkness had already thickened around midnight, but Annele's eyes were still wide open. She was thinking:

The night before Pentecost! All the paths have now been swept, in all the farms the windowsills and doors, all the ceilings, are decorated with mountain ash, crab apple, and lilac branches. The birch boughs rustle mysteriously whenever anyone accidentally touches them, stretching out a hand deep in a dream. But the people are peacefully sleeping in their white linen shirts, they don't know what the birch boughs are saying to the mountain ashes, lilacs, and guelder roses, or how they flood the air with sweet aromas. How can they sleep so calmly? How can they not long to hear what is in those aromas, in those flowers, and what tales they have to tell?

The night before Pentecost! The fields are drenched with dew, the forests and gardens full of blossoms and leaves. All the buds are swelling apace so as to be able to open with the morning sun.

She didn't know what heaviness this was, what exactly it was she wanted, what exactly she was grieving for, to cause such a huge wave to surge in her throat with a deep sob. She got scared, abruptly held her breath, bit her tongue. But Mother's head already loomed from the big bed.

"What is it, lass, are you sick?"

Annele was quiet as a mouse.

"Is anything hurting you?"

"Yes, and even if I say I'm hurting, Mother will answer: You've got growing pains," thought the girl.

What is she to say? She doesn't know it herself. Is she sobbing because there are no birch boughs? If she were to say that, Mother would laugh heartily. And she'd be perfectly right to laugh at her. No, Annele mustn't admit what a little silly she is. Better that she should burrow deeper under the sheet and pretend to be asleep.

Meanwhile, out in the fields, a great Pentecost Eve grows apace.

Delicacies

It's exactly noon. Annele is lying face down in the little yard fighting with sleep. Of course she could go take a nap, but she's thinking: how can I take a nap? – What about Pentecost? It must be lived to the full, as long as possible. But her eyes have an overwhelming desire to close. This morning Father didn't let her sleep late as he usually does on Sunday mornings, for today Father is going to church and paying a visit to distant Spring Farm. He and Brother left early. But regardless of all this: she mustn't sleep away Pentecost. And she turns around quickly to face the sun.

But what should she do? How can she spend her precious leisure time?

If this were Spring Farm, she'd know. There'd be a hundred paths to run down, a hundred places to go to and discover what new miracles have appeared the night before Pentecost.

For today is a special day, and special things must surely have happened on a day like this.

No matter how hard she thinks, however: there's nothing unusual to find on the barrens.

Often when Annele suddenly has a hankering for something, for the way things used to be in the old days, Mother says: "What's the use of talking about that, lass? Those are delicacies."

"What are delicacies?"

Mother called even *pūtelis* a delicacy, but nobody called it that at Spring Farm. At Spring Farm it was easy to get it, for Granny would make *pūtelis* every day for an afternoon snack. It was no big thing. But here you couldn't have any.

Was everything you couldn't get a delicacy? Including all the things children weren't allowed to have?

And was a delicacy something bad or sinful?

Be that as it may, Annele would have loved to have some kind of delicacy right now. She couldn't really say what it was her young appetite craved. Anything would have been fine with her.

Either a great big spoonful of *pūtelis*, or a handful of juicy sorrel, or those hard green gooseberry buttons that a person could grab by the handful, hanging from every bush at Spring Farm this time of year, or even – oh, doubtless in some sunny spot strawberries might already be getting ripe, the first little white buttons with rosy cheeks!

Lilies of the valley, wood hyacinths, guelder roses! And strawberries in between! Maybe the woods at Spring Farm were already white and red with them. The lusciousness, the fragrant smells!

When Annele thought of it, she suddenly felt such a craving for these delicacies that she was aflame with it.

Her mouth was ablaze, burning, like shaggy Citron's mouth at Spring Farm when he insistently ran back and forth around the girl, yelping loudly and demanding her bread and butter. Her mouth could have swallowed pretty near the whole forest of Spring Farm.

A funny thing, these delicacies! Where did these cravings come from?

At night, too, one such craving drove sobs into her throat, like water through a floodgate. At those times her mouth wanted nothing, but the craving was huge nonetheless, and burned like fire.

It ardently longed for rooms bedecked with greenery, it wanted birch boughs, wanted the great blue night of Pentecost and something else as well, something Annele had no words for; and her heart stung with pain that she had none of these things.

That almost felt the same as now and yet quite different. What was it that longed for those other things?

"I guess that must have been my soul," thinks the girl.

She's still not clear about the soul – what it is, or why it has different cravings than her mouth. For a while, lying on the lawn, she floats as if over blue waters, in search of the soul, but the capricious impulses of her flesh refuse to be silent, keep urging her: "Don't lie around like this, Annele, do something."

Yes, but what's she supposed to do?

And as the girl turns this way and that as though looking for a way out, she catches sight of – a door. A new door, without a lock, just latched shut and stopped with a wooden plug. What door is this?

How could Annele, always so sharp-eyed, have missed seeing that Father has built a small lean-to pantry under the wide eaves of the little house? It had been finished the day before yesterday, and was made of new white boards. It smelled like the forest.

It was really a wonder that Annele had not opened this door yet!

Now was her chance to do it.

But what about Mother? What would she say? Wonder if you could go in there without permission?

Mother was taking a nap somewhere. Let her sleep! Annele would just take a peek to see what was in the little lean-to.

The door opened as easy as could be. The latch slipped out of her hands by itself. The little pantry was snug as a little glove, but cool. A shimmering white shelf met her eyes. On the shelf little jars and bowls stood in a row. What could be in them? Annele's eyes couldn't reach that high. That little brown pot with the handles – now there was something the girl was familiar with. She could have sworn it was the pot that held the cream. When Mother skimmed the milk containers, she always put all the fresh, velvet-smooth, sweet top milk in it.

Cream – yumm, cream! Shivers of anticipation ran through Annele and suddenly tossed a great craving for cream into her, like fire tossed into straw. Why, cream was the sweetest craving of all! It swallowed all her other rambling and undefined cravings for sorrel or hard gooseberry buttons, because the craving for cream could be satisfied right here, on the spot.

True, if you pressed even the tip of your little finger into such a surface of smooth, velvety milk, the mark was impossible to eradicate. But who would notice such a mark in a whole pot of cream with an uneven surface, when the tendency was always to run one gap into the others? Oh, there was no need to worry! – And besides, it was no big deal! It was only one little fingertip's worth of cream! Because she wasn't going to take more than that.

But it wasn't so easy to take the little pot off the shelf. Annele stretched from her feet to her fingertips, tried to roll the little pot closer to her now on one side, then on the other, but it wouldn't budge.

The little pot seemed to be terribly heavy and disobedient.

All right, if it didn't come of its own accord, she'd use force. Annele impatiently pushed with all her strength and suddenly, quite unexpectedly, it yielded. Lightly, like a balloon filled with air, it jumped into her hands, lurched out of her hands onto her shoulder, rolled dancing off her shoulder down her back and spun into a corner.

Not a drop had spilled?

Well, what did that mean, was the little pot empty?

There it lay, on its side.

Sure enough, it was empty!

The girl retrieved it from the corner. There was a big hole in its side.

Annele went hot and cold all over. She had broken the pot.

An empty pot, too! Empty!

A fine delicacy, indeed!

What if Mother found it like this? Mercy! Annele knew what that would mean. After all, you couldn't buy a pot every day.

There lay the broken-off piece.

For a while she stood there helplessly, the shard in one hand, the pot in the other. How could she join together what had split apart forever?

It was no longer possible, but it *must* be possible. If you joined one to the other, the broken-off piece fit into the whole the way a hand fits a glove. But would it stay that way?

It didn't, darn it!

Mother, of course, could make the two parts stay together. Mother knew how to repair pots and bowls. She would drill a hole with an awl in one edge, then the other, sew together the broken edges with coarse thread, putty the crack with bread, put it in the sun to dry, and the pot was as good as new. But did Annele dare go to Mother and tell her everything? No, she couldn't. She'd die of shame.

Some sort of noise suddenly boomed in her ears. Or perhaps it was fear taking hold of her! But suddenly a clever solution presented itself. She must put the little pot back in such a way that you wouldn't notice. Yes, that was it. Then everything would be all right. – Desperately holding the broken-off piece to the cracked part, the girl again stretched full length to reach the shelf, and it really did seem that she had suddenly grown taller, that as she struggled with supernatural strength the impossible became possible; the little pot was once more back on the shelf standing there in such a way that from the side you couldn't tell there'd been a catastrophe. Now that it was successfully in place, the girl shot out the door quick as a flash. She dropped the latch on the hook, put the plug back in place, looked around quickly: silence, as before. No one had seen or heard.

You'd have thought all was well now, but she fled. Away, away from this place. With great leaps and on tiptoe, as far as she could run, she darted off like a bat.

Her great craving, too, had flown away like a bat. Not for a moment had it even occurred to her to be interested in the other pots that were on the shelf.

No, no, no! That was all over! Just as she had recently been burned by her craving, she now burned with shame. Shame, shame!

She fled behind the barnyard, but that wasn't very far, she ran to the new ditch Father had dug, raced as far as she could along that same ditch so only her head showed as she ran.

But it didn't make her feel any better. Shame dogged her footsteps.

It was all awful, awful, awful.

Awful right from the start – how she'd caught sight of the door, how she'd stealthily opened it, how she'd tried to get hold of the little pot, how she'd tried to make it look as though it wasn't broken, how she'd latched the door again so nobody would notice, and how she now had to run, run away!

It was all awful, awful!

Her craving for cream and all her other cravings had turned into such bitterness in her mouth that she had to spit it out. But the bitterness would not go away.

For a long time the girl's head moved down the ditch, but how long could she keep running away? Her mother was calling. Annele had to take the cattle out to pasture.

Obedient, she came running at once. She watched her mother on the sly. Did she already know about the mischief?

Mother was in a good mood. She offered to bring the afternoon snack out to the pasture herself.

Just as at any other time Annele would have looked forward to this occasion with the greatest pleasure, so she now awaited it with a sudden sense of panic. But when Mother came, Annele calmed down for a while. No need to worry yet. Mother had apparently not been in the pantry yet, and did not know. Everything was sure to turn out all right.

But it didn't. The more time passed, the more she felt the unpleasant incident in her very bones. If Mother had asked her now, "Are you in pain?" and, hearing the girl answer "Yes!" had told her, "Those are growing pains," Annele would have found it impossible to believe her. On the contrary, she felt that when the little pot fell, she herself had dropped to the ground and shrunk till she was as small as could be.

The next morning Father wanted to let her sleep in. But Annele heard him leave early, she watched her mother through half-open lids come in and go outside again several times. She kept watching closely what Mother's mouth and eyes would say. Would she look in her direction sternly and reproachfully? You bad girl, what have you done?

She tossed and turned a while longer, half asleep, then got dressed quietly and went to the pasture. From a distance she heard Father singing in a lovely sonorous voice, "Go forth, my heart, rejoice, rejoice!"

At any other time the girl's heart would have leaped for joy to hear Father sing, for now that they lived in the barrens he so rarely sang anymore, but today it felt as though she had no right to take pleasure in the sonorous loveliness of the hymn.

"What's this? Why have you come so early?" Father asked in surprise. "Have you slept your fill so soon?"

"I wasn't sleepy anymore," the girl said softly.

"Now I know you're fibbing! I'd believe you if you said you weren't hungry, but don't tell me you ever get enough sleep, you little grasshopper you! I'm sure it's not easy getting up in the morning, how well I know that from my own experience. You're still too young, I know it."

And Father looked at the girl with so much love.

Annele's eyes filled with tears. It was so nice that Father realized how hard she fought sleep every morning. But she was dejected and avoided Father's eyes.

Whenever a head moved across the vast barrens, Annele would catch sight of it at once. After the afternoon snack, one such head appeared behind the hill in the direction of Brook Farm. Even before the traveler's feet became visible, Annele knew who it was. It was Jānis, who worked as a farmhand at Brook Farm and came to visit Father almost every Sunday.

"A decent young fellow!" Annele had heard Father say of him one night, as he watched Jānis slowly disappear in the distance.

"And good-looking, too. It'll be a lucky girl that gets him some day," Mother had answered.

Since Annele never stopped waiting what the day would bring, she always looked forward to Jānis's visits. "Come Sunday, Jānis will be here," she would think in joyful anticipation even before the week was over, for Jānis was almost their only visitor on the barrens, and a nice one at that.

He was a strapping young man, about as tall as Father, with lovely blue eyes and bright yellow hair, always smiling, with a gentle sense of humor. When he came, he would shake hands with all of them, one by one, and also inquire how Annele was doing, as though she were a grown-up, and remember even the next time he came her conversation and her words. Annele liked that.

But this time she didn't want to meet the visitor. She quickly rounded up the animals and drove them a long way away. But from afar she watched and saw everything. Father, too, had seen the visitor coming, went out to meet him. With slow, Sunday steps they approached each other. Annele knew they were both smiling. Now they shook hands, stood, and talked. Father lit his pipe, but Jānis did not smoke. Now Father took the visitor around the field. The ground had been broken and sown this spring, and was now green, thick as homespun cloth. Then they walked over to the ditch. Father showed how much he had dug during the week.

They sat down at the edge of the ditch, and Father would stretch out his arm from time to time, pointing now in the direction of Homefield Farm, now toward Fork Farm. The visitor, too, kept pointing the same way. Annele knew they were talking about the surrounding farms. What the people were like there, and how they lived. It would have been a treat to hear all this, like eating a sweet roll, and she could easily have done so. The cattle could have grazed all around them, for there was plenty of grass, and she could have sat next to them by the ditch and listened to the two of them talking. Father would not only not have chased her away, he would have put his arm around her shoulders and pressed her to him affectionately, and Jānis might have patted her on the head. But now there was nothing doing. How could she face Jānis, who was such a decent young fellow, while she had done so much incorrigible mischief?

When the men had had their fill of sitting at the edge of the ditch, they went inside the house. Now they'd have a bit to eat and talk about distant countries and foreign nations, about wartime and peacetime, and about what it had been like when their parents and grandparents were young.

Annele knows what that's like. She sees the men sitting down at the little table, sees Jānis breaking a flatcake, putting a little lump of butter on each bite of bread, talking pleasantly all the while, and telling stories, as though it wasn't the eating that mattered most, but the lovely conversation, which moves so easily and smoothly when he talks with Father, as though little clay balls were being tossed back and forth between them in a game.

No matter which direction Annele ran in around the cattle, she kept in view the door of the house, and she had a feeling that the visitor had overstayed his time. Finally all three came outside. They stood still outside the front door.

Mother said something, waved her hand in the direction of the pasture.

They all looked in Annele's direction.

That stung her like a burning blade of steel. What was wrong? Why were they looking in the direction of the pasture? What were they talking about? Annele, what else? There was no doubt about it. Mother had discovered everything and was now telling them all about Annele's mischief. After all, grown-ups are pitiless when it comes to children. Oh dear, oh dear! Now the whole world would know! How would she face people now?

Jānis always had sympathy for her. Just last time he had said, "Isn't it too hard for the little one? Out with the cattle every day." And when Mother had said that Annele was doing a good job, he had smiled such a lovely smile: "That's all right then! She'll be a hard worker one of these days!" And now? What could he say now? He'd think it wasn't even worth looking at a girl like her anymore.

Jānis left, walking along the new ditch, and Father accompanied him. He walked with him a long way. Their heads vanished beyond the hill.

Annele, too, would like to go away somewhere and not come back. Over there, beyond the corner of the forest, in which is submerged a mysterious and strange forester's house – Owl Farm. They say that once, late at night, the mistress of this farm left and never returned. Annele's heart is heavy. She understands that you can go far, far, far away and not come back.

The sun is near the horizon. It's time to take the cattle home, but Annele is by the furthermost boundary, by the shrubs where the cranes are. She doesn't like being near the house. If only she could crawl into the new ditch like an earthworm, the very bottom of the ditch, and vanish.

Father has walked Jānis almost as far as Brook Farm, for it's taken him all this time to come over the hill. But he doesn't go home. He turns and comes straight toward Annele, carrying his cap in his hand. There's something in the cap. Now he's smiling, close by.

"Come here, lass! Look what I've got."

In the cap is a tiny puppy the size of a fist. Black all over, with one white eye.

"Oh Dad, how nice! Who gave him to you?"

"Jānis. He told me to come with him and gave it to me. We said he'd be a companion for you."

"Where? When you were standing by the front door?" Annele asked and felt herself blushing all over.

"What front door?" Father didn't understand.

The girl blushed even more, bent down to the puppy, which Father had put on the ground. She was so ashamed. No one had accused her, no one had said anything bad about her, but she herself had imagined the very worst. It all came from the bad things she had done today. Father ran a little distance, and the puppy lolloped after him with his stubby little legs, couldn't catch up with him, rolled over like a ball of yarn, and whined piteously. The girl picked him up in her arms, squeezed him as she petted him, but he now gave such a howl that she was startled and hurriedly put him back in the grass.

"What makes him howl like that?"

"You squeezed him too hard, and around his ears, too, where it hurts most. He's still vulnerable and weak like all young creatures."

"Does that hurt young creatures so much?"

"You wait – if I were to squeeze you good and hard between these palms, I wonder what you'd say!" Father began to laugh, showing his palms, deliberately large.

Young creatures hurt. – Yes, Father really knows! If she were to tell him what happened yesterday – wonder what he'd say then.

"What shall we call the little tyke? What do you say, lass?" Father asked.

"Let's call him Krancis, shall we?"

No answer.

Father picked up the puppy and put it back in his cap.

"Let's give him a drink of milk at home and then he can sleep."

He turned homeward, but looked back in surprise when the girl suddenly raced by him quick as a flash. She had caught sight of Mother, who was coming to call her home.

She ran and ran until, out of breath, she ran smack into Mother.

"Mother, Mother, I broke that little pot."

"What pot?"

"The one with the brown handles."

Mother thought for a moment.

"Oh, that one! It had a crack already. I didn't pour milk into it anymore – I was planning to repair it as soon as I had a free moment. – But tell me how – how did you get a hold of the pot? How did you break it?"

Now Annele has to tell Mother. And she does. God only knows if she really tells her all about her craving for cream or not. One thing is sure – that night she jumps around the little cabin on the barrens on one foot, then on the other, over and over again. She feels such relief, such great relief!

But what about Mother? What was it Mother said?

She just gave Annele's shoulders a good shake and laughed: "That's the way things sometimes go when you're a child!"

Mother was kind, so kind.

People Arrive

Right after Pentecost three wagons full of people arrived from Edgefield Farm. Annele was watching her herd by the roadside and saw them. At the head of the column drove the oldest son of the master of Edgefield Farm, Aldis Laukmalis, and one of the maids who had brought the sheep after St. George's Day. In the second wagon was Krists Laukmalis, the farmer's second son, with Ģelžu Miķelis, while four men or so sat in the third wagon. The fields had now been sown, while the harvest was still a long way off. In the meantime the pens in the barnyard at New Farm needed to be finished.

When the wagons had come closest to the place where Annele stood like a pillar of salt watching the passers-by, Aldis pulled up and called out:

"Hey, girl, aren't you bored?"

He lifted a book with a black cover from the front of the wagon. It was three times as big as a Bible.

"They say you're a great reader. Here's something for you to read."

Annele's shoulders rose in a shrug.

What was this book to her!

Aldis rocked the book in his hands, though it seemed to weigh pounds and pounds, tossed it back in the wagon and pulled on the reins. The other drivers had already driven past him. He was in no hurry to catch up with them. Slowly he drove into New Farm, talking with the young maidservant the whole time.

The men got to work soon. They sawed, hewed, chopped, planed. Only Krists watched, his hands stuck in his pockets. He hadn't come to work. He was supposed to drive back the spare horses, and deliver needed materials, and food as well, in a few days. He was given easy work and coddled in all sorts of ways, for he was said to be sickly.

Although Krists had an easier life, Annele had the feeling that Aldis was much more cheerful and happy. Aldis had wonderful eyes that were always laughing and a lithe body – indeed, when you really took a good look, Aldis was almost more handsome than Jānis of Brook Farm. Only he was a little bit shorter. But when all was said and done, Jānis was kinder. And that was important in Annele's opinion.

As the work continued, Aldis and Annele's father were always in the lead. When a log had to be lifted, Father would call, "Aldi, take the other end!" With Aldis, every job went smoothly. While others sweated and toiled, Aldis would whistle.

It was quite a sight to see the building grow. They hammered in place the cross-beams, they raised the rafters. Bundles of white straw lay in a pile – they would be used to thatch the roof.

Father spread the straw and tied it, while Aldis would toss him the bundles. Aldis ran across the frame of rafters like a cat, sometimes simply balancing with his arms, looking into the distance all the while. Annele liked to watch the roof growing higher and higher. Others watched, too – Anlīze the maid, every time she ran across the yard. Of course, she couldn't stand and watch like Annele when the latter came home from herding; Anlīze had to prepare food and wash shirts for all the men who were working on the building. That was why she had been sent from Edgefield Farm. But she was just as quick at her chores as Aldis – said Mother – and that was why she could have a quick look now and then to see the men at work, and to warn Aldis:

"Oh Aldi, do hold on! Be careful you don't fall!"

"I can even stand on one leg if you like," Aldis frightened her, balancing on a rafter.

"Oh Aldi, I'm scared!"

Then Father, too, began to scold:

"Don't be silly, Aldi, and don't make such a fool of yourself! Remember, this place will belong to you some day."

"Not me. I don't like it here. Let Krists have this farm. My place is out in the world," Aldis waved his hand in a dismissive gesture.

But where had Aldis put the book he had brought with him? Annele searched every corner and every hiding place, of which there were not too many at the new farm, but she couldn't find it. Finally, when the pile of straw got smaller and smaller as the bundles climbed up on the roof, she caught sight of what looked like a herdsman's hut made of white boards. That's where Aldis slept. A white pillow, a straw mattress, a striped wool blanket, and the big book at the head end. Probably Aldis leafed through it during the noon break.

For a long time Annele hesitated: what should she do? Should she crawl into the hut or not; take the book or not? Was it all right to do this if Aldis hadn't given it to her? But hadn't he himself showed it to her and tempted her, hadn't he in a way promised it to her, calling her a great reader? Annele held on to that promise. For no craving is as strong as the craving for books. And yet it is different from other cravings.

It couldn't be a sin, could it? A book wasn't something you'd eat up. You could put it back again and no one would notice what had been done to it. Who'd be harmed if she took it? No one, of course.

But then why not ask Aldis? Maybe he'd let her have it.

Yes, but was it so easy to ask? You never knew how to address him: by his first or last name. True, he was a relative, but he was a grown-up; either way seemed incorrect.

Thus Annele pondered and coveted for a long time, then finally quickly did the deed. She hardly knew how it had happened, but all of a sudden she had surreptitiously approached Aldis's book, had tucked it under her arm, and was stealing away from the barnyard side of the house, not realizing that Aldis's alert eyes had watched everything from the roof, where he was sitting spreading bundles of straw.

"Hey, folks, catch the goose thief!" Aldis suddenly exclaimed.

Goose thief? What goose thief? Startled, Annele froze. Having taken one step, she remained riveted to the spot. And then she saw everyone's faces turned in her direction and everyone's eyes laughing. Now she knew where the goose thief was. The book began to slip. Annele's knees wobbled as she tried to hold on to the weight of it. She was at a loss what to do.

But Aldis had simply intended to give her a fright and to tease her a bit. When he saw he had succeeded, he laughed:

"All right, take it away, take it! Enjoy your roast goose!"

And so she had managed to get past Aldis, but would she be as lucky with Mother if she tried to take the book along to the pasture? Annele slipped her heavy cloak over her shoulders, then put her basket over one arm and thrust the book under the other.

Mother saw her off as she left for the pasture.

"My, are you broad today," Mother exclaimed in surprise, "and wearing your cloak, too? What are you dragging that heavy thing along for?"

"There's going to be rain," Annele remarked shyly and went running off, her elbows tucked in under the cloak like rain-soaked wings. She didn't want Mother to see or hear what she was guarding there.

What a strange book it was! As soon as you opened it, it said, "Latvian News", and every couple of pages again it said, "Latvian News." And on and on, like fence posts between sections of fence: "Latvian News."

It wasn't a real book that you could read with bated breath from end to end.

It was more like a pile of cinders in which the stepmother had spilled peas in order to torment Cinderella. There were few grains whose taste Annele enjoyed. But she searched it tirelessly, examining and later finding good even those grains that had initially seemed wormy and half-eaten.

The cranes were no longer afraid of Annele, but something was scaring them from the other direction. Several times a day the sentry would warn them: watch out! Like a great cloud, they would then rise in the air, circling the bushes in a great arc, alighting again, only to take wing once more soon. What was it that scared them so?

And then one day the person who had been scaring them appeared. A man was coming through the bushes, jumping from hummock to hummock. After jumping over the ditch, he walked straight toward Annele.

He came, quick and supple as a young man, but he wasn't as young as you might have thought from the way he walked. A short, skinny little man. His cap with its shiny visor flashed in the sun, his shirt was white, without a bandanna; his stockings were bright blue, tied with garters about his knees, and when he raised his feet elegantly, one couldn't help noticing them.

His talk was as loud as a trumpet.

"Good day to you, herd girl! What's that under your arm pulling your sides out of shape?"

Annele blushed. She hoped he wouldn't start talking about the goose.

But the man was already answering his own question after barely glancing at the book.

"Old issues of the *Latvian News*. I see, I see. Come on, what are you doing with that mishmash? You'll get twisted out of shape lugging that around. If you're a book lover, you can get any amount of books from me. Every week, I can bring you a whole pile from the pastor's house."

The herd girl appeared to have no mouth, only eyes. So the stranger went on chattering.

"Who do you think I am, eh? Your next-door neighbor. From that farm over there."

"Where?" Annele asked in surprise, for he was pointing straight into the bushes.

"Come over here. I'll show you! – Throw that book away!" he called, seeing that the girl had a heavy weight to lug.

They both jumped across the ditch.

"This is the boundary. We dug it even before St. George's Day. The hired hands came and got it done before you could say Jack Robinson. We don't dillydally."

Annele had the feeling that the stranger had wanted to add something to the last sentence, but hadn't.

Could it be that he had meant to say: "We don't dillydally like your father and the people at your house?" Well, in that case he'd better watch out!

"D'you see those buildings? That's my farm," pointed the stranger.

They were standing on a little hill. Yes, from here, a good distance beyond the bushes, you could see two fine new brick buildings with red roofs.

"Oh, those," Annele exclaimed in surprise. "I had no idea they were there."

"The shrubs are in the way, but come fall we'll get rid of them all, then you'll have a clear view."

"The bushes are going to be chopped down?"

"We'll chop them down so the chips will fly!"

"But what will happen to the cranes?"

"The cranes will go kerflooey!" the stranger laughed.

"The cranes will go kerflooey!" Annele exclaimed, shocked.

She was hearing this word for the first time, but she realized it boded the cranes no good.

"Oh, those lovely birds!" she lamented.

"Lovely birds!" the stranger rebuked her contemptuously. "A child talks like a child. What use are they to you? What use are they to me? Well, there you are then! Wild birds and wild animals are no use to anyone. Cows and sheep, now – they're good for something."

Annele hated the way the stranger talked. It's a good thing that she saw Pearl, head raised, going off up to some sort of mischief with the whole herd after her. So she ran to ward her off without answering the stranger.

He called after her:

"You're Krišjānis's daughter, aren't you? Is your father home?"

Receiving no answer from Annele, elegantly lifting his feet, he went on his way and without stopping added, over his shoulder:

"You will get those books!"

Annele burst out laughing.

A funny neighbor he'd turned out to be!

It's nice when you see people, though. Annele's eyes are always hungry for them, and when they look in the direction of the road, what is it they expect to see? People, of course! There are few to see in the barrens. She wouldn't even mind if Simkus with his hacking cough came trudging along, carrying his bundle of kerchiefs, or Bungatiņš with his wooden leg. Annele wouldn't even have minded seeing the tall mute beggar who was always called on at Spring Farm if people wanted to frighten little children. "Just you wait – the Mute will come, clap you under his arm and carry you off into the woods!" they were told. And there wasn't a child that wasn't struck dumb when the Mute was mentioned.

The Mute was a man in the prime of life with a broad, crimson red face. His tall figure was made even taller by a bumpy black top hat that he had inherited in god knows what mysterious way. His cudgel, too, was longer and stouter than the canes of other beggars because, since he couldn't hear dogs barking, he would swing the cudgel around him in circles when he entered a farmstead so the dogs could not pounce upon his shins. When the Mute entered and stood in a corner, he would start to yell fiercely and to show by signs that he wanted people to give him bread. He knew no other language, could do no work other than going begging, though he was so strong he could have moved mountains. He always acted fierce, even bestial, and threatened children with his cudgel. Yet he never hurt anyone. As he walked down the road, all by himself, he would yell, waving his hands and gesticulating. It was clear that at such times he was telling himself something.

She was sorry for the Mute. Sorry for all those who had no friends. Annele, too, was friendless.

How nice it would have been if there was a girl or boy her age in the barrens. But there were none.

It was so sultry and hot today. Here was something she could have talked about with somebody.

As the cows grazed, they were moving in the direction of Fork Farm.

Along the edge of the little hill the flaxen-haired head of the boy from Fork Farm slides past every day. When Annele brings her herd closer, he, too, climbs higher. His peaked cap is down over his ears, his whip is raised above his head. As soon as any of Annele's sheep even tries to approach him – flick! – there goes the whip, accompanied by a stern: "Whoa there! Don't you have eyes in your head?"

There they stand, facing each other.

Click-clack! Click-clack! The pebbles skip in twos, in threes. That's something he's good at.

It's like he was mute, that boy.

Click-clack! Click-clack!

How long are they going to stand there?

"And you? Can't you say something?" some wise voice says to Annele.

What am I supposed to say to him?

Click-clack! Click-clack!

Suddenly the boy starts. The pebbles are scattered. In his fright he throws up his hands:

"Look what's behind you!"

That same moment there is a flash of lightning. A thunderclap that seems to rend the sky.

A thunderstorm. Almost right overhead.

The boy from Fork Farm vanishes behind the hill with his sheep.

"Run home, run home!" the voice of fear urges Annele.

But no. Why, the sun is still as hot as an oven. There's no sign yet of the white mist of rain, is there? There's still time! And later there won't be a chance to see what she sees now!

The storm approaches as fast as the wind. Like bundles of tow, clouds spin and twist. Jagged spears fling lightnings, hurl themselves at the sun. Bury it. Thunderclaps bounce rumbling off one mountain range of clouds, fall into abysses, race up other mountain ranges, hail new celestial voices that do their work below, booming and deep. It's all still gathering. Not a leaf stirs. The thunder-wielding blacksmiths unstop the wells of the sky. They push and they shove. The locks are cracking! The bolts are breaking! Any minute now it'll be open!

Annele no longer remembers the thunderstorm she experienced at Spring Farm. There, she never got to see what she can see here. The wide expanse of the sky was covered by forests there. Oh, the wonderful celestial games that thunderclaps and lightnings play here! It seemed to Annele as though the ground and the grass were contracting into themselves. As though expecting a blow, the cattle jerked their heads skyward, slowly mooed as though asking a question, but then went on eating, snuffling greedily, as though they had to hurry and fill their stomachs before a catastrophe descended on them.

Lightly, like a rider on a galloping horse, a cloud suddenly shot up from the horizon, raced toward the middle of the sky. As it raced, it grew. It pulled into itself other clouds, thunderclaps, lightnings. It grew and grew, pulled into itself the forest, the fields. The air gave a sudden roar as though from a thousand throats. It felt as if the treetops were breaking like reeds, never to rise again.

Everything disappeared in a foaming rapid. The whirlwind was here.

"Go home, go home!"

It was too late to shout. With hissing whips the whirlwind encircled the cattle, drove them into a pile, lifted them as if on wings, dragged them with it.

She ran ahead to turn them back. She called, she shouted. The whirlwind tossed her aside, jets of rain as though from a suddenly opened sluice hurled her to the ground.

"The cattle will be done for," the girl whispered close to tears.

A rider galloped out of the farmstead and vanished in the raging storm. It was Father. Who else.

Now things would turn out right.

"Hey, girl, where're your cattle?" she heard shouts from under the eaves of the new cattle pens, where the workmen had fled to take shelter.

She didn't pay attention. It was none of their business!

In the house she stopped by the door, as though ashamed of the rivulets of water that flowed from her head, her hands, her feet.

"Where's your wrap?" sternly asked Mother.

"Who cares about the wrap, but where's your goose?" called Aldis from the corner. He himself was not visible, for the room was dark as night, but his voice was bright and mocking.

Shivers ran down Annele's back.

The book – yes, where was the book now? At the place where she had talked with the new neighbor. That's where it lay. That's where the rain was making a sodden mess of it.

Annele rushed to the door.

"I'll save it, I'll save it," she exclaimed.

Aldis's hands held fast the handle of the door.

"You're not going to save a thing, silly girl. That goose of yours isn't fit for a roast anymore, just porridge."

That's how Aldis laughed, though outside the thunder rolled and the lightning flashed. It would have been better if he too had thundered and flung lightnings. But now he was laughing. Laughing at Annele.

And she deserved to be laughed at. The cattle were scattered far and wide, her wrap was in the bushes, the book out in the rain, and look how she streamed water like a brook from every seam – nobody would praise her for any of this. Just as Father had saved her from the storm at Spring Farm, so he had saved her again this time. She should have been big and smart by now, but that was wishful thinking. Wonder where the cattle would be now if it hadn't been for Father? It was bitter to think about how badly she had failed.

As soon as the storm had given full vent to its fury and vanished in the distance, Annele ran to get her book. What she found were only pitiful remains of it. The whirlwind had torn it out of its covers, had shredded the pages, had scattered them, while the gush of rain had soaked them and turned them to rags. Until late in the evening she tried hard to make a complete whole out of the scattered shreds, but in vain.

It was true that she had grown bored with the old newspapers long ago. She had turned over the pages impatiently, like a bundle of straw that's already been threshed, searching for a tasty grain, but hadn't found much of anything. What that newspaper man wrote about Englishmen, Austrians, and Frenchmen seemed a complete waste of time to her, but there were few stories about people in the old pages. Yet now that they had fallen apart and been swept away along with the whirl-wind, she felt there must have been something good, something undiscovered in them that they had carried away with them like an unfathomable mystery, and she felt regretful.

Laukmalis and Krists came with two horse-drawn carts to take back the workmen to Edgefield Farm, for haymaking had begun there, and after that came the other big jobs of summer. The cattle pens now had a roof. They could not be completely finished until fall. Laukmalis walked through the new building, inspected it thoroughly inside and out to see the work the men had done, but didn't say a word. Krists walked behind his father, his hands in his trouser pockets, whistling through his teeth. Aldis whistled too, drove nails into boards, and whistled. Annele liked that, and yet when Krists would whistle, she hated it. For some reason it felt as though by his whistling Krists was saying to Aldis, "You wait, you're going to get it, and then you'll stop your whistling."

The men had lunch and went to take a midday nap. During this heat one couldn't drive the long distance. Anlīze the maid put away the dishes, put the things in baskets, shook out Aldis's pillows and blankets, tied them in a bundle, got everything ready so that later they could set off, for that evening they were supposed to mow the first swaths of hay in the meadows of Edgefield Farm. Mother, too, rummaged through Father's shirts and trousers to pick the ones that were whitest and in the best state of repair, so he'd look respectable, white as a swan in the meadows – for Father was going with the others to help with haymaking.

When there was such a great to-do getting ready, Annele couldn't take a nap either, could she? However, as she in her restlessness raced into the house from the outside to watch if anything unusual was happening there as well, Father stationed himself in the open doorway to keep her out and said reprovingly, "Children shouldn't poke their noses everywhere," – turned her around and pushed her back the way she had come from.

Any harsher word from Father hurt Annele. After all, she hadn't meant to do anything bad. And she couldn't help it that under Father's arm she had seen Aldis, Krists, and Laukmalis inside the house. Laukmalis was talking to Aldis. But Aldis stood there with his head down. Was his father scolding him? Krists was sitting on the bench, his legs stretched out and his hands in his trouser pockets. He was no longer whistling, but his jutting chin seemed to say that it knew a whole lot of things.

Aldis soon came outside. He was very busy. He greased the wheels, got together all the horses' gear. His cap was down low over his eyes, and he didn't talk to anybody.

Father harnessed his horse by the cattle pens. Annele sat on the logs and heard Mother talking with Father. Some of the words slipped her memory, while others remained behind, and preoccupied her a great deal.

"How could Anlīze behave that way? Such a decent young woman, such an upright young woman, what does she want with a fellow like him," said Mother.

"But what about Aldis?" asked Father in turn.

"Oh, who cares about Aldis! A young cockerel like him. Frivolous, thoughtless. And he'll find a warm welcome everywhere."

That's what Father and Mother said to each other.

Annele was already out in the pasture when the men left. In the first wagon sat Laukmalis with his two sons. The farmer held the reins of the horse himself, and Aldis could have looked in Annele's direction as he had done the day he arrived, but he didn't. Anlīze with the baskets and sacks sat next to Ģelžu Miķelis, who talked without a break and pointed with the end of his whip at distant homesteads in the vicinity. But he was the one who did all the talking. Anlīze, like Aldis, stared straight ahead and did not look up. Both her hands lay in her lap.

Anlīze!

What sort of a person was she? Annele began to think. She had the feeling that up to that point she hadn't properly paid attention to Anlīze, but that now she did see her. Anlīze did her work quickly and nimbly, but she did not talk much, and laughed even less. Mother said she was upright and decent. So then would she and Aldis have a wedding just like Ingus and Karlīne that time at Spring Farm?

No they wouldn't! Annele shook her head. She felt that in this case things were not as they should be. Ingus was full of darkness while Karlīne was light, that's the way a couple should be. But look at Aldis and Anlīze! What kind of a match were they? No match at all. Aldis had neither the girth nor the height that Ingus had. He didn't even shave the way Ingus and the other married men used to do every Saturday night, and he didn't have a real tobacco pipe either, the kind with a porcelain bowl. What's a young lad like you doing with that, Father had said as though reprimanding him one night when Aldis had taken his pipe. No, Aldis was not a man yet.

And Anlīze was full of darkness. She rarely laughed. She walked heavily and turned slowly. But why was that? Annele thought back a way. It seemed like Anlīze had always been sad.

Sad? That's right, Anlīze was sad. Then somebody must have been hurting her, like people did the Mute.

Why, that must be it! – It must be sad for Anlīze that she and Aldis had arrived in the same wagon, and were leaving each in a separate one. Krists's whistling, too, must bode Anlīze no good, or the fact that Father hadn't allowed Annele inside where Papa Laukmalis, Aldis, and Krists were; and what they had discussed wouldn't have given Anlīze any comfort, and neither would what Father and Mother had said to each other. Yes, that was it! Papa Laukmalis would no doubt look for an opportunity to give Anlīze a scolding, just as he had scolded Aldis. And if he didn't, then maybe Momma Laukmale would. And even if she didn't exactly give Anlīze a scolding, she would talk to her curtly and nothing Anlīze did would please her, so what kind of a life would Anlīze have at Edgefield Farm! Maybe that's what had been on her mind when she left. She hadn't listened to a word Ģelžu Miķelis was saying, and her hands had lain so heavily in her lap.

But Annele didn't like to dwell too long on a sad Anlīze, she preferred a happy Anlīze. And that was something she could have.

There was nothing to stop her from planning a wedding for Anlīze and Aldis, was there? Papa and Momma Laukmalis had better not interfere! She decorated the big room at Edgefield Farm with oaks and birch branches, with the most magnificent flowers that were growing in the water meadows of the Tērvete River and in the big pastures of Edgefield Farm just now, she harnessed the finest horses Edgefield Farm had to the brown buggy, and that's where Anlīze and Aldis now sat. They were quite different from the two who had just come back from New Farm. Aldis was a strapping, strong figure of a man and Anlīze was light as a swallow. She was a perfect match for Aldis. Annele sent them off to church, while she herself set long tables for them with white linen cloths from Mother's trunk, for Momma Laukmale refused to give them any tablecloths.

So Annele spent all afternoon with Anlīze and Aldis, seeing them off and waiting for them to get back. She walked down lovely long paths of thought with other people she had met at Spring Farm, each of whom had a place in the chambers of her heart. Spending time with people in her imagination was her favorite game in these bare barrens where scarcely a soul ever strayed.

Fourfooted Friends

Krančelis was growing. Three times a day Annele supplied him with milk. For this he was a grateful and true friend to her. Of course he trailed after the other members of the household too, but only when Annele wasn't home. As soon as she appeared, Krančelis greeted her with joyful barking. As his coat filled out, so did his voice. When Annele came, he wouldn't leave her side for a moment, working away with the sharp teeth of his friendship on her *pastalas*, her stockings, and the hem of her skirt till they looked like the fringe at the ends of a towel. For this reason Annele was forced to be somewhat restrained and often had to harshly interrupt Krančelis's outbursts of joy. She would then grab him by the loose skin on the scruff of his neck and lug him over to the place where he slept. Krančelis would realize that the fun was over. A few more whimpers and he'd doze off.

He could never get enough sleep, but his restless spirit would rouse him at the least little noise and call, "Krančel, watch what's happening in the world!"

When Annele drove the herd out to the pasture, Krančelis would lift his nose from where he lay and beg, howling: me too, me too, me too! Annele wouldn't have minded, but Mother sternly said, "A dog has to watch the farm. No running off to the pasture." Then both wishful thinkers knew they must obey, and Mother had only to make a threatening gesture before Krančelis pulled in his back pasterns and scampered off to his safe place.

Krančelis had a while to wait till his pasterns would grow so strong that he would have no more need for obedience.

And one day that time had come. Krančelis came somersaulting over from the house with an old *pastala* in his teeth. Annele ran to meet him, tried to chase him back, but he wouldn't obey. He snarled, barked, growled, jumping backward one moment, then running off a short distance. Joyfully wagging his stubby tail, tilting his head, he'd give his gracious permission, as if to say: Go on, you take it now, see if you can! only to grab the *pastala* in his teeth again soon ever so tightly, growling the whole time and challenging her: "Come on, Annele, grab a hold of the other side with your teeth – we're going to have a fine tug of war, the two of us."

Annele tried, if not with her teeth then at least with her nails – she teased and tricked the little dog, now whirling the *pastala* through the air, now throwing it away, now dragging along the ground the old piece of leather which the puppy's white teeth held on to like newly forged iron. Krančelis didn't take it amiss, but kept leading the girl on so she would appease his insatiable desire for frisking around.

Krančelis now ran with her to the pasture every day. And since Mother either didn't notice or deliberately made no objection, it was now an established fact: Krančelis was her fellow herder.

Of course initially, because he was always ready to frisk and frolic, he was a better playmate than a herder.

Annele's favorite was the year-old heifer Dapple. Her skin was brown and so shiny it looked polished. She allowed Annele to hug her head and to lean her cheek against Dapple's warm neck. Krančelis didn't like all this cuddling. Barking fiercely, he would jump up and down around Dapple, but all it took was for her to roll her big velvety eyes and to turn her sharp, budding little horns against him, and Krančelis would take to his heels, his tail between his legs. The sheep, too, were just as scary, especially the horned ram from Edgefield Farm, who would come running straight for Krančelis, swaggeringly pawing the ground with the hobnailed boots that were his hoofs.

The sheep from Edgefield Farm all seemed alike to Annele. They were equally greedy, equally disobedient, equally vociferous and fearful. Besides, the flock was too large for Annele to get to know every one of them. They kept to themselves and often went off on their own on some kind of mischief. The barrens could not satisfy them, for they were used to better, though much more cramped, pastures. And so they would stray, stealing mostly in the direction of Fork Farm, just for a chance to grab a mouthful of Fork Farm oats or clover. Annele often had to run and ward them off. Krančelis ran with her and learned. And then came the big day when his new skill – his sudden bark – made the sheep run, run so fast that it seemed a sudden whirlwind had swept them up off the ground and tossed them into a heap. All you could see were their fat backsides with their woolly little tails. The swaggering ram raised his horns from the very middle of them, that's how scared he was. Annele laughed aloud, Krančelis wagged his tail, happy and triumphant. The girl petted him.

Annele's five ewes and their lambs, of course, were nearer and dearer to her. One in particular enjoyed her special favor. She had lambed late, after St. George's Day. The lamb just wouldn't gain weight or strength. When the weather was cold and rainy, it stood trembling, hunched on its long legs like little posts. It wasn't able to run with the herd. The big ewe would then stay behind with it, bleating piteously. What choice did Annele have but to pick up the lamb in her arms and carry it? The big ewe soon began to join the herd and no longer paid much attention to her child. Annele would gather the best grass for the lamb, feed it with her morning bread, and bundle it in her wrap on rainy days. But the lamb was somehow sad, and remained so. "If it cheers up, it'll be a survivor, if not, then there's nothing to be done," speculated Annele and tried every way she could to raise the spirits of the little woebegone creature. Krančelis was her foremost helper. Tirelessly, he came dragging sticks, old pieces of leather, bones, and all kinds of trash in an attempt to encourage the lamb to play the same kind of game that he had played with Annele for hours on end. He frisked in front of the lamb barking and romping about, or else tugging its curly fleece now on one side, now on the other, trying to snatch its little tail, all apparently in fun though, with blunt teeth, so as not to hurt the sickly little creature.

This ceaseless effort was not without success. The lamb began to pay attention to Krančelis's jumping and barking, and when, for the first time, head tilted and ears laid back, it ran right at Krančelis, trying to butt him to death with its ridiculously minuscule little horns, Annele burst out laughing with joy, while Krančelis, even louder, barked joyfully. From that day onward, albeit slowly, the little lamb grew more and more sturdy and plump.

One afternoon Mother sent out the big brood sow with the rest of the cattle to get the numbness out of the sow's feet. They'd lost almost all feeling and strength since the sow always lay in her sty. Though she could barely keep her balance on her short, stubby feet, the heavy grunter was a real troublemaker in the herd. With her snout she would push the sheep to their feet when they were lying down for a rest, and she'd go for the cows and try to tear the grass from their very mouths, but when the cows would threaten her with their horns, she'd squeal as though she were being led to slaughter. She would do the same thing when Annele ran to turn her back and keep her from straying. Then she would growl so fiercely and toss her head in protest, enough to scare a person to death. She would constantly walk around grunting and burrowing with her fat snout everywhere. Even when she would stretch out on her side in the sun and stretch out her short little legs, she'd gurgle full of restlessness: snork, snork, I guess everything's all right, but I want it to be even better. I'm not satisfied, not satisfied at all.

Once, when Annele had become engrossed in a book for a short while, she was suddenly startled by agitation among the cattle. Seemingly upset by something unexpected, the sheep huddled together, bleated piteously, trembled; the cows mooed loudly, Krančelis all but dived into the herd, barking at the top of his lungs.

What had happened? Annele jumped to her feet and caught sight of something horrible.

The big sow had grabbed her delicate little white lamb in her teeth. Her sharp tusks, dripping with blood, had fastened themselves deep into the little fleecy back. The lamb's legs and head hung limply, as though already lifeless. Not a sound came from his half-open mouth, in which his little pink tongue was already going out like a tiny flame.

The girl screamed, wailed, ran toward the sow, hit her with a switch. Krančelis barked and howled like crazy, but the sow came at them like a horrible monster, refusing to turn aside, growling fiercely, worrying and shaking the little lifeless creature in her tusks.

Krančelis, his tail between his legs, fleeing in apparent terror, raced in the direction of the farm, and Annele followed him, shouting for her mother.

There was so much noise they couldn't help hearing it at the farm. And so Mother came outside and set off for the pasture at a run. Even from a distance she saw what was going on. Annele had fallen face down, and was weeping loudly. She didn't want to hear or see any more. Mother took away the dead lamb, and no longer let the sow go out in the pasture.

All afternoon Annele cried. Krančelis lay cuddled against her, now giving a short growl, now whining, now nuzzling her face or licking her hands, uneasy, showing how worried he was at not being able to raise Annele's spirits.

The girl petted him gratefully.

"What's the use, Krančeli, what's the use? The little lamb is gone, and he'll never ever return."

With sharp regret she blamed herself as well.

"If only I had looked up a tiny little moment earlier, it wouldn't have happened," she kept lamenting.

—※—

It was the middle of summer. Crack-crack! Crack-crack! – there was a burst of reports behind the forest.

"What's that crackling?"

"They're shooting, I guess. The duck hunt must have started. They say there are lots of ducks in the lake behind the forest."

"The lake? What lake? A real lake?"

"I don't know. That's what they say."

"Are they shooting ducks? How do they shoot them?"

Mother laughed.

"How can I tell you? I've never been to a duck hunt."

Crack – crack! Crack – crack!

Great flocks of birds were speeding across the barrens. Flap, flap, swiftly, swiftly, their beating wings made small waves of air.

There was great agitation behind the forest. Birds fled to save their lives.

Suddenly one of them began to revolve in the air, to fall. Slowly, then faster and faster, like a withered leaf from a tree, it came down with sloping wing. Not far from Annele, it fell to earth. Wings flailing the air, it rose again – fell, rose – fell, then remained nestled against the ground, its neck outstretched.

"Bird, dear bird, what happened to you, little bird?"

Annele ran up to it, lifted it up. Its head hung dangling down, its wings shimmered like the most expensive silk, the tender, downy breast was warm as warm, and in it, like a little clock, the little heart was still beating at feverish speed. Annele hugged it to her breast: "Little bird, my little bird." Blood dripped on her fingers.

"Blood!"

Annele hurried home. Maybe Mother would know, maybe she could save it.

"Mother, Mother!"

"What is it now?"

"A bird, covered in blood."

"A wild duck. Those hunters are all the same. They shoot and can't finish the job. One of its wings is smashed."

"Why do they have to shoot?"

"Go ask them."

"We've got to help it, Mommy!"

"It's beyond help."

The bird suddenly convulsed in the girl's arms. It died.

"Another life gone," she wailed plaintively. And then, full of rage: "I never ever want to set eyes on such hunters!"

The Magic of the Barrens

Whatever direction the winds come from, they roam freely across the barrens, and nothing stands in their way. Only the big boulder in the middle of the barrens offers a bit of shelter from them. One of its sides is sheer as a cliff, the other is bumpy and steep. The winds in their course have to make a detour around it. The boulder splits them and separates them, like the last couple in the children's game, and it is only beyond its shadow that they are able to join hands once again. The big boulder is Annele's mighty fortress, a favorite place for dreams and games, a faithful companion in whose shelter it is pleasant to while away the time.

Winds, too, are wonderful companions. There are many of them, all different, and they have many stories to tell, all different.

There's a sudden hiss in the air, the sickly grass of the barrens bends down, and the wind is here.

"Where do you come from?"

"Fork Farm."

"Are the cherries red at Fork Farm already?"

"Whole orchards full, whole orchards full. Red as beads, sweet as sugar. The boy from Fork Farm has his pockets full, and you haven't got any. Make friends with him and you'll get some too."

"Oh, who cares? I don't need that boy's cherries."

But the wind is long gone.

And another day, there's another one.

"Here I am, Annele."

"Were do you come from?"

"Spring Farm."

"How's Granny, how are the orchards, how's the forest, how's the river, how're the meadows?"

"Dear, lovely, full of blossoms, full of fruit. Come and visit, come and visit!"

And another day the wind runs by from a different direction.

"Where do you come from?"

"Bridefields Farm."

"Is that a fine farm?"

"It certainly is, it certainly is. White windows, high lintels, carved gates, a house that's snug and cozy."

And then comes a wind that is warm as down and soft as velvet. It's just a breeze.

It comes when the sky is high as a vault and blue as cornflowers in their first bloom and when there are tiny white clouds in the depths of the sky like tiny scattered bits of wool. This is a wind that is a rare, rare, rare visitor indeed, and Annele asks it:

"Where do you come from?"

"Paradise."

"Paradise! What's paradise like?"

"Sun hills, moon palaces, red roses, white roses."

And in an instant it's gone.

The winds are the servants of the clouds. They bring the clouds and take them away. Slowly during the morning, clouds float past with white, light sails, chasing black shadow boats across the barrens. Occasionally one cloud will collide with another, and then both shatter, disintegrate like two eggshells, vanish like smoke in the azure of the sky. Sometimes a cloud collapses like a tired wayfarer in the field of the sky, letting others pass by so they can go on their way. Soon another tired wayfarer joins it. Then a third and a fourth. Massed together, they expand in all sorts of ways – some horned, some angular. They form shapes: one like a Jew with a long white beard, a second like a mighty bird with outspread wings and a crooked beak, a third like a beautiful maiden with long hair and a gauzy gown. But look: hey presto! the beautiful maiden changes into a bearded Jew or a robber chieftain with a rooster's feather on his cap, and the mighty bird has shrunk to a mouse fleeing from a cat. Clouds can't ever quiet down, although they seem to be standing still. They are changeable, fidgety, playful like children.

Only those mighty clouds that have spent the day wandering all over the world with the thunderstorms are quieter and calmer. Their backs round, or angular and sharp, or carved in straight lines, they lie there after their day of hard work facing the sun like a huge mountain range. Red, rosy, or white as snow, they rise one after another with bottomless ravines and precipices between them. On their sharp-edged backs they carry towers and castles, and drawbridges span the ravines. Among these cloud castles, towers, staircases, and drawbridges Annele could let the heroes of all kinds of legends and stories accomplish their feats, and she was never tired of inventing new adventures for them.

Mighty deeds of valor were being performed in other parts of the world, and no one in the barrens had even an inkling of them.

⌁

Annele is sitting and thinking. The shadow of her head is wide and lies on her knees. The sun shrinks the shadow shorter and shorter.

She thinks about land, what else. The barrens are far too bare and poor. It's high time the flowers came out, but there's no sign of them. The grass, too, isn't getting any taller. There are places where large areas are covered with nothing but thistles. You'd better not try to walk barefoot there!

Father says this bare land is a gold mine. All right, it was a figure of speech. The gold mine, no doubt, is rye, wheat, barley, and potatoes. And maybe the clover field, too. Of course that's all very well! But that wasn't all. All of that was visible on the surface, but the earth was so big, and it was impossible that a piece of land like this should contain no more than that. Didn't the depths of the earth contain the Underground Kingdom, with cities, houses, lakes, forests, and magic gardens, as legends would have it? Did the great mountains of the world really have boundless grotto palaces whose walls were made of gold and jewels, and in which were gathered treasure troves so great there were none like them above ground? Did all these riches belong to the mountain spirits, and were they guarded by dwarves? Who could tell? Maybe the Pērkons girls, who now lived on the other side of the earth, in America, knew more about this. It was hardly likely, though. Čiepiņa certainly didn't even know the earth was round. And maybe it didn't matter to Čiepiņa.

But everything mattered to Annele. From morning till night she constantly felt her clothes, her hands, her braids being tugged by those same winds, by the sky and the sun and the piece of land they called the barrens. She felt them urging her constantly: guess my riddle, guess my riddle! But more than anything she wanted to know what was behind everything she saw and heard and felt and touched. Behind it all, behind it all! The thing she hungered for constantly, thirsted, wished for. In her childish way she imagined that everything she saw, felt, and knew was like the antennae of some large insect, while the insect itself remained invisible and unknown. Who are you, who are you, you? But no answer came. Fine. The insect, too, was only a figure of speech, of course. But was there anyone who knew more than this? Maybe the rainbow, which in an instant built its magic bridge in piles of clouds, maybe the wind, which dismantled and unraveled the image of the world and rearranged it again, maybe the cranes, who so jealously guarded their kingdom from human eyes. To Annele everything she saw and did not comprehend seemed wiser than a human being. And sometimes it felt as though there were only a thin little layer between what she saw and what she didn't see, and between what she knew and what she didn't know, like the thin sheet of ice over the brook in autumn. If only she could break it. She could with her thoughts. But thoughts don't endure. There is a place to which thoughts refuse to accompany you, where they themselves are at their wits' end.

But would she ever know everything anyway? Look, if you climb a bit higher: the very last little blue stripe on the horizon is never ever the last. There's one more beyond it, and another beyond that, like the waves in that little lake in the slough – as soon as one vanished and sank, a new one would rise in its stead, constantly, endlessly. Infinity!

Infinity! This was another one of those words you couldn't figure out no matter how much you thought. Endless and boundless! Where was there a thing you could call infinite? No beginning or end! When you began thinking about it, you'd shrink like a mote of dust while the thoughts expanded to such a huge size it felt as if they wanted to rend the blue canvas of the sky like a balloon filled with air. Infinity exists, but to think about it is like banging your head against a wall.

Thoughts!

Wonderful friends, persistent companions. The minute you open your eyes, they're there. Changeable like clouds, quick as breath and sometimes heavy as clods of dirt, when you're struggling with questions that don't allow themselves to be cracked, like petrified nuts. And they don't leave you alone, and you can't shake them off. Then, quick! you must start singing, and your heart is free again.

The boy from Fork Farm mustn't hear Annele's song. Because what does that rascal do? He impales Annele's songs on a spit, as it were, twists them, tortures them, plays the clown, what comes out is neither fish nor fowl, for he only knows how to yell, he can't sing. It's far better to keep your distance from a boy like that, somewhere where you can give your voice free rein, sing as loud and as far as you want. Fill your lungs full of breath like a bellows and then sing one verse of a song all in one go. Let the boy from Fork Farm try that – he won't be able to do it.

There are different days for different songs. Sunday morning is for sacred hymns. But they don't sound right in the barrens. They want to be sung together with other voices or with the rustling of the forest, or with the trumpets of an organ. When you sing them by yourself, they sound like a beggar's litanies. Cheerful songs are something else. They could compete with choirs of little birds, of whom there was a great abundance in the barrens, for in hatching season half a dozen little yellow open beaks would jump out toward you from every hoofprint on the ground.

It wasn't all that easy to add to one's collection of songs in the barrens. Father and Mother, who knew hundreds of songs, each went about their own work. There was no one to sing with, and so their songs had grown silent, songs that had seemed to grow up new every day like flowers in the forests and fields. Now Annele had to look for songs in books. In the school holidays Brother had left her a thick German book chock-full of the longest songs. For many of them Annele also knew the melody, for Brother used to sing them, but now, since she had listened to them by fits and starts, they were in her head like a scattered string of beads that she had to re-assemble. Drumming on the top of her head and her forehead with her fingers, the girl searched for trills and modulations until they finally escaped as if from a prison, found the word that matched them, and now her voice could run up and down them as if they were a staircase. Now that she had found the melody, the words, too, were easier to understand – they had been obscure as Annele read them in the foreign language.

> "Preisend mit viel schönen Re-eden
> Ihrer Länder Wert und Za-a-a-ahl,
> Ihrer Länder Wert und Zahl,
> Sassen viele deutsche Fürsten,
> Sassen viele deutsche Fürsten
> Einst zu Worms im Kaisersa-a-al,
> Einst zu Wo-o-orms im Kaisersaal."

And as these many German princes had endless conversations, arguments, and struggles in this long song, Annele had the feeling they were fluttering before her eyes in their wide cloaks and with glistening crowns on their heads. Full of enthusiasm at the words of the song, she fought the battles of the noble-minded and magnanimous princes against the base-hearted and ignominious ones, and with deep satisfaction she brought everything to a good conclusion.

There were special songs for when she was in a mischievous frame of mind. They weren't in any book, and she didn't have to learn them. Like naughty children in a forbidden orchard, they sneaked into her head all by themselves. There were Joskelis's songs, there were the high-spirited songs her sister and brother would bring home during the holidays. There were mocking songs by country people about the gentry, by journeymen and apprentices about their masters, there were songs in which the old patriarchs of the Bible, Abraham, Isaac, and Jacob, spun like tops through lines where the syllables were all chopped up. All this was inside Annele's head. To the sound of songs like those, she could skip in rhythm with all her might, supported by Krančelis, who interpreted each movement that was fast or out of the ordinary as an invitation to have a good romp and to let off steam in the sheer joy of his young limbs, barking, howling, and turning somersaults. The cows didn't let this hullabaloo deter them from the work of eating, but the sheep, with the impetuousness of a sudden fright, ran and huddled together. Their heads jerked up, and without stopping the mills of chewing their cud, they looked reproachfully and sternly at the two who had disturbed their routine, as though to say, "Now listen! What kind of crazy behavior is this?"

She'd sung all the songs many times through, and yet something wasn't as it should be. There was still a multitude of words and sounds forcing their way out of her. Then Annele let them go as they wished and whatever way they came out on her tongue. At such times she didn't even want Krančelis to listen to them, that's how different these words sounded. But they opened up her heart and flooded her breast with enthusiasm and her eyes with tears of joy, and in them were the sun, the winds, the sky, the clouds, and also a tiny, tiny bit of the invisible power that was behind all things.

The sky was like a deep blue lake. The whiteness of the clouds shone in it like snow. Cloud shadows, so light and joyful, were scattered across the barrens, passed over Annele's hands. If only she could have caught every one of them like a bird! The mirror that was the little lake behind the farm now vanished as though wiped away by a black hand, now began to glitter like a sparkling crystal bowl. As for the birch groves in the distance, it seemed as if someone were playfully throwing them into the sunshine, then jerking them back into the shadows once more. And yet there was no wind, but only a gentle warm breeze at this early hour.

The dew had not been shaken off the grass yet. Only one row of footsteps ran in the direction of the house. That's the direction in which Father had walked after herding the cattle while Annele slept in this Sunday morning.

Sunday morning! Was it just that it was Sunday morning? No, something unprecedented had taken place.

Annele threw down the wrap, threw down her head scarf, turned to face the caressing breeze, ran and fell into the grass of the barrens as into a mother's arms.

She nestled her cheek against the earth. Listening. What would she hear? Something wonderful for sure. The earth was fragrant. The air was fragrant. Where did such flowers bloom? Where? Where?

Her heart beat restlessly. What was it? What was happening? – Nothing but the passing shadow of a bird. And the soughing of trees in the distance.

Let them sough. Let them sough for a long, long time. The tips of grasses – the tips of grasses and a blue sky. Nothing else.

How could she daydream like this and forget her duties?

Woof-woof!

Krančelis yowled for help. He was awake. Fighting against a superior force. He hurled himself at the cows' tails, at their horns, as they thundered by like an army bound for forbidden territory. The bushes rushed by like a stream.

Annele struggled through the bushes, sank in the bog, jumped from alder stump to stump, and suddenly found herself up to her knees in thick grass.

This is where the cows were. Scattered, all of them, hungrily snatching for grass. Whenever their heads jerked up, grass stalks hung from them, pulled up by the roots; before they even managed to swallow that, they'd run and snatch more, quickly storing it in the compartments of their stomachs. Krančelis couldn't do a thing. Nose and tail raised, he swam in the tall grass as in a lake, hissing, blinking his eyes, for the panicles of the grasses and the flower heads lashed him like rods. It was high time for Annele to come with her switch. The cows had already caught sight of the herder. They already knew they'd done something bad. They braced themselves and jumped backward without waiting for a harsh punishment. Back into the bushes. As soon as Krančelis was back on firm ground, his barks wound themselves around the cows like the thongs of whips.

Meanwhile the herd girl herself no sooner waded into the grass than she stood still as if spellbound. What a place this was! What a meadow! It lay in the elbow of the forest as though on a pillow. Trees, their branches sunk into the grass, guarded it. It was like a huge bowl full of moisture, blossoms, sun-drenched scents.

She opened her arms, then pressed them to her over her breast. And began to pick the flowers avidly. She plucked them, pressed them to her breast, snuggled them against her cheek, and went on plucking.

At the edge of the forest, a cuckoo began to call. The girl was startled. And instantly left the flowers alone.

Oh dear, what am I doing? Just as greedy as the cows!

No! Let the flowers be, let them grow. There must be no gap. For never before had she seen such a beautiful meadow, so green a forest, so bright a sun, such large blossoms. Here it was, the thing she'd been expecting all morning. Let it grow untouched. Silent. Beautiful. Holy.

Summer?

Here it was. The real, true summer.

The moon was high in the sky. The pointed sickle had already bent together its horns, all that was left was a narrow rim. Once it was filled with light, the moon would be full.

Annele ran out on the barrens in the very circle of light. Not a cloud in the sky. Fields, farmstead, hills, all under the blue sheet of moonlight. The air was vibrating spookily. She swerved toward her shadow. It was black, as if sketched on the ground with charcoal. When she bent over suddenly, it shrank at her feet. When she flung herself to one side, to the other, the shadow skipped toward her as though playing with her and mimicking her. It was light as could be. She could play with it to her heart's content. Annele turned round and round, whirled, waved her arms about, fluttered them like wings, wreathing and entwining herself in her own aliveness and agility in order to see herself mirrored in her shadow. And the shadow, its rhythm fleetingly light, grotesque, drew her on into wilder and wilder recklessness and gaiety, caused her to invent ever new and impossible movements, turns, steps, and finally felt like a living creature, a kind of spooky playmate, whose nimble muteness drew loud laughter and shrieks of joy from her breast.

This hullabaloo was heard by Krančelis, who shot out into the barrens like a spinning top when you let go of it, rolling a ball of black shadows. In this blue infinity both of them felt like running.

But suddenly Annele's feet stopped as though a fence had been raised in front of her.

There was the forest. And beyond the forest, the lake, a lake sent by God.*

The thought of it suddenly transformed everything. This was no longer an ordinary forest, but a pinewoods out of a fairy tale; not the barrens by moonlight, but the infinite space of legend.

Who had seen it – this lake? Father had replied that it was like any other lake, while Miķelis, on being asked what a lake sent by God looked like, had simply said: – A puddle!

Such answers are not enough to satisfy Annele. How can a lake sent by God be just like any other lake, or even look like a puddle? Others lie nestled in their shores from eternity to eternity, but a lake sent by God suddenly, one fine day, begins to swirl, to ripple, to billow, to hiss, to rise up from its shores and to soar upwards suddenly into the air. Once there it roars like a "sea of water," looking for a place to land. They say this is what happened to the lake on the other side of the forest. For three days and three nights, they say, it lay in the air, until a young woman happened to say: it roars like a Slough. At once the lake descended, drowned the young woman, buried farms and fields. It's been lying there since time immemorial now, but it's raring to rise in the sky at any time. Maybe at this very moment, this bright moonlit night, when people have gone home back to their houses, while outside invisible and unknown forces go into action.

Krančelis growls, shakes his head, growls.

"What's that over there, Krančel, what's that over there?" The girl picks up the puppy and puts him in the crook of her arm.

The farmstead is far away. The new, unweathered roof flows together with the moonlight and seems to have vanished from the face of the earth. The buildings have shrunk to the size of little loaves.

Motionless, lifeless, the shadow lies next to Annele. The blue sheet of moonlight goes shimmering and rippling far, far into the distance.

Krančelis whimpers, restlessly moving his head from side to side, snorts, sniffs the distance. Utters a quick sound: "What's that over there? What's that over there?"

"The barrens, Krančel, the barrens," Annele reassures him, but her voice sounds kind of funny.

"Woof, woof! There *is* something here!" Krančelis scrambles to his front feet and would have jumped across Annele's arms if she hadn't held on to him in time.

*According to Latvian popular belief, there are lakes that fly through the air waiting for someone to say their name; when anyone utters the lake's name, the lake descends at that spot.

What is it that's here, on the barrens? The land has been lying here for thousands of years now. Thousands of feet have crossed it. Going back and forth. Back and forth. What happened to them? Could it be that they return on a blue moonlit night? Could this be the sound of their footsteps? Suppose she suddenly caught sight of them, suppose something happened to make her hair stand on end maybe? Annele can't see anything yet, but Krančelis can, Krančelis is restless.

"Krančel!"

Yes, something out there shimmers, moves about, is alive.

"Woof, woof! Let go! I'll catch it!" Krančelis struggles across her arms.

"There's nothing there. Nothing. The barrens, Krančel, just the barrens."

Two hearts beat side by side.

And the very next moment Annele does a sudden about-face, and off she runs.

The Birthday

Warm, warm were the days of September. The barrens were spun full of threads of white gossamer. At noon these would rise from the ground and sway in the air, shimmering faintly like silken sails set free. Annele ran around blowing them into the wind: let them go off to the warm countries!

The cranes were getting more and more restless day by day. In the cranes' marsh there was the sound of axes chopping. The veil of shrubs began to have holes, became thinner and thinner, and one morning you could already clearly see the two stately buildings on the neighbor's farm. He himself leapt from hummock to hummock cutting down alder bushes like reeds. The cranes stretched their beautiful necks, assembled by calling to each other, flew away and flew back over, as though waiting to see whether the human scarecrow would vanish at some point. In vain! It looked as though he were planning to get rid of every single bush and to lay level every single hummock, to drive away the cranes. "Be off, be off! There's no room for you here anymore. The plow and the harrow must break this ground!"

"I just wish he couldn't hurt the cranes," Annele thought defiantly, for she was wholeheartedly on the side of the cranes.

One sunny morning the cranes all rose in the air above the marsh. Restlessly and in confusion they flew, called to each other. One crane in particular flew round and round the others several times, calling the whole time, as though anxious whether all of them had risen from the marsh. Then it flew to take the lead. The others took their places in a vee, like two wings. They began to glide toward the sun.

Gentle, mysterious, their calls rang out at the head, the center, the ends of the line. In rhythm as it were. What were they calling? "Goodbye, goodbye!"

Annele stretched out her arms. Cranes! Beautiful, wise cranes! If only she knew how to fly like that! She didn't take her eyes off them until the slender world travelers sank out of sight behind a white cloud.

⟡

"Good morning, girl, how's it going?"

There was the neighbor, a switch in his hand and wearing the same blue stockings as in spring, as bright as if he had just put them on. He himself was sunburned as brown as a Gypsy and a lot thinner. That's how hard he'd been slaving away.

"I'm looking for workers. Maybe you'd like to come too, and help out with the potato harvest?" he now asked in his vivacious way of talking.

Annele didn't know what to say. She had a hard time talking to strangers. And besides the neighbor hadn't brought the books either. She was all for keeping promises.

The neighbor seemed to guess what she was thinking.

"You're going to get those books. Once the working season is over, I'll drive over to the pastor's house and bring some."

So he was planning to bring the books from the pastor's house! Then they wouldn't amount to much. The books from the pastor's house were brought to Annele by Līziņa, and she'd read all of them by now. Still, she didn't say a word, for the neighbor meant well.

"Well, how about it? Would you like to come?" the neighbor persisted.

"Where?"

"To the fields of River Estate. I've got potatoes planted there. You can work to your heart's content gathering them."

Yes, she'd be glad to go.

"Mother won't let me, though."

"Oh, I'm sure she will," the neighbor tossed his chin with conviction, flicked his switch and went off toward New Farm, swaying his hips slightly.

On his way back, he called out from a distance:

"Listen, girl, come on over to my house early tonight, will you? Your mother says it's all right."

"My mother says it's all right?" the girl was surprised.

And it was quite true. Toward evening Mother sent a herder to take Annele's place – an old woman from a nearby farm who had no steady employment. She was disabled, and a couple of times this summer Annele's mother, too, had given her an occasional loaf of bread to take home. This time she had come over perhaps with the same request, and she was only too happy to let Annele take the momentous trip to the estate.

Mother now told Annele to get ready at once: to bathe, to braid her hair tight, for early tomorrow morning there'd no longer be time for all that – they'd have to leave at daybreak. She gave her permission to wear her Sunday clothes, to put on the new rose-colored headscarf, but to take the old *pastalas* she wore every day, for they'd get full of mud anyhow as she waded along the furrows. For a basket Mother gave her her own handbasket, because an unfamiliar one might be too heavy or much too light for her, and the other people might laugh at a potato picker like her. Mother was unusually kind and benevolent. When she had given her all sorts of good admonitions on how to behave in a strange house and how to do a good job, she finally said the nicest thing of all:

"Well, if tomorrow wasn't such a special day for you, I wouldn't let you go."

"What special day?"

"Tomorrow's your ninth birthday," Mother said as though she were handing her a gift.

Birthday? Annele didn't understand. What kind of a day was that? Her ninth birthday! Was it so important she had to be told? Perhaps it was! For after all tomorrow she had an important job to do: she was going to help with the potato harvest, just like a grown-up. That alone made it apparent that the ninth must be a splendid sort of day, even though it was Annele's very first.

Aware of this ninth birthday, her spirit elated and courageous, the girl hurried over to the neighbor's house. The sun was setting by the boundary ditch. She followed the little zigzag footpath through the bushes that had been trodden by the neighbor. It was true she was also overcome by an old sense of diffidence: how on earth would she enter the strange farm? What would she say? What would she do? But remembering that tomorrow she would be nine years old, Annele grew ashamed of such diffidence and decided to act her age.

It's interesting that things and places always look different from a distance than they do up close. The neighbor's farm, too, did not tally in the least with the farm as she had imagined it, and now she was forced to rearrange quite a few things. There was a lot about it she found less agreeable than her fantasy image, and she seemed to be arguing about it with someone: no, that's not the way it is. There was no way it could be like that. The buildings were stately all right. Behind the farm the little hill sloped downward, and at the bottom two more newly begun buildings came in sight. In the yard, in front of the windows, there was a flowerbed with dahlias and asters, but these had been partly choked by nettles and weeds. The yard was littered, the paths had not been swept.

Annele was so busy observing and looking at all this that she quite forgot to go into the house. Now she was startled by a voice that called:

"What sort of a girl is that, huh? Gawking, like she's never seen a farm! Come here to play the spy, has she?"

Behind the flowerbed, in the open door, stood a woman. Young, rather heavyset. The black print headscarf she wore seemed to have been boldly tossed on – it concealed one ear, while a strand of hair hung over the other, down behind the jacket collar. This must be the mistress of the farm.

"Good evening! I came – –" Annele said hesitantly.

The woman had stuck her hand under the scarf and was scratching the nape of her neck.

"Are you the gal that wants to go along to the estate fields?"

Wants to, wants to?! Why, it was the neighbor who had come, had invited her of his own accord. Annele was surprised, but not a word crossed her lips.

The woman didn't wait for an answer. She turned around and went inside. Annele followed her. The mistress left again by another door, and the girl remained alone.

The room was big, the windows bright, the walls whitewashed, but the window-panes were flyspecked as thick as thick. The sheet that covered the table looked as if it hadn't been washed for a year, and on it were all kinds of dishes, some clean, some unwashed, some with scraps of food on them, as well as different articles of clothing, a crumpled scarf, a baby's socks, diapers. The bed had a balled-up sheet in one corner from last night, and wisps of straw had dropped out of the pallet onto the floor. The table was big, with shiny legs, the bed had a high head- and footboard, there was a varnished dresser along one wall, and chairs along the others. But all of them had something on top of them: either a sieve, or a hamper full of flour, or a scoop, or diapers, which were in every corner. The only free space for a person to stand was in the very middle of the room. Annele was amazed. Her little room at home was twice as small, but seemed to be much bigger, cleaner, and richer.

Behind the door through which the mistress had left, she could hear the voices of two women.

"A man like him thinks just like a child. Going from farm to farm looking for gals to gather potatoes. What can a little kid like that do?" said one. Annele recognized the mistress.

"Still, she does have two hands. And there's never enough of those. A child and an old person sometimes do a lot more than the loafers you've managed to hire as a farmhand and maidservant."

"Who hired those loafers? Not me. It was him, your clever son."

"What my son has done is done, but when *you* do something, somebody's got to pick up after you."

"But I've got everybody to think about. I'm the one that has to take care of everybody and stuff those big haversacks. How'm I going to manage to feed everyone tomorrow, butter and bread and all?"

At these words something heavy dropped on the ground. Annele did an about-face, with a single thought in her mind: "Got to get to the door! Home!"

What did she need the neighbors' bread for, or their butter? Or their potatoes?

But in front of the door stood the neighbor, who'd just come inside.

"Ah, how nice that you've come. Let's have some tea, let's have some tea. I've got a treat for you, some jam, huh? Bet she's made some. I brought home some sugar." He began to clear the table, putting the things that had been thrown on it into the bed, on the windowsills and chairs.

Annele could no longer run away. What would the neighbor say, what would Mother and Father say at home? And what would she tell them? Here she was, allowed to visit a stranger's home for the first time, and all she could think of was scurrying back home.

The farmer went out the door behind which the mistress was making such a racket. He spoke curtly.

"Where's the tea? Not made yet? Let's have some, let's have some! Where's the jam you cooked? Give it here! Give us some bread! Give us some butter!"

"Whoa, whoa there! Where's the fire? I don't have ten hands. There's the servants and cattle and kids, there's haversacks to be filled for the road."

"The cattle are fed by the maid, and Mother takes care of the kids – all you've got to do is attend to the food! Shame on you!"

"Who am I supposed to be ashamed of? That snotty chit of a girl?"

Annele put her hands over her ears. She didn't want to hear. Behind that door they were all bickering.

The farmer came in, carrying a little brown mug and a glass in one hand, and a black kettle in the other; he poured a hot dark liquid, first into the mug for Annele, then into the glass for himself. Behind him an elderly woman brought in some bread and a rather large pot whose rim was smeared.

"Here's the jam. – Floundering around like a bat in a bundle of tow."

She didn't say another word, but walked outside.

"Bring some butter, too, Mother," the farmer called after her.

"She's not going to go for butter, you can rest assured about that," replied the mother.

"Well, we'll manage just with jam, right, girl?" the farmer cheerfully invited Annele to express her agreement.

Annele suspected that the mistress didn't like to give away anything willingly, and she didn't want to eat anything, but also couldn't not eat so as not to hurt the farmer's feelings. He had managed to find a candle stub and lit it, for it was already getting dark in the room, and had then cut off a big slice of bread and spread it with a thick layer of jam. The bread was sour, underbaked and hard as a whetstone, while the jam was bluish black and bitter. But the farmer ate with relish, quickly, and immediately hurried outside again.

The mistress came in, picked up a couple of the things that were scattered on the bed and the chairs, put them back again, rummaged around in the dresser, apparently didn't find what she was looking for, came to the table.

Annele had the feeling that the mistress was looking only at her; she unwillingly bit into her bread, rolled it around in her mouth, couldn't swallow, every bite had a sharp aftertaste of iron. Finally she put the bread on the table and no longer touched it. The mistress picked it up. "I can certainly see what a fussy eater you are." Annele thought, Now she'll clear away the dishes, but everything was left where it was. She left as she had come.

The farmer's mother brought in a straw pallet, pushed a few chairs together along the wall, threw the little pallet across them: "You can sleep here. Where else can we put you?" – She blew out the candle stub in the bottleneck and left.

Annele thought for a while, waited a bit, not knowing what to do. But nobody came, there was no alternative but to lie down. Without taking off her clothes she stretched out on the pallet. There was no blanket, no pillow, and she dared not move for fear the chairs would slide each in a different direction. In the window loomed the nearby building, cold and rejecting – sadness weighed on her eyelids at this strange house where Annele felt so alone, alone – like someone banished to a wilderness. At last, however, darkness pressed her eyes shut, and she slept for a while.

Suddenly she awoke. The door to the kitchen opened, and candlelight sharply pierced the darkness of the room. The light was followed by the mistress, carrying a stuffed sack. She put the sack and a candle end on the table, sat down on a chair next to it, raised her foot and put it on the table as well, and began unrolling from it a long strip of dirty rag that gave off a foul odor. There was a deep, festering sore on her foot, with swollen edges.

The mistress took the candle end in one hand, and with the other began to squeeze the sore, her lips pressed together, sucking in her breath and looking around helplessly. She caught sight of Annele's eyes.

"It hurts. It hurts awful bad. I did tie on some cow manure, but it hurts like the dickens."

"On a sore like that, my mother puts bacon or pot cheese, or onions. There are also different kinds of herbs, but I don't know them."

"Oh, come on," the mistress said incredulously, "bacon, pot cheese, onions! As though you had to feed a sore like this!"

"How can she not know a thing that everybody else knows?" Annele wondered. And added a further instruction:

"And the sore has to be cleaned. It's got to be thoroughly washed with hot water and soap. The sore itself and the whole foot."

"Come on! What good can water do?"

"Yes, water! And if remedies don't work anymore at all, you have to pour the sore," Annele eagerly continued, for she had seen sores being healed.

"Pour? How do you do that?" the mistress asked curiously.

"My father had a sore on his foot that went to the bone. It just wouldn't heal at all. Some wool from his sock had gotten into the sore. When that happens, it doesn't heal. And then they started pouring it, and it healed within a week. And this is how you do it, you see: you boil a bucketful of water and let it cool till it's bearable, then take two ears of rye – they're boiled in water, too, till they're nice and clean – then put them on the sore and begin pouring the hot water over them with a dipper. And you just pour and pour for hours till the ears of rye draw the bits of wool out of the sore and it heals!"

"Come on, you don't think I'm going to fall for that, do you?" the mistress shook her head in disbelief, "I bet it's one of those superstitions, the kind they print in almanacs. – Oh damn, how it hurts!" she suddenly pressed her lips together again drawing in her breath, at which her mouth, illumined by the candle near it, expanded into something so huge and funny, detached from the other features of her face, which had vanished in the shadows, that Annele barely managed to turn her head the other way and bite her teeth into the pallet so as not to burst out laughing. But when she looked at the mistress again, she sat seemingly lost in thought, rocking her foot in both hands and looking at the candle pensively. Annele grew ashamed that she had laughed like that.

"Another thing that works is if you pound plantain leaves with the butt of an axe and then put them on the sore. They take away the heat, too, and make the wound heal," she hastened to make up for her naughtiness.

"Sure, sure, as if I had the time to fool around with all that rubbishy nonsense," the mistress said sullenly and again began to wrap her foot in the same dirty rags. Then she rose with difficulty and went outside. By the door she put her hand in front of the candle and blew it out. There was black darkness outside. Annele had the feeling that the mistress was dark herself and was entering darkness, and for some reason her heart suddenly felt a stab of pain.

The light outside was gray and dim when they came to wake Annele. She was chilled to the bone. And she didn't get warm during the ride, either, for a thick mist made the air damp and cool.

The field at the estate was big, with endless long furrows. As far as you could see in the mist, people were moving around like ants everywhere. The potatoes here had been planted for the servants and employees of the estate, and today was harvesting day, which is why they were all hurrying to harvest their share. Just last year, the

neighbor had had the overseer's job at the estate – that was why it was so easy for him to build his farm, and that was why he had still been given his potato acres in the estate's fields.

Annele ran quick as a little partridge: to the pile with two baskets, and back again with two. She'd been given the other basket by the neighbor's wife. She was ahead of the others with her row, she didn't want people to think she couldn't keep up with the others, that the neighbor's wife had to give her food from her haversack for nothing.

Suddenly the thick mist parted and out floated the sun, white and fiery. Commanding as a queen it took its place in the vast field of the heavens.

Was this ever beautiful! Everything was lit up. The big manor house with its fine white buildings, the row of red maples along the white highway, the yellow cluster of birches at the bend of the forest, and the mighty forest itself, ever green, which seemed to embrace all the rest in its wide, dark arms. The men stripped to their shirt-sleeves, for the sun hovered above the ground as it were, caressing and warming it so gently. Their hands worked twice as fast, their feet ran twice as fast now that for a moment they could gaze on the loveliness of the earth that they'd missed so long and that was so dear to their hearts.

At the manor house, the bell rang for the noon meal, and as if by magic everybody stopped work and hurried to the bread sacks. The neighbor, quick at eating and quick at work, was already by the wagon, unharnessed the horses from the plow, fed them. The farmhand and the maidservant sat down by the pile of potatoes waiting for their meal, but the mistress still loitered far down her furrow, apparently wanting to finish it. "Hey, why doesn't she come?" called the maidservant impatiently, clapping her hands. The farmer, too, walked toward her down the furrow, though not far, stopped, waited. Then she finally came, too, looking as if she were entangled in a heavy long skirt that was so ample it had close to a hundred folds. The master, his hands in his trouser pockets – as though there was no other way to keep them from working – said nothing, though his eyes roved uneasily.

Now the mistress untied the sack and slowly took from it bread, butter, meat, but all eyes eagerly looked at the wagon, in which there was yet another big tin container and a bowl. That container in itself was a conspicuous thing – it came from the manor, there were none like it in the farm households. It was prudent and thoughtful of the mistress that she had thought of making gruel. Now they could enjoy it with no less pleasure than in summer.

When the gruel had been poured into the bowl, the mistress began rummaging around in the sack, in the wagon, among the folds of her full skirt, faster and faster, with more and more agitation; she gave the sack a good shake, turned it inside out, shook it out again. Her arms dropped to her sides. "Oh well, those stinkers got left behind on the table at home," she said, visibly disappointed. It was the spoons she had been looking for and failed to find.

Again Annele burst out laughing. She quickly hid her laughter under her headscarf. But the neighbor's wife did look so funny as she expressed her openmouthed surprise that the spoons should have been in the haversack but that those stinkers had been left behind on the table at home. And she'd called the spoons "stinkers." What a funny woman!

"There aren't any spoons, but there *is* some gruel," the farmhand said curtly, picked up the bowl and raised it to his lips; two little rivulets flowed past his mustache from the corners of his lips; the maidservant laughed, pushed him away to keep him from slurping it all, a large part of the contents of the bowl was spilled on the ground, the maid took the rest and drank it, and only the dregs were left in the bowl, with no way to get at them.

The mistress filled the bowl again. "Go ahead, you have a drink, too," she urged her husband.

The farmer rose, wiped his knife on his trousers, collapsed the blade into the haft, put it in his pocket and left without a word.

At that moment, wild excitement and laughter dropped like a rocket into all the little groups who were eating their meal everywhere around them. They all jumped to their feet. From one pile of potatoes, out of the blue, a little hare had jumped out and was now making a run for it. And after it went all those young legs that had pins and needles in them from squatting in the furrows, and now leapt up as though a call had gone out: run to your heart's content! Every little group the hare shot past jumped to their feet at once and ran after it. As though the quick little hare were pulling all the young people behind him, tied to a string: the farmhands, maids, boys, and girls. Till one by one they got exhausted and, laughing, gave it up as hopeless. But when the little hare was out of danger, it turned back to face its pursuers, sat on its hind legs, ears erect, and waited defiantly: Come on, over here! Indeed, who could hurt it now? There it sat on the hill like the king of the forest himself. The sun flashed on its white chest, and the forest, weaving a vast garland, stood there as if to guard it and to threaten its attackers.

"They didn't catch it, they didn't catch it!" Annele rejoiced, taking part in this noontime hullabaloo with her eyes, her ears, and her whole being.

Behind her, somebody was speaking. It was the mistress.

"Did you see that? Running off again like his mouth was frozen shut, and not enough to eat or to drink. Now I ask you, couldn't he have taken a sip like that farmhand? Oh no! So what if there were no spoons? But no! And it's always like that, always. It's like I can't do anything right. I put on a long skirt, 'n' he goes: Why d'you waddle around like a duck? I put on a short skirt: What's with your skirt? Did the dogs chew it off? And it's always like that. Why can't things be all right? But no! What do I do with a husband like that? It's a crying shame!"

Annele looked around. Who was the mistress talking to? Nobody. There was nobody there. The farmhand and the maid had left to join the folks who were chasing the hare. But the mistress was looking Annele straight in the eye.

Is she speaking to me? Saying something to me? The girl suddenly felt scared. She flushed. Was she a grown-up, to be spoken to like this? She didn't know what to do with the mistress's words. Was it sorrow that weighed on the mistress and that she was pouring out to Annele? Cold and heavy it lay on her, pity suddenly filled her heart. Shame for having laughed at the mistress just a while ago. Yes, these neighbors were different, and so was their farm.

It was a good thing the farmer came back with his quick stride.

"To work, to work! Let's buckle down so we can get back on the road early. There's not a lot left to do, is there?"

But this "not a lot" refused to go at all well. At least so it seemed to Annele. When she carried her baskets to empty them, her legs would wobble kind of strangely, rubbing together at the knees. And the furrows seemed to be two, three times as long. She thought she'd never get to the end. And the afternoon seemed as long as the longest day of summer. No matter how often she peeked at the sun, it seemed to be standing still.

And then suddenly – look! – it was already down by the treetops. The maples were turning red, and the tips of the forest trees. The last furrow had been harvested, already the harrow had passed across it. Home! Home!

Her feet are happy again, her heart. Home! Annele feels a whole eternity has passed since she was home. Dear Father! Dear Mother! Krančelis! How they'll be waiting for her! Like a traveler from distant lands. After a big job of work successfully completed. How dear, how dear they are!

Quickly the fall evening grows dark. By the time they load the sacks, harness the horses, it's night. Annele rides in the first wagon with the neighbor and his wife. In a hollow between two sacks the mistress spreads a couple of empty sacks and invites the girl to stretch out, for – she says – Annele won't be able to keep her eyes open the whole long ride anyway. It wasn't an easy day, after all, she says, for a little polecat like her.

Annele is surprised how gently the mistress speaks now. Now the master, too, praises her for being a hard worker who didn't stay too far behind the grown-ups. They both speak harmoniously and kindly.

Annele's mind resists, of course, it wants to share all tribulations with the grown-ups, even a sleepless night, but her feet lie down by themselves. The mistress tosses her her own shawl, and the rhythm of the rolling wheels begins to lull her. The hoofbeats seem to sink into cotton wool, the muttering voices of the people in the wagon. Uphill – downhill, uphill – downhill rocks the wagon.

But suddenly something forgotten tears open her eyes almost by force. There was something, wasn't there? – – – something especially noteworthy about today – – what was it?

Her eyes watch the stars. Wonderful, shining stars above the tops of black pines. The treetops rise and fall, come toward her, are left behind, while the stars follow her without turning away, looking into her eyes. And it is they who guess what day it is today.

"Hey, did you forget? It's your birthday today, remember?" say the stars.

"Birthday!" Annele nearly exclaims out loud. Her first birthday.

And so lovely, so lovely! How warm the sun was. And the big job she'd completed. And now the stars! Dear stars! Millions and millions!

Wedding Shoes

What rider is this racing into the yard? – Annele stares. He raced inside and, making his fine horse prance, lingered in the middle of the courtyard for a while as the horse shifted from leg to leg. Now he takes his leave, doffing his cap with a long arm, swings his horse around and gallops away in the direction of Fork Farm. His cap is over one ear, and there's a big red paper rose pinned to the cap right by the visor. The visor gleams all black and new. He races past the girl, and she follows him with her eyes as far as she can see.

Mother brings her the noon meal.

"Mother, Mother, what rider was that?"

"He brought an invitation to a wedding."

"How did he do that?"

"Greetings from the bridegroom and the bride, and the wedding is Sunday morning."

"What wedding?"

"At Spring Farm. Don't you know Uncle Ansis is getting married on Sunday?"

"Uncle Avots? Uncle Ansis?" Annele claps her hands in surprise, then bends over at the waist and laughs and laughs.

"Hey, what are you laughing about? Is it so funny that Uncle is getting married? It's about time, you know."

"I don't know. I don't know. But how come he sends around a farmhand to have him invite our father? Why, Father and he are brothers."

"So what if they're brothers? A person can't go to a wedding uninvited. This is the second week that young fellow's been riding around. The invitations have gone out to parish after parish. Relatives of relatives, friends of friends. All over the place."

"Heavens – what an awful lot! What about children, though? Are children also invited? Me, too?"

"People bring their children as well. In their laps like little pots with handles," Mother laughs.

Annele laughs, too. Here's some fun again for a change!

"But what's it like at a wedding?"

"Guess we have to go and see for ourselves."

All this is to Annele's liking. She knows that if Mother is laughing like this and looking forward to the wedding, she might take Annele, too.

Good things seldom come alone. Toward the end of the week, Ģelžu Miķelis came with the two maidservants from Edgefield Farm. Miķelis came to help Father and also so there'd be somebody to watch the house and look after the animals while the people of the household went to the wedding; but the two maidservants had come along to drive home the Edgefield flock of sheep from the summer pasture. At Edgefield Farm all the fields had been harvested, and thus there were now pastures, much grassier and fatter than in the barrens; they needed to be grazed in a hurry before the frost came.

With a rush of joy, Annele watched the maids' arrival.

"I'm done, I'm done! That job is finished now. The sheep are healthy, not one has the least little bruise." Annele could hand them over with a clear conscience. And then she'd be free of them.

Both maids were strangers to her. The younger one, who had sparkling black eyes, was carrying something under her arm.

"A herder deserves to be paid. Here's what you've earned. The mistress told me to bring this for you."

Annele fingered the little parcel, which was wrapped in paper and tied with a string.

Shoes! And shoes were just what she needed, with Uncle's wedding just around the corner. Why, if you had no shoes you couldn't even go to a wedding! God was certainly provident!

Oh summer, summer! Like a supple willow switch it had bent to form a ring with two ends: one was the day when the Edgefield sheep were brought to New Farm, and the second was here now, the day they were driven home. Right here, in the pasture, Anlīze had given her Momma Laukmale's present and promised her a pair of shoes as her herder's pay.

"But where's Anlīze?" she asked the maids.

"Anlīze? Why should you care!" laughed the stranger. "Better separate those sheep of yours."

"This way, this way, sheep, this way!" Annele tried to separate them, but the sheep, which had grown accustomed to sharing the same pasture and the same sheepfold all summer, would not separate no matter what, and had to be driven into the sheepfolds to be separated.

This all took place amid much bleating on the part of the sheep, laughing on the part of the maids, and lots of running and chasing back and forth on everyone's part.

She didn't manage to get a closer look at her new possession until late that night when the day's work was over. Don't anyone dare get in my way, thought Annele as she raced excitedly to the little bundle wrapped in gray paper.

But her joy passed in a twinkling, like a straw fire. Annele picked up one shoe, then the other. Her face fell. Black, hard, and heavy like blocks of wood – that's what the shoes were like.

"Why're you standing there like that?" asked Mother.

"They're not shoes at all," Annele said dejectedly.

"Then what are they?"

"Blocks of wood," the girl muttered sulkily.

"Well, what did you think the shoes would look like?"

"Like Līziņa's shoes, soft and supple like stockings."

"Līziņa has city shoes. You won't get anywhere with those in the country. Here you've got to wade through the mud and across plowed fields. You need strong shoes. They'll be your school shoes, too."

"I'm not going to wear those," the girl said stubbornly and pushed the shoes away.

This exasperated her mother

"Well, have it your way. But if you don't wear them, you can't go to the wedding. I'm certainly not buying you another pair."

Oh yes! The wedding! Darn! The wedding! How could she show up at the wedding with shoes like that? But where would she get another pair? Oh dear, oh dear!

Her mother came in again after her outdoor chores and saw the girl still standing there, shedding tears at the wages she'd earned this summer. She regretted her harshness.

"Well, what are you standing there for? Try those shoes on first, why don't you? Maybe they're just fine."

The girl had to sit down and try on the shoes. It didn't do much good. Perhaps the shoes actually did fit somebody – but they certainly didn't fit Annele. When her foot rose, they didn't rise with it, and when her foot bent, they didn't bend with it. Whenever she took a step, the shoe – clatter, clatter, clatter! – came away from her heel, while some-

thing began to squeeze and pinch her toes dreadfully.

But Mother wanted the shoes to fit.

"That's all right, that's all right! I'm sure they'll start feeling comfortable in no time," she soothed Annele. "Considering that the shoes were not bought to measure, they're perfectly fine. They're a bit wide in the heel, that's all right, we'll put on two pairs of socks and stuff a little wad of cotton wool between the two socks, that'll fill it out."

"It's hurting my toes!"

"That's because your foot slides forward. When we fix the heel in place, it's not going to slide anywhere. And anyway what made you think you could flutter around with those shoes the way you do with your *pastalas*?" she added impatiently. "Don't think that you're the only one that has this problem. I can't tell you the number of people that come home from a wedding with their feet all raw! D'you know why? 'Cause their shoes rubbed them raw. Let's give them a good greasing with tallow, and you break them in a bit every day – by Sunday they'll be as soft as suede."

Realizing that her mother very much wanted Annele to be able to go to the wedding, and wishing this herself as well, Annele no longer dared to say anything bad about the shoes; indeed, as she lay in her bed and saw the shoes standing by the wall so peacefully and harmoniously, snuggling up against each other, it was hard for her to imagine that they were so wicked as not to yield to her feet, which were bursting to go to the wedding.

But every time Annele tried to stick her feet into the new shoes, her entire being was filled with the most ardent desire to get her feet out of them again as quickly as possible. Then she would flush with rage and call them all kinds of unflattering names.

On Sunday morning they all got up early. They had quite a distance to travel. The morning was almost as nice as it had been the time people at Spring Farm were getting ready to go to holy communion; you might say it was even nicer, for nobody was trying to make a solemn face or talking in a low voice, but everybody was elated and happy, talking, joking, and Father was even singing, "Where are you going, little rooster of mine?" Father looked so handsome in his new gray jacket and white dicky with its high collar, around which Mother tied a wide black silk tie with a knot so elaborate Father could neither tie or untie it himself. He said that now he was like a prisoner in chains, but his blue eyes laughed merrily.

"What are you so happy about? You're not at the wedding yet," scolded Mother, but she, too, had a smiling face.

"I'm happy that my wedding jacket still fits me."

"Don't you stretch those pockets even wider," Mother lightly slapped his hands in the trouser pockets.

"I'm just checking to see if they're still wide enough to hide my rough laborer's hands from those fine wedding guests."

Now Mother, too, began to get ready. To Annele's great amazement she put on a new alpaca dress, black and shiny like silk. On her head she put not the big embroidered bonnet, but a small German-style bonnet pinned up in the latest fashion. Over her shoulders she put the rainbow-colored silk shawl, the prettiest of all. Now she was fit to be seen at a wedding!

Father went out to see how far Miķelis had gotten with the horse. Annele, who had been running around barefoot all this time, now quickly, quickly put on her shoes with Mother's help. For some reason the two of them, as though by mutual agreement, hid this business from Father, as though by telling him they would diminish the wedding pleasures and spoil this morning's lovely harmony. It was better that Father should not know that Annele's shoes did not fit properly.

A good-sized wad of wool, stuffed into the heel between two socks, secured it in place quite firmly, and the fact that other empty spaces had also been filled here and there didn't allow the shoe to rub; only the tops of the shoes, hard as wood and flat, squeezed Annele's feet terribly and could in no way be corrected.

"Is that all right now?" asked Mother, and Annele replied that it was all right. There was no time to complain anymore. She herself believed it was all right. She tried to pick up her feet the way she had seen men kneading clay for new buildings. That way the joints didn't have to move so much. And she stopped thinking about the shoes. She thought about the wedding, the first she'd ever gone to in her life, she thought about Spring Farm, which she hadn't seen for half a year, she thought of Lulīte of Black Earth Farm and all her little sisters who would by now have grown bigger and smarter.

The horse was harnessed to the brown board wagon, and on the seat shone Mother's beautiful striped wool blanket. Miķelis held the reins while the wedding guests got in, then handed them to Father, taking a moment to check the harness to see if all the straps were all right, and running his hand over Gray's back, though it had already been brushed till it gleamed like silk, then accompanied the travelers on their journey with his kindly smile.

The morning was dry and clear. Splinters from last night's frost under a thin sheet of ice broke with a tinkling sound. The orchards were full of golden leaves. Like slow drops of water these detached themselves and flowed from the treetops, which had already been stripped almost bare and, each branching in its own individual way, joyfully stretched toward the serene morning sky as though relieved. The lower branches, too, and the golden carpet below the trees, stood out against the eastern sky with their rich dark glow. But here and there the calm mirrors of ponds in gilt frames flashed past the travelers.

Bells were beginning to tinkle on the highway. By the time the party reached the crossroads, they were coming from the east, the west, the north, poured together into one flood of sound, and flowed toward the south.

Wedding guests, wedding guests!

Whenever anyone came up from behind, they'd pass them and be in front of them in no time.

"Why don't you pull on the reins a bit, too, and show Gray the whip," Mother urged.

Annele would also have been thrilled to race along with all the bells, but Father was never one to race a horse, and just left his whip in the wagon. "Never mind, never mind, we'll get to the same place, don't you worry," he laughed.

Now eight hoofs and four bells struck in rhythm – a buggy drawn by two horses was passing them. The people in the wagon took a haughty look at the little gray horse and flew by like the wind.

"Fine horses!" praised Father.

"Yes, the person who owns those has a reason to be glad," said Mother.

"Rejoice in another's luck, and another's good fortune will be yours," replied Father.

"Yes, yes, that's what I always say, too, but –"

"But – well, but you see how our Gray is galloping, as though he had new blood in his veins. Aren't we following in the wake of their good fortune?"

All three of them laughed merrily. It was true that as the fine buggy was speeding by, Gray had suddenly lowered his head to his breast, snorted, shaken his head and ears, and begun racing after it at an easy trot like the finest racehorse.

"Rejoice in another's luck, and another's good fortune will be yours," Annele sang, but the rhythm of the wheels as they rolled along quickly broke up her singing. She didn't care. This was more like it. The faster, the better.

Not quite at the same time as the elegant buggy but soon after it our wedding party, too, drove into Spring Farm. The house, the yard were full of people. Horses had been tied to all the fences, pawing the ground, neighing, nickering softly. People were talking loudly and excitedly, as though calling to each other across great distances. Red-faced young fellows, white silk ribbons fluttering around their shoulders, ran in and out bareheaded. Now and then a little white dress would quickly dart outside, then disappear again hurriedly. Older men dressed in heavy homespun walked slowly across the threshold into the room at the other end of the house, where there was a table for the men, with smoking, brandy, and snacks.

Annele was immediately surrounded by a large crowd of children of all sizes and ages. There were Lulīte and her sisters, who always held hands like beads on a string, there was Ancīte from Edgefield Farm, there were the children of many relatives and friends. Through them all though, as though he didn't know what to do with his legs and his arms, darted a pudgy boy with a snub, turned-up nose and protruding calf eyes.

"Who's that girl?" he asked, quickly knotting Lulīte's scarf and hanging his whole weight from the scarf as if it was a swing. Lulīte began to choke, and she screamed.

"Will you leave me alone, you devil!" – she pushed and chased the boy away.

"Who's that girl? What kind of dress is that?"

The boy danced around Annele, and tore from her hands the overcoat she had half taken off.

"A poor sort of girl. A poor sort of dress," the boy puckered his lips scornfully, pointed his finger at Annele as he looked at the others, rolling his eyes so everybody laughed. Only Lulīte didn't.

"Don't listen to him. He's nasty. Your dress is pretty."

"Pretty as a peddler's rags, pretty as old Kate's bag of chaff." The boy jumped around, bouncing up and down on one leg.

Now Lulīte, too, laughed.

Annele's feelings were hurt. Here was her dress, which she had thought was pretty as a picture. Now they were making fun of it. The other girls actually did have more colorful and expensive dresses. The Laukmalis girl and Lulīte even had flounces at the neck and wrists, which looked particularly lovely.

"Don't you look at mine! It's made out of an old one of Mother's. And even though it's more elegant, not one girl here has one as beautifully made as yours," Lulīte comforted her.

"Say, who's that boy?" asked Annele.

"That's Anšelis from Mole Farm, Uncle Ansis's godson. He's a real rascal. Mother says he takes after his godfather."

The girls now joined hands and went to look at the wedding. Lulīte had already seen everything and reported that twelve bridesmaids, all in white dresses, were in the same room with the bride but wouldn't show themselves to anyone before the wedding party set off for church.

In the entryway women stood packed like sardines. Their skirts were twice as full as they themselves, and when the girls squeezed through, the women scolded that children shouldn't always get in the grown-ups' way.

"So what are kids supposed to do?" Lulīte replied, though not very loudly, and just continued to elbow her way forward. She whispered to Annele that these women were not farmers' wives, overseers, or people of quality, so why should she listen to them. No doubt they were hired women from neighboring farms or even women who had no employment. Lulīte wanted Annele to see her mother, who, she said, was wearing new silk shawls, and would put on different ones that night.

The big servants' living room had been cleared, leaving only bare walls with a long table the whole length of the room and narrow, newly made benches close to the wall. On these benches sat the farmers' wives and mothers one right next to the other. Annele's mother, with her rainbow silk shawl on a bright blue background and with blue fringes, and wearing her fashionable little bonnet, looked very elegant, while the mistress of Black Earth Farm wasn't half as fine, though her shawl was new and bright, much too bright, it stung your eyes. Momma Laukmale had a flounced bonnet and a yellow silk scarf tied over it, while over her shoulders she wore one of those unusual shawls that were the envy of all the other farmers' wives. The other women, too, were a sight to see, but the girls liked their own mothers best.

"My mother is the prettiest of all," said Lulīte.

"Not at all – my mother is," Annele was about to say, but she thought better of it, since Lulīte was a nice girl, and besides had defended her against the naughty boy, and so she allowed Lulīte's mother to be the prettiest.

"My sister Līziņa's going to be the prettiest bridesmaid, though," she boasted.

Lulīte agreed. After all, she herself didn't have an older sister.

Now people began to crowd around the tables. Some got up, others sat down. Soon they'd have to leave for church.

Anšelis wriggled through the wedding guests like a slowworm. He looked for the kids, waved his arm, calling everybody to run to the pavilion.

The "pavilion" was a big canvas tent of the type you see at fairs. It had been specially set up in the Spring Farm orchard for the present occasion. Inside were long tables and rough splintery benches, just like the ones in the house. Whenever the grown-ups didn't want the children underfoot, they would say, "What are you doing here? Run to the pavilion!" Thus the children believed the pavilion had been built just for them, and looked upon it as theirs.

The children ran into the pavilion. Anšelis jumped on a bench, for he was so small he disappeared from sight among the rest, and shouted:

"Kids, you know what? The grown-ups are off to church soon, but we can run straight across the hill and wait for rolls."

"Who needs more rolls! What a stupid idea! We've got whole tables full of them here," drawled Lulīte's brother Kristaps, who was big and slow. He didn't like Anšelis's fidgetiness.

"Gee, you don't even know what I'm talking about!" Anšelis retorted. "You think we need rolls? All we want is the run. Kids, who wants to come?"

All of them, all, surrounded Anšelis. They all wanted to come.

Anšelis ran to the hired hands' klēts, and the children after him like wild geese. In this klēts were the household's working clothes, which they did not need today. Sheepskin jackets, quilted vests, woolen wraps, blankets. They all grabbed whatever they could get, threw it over their heads and muffled their faces so they wouldn't be recognized. That's what Anšelis told them to do. Then they all ran off behind the farm buildings, for in the yard the wedding guests were already beginning to gather and to get ready for the ride to church. The farmhands who had come along to be the drivers of the more genteel farmers drove up with the buggies, cracking their whips defiantly, the well-fed horses pawed the ground, stamped their hoofs, snorted and shook their heads, and the harness bells began to jingle, while their clappers clicked without interruption.

The church was not far from Spring Farm. If you went straight through the woods, it was no more than two miles or so. As a result there'd be no dashing ride for the wedding party, which is why it had been decided to take a sweeping detour around the fields so that the line of drivers could stretch out as in a polonaise and then appear on the highway in all its magnificence. There were also triumphal arches, one where the fields of Spring Farm ended, the other at the entrance to the highway.

When the children reached the top of the hill, they heard the line of wagons and buggies begin to move. The wagons rumbled, there was a clattering of hooves, a tinkling of bells, and a jingling of harness bells, and all of this flowed together in a vast jangling cloud that reached them quick as the wind through the clear autumn air. Though the drivers had to take a sharp curve down below until they reached the end of the road and then had to drive up the steep hill, the children had barely had time to reach the highway and to throw themselves in the ditch when the first horses' heads appeared over the hill. This was the driver who was in charge of the buggy that carried the bride and groom, the same man who had fed his black horses for four weeks until they were so sleek not a drop of water would stay on their back. As they raced up the hill, the horses had been startled by the children, who were waiting for their rolls squatting in the ditch on the other side of the road, and now they snorted as they pulled along and tossed the buggy like a feather. In the buggy, Uncle Ansis rose to his feet, seized hold of the reins and stopped the horses with one jerk. Strong as a bear – that was Uncle. The horses reared on their hind legs, dug in their front legs in the gravel of the road, continued at a gallop a while longer, and then slowed down to a smooth canter. Uncle sat down. His gleaming wide eyes flashed like steel, and his mouth was stern. Now she could no longer see anything, for she had to protect her eyes. Rolls and flatcakes came raining down from the wagons of the wedding party. The wedding guests were in a hurry to get rid of them, since they saw the ditch full of expectant children and had no hope of meeting up with any more, as the church was quite close by. Annele was dying to see them all, the wrap slid off her head, and she forgot to be careful not to show her face. But the horses were running too fast. From one wagon, a woman stared long and attentively, and looked back as if she couldn't believe her eyes. It was Mother.

"Gee, I wonder if this was really a good idea," Annele suddenly thought.

At the very edge of the ditch, off to the side, like a big bug, a horse and wagon had been waiting for the wedding party to race past. Now the horse continued trotting slowly in the direction of Spring Farm. In the wagon sat an older woman swathed in many shawls.

"Rolls, rolls! Who's got rolls?" called Anšelis, standing in the middle of the road. He took the handfuls of rolls he was given and threw them after the woman in the wagon. Some of them hit her back, others fell into the wagon, others flew past and rolled down the road.

The woman turned around and shook her whip at them.

"Oh children, children! What a godless lot you are! Spoiled, naughty children. Throwing about God's gift! Rolling God's gift down the road like a toy! Just you wait!"

She scolded and threatened them for a long time, until the horse carried her away and the wind bore away her words.

Anšelis didn't listen, but took to his heels. And all the rest after him one by one. Only Annele suddenly couldn't move. Her feet hurt as if they were on fire, and she flattened herself against the ground. The wads of wool that were supposed to stay in the places that pinched had moved and gone further up. The thing to do now was to get them back in place, but this neither Annele nor Lulīte, who as a true and loyal friend would not abandon her in her trouble, knew how to do.

"Wait, wait!" Lulīte called. "Help Annele!"

"Look, kids, look at those blocks of wood that girl has on her feet! Are you a cripple?" Anšelis jumped around pointing at the wads of wool that had been stuffed in Annele's shoes. "So why'd you come crawling to the wedding if you don't have proper shoes?"

Everybody laughed, but Annele's eyes filled with tears. So that's what that boy was like. Even though she had gone running to catch rolls with him, he had no sympathy with her at all, but just made fun of her and teased her.

She and Lulīte were the very last to get back to Spring Farm. The other children and Anšelis had already put back their disguise clothes in the farmhands' *klēts*, and they too went there by a roundabout route. Just then, the woman whose back

Anšelis had pelted with rolls came driving in from the other direction. Anšelis, his hands in his pants pockets, was walking around the yard like an overseer.

"Listen, aren't you that rascal that was throwing God's gift all over the place?" the woman, who was a distant relative from near the Lithuanian border, shook one uplifted finger and a roll at Anšelis. Anšelis shrugged his shoulders till they were up to his ears and turned his neck between them from side to side as if to say: what does that woman want from me? I don't understand a thing.

"But those gals were definitely there," the stranger pointed at the two girls, who were timidly creeping out of the farmhands' *klēts*.

"Yes, yes, they were certainly there. Awful girls," said Anšelis.

The girls slammed the door and fled.

"See what idiots they are?" Anšelis called after them.

Who had first mentioned that the children of the wedding guests themselves had lain in wait in a ditch by the highway waiting for rolls? Be that as it may, the wedding guests now knew. The mothers questioned their children. Anšelis protested his innocence so hard that his ears were burning, and his mother believed him, too. So what if the others had run to the highway? Not her boy! The other culprits all kept silent. You'd have thought they were mute. But Annele couldn't conceal anything from her mother. Yes, she said, she had been there. "Oh dear, oh dear, child, I never thought you'd disgrace me so!" Mother scolded her and thus spoiled all of Annele's pleasure in the wedding, for if Mother felt disgraced then wasn't it even more disgraceful that Annele had gotten into mischief and then mingled with these strangers who might be pointing their fingers at her?

Lulīte disagreed.

"If you keep listening to the grown-ups, you'll never manage to get into mischief at all. Why don't we go and look at the bride instead?"

The girls fought their way through the throng of wedding guests. There, people were already sitting down to eat. At the very end of the table, against the wall of the farmhands' corner of the house which was decorated all over with garlands, paper tassels, little flags, and roses, sat Uncle Ansis and a beautiful young woman with big brown eyes and cheeks like apples. In front of them burned two tall white candles, though it was still day outside. To the right of the bride twelve bridesmaids sat in a row all dressed in white, and on the other side facing each was a groomsman with a nosegay of myrtle and long white silk ribbons on his right shoulder. The bridesmaids would put tiny bits of food on their plates and just nibble at it a bit, for they were tightly laced into their bodices, while around their hips their gowns ballooned like clouds. They had little garlands of flowers on their heads, each one different. Alma from Gladden Farm had red poppies, while Līziņa had apple blossoms.

"They're all pretty, but Līziņa is prettiest of all," said Annele just as she had before.

"That's true. There's not one bridesmaid as pretty as Līziņa," agreed Lulīte, after examining the bridesmaids with a critical eye.

The young couple rose and with them their entire table. Immediately others sat down at the table. They'd been waiting their turn. Twelve musicians began to blow so loudly that the thick walls of Spring Farm shook, and in the small space that had been cleared in the large room, the new husband led out his bride and was the first to begin the dance. Behind him the twelve white bridesmaids and their groomsmen turned round and round, round and round, like white foam wheels with black hubs in the middle. Now other full-skirted figures joined the dance: blue, green, red, yellow. The rooms were so small they had to turn round and round in the same spot. The trumpets blared, people were yelling at the top of their lungs in order to be heard by their neighbors, and from the adjacent rooms came the same deafening noise, for there the men were sitting around the tables playing cards, telling jokes, arguing, teasing each other, laughing, and drinking. Outside, facing each of the windows, a dog sat howling lustily. The Spring Farm dog, shaggy Citron, had called together his brothers to share the good things that dropped from the wedding tables, and in return they helped him bear his sorrows, howling with him enough to wake the dead. Now and then the musicians relaxed their puffed-up cheeks for a little while, wiped their perspiration, drank a tankard of beer, and let loose again. While they took a break, the maids would sprinkle the clay floor from big dippers. But as soon as the dancers began stamping around again, the dust would swirl like mist.

Nimble as a goat, Anšelis elbowed his way through the guests looking for the children. When he found one, he'd tell them, "What are you standing around for gaping? We're going to have our own ball! To the pavilion, everybody!"

No matter what escapades Anšelis had been responsible for, all he had to do was call and everybody appeared. In the pavilion the children had more space than all the guests and musicians combined had in the house. They could hear the music from the house, muffled but still loud enough to be earsplitting, and the dogs, which had been chased away from the windows, sat in the corner of the orchard, howling with the trumpets as loudly as they could. Anšelis arranged the children in pairs and organized a *française*. He whirled around himself, flinging himself toward the right, then toward the left, and flung the others, bowed, taught the others to bow, but was much too impatient, stern, and insistent and, most importantly, was no good at dancing himself. When he would call "mill!" all the children knew what to do, but when he would call "chai," no one knew. "Chai" stood for "chaine," a chain or braid, one of the favorite figures of the *française*. Anšelis had watched it and thought he could carry out what he had seen, but failed miserably. Nothing came of the chain. Instead there was a fight, for the boys couldn't stand being called "bears" and "clods" by a teacher who was himself no good at dancing. Anšelis got a sound beating and escaped behind the pavilion. From the outside Anšelis's plump little cheeks, snub nose, and a long, stuck-out tongue pressed themselves into the canvas of the tent. That was his revenge.

No one ever found out whose punishing hand it was that rose to the challenge. It only took a moment. The face vanished, followed by a horrible yell: "My nose! My nose!"

"Now Anšelis's nose is done for!" said Lulīte, frightened, and they all became motionless with fear, for all of them felt guilty. Anšelis yelled at the top of his voice, and with his bloody nose ran to look for his mother.

The children ran into the corner of the pavilion like lambs fleeing from a wolf. Where else could they go? Outside it was night, and Anšelis was with the guests.

Anšelis's mother came in, stern as a judge. Who did it? Who dared? Who aimed for it? Who hit it?

Anšelis wiped his nose, which was no longer bleeding too much, and kept pointing: this one and that one. This one and that one. They were all to blame.

If they were all to blame, Anšelis's mother scolded them all, and so they all became Anšelis's enemies.

"I don't want to play with kids like that," he squalled, sobbing.

"All right, all right, we're leaving, we're leaving. I'm certainly not going to let my son be beaten almost to death by such riffraff," said his mother looking around fiercely, and led away the apple of her eye.

This was the finale of all the wedding pleasures.

In all this hullabaloo, someone had stepped on Annele's feet, and they hurt so badly that she had only one wish: to go home!

Limping, she crept through the house and found her father in one of the small rooms at the farmer's end, shrouded in blue smoke that was so thick you could have cut it with a knife. Father was smoking his pipe and watching a card game. All the conversations had been finished, all the jokes told, and even the laughter was slower. Knock, knock! – the players' fists hit the table. The girl came up to her father and nestled her head against him.

"Yes, yes, lass, we're leaving in a minute," he answered, guessing her thoughts.

Granny, who had been up all night like a benevolent spirit, seeing to it that no one went hungry or left empty-handed without wedding rolls, came over and put a white sack full of wedding bread in the wagon. "You are coming back again around nightfall tomorrow, aren't you?" she asked.

"Tomorrow? I doubt it. Tomorrow's a workday for us. And anyway, will you have enough rolls?"

"They're just baking new ones in the ovens," Granny answered.

Gray began to canter.

Trumpets sound, then abate. The sound becomes softer and softer. As though blown away by the breeze – finally a last trumpet suddenly peals, and that's the end. Night embraces the travelers soft and silent like a mother who's been waiting outside for her family.

The girl moans and fidgets, moans and fidgets. She can't sit still.

"What's wrong with you?" Mother asks impatiently.

"The shoes," is her barely audible reply.

"The shoes, the shoes! The shoes are fine. It's just your feet that are no good. You're always complaining about them."

"But why don't I have proper ones?"

"Proper ones? What's the difference, as long as they're shoes? Seems like you have the feet of a princess," Mother scolds her and adds: "How come they were fine this morning when you left for the wedding?"

"Shoes? Shoes? What about your shoes?" Father asks as well now, and feels Annele's feet. "You know what? These are nothing but blocks of wood. Take them off!"

Annele doesn't have to be told twice.

"We'll give those blocks back to the peddler," laughs Father, takes Annele's feet in his lap and hides them under his fur coat. Then, in a comical voice, he recites the well-known anecdote:

"Where're you off to?"

"To the wedding, to the wedding!" he answers in a snappy voice, bouncing the girl's feet up and down.

"Where have you come from?"

"From the wedding! From the d-a-amn wedding!" he imitates the growly voice of someone who has a hangover.

They all laugh. Annele loudest of all.

"Well now, this is how you should come home from a wedding!" says Father and pulls on the reins. Snorting joyfully, Gray begins to run, and the road turns brighter and brighter as a barely perceptible glow appears in the east.

Autumn

The wind that had one dark morning suddenly started blowing from the corner of the forest where the mysterious forest ranger's farm lay was harsh and relentless. It had come to stay, and had no intention of changing. It blew away the last vestiges of summer. The corner of the forest was like a magician's cauldron, running over, boiling, sending endless mountains of clouds across the barrens. All the steam, it seemed, was first spun into a thick, gray mass of rain in that corner, and then some invisible mower of clouds tossed it across the world in thick spouting swaths. It never changed, morning, noon, or night. Each day came with a new blanket of forgetfulness to cover what had once been. The silvery light of summer, the velvety cries of the cranes, lighthearted footsteps, and a lighthearted mind – gone, all gone now!

In the mornings Annele would leave the house carefully bundled up in her wrap, which during the summer had been forgotten in a different corner of the barrens every day. The wrap never had time to get dry overnight, it was heavy, pulled her head back, smelled like lye, but nevertheless protected her somewhat, and warmed the wind that tirelessly tried to get at her young limbs, sharp as nettles.

The pasture lay into the wind. But the animals hated the sharp switches of rain in their eyes. Their heads tilted to one side, the sheep bleating piteously, the whole herd steered toward Fork Farm, and Annele gave in to their wisdom, spread out her wrap like a sail into the wind, and followed without resistance. Not until they reached the boundary road did she run ahead to turn them aside. Just as before, they all now headed back, heads tilted to one side, straight for the forest. Here their rear was somewhat protected. The sheep made for the bushes, but the effect of the rain was far worse here: dripping, rolling spouts of pearls from every little twig abundantly added to the bounty from the sky. Complaining incessantly and murmuring piteously, the sheep would hastily snatch a mouthful of grass here and there, but refused to graze anywhere for a longer period. The chilly dampness kept both the animals and their human herder in constant motion.

The workday dragged on without interruption from morning till night, for now the animals were no longer driven home at noon. The fields were empty, and the roads. You could look and look forever without seeing another human being. In vain Annele's eyes searched for the flaxen-headed boy from Fork Farm as well. At Fork Farm, as at any well-established farm, there was probably enough fodder, and the cattle were already being kept in the stables. Envy stung her that even this boy was not outside. Why did he have it so good when Annele didn't?

Sometimes the sky can be deceptive, too. For a short time the thick mass of clouds turns paler, the raindrops fall less frequently, stop altogether. If a bird flies up now, as I count to ten, fifteen, no, twenty, then the rain will stop by the end of the day and we'll have nice weather again. And Annele counts: twenty, fifty, a hundred, two hundred – but the sky is still deserted. And when she has long since given up hope, a black dot emerges among the clouds, sticks it out for a while, tossing in the face of the storm and then drops like a rock, its wings drawn back.

An hour has sixty minutes, a minute has sixty seconds; sixty steps – and one minute is over. Once, twice, three times sixty – how endlessly far you have to walk till you've walked an hour. And in the middle Annele always loses count. Then she has to start from scratch. Surely by now the hour must have passed, or even two or three, she's done so much counting, yet it seems that time hasn't moved on a bit. In the sky, even though overcast, there is none of that brightness that indicates noon, and so she can't have a taste of her noonday bread yet. Otherwise the rest of the day might turn out much too long. The wind hisses, and rain falls ceaselessly, ceaselessly with a small, choppy noise on her head, on her clothes. She can't read, can't knit. As for songs – they're always at hand, of course, but what is she to do with them? The rain is constantly in the way, it won't let a song through. Fearfully the song shrinks back and clings to the singer, weighs on her.

The cattle are getting restless. They struggle to go home. To drive them back, into the wind, is no longer possible. The cattle sense that evening is approaching. You can stand in their way and intercept them, but the whole herd slides past, impossible to stop. By the time they reach the gate, it's almost twilight, too. Dusk falls quickly. Day is over, faster than expected.

The fire is burning in the little cookstove. Annele looks into its mouth, hunkering there like a little hare, wet herder clothes and all. Warmth begins to creep into her limbs, and the warmer she gets, the more a cloud of steam begins to surround her. Krančelis presses close to her with his furry coat, whining and asking her to forgive him. He's been a faithless friend, saving his own skin today.

"Forgive me, Annele, forgive me, you do understand, don't you? When it's raining I can't go with you. I prefer being inside my kennel in the dry straw."

Yes, Annele can understand that.

One day the roosters crow in the afternoon, crow late in the evening. You can hear big Goldencrest even in the house. "Listen to that loudmouth!" Mother is glad. "Now we'll finally have a change in the weather. Now we'll finally get to see the sun again."

The rain is over at last, but there is no sun. Instead, there are thick walls of fog, which no wind comes to break up. A hundred paces from the farm, and you can no longer see the house. A dried-up thistle leaps up out of the fog, thick as a shrub, filled with countless reddish brown beads – all the grasses in the barrens wear this heavy jewelry of tears. Wherever the cattle go, they leave black rows of tracks. Annele's *pastalas* are soaking wet. Neither the herder nor the herd feel like stopping, but where will they find a better place? Wherever they go, the fog locks them inside an eerie solitude, where they can no longer see the farm, nor the surroundings, nor a single living creature.

Suddenly the blows of a crowbar split the fog. A small fire flickers dimly. Annele's heart suddenly trembles with joy. The barrens are alive.

The little fire is burning on the head of the big boulder. All around, down to its very feet, the boulder has been laid bare by means of a deep ditch, which is slowly oozing full of brown water. Father is working nearby and seemingly does not even see the crowd of new arrivals that now surround his fire. Father is doing important work. At times like this he is not in the habit of looking, or talking for that matter. If she were to ask him a question, she can already tell what his answer would be. "Ask your eyes," is what Father would say. He looks fierce as could be, but the boulder, too, seems fierce, and they seem to be at war with each other. The boulder must perish, that's been decided. But Annele is sorry for the boulder. All summer it has been her good friend and shelter from the winds. What would the barrens be without it! I wish it was impossible to hurt it, she thinks, but she herself can't accept such thoughts, for in that case Father's work would be futile.

And besides Father isn't going to give in. Out of the question. He's going to finish what he's started.

Here's a little stack of white, dry wood, covered with resin like drops of honey. If you add this wood to the fire, flames shoot up crackling, sending up streams of sparks. Annele puts her hand on the boulder: the stone is hot as a stove. Father grabs the crowbar, hits the boulder a couple of times on the forehead, shakes his head. Not enough yet. Weighing them in his hands, he selects even heavier logs matted with resin. Now the flames shoot even higher. Jumping this way and that, Father's feet sink up to their knees in the brown water, his face is sooty with the black smoke from the resin, and big drops of sweat run down it, leaving little white tracks. Thus he throws log after log, raps with his crowbar, pokes the fire: the flames roar, resin rains down snorting like foam overflowing a kettle, the fog pushes back the smoke, sparks come floating down. Like hell itself. But Annele likes this hell. She can't stir from the spot.

But now Father has caught sight of her. Sternly he shouts:

"Run! Drive the cattle further away! Turn your back! Wrap something around your head!"

A stupefying explosion! The flock of sheep vanishes quick as a flash. Around the boulder, something falls crackling like hail. But the blows of the crowbar fall among this hail hurriedly, without interruption.

When Annele returns to the boulder, Father stands there wiping his perspiration on his sleeve.

"Finished! Come and take a look!"

There lies the boulder, split crisscross right down the middle. Shattered in all four directions it lies in its own grave. A layer of countless fragments covers the ground.

"Oh dear!" exclaims Annele.

"Yes, how about that?" Father looks at her smiling and happy. He stands there in his shirtsleeves as though it were summer, arms crossed, having a bit of a rest, then grabs the crowbar again, strikes at the open cracks, throws the fragments across the edge of the little ditch.

"Take a look at that. Doesn't it look like a big pumpkin split in half?"

"Yes, and inside it's so sparkly and shiny. You'd never have thought it would be, judging from the outside. It was so gray."

"That's granite for you. On the outside the wind and the rain had rubbed it smooth and gray, but inside it's fresh and pink like young flesh."

"Is the boulder alive, then?" Annele asks now, timidly trying to meet her father's eyes.

But Father no longer replies. Merrily and swiftly, the rhythm of his work flows on. Each split-off fragment must now be broken up into smaller pieces. Again the fire roars, the resin rains down, smoke rises into the air, flakes of soot descend, the crowbar rings out.

Annele collects the little splinters that glow pink in the gray grass. Each splinter is made up of countless smaller ones. And they're all put together as though someone had done it with a careful hand. One is bright red, another greenish, another silvery gray, another bluish. And each one radiates a sort of tiny little gleam, but all of them together glow so intensely that it makes Annele want to touch them to see if they are warm.

How beautiful the stone is inside! But surely precious stones must be a thousand times more beautiful? And precious stones are hidden in the earth. So the earth really is full of marvels. Maybe right here, under her feet, the barrens hide wonders that cannot be expressed by mortal men. Why don't people look for them? She's never heard of any present-day person who's been in the Lower World and seen anything remarkable. All the stories about wondrous things begin with the words "my great-grandfather on my father's side." Marvels appear no later than great-grandfather's time. Everything that has happened, happened in the old days. Marvels are scared of the present. Wonder if there will ever be a time when they appear again? Annele would love to live to see that day!

Mother comes through the fog bringing the midday meal. She puts it on the split boulder, looks at everything, and clasps her hands with surprise.

"Husband, husband, look at what you've done! Why do you struggle here all alone like a giant? You'll overstrain yourself, see if you don't, and get sick."

She realizes that Father is working in his shirtsleeves, and scolds anxiously:

"Have you lost your mind? In your shirtsleeves, as though it was haymaking season! While the fog soaks everything like lead."

"But I've got fires all around me here! And even if some part of the body draws the cold, it doesn't matter. If you keep on working, your blood distributes any ill effects," Father says merrily.

The bowl of food, the spoons, the bread have been placed on the pink stone as though on a tray.

"Just yesterday the insides of the stone thought they'd never ever see the sun, and now we're using them as our table," said Annele.

"Yes, and soon this giant of a boulder will make the foundation of new buildings. We'll build a threshing barn, we'll build a house. This will all come in useful," Father said, smoothing back his hair with one hand and straightening his shirt collar and sleeves before he picked up the bread.

"Sure you'll build them, but d'you think the buildings will be yours, or that you'll spend your life in them?" said Mother and sighed.

"Am I the only person on earth? If I don't live in them, somebody else will. Just like I've lived within walls built by other people. A person has to take care of other people."

Fierce and quick, Mother replies:

"A person has to do his work, but you go to extremes. You don't ask: am I strong enough to do this or not, you just rush in like a bear."

"And I get a few things done with God's help," Father says, smiling calmly and breaking his bread.

"Oh yes, your brothers are smart. Just like it says in the stories."

"What if they are, Mother? I'm no slave who can be pushed around, though. It's what I want to do myself – I like working hard like this. At Spring Farm everything was done the old way, and I was getting bored with it. But here, almost every day, there's something new to do, where you can use your strength and intelligence. Having fields and buildings grow under your hands – isn't that worth something?"

"Yes, and I only wish they were ours," Mother sighed, but there was no answer. Father changed the subject.

"I think it's time to stop taking the animals out to pasture. No need to get the child soaked for days on end. Why, the barrens are bare as the palm of your hand."

Mother agreed.

She had also thought so. The neighbors, who had better pastures, had had their cattle in the barns for a couple of weeks now. It was late in the season, and the snow might start falling any day now.

"If only the snow would hurry up and come soon. Then Miķelis will come and bring a second horse to help, and we can begin collecting rocks all over the barrens. We'll drag this treasure home, too. There'll be fine rides for you – you wait and see!" Father claps Annele on her shoulder to cheer her up.

The People of the Afterlife

When people have lived their life, they pass away into the afterlife. What do they do there, how do they live? We can only guess – no one is destined to know the real truth. We know only as much about those who have passed over into the afterlife as they have left us to remember them by here on earth. Some leave behind a great memory, others one of little consequence, and some vanish like smoke in the wind, and no one remembers the place they occupied in life. You can leave behind a good or a bad memory. People recall those who leave a good memory for a long time, while a bad memory is bitter in people's mouth.

Among the people of the afterlife, Annele has friends she often thinks about. One of them is dear Eņģele, the woman with the strange name that Mother has told her so much about. The times in which Eņģele lived seem so far away. On dark autumn nights, so the story goes, she went to the manor to thresh, walking through the woods with a trembling heart, reciting the Lord's Prayer and crossing herself as she passed the fearful haunts of ghosts, and graveyards. Eņģele had a heavy burden to bear and worked very hard. Those were the days of slavery. But her story is not just a tale of woe. As Mother tells the story, Eņģele was able to laugh like a child with children, knew songs, fairytales, and legends, knew the good or bad uses of every flower that bloomed in the valleys of Tauraģe, and knew how to interpret the language of each bird. Mother keeps mentioning Tauraģe, her childhood home, and the lovely river banks where she roamed with Eņģele listening to her wise talk. To Annele these banks seem like a far-off legendary country. She sometimes even doubts whether she could find them if she went and looked for them. Perhaps places, too, pass away just like people. Mother, too, remembers Tauraģe only from her childhood. When Annele once asked her if she had been there at a later date, Mother said: "Not since I was young. – And anyway, I doubt that it would still be there."

Mother didn't go on to explain what this "it" was.

Eņģele hasn't left much of a mark. Annele knows of no one who saw her or knew her. Only Mother speaks of her, and as for Annele, she won't forget Eņģele as long as she lives. Sometimes it feels as though Eņģele is suddenly near. As Annele sits in the barrens and the wind rustles around her, suddenly a shadow seems to appear at her side, and someone seems to ask:

"Are you my Luzīte's daughter?"

And something that feels like a breeze seems to caress her hair.

"You go ahead and grow! Grow up to be a decent person. Don't put your parents to shame."

Then she is gone.

And Annele suddenly feels a strange sort of pang in her heart, but not the least bit of fear.

Another person from the afterlife who gives Annele even more food for thought is Pastor Zimmermann. His memory is great. When they started talking about him at Spring Farm, it took all night, for everyone wanted to give his own perspective on all the important events that involved the pastor. What Annele enjoyed most was when her father would give his account of things. Not just because he knew much more than the others, but also because his story was so unusual and stirring that the words and the language seemed quite different from those used in ordinary speech. Almost as though he were reading the Bible.

Pastor Zimmermann lies right by the church under a gray stone cross. On the cross it says, "Pastor Zimmermann, d. anno 1848."

Every Sunday his grave is decorated at all four corners with tightly tied bouquets of flowers.

The first time Annele was in church, Mother took her to this grave.

"And this is where Pastor Zimmermann is buried."

"Who brings him those flowers?" asked Annele.

"Those who saw him and knew him bring him flowers. How could you not bring flowers for Pastor Zimmermann?"

The days are beginning to shrink shorter and shorter. Darkness comes quickly, black as soot. Light is so expensive. The candle that was bought in town melts quickly. But Mother has already rendered some tallow, and today she herself will begin dipping candles. The wicks of the candles, made of soft cotton yarn, have been strung in a row from a piece of long, white kindling. Carefully she dips the wicks in a bowl filled to the brim with hot tallow; just as carefully she pulls them out and hangs them over a nearby empty kettle to let them drip. And on and on, row by row. When a candle has finished dripping and has set, it is dipped again, and this is done until the candle is thick enough. Mother doesn't make them too thick, so as to save tallow, for winter is so long.

Father can no longer see enough to weave and gets down from his bench. But there is no candle to burn yet. Though candle dipping is a lovely job, Mother doesn't ask Annele to help. So Annele now pesters Father to tell her a story.

"What shall I tell you about?"

"About Pastor Zimmermann."

"What, again?"

"You haven't told me the whole story."

"Haven't I though!"

"From start to finish, I mean!"

And Father begins pacing through the little room. Three steps one way, three steps back the other way. On his face is a sort of quiet, serene smile. And then he says as if speaking to himself: "Yes, yes indeed, there's never been another pastor like him, and there never will be!"

"Tell us how he confirmed you."

"How can I explain that to you, child? It says in the Scripture that the devil took the Savior to a high mountain and showed him all the glory of the world; and so I have to say that in confirmation class Pastor Zimmermann took us to such a high mountain and showed us the glory of God. He was like fire. He kept us till midnight. But none of us felt like dozing. Nobody dared to in church, either. No matter how hard we had been working. And how could anyone have dozed there! Why, it was as if he bore us aloft on wings!

"Often we couldn't understand him. We listened trembling, but we didn't understand. But none of us dared stray some place else with our thoughts, nor ask questions."

"Why didn't you understand him?"

"Can you understand a storm as it roars through the forest and sweeps a path behind it; can you understand when birds call to each other at dawn and every little blade of grass looks at the sun with diamond eyes, can you understand when you go outside on a spring day and see a life of miracles where there wasn't a thing the day before? And there, too, you don't dare stray some place else with your thoughts – that's how strong it all is, everything you see.

"And the same thing was true of him.

"His face was full of love and severity, like thunder and sunlight, his face was like the face of heaven.

"Once he had been talking to us till late into the night. And then suddenly fallen silent. Put his head on the book and seemed to be asleep. But one of us started fooling around and jeering. Others too. And then all of a sudden the pastor jumps to his feet and looks at us. Doesn't say a word, just looks at us. And we start shaking, like leaves, all of us."

"Were you scared?"

"Not scared. Not as though he could hurt us. He never hurt a soul. But here's what I figured out later: because we disturbed him. He was with himself, with his thoughts and torments."

"What does that mean – with his torments?"

Father did not answer, and the girl continued asking questions:

"But where was he from?"

"I don't rightly know. There's few that know, maybe. People even said he was one of our own. And he certainly talked like people hereabouts. It's just that as long as I've been aware of him, whenever his name was even mentioned it was like praying to God. And when we children were taught something, or taught a lesson, the last thing we were told was always: Just wait till you start going to Pastor Zimmermann! And it meant something like: Just wait, that's when you'll be washed clean and purified, that's when you'll become new beings. And nobody left him empty-handed. He gave to everybody."

"What did he give?"

"You mean bread? That went without saying. I myself, when I was studying for my confirmation, saw a woman come for a bushel of rye seed. Give her some, he said to the overseer. The overseer goes into the *klēts*: there is none. He himself didn't even have a bushel of rye left over. That's the way he lived. But what is bread, after all? He lived only for others. He gave away everything he had, and he gave himself away, too. In his rooms there were no unnecessary luxuries. I guess he had no relatives either, and he never married. And he was tall as an oak and a fine figure of a man!

"If you could go around to all the people who saw him and ask them, each of them could tell you something special about him. For he drew people to him with great love and transformed them. He inspired each of them with his spirit, and they matured the way fruit matures when it hangs in the sun.

"In those days the gentry were like gods, there was no way you could touch them. Take our squire, he was very severe, hard, and unapproachable. At that time he married a young wife, but d'you think a person was even allowed to touch the hem of her clothes? What do you think peasants were worth in those days? The estate managers and overseers would torture them. When I was a little boy, our house burned down. In those days the manor owned everything, and the manor wouldn't build us another house. They threw together some kind of clay shack, and that's where we lived. There was no stove or hearth, the water ran down the walls. But that's where we were born and where we grew up. We grew up like young wolf cubs. When there got to be more of us, bunks were put up along the walls, one above another, up to the ceiling. The bigger kids always had to move to the top bunks. The cooking fire was further up the hill, where a second shack had been slapped together for the purpose. There, during the threshing season, my mother, your granny, had to go at cockcrow to light a fire and cook breakfast. Often the coals under the ashes had long since gone out from the rain or snow that blew in down the chimney; and then it would take a long time to strike a fire and light it again. The winters were very severe, and water had to be carried a long distance from the spring down the hill. And so it went for ten years. That's when Granny's back got stooped.

"And then one day, I remember it as though it had been today, the pastor drove into the yard. That's the way he used to arrive, suddenly, when nobody was expecting him. He looked at everything. He walks into the cooking shack, where we're all hunkering frozen around the fire like little Gypsies. The smoke is so bad you can't breathe. Can people be living like this, does the squire know you have to live this way? And his eyes flash like two suns. The squire? Father – my father – just shrugs his shoulders. Then the pastor doesn't say any more, just examines everything, asks all kinds of questions and drives away. He doesn't offer any consolation or make any promises. The following week, though, carpenters arrive with workers, start measuring and digging and building, and build the house that's still there at Spring Farm.

"It was about that time that the squire's young wife became like a human being in her dealings with the peasants. But when something good would come, everyone knew where it came from and through whom. *He* was the one who stood between the people and the gentry and held their hearts in his hand and directed them like streams of water. But he did not seek advantage for himself, nor honor for his name. This was why evil and gossip were consumed like straw in the face of the purity of his heart.

"But helping people materially was by no means all he did. He had words, words that were like the bread of life! The pastor looked forward to Sunday as though it was a festival, and the church was thronged with listeners then. People would come from miles around. During the workweek they had worked till they were ready to drop, then they stood during the service, and there's many among them that didn't get home till sunset. But if they just got to hear his words, to look at his face, they'd each go home as though they'd been given great wealth."

Father falls silent as if he were already finished.

"And then, Daddy, what happened to him then?"

"You already know that."

"I do, but I want you to tell me the rest!"

"Then came that terrible year of the chol'ra. There was a great heat wave and drought, and there were rumors that in Jelgava people were dropping on the streets like falling leaves. The disease would suddenly fall on people at random, like the noose of a snare. People turned into wild beasts, without pity. Where the disease attacked, it was said, children would flee from their parents and abandon them, parents would flee from their children. In the streets, rumor had it, black-faced, sooty men were running about. They were terrible men, who were not afraid of the devil himself. Drunk, and for a lot of money, they would pick up the fallen people, load them onto big carts and then take them to an out-of-the-way place, far outside of town. There, deep pits had been dug beforehand, and that's where they'd throw the bodies. People who had been in Jelgava said they had seen such wagons stacked full of dead bodies one on top of the other; the women's long hair, they said, would get caught in the wheels. One person had more terrible stories to tell than another. Normally no one would travel to town, only if the manor sent them. And this is what happened: those who covered their faces and had not the least bit to eat or drink in the accursed town stayed healthy, while anyone who had eaten a meal there or had entered into closer dealings with the townspeople was lost.

"And then the news came that the pastor had gone to Jelgava. Some said he was making the rounds day and night helping the sick, others had seen him following a wagon loaded with those who had died of the disease, accompanying them to their last resting place, going from one grave to another. For his heart had been deeply moved to compassion for them, thrown into pits like animals without a blessing and without God's word. Many people had followed him, but had not dared to approach the graves. They had stood at a distance and listened to the mighty words he spoke.

"And then one morning a new rumor flew from farm to farm: the pastor was back. He had come back in the middle of the night and called the housekeeper, telling her to heat water for a bath. But then he had given strict injunctions that no one should come near him, not even enter the same room where he was. He had locked the door and let no one else inside.

"When people heard that, they all stopped in their tracks. Their hearts trembled. None of them gave a thought to their work now. They foresaw and expected a sad ending.

"And by the evening of that same day, even people in the most distant farms knew the pastor was dead.

"That same night they dug a grave by the church, brought his body and placed it inside. For three days and three nights the grave stood open. It was the peak of the harvest season, but for three days and three nights the churchyard was packed with people. Those who weren't able to go by day would go by night. And when you'd go inside, the churchyard would rustle and sway with the crowd's sobbing and weeping, which would abate at one end and start up again at the other. He was strewn with tears, strewn with flowers.

"On the third day some pastors came from the neighboring congregations to bury him. And everyone bore witness that they had never heard such great sorrow and seen such great love as was shown here by a congregation for its pastor.

"But then, of course, it isn't everyone that's chosen by God and sent by God."

Here Father's story ended like a legend from distant times. The little room had become dark. Only the four windowpanes glowed palely in the mullion. But Annele felt as though some great stream were carrying her above deep waters and as though its waves proudly proclaimed, "See, that's the kind of person that lived once."

And she can't stop thinking about this man. It's lovely, lovely that such a person has lived. She walks his daily rounds and relives everything that happened. She follows him inside through the majestic door of the mansion, straight to her ladyship sitting in the hall of mirrors in her blue silk gown, and hears the pastor say: "You're living the good life while the ordinary people are having a hard, hard time, and nobody thinks about them. You must help the people." And he refuses to budge until he gets help for the people. She walks with the pastor through the hot, parched streets of Jelgava, where people are "dropping like flies" of the dread epidemic. She stands with him by a big grave in which many of the dead have been thrown because there are no coffins for individual persons anymore, or anyone to bury them, and she hears the pastor speaking, but she cannot understand his words. She is in the pastor's room late at night with the confirmation class. And she sees the pastor's head sink down on the desk, and the children think he has fallen asleep. But he's not asleep at all. He is within himself with his thoughts and with his torments, as Father said. Those are words that always make her stop like a too-high threshold. Annele knows that beyond the things that are happening and that people see is something else that you cannot see and cannot comprehend. And that is what she has to think about most. That's where the big why? why? why?s begin, which nobody answers, but to which you have to find your own answers.

The door opens, and Mother comes in with a bright little candle in her hand. She had taken one row of newly dipped candles outside so they would set sooner, and now they are ready.

"Look, the first candle we've dipped this fall and in these barrens. Let's hope it burns brightly!" she says with a smile and puts the candle on the table. They all sit in silence and reverently gaze at the little flame.

The little candle burns and melts, crackling like a piece of resinous fir wood. Soon it will be half burned, soon it will be all gone.

"A candle is like a human being. It gives its brightness as it dwindles and goes out itself," unexpectedly says Father.

"Like Pastor Zimmermann, right, Dad?" asks Annele.

Father looks at the candle pensively and does not answer.

The Holiday Season

At the end of November, a strong gale came and tore to shreds the fogs that had been spun over the weeks, rolled them up into swaths and threw them beyond the horizon. Night tucked an endless sheet of stars around earth's black bed. But the ground froze and crackled. When all the ditches and sloughs had frozen over, soft gray clouds rose in the sky and began sprinkling snow as though from a bottomless sack, day and night. When Annele went out one morning with a clear winter sun, everything was white. You could no longer see distant farms, or trees, or shrubs. Only the nearby railroad track stood out like a line drawn in ink on white paper. Along this line, as always, at set times, the train raced along panting and out of breath, spitting sparks; as it rushed into the woods, it gave a god-awful scream – and then, as though it had fallen into some pit, grunted and hissed for a while, then screamed again and, puffing softly, sank into silence like a coal that goes out when thrown into water. And again the vast barrens and the little railroad station in the middle of the forest lay there without a sign of life.

Around Annele's house, there were only three beaten paths: to the well, to the barn, and to the woodpile; the other paths were covered with snow, and no one came to the farm along them anymore. Softly, the days passed as in a fairy tale. By the only window, Father's loom had been set up, and the rhythmic beat of the shuttle mingled with the noise of Mother's spinning wheel rumbling gently and rising and falling in waves. Mother at her work had to make do with less light, as did Annele, whose spinning wheel and big reel had been crowded almost completely into a corner. It makes no difference to Annele. Her eyes are bright and so sharp she can see a needle in the dark. Here, too, her job is to supply Father with spools for weaving, and she is just as responsible for this as the grown-ups for their work. Every night she counts how many unusable spools, where the yarn had slipped off or been badly wound, Father has tossed back into her little workbasket. Then she knows by how much she has grown, by how much her soundness of judgment has increased, for of course Father never scolds when the work has been badly done, he just says, "That's all right! Tomorrow is another day. Your judgment will get sounder with time."

Sometimes Father suddenly stopped working. One hand, as if forgotten, still lay on the woven cloth, the other one, the one that held the shuttle, dropped at his side, as he himself, head turned toward the window, gazed out over the snowy plain. Then he began to weave once more with such loud urgency as though he were racing to the top of a hill, his cheeks flushed with joy. At other times, again sitting thoughtfully, he'd start talking about people, about the weather, about life, and Annele had the feeling listening to him as though he had just traveled all over some distant new region and was now recounting his experiences, which he could never finish telling.

When dusk fell, work came to a stop. Annele now had a chance to run about outside. Outside the door, her friend Krančelis awaited her, his one white eye laughing and the other black one weeping, flung his paws at her chest and his nose in her face, while Annele grabbed him by both ears, gently so it wouldn't hurt, and kissed him on his soft forehead. "Little puppy, little puppy, you'll never grow up to be a big dog," she said pityingly. "Who cares!" snorted Krančelis and went loping off, casting big circles, toward the slough, thus tempting Annele to follow him. On the slough, ice glinted in narrow strips, swept clear of snow by the wind and polished like a mirror. Annele would no sooner go gliding across on her *pastalas* like skates, balancing her arms like the sails of a windmill, than she stopped short at the other end, so very slippery was the ice. And Annele glided back and forth, back and forth, until her craving was somewhat relieved, while Krančelis hunkered at the edge admiring her, his black eye piteously tilted, whining dolefully now and then.

"Your turn now, Krančeli! C'me here, c'me here!" Annele called.

"I can't," whined Krančelis, "neither one foot, nor the other, nor the third, nor the fourth wants to stay in place. They just won't stay in place."

"C'me here, c'me here!" Annele stood in the middle of the slough and slapped both her knees, coaxing him.

"Have mercy, have mercy, Annele, I can't!"

"You're gonna be sorry if you don't," Annele threatened. "Well, get a move on!"

"Have mercy, have mercy, I can't!" Krančelis begged even more imploringly, flung himself down on his back and showed his four helpless feet.

Here came Annele, though.

"There's not going be any mercy," she said, wrapped the little dog around her arm a couple of times and then rolled him head over heels across the ice until he tumbled into a snowdrift. But she didn't gain the upper hand a second time. As soon as, laughing loudly, she made a move in his direction, Krančelis was up like a flash, and took to his heels with his tail between his legs.

It was already dark. At the end of the house, Mother stood and called:

"Come home, Annele, come home! Are you planning to tear around all night?"

"I hope I don't get a scolding because of those *pastalas*," Annele thought anxiously and, picking up one foot, felt it carefully to see if the ice had rubbed a hole in her *pastala*, but no: it was all right.

That same moment, she felt a push and tumbled into the snow. Krančelis was on top of her.

"You rascal," Annele scolded, "look how he paid me back." And with both hands she warded off Krančelis's nose, which was all over her face, begging and apologizing: "Come on, Annele, I'm all right and you're all right. And tomorrow we'll go back to the ice, just think of the fun we're going to have! We can be as wild as we like!"

By now, Annele felt she had been living in the snowed-in house with her parents for a hundred years. Especially at night, when the loom and the spinning wheels were silent and all three inhabitants, huddled around the little light, were doing noiseless chores. Then, Annele was allowed to read, but when the book, which she had read several times, no longer appealed to her, she went to the window, and through a thawed spot as wide as her palm looked outside for a long time intently. Then the world under the night sky seemed to her like a mysterious door through which, at any moment, something strange and unusual must come forth. She looked until her eyes grew tired, but there was no sign of anything.

One night, though, in that dusky expanse, under a new rim of moon pointed as a horn, she actually did catch sight of three black dots moving and approaching.

"Somebody's coming! Moving! Coming this way!" Annele excitedly announced to the room.

"Who's coming?" wondered Mother and came to the window. After watching for a while, she said anxiously: "Yes, they really are coming this way! Wonder who it could be?" She went back into the room, returned to the window, looked out again. The travelers were not far now. They came straight across the barrens, wading through deep snow. You could hear their voices now. Loud, boastfully clamorous, talking at the same time, in words and in a language that were incomprehensible. Big cudgels whooshed through the air. Annele had the feeling they could be heard across the barrens all the way to the last boundary. And that the entire barrens were startled, woken up from their sleep. – What sort of men were these?

"Maybe we ought to put out the light," said Mother.

"I'll go out and meet them, then we'll see who it is." Father calmly took his cap, and Annele, who didn't have time to intercept him, delay, and protect him, flattened herself against the doorpost: oh dear! Suppose they are wicked people! Suppose they hurt Father! Then she hears them – merry, bright voices and laughter. Already she feels relieved. They can't be wicked. And then here they come, making all the walls echo, shake the snow from their feet outside, and burst into the house with a wide stream of icy cold air.

"Look, here's your robbers for you!" says Father, laughing as he brings the guests inside. And all three newcomers laugh, their mouths wide open.

"Scared you, huh?" asks the shortest of the men, bragging, playing the hero.

"You did, we were terribly scared," Mother answers jokingly, for of course that's exactly what they want to hear. And again they all guffaw heartily.

And Annele now sees that one of them, the tall one, is Jānis from Brook Farm, the two others are about the size of tall herd boys.

"Herd boys? Not by a long shot!" one of them retorts in answer to Mother's question. "Why, this spring we'll be through with school, then it's confirmation class, and off to work as hired hands. Plenty of strength in these bones, huh?" And he thumps his fist against his chest. "That's strength for you! Booms like a barrel!"

Mother inquires where they're going.

Where else but to visit the new cottagers. To give them a bit of a scare, have a little chat. Don't take it amiss. What else is there to do, these long winter evenings?

All of them, their clothes and shoes chilled by the winter wind, sit down around the table. Father and Jānis smoke a pipe together, but not the young boys. They say tobacco makes them woozy. The little lamp burns in the middle, flooding their faces with its pale light. Annele can't look her fill at these unprecedented strangers. How Jānis's long yellow curly hair twines around his forehead and cheeks! He's only smoking to be polite. When Father is talking, Jānis listens attentively and smiles, covering the pipe with his hand, and when answering a question or saying something himself, he always looks at Mother and at Annele, too, so courteously and with such bright sincerity: How about it, do you agree? As though Annele were a grown-up or something. When that happens, Annele doesn't know if she dares to look him in the eyes or not, and always turns away and looks at the wall. It's different with the younger fellows. They don't even look in Annele's direction. And also they don't have much to say, but wait with their mouths open for Jānis or Father to say something. Then they roar: Yes! – and forget to clap their mouths shut, so that the light that shines in shows everyone their red tongues and white teeth. Everyone is feeling cheerful and happy. Here are the loud voices that scared the entire barrens. Trapped between the four walls of New Farm as though in a cage!

No matter how closely and attentively Annele watches all this, the conversation begins to get hard to understand, and as soon as she stretches out on her bed a bit to rest her feet, which seem so heavy, the conversation suddenly seems to drop behind some kind of wall. Only much later she hears somebody say:

"Yes, soon, soon! We'll be back at Christmas. Why, Christmas is just around the corner."

"Christmas, Christmas is just around the corner!" is Annele's first thought as she wakes up the next morning. The loom and the spinning wheels are silent. Father is shod for the road – hip boots, and a big fat cudgel in his hand. "Go on, be off with you," Mother bids him good-humoredly, "maybe you'll bring back a Christmas present." What present? wonders Annele. – "You'll see!"

Annele can now run outside to slide on the ice bright and early, but she has no peace of mind anywhere; while she's busy on the ice, something important may happen inside and pass by unnoticed; when she runs inside, on the other hand, the outdoors beckons to her so pleasantly and temptingly. Everything looks festive: the glistening snow-covered hills, rolling into the distance like the frozen waves of a lake, flocks of jackdaws as they fly screaming to their nests in the bare birch groves on the horizon, columns of smoke rising from distant chimneys where people are living and getting ready for the holidays.

Krančelis sits facing in the direction of the railroad, ears pricked, refusing to stir no matter how much she calls him and beckons to him. He just throws back his head and gives a short bark. "I know, I know, but leave me alone. I've got a job to do." When Annele comes running back from the slough for the third time, Krančelis is off like a bullet to meet someone who is approaching quickly, dressed in a short, knee-length coat, with a bundle on his shoulders. Oh joy, oh joy! Why, it's Annele's big brother! He is coming from the train, from his school in town. Annele rushes back to Mother with her urgent news, so Mother can go meet him. Annele herself doesn't know what to do. Should she go, too, or wait at a distance, or hide altogether somewhere in the house? How can she be the first to put herself forward, what is she supposed to do, what should she talk about? All that comes from outside is so oddly unfamiliar and distant. Wonder what he's like now, this brother of hers? Even taller, even smarter than he was in summer, while Annele is still the same little silly. Oh dear, oh dear!

Shyly she shakes hands with her brother as though he were a stranger. How he takes off his cap, how he talks, laughs, moves, strokes his hair back from his forehead, how he unties his bundle. Wonder if there's anything nice inside? Especially books, of course! Annele immediately sees which ones are old friends and which ones are more recent additions – how she'd like to feel them and see how thick they are, what the cover looks like, whether it can be read in her familiar Latvian or in a foreign tongue, whether the words come in rhyming verse or just plain, and whether there are pictures inside. And what's Brother going to do with them all: will he take them all with him again when he leaves or leave them at home, and will he even allow her to look at them? Can Annele be so well-behaved that he'll let her? Annele would have loved to get the answers to these questions all at once, but her mouth would not open, no matter how hard she tried. Not until her brother had changed into some old clothes he had left behind at home, and Mother gave him something to eat, did Annele blurt out a question:

"How long is it till Christmas?"

"Three more days from morning till night," Brother said, laying down his spoon, and immediately ran outside.

When he had brought in a supply of firewood and water for Mother, but Father was not back yet, Brother put on Mother's short sheepskin jacket and went out to meet him. They came back toward dusk, and Father, after tossing down a heavy burden, wiped his brow.

"So you got it?" Mother said joyfully and felt the burden. Annele, too, quickly touched it with one finger. Soft! Oh the riches, the abundance that now came from all sides into the little house on the barrens! It crushed her heart! She didn't know what to do with herself.

Next day Brother walked around bundled up like a lumberjack as he looked for an axe. By now Annele had gotten quite accustomed to him again, and she followed him closely. An axe? What on earth for? she wanted to know. Her mouth had thawed

to all sorts of relentless questions, there was no getting rid of her. All morning she tormented her brother. Their conversation followed a pattern:

"Where are you going?"

"Going to the woods."

"What're you going to do there?"

"Chop down a tree."

"What sort of tree?"

"You don't have to know that."

If she doesn't have to know, she doesn't need to, but Annele does need to go with Brother, no matter what. She whines and pesters now Mother, now Brother; the former so she'll let her go, the latter so he'll take her along, but her wheedling meets with no success. Brother doesn't want this sort of companion, who'll only be in the way, and Mother can't understand what it is in the woods that makes her want to go so badly.

What is in the woods? Really, what funny questions the grown-ups ask! Why, the woods! Trees she hasn't seen for ever so long. Near the farm there's not a tree, not the least little shrub. The switches that were stuck in the ground this fall so you could see the road during a blizzard don't deserve the name of trees. And how Annele wants to see the woods, how very, very much!

When Father intervenes, matters suddenly take a favorable turn. Why not let the child have such an innocent pleasure? As long as she gets dressed nice and warm, she can go, he decides. And what he says, goes.

Neither Mother nor Brother object much anymore. Only Annele must make big promises: not to untie her shawl, not to get cold, not to run in the snow on purpose but always to step in her brother's footsteps and to obey his every command.

When they start walking, Annele realizes that it will be hard to follow on his heels, for the strides Brother takes are as long as Annele's stubbornness was great when she insisted on coming. But that's all right! She can stand it.

Krančelis has been strictly forbidden to follow. He's agreed, wagging his tail and his head, but look! – they've hardly walked a hundred steps when the dog is ahead of them. His front paws stretched in front of him on the snow, tail thrashing, so devoted and friendly: "See? I was first!"

Brother is stern with Krančelis:

"Oh, so that's how you obey me? Get back home right this minute! That's the place for a dog!" And a snowball made behind his back hit Krančelis broadside. Whirling round and round in circles, he took off in the direction of home. Annele stopped walking and turned her head back a tiny little bit. That was all it took. At once, the dog was back. All wrongs were forgotten. He flattened himself against Annele's hand, then, crawling on his belly, approached Brother. "Well, all right," said Brother. He stroked the dog's soft head. Krančelis went tumbling through the snow, ran into the woods barking furiously, scared the jackdaws off their nests, frightened a hare, which went loping across the field as though the devil himself were after it. That's the kind of warrior Krančelis was.

Easily, sliding all the way, they flew across the frozen meadow that had been flooded all fall, and entered the woods. After they had walked a short while, Brother said: "Now you stay here and wait till I come back." And he vanished in a thicket.

For a while Annele stood there surprised: What was this? Wait here, that's all? What was the good of coming to the woods, then? How could she stand still when every urge she had, every thought, was to rush forward? Into the woods.

But what about her promise to Brother that she'll obey his every command? Well, that's all right. She'll just go beyond the next tree and come back at once. But once she has gone beyond that tree, she wants to see what's beyond the next one. The woods are like a huge enchanted palace with countless doors and exits; as soon as you enter through one, you're practically pulled further through a second one: just a few steps and she'll soon see what other lovely and good things she's missed.

Oh, the fir trees, all those fir trees! Thousands, arched, slim as towers, intersecting somewhere high in the sky! Spreading their broad-winged snowy cloaks, protecting the tiny baby firs. "How beautiful, how beautiful!" Annele whispers, not knowing what it is that is beautiful: the light that pours down the branches, shimmering in the treetops, gleaming in the snowdrifts, growing dark in the thicket like a brook swallowed by the ground, or the silence that seems to hum from one end of the sky to the other like an uninterrupted diamond string, or the nearness and loving kindness of all these tall, lofty trees: We're all around you, Annele, little human sister! – Crisscross through the dear home of the trees walked Annele till she came out in one place that was like a stately hall adorned with pillars all round. A hushed solemn glitter, as though made ready for the holidays. "This must be it – the forest Christmas!" thought Annele as her eyes moved upward, through the tips of the branches that gleamed, gilded like the treetops, in a light rosy haze. Why, it's evening! – remembered Annele, shivering suddenly. "I'll just follow my own footsteps back, and I'm sure I'll get to the right spot." But once she goes back deeper into the thicket, the girl sees that a number of tracks have crossed there, and no longer knows which way to turn. This could turn out badly, if it were not for a loud bark that suddenly seems to drop out of the blue. There comes Krančelis, winding his way through the trees like a ball of yarn, sniffing the trail. With leaps of joy, he slams into Annele's chest, pushing her down into the snow. Then, having quickly sniffed out the way to the huge hall of the forest, and convincing himself that Annele has indeed been there and that so far all is as it should be, he barks at the fir trees in their splendid semicircle of pyramids as though to say: You've grown all you could, I'm satisfied with you, nimbly jumps back, grabs Annele by her shawl, growls, and shakes it to let her know that it's time to stop the nonsense and to head for the open fields as fast as their legs can carry them. And thus, indulging in all sorts of additional pleasures as well, like chasing or barking at squirrels, hares, and jackdaws, Krančelis does not lose sight of his chief responsibility, and unerringly and faithfully leads Annele out into the open.

There stands Brother with a big bundle of junipers tied with bast, and now Annele gets a scolding. And that's nothing – there's more to come from Mother, he says, just you wait. Now she had to walk in front and tread in the footsteps they'd made before. When they reached the top of the little hill, a huge round moon rose and began to climb toward them. Annele's hands were so icy cold that tears came into her eyes when she sucked in her breath. It didn't matter though. She'd seen the woods, the wonderful woods. And she wasn't worried that Brother might tell Mother. There was no way he would tell on her! And he didn't.

⌒╫⌒

Saturday before Christmas calls Annele awake. Something heavy is lying on her legs. A big white board has been placed across the bed, full of freshly baked flatcakes, sweet pretzels, and crescent rolls. And who's that standing by the stove next to Mother, with those thick golden gleaming braids? Līziņa! Annele gives a loud scream, frightening horribly the two women baking flatcakes. Līziņa comes running over to the bed and gives Annele a kiss, holding her hands, sticky with dough, behind her back: "Oh you girl, girl! Better get up quick and run outside so you don't get in our way!" – "Yes," Annele says, but she dawdles a while longer. She needs a little more time to think about something nice: her beloved big sister has arrived during the night. The closer the holiday comes, the holier it becomes.

All day, Annele is outside. For lunch she gets a big hot meat pie and that's all. Krančelis is no good as a playmate today. Growling and fighting the whole world, he either chews up his bones practically on the spot, or drags them off to hide them in snowdrifts, having a hard time finding places that are deep enough and good enough to satisfy him completely, which is why he has to move his treasures several times. It takes him all day. Tired out from his great efforts, having eaten his fill, he lazily stretches out on a bundle of straw in front of the barn at last, and when Annele keeps inviting him to run to the slough, he yells back only at intervals: "Woof! Leave me alone! What do you take me for, a puppy?"

The distant chimneys that have been working furiously all day have stopped smoking. The blaze of the sunset has died down. Slowly, the moon begins to glow; it's been standing in the evening sky for a long time, waiting for the great luminary of the day to vanish. The horizon closes like a blue steel ring.

Christmas has arrived.

"Annele, Annele! Quick, quick!"

A fluttering white headscarf: her big sister is calling.

What's the big hurry? What's happened?

Still, to keep them from waiting in vain, Annele runs home in joyful awe, full of expectation. – Something must be up.

She opens the door and stops on the threshold. What a miracle, what an unprecedented miracle! In the middle of the room there's the loveliest spruce with seven shining stars! The walls and the corners seem to have vanished, melted away, buried in soft black moss. There's only the spruce, growing upward, flashing gold and silver among branches filled with the twilight of night.

Annele looks questioningly into smiling faces, into eyes that gleam moist. Oh, so that was it! Her brother's burden tied with bast, her sister's many mysterious little bundles wrapped in colored paper. All for Annele! And for her first enchanting tree!

Oh Christmas, Christmas! What is she to say now? Her lips are silent, her heart beats with happiness. Wonder if this will go on for a long, long time? –

And Annele seems to hear the great night murmuring and rustling somewhere and the whole world's answer: Yes, for a long time! For ever and ever!

But when she wakes up again another morning, Christmas is gone. Gone with seven-league boots, thousands of miles away. Christmas will circle around hundreds of suns and won't be back on the snowy barrens knocking at Annele's door till another year has gone by.

New Year's Eve arrives out of breath. Like a mysterious magician. When dusk begins to fall, they sing Father's favorite evening hymn about the impermanence of all living things.

"And just as season follows season
Or floods abate and then run dry,
We too shall vanish from the earth
Before our minds can comprehend it."

This is truly fitting for New Year's Eve.

Then everybody sits for a while in silent meditation, and then it's time for the fun to begin. Sister carries in a big bowl full of clear water, then throws in gilded nutshells with the remaining stubs of the candles from the Christmas tree stuck inside them. She churns and stirs up the water, and now the little golden ships of fortune with their flaming masts can start predicting what the future has in store.

Annele likes this lovely game. Will the little ships that were destined for each other meet in calm waters and then continue their journey together, inseparable, or will they merely encounter each other in the raging billows for a short while, only to be tossed past coasts and cliffs, forever apart? Will the tiny life flame of one be extinguished in the meantime, which would be just like being engulfed by the abyss? And how sorry, how sorry she'd be for the poor flame that was left behind! Or will each go staggering down its own current, never catching sight, for all its flaming eye, of its dear friend, never reaching its companion?

They led about different destinies on the little ships until they ran out of candle stubs. Then it was time to go to bed.

No, first they must go outside to listen to what the New Year says.

Arm in arm, close to each other, the two sisters waded out in the snow on the barrens, stopped and listened for a long time. Krančelis hunkered down next to them, pricking his ears. The moon had not risen yet. Annele had the feeling that from all directions night was looking at her, its eyes deep with wonder. Things were as usual, and yet they weren't. It was as though a wonderful voice were calling her from somewhere, a voice to which her heart responded fervently and jubilantly. A sort of huge surging wave tossed her up in what felt like a really high swing that went swooshing between the sky and the earth. But she was safe, so safe. Nothing could happen to her. And the sun, the moon, the stars, and everybody Annele loved were on the swing with her. But she didn't know what she was so happy about. She grabbed Krančelis by the scruff of his neck. Shook him.

"This will be a lovely year. My heart is so glad."

"Woof!" responded Krančelis. "Woof! It will, it will!"

The Epiphany Snowstorm

Epiphany fell on a Friday, and so it turned out that there were four nights of celebration. On Christmas Day, Līziņa had suggested to Brother that they should spend Epiphany visiting Uncle Zanders, who lived a few miles on the other side of Dobele. They could go there on Epiphany and return on the Saturday after the holiday. That Sunday, Līziņa planned to return to Jelgava.

Both of them were eager to go. On the morning of Epiphany, Father accompanied them quite a distance through the forest, showing them a short cut. When he came back, he was pleased: the sled had gone like greased lightning. The road had been driven pretty smooth by wood carters. More than a week already, the weather had stayed clear and frosty. The air sparkled. At night the sun set red, as if during a heat wave.

The following day snow began to fall, though it was still freezing. Gusts of wind swept the barrens, whirling up a fog of white dust here and there. It didn't take long for the wind to turn into a storm. Eddies of snow swirled across the barrens. With thick spurts, the storm tossed swaths of snow around the little house. It piled up drifts as high as the rafters. Howling, it fell into the drifts, pulled at them, tore them to shreds as though trying to throw them back into the clouds again like a child's toys. A white confusion of snow raged everywhere. It was the kind of weather when sky and earth are fused into one. People who had no business outside kept within doors.

Around noon, a blue crack of sky would suddenly open once in a while, but the galloping clouds would immediately cover it up with hail and snow.

Full of worry, Mother would glance out the little window now and then, shake her head, sigh. She couldn't stop thinking about the children, who were supposed to return from their visit as had been agreed. Finally she blurted out:

"I'm worried, I'm worried. In weather like this, where would they go if they've set out for home? No way a person can see the road, or a horse can wade through the drifts."

Father was calm.

"Who'd let them out on the road in this kind of weather? A good master wouldn't even chase his dog outside, so why should my own brother let my children drive off, when it's their first visit to his house since they grew up. His wife, too, is just as good a mother as you are, and she's got children of her own. No, no, you're wasting your time worrying. You'll see: the blizzard will subside, and they'll be back, even if it's in the evening. And even if it's night. The night is still bright toward the east."

But the storm grew more violent by the hour. It hurled itself against the house like something demented. It howled around the corners, tore at the roof, whistled in the chimney like an infuriated wild beast that has encountered an obstruction – the mote of dust that the little house on the barrens was compared to it. Pull it down, tear it into shreds, trample it, toss it away, in order to be able to roar and howl unimpeded as it galloped past along with the gray clouds whose great race across the vast plains of the sky is barred by no obstacles.

Toward evening Annele's parents went out to take care of the animals, to bring in firewood and water. The last time Father came in, Krančelis, too, rolled inside between his feet. He pushed his nose in Annele's face, barked, whined, sniffed things, shook himself so hard that a white cloud of snow rose from his thick fur, crept into the darkest corner for fear they'd chase him outside. Father said the poor little dog's kennel had been completely snowed in, and when Krančelis had caught sight of him, he'd been so overjoyed he had landed on Father's shoulder with one leap. There was only one way to reward a feat of such daring and skill: he must be brought inside the house. Father, too, had his hair and eyebrows and neck and ears all covered with snow. Mother shook out her shawl, which had a little snowdrift in each fold that in the heat of the room had already managed to roll up into lumps. The two of them stood there shaking themselves off, filling the room with a snowy breath that gave Annele goose bumps. She watched with pleasure as Mother lit the kitchen stove early and put supper on to cook. Sitting in front of the stove and watching the fire was a task she would enjoy today. But her sense of comfort was slow to come. The chimney was full of snow. The wind would not stop puffing and panting in it, pushing the smoke back inside. Mother helped the fire every way she knew how – with dry kindling, birch bark, resinous wood that gave a quick flame, but for a long time her efforts were in vain. Then she threw open the door. A jet of wind rushed in the door and into the open mouth of the stove. That helped. Ashes sprayed, the flames subsided, but immediately shot up again, roaring joyfully, and in a moment they had consumed the birch bark and dry kindling, and were grabbing mouthfuls of wood, which crackled asking: "Is it burning yet?" – "It is, it is, it is," called the roaring flames, shrinking back and up toward the chimney like laughing witches.

Mother slammed the door in a hurry. There was no more smoke, to be sure, but in that brief moment the house had cooled off like a kennel. Krančelis protested with a groan.

He lay under the parents' bed, head stretched out on his front paws. As soon as he had had a quick nap he began blinking his eyes alertly. He found all the activity around the fire mighty interesting, but being an experienced dog preferred not to draw the attention of some bossy human to himself at the wrong time. He could get punched in the ribs, or at the very least be told to scram or get out from underfoot. Neither was pleasant.

Near the mouth of the stove squatted Annele. Right in the middle of that red glow that dawned with ever-changing, fluid outlines over the room. The warmth was spreading.

The time had come now for Krančelis to crawl out from under the bed. Lazily he rose. He extended both pairs of legs as far as they would go, stretched, yawned, and then slowly headed straight for Annele and hunkered down close beside her.

"Fire, Krančel!" Annele said cheerfully. "Khmm!" Krančelis, his mouth open, barely managed to answer in his dog language. It was not a bark, but much more. It expressed joy, agreement, invitation, flattery, pleading, attention, warning, and whatever else Krančelis needed to say. It served him instead of many different sorts of words that God had not put into his mouth. In every case, Annele interpreted this "khmm" differently. This time it was a happy "yes," underlined by a vigorous thump of his tail.

Annele clasped the little dog's head and spoke to him lovingly.

"A little flame, Krančel, that's right! Look how funny it is! Wherever the fire comes close, a little flame man jumps out. And another, a third, a fourth and fifth and sixth behind it! Can you count them all? No, you can't! They live deep, deep inside that red glow. They live there waiting. When it's their turn, they jump out, like at a dance. But you think there's nothing down there but the neck of the stove, and that's all! No, no, Krančel! That's not the way it is at all. By the same token, when you were lying in the kennel and the blizzard was blowing all around, you might have thought: There are only as many snowflakes as I can see around my nose. But you know how many there are? There are millions and billions and trillions of them. So many snowflakes nobody on earth can count them, even if they live a thousand years. Just think, right now the whole world is like a huge, huge, huge sack of very fine flour. And everything's inside that sack: Fork Farm, Spring Farm, Žagare, Dobele, Jelgava, Rīga. And far, far beyond those places. And then here comes this giant with his head in the clouds and grabs a flail as big as the big forest at Abo Estate, and takes a whack at the sack. You can imagine the dust that raises. So thick you can't keep your eyes open!"

"Khem, khem!" sneezes Krančelis.

"Yes, and then – "

"Khem, khem!" Krančelis is waiting.

"Yes, and then – "

And then the sack suddenly bursts and Annele is outside. So completely outside that she is not aware whether it is her hand or someone else's holding on to Krančelis's fur. She herself is in a big slough full of green grass and forget-me-nots. And the sky, too, is like a single forget-me-not flower. Strawberries are blooming in the ditch. The sun burns overhead like an enormous candle. She decides to run and look if there are any red berries. She runs and sees that the torn sack of snow is rolling away in a cloud of white dust. And there it lies at the horizon like a huge snowball. But then it turns out to be nothing but the white orchards of Spring Farm. Gray rooftops, with the white orchards behind them.

"Khem, khem," Krančelis growls. "Why aren't you talking anymore?"

"Yes, Krančel, trillions and trillions – "

But then her thoughts leap to another unbelievable number. How is it that the count at the big estate can have an income of twenty-five rubles an hour? This figure has preoccupied her ever since she heard someone talking about it at Spring Farm. If it had been only Anyus who spoke about it, she might not believe it, for Anyus often boasted about her master and mistress; but others said so, too. Just think of it: whether he's eating or drinking, driving or sleeping, dancing in his mansions or shooting hares in the woods – by day and by night, for weeks and months and years, as soon as each hour is over, there's twenty-five rubles on the table. And all that time the count doesn't have to lift a finger. The rubles simply "come in." When you know how rare these rubles are, it seems like magic.

A ruble is a mountaintop that it takes a hundred steps to reach. Count them: a hundred. But nobody counts them and gives them to you. If you want to get a ruble, you have to put together these hundred steps by yourself. In other words: you've got to scrape them together.

To scrape together a ruble. How often Annele has heard that expression. The rubles must now be scraped together painstakingly so Brother can go to the big school in Jelgava. Annele knows how Mother has to scrimp and save, of how many eggs, of how many pounds of butter she must stint her eaters so that those pounds, once they have somehow been transported to town, can scrape together that mighty ruble. Līziņa scrapes too. Father even tried to give up his pipe for a while so as not to have to spend those precious kopecks. But he didn't succeed. Dejected, he confessed that it would be easier to give up food. It wasn't as though Father used a lot of to-bacco. The flowers of fringed field clover, cherry leaves, and other fragrant herbs he had collected in summer, dried, chopped up, and mixed with a pinch of real tobacco – that was Father's tobacco. The smoke was light, fragrant, ethereal. The little room kept its scent, as though it had been perfumed with precious incense.

Talk about scraping together a ruble would always reach a point when Mother would say:

"If only you'd saved something when you were younger."

Father shrugged helplessly:

"You know yourself how hard it is to save."

And then Mother would start in about debtors:

"Ah yes! How can you save anything, you with your light hand? The whole world is full of people who owe you money. Whenever anybody asks, you go: Here!"

"Am I some kind of millionaire that the whole world is full of people who're in my debt?" Father chuckled easily. "Believe me, dear wife. I wouldn't be surprised if those are just kopeck debtors."

"Are kopecks something you can pick up on the ground? You know that if you don't save the kopecks, you'll never manage to get a ruble. Of course you don't tell *me*. Other people tell me. When you men happen to go somewhere together, to town, or to do road construction, off to work, and if the need arises, who do people turn to? To you. Lend me some, Krišjān! And Krišjānis lends it to them if he has a ko-peck to call his own. Couldn't you just be firm one of these days and say: No, and there's an end to it!"

"You're funny, Mother. If he has no money and I do, and he asks me, how can I turn him down?"

"But who's going to pay you back? You tossed it into the wind, and the wind should pay you back. Only the wind."

"We know all that," Father said placidly. "What are we arguing about, then?"

"About people who laugh and take the sweat of your brow, while you begrudge yourself a pipe of tobacco, or a sweet roll for your child," said Mother.

"Dear wife, since when have tobacco and sweet rolls been a misfortune? We've never lacked for bread, though. Tell me – don't we have reason to be grateful to God?"

"How you talk, husband! Bread isn't everything, you know. Look: the children are growing up, but we don't have a single thing to give as a dowry to the big girl, for instance, should the occasion arise. I've been harping and harping that you should have someone build us a little cabinet one year, a couple of chairs another year, a dresser the third, and if we'd tried to do that, we'd have quite a lot of stuff on hand by now."

"It's not that I..." Father begins again, no longer as sure of himself, and then ends sort of softly with his usual: "We'll get it when we need it."

"When are we going to get it? – Now there are schools to deal with. We don't know how much the boy's going to need. And is the little one to get nothing at all?"

Father did not respond, but Mother could not end the conversation so soon. She had to finish saying what was on her mind, so there'd be peace for a while. For in addition to kopeck debtors Father also had ruble debtors. Two in particular were always mentioned. One had borrowed a ruble from Father, the other three rubles even, and – like the others – had solemnly sworn to repay the debt, but had forgotten to do it. Father defended them.

"If the man had the money, I'm sure he wouldn't remain in my debt," he used to say. Whereupon Mother would say, "That man has ten times the money, but why should he repay you if you don't ask him?"

"How can I ask him? No, I can't cause the man such embarrassment if he doesn't have the good sense to do it himself."

Another time, Father answered Mother's objections by saying, "Come on, Mother, do you really think we'd be richer if we got those few paltry rubles?"

It took Mother a long time to get over those "paltry rubles."

Annele realized that Father was more optimistic, more carefree than Mother, and that each of them saw the events of their life differently.

Schools. That was a touchy subject. When schools were mentioned, her heart suddenly gave a pang as though it were sick. That distant, unfulfillable longing! Like distant hills that never came closer.

But didn't Father understand this longing? Of course he did. Why else did he turn away and no longer answer? His heart was aching, too.

If only she had one of those rubles in her pocket that can never be spent, like a strawberry that you can keep picking forever. How lovely life would be then! Schools within her reach. Who'd stop her from going if she could pay for them?

In the meantime, a ruble was no small thing. Once it was spent, no magic power – as in the fairy tale – could make it hop back in your pocket. You had to keep "scraping it together." How she wished she could help her parents with this work.

For herding sheep, in all fairness, she should have been paid one such ruble. There had been close to a hundred sheep, and even if she was only paid a kopeck a head, it would come to a ruble. But now, in lieu of payment, they'd brought her those shoes she couldn't wear that moldered on top of the wardrobe like two grumpy mushrooms. It was just her luck!

Annele was daydreaming, but her ears were alert. Her ears sensed Mother's worry and Father's calm. Even though they exchanged only a few words, most of which fell to Mother. She was constantly worried about the severe weather, about the children who hadn't returned. It seemed as if she trembled with each repeated squall of blizzard that raced across the barrens. Father placed only two words like a wall to confront this trembling: "Don't worry!"

But was that enough?

Quietly, they had supper and went to bed. They had to hurry so they could get under the blankets while there was still a bit of warmth. The room grew cold quickly. The warmth was swallowed by the storm, which pushed its breath under the door, through the window, through every chink. It battled round the house so fiercely that it seemed it had been waiting on purpose till everybody went to bed. It pulled at one corner, at another, at the very middle. The chimney howled cruelly, but the walls held.

Annele curled up on her pallet like a snail. A blanket over her head. She kept blowing warm breath until her hands and feet got warm. Father's sheepskin jacket, thrown over the blankets, did its share. And she really needed it. Cold rose from the clay floor just below, stinging like nettles.

Sleep refused to come. Her parents were still talking, too.

"Well, this day's worries are over," said Father.

"But my mind is not at rest. Even if it stops and they leave tomorrow morning, how are they going to wade through those snowdrifts? With a horse like that!"

"Come on, Gray is nothing to sneeze at!"

"He's just a stack of bones!"

"I hope you'll take that back, Mother. To the best of my ability, I've fattened Gray up quite a bit."

"There's no way to fatten up the likes of him. A walking skeleton is a walking skeleton!"

"He looks good to me," said Father.

Annele agreed with her father. She, too, thought Gray was a fine figure of a horse. But Mother had meant to say something quite different. And then she did:

"That's because everything looks good to you. D'you think Laukmalis had no other horse? But he knew on whom he could fob off a Gypsy's hack like Gray. I bet another man would have told him where to get off. But you take everything they give you, because you won't put your foot down like a man."

"You're mistaken, Mother."

"What do you mean, I'm mistaken? Isn't that true? Who else would have come to live and toil in this wilderness, and to crawl into this den of wolves?"

"Why do they have to talk like that?" Annele thinks. Her heart is split between Father and Mother, but it feels like the greater share falls to Father. She does not criticize. She does not want Father to be different. She loves him the way he is. But so often she also feels very sorry for him. Perhaps you feel sorry like this for everything you love.

And Annele knows that Mother, too, feels sorry for Father. Even if she sometimes scolds and would like everything to be different. Annele always thinks of that time at Spring Farm when late one cold evening a traveler from foreign parts showed up and asked for directions. And how Father quickly went off to show him the way. He'd run quite a distance with the stranger, without a jacket or cap, and his hair had fluttered in the breeze. Annele hadn't seen it with her own eyes, but Mother had told the story. Bitter and curt. What did Father have to rush for, why, he hadn't even had time to get dressed properly! Couldn't that German have waited? After all, he'd been the one that came with a request, and not the other way around. Was he, who'd come in from outside, more deserving than Father, that Father had to run, at the drop of a hat, as if there was a fire?

And Mother had said a lot more – bitter and curt.

Then old Anyus, who defended the entire "gentry" class, had taken her pipe out of her mouth and said sternly: "If you are a person of lowly origins, you have to do that." Mother had contradicted her and had thus driven old Anyus into even greater sternness, so that, raising her voice, she'd warned Mother to beware lest the demon of stubbornness and pride take up his residence in her heart. "Blessed are they," Anyus had said, "who become aware of his goading in time and drive him out with a poker. And watch out that that horrible dragon who stands there with his head raised looking for a place to take up his abode doesn't creep into the child's heart! Here stands the girl devouring every word her mother, in her godless way, says against the gentry." Whereupon old Anyus had looked severely at that very same girl with her round, condemning eyes.

But Annele's heart was like a watchful bird on a branch. Maybe that demon of stubbornness and pride had already entered her, for she liked what Mother said, but didn't like what old Anyus said at all. Why the harangue about this "gentry" of hers? Annele felt there were no real people among the gentry at all, they were like cake, which doesn't really satisfy your hunger; whereas ordinary folks – ordinary folks were something quite different.

Lowly! Her father, lowly! You wait and see, Anyus! Father can stand at the top of a mountain, at the very summit!

〜✦〜

That night Annele saw a dream. The fairy-tale ruble, the one that can never be spent, was in her hand: as soon as she put one down, another was in her palm. And so she piled up stacks and stacks of them. White, shiny, but cold as ice. And then suddenly she couldn't anymore. Her fingers were stiff. The ruble rolled away.

She woke up.

Her feet were bare. Her hands were bare up to the elbows. Father's jacket was on the floor. Oooh, how cold, how cold!

She curled up tight and uncovered her eyes. There was something unusual about the room. The light of the white, shiny ruble. On the wall, spookily large, the shadows of the crossbeams of the loom lay crisscross. The iron fittings on the green trunk with the red roosters gleamed like silver bands. Even the old brown wardrobe that always stood there so sadly subservient now looked as though it had put on a soft velvet jacket.

Annele sat up quickly and looked out the little window. The snow-clogged panes shone and glinted. The moon was shining outside. The storm was no longer pushing at the corners of the house, the chimney no longer howled. Stillness had spread across the barrens.

The blizzard was over. As quickly as it had come, it had left again.

Morning dawned bright. The sun rose and swept away the shadows as though with a fiery broom. The barrens blazed up like a huge lighter. Far, far into the distance stretched the open space with its glittering mounds of snow. Krančelis leaped over them – rolled about, disappeared up to the tip of his tail, thrashed about sputtering in the porous snow, howled, whined, barked with joy.

Now there was work to be done outside. Clearing the snowdrift out of the doorway, shoveling paths, tending the cattle. Their steps were hurried, their hands quick.

The morning passed by. Annele was surprised. Today her parents were strangely silent. Of course, it was Sunday, and each of them had a book in their hands. But in between times they could surely have talked about why the travelers hadn't returned yet. Yesterday, there had been no end to their talk, today they were silent. Annele knew it was because their worry had now settled deeper into their bones.

They did the noon chores and came back into the house. And again they did not talk, as though angry at each other.

The sun was just about to set over the forest when Father suddenly rose to his feet, got his tall boots, put on his sheepskin jacket and took the fat cudgel from the woods at Spring Farm in his hand.

"You're going to meet them?" Mother asked.

"I have to see what's up. What the road through the woods is like."

Father left, but Krančelis remained sitting at the end of the house as though turned to stone, deaf to all questions and invitations.

Annele had had time to level many snowdrifts, to trample many paths over again, when Krančelis gave the first signal.

"Somebody's coming!"

Mother came out of the house.

"What? Is it the sleigh?"

Not the sleigh – it was Father coming back.

He came lightly, as if some heavenly spirit were carrying him across the snow. His face was bright and cheerful.

"Well, so what's up?" Mother called uncomprehending from a distance.

"What's up, dear wife, is that I realized how little faith we have, how little we know. I rushed off to the woods, and turned around like a fool. You see, it occurred to me that the children will be smarter than us and take the big detour road which will have been well traveled. And you worried in vain and tormented yourself in vain day and night. You know the proverb: Nothing has ever happened to you but what God has ordained."

"Yes, yes, I know," Mother answered grudgingly. "But that doesn't help. And what good did it do for you to run all the way to the woods?"

"What good did it do? My heart became light. And if my eyes don't trick me, something is rising, moving this way from the bottom lands of Fork Farm – it must be them."

Peering keenly, Father looked in the direction of Fork Farm. The sun had disappeared behind the forest. The horizon was submerged in shadows, but in one spot, through what looked like a blue gate, it let through a moving sleigh.

Krančelis couldn't understand why Father was on the lookout. His master had left and returned again. He was satisfied.

"Krančel, how come you don't see them?" Annele said reproachfully.

"Woof, woof!" Yes, now he finally saw them. It was as if a stone had dropped on his dog consciousness. How could he have forgotten that Gray and the big children were not at home! He must blot out this disgrace. Howling and barking, he raced across the barrens and vanished among the snowdrifts.

The three of them waiting there laughed. Their laughter rang out in the soft silence of dusk. The barrens themselves now seemed to be full and sonorous. Everybody felt good.

"Just don't tell the children we were so foolishly worried," warned Father.

"Why should I go and tell them?" Mother replied mollified, having shaken off her worries.

The sleigh came across the barrens loud and swift, making its way around the snowdrifts. Gray neighed and snorted, Krančelis leaped around him, barking merrily, while the two in the sleigh were laughing, exclaiming, and talking at the same time. When they had raced into the yard and had both jumped out, each into their own snowdrift, Gray neighed softly and turned his head toward Father, who was the first to fondle him, lightly stroking and then slapping the horse's trembling haunch.

"I hope you weren't hard on my Gray."

"Not at all," the returnees protested. The highway, they said, had already been well traveled, though after the turnoff there had been only the track of one sleigh, and nothing at all once they had passed Fork Farm, so that the snowdrifts in some places had been up to the horse's belly; otherwise, though, everything had gone well, very well.

When Gray has been unharnessed and fed, and there is deep darkness outside, they all sit around the table, the little lamp is burning and there is no end to the travelers' stories about what a good time they've had. How happy the relatives were about their arrival, and what a lovely day they had picked for their visit, since a nearby neighbor of Uncle's was getting married. They spent every night of their visit at this wedding, staying up till dawn. There were lots of young people, lots of city people and important persons from the vicinity. But the one who surpassed them all was a young wealthy crown farmer, who alone tossed one silver ruble at a time to the musicians. And this young gentleman no sooner caught sight of Līziņa than he refused to budge from her side. Dancing only with her, he refused to let her out of his arms all night, so to speak.

It is mostly Brother who tells these stories, especially the one about the crown farmer, and as he speaks he glances at Līziņa a little oddly, giving a wink with one eye half-closed. Maybe the others don't notice, but Annele can see it clearly, and thinks something else happened during the visit, something special that the half-closed eye seems to know about.

Līziņa doesn't want him to tell the stories. She slaps his hands.

"What silly things you say! It's all nonsense."

"Aha, you don't want to hear the truth," Brother dodges her slaps with a laugh.

"Who is that crown farmer, and what's his name?" Father wants to know.

When Brother says the crown farmer's name, it turns out he lives quite close by. Father knows the man himself, his farm, and his family. A grand family, a big farm, and great wealth. Only one sister. She's already married, and her dowry's been paid. The man can live like the squire of an average estate.

"There's no sense setting your cap at people like that! Not a hope!" Mother sighs.

"Does he know you're not some heiress, but a poor farmhand's daughter?" Father now asks Līziņa directly, and it seems to Annele that his voice is unusually stern.

"Oh, what does he need to know for? And anyway, why do we have to talk about him?" Līziņa responds curtly, as if irritated. She jumps up and leaves the table. Nor does anybody continue talking about the crown farmer.

But Annele is thinking. She is in the great big room at the unknown farm with the roar, chatter, laughter, and movement of many people around her, and Līziņa is among them, while a stranger keeps circling and circling around her, and Annele can't understand what it is the stranger really wants. She isn't kindly disposed toward him, that's for sure.

Līziņa isn't cheerful anymore, either. While Mother is making supper, and Father and Brother, sitting on the bed, talk about Uncle Zanders – how his crops are doing, what sort of horses he has, how trading is going in Dobele – Līziņa, bent over the table, is measuring something in a hurry and sewing, for she has to leave early next morning. Annele deliberately romps around with Krančelis: wonder if she'll glance in Annele's direction, burst out laughing? No, she neither hears nor sees. Her long black lashes have dropped on her cheeks, her nostrils rise and fall quickly as she breathes, but her lips are pinched together so tight it seems she has no intention of talking at all. She sews for a while, sews, stops suddenly, her white fingers quickly, quickly drum against the table; sews for a while, sews – and drums again.

It's not like other times, but Annele already knows: no time is like other times.

The Rīga Cousin

The days are long, the days are short. They are long when they go by trailing one after the other like snails. Gray, empty. And they seem short when they have run past without leaving a single memorable incident. Gray, empty. There was no shortage of such days in the barrens.

One evening as fall approached Mother said: "Your aunt from Rīga and Mildiņa and Einītis have arrived at Chisel Farm. They'll be coming to see us as well, the very next day maybe."

That was good news. Annele walked on air thinking happy thoughts: "Good, good. Now people will come to the barrens."

Much too early on the following day she started waiting. Her impatience wore her out, and by the time they actually did come – she saw three heads like little dots moving along the edge of the ditch – Annele was in a critical frame of mind.

"Don't tell me they're coming along the ditch! Don't they realize it goes straight into the wheat field? How come they don't see that it ends there and that you can't go any further?"

She signaled, called, waved her arm. The approaching figures did not see her.

"They can only see what's right in front of their eyes. No further."

She couldn't run and meet them, for a herd girl cannot leave her job.

"Oh, for goodness' sake! Townspeople!" Annele shook her head.

Mother had caught sight of them. She ran out to meet them. Now they knew which direction to turn.

Annele understood: the visitors needed to rest, to have a good talk and a bite to eat, but it all took much too long. Still, Milda could have run out to the pasture hours ago.

She didn't come till it was almost evening.

She didn't come skipping, as Annele would have done on a similar occasion, but walking slowly and with dignity like the city girl she was. If that was the way it was, Annele also restrained herself and allowed the visitor to come quite close before she ran to meet her.

The girls shook hands and kissed.

"How are things going?" asked Milda.

"See for yourself," Annele answered.

That subject was exhausted.

"My, you've grown tall," Annele inspected her cousin, who looked pale and lanky.

"It's just my high absetzes, other than that I'm no taller than you are."

"What's 'absetzes'?"

Milda pointed to her heels.

"Let's measure how tall we are!" said Annele.

They stood back to back and measured themselves. For some reason Milda did not want to show that she was taller, even by a tiny little bit.

"You're wearing *pastalas*, that's why." Milda looked at Annele's feet. "I'd never wear *pastalas*. They make your foot big and clumsy."

Blushing to the roots of her hair, Annele took a look. Did Milda have to talk like that?

She didn't answer Milda. She had to run and turn back the cows which, realizing the herder was preoccupied, had at once decided to run off on their own. When Annele came back, Milda was still standing in the same spot, her nose turned up somewhat.

"It shtörs me," she said.

"What's 'shtörs'?"

"Bothers me, I mean."

"What bothers you?"

"You don't understand anything, do you?" Milda retorted.

Annele did understand, but Milda's way of talking irritated her.

Now she caught sight of her aunt and Einītis, and ran to meet them.

Mildiņa's mother was tall, kind, and bright, but a little helpless. A tiny bit stooped. More from habit than because she couldn't straighten her back. Her blue eyes under the thick black eyebrows, always smiling, had an observant and warmhearted gaze.

Einītis clung to his mother's skirt. He was not much shorter than Mildiņa, but everybody considered him sickly and small.

His hair was the color of flax, and his eyebrows and eyelashes, which were practically invisible, were just as white. His eyelids always looked red. The boy was as frail as an egg. As soon as anybody touched a finger to him, he began sniveling. Annele didn't know what to do with him. To her, Mildiņa always seemed to be a closer relative than this boy, who gave grumpy answers.

"My Einītis is on the sickly side, you know," said Aunt. She felt sorry for him and spoiled him. But Annele's mother thought that when Einītis was born he hadn't been properly thrashed with birch branches in the sauna. That was all it was, she said. Aunt, being a person with modern views, had refused to believe in such foolish customs.

Aunt pats Annele's head and kisses her, compliments her on being a herder, and presses a little bundle into her hand. In it is a pretzel and a few cubes of brown sugar.

"Why did you run away empty-handed like that? You were supposed to bring your cousin her present, you know," she scolds Mildiņa.

Then she questions Annele about the herd: what sort of cows, their names, how much milk do they give?

Annele is only too glad to tell her: Acorn and Pearl are the full-grown cows, good milkers. Acorn's very independent, and you always have to keep an eye on her. Wherever she goes, the whole herd follows. She can smell a meadow or a wheat field a mile away. Head raised, she then bellows stubbornly and demands to go in that direction. When you turn her back, she acts surprised, turning her horns this way and that. She'll obey, mind you, but only that one time: as soon as you lose sight of her, you don't know where she'll end up. Pearl isn't a blockhead like Acorn. She's incapable of thinking up tricks. She eats what's there to eat and finds a larger share than Acorn, who sometimes ends up with her belly empty as she runs after tidbits. That's why she gives less milk.

Poppy and Brownie are still in their childhood. Poppy is only one year old, while Brownie is three. Brownie is the prettiest of the cows. Annele's favorite. Small, beautifully curved horns, a coat like silk. Her wide, moist eyes are so wise. She watches and waits for Annele to come, embrace her neck, nestle her head against her, tickle her behind the ears. Annele invites Milda to see how sweet Brownie is.

"Oh, ugh!" Milda shakes her head.

Annele sees that her visitors are only listening with half an ear, and, dumb-founded, she suddenly flushes for forgetting herself and chattering too much.

That day the visitors are still like company, while the next day they seem at home. To save her city clothes, Milda gets to wear Annele's dress, and Aunt, too, puts on Mother's Sunday skirt and instead of shoes she wears *pastalas*, which are easier on her feet. Milda refuses to wear *pastalas*. She says the strings bite into her calves. She'd rather go barefoot.

Aunt would love to do some sewing or mending. But there's nothing to sew, for there's no cloth to make anything new, and Mother's already finished the mending herself. So now both sisters try to figure out what sort of work will be given to the vis-itor, for she doesn't want to be without work.

Finally they figure it out, and Aunt begins to work. On her knees is a piece of old homespun cloth that was once the back of one of Father's jackets. On it, with chalk, she draws all sorts of coils and curlicues, and along these she later carefully guides a needle threaded with a length of colored yarn. The result is garlands, stalks, leaves, and flowers. It will be a rug by Mother's bedside or a wall hanging. They can put it wherever they like. It's beautiful, wherever it's placed.

As soon as Annele drives the herd home at noon, she immediately hastens to see how many flowers have appeared on the threadbare piece of cloth. In the middle of the yard there is a stack of lumber. This is where Aunt sits, hunched in the short shadow of the boards. She's come to the country for the clean air and the greenery, which is why she doesn't sit indoors, but there is no greenery except the green grass that has been growing undisturbed in the gaps between the boards since spring. Annele squats on the ground next to her and watches the needle running back and forth diligently with its colored yarn. Her aunt interrupts her work and strokes Annele's head with a pale, delicate hand. Then they both inspect the embroidered roses. They're all alike, with a bit of red in the middle, a bit of green in the leaves, but all the rest is gray, for Aunt's supply of yarn consists largely of gray yarn from unrav-eled old stockings. Annele thinks that the roses should really look different, but she keeps this to herself. There is no colored wool, and that is why it is impossible to create miracles.

It's nice to sit with this aunt from Rīga for a while and have a chat. Annele has so much to tell about Acorn, Brownie, Krančelis, about cranes and peewits; about Goldencrest, the king over the hens; about the big rock Father blew up in fall, and how it was cemented into the foundation for the threshing barn; about Aldis, Krists, Miķelis, and the other men who've been coming to New Farm to put up buildings. There's no one else she can tell, for the others already know, while this is all new to her Rīga aunt; and she must enjoy listening, for she keeps asking question after ques-tion, but sometimes clasps her hands one on top of the other and laughs till tears spurt into her eyes. At such times the girl looks at her perplexed: What is her aunt laughing about? But soon she forgets again, she herself enjoys the words set free like a brook, and the fact that when she tells it again everything seems different than when she actually saw it with her eyes.

City people sleep late. That's their custom. Annele has sung her fill, read a book till she can read no more, measured the shadow several times, according to which it's long past breakfast time, has upbraided her cousin in a solitary monologue because she is way overdue bringing breakfast, as they had agreed yesterday, – and then finally she comes, as though on a long march, without hurrying the least bit.

"Too slow," Annele criticizes.

"Why do you graze them so far away?" are her cousin's first words.

"Don't you know? Why, I graze them where the grass is."

"But then you could have run to meet me when you saw me coming."

"Herders have to stay with their herd," Annele declares firmly.

The herder now sits down to her meal and instructs Milda:

"Milda, run and turn back Acorn."

But Acorn knows quite well what sort of herder follows her with seemingly hobbled steps, and Milda is left gaping as the cow's raised tail snakes past her eyes. Annele catches her troublemaker with one leg over the ditch of Fork Farm.

"I told you: run, but you creep like an earthworm. That's no way to herd," Annele instructs her cousin.

Milda wrinkles her nose.

"I'm no country girl – I'm not used to running about. Nobody runs like that in town."

"Funny!" Annele gives a laugh, not knowing how to respond.

The cattle don't let the herder eat in peace.

"You really could turn back those sheep."

"There you go, sending me again," Milda acts surprised. "How come I'm always supposed to go to turn them back for you? It's not a bit interesting. Or genteel for that matter."

As though she had been slapped in the face, Annele jumps to her feet and attends to her duty.

"Was that the way it really was, did I always send Milda to turn the herd back? No, that's not true! Not always, anyway. Only once in a while. And is that why I'm not genteel? That's not true! – Well, maybe, maybe it is. After all, she's company. It isn't proper. And what did I have to do that for? I'm just getting lazy, that's all."

Annele never again sends her visitor to turn back the animals.

With her cousin, things often turn out differently than expected. What she likes, Annele dislikes, and vice versa. It's the same with Rīga, which is what most of their talk is about. It turns out differently than it should. Annele listens and listens, but she's not satisfied. She doesn't like Milda's Rīga as much as the Rīga she's imagined herself, but Milda can't stand objections: "You don't know anything about it! Have you ever seen Rīga?"

She's never seen Rīga, not exactly, but that's no reason for her not to know anything about it. She knows the whole long song "Rīga, Rīga, so they say" by heart. Milda's never even heard of it. She listens and shakes her head: W-e-e-l-l, I guess a song like that is good enough for country people.

Annele can see Rīga. It is a distant, white-towered, mighty city, shining in eternal sunlight.

What are these towers like? What does Milda know about them?

Towers? Oh, sure. There are some – St. Peter's, St. James's, the cathedral's. Each and every one of them is black and old, with roosters sitting on top. What's there to say about the towers?

Whereas the magnificent buildings, the gleaming shop windows, the fine gentlemen, the lovely ladies are a different matter! And the way the ladies walk: on high heels, with only their toes touching the ground. One hand lifting the train of the skirt, a parasol in the other, head elegantly thrown back, for the hat on its high chignon is pinned so it slopes toward the tip of the nose. The genteel fashion of the ladies is to raise their eyebrows, to pinch their lips together so their mouth looks small. And the genteel fashion of the gentlemen, on the other hand, is to walk about with shiny top hats on their heads, their mustaches twirled, their beards brushed out in both directions, jackets buttoned at the waist, a thin little cane in one hand. When gentlemen greet ladies, the top hat leaps up in a hand elegantly thrown back, the gentleman turns toward the lady, both of them smile, look into each other's eyes, bat their eyelashes, say: Moyn, moyn! This is all acted out by Milda, who turns this way and that, bows, makes faces, rolls her eyes. And in this Rīga there are gentlemen who, if Milda happens to pass by going the other way, look at her, look so hard that it seems their eyes are stuck in their eyelids with amazement. And this happens not once or twice, oh no: it happens quite often that gentlemen pass by practically staring. It seems as though Milda herself were the great city of Rīga then, and as though gentlemen revolved around looking at her like she was the moon.

"Looking at you? Well, why do those gentlemen look at you like that?" Annele is puzzled.

"Gee, how would I know?" Milda tosses her head back haughtily.

The sun is beginning to burn worse and worse. Milda protects the back of her head with both hands, but it does no good. And since they've had quite a long talk, she returns to the house, walking somewhat more hastily but still elegantly.

Annele watches as Milda leaves. Head leaning back sideways a bit, feet in rhythm, swaying at the hips. That must be the way Rīga ladies walk.

She keeps remembering the stories. Ladies, gentlemen, and Milda herself. How come she kept mentioning that the gentlemen look at her? Why do they look at her like that?

Well, if they look at her, they must like her. And if they like her, she must be beautiful.

So Milda is beautiful?

Yes, if you add up everything Milda has said about herself, or rather, the things she says others say about her, the end result is that Milda really is beautiful. She has a patrician nose, a tiny little red mouth, dark, curly hair, blue eyes which under their black lashes sometimes dilate till they are so large that the whites hold the dark pupils in a wide embrace; this happens especially when she shows how the gentlemen look at her. Not all at once, but bit by bit it's all come to light, and not all at once, but slowly, bit by bit, it has become clear to Annele that she is not like Milda. Not by a long shot! She has neither a patrician nose, nor a tiny little coin of a mouth, nor hair as curly as Milda's, nor lashes as long. And if Milda with all these traits is beautiful, while Annele lacks them, then it's clear as daylight that Annele is not beautiful. Once she reaches this conclusion, Annele feels a bit like laughing. "Funny," she says. But the laughter soon passes. It comes down like a fine icy drizzle from head to foot, and it no longer seems like laughter at all, the way it gnaws strangely at her arms and legs, and turns bitter in her mouth as if she had bitten into a sour apple.

She's not pretty, not pretty. Can that really be true, though? She doesn't want to believe it.

There is one little mirror at home on the wall. It's useful when you want to see if your hair's been parted straight. It doesn't show your whole face.

She could ask somebody. But who? Mother would laugh and make some kind of joke, but she's embarrassed to ask Father. How can you ask a question like that?

But the girl can't stop thinking about it. She is sitting with Aunt, talking about this and that, and then – quite quickly and suddenly:

"Aren't I pretty at all?"

"You? What's wrong with the way you look?" Aunt asks her in turn.

That's not a satisfactory answer.

"But Mildiņa is prettier, right?"

"Depends on who's looking. Each of you has her own beauty."

"You're awfully ugly. Your nose is spotted."

That's Einis, who never has a kind word for Annele.

"His own nose is spotted as a peewit's egg," laughs Aunt.

Annele thinks for a while and then says:

"Oh, to hell with being pretty! What do I need to be pretty for?"

Another time when the girls talk about Rīga, it's a different Rīga. It's called Sand Hills. That's where Milda lives. And Milda, too, is different then. Not the proud Rīga lady with her head thrown back, but quite a simple girl. And the Sand Hills are extremely interesting. There's no end of work. New streets are being drawn, lots are being measured for big and small buildings, foundations are being dug, building materials brought in. In the Sand Hills, Rīga grows the same way as New Farm is growing here. Only there, building after building goes up with incredible speed, and people teem like ants. Not like here, when they only get to the construction work at those times when there's no more work in the fields. In Rīga there are hundreds of people who do nothing but construction work. – Along the newly drawn streets they buy a plot of land, and then houses shoot up like mushrooms. Then people walk at a half-run, and you'd think the building was being done by machines. And these houses are being built not by some kind of fine gentlemen or Germans, but by ordinary moujiks. Peons.

What kind of words are those, wonders Annele, for this is the first time she's heard many of Milda's expressions. Milda explains that these peons are plain and simple Latvians who've saved up some money and are now flaunting their houses in Sand Hills. Why, soon they'll own half of Rīga. One of them particularly, a bachelor by the name of Namdaris, has as much money as the devil has chaff. He owns a whole street, says Milda. He's built close to twenty houses. And as soon as one is finished, right away it's as full as a beehive. For the apartments are exactly the kind that people in Sand Hills are looking for: a nice room with a big window, while the hallway, which has many little kitchens, is shared by all the tenants. Everything's spacious, comfortable, clean, and airy. Milda's parents, too, are planning to move there in fall from their dreadful basement apartment. Namdaris knows Mama and occasionally drops in and then boasts that in his buildings everybody will feel as if they were in paradise.

Namdaris, says Milda, never talks about anything but his buildings, or about how he's going to find a wife as soon as he finishes the construction work. Milda's mama then advises him that he shouldn't put off getting married. As soon as he finishes the buildings, her mama says, money will start coming in, but the more money comes in, the more he'll want to build more buildings, for the people who need them keep coming in droves, like flies in summer. And her mama says he could go on slaving like this till his hair turns gray, when it will be too late to get married. Yes, Namdaris apparently has given it some thought, and he actually is looking for a wife, but while he's been looking, a year or two have gone by, and the young woman he had in mind is married by now, while another, who was left on the shelf and waited, is too old for him now.

Thus Milda tells her stories with her quick little Rīga tongue, and her mouth is full of laughter. As for Namdaris himself, she says he's pretty stooped and stiff; his beard is already showing signs of gray; he's old, around thirty or more, and the way he looks and looks! Of course he almost devours Milda too with his eyes, maybe waiting for her to grow up. But she wouldn't. She'd never marry a bag of bones, a skinflint like him, all the girls should turn a fellow like him down! She'd be the first to turn him down, Milda says. Papa thinks so too. Papa can't stand the sight of Namdaris. He's always grumbling, says Milda, that an idiot like Namdaris is so brazenly lucky that he can, as it were, pick money up off the ground. But Milda's mama defends Namdaris. She says it's not a bad thing for a person to try hard. A person who tries hard is going to get somewhere. Namdaris knows how to make money, but that doesn't make him a bad person, says her mama.

No, he's not a bad person, acknowledges Milda. Other builders are a lot worse. He doesn't charge exorbitant rents, and he allows you to carry away the wood chips from his new buildings for free. In spring, when the carpenters cut and trimmed the logs and there were scads of wood chips, crowds of women, but mostly children, came all day long. They arrived with empty sacks and left in a row like peddlers, though they carried their sacks not on their backs, but on their heads.

Milda, too, went out collecting chips all spring. The woodshed is packed full with firewood, all of it brought by Milda. Mama has a stitch in her side, she can't lift or carry, and Einis is still little and delicate, and besides Mama finds excuses for him. But firewood is so expensive, and this is where you can get it for free. Who but Milda can go and collect the chips?

When Milda reaches the part about carrying wood chips, her voice gets dark and plaintive. That in itself is enough to make one surmise what this Rīga where Milda lives is like, and what her life there is like. At the crack of dawn, her mama rouses her from her sleep. She has to hurry so other firewood gatherers don't pick out and walk off with the larger scraps of wood. Out the door, quick. No time to think of breakfast. And it's not as though she ever gets there first. The construction site is crowded. Some of the construction workers are rude, they chase away the kids from underfoot so they won't interfere with the work, others say nothing. They're the best. But the people who give Milda the hardest time are the boys, whom she calls street urchins. They rarely come singly like the girls, but in groups, and they stick together. They pick out the thickest scraps, log ends, little blocks of wood, all the biggest and best stuff, and put it in a pile. And whatever is in the pile is theirs. While some of them lug their sacks home, the others stay by the pile watching it. Don't even go close if you're a girl. They curse, whistle, push, pinch, pull the girls' braids. Sometimes the noise is enough to split your eardrums. Then it's a good thing when Namdaris arrives. He doesn't give the boys free rein. The pile they've stacked up doesn't do them a bit of good. As for the boys, Namdaris tells them to share all the wood equally. If anybody contradicts him or even starts to swear, Namdaris sends him packing. Then every child can take home scraps from his own pile till nightfall, and nobody is allowed to touch it anymore.

Yes indeed! Hunting for wood scraps is hell for the children in the outskirts of Rīga.

At the end of the day, the top of your head burns like fire from the pressure of the sack, and during the night, every time she wakes up, Milda touches her head to see if she's lost all her hair from all that carrying, but no: her hair is as full and curly as it's always been.

"Yes, don't think that life in Rīga is easy," Milda says then, shaking her head with a sort of grown-up superiority. "You know, you've got it easy here in the country! Your mother goes in the garden, pulls a few potatoes, picks some beets; she goes in the *klēts*, grabs some flour; goes in the pantry, and there's cream and butter, and milk. More than enough for everybody. Look at us, though. No *klēts*, no pantry. It's all at the store, and it all costs money. And when you buy stuff on credit, they don't give you the best, but the worst. Papa earns so little, so little. When the month is over, it's all been eaten up in advance, and we never manage to get out of debt. Papa is capable of filling a much more important job, but they don't give him one. As soon as a better job opens up, they pick somebody else, some complete idiot, a totally useless person, and Papa has to do without. Whenever he's home from work, Papa does nothing but grumble and grouse, but it's no use. Mama thinks Papa would have a better chance if he was kinder and more accommodating, but he isn't capable of it. It's not easy with Papa, but that's the way it is."

When Milda is in a good mood, the girls sing together. It's true that Milda can't go down as low or go up as high as Annele, but hers is a rich middle range sound, and their voices intertwine very nicely. Not for long though. The songs that appeal to Annele don't appeal to Milda. When it comes to folk songs, she shakes her head. Neither "Blow, wind," nor "I lost my fine horse," nor "Far, far at night," nor "Pine tree, pine tree, where are your branches?" which sound so lovely and echo so far away over the barren, find favor in Milda's eyes. Milda says they're not taught at her school, and songs that aren't taught at her school are just for common people. She wants Annele to learn "Guter Mond," "Aus dem Himmel ferne," and "Es braust ein Ruf wie Donnerhall." But if Milda doesn't accept Annele's songs, then Annele

doesn't accept Milda's. To Annele "Guter Mond" and "Aus dem Himmel ferne" are
nothing but screeching, a silly German business, while she simply can't get that
donnerhall into her head. She tells Milda in no uncertain terms. Milda can teach her
as much as she likes, Annele stops up her ears and refuses to listen.

"You can't get it into your head because you're not very bright. People who are
bright learn easily."

"So what if I'm not bright!"

Then Milda angrily turns on her heel and runs home.

Once Milda is gone, Annele drives her herd a good long distance away and now
tries to sing the songs Milda taught her. Yes, she can do it pretty well. Only that
donnerhall still limps along. She doesn't understand what the words mean. But the
last lines go meandering off, to end up lodged in her head: "Lieb Vaterland, magst
ruhig sein, fest steht und treu die Wa-a-acht am Rhein."

Milda comes to the pasture less and less often. When the sun is oppressively hot,
she doesn't feel like it; when it is cloudy and drizzling, she doesn't feel like it. Now
Annele listens to her talk of Rīga with only half an ear, and no longer accepts those
fine city manners. As the days go by, Milda increasingly points up the distance between her and a plain country girl like Annele. But when Milda scolds her, saying:
"See what sort of a person you are?" – Annele stubbornly tosses her head: "So what?"
And once, when Milda has again been forced to point out to Annele that refined
people don't do thus and so, Annele suddenly turns against her and says: "Go to hell,
and take your refinement with you!"

This is too much for Milda. She tries to think of an answer and can't think of
one so quickly. Here's what she finally says: "Well, what other language can you expect from a girl that spends her life among sheep and pigs?"

And so now their conversations are at an end, too.

In the barrens, there's little greenery for the Rīga guests, and so they start to talk
about having to go back to Chisel Farm. There you've got the woods with all sorts of
berries right outside the door, and in the orchard apples and other fruit are starting
to ripen, and so one fine morning Annele sees all three of them go off in the direction
of Chisel Farm. Mother accompanies them, a white bundle under her arm.

This takes Annele by surprise. Though they'd been talking about leaving, she
didn't believe it would be so soon. And surely they could have said goodbye to her.
True, this morning, when she left with the herd, the Rīga relatives were still fast
asleep in the barn, but Milda could surely have run to the pasture for a while. It
hadn't even occurred to her. As though Annele didn't even exist.

Tears come into her eyes out of bitterness or regret. Her regret is stronger, however, and gains the upper hand. Step by step she follows the walking figures with her
eyes. By the boundary ditch they stop, talk for a while, Mother gives Milda her little
white bundle and turns back. Annele has the impression that her aunt waves her
hand in the direction of her herd. Milda doesn't even look up. Now they are vanishing on the other side of the pale field of rye. Now you still see their heads, now
they vanish, then disappear completely.

It's sad that they leave and disappear like this. Annele has the feeling that the visitors left sadder than when they arrived. Maybe things were different for them here than they had expected. It was probably all because Annele was not as kind, as friendly and nice as she should have been toward them.

Mother had seen her company off with a little white bundle. In it were meat and butter to take to Rīga. Annele remembers from her earliest childhood, when Milda's parents still lived in the country, how Mother always went to see them with such bundles. Always, she'd leave with her hands full, and return empty-handed. Life was hard for Milda's parents. Why was this so? Annele didn't understand.

Milda will go to Rīga, and again she will have to carry wood scraps to get firewood. Annele has no need to worry about firewood – Father brought home a load last winter. And it's just as Milda said: Annele has potatoes and bread, butter and milk, and, nicest of all, she has a father who never grumbles or scolds; of course sometimes he doesn't talk and doesn't answer while he's working on something, but when he talks he's as nice and loving as the sun. Come to think of it, Annele really does have a much better life than Milda in that fine Rīga of hers.

Fear

When she drove the herd home at noon, Annele learned that the Rīga visitors would stay on at Chisel Farm for a while longer. And so it had been arranged that in a few weeks Mother and Father would go to Jelgava to visit the older children and bring some food for Brother, who had already gone back to his school with Uncle from Spring Farm. That would be when Milda would come back to the barrens for a couple more days to keep Annele company.

And that's what happened.

During those weeks, the days had already become perceptibly shorter, and the nights dark. When Mother, dressed for the road, woke Annele, reminding her once more of all the household chores and telling her to be sure and close the door, it might have been midnight, or late in the evening maybe, for the sooner you set off for a destination as distant as Jelgava the better; why, the bumpy dirt road from the house to the highway took close to an hour, and Gray was never one to canter a lot.

Father was waiting outside. He called. The horse was harnessed. Mother hurriedly tied her shawl across her chest, cast a glance around the room to see if she had forgotten anything. Instructed the girl: "You two can get into the big bed now, it'll be warmer and safer there. Bolt the door. And don't be afraid. Who would ever come all the way out here, miles and miles away from anywhere? It's never happened before."

The door had a wooden bolt carved by Father himself. As Annele shot the bolt, she could hear that her parents were already in the wagon, still talking quietly, Gray snorted a bit, Father stirred the reins, urged the horse, Krančelis, too lazy to show astonishment or surprise at such an unaccustomed night drive, whimpered piteously a few times, but stayed in his kennel. Annele felt it would be inappropriate to take advantage of her privilege and crawl into her parents' bed while Milda remained alone in the bed they shared. So she went back and lay down next to Milda, who was fast asleep.

Somewhere off in the darkness, in the direction of Fork Farm, there was still the rattling of the wagon. Sometimes the noise was louder, as though coming closer, at other times it was weaker, as though waning, but she could hear it. The wheels bouncing over the bumps sounded like distant faint blows on the ground. They rolled and rolled and rolled. Rat-tat-tat! Rat-tat-tat! Amazing how long you could hear them! Now they rumbled over the little bridge across the boundary ditch, then once more began to thunder more loudly, for they were on a hard road. And then suddenly everything was silent.

Annele raised her head, listened as hard as she could. She couldn't hear another sound. Time to put her head on the pillow and sleep.

Odd, though! Her head was turned now toward Milda, now toward the wall, then back toward Milda, but she couldn't sleep.

Milda was snoring too loudly. One snore like that, and sleep was gone in a flash. She stopped up her ears, but in vain. She could still hear it.

Well, so what if sleep wouldn't come! She pushed away the blanket and began to think. Her mother's words still rang in her ears. "Don't be afraid."

And suddenly she knew that it was these words and these words alone that had been in her ears all this time. Not Milda's snoring. "Don't be afraid, don't be afraid!" Just those words, all the time.

Why had Mother said: Don't be afraid? Afraid? What was that? Why, they'd never thought or talked about fear. Milda had come so Annele wouldn't be bored all by herself. And was there any safety in being with her? She was such a heavy sleeper she didn't know if it was morning or night, as she said herself. Annele would be better off with Krančelis. Should she open the door and call the dog? Not because she was afraid, but for company's sake. He'd prefer being inside, too. And if anything was wrong, he'd respond. Why, he could hear a bird's wing in the air.

She'd already pushed back the bolt, and now all she had to do was throw open the door, but suddenly it felt as if somebody had slapped her hand, and the bolt shot back again. For: suppose somebody was standing outside at this very moment, waiting to slip into the house as soon as the door was opened? Or suppose he responded to her calling the dog with a strange, unfamiliar voice? What then? These thoughts flashed into the girl's head like lightning, but she immediately tried to dismiss them. Nonsense, nonsense! Why should anybody stand there, or wait, or respond to her call? There was nobody there! And even if anyone *was* there, Krančelis would have barked.

But suppose Krančelis had been killed with a sausage filled with a deadly poison? Yes, what if he had been poisoned?

Her heart convulsed, became numb. But Annele shook off the numbness.

Nonsense, nonsense! The silly thoughts that came into your mind! Everything was silent. Krančelis was in his kennel guarding the house. And that was all right. She'd leave him there. The house was no place for a dog.

Annele crawled back into bed. She curled up, stiff with cold. She decided to sleep, just sleep. When she woke up, morning would be here, and with it the secure chores of the day.

But how could she sleep if Milda snored like that? Every time she snored something would go crack in her throat. Annele began to count these cracks. "Once I reach a hundred, I'll be asleep," she thought. Crack – crack! One – two – three – –

She hadn't even counted to ten when her thoughts had sped elsewhere. Her thoughts raced around the chilly emptiness in which the barrens now lay, with New Farm in the center of it and Annele inside. Never before had this empty space seemed so vast, lonely, and cold to Annele. As though Father's wagon with its wheels as it rolled away had swept all life and warmth from it. Empty and yet somehow not really empty. Something alien and incomprehensible had edged closer. It lurked there silently.

"You're afraid," a voice seemed to whisper somewhere.

"What nonsense! What would I be afraid of?" Annele responded to the whisperer.

"You're afraid, you're afraid," the whisperer taunted her.

It wasn't the first time Father and Mother had been away from home. Last fall they had gone to church and returned quite late, while in spring, again after driving to church and then paying a short visit to Spring Farm, they had returned when it was pitch dark. So that she would not have to sit around idly waiting, the girl had at nightfall gone out to tend to the cattle as best she could. And in the big barn she had gone straight into that black, menacing corner to grab an armful of straw. And as she came back from the stables, she had walked not the least bit faster, though her heart, throbbing fast, had urged her to do so, for the darkness in back of her seemed to be right on her heels.

If she hadn't been scared then, she surely wasn't scared now. Fiddlesticks! Besides, with Milda here, there were two of them now!

But why couldn't she sleep? She had the feeling she had been lying there sleepless for hours and hours. Where might her parents be by now? If they had gone by one highway, they might be near Lipsts, if by the other, they were probably on the other side of Zaļā Muiža. But in that case it should be dawn soon.

Quickly she opened her eyes. Was it daybreak yet? No! The darkness seemed even blacker and thicker. Oppressively heavy. So she could sleep some more. Sleep peacefully.

But whenever her eyelids were about to sink into oblivion, some sort of noise – she wasn't sure if it was familiar or unfamiliar – would tear them open again: now something would crack in the wall, or the door would rattle, or something would sweep across the roof with a hiss.

"A mouse." – "The wind." – "Just something in my ears," Annele would then quickly dismiss such noises.

Listen! Now she could clearly hear Krančelis suddenly beginning to growl in his kennel. More slowly. More fiercely. Quite fiercely now. The dog's four paws softly padded down the trodden path. The dog was running this way. At the end of the house, his accustomed observation point, he hunkered down and uttered a long howl. Growling and snarling he ran around the house, squatted down again and now sent an uninterrupted series of warning calls in the direction of Fork Farm.

Annele raised her head. Listened. In that direction, there seemed to be the sound of a wagon rattling. Far away, seemingly tossed this way by a gust of wind, the barking of dogs began to abate as though shrouded in fog. So Krančelis hadn't been dreaming. There really *was* something moving, driving out there.

And it was coming closer. It didn't turn off down the boundary road in either direction, but rumbled across the little bridge and was now on the barrens. There was no road here but the one that led straight to New Farm.

Was it her parents returning? Had something happened?

No! If it had been her parents, Krančelis wouldn't be barking so fiercely. He'd have run to meet them. And this wasn't the firm, distinct rattling of the board wagon that had accompanied her parents' departure. Whoever it was that was coming was poking along, in what sounded like a manure cart.

Annele jumped out of bed and went to the window. The darkness was so thick it covered everything. It was midnight, maybe.

Nevertheless she could see a tangled mass of black in the barrens. Maybe it was moving, maybe standing still. Barking, Krančelis vanished in the darkness, and barking and fleeing he rushed back, escaping behind the house.

Milda's snores suddenly broke off. She sat up abruptly. Half bewildered, half frightened as she was, the questions just tumbled from her lips.

"What is it? Why are you running about, why don't you let me sleep? What's that dog barking for? Where're your parents? Have they left? What's going on here? There's somebody driving this way, can't you hear them? Who's that coming? Why are you looking out the window? Come here! I'm scared. Who's that coming?"

"I don't know," Annele answered from the window.

"What? You don't know?"

"No! How should I know?"

"Well, who should know if not you? Am I supposed to know who's prowling around on your barrens? Maybe it's a total stranger."

"It probably is a stranger," Annele said hesitantly.

"A stranger!" Milda exclaimed, hearing her suspicions confirmed, and then, in a whisper, pronounced her opinion:

"Well, then it can only be a robber or a murderer."

"Don't talk nonsense!" Annele retorted, angry that similar thoughts had just crossed her own mind. "Why on earth would a robber turn up in this place?"

"What do you know about it?" Milda couldn't stand being contradicted. "Every ditch is full of robbers. I bet he was sitting hiding in the bushes and saw your old folks driving by. And I bet he thought this was his chance. Nobody but kids at home."

"How could he know that? And what would there be for him to steal here?"

"But this is an isolated and faraway place. Just the place for a robber. He can load his wagon and drive away, and no one will be the wiser. The things burglars do sometimes! You country people are much too naive. Like your father and mother. How can they leave kids alone in the middle of the night and in a wasteland like this!"

"Don't yell! It's too late now!"

"Am I yelling? You're the one that's yelling! Get away from the window so he doesn't see there's people here. Come on! I'm scared!"

Annele finds her clothes and starts getting dressed. Milda hurriedly follows suit. Exclaiming between sobs: "It's no use. It's not as though we can run away anywhere!"

Slowly but inexorably the wagon approaches. The dog is frantic. Milda stops up her ears. Complains:

"Oh, why did I have to come here yesterday! Mama absolutely didn't want me to. She had a premonition. But that's what comes of only thinking of others! Why didn't I stay at Chisel Farm? What do we care? Let them drive off, let them go wherever they like! But what do I do now? I'll never see Mama, or Papa, or Einītis again!"

"Don't think that way. Maybe it isn't a bad person at all. Maybe he's just lost his way and is looking for a place to spend the night," Annele reassured her.

"A place to spend the night? Sure. Tell me about it! Are you saying he's passed by all the big farms and come here into your wasteland to look for a place to spend the night?"

She was right.

Suddenly Krančelis abruptly broke off his big barking. The wagon was close, but they could no longer hear the dog.

"What does that mean? If the dog isn't barking anymore, it must be somebody he knows."

"Somebody he knows really well, sure! I bet he shoved something down the dog's throat, and now he's done for. There's plenty of stories about such things in the papers."

The wagon rumbled past the end of the house. The girls held their breath. They could distinctly hear the dog jumping about the wagon, and the driver's voice muttering something in response. Annele whispered to express her joy that no harm had been done to Krančelis yet.

"You really think it happens that quickly?" Milda whispered back. "The sausage with the poison is sweet and delicious, and then the dog jumps up and down asking for more. But just wait: all of a sudden his throat will contract. He'll gasp for breath one more time, he'll give a sudden howl, and then he'll collapse and that's the end of him! You wait, it won't be long now."

"Nonsense! It's not going to happen."

"Wait, where's he going now?" Milda pricked up her ears.

The wagon slowly rumbled away and stopped.

"To the stables."

"The stables!" Milda exclaimed, pleased. "Well, then I know. Then he's come to steal cattle and won't even come to the house. That's good. Let's just be quiet, pretend we're asleep, let him do whatever he likes."

Annele got angry.

"Don't talk nonsense! How can a single person steal the cattle and cart them away? That will never happen!"

"Are you going to tell him what to do and what not to do? – Have you got any fattened pigs in the pigsty?"

"We do have one young porker."

"There you go! Then that's all he needs. He's going to kill it, throw it in the wagon, and leave before you can say knife," Milda stated with deep conviction.

"You talk like a child. You haven't the slightest idea how to deal with animals. He could no more overpower a porker single-handedly than he could lift it into the wagon."

"Well, you're not going to tell him how," Milda flew into a rage. "You're just sorry for your animals, that's all. As far as you're concerned he can come and bump off the two of us."

"Bump off, bump off. What sort of expression is that?" Annele now argues back. "Why'nt you listen to what he's doing out there? I think he's unharnessing the horse."

All sorts of sounds came from the stables. There was the muttering of a human voice, somebody called "Whoa!" or "Easy there!" A horse stamped its feet. Now the shafts dropped, the harness was taken off the horse, then the collar, now it was led out from between the shafts, there was no doubt that the horse had been unharnessed and the person who had arrived acted as though he was at home. There was not a sound from the dog.

Milda expressed her thoughts about this.

"The dog is dead. I've been telling you all this time. But do you believe me? You always want to be the smart one. But look what's happening now."

Feet pounded the path.

"Oh dear! He's coming this way!" exclaimed Annele.

At that moment a stupefying scream assailed her ears. At the top of her lungs, Milda shouted:

"Help, help! Save us! Murderers! Save us, everybody!"

She herself did not know who this everybody that would save them could be. Would those be some sort of invisible spirits somewhere close by, or could her cries be heard at Fork Farm or even at Chisel Farm, and would these helpers come with lightning speed, or perhaps could she with her scream hurl back the unknown monster as though with a slingshot? She didn't think.

In one breath, she yelled for help as loud as she could, in the next warned Annele in a whisper not to open the door for God's sake, urged her to push the table, chairs, benches, the big chest, the wardrobe in front of it, but of course the girls didn't manage to do any of this, for a fist hammered against the door, a hand impatiently rattled the doorknob. Milda shrieked her last "Help!" – threw herself into the bed and covered her head. But on the other side of the door someone was calling:

"Who'th that thcreaming? Rithe and thine, rithe and thine!"

A familiar lisping voice.

"Miķelis!" Annele exclaimed with such a rush of joy that her head was flung back from laughing so hard. "Don't be scared, Milda dear! It's Ģelžu Miķelis from Edgefield Farm. He can't pronounce the letter 's'."

Milda flung away the pillow.

"What Miķelis? Don't let him in, don't let him in!"

Annele had already unbolted the door.

Miķelis loomed in the doorway, scolding:

"What are you thquealing about, you thilly girl?"

"Nobody was squealing," Annele defended herself. "I have company, and she had a nightmare."

There was no way the girl was going to confess how terrified they had been.

"Well yeth, I'm pretty tired too," Miķelis said with a yawn. "I thnoozed and nodded all the way here."

Miķelis wanted the barn key so he could feed his horse and crawl in the hay for the night. While Annele was looking for the key, he told her longwindedly how yesterday morning already Papa Laukmalis had told him to go to New Farm so the girl wouldn't be alone when her father and mother went to Jelgava. And how Miķelis, thinking, "I will, I will, tonight!" had then gone to buy a piglet at the Žagare fair that had happened to take place yesterday; how he hadn't bought a piglet to be sure, but had taken a drop too much and hadn't gotten home till sunset, and how it wasn't until then that he had remembered what he had been told to do. Then he had thought it all over, decided what to do, had a bite to eat, gotten everything together and ready, harnessed the horse, and by the time he left the farmstead it had already been so dark that the dogs at his own farm no longer knew him, but barked at him as though he was a stranger. And so he had driven along, struggling with sleep, cooling his head, and fighting against all kinds of calamities: one time he had barely missed getting killed when he ran into a milestone, another he'd almost driven into the ditch, and a third time he'd turned down the wrong road, for that stinker of a horse, he said, was a Jewish peddler's nag, which was accustomed to turn down every country lane. The peddler had left it, worked almost to death, to graze in a field at Edgefield Farm, where it had recovered nicely, and Papa, sparing his own horses, had told Miķelis to take it for the night drive. And Miķelis, you see, doesn't say anything, he does what he's told, but it isn't his fault that he didn't show up till now, way after midnight. Whatever people say, it's not his fault.

Milda pretends that she's asleep and can't hear anything, but as soon as Miķelis is gone and the door is bolted, she sits up and sternly asks:

"And you had no idea this idiot was on his way here?"

"Miķelis is not an idiot, he just can't pronounce the letter 's'," Annele defends herself.

"I don't care. But you did know he was coming, and you just wanted me to be scared."

What nonsense Milda talked! Annele was shocked.

"How could I have known if I was scared myself? You saw me, I know you did."

"You weren't scared at all. You were just pretending you were. But you weren't screaming, or shaking."

Annele had no idea how to refute these suspicions.

"And I suppose your father didn't know either and didn't tell you?" Milda continued her inquisition.

"Maybe Father and Papa Laukmalis had planned it, but when Miķelis didn't show up yesterday Father thought Laukmalis had forgotten to send him, and so preferred not to tell us so as not to scare us for nothing because we had to stay by ourselves," was Annele's explanation of the incident with Miķelis.

"Typical peasants," concluded Milda haughtily. "There's no *ordnung* in anything they do."

"Ordnung, ordnung," repeated Annele. It was a word she was not familiar with.

But she didn't have a chance to ask Milda before sleep overwhelmed her.

Joys and Sorrows

Winter and summer, winter and summer. Herding the cattle, herding the cattle! And time passes. Is spring back already?

Flutes of ice.

Thin, fat, jagged, fringed, transparent like lace fringes they hang from the eaves. Here comes the sun. The flutes of ice begin to drip amber drops:

Pat, pat, pat!

Like honey from hanging honeycombs.

February is getting ready to clear out. At Candlemas there was such a thaw that there was enough not only for a pigeon but for an ox to quench his thirst. That means an early spring. Though of course it was bitter cold for a few more weeks after that. Now, though, the sun wears away the ice day by day.

Pat, pat, pat!

A sunny, sunny morning.

"Come on, let's go to the barn," Mother urges Annele. Smiling, mysterious.

As soon as they open the door, the barn suddenly comes to life: the lambs murmur, the sheep bleat, the cows low, the piglets grunt. Mother answers them all: "Easy, easy now! Wait! It isn't your turn yet."

When they entered they left the door wide open. The sun rushes in after them in a broad stream. Let it rush, let it bring warmth. After all, this is no longer winter, when the warmth of the barn had to be preserved like something precious. A bit of outside air can only do the cattle good now.

The cows are all on their feet, waiting and lowing, their heads turned toward their caretaker. Brownie alone lies on a big armful of yellow straw like loose rumpled pillows. She too would like to get up, but she can't. She just helplessly turns her head this way and that. And Mother pats her and reassures her: "You just lie there, stay down, Brownie dear, stay down!"

Annele has already caught sight of the reason for Brownie's lying down. Next to Brownie, alertly raised, a second head looks at her, a white star on its forehead.

"Look, Mother, Brownie's got a little calf!" the girl claps her hands with joy.

"Yes, how about that! Brownie's a mother too now. Well, how d'you like the little heifer? She's a healthy and strong little thing. We're going to raise her."

"She's beautiful, beautiful! She'll be just like Brownie."

Annele caresses the silky coat, but Brownie looks at her mistrustfully and tosses her horns in Annele's direction with a snort.

"Brownie doesn't recognize me anymore. She's trying to butt me."

"She's afraid you'll hurt her child. Well, what shall we call our new little heifer?"

"Star. She's got a star on her forehead."

"All right, Star it is. And she's going to be your cow. When she starts giving milk, we'll save the butter and sell it, and the profit will go towards school for you."

Annele's eyes begin to sparkle. School, school! But when will that be? Star has barely been born, when will she give milk? One year, two years, three years. – Is that how long she is supposed to wait for school?

"What can we do? Father's income is hardly enough for our daily bread. So all we've got is the cattle to give us that extra penny. But how long for? The bigger the fields get, the less pasture there'll be. And when there's no more pasture, who's going to let their farmhand keep this many animals, even if the farmhand happens to be a close relative? The homestead is growing bigger by leaps and bounds, too. Going to build the threshing barn this summer, and the farmhouse next summer. And when there's a nest the bird will come too. If it's Aldis, then I don't really mind, but if it should turn out to be Krists – who knows what either of them is planning to do! They haven't had a chance to live yet, or to be in charge of a place." So says Mother.

When they have seen to the cattle, milked the cows, and petted the curly lambs, of which almost every ewe has two, Mother hurries her outside and locks the barn.

The eaves are now no longer dripping, but literally streaming. The sun now hangs directly overhead. A clear little rivulet collects down below and spreads and runs on. The ice on the slough glistens as though it had been crying. Between the drifts, where the snow is shallower, there's something swelling, thrust out like a workingman's grimy fist. The further you run into the barrens, the more of those you see. Some snowdrifts still bear your weight, while into some you sink up to your knees – they're brittle as birch bark. The wind blows, the sun is warm, and between the two of them they use up the snow as fast as they can. Soon the barrens will be clear, shoots of grass will appear, and the animals will be let outside for the first time. How loud, how excited they will be then! The cows, muzzles in the air, will break into prolonged joyful mooing, the sheep will murmur to each other in their own language, and the lambs, outside for the first time in their lives, will gambol on all fours like wild things. Just the thought of it makes Annele burst out laughing. What a day that will be, like a holiday! Set free from the dark house, out of the cramped four walls, in the wide-open barrens all day long with the peewits, the larks, the cranes, with the winds and the racing clouds! Yes, what a life that will be!

The week after Easter, Laukmalis arrived. The first thing he talked about was the terrible mud. All the roads were thawed, the wagon had sunk in up to its hubs, the horse had the devil of a time pulling it out. The barren land especially, with its clayey soil, was hell itself to cross.

"But to make up for it everything here on your land will grow like wild," Father reassures the visitor.

The men now inspect the materials that have been brought in during the winter for the new buildings. The ground has thawed now and – who knows? – they might begin to dig the foundation for the threshing barn as early as next week. Just so as the roads are dry enough to bring the craftsmen and workers from Edgefield Farm. Later the men make the rounds of the fields, jumping across the ditches that now criss-cross the land and have seeped full of the clayey water of spring. Krančelis follows them, chasing peewits that flutter screaming around him and almost settle on his nose like flies. By one of the wider ditches he stops, whines, barks, and begs till Father comes and lifts him across. What can you do with a dog like Krančelis? Why, he's as helpless as a baby. In the meantime, Mother has fried some chops and eggs and made some tea. When the men return, she immediately serves the food. The visitor eats at a leisurely pace, answering all sorts of questions in between times: what is each of the people at his farm doing, how are things at Spring Farm, and at Black Earth Farm? He thanks them for inquiring. At Edgefield Farm, everything is as usual, while at Spring Farm, and at Black Earth Farm, they're expecting new sons or daughters.

"Is that right?" says Father, and no more.

Now Mother remarks that Laukmalis could have brought his Ancīte along on the trip. Her girl, too, would have found it entertaining, for she sees no children her age all winter long. Laukmalis listens, keeps silent for a while, grins as though pleased about something, and finally says:

"It's a long way, and mud everywhere. No journey for a child." But then goes on:

"You know, my daughter won't be able to go gallivanting around all over the place anymore. She's a bit tied down now. Starting school."

"Which school?" asks Mother.

"Not the parish school yet, oh no. She's learning with her young ladyship, right here at the manor house. Studying the language. Writing, speaking. See, at the manor house they talk nothing but German. And when she goes to Forstmann later on, it'll be easy as falling off a log."

"True, true," says Mother, and her face grows sad, for she is thinking, "I wish my child was so lucky!"

"Guess it can't be helped that my sons didn't have too good an education, but it's going to be different with my daughter," says Laukmalis importantly. "After all it would be a disgrace if you, a farmhand, could send your son to Jelgava and I couldn't send my daughter. No, no! We've made our decision. When she finishes the parish school, our daughter is going to Jelgava and study to be a guviness, and then I'll buy her a blue silk dress."

Even the first words about Ancīte going to school had been like a stab with a dull knife into Annele's heart, and then stab followed stab: about learning German, about the Jelgava school, and becoming a guviness, and finally about the blue silk dress.

None of this, none of all this is for Annele.

It is true that she doesn't know what a guviness really is, but no doubt it is something high and mighty. Ancīte Laukmalis is walking down a new path, while Annele has to stay by the wayside. Indeed, it even seems to her that Ancīte has taken wing and is soaring above her, like those great strange birds that flew across the bar-rens yesterday with a mighty beating of wings, and of which Mother said that they must be wild swans. As she watched them disappear, she felt sort of funny, as though she would burst out crying, and now she actually does. She feels tears rise into her eye sockets and choke her throat. So as not to break into sobs and disgrace herself in front of the grown-ups, she jumps up and rushes out the door. After she runs to the end of the house, a few deep sobs manage to escape, but then she clenches her tears in her chest and pushes them back inside. What's the good of crying? Is that going to change anything?

Such restlessness in her feet, such restlessness in her chest. She feels like running somewhere, like catching up with something. Catching up with Ancīte so she doesn't go too far, learn too much wisdom. Oh schools, schools! If the way to them were open, she wouldn't mind walking to the end of the world, she'd fly like a bird, nothing would be too hard.

Annele goes off to carry her heavy heart around the little lake. Now that spring is here, the peewits' screams all around the lake announce their incessant fear for their nests and their children. They never get smart like the skylarks, who rend the air with their songs too far up to see, without a single worry for their nests, placed in a horse's hoofprint or a furrow's crust. The birds and their fates are unlike each other.

Puny marsh marigolds, tiny bird's-eye primroses grow in the swamp around the slough. It's no use looking for the kind of flowers that grow in the meadows of Spring Farm. Father hasn't had a chance to dig ditches and drain the ground of excess water. Once he does that, there will be flowers – big, colorful, and beautiful. All flowers do not have the same fate either.

And the same way all children, all people, too, do not have the same destiny. That's a lesson every new day teaches Annele.

When Mother awakened Annele in the morning, the first thing Annele would say was, What's the weather today? And Mother always had something good to say. If there was sun, it was a sun the like of which had never been seen before: it soared right above the earth's surface. If there was rain, it was a nice, warm, gentle rain that barely drizzled, moistened the ground, and made everything grow by leaps and bounds. If there was a storm with rain, it was always a good kind of storm that chases away clouds and gives back the sun. But if it had already been raining for two, three, or more days on end, then the morning on which Mother woke Annele was the very morning that would now give back the sun and put an end to all their troubles. The weather was always good and it was just waiting for the little herd girl to come outside in order to pour its blessings on her. She just needed to be good herself.

Oh mornings, mornings with your early rising! Annele suspected that her mother just plain didn't allow her to sleep till the appointed time. She'd always shout for Annele to get up just when she had waded into the deepest river of sleep. Her head heard alright, but her feet and her hands wouldn't obey or get up at all, they lay there like logs. And that was why every morning there would be all those questions about the weather. For at least as long as she was talking to Mother, Annele could play for time and abandon herself to sleep. And after that, she could maybe wait a little while to see if Mother had any more to say. Of course she didn't! Mother was quick as lightning and as usual, once she had praised the day that lay ahead, she called, "Get up, get up!" She herself was already out the door, and at almost that same moment the cows, too, began to bellow in the open barn door. No more loafing and lying about. She had to do as all those legendary children did that Mother was always setting up as examples for her girl. Out of bed like a shot, head into cold water, and get dressed in no time, putting off a more thorough bath and the brushing of her hair till evening.

Once she was out on the barrens and measured her shadow, it was not longer than other mornings at all. She couldn't reproach Mother for waking her too early. But maybe she woke her too early every morning?

Noon.

"Go take a nap, take a nap, lass! Or you won't be able to get up in the morning."

What is Mother talking about! Has there been one morning when Annele hasn't been able to get up? Just because she is a little sleepy in the mornings is no reason to waste in sleep precious time when there is the freedom to do whatever she likes.

So many different things to do. The first place she goes is to the flowerbeds in the kitchen garden. How are they doing? Here there are clumps of sage, southernwood, tansy, and dahlias and hollyhocks grow lush; seedlings and cuttings of all these plants have been brought over from neighboring farms, for that is how flowers travel from house to house, like friends sent by God. But more than all the rest Annele is concerned about the bed that has been seeded with unknown flower seeds. The seeds were brought at Easter by Līziņa, and now they have come up: elongated, round, long-stemmed, bushy, fringed, sinewy. Touching them delicately with her fingertips, Annele feels the little knots along their stalks: Are there any buds yet, maybe? There aren't any. She must wait, wait patiently.

The sun is boiling hot.

Not a sound outside, not even the faintest breeze in the air.

The gate creaks.

"Oh dear, what a noise!" Annele is startled.

Nobody heard. Everybody is taking their midday rest. Only Krančelis reproachfully begins to whine in his kennel.

"Don't go walking around right at noon, Annele. Can't you see that I can't come with you? I'm dying with the heat." And he pants with his tongue hanging out.

"You just sleep, go on, sleep! I don't need you."

Only her shadow accompanies her. Shrunk to the size of a ball at her very feet.

The big ditch in the rye field. The first ditch Father dug. It's in bloom! Like a wonderfully embroidered beaded belt it unrolls through the rye. All the flowers there are in fields and meadows have found their home here. Thick, juicy grass, untouched by the mouths of cattle or human hands. Who knows, maybe there are even strawberries among the flowers.

There are, there are!

Bent over the fragrant fruit of the earth, the girl stops and listens. And thinks. What is all this? Silence? But it hums and sings. Star upon star, daisies and corn cockles have burst into bloom! And the poppies, with their short half day of life, sparkle and glitter. And the rye field with its greenish-brown forest of stalks! It is all full of fragrance, it hums, glows, blossoms, breathes. Meanwhile, the working people are fast asleep, sleeping the heavy sleep of fatigue where they sank down in a cool room.

The people don't know how holy and full is the noon hour. How sweet the fragrance of the sun is, how sonorous the breath of the earth. How lovely the summer can be, right here in a ditch full of flowers, in the middle of the rye in the vast barrens. Lovely summer!

On Sunday afternoon, Mother comes out to the pasture to talk to the girl, to let the cows graze in less accessible spots so they'll eat their Sunday share of grass. Mother catches sight of Annele with a book under her arm and says:

"That's right, you go ahead and study! Now's a good time to get some book learning. Come winter you'll be going to school."

"What? This very winter?" exclaims Annele.

"That's right. You see how the time has gone by. This summer, too, will pass, your days as a herd girl will be over, and here you were thinking they would never end. Thus one's whole life passes like a morning dream," she says. As though she were quoting a verse from a sad song.

What a surprise! What sudden joy! Annele doesn't know what to say. There's also a feeling of regret. Because herding is over? Can it really be over? Never to return?

"All right, so I'll go to school in winter, but what about next summer? Back to herding?"

"We hope not. When Laukmalis was here, we talked about that with Father. Next summer he's planning to hire one more man, for Father can no longer handle the work here on his own. And if this man happens to have children, the herding will be part of his contract. Then you can go to summer school."

"But suppose the man has no children?"

"I wouldn't think Laukmalis will take on a man like that," Mother shakes her head in disbelief.

"Summer school! Isn't that where you learn twice as much as in winter school?"

"That's what they say."

"Mother, Mother, I wonder if all this is true?"

"Let's hope so, child. You've certainly earned that school."

Wherever Annele goes, whatever she does, she thinks of nothing but school now. She has counted up the months, weeks, and days. Every night, one day is subtracted from that empty period during which there is no school yet. They certainly pass slowly, those days, but once one has been lived to the full it has been conquered. And they do not pass in vain. Now is her chance to go over all the books, all the subjects that serve as a kind of foundation for school.

The Bible stories are in her head as solid as a rock, the catechism and the Ten Commandments are firm as well, except that she always falters a bit on the question, "What is that?" Annele doesn't understand why this question should always be stuck in the middle of everything. It sometimes makes your answer about a commandment come out quite differently than you think. That's why she often gets muddled. She knows her multiplication tables inside out, whether she recites them from the beginning to the end or backwards – from the end to the beginning. But the highest mountain she has had to climb is Spiess's German *Translator*. Annele has worked her way more than halfway through the book, and was hoping to get all the way to the end by fall. She didn't feel too confident on this terrain at all. The *Translator* was like thorny shrubbery that pricked and poked you and often led you astray. When you thought that from now on everything would go smoothly and nicely, you would suddenly be brought to a standstill and stumble as though over an insurmountable obstacle, and you would have to retrace your steps once more. Annele battled her way through this *Translator* with militant fervor. It had to be conquered like fate. She knew that. Every child that wanted to get to the top had to go through the *Translator*. Only then came the level and sunny plain of *Two Hundred Assignments*.

The *Translator* is her daily, bitter toil, while *Two Hundred Assignments* are Annele's Sunday pleasure, a sugarplum for her avid tongue that she will not be allowed to eat properly until later. The little book is half as thick as the *Translator*, and the very fact that it is so light gives one the impression that it is work that can be dealt with quickly. It contains little stories, rhymes, fairy tales. For the most part, Annele is able to understand them, but if she is confronted with an unfamiliar word anywhere, she circles it with her thoughts until at last she guesses what it is. And it all stays in her memory easily. Once she is through with the *Translator, Two Hundred Assignments* will fall into her lap of their own accord like ripe apples.

As she studies, Annele thinks time and time again about her future teacher. She's never seen him yet, but from what others have told her she knows he is a stately and stern man as tall as her father, with big blue eyes, who catches the boys at their pranks, and before whose upraised finger and – often! – upraised ruler the whole classroom sometimes quakes. When she thinks about that, she has a funny itchy feeling inside. But Annele rejects her fear. The teacher is not only strict, he is also good and kind. And besides, Annele is not a child that will stand there with her finger in her mouth and not know anything. Yes, it's much more likely that the teacher will be amazed by her: Wonder where that girl managed to learn so much? And then there will be the times when all the children will be lined up around the teacher's desk and they'll have to recite a lesson. But nobody will really know the answer. Now one, now another will stammer a reply. Then the teacher with his bright eyes will look closely at the whole line and catch sight of Annele. "I want that girl from the barrens to answer," he'll point at her, because he won't be able to remember Annele's name out of all those children right away. And Annele will recite the assignment as slick as a whistle. She won't stumble once. And then the teacher will say: "Good. That girl from the barrens can come right to the front and sit in the first row."

But the first row is only for those children who are better at their studies than all the others.

Oh wonderful time to come!

All that has happened up to this point now seems to have gone into hiding, from joy at the approaching school year, from the fever and restlessness of preparation. All her former tasks now seem to be done as though out of habit, her heart is no longer in them.

The season was moving toward fall. Each day the sun bent its fiery bow shorter. The wind brought the smell of ripe ears of grain from the fields. In the nearby forest unusual noises were heard. Dogs howled, trumpets droned, shots rang out. One day on the hill by the forest what looked like a great ball of yarn suddenly popped up and, howling dreadfully, rushed toward Annele as fast as the wind. It was Krančelis, who would now so often steal away and disappear for long periods of time. He ran up to her, trembled and shook with terror in his eyes, dropped on his belly, crawled on it whining, yowling, as though afraid of severe punishment. When the girl bent down to him, he did not believe her benevolence, but leaped backwards, as though expecting something horrible. For a long time the girl coaxed, called, while the dog, moaning, submitted to her caress, crawled closer, licked her hands.

"What was it, Krančel, what happened, puppy?"

He had been forgiven. But for what? What was the terrible thing he had experienced in the forest? What sin had he committed that he had to beg for her forgiveness? Whatever it had been, Annele took advantage of the incident, persuading and warning her four-footed friend to stop running around in strange places and especially to avoid the forest where he could get into trouble, for there were all kinds of danger lying in wait for him there.

Krančelis was grateful and much obliged for everything, showing this with sudden leaps, loud barking, and joyful sprints round and round in circles. All day long he was a trusty watchdog and companion, instantly stopped the least attempt of the sheep to get into mischief, anticipated Annele's every wish, demonstrated his playfulness, his agility, and skill; in short, that day Krančelis behaved in such an exemplary fashion that he deserved the highest praise, but the following day the dog was again gone all morning. When Annele brought back the cattle at noon, her first words were:

"Where's Krančelis?"

"No sign of him."

"I just hope nothing's happened to him."

"Why should anything happen to him?" Mother replied nonchalantly. "He's simply gotten used to roaming around lately. In the forest, the hunters are shooting, blowing their trumpets. That makes him excited. A mutt's a mutt. He's part greyhound himself, and now he's itching to run with the dogs and track down the game. He's sure to turn up again."

But that night, too, his food was still untouched, the kennel empty. The dog hadn't returned.

"Krančelis is gone," Annele told each of the members of the household, expecting a favorable reply. But Krančelis's fate did not concern the grown-ups. Miķelis even laughed: "Bet he's kicked the bucket, that Krančelis of yours. And no wonder. What did he run into a trap for? He got what he asked for."

Only Father consoled her.

"Don't worry! He's probably gone off with the hunters' dogs. He'll be back, you'll see."

Krančelis wasn't back – not on the morning of the next day, nor at night, when she brought home the cattle.

"Now Krančelis is dead and gone," Annele said, shaking her head ponderously.

"It does seem that way, doesn't it?"

When Mother, too, confirmed it, Annele couldn't bear it anymore, threw down what she had in her hand, and ran toward the forest.

The lovely meadow was all mowed and dry. There she stopped short. She called, shouted, coaxed. Wasn't it all in vain, though? That's what she had been doing for the past two days. Maybe the dog was lying somewhere with a gunshot wound. Maybe he could still give a whine, a short howl. In the evening silence, she would even have heard the grass grow. But everything remained silent. The forest had taken Krančelis.

The darkness thickened.

"Krančeli, my friend, Krančeli, my friend," the girl whispered and then sadly returned home. Across the barrens where Krančelis's brief life had been spent.

"Krančeli, my friend, my friend!"

Not What She Expected

School, school!

Here it is at last. Annele enters it like a sanctuary. Big doors, big windows, wide stairs. And rooms like beehives. Clack, clack! – steps ring out on the brick floor of the entryway. Patter, patter! go countless boots on the wood floors of the huge rooms, and *pastalas* shuffle with a rustling sound. The classrooms, the entryway, the stairway are packed with schoolchildren and the people accompanying them – calling, chattering, talking, buzzing. The quieter and more timid ones stand along the walls or in corners waiting for the dust to settle, for the vast majority to leave so that they, too, can then do all that needs to be done today: go in and register with the teacher, pick a place to sleep, take a look to see which seat in the classroom would be best to have – not too close to the teacher. The bolder and more enterprising kids go rumbling like a thundercloud – now downstairs, now upstairs and, outyelling each other, tell the others what they have seen. What's different from home, what's similar, and what is the same. Before Annele knows it, she is holding hands with some girl, and like a wave they surge up the stairs, colliding head-on with a wave that flows the other way. A girl with a green speckled headscarf is pulling her forward. Without seeing a thing they run through the girls' dormitory and washroom, and then across the hall into the boys' dormitory. Here, too, there is hustle and bustle, noise, chatter. In the washroom a tin trough goes round the walls. There are holes in the bottom of the trough. The strange girl is already familiar with all this. Goodness knows how often she has been here today. With one girl or another. "You want to see running water?" she asks, and at once turns the handle of the faucet in the corner. The water barely flows, for the tank is empty. The strange girl guides the water with her finger towards the place where the holes are, demonstrating how the water spurts when the boys wash themselves in the mornings, like rain pouring off the roof. One section of the tin is loose. The girl tugs on it hard. The tin rattles. She gives it another tug. – Who knows how many times it's been tugged that way! The section of tin suddenly comes off and is left in her hand. The girl gets scared, flashes a quick glance in all directions to see if there are any witnesses to her mischief.

"You're going to catch it!" the girl threatens Annele, throws down the piece of tin, pulls her hand out of Annele's hand, and is gone in an instant. Annele flushes from the shock, from shame, from not knowing what to do. Jostling each other, noisily, a group of boys crosses the room. Nobody has seen a thing. Very well, just leave that tin where it is!

Downstairs, Father is waiting. He takes the girl's hand.

"Don't go running off anymore! It's our turn. Let's go see the teacher."

Annele's knees start shaking. What is he going to ask her? How will she manage to recite without making mistakes? And now there's the business with the tin.

The teacher is sitting at a large desk writing. He has a big head with bushy hair that hangs over his forehead. He barely glances at Annele and her father.

"Anna Avots? What farm is she from? Oh – Krišjānis's daughter. Date of birth? Mother's name? Can she read? – Good. Next!"

"Where will the child be sleeping?" Father asks.

"Upstairs. Take the next empty bed. She'll see once she gets there. Picking and choosing is not allowed."

Yes. Father understands right away. The teacher is very busy today. He can't enter into conversation with every child, even though that child should happen to be his own little girl.

From the wagon Father brings the little brown trunk that has already accompanied the big children to school in the past, and now the two of them go upstairs. The little brown beds are lined up in long rows. In the middle there's a narrow walkway. Up to the middle of the room, the beds have already been made up. On many of them fathers and mothers sit talking and giving instructions to the children standing next to them.

The boys and girls mingle pell-mell, for they haven't yet been officially told that the boys are not allowed to come into the girls' room, and vice versa.

Annele covers her little bed with the blanket given to her by her mother, and puts the pillow on it. The bed is long, but the pallet is short. Part of the boards are left bare, for even the blanket is not long enough, no matter how much you stretch it. The bare boards will freeze her feet.

Once everything is in place, she and Father sit down on the little bed and for a while listen to the others' conversations, as though there was nothing more for them to talk about. Then Father rises to his feet. It is almost night, but home is far away.

"Be a credit to your family, lass," Father says, and his big warm hand clasps the girl's head for a moment as though blessing her. His lips speak inaudible words. Then he puts on his cap. Annele goes with him down the stairs, but he doesn't look back anymore.

Now Annele again roams through the large rooms, first upstairs, then downstairs; she stands around now here, now there. There are so many, so many children, they walk in twos, in threes, and in larger groups, but she's never seen any of them before, what is she to do with herself? There comes that girl with the green speckled scarf with whom she ran hand in hand a little while ago. There's somebody she knows. Now the girl is walking hand in hand with another girl. Annele runs toward her, holds her by the sleeve. But the strange girl looks at her distantly, as though she had never seen Annele before, angrily pulls her sleeve free and walks off with her friend. And Annele might imagine she'd only seen her in a dream if the memory of the piece of tin that this same girl tore off in the washroom were not so clear in her mind.

It's getting dark. From the outside, a group of boys come in, their cheeks windblown. They walk with a dashing stride and speak boldly. In their own group they cluster around a boy who is half a head taller than the others. The prefect, the prefect, the prefect! That word is constantly on their lips.

The prefect is that tall boy. He and the others around him are the summer scholars.

The prefect sees that it is already dark in the classroom, jumps on the desk and reaches for the lamp. Following each of his movements attentively, the boys stand around him: maybe he'll need some service, or a match will drop, or his foot will slip on the sloping desk? At any moment they'll be ready to prop him up and keep him from falling. But the prefect is sure of himself. He even stretches on tiptoe and, once the lamp is lit, swings his arms and with an elegant leap jumps down over the others' heads into the narrow walkway.

The first graders, necks outstretched, crowd around the lamp. Few of them have ever seen anything as big and bright in their lifetime.

The prefect is by the big blackboard. It's crisscrossed with chalk lines. The piece of chalk has been smashed into fragments.

"Who did that?" the prefect calls sternly into the classroom and, impatient at not receiving an answer, at once continues: "Well, you'd better make sure this is the first and last time. I'll let it go today, but tomorrow, if anybody's caught they'll get rapped on the knuckles but good! You're not herding cows anymore, you're at school, understand?"

Maybe they do understand him. The racket abates at once. But he shouts even louder:

"Quiet now! Come to order! To your desks!"

There is a sudden rustle, like a swath when the scythe cuts it. Everyone is seated, only the prefect is on his feet waiting for everybody to quiet down. What does the prefect have to say?

"In a moment you're going to supper, understand? And after that upstairs and to bed. And don't think you can blather and gossip and dawdle. This is not a horse pasture but a school, understand? And don't think you can splash people in the washroom tomorrow morning, and go wasting water. That's not what water is for, understand? Today we brought up the water for you, but tomorrow you'll all take turns, and you're going to have to bring water for the boys and girls both, because the girls have chores in the kitchen and with the dishes. Understand?"

Next door someone was ringing a big sleigh bell.

A rather big girl ran into the classroom.

"Suppertime, suppertime!"

On the dining tables steamed great bowls full of unpeeled potatoes, and in the smaller bowls were cut-up pieces of herring. Those who had no knife to peel the potatoes did it with the help of their teeth and nails. Every mouth was in motion.

Annele was not fond of herring. At home they rarely got it, and when they did she would leave it untouched. But now she thought she shouldn't. The herring was red and dry, so salty her tongue burned. Annele stealthily looked at her neighbors: were the other children eating it? Some were, while some pushed it under the potato skins on the table. If that's the way it was, Annele would do the same with her piece. She did finish her potato, which was split in the middle and mealy. She didn't want any more.

What was it she did want? She couldn't say. Something irksomely heavy had come over her. Her heart was sad and full of longing. She hated the tables littered with potato skins. And why were they brown? At home the table was as white as chalk. After every meal, Mother scrubbed it with a twist of straw and some sand. Also at home potato skins were not left lying about like this, but were immediately put away into a separate little bowl. Here there was no such order. Here they showed no respect for God's gift, as they ought to have done. She herself had hidden her piece of herring. Just like the others. Why didn't anyone keep an eye on them? Something wasn't right. Something gnawed at her, something seemed too cramped somehow. Vast darkness was looking in through the wide window. So unaccustomed and unfamiliar. Not even one potted plant was there to love her. At home on her little windowsill, Annele had two: a geranium and a little myrtle. Every time she watered them she would count the new leaves. Now they stand there. Silent and lonely. Maybe Father has already returned. Who will run and greet him? Annele isn't there anymore. Now he and Mother are sitting down to eat. Father is telling her about the school, and Mother is saying: "Yes, now we're all alone on these barrens."

A sharp bitterness stings her eyes. She cannot bear to look out the window anymore. Abruptly she turns her head the other way. That's where the boys' tables are. Just as they do in class, the boys sit on the left, the girls on the right. And one boy says, loudly: "Salty herrings, boy, are they salty! Look, the salt is spurting out the girls' eyes!"

The boys' table laughs, while Annele, startled, quickly looks down. Was the boy talking about her? Sure, who else?

The summer children sit in the same classroom as the first-graders. They take up one third of the seats, and sit separately. Annele sits in the eighth bench. That's where the rows of the little kids begin. Those continue a long way in back of her, as far as the door. Bent over their writing slates so low you can only see their backs, the little kids copy the letters that the teacher, explaining and clarifying, has slowly traced on the big board, so that everyone can get a good look how to do it.

Annele's little slate has long since been full. Why should she write out those letters? It is child's play as far as she is concerned. She has nothing to do, and so she allows her eyes to roam about. The first to attract her attention is the teacher. He is tall, a fine figure of a man, and holds himself erect. His ruddy face is large, his eyes are stern and piercing. He only sits on his chair behind his desk when he calls the children to the front to recite, but while they write or study, he walks, hands clasped behind his back, down the center aisle from one end to the other with big even steps. His boots squeak, the right one more than the left. Once he reaches the classroom door, he turns on this squeakier heel and comes back. Then Annele no longer dares to look at him, but hangs her head. At other times, he dictates sentences to the summer children, and then they write. Then, for a change, the teacher takes his hands – big, soft, white hands – off his back and, pushing back his jacket, puts them in his trouser pockets. Annele now notices that the trouser pockets are slightly frayed, and quickly looks the other way, so that the teacher should not be displeased when he realizes she has noticed this.

At other times the teacher quickly, as though reminded of something, interrupts his pacing and goes into the classroom next door. In the next room there are children who will soon be confirmed, and they are taught by the sexton, who does not live at the school but comes in the mornings and leaves again at night. The sexton is German and has a funny way of talking. He teaches the commandments and Bible stories. Annele isn't interested in this class. In her eyes the sexton is a sexton, not a teacher at all. Only the man who teaches in this classroom of hers is a real teacher.

As soon as the teacher leaves, the class begins to buzz, as though a breeze had passed through leafy branches. Heads are up and eyes go around the room. Only the prefect, the very first on the first bench on the boys' side, sits as usual, bent over his notebook. His head quickly turns this way, then that, but since there is not a lot of noise, he does not consider it necessary to pay too much attention to this buzzing. From where she sits, Annele has a good view of the first benches on the boys' side. Next to the prefect sit two boys with blond bushy hair. It is immediately apparent that they are brothers. They both have the same type of hair, thick and shaggy, and their faces, too, resemble each other, only one has a thin face, and the other a fat one.

Annele doesn't like the one with the fat face, while she thinks the one with the thin face is the handsomest boy in the whole school.

The girls' prefect is Emma Dzelzskalns. She decides which girls must take their turn to go help in the kitchen and with the tables. She is slim and pretty, her eyes are brown, and she goes around with her nose in the air. The girls crowd around her, happy if they can do something to please her, if Emma says a kind word to them. But she rarely does. She has nothing to say to the first-graders at all, she only tells them what to do.

The summer children! All the little kids put together do not add up to one of them. As Annele sees it, they are the gentry as compared to the common folk. They walk around in their own cliques, they have their laughter, their conversations, their secrets. They surround the teacher the way vassals do a king. When the teacher addresses his remarks or instructions to them, he does so in a muffled voice, as is appropriate when talking to his own people, and largely in German, especially with Emma Dzelzskalns, who often simply remains seated when answering the teacher, and doesn't jump to her feet like the little kids when they have to respond to the teacher's questions.

In no time at all, Annele is done with her letters, and then her hungry eyes stealthily roam around the classroom and greedily absorb and utilize every little detail. Suddenly the teacher becomes aware of this. He stops pacing, comes and stands at the end of her bench.

"Why aren't you writing?"

"I've already filled the slate."

"Show me!"

The teacher looks at one side of the slate, then the other. For a fairly long time, it seems to Annele. "Now he'll know everything," she thinks.

"You already know all the letters?"

"Yes."

"Who taught you?"

Who did teach her? Annele doesn't really know. She answers at random: "My brother!"

The teacher gives back the slate.

"Then you can copy from the book."

Annele now copies from the book: "The cat and the mouse." "The dog and the bone." "The plowman and the plowshare." She writes and secretly shrugs her shoulders. Such work seems futile to her. How long is she to do this?

She is not making progress in school, she is dragging backwards. During the time she spends writing, she could be learning all the things the teacher assigns to the summer children. If only the teacher would let her join them. If only the teacher knew and realized that she is so far ahead with her studies.

But how is she to tell the teacher? The one occasion when the teacher talked to her is over. That's when she should have told him. But how? It was so quiet in the classroom then that you could hear the grating of the slate pencils. If she had said anything, every ear would have perked up, and goodness knows what would have come of it. It is easy to study, but it's hard to talk to the teacher.

You can in silence. And in the silence Annele begs, like saying a prayer.

"Dear teacher, do let me join the summer children. You'll see how hard I'll study. I can do the *Translator*, you know, and I'm finished learning *Two Hundred Assignments* as well. I can understand everything you've been telling the summer children. Why can't I study with them? I do so want to study. Ahead of everybody. More and more. Dear, dear teacher, do let me move ahead, please!"

This is the prayer that burns in Annele's eyes as they look at the teacher, although her lips are silent.

"Well, Avots, you're looking around again. Is your slate full already?" the teacher, who now remembers Annele's name, asks from his desk.

"Yes," the girl whispers barely audibly.

"Come and show me!"

Annele goes. Her heart seems to tremble in her throat. Now is her chance, when the teacher asks her a question. Now she can tell him everything she didn't tell him before. The words she was thinking just now.

The teacher looks at one side, then the other. But where are Annele's words that she was planning to tell her teacher? She can't remember even one. As if in despair, as though she wanted to peel the words from her mouth like kernels from a nutshell, she presses her fist to her lips. How should she begin? How should she begin?

The teacher quickly glances at her, frowns, sternly calls:

"Don't bite your nails!"

Annele winces. What the teacher has said is so unexpected and impossible!

"But I'm not doing that!"

"What do you mean, you're not doing that? Do you think I'm blind?"

Annele dares not say that. But she hasn't done anything wrong. She's given the teacher no reason to be angry.

"I didn't do that!"

"Don't contradict!"

Annele stands there mute.

Yes, now it's all over. She knows now that she'll never be able to ask the teacher to let her learn with the summer children. Never, never.

The teacher gives her back the slate. He is annoyed.

"You've copied everything correctly, but your handwriting is totally useless. Who taught you to write like that?"

"I did."

"You're going to have to learn to write better than that. Tomorrow you shall come to me for a notebook, and there you will have model sentences to copy so you can learn to write properly. Penmanship. Do you understand?"

As Annele returns to her desk, her eyes automatically dart toward where the blond boy has his seat. He looks at her, baring his white teeth in a grin. "Don't bite your nails!" says his grin.

Well! She's never, ever going to look at that boy again.

When she takes her seat, she has the feeling that many heads are turned in her direction with many grins. And they all go, "Don't bite your nails!"

Her face is burning hot. And inside her chest it's so tight that she feels she can't breathe. She has been scolded in front of the entire class, but she's not conscious of having done anything wrong. Did the teacher really think she had? And if he thought it was true, couldn't he have said quietly and lovingly, as Father used to at such times: "Don't do that, lass, that's not nice." Instead he did it so everybody could hear. So everybody stays on one side, while she, the one who's been scolded, is the only one on the other side. Is she guilty or innocent? No one asks her or believes her. She alone knows. And she knows the teacher has been unjust. The teacher! Everything has turned out differently than she expected. The teacher seems to have receded far, far into the distance. He has become inaccessible to Annele.

Annele buys the copybook from the teacher. She riffles through it.

"Mother makes muffins. The gypsy grabs a goose. The willows wave in the wind."

She counts the lines. There are lots of them, and she has to fill them all. Ten times, one after the other, she must learn to trace the letters and words the same way as they are written in the model sentence on the first line.

"The gypsy grabs a goose. The willows wave in the wind."

On the first line she succeeds in tracing the letters more or less the way they are written at the top, the second is barely all right, but the further down the page, the more the letters go as they please, taking the writer along her own path.

The teacher is not satisfied.

"Other children are making progress, but you're not."

He shows the class several copybooks with beautiful copperplate writing. These belong to the summer children.

"That's the way you should write," he says.

For Annele, his words go in one ear and out the other. She is incapable of learning copperplate writing, and that's all there's to it. She no longer struggles with this task – it is unattainable. However, she tries all the more to take in what the teacher teaches the summer children. To commit this to memory is as simple as ABC. But even that doesn't amount to much, and she always feels a kind of hunger: when will there be more?

The students' dormitories are big and cold. At night the children gather here twittering like flocks of sparrows. Before the teacher shows up, they must quickly, quickly make use of the time. There is tussling and wrestling, laughter and shouting, and pillows flying through the air. From the many mouths, the breath rises like smoke, but soon you can't see it anymore. The air has warmed up. Then there is the sound of the teacher's steps on the stairs. As fast as they can, they all scramble into bed. It's true that the teacher first goes into the boys' dormitory: once, twice, three times from one end to the other, but right after that he comes to check on the girls. Then they must all be in their beds. When the teacher has inspected the girls' dormitory, he goes back to the boys one more time until things have calmed down there as well, then stands listening at the top of the stairs a while longer, and then his steps can be heard pounding down the stairs. Everyone draws a sigh of relief. Now they can still whisper with their nearest neighbor, share some special secret, or discuss something that happened during the day. But often it happens that a loud burst of laughter or a shout suddenly goes up like a rocket from some corner. All heads bob up. They listen. And often one of these little bursts of laughter goes tittering through all the beds like an infectious disease, only softly, softly, tossed from hand to hand, for below the girls' dormitory are the teacher's quarters.

A couple of times a month the Jew Meirītis comes to visit the school. He has a small pony, and a small store of merchandise. "Lace, caps, pins." He can't do any business in the school. Although it's crammed full of people, none of them have any money. Nor does he ever offer his merchandise to the students. He tends to keep to the teacher's end of the school, and always arranges things so that he can stay the night. Though Meirītis is travelling around as a peddler, he is not like the other peddlers. He only visits places where more refined people live, and he is always welcomed like a guest, given a good bed to sleep in and good food to eat. The teacher and Meirītis have tea together. There is a rumor that he was once a rich man, and is still refined and generally intelligent. The teacher and Meirītis spend whole evenings talking together.

When the teacher comes upstairs to put the children to bed, Meirītis shuffles after him. Three steps behind the tall, erect teacher, who walks with his hands clasped behind his back as usual, comes Meirītis – a tiny little man with a little white beard, dressed in a long black caftan, with a little black skullcap on his head. The girls vanish beneath their blankets, because they have to bite their tongues with laughing. Meirītis is constantly in the middle of a story – turning and twisting, fidgeting, waving his hands about, shrugging his shoulders, while the teacher only interjects an occasional word, and sometimes it seems he hasn't been listening at all. But Meirītis isn't upset by that. Sometimes his voice becomes so soft that it is nothing but a muttering into his white beard. No doubt that is how he talks to himself as he travels the long country roads in his wagon. No one answers him, nor does he need an answer. He remarks on everything he sees in his own dialect.

The teacher leaves the girls' dormitory, but on his way back he goes past the top of the stairs and reenters the room just as the girl in the bed next to Annele's has asked the girls a riddle: "Guess my riddle – a big white ram with a little black tail," and shouts "No, no, no!" in response to all guesses. Then the girls come up with the absurdest, most daring answers, and one bold voice exclaims: "That's the teacher followed by Meirītis." The laughter and hullabaloo that follows is so out of the ordinary that the teacher has heard it, too, and now returns to check what is going on. But as soon as he crosses the threshold, the girls immediately dive under the covers like ducks under water. The blankets quake, the blankets rise and fall with suppressed laughter. Annele burrows deeper under her hair. Her pallet is short, her blanket thin. Therefore at night she usually unbraids her hair and spreads it over her. Her hair is long and thick. When she draws her knees up to her chest, it reaches her feet. Now, when Meirītis comes up to her bed, he lets the teacher continue on his rounds, puts his wrinkled, bony hands on the foot of the bed and, swaying his head, blows "Oy, oy, oy!" in a singsong tone through his long nose. The nearby beds are suddenly shaken as though by an earthquake. It is a seismic wave whose vibrations reach the furthermost corner. The teacher's eyes, full of distrust, scan all the beds that gurgle like hidden brooks; he finds no reason to call, "Silence!" but just to be on the safe side he turns back at the door to walk through the room once more.

And, just as he did the first time, Meirītis stops at this one bed again, with his head swaying, going, "Oy, oy, oy!"

The tall teacher and short little Meirītis are gone! Peace, peace! Quick as a flash, the girls pull the blankets off their heads. They're almost choking with the heat and with the desire to laugh. But now that the teacher has left, the shivers of laughter, too, have vanished into thin air and no longer sting them inside.

"Tell me, why did that Meirītis always stop at my bed and go, 'Oy, oy, oy'? What did he want?" wonders Annele.

"Don't you see?" answers Minnīte. "Why, you look like a spook with that jungle of hair. A real witch of the woods, you know! The man looks and looks from one end to the other, and he can't figure out where the spook's head and where the feet are. That's why he was oy-oy-oying and shaking his white head with his black skullcap."

They've had their noon meal, and now the long recess begins. It's going to be longer than usual, for the teacher has company. The boys have already gotten wind of it, and they've hardly eaten their last bite of food when they pour out the door like a snowslide down a hill. Off to the banks of the Tērvete River behind the school. A big war is supposed to start there today between the "Turks" and the "Russians," for new snow has fallen overnight. The "Russians" are below, in the osiers along the bank, in good positions. They are largely recruited from among the bigger boys – the summer scholars and the sexton's class. On the hill are the "Turks," the small fry, first- and second-grade boys. They have to be the Turks, for being Russians is the privilege of the big boys. Though they are small fry, there are twice as many of them as there are Russians. And they have lots of courage. They are quick, nimble, and for every bullet they'll throw back three. That's how many of them there are. In closed ranks like a cloud of mosquitoes they launch their attack down the hill with a thundering "Hurrah!" But the enemy's bullets hurt. The snow along the bank is old and has become hard. And the hands of the "Russians" are twice as big and strong. The river is right there within reach and is full of rapids and places that never freeze, where the water bubbles over the pebbles. Heavy charges start coming at the "Turks." They protect their heads and eyes, but their arms and legs are in for a bad time. Suddenly one of them gets hit on the forehead and lets out a yell like a trumpet call. This provokes a storm of protest among the other "Turks" as well.

"Rocks, rocks! They're throwing rocks. They're not fighting fair! They're criminals! They're throwing rocks!"

The girls stand at the top of the hill, hands under their woolen shawls. They are not allowed to join the fighting, but they *can* yell at the top of their lungs. And yell they do, threatening the enemy that they mustn't hurt the little boys, mustn't use rocks, must aim neither at heads nor noses nor eyes, or else the girls will at once go and complain to the teacher.

If they want to get the teacher involved, then that's no proper war anymore. The "Russians" stop fighting. They say none of them threw a rock. It's just that their strong bullets "have a bite," because they are real fighters, not softies with porridge instead of bones.

The "Turks" can't let such an insult go unchallenged. Not one of their men has porridge instead of bones. Their hearts are stout. They've already reformed their ranks. They dare the "Russians" to come.

The "Russians" refuse point-blank.

The "Turks" are forced to send ambassadors with a new offer of war, in short, they have to beg them to restart military operations. They have to beg for a long time. Finally the "Russians" give their response.

"All right. But only if you get rid of that crybaby! Let him go join the girls."

The "crybaby" stands firm, as though he was rooted in the ground. Three "Turkish" men can't budge him. Finally, with the help of reinforcements, he is removed and tossed into a cluster of girls.

It is an unheard-of injustice and wrong. The "crybaby" can swear to it that the other side threw a rock that had been broken out of the river. He's got a bump on his forehead. And he's not going to stand for it. As soon as the battlefield is cleared, he plans to look for the rock and then go straight to the teacher.

Yes. The girls are going to help him. The girls will go with him as witnesses. One and all.

Annele has kitchen duty today. She's been picked together with Minnīte Skuja and two more of the little girls. The other four are big girls. One of the summer girls, Emma Dzelzskalns, proud and imperious as a queen, is in charge of them. The little girls must put the dining room back in order: they must clear away the dishes, clean the tables and the floors. Emma sees to it that everything is so clean there isn't a speck of dust. If she sees the least little bit of dirt, she goes, "Sweep it again."

As they work, Minnīte stays by Annele's side, but her thoughts are outside with the warring parties. Every time she carries a pile of dishes out into the kitchen, throwing them down so hurriedly that they fall every which way, she's back at one window, then another. She can see and hear not only with her eyes and ears, but with her feet, her hands, her whole nimble body. She knows everything that's going on by the river, like a general from afar, or at least she thinks she knows everything and shouts the information into the ears of the other girls. When the loudest hurrahs ring out on the river bank, she refuses to budge from the window, let the dishes walk to the kitchen with the other girls' feet if they like, that's none of her business anymore.

"To the windows, girls, to the windows! Will you look at that! They're running this way from the river. Calling the teacher. There's scads of boys killed. With their ears off. Broken noses. Blood running in streams. I knew that would happen. I bet the big boys were throwing sticks, or rocks. Look at the teacher come running. He hasn't even had time to put on his cap. Gee, are the boys going to get a thrashing!" Minnīte gloats as she shouts all this.

The teacher really does hurriedly run to the battlefield, accompanied by a small group of excited girls all speaking at once, among them the "crybaby" with the bump on his forehead. Minnīte is at once ready to drop everything and run after them, to see what's happened on the riverbank, but by the door, just in time, Emma

Dzelzskalns grabs her by the shoulder. She too had run inside the classroom to watch the tumult of the battle on the riverbank, but is now back at the height of her duties and frowning sternly. As she continues to hold Minnīte by the shoulder, she reprimands her:

"What's going on here? That's no way to work! Were you assigned to stand and look out the windows or run around? Is the dining room clean? Are the dishes where they're supposed to be?"

"The dining room is clean. We cleared everything away. Let go!" Minnīte shakes her shoulder.

"All right then, go clean the cauldron, on the double! That hasn't been done yet."

Emma catches sight of Annele nearby. She orders her as well:

"Skuja, Avote, both of you clean the cauldron!"

The two girls look at each other incredulously.

"What? Us? That's not our job. The big girls have always done that!" Minnīte exclaims in surprise.

"You're big enough."

"But we don't have to do that. I won't do it."

"I won't either," Annele tosses her head back. "We've already done our job. We can't reach the bottom of the cauldron."

"I'll be the one to decide whether you can do it or not. I'm in charge here, not you."

With one quick twist, Minnīte frees her shoulder from Emma's grasp.

"You can't tell us what to do. You're a girl just like us."

"You're not supposed to be unjust. You've got to act according to the rules," says Annele.

"You aren't the teacher, you're just a girl," persists Minnīte.

"That's all I need – you brats telling me what I'm allowed or not allowed to do. Start on the cauldron, and make it snappy!"

The two girls raise their heads even more stubbornly.

"We're not going, so there! And especially not because *you* told us to!"

"All right. Then I'll report you to the teacher."

"We'll report you first. Look, there comes the teacher now!" Minnīte exclaims and makes for the door. The teacher comes past the windows, walking quickly, flushed after passing judgment on the warriors. Then come the boys, followed by the girls. They're all quiet, and return to class without further ado. A couple of the boys have had their hair pulled out, but there are no visible bumps or injuries.

Emma has grabbed Minnīte near the very door, and is holding on to her. But Minnīte doesn't hurt as much as her cries would make one believe.

"Teacher, teacher, Dzelzskalns is squeezing my shoulder!"

"Shut up at once, or I really will report you!"

"I'll report you first. Teacher, teacher!"

The teacher is just going past. The door bursts open, and he is in the kitchen.

"What's going on here?"

"They're disobedient," Emma points at the little girls. And before Minnīte has had a chance to open her quick mouth, Annele interjects:

"No. We aren't disobedient, but Dzelzskalns is unjust."

The teacher frowns.

"What has she been doing?"

And, turning to Emma, tells her in German: "Tell me!"

Annele gives up hope.

Some justice! Once they start speaking German, she knows whose side justice will be on.

But Emma has to tell everything the way it happened, even though she chooses her words as much in her favor as possible. And the teacher does not side with her by any means. You have to act according to the rules, and you can't start a new order on your own responsibility. The little girls are little, no matter how tall they might be. And you mustn't ill-treat them.

Annele understands everything the teacher says, but Minnīte just sees how Emma flushes, drops her eyes, and, after the teacher leaves, quickly disappears from the kitchen. That's enough for her. Annele, on the other hand, feels her head and shoulders lift, and it's as if the teacher were the one lifting them, and rising higher himself as well. In spite of everything, the teacher has proved to be kind and wise, and fair. He didn't listen to Emma, but judged the case as was right. Annele is completely satisfied with this great day of judgment.

It is hard to believe how quickly time passes. Before you know it, winter began to shrink. During the cold moonlit nights, there was an eerie sort of frosty glow, like the shimmering of a faraway spring. On nights like this, the chilly stream of air that freely flowed through the large room, barely scared away by the breath from those many lungs, would often suddenly rouse Annele from her sleep. Outside night shimmered like a great, mysterious spinner from whose distaff unrolled magic threads in which, as in a net, she caught fields, forests, and farms. Everything was different than in the daytime, silent but full of deep life. Stars looked in through the large windows. A black strip of forest was like a line drawn under the star-filled luminous sky. It was sweeter than sleep at such times, Annele felt, to lie there with her eyes open and think about what things were like out there in the world and here at school.

With what delight she had entered school back in fall. And now, in a few short weeks, this winter would be over. Had she achieved what she had hoped for? No. Often she had the feeling she was going back over the same familiar ground. She had imagined that in no time at all she would learn everything that was taught in school, everything the teacher knew. But the teacher was still walking through the classrooms day after day, his hands clasped behind his back, imposing and unapproachable, and it seemed he had nothing to give to Annele.

And yet, looking at it from another perspective, she *has* made progress, big, bold strides in fact. Look at how much she now knows that she didn't know before. Somewhere, there is a little shining light that keeps growing larger. It comes all by itself. Often, you've worn yourself out thinking about something, and suddenly it opens like a book, and everything is clear. No need to ask anybody. As Mother told Annele when she was still little and asked a question the grown-ups didn't want to answer: "Wait, when you grasp the world, you'll understand all by yourself." Yes, now she sees that she is beginning to "grasp the world" more and more deeply. Sometimes this growing awareness is bitter, but sometimes it is wonderfully sweet and pleasant. Something opens up, and it could probably not be expressed in words, only understood with a kind of deep tenderness. Like the snowy moonlit outdoors just now, the bright night, the forest, and the girls sleeping around her. And, further away, Father and Mother in the little house on the barrens, her sister and brother in far-off Jelgava. It's all familiar to her, of course, but at other times it appears quite different, just as a little light you hold in your hand shows every object differently. And that's the tenderness inside her. Perhaps the best way to "grasp the world" is by means of this tenderness. And the deeper the girl goes in her thoughts, the more immeasurable this tenderness inside her seems, the more boundless the world, the more passionate her joy at being able to "grasp the world" more and more completely.

And now the day has arrived when they have no more homework to do for the next day. All that happens tomorrow will be the distribution of the report cards, and school will be closed. The children have all afternoon off. No more preparation for lessons, no exercises to do. The teacher no longer watches over them vigilantly. He is sitting in his room writing report cards. He'll be at his task until midnight. The boys' prefect is helping him.

Loud, free, excited, the boys and girls rush pell-mell down the riverbank. The thawed-out ground sways, their feet sink into many a mud puddle, but who cares? The blackbirds are whistling, the pussy willows are in bloom. The Tērvete River races past them roaring, fierce, grayish brown. The girls follow the rhythm of the rushing river like birds. In sheltered spots, here and there, marsh marigolds are already in bloom, while in the bushes you can pick handfuls of hepaticas. For a while, the boys mill around their winter battlegrounds, where victories were won and defeats were endured. Now they have different games. Boxing, wrestling, racing. Today, though, there are no more disagreements. Every incident is resolved easily and quickly. Across the plowed fields blow the breezes of spring.

Their joy at being free is indomitable. When, at sunset, it flows from the outdoors back into the school building, it rumbles like thunder, and its roar reaches the teacher's end of the school. The teacher sends the prefect with threats, but who's going to obey those? The power of the school is at an end. Are they going to be kept after school for this tomorrow? So what! It's the last day in any case.

The prefect comes back a little later, and now there is a book in his hand. The book is from the teacher. It's fun to read. One of the children must read, and the others can listen. Those are the teacher's instructions.

"Let's have the book!"

"Who's going to read?"

"If you give it to somebody, they'll read it."

"I'll give the book to the person who's going to read aloud. No one else. That's what the teacher said to do."

Silence. The prefect is waiting.

"Come on, let's have some volunteers!"

"Funny! Why should anybody volunteer? Give the book to one person, and let them read," a wise guy remarks.

"All right then, here, you read!" the prefect passes the book to the speaker.

"Me? Why me? Let Biela read!"

Biela is one of the blond brothers who sit in the first row next to the prefect.

"Leave me alone, will you?" Biela holds up both hands in protest.

"He can't read at all. He whistles like a steam engine after each word," exclaims another wise guy.

"He says every word twice so he can figure out the next one in the meantime," pipes up another.

"He flounders through a book like a chicken through a tangle of yarn," adds a third.

And so it goes with every one of the boys. None can pass the severe barrage of criticism that breaks out around him as soon as the prefect offers him the book.

The boys refuse to read. Not Biela, nor the others from the first row. Let alone the rest. Let the girls read. What are they there for? Can't Emma Dzelzskalns read? She's head of the class! She's so good at German. Let her do as she's told now – her that's always so good and obedient.

Emma tosses her head proudly.

"Me, read aloud to you? I wouldn't even dream of it! I'm going upstairs to pack."

The other summer girls, too, have to go and pack. If Emma won't read, why should they be the ones to read?

"Then I know. Let Anna Avots read then," exclaims Minnīte, who refuses to budge from the side of the prefect with his book. She wants to see what it is about.

"You want to read?" the prefect somewhat dubiously raises the hand with the book toward Annele.

"Yes, yes, she's got a high-pitched voice," Minnīte hastens to add.

"I don't know," Annele hesitates.

"Of course she's going to read! She's got a high-pitched voice, and she'll rattle it off as easy as anything. She can read, and we can all listen."

The prefect weighs the book in his hand, seemingly not too pleased.

"D'you want it or don't you?"

Annele gets scared. Suppose he takes the book back again?

"Let me have it!"

"Be careful! You mustn't get the book dirty, or bend the corners, or tear the pages. I'm giving it to you, and you're the one who's expected to give it back."

"Come on, give it to her! You think she doesn't know?" Minnīte interjects impatiently.

Annele sits in the middle of the classroom under the big lamp. Minnīte is right by her side. The other girls around her. The big boys further away, on purpose – they, of course, are not going to listen to what a brat of a first-grade girl reads aloud.

The book is still quite new. The pages stick and rustle like silk. There are many stories inside, and lots of titles. What should she read?

"A really nice one," wishes Minnīte.

"Open the book and read whatever is there," suggests another girl.

The book opens to the story "The Hero of Tērvete."

"What Tērvete is that? The same old Tērvete that flows past our school?" asks Minnīte.

Yes, it's the same one.

Annele reads. About their Latvian ancestors who lived in villages, while their chieftains lived in castles. How they had rich fields and big herds of cattle. How then foreign warriors came in ships, burned, robbed, murdered, and forced others to accept baptism. But the ancestors washed off the baptism in the rivers and rose against their oppressors time and time again. How then more warriors came in big hordes, and how they had weapons that the ancestors were not familiar with. And, whatever the enemy couldn't do by force of arms or fire, they did by trickery. They invited the Latvian chieftains to a meeting, but then overpowered them, drove them into a barn, and then set the barn on fire. That's how they destroyed the chieftains, and now they could easily conquer the scattered and disorganized people. But the ones who resisted the foreign invaders the longest were the people of Zemgale. For a hundred years, they fought for their freedom. They had mighty chieftains.

The most famous of them all was Viesturis, who ruled in Zemgale and lived in the castle of Tērvete. Another powerful warrior who came to join Viesturis was Nameitis. Finally, when the people of Zemgale were outnumbered by the vast numbers of enemies, they still did not submit, but preferred to burn their castles and go into exile abroad.

Annele's heart is aflame and her thoughts are aflame. They are uplifted by a sudden surge. Impetuous, stormy her thoughts flood over her. Latvians. Ancestors. Free. Free heroes, her thoughts proclaim. As though in her heart a thousand eyes and ears had awakened, which see and hear this distant past. What times those were. What pride and what power. Life and death struggles have raged right here on the soil of her dear native land. Her eye, quick as lightning, darts outside the big windows: is anything visible, or audible? – It all seems so vivid and alive.

The horizon lies in a glittering ring. The world is silent. That glorious time is far, far away.

"Why aren't you reading? Read, read, Avote!"

They've all pressed close to her, girls and boys both. Their mingled breath is like the rustle of leaves and warms the air like steam.

"Read, Avote, read!"

The voice suddenly breaks off. Who's that in the doorway? For some time now, the teacher has been standing there listening. And for a brief moment, but deeply, deeply, Annele now looks into those eyes whose attention she had so hoped to attract when she came to school in fall, yet which she had failed to attract. And now the look in his eyes is searching, as it were, and surprised, as though he wanted to ask: Who's that girl reading there, and where did she come from?

Father hasn't had time to come and get Annele. Instead, Miķelis is here, and so early that no other child's ride home has arrived yet. Annele's eyes grow dark.

"It couldn't be helped," explains Miķelis. Spring is here, with all the work that entails, Miķelis himself still needs to go to Edgefield Farm, he's got ten different chores to do. And that's why he's just going to pick up Annele's things, while she herself is to walk. Besides, it's no pleasure driving through these mud holes. Bumpy isn't even the word for it. Let Annele just walk along the road, and by nightfall he'll catch up with her and take her home.

Her first report card. Arithmetic – good. Geography – good. Religion – good. Penmanship – fair. This is really terrible. "Fair" is the same as "bad." How awful to get a "fair" on your report card. Latvian – very good. The word "very" has been underlined. "Maybe that's because the teacher heard me reading that night," thinks Annele.

There's a cool spring wind blowing. At a run, Annele hurries away from the school together with a little group of other students. They stop in a cluster by the forest and look back. There, behind them, is the stately school building with its red tiled roof. Like a mother sending her children out into the world. Annele feels a sharp pain inside. She is sorry to leave the school, but even sorrier that school wasn't what she expected, was not a more loving mother.

The little group melts away quickly, like a snowball in a fist. The students who live in nearby farms run off without even saying goodbye, alongside roads, splashing through the mud. Finally only one girl is still walking with Annele, but when they reach the top of the hill she, too, disappears. She has turned off along a boundary path that goes straight up the hill to a farm, and does not look back.

And so those who were the most vivid in her memory are gone too: Minnīte Skuja, Emma Dzelzskalns, the prefect, the two blond brothers; gone without a look backward. Will she ever meet them again? Who knows? She walks alone down the long, long highway. Miķelis does not catch up with her until she is almost home.

The New Herder

It has now been decided – Annele will go to summer school. The new man who will come to be Father's helper, and whose name is Auka, has four boys. The oldest is ten, and so he will be the herder in Annele's place.

But where are they going to live? Annele can't understand. The foundation for the big farmhouse is only just being dug, and it is impossible to squeeze any more people into the small cabin than already live there.

"A place to live? Ith that all you're worried about?" laughs Miķelis. "There'th room to thpare in the wagon shed. It'll be pretty cool to thtart with, but thummer'll be here thoon. How do you think Gypthieth manage?"

On St. George's Day, Auka arrived with two small wagons. In one there was a bed, a trunk, several trestles, the second contained mostly children. Four heads stirred in the wagon, and one was at the mother's breast. It was only a few days old and belonged to the youngest of Auka's offspring.

Miķelis stood in the yard to welcome the new arrivals. "Gypthieth, that'th all they are. What a racket there'th going to be now."

The children were lifted out of the wagon, then a sheep with two lambs. Those were all the animals the Aukas had. The man did say that later on he would go and bring a heifer that had been promised him by his relatives, but she could not be expected to give milk before the year was out.

"So many children and not a drop of milk," said Mother pityingly.

The young Aukas, from top to bottom, were called: Kristapelis, Jancis, Pēcis, Ansītis. The youngest hadn't been christened yet. Father Auka lamented that they had run out of godfathers and names among their relatives, and that they'd have to get one in Lithuania, where his brother Mārtiņš lived. That's where he also hoped to get the heifer.

Mother Auka couldn't budge a step. The children clung to her skirt. Hiding their faces in its folds, they squealed like stuck pigs: "I'm scared, I'm scared!" Scared of what? Of the strangers, the buildings, the rooster which, hoping for spilled grain, brings his hens closer to the wagon, of a pile of boards in the yard, of the winds that whistle around the corners of the buildings, of a faraway train that runs out of the forest huffing and puffing with its cloud of white smoke and rushes away into the distance, who knows where; in short, there is not a single occurrence or object on the barrens that does not inspire them with the greatest horror, which they then give vent to with eruptions of earsplitting screams. Aukiene scolds, yells, shakes them off like leeches attached to her flesh; when that does no good, she cuffs one of them soundly and throws him down in the middle of the yard, and the same with the second and third, until all of them, bundled in woolen shawls, piled up in a heap, kick and squeal like piglets stuffed into sacks.

Aukiene is full of steam and nervous energy. She does not know what to pick up, what to leave where it is. She does everything by fits and starts. She snatches, grabs, carries, hurls. She helps empty the wagons. Runs into the wagon shed with some object, flings it into a corner, throws the next one right on top of it. Without saying a word, her husband takes the same object and carries it into another corner. His wife does not like that. She wants to tear the object from her husband's hands. He won't let her. So they wrestle for the object, pulling each in a different direction until the husband gains the upper hand. He cannot be budged, though he is shorter than his wife by a head. Now that he has the upper hand, he stands there, legs apart, and says fiercely: "I'll take the strap to you, you wait!"

The same way he also confronts the screaming pile of the kids in the yard, suddenly stretching fiercely and menacingly reaching for his trouser belt: "I'll take the strap to you, you wait!"

Still, that's as far as it goes. He does not unbuckle his trouser belt, nor do the children pay attention to his threats; only when their mother approaches does the three little ones' squalling suddenly come to a stop, and with fearful but sharply observant eyes they try to read their mother's face: What's going to happen now? Will it be good or bad?

The first to bear the brunt of this wrath is Kristapelis, so that his ears flush as red as Goldencrest's cockscomb, for his ears always have to atone for all his sins.

"Well, big boy? Got mould in your ears? Can't you keep the little kids quiet? Standing there like a post!"

Keep the little kids quiet! What does Kristapelis care about keeping them quiet? He just stands there. Grumpy, indifferent, motionless like an old man. While the little kids go on blubbering.

"Maybe the children are hungry if they cry that way. They don't know what's the matter with them, maybe," says Annele's mother.

"Why should they be hungry! I cooked a couple of pounds of peas yesterday. They were nibbling on them all the way here. That ought to be enough for them!"

Aukiene produces some peas in a sieve. But Jancis, Pēteris, and Ansītis, as though mortally insulted, kick at the sieve.

Annele's mother comes with a bowl of porridge.

"Look what I've got!" she invites the little ones temptingly, and four necks stretch toward her, four pairs of eyes begin to gleam. Here comes the big feast.

They have one spoon between them. It makes the rounds much too slowly. Once it reaches one of them, it stays there. Kristapelis in particular, with the privileges bestowed on him as the firstborn, takes one, two, three turns all at once. The spoon slides with a squeaking sound along the bottom of the dish, stirring up the fattest lumps, which disappear down the gaping hole that is Kristapelis's mouth. The little ones realize that their rights are in jeopardy. The stronger ones among them still manage to get something, but Ansītis has the worst time of them all. After vainly struggling to get the spoon, all he can think of doing is to kick at the bowl, to pummel his brothers' elbows with his fists, and to keep repeating with his lisping little mouth: "Don't dwink the powwidge if you don't eat the peath, don't dwink the powwidge if you don't eat the peath." And so on to the point of weeping and sobbing.

Out runs the boys' mother with true gale force. Fisticuffs fall like rain. Mostly on Kristapelis's shoulders – ducking his head, he makes his escape. Now the little ones could eat their fill of porridge in peace, but Pēteris and Jancis soon lose interest now that their big brother, the bully, is gone; and, leaving the spoon and the whole delicacy to Ansītis, they run off after Kristapelis. Ansītis now has time to splash around the bowl with the spoon. He fishes out the lumps, and they do find their way to his mouth, while the porridge begins to spill wherever it pleases: one spoonful runs down the tip of his nose, another behind his collar, and with the third he tries to figure out what happens when he pours it down the folds of his rompers. By then Aukiene has noticed this, and at once puts an end to the lovely game with a merciless slap.

The fingers of the newly arrived boys don't keep still for a moment. They pick away at New Farm wherever and whatever way they can. They pull up the grass in the yard, peel pebbles out of the paths so that they become bumpy and people stumble as they walk along them, they bore pits in the new wall of the barnyard, digging their noses into the chalky dust which seems delicious to their young bones. But when they finally began to tear splinters from the walls of the house as well, their father's stern voice came from some corner of the yard: "I'll take the strap to you, you wait!" At this the little vandals shrank into themselves, motionless as insects when a human shadow falls on them, and suddenly they had vanished from that spot, to resume their activity all the more energetically in some other place, more remote from human eyes. Annele's father now hastened to make a gate for the garden and a solid door for the pantry lean-to, reinforced with wickerwork and bolts. Nothing could be safe from such active hands. When they were punished and forced to sit quietly, quietly – will you look at that? – they'd start scuffling among themselves like kittens: they'd slap and scratch each other, throw sand in each other's eyes, until their mother again came running like a raging whirlwind over their tow-haired heads. Yet a beating was never as severe as her threats. There might be a slap or two that hardly bothered the little boys. But when their mother threatened them with the terrible Jew who walks around with a sack and catches naughty children, with the Mute Beggar who would be here any moment now, his cane raised, with the Evil One himself who stood waiting around the corner with fiery pitchforks, the little kids screamed so hard, hiding their faces in their mother's skirts or practically crawling into the ground, their fists pressing their eyes shut, that it was pitiful to see them. It was because of these threats that, whenever the children saw anyone driving or walking past even at a great distance, they immediately dropped everything and, unanimously huddling close together and screaming at the top of their lungs, ran to hide in the shed in the darkest corner under their parents' bed. At such times the children would not be comforted, allowed no one near them, and no amount of promises could entice them to come out. They had no friend to confide in. Their oldest brother Kristapelis teased them on purpose. In his mouth the mother's threats turned into horror. When Kristapelis stayed close to his little brothers, he was usually up to no good. There was bound to be a big fight and horrible screaming. And whenever his mother appeared anywhere, Kristapelis took to his heels, well aware that the first blow would be for him. And it always did seem as though he had deserved it.

But was this really true? Kristapelis was the oldest – he seemed much older than his years. He was always the "big one," held responsible even for the mischief of the little ones. He was not allowed any childish pleasures. In his hands some harmless game that the little kids could indulge in to their heart's content was "mischief." As soon as his mother caught sight of it, there would be a harsh reprimand: "What are you doing, up to mischief again? Go look after the child!"

The child, oh yes. The little Auka baby, for whom big Auka was planning to find a godfather in Lithuania, was the thorn in Kristapelis's flesh. He tried to avoid the baby as much as possible. Nobody could understand how the boy could find a hiding place at New Farm, where there were neither trees nor shrubs, and Aukiene couldn't understand it either. Where could he have disappeared to? It could only be behind the buildings. But as soon as Aukiene looked around one corner, Kristapelis like an arrow had shot behind the next, and so she often had to race around all the buildings in a kind of circle dance, but did not find Kristapelis.

The wind loved the barrens. It was especially rough and harshly joyful in spring. It tumbled in through all the doors, rattled at all the windowpanes. Howling and whistling it crept through the chinks of the wagon shed where Kristapelis squeezed, pawed, dandled, tossed his little brother, unable to get him to stop crying.

"All right then, I'll show you!" the boy said spitefully and pulled the screaming child into the open door of the shed, where the wind slammed its mouth shut like the blow of a hammer. Swallowing the wind it had suddenly inhaled, the child suddenly stopped breathing, and could not get its wind back for a long time, turning blue and stiff, so that Kristapelis panicked, threw it down in the bed and ran for his mother. Aukiene didn't miss a chance to make one of her terrible threats against Kristapelis: "If the child is dead, I'm going to kill you." Kristapelis ran off and hid, and when he dared to show up again, his eyes were red. His mother said: "Well, tomorrow you won't bother me anymore. Then you can run around herding the cattle."

Kristapelis scowled as he watched his mother hurrying off. "I would ten times rather herd cattle than look after that brat," he muttered, for he did not dare say it out loud.

What kind of people were these that had come to live in the barren! They came and went, argued, went about their business with loud voices and loud restlessness. Annele felt as though this was no longer her own home, as though her own father and mother had become tiny and almost invisible in the face of these parents who were like enemies toward their own children, always in a state of war. Less so Auka himself – all of his severity consisted practically only in threatening to use the strap – but Aukiene looked as though she were always running from a battlefield – disheveled, jumpy, she constantly had harsh words upon her lips. Annele wasn't as sorry for the little ones. They were so funny, with their big pea-sized tears that would now flow down their dirty little cheeks when they cried, now run salty as could be into their mouths opened wide in laughter; in spite of everything they got to do pretty much what they felt like doing, which was by no means possible for Kristapelis. And Kristapelis would now be the one who would have to replace Annele, herding the cattle while she went to summer school. It had all turned out so strange. She had always sadly thought: How come Ancīte can go to school and I have to herd sheep? And now she herself would be going to school, and Kristapelis would have to herd the sheep.

She must find out what Kristapelis thinks of all this. And, as soon as she has overcome her first diffidence, she starts a conversation with him:

"Do you like being a herder?"

"What did you say?"

"Do you like herding cattle?"

"What's there to like? If I have to go, I'll go."

And that's the end of their conversation.

Annele is worried. How will this boy manage herding on the barrens? He can't join up with other herders, he probably doesn't know how to knit or do any other work, there's been no dog on the barren since Krančelis disappeared, nor is there a river with osiers, near which boys like to spend their time, and as for books, no doubt he doesn't have any – so how is he going to pass his day?

"You know what, I'll bring you a book," she decides without further ado to cheer up Kristapelis a bit, runs off to return shortly with a copy of *School Bread* that is pretty tattered though still in one piece. She can manage without it now, and it seems the one most appropriate for Kristapelis.

"It's lovely reading. Little stories and fables. You can read it for hours on end, and you won't be bored."

Without raising his head, Kristapelis scowls. Can't he move his hand just a little bit, wonders Annele, bringing the book closer and closer to the boy's eyes. He sits like an old man, propping the elbows of his crossed arms on his knees. When Annele seems too close to him, he jerks one elbow upwards, and *School Bread* drops from the girl's hands. And he growls: "Leave me alone. What do I need your dumb old book for?"

Annele is dumbfounded.

"Maybe you don't know how to read," it suddenly occurs to her.

"It's none of your damn business whether I can read or not," Kristapelis replies matter-of-factly, putting his hands in his pants pockets and looking at the girl disdainfully.

⁓⫯⊸

The day after St. George's Day Kristapelis starts on his job. Since it is Sunday, the whole household is in the yard watching the cattle leave the barns for the first time. It is a big, important day, the day that sharply separates two seasons. Now winter has truly turned away its gloomy face, and summer approaches, smiling sweetly. The cattle come out of the barns excited, stunned by the bright light, intoxicated by the strong air of spring. The lambs bleat piteously, frisk, run around as though they had lost their heads, no longer recognizing their mothers, so that the latter also need to call, to comfort, to nuzzle, and the air is full of the bleating of sheep like the confused language of Babel. The cows come outside looking dignified, careful, a little wobbly, a little unsure, getting rid of the numbness in their legs after standing a whole long winter, then bolt, tails raised, legs in the air, as though pursued by the Evil One himself. They recoil, calm down, sniff the ground, get the feel of it: Is it still the same as last summer? With a snort they make as if to butt at each other with their horns, not that the butting amounts to much, and finally, horns uplifted, sniff the air for a long time until, from their outstretched noses as though from huge trombones, they send long, uninterrupted moos of joy in all directions. This is their great spring song. Now Kristapelis, too, arrives, cap over his forehead, his herder's bag around his neck, a long whip in one hand.

"A whip," wonders Annele. "What's he going to do with a whip?"

"He'th thertainly not going to pet your lambth with it. He'll give 'em a good hiding," laughs Miķelis.

And, as if to confirm Miķelis's words, Kristapelis sends the whip whistling in one long whack across the backs of the lambs, then deftly flicks it aside and cracks it at their feet. Bleating piteously, they jump suddenly, and some continue to hop on three legs for a good long while.

Annele shakes her head. So that's the kind of herder he is.

She's never approved of whips. Her weapon as a herder has been a switch with soft branches that was worn down to a stump by evening, mostly from whacking thistles, which she has been trying to eradicate from the barren. At most, naughty Pearl has sometimes gotten a few good smacks on the legs, while Brownie has hardly known the taste of the switch. Now the animals will be subjected to a different kind of discipline.

When the cattle come home from the pasture, little Star has a bump on her forehead. She rubs her forehead against Mother's shin, but won't allow her to touch it. There are no flies, no gadflies yet, how did she get that bump?

When asked, Kristapelis shrugs his shoulders. He doesn't know a thing, it's not his fault.

But Jancis knows. "I'm going to tell," he boasts.

Kristapelis sticks out his tongue at him and quickly disappears.

Then Jancis does tell. Kristapelis has a slingshot, and he shoots at the cows' foreheads with little pebbles. He can't hit the other ones, but little Star has a blaze, and so he managed to hit her.

Annele's mother claps her hands with shock. What's to be done with a herder like that! Why, he's going to kill all the cattle! His mother's got to be told at once.

"Wait, wait," Father restrains her, "I'll go and talk to the boy."

Annele's father goes and talks with Kristapelis. No one knows what they speak about. When Father returns, he says: "That boy isn't bad, he's just been knocked about a bit. Is there anyone that says a kind word to him? No. So what can you expect? You've got to talk kindly to a child. Put a bit of butter in his lunch, that's something he'll understand."

"A herder deserves to be well fed. I don't have to be told," answers Mother.

"And whatever we accomplish with kindness will work. Violence will certainly get us nowhere," says Father. "Don't you see? The only way the boy's father and mother know how to deal with him is to slap him and threaten him with the strap. What good does that do a child? No good at all."

So Kristapelis's mother is not told about his mischief, but he still comes out of his hiding place with red eyes. And when Annele's mother brings out a bowl of milk porridge that night, he lets everyone take their turn with the spoon as is only fair and makes sure everyone gets their share.

It became a tradition for Mother's porridge bowl to walk to the Aukas' place every day as long as Mother herself had anything to pour into it.

Summer School

There had never been such a lovely spring on the barren. When Annele ran outside early in the mornings on her way to school, she felt as happy and free as the larks in the sky. And now the larks were in charge on the barrens as well. Ditches crisscrossed the slough, and the ground around it had been broken in fall; at the moment it was being gotten ready for sowing the spring crop. The peewits no longer had anywhere to stay. There were still one or two families that had built their nests according to old custom in damper spots, under slices of turf, but the plowman's comings and goings disturbed them so much that from early morning till late at night, out of breath, they were forced to sound their doleful songs. What had happened to their many-headed tribes of relatives? Nobody knew. The dominion of the birds on the barrens was drawing to a close. The cranes, too, had lost their home. The bushes on the neighbor's land had been cut down, the ground drained. The land lay plowed, with black furrows that had an oily sheen, waiting for seed. The cranes did occasionally fly across the barrens with their gentle calls, their great wings flapping, but always high up, as though they had chosen new itineraries. Annele followed them with her eyes as far as the horizon. Where had they found a new home?

Her way to school was against the sun. The sun wasn't very high yet. Classes started at eight, but respectable students were at their desks in good time. The earliest to arrive were often those who lived furthest away. Annele had over three miles to walk to school, and so her mother woke her every morning not much later than formerly, when Annele was a herder. She would wake her and urge her to hurry, but Annele urged herself on happily, too. She was going to school! This was such a different life – different food for her heart, different responsibilities. She felt she had been raised to a different status because she had the good fortune of being able to go to summer school. Wherever cattle grazed by the roadside, children were there herding them. Some as old as Annele, some younger or older. They could not go to summer school, but Annele could. She was grateful, grateful to Father and Mother.

From the little rise, Annele enjoyed taking one more look back at her home. There it lay in the lowest part of the barrens, as if on a great big tray. Now it could definitely be called a farm. The construction of the barnyard and threshing floor was finished at last, and this summer the farmhouse was being built. It would be finished by fall. The rest of the buildings had thick white thatched roofs, but the farmhouse would be shingled. The first little cabin would then become a *klēts* until fine new *klētis* would be built with tiled roofs. After that, at their leisure, they could build all the smaller buildings. But first they would plant an apple orchard. A big square had already been measured on the south side, and ditches dug all around it. The trees would be the glory of the farm, and all would be as it should; then the farm would not be distinguishable from others that had been built in the old days.

When Annele looks back from the rise, she does not think about the farm much. The blueprint of the farm has been in her head for ever so long, and she's figured it all out. When she looks back, she is trying to see if she can catch sight of her father. Like looking for a light in a farmhouse when you're on the highway at night. Where the light is, it feels homey and good.

And it feels good wherever Father is. That's where the light of the new farm is, that's where its heart is. There's not a ditch in the fields that he didn't dig; not a field he didn't plow, work into fertile ground, and sow; not a foundation for the new buildings that he didn't dig; not a wall he didn't build; not a roof he didn't thatch. It seems to Annele that everything she sees on the barren has grown from her father's hands. Others have come and gone, but they didn't care whether this job or another got done today or tomorrow. They worked with their hands, not with their thoughts and their hearts. When they were finished with one stage of a job, they'd stand around waiting to see what Father would do. They followed his instructions, for they could see only one tiny section of the work that had to be done, while Father carried it all in his mind. He never had time to stop and chat. But when he was alone at some lonely task, it sometimes happened that he suddenly stopped what he was doing, seemingly forgot himself, hands clasped on his chest, looking somewhere off into the fields of the sky with a bright, rapturous face as his lips softly talked to someone.

"Who taught Father how to do everything?" Annele once wanted to know.

"I don't think anybody taught me. I kept my eyes open and watched. All of life is a school."

Father had never had a single day of schooling. Granny's hymnbook had been her sons' school. Annele remembers it, this strange book where every hymn began with a huge capital letter painted red, so that the entire first verse of the hymn seemed to be lying in the lap of this letter. At the top of every page there was a little picture with little reclining angels all intertwined. When Annele first saw it, it had already lost its covers, and a good many pages had vanished goodness knows where, but once it had had a strong pigskin binding with brass hasps; however, the Avots sons had torn these strong, lovely clothes off its back as they struggled with their letters.

On the other side of the rise is Brook Farm. The nicest spot on the way to school. A bubbling little silvery watercourse. A little path through grass full of forget-me-nots and anemones. It winds its way toward a grove of white birches. What does it look like there? She'd love to have a look. To see. But somebody from Brook Farm might make his appearance. "What are you doing here, girl? You're supposed to be on your way to school." She can stand on the little footbridge for a while. That belongs to everyone. Her eyes can linger on all this loveliness, she can listen to the songs of the birds, watch the river skipping over the pebbles with silver shoes.

A lovely river. Where does it come from? Along its course, in the gently sloping valley, are farm upon farm, splendid as can be. Birch groves, orchards. White with blossoms.

Rye fields. Clearings. The highway. The bright, large eye of the millpond. And suddenly it occurs to Annele that she has lingered too long in the morning's loveliness, that she'll be late for school. Such a rich morning. It feels as though she's experienced so much. But now she must run for sure. She must run.

The students are standing in little groups. There's still plenty of time. Sludinātājs hasn't arrived yet.

The summer school is by no means nice to look at. It lies beneath the muddy eyelid of the millpond, right by the crossroad. With its tall, black chimney it looks like a grumpy night watchman who hasn't had enough sleep, and it has had many restless nights in its life, for it was once a public house. It has remained the same in outward appearance, only the inside furnishings have been somewhat adapted to the present needs of the school. At the tavern end one large classroom and the teacher's lodgings have been put in; the former stable for horses has remained unused.

"Sludinātājs is coming, Sludinātājs is coming!"

The students stir. Time to go into the classroom.

Here comes Sludinātājs, long-legged, quick to see things, seeming to read the school yard as if to find out: Is anybody standing around, is anybody getting into mischief?

He is immediately joined by three tall boys, brothers, wearing identical reddish-brown cardigans. All four of them go to the first row of desks in the classroom, lordly, like self-confident patricians.

Sludinātājs is not a boy anymore, but rather a young man. He has a white ironed dickey and a tie, while the reddish-brown brothers have the same white bandannas as the rest of the boys. Sludinātājs is the only son of rich farmers. He acts so smart, as though he were only coming to school out of politeness. Maybe he's going to go to school in town, and the teacher is preparing him for some higher grade. It is certainly possible, but nobody knows a thing about it.

Is Sludinātājs the prefect? That isn't clear either. The teacher has not appointed anyone as a prefect, and yet Sludinātājs does have special privileges. His brown, flashing eyes are everywhere, and sting like wasps. They never caress anyone, but always sting. And this sting is mockery, or worse – ridicule. It makes everyone flinch, as though struck by a switch. And these switches are the kind that prefer to strike on the sly. You'll be sorry if you cannot, or don't know how to, dodge them. Annele, too, doesn't know how to do this. With astonishment, but even more with a sense of shock, she winces one day as Sludinātājs's group passes by and she hears a word behind her like a rock flung on the ground. She does not understand it, but suspects that the word has some connection with her. Look at the way it's always uttered when she appears. Or the way the smaller boys repeat it, looking at her meaningfully. For it is every little squirt's highest ambition to be in some sort of agreement with Sludinātājs and his supporters. Exactly the way it was with the prefect in winter school.

Once as she and Lūcīte Pirtskalns go past a group of boys from which the familiar mocking calls can be heard, Lūcīte quickly pulls her past them and away.

"Don't you listen to those boys and their drivel," Lūcīte instructs her. "That's Sludinātājs for you, he makes up nicknames for everybody. They ought to make fun of him with that funny name of his, but he makes fun of others. And they leave him alone because everybody's scared to start a fight with him. That isn't right, but that's the way it is. Especially girls – as soon as a new girl comes to school, he starts bothering her. Right now you're the newest, and this is the way it will go on for a while until they get bored. I've been at this school for a long time, and now they leave me alone. You'd better pretend you don't even notice. Or tell them: 'Bark all you want, doggy, just as long as you don't bite me!' But if they see that your eyes are red from crying, no mouse hole will be deep enough to hide you. That's happened to more than one girl. Then in the end you have to report him to the teacher."

"No, no, not that," Annele quickly replies.

Lūcīte Pirtskalns sits next to Annele. She's on Annele's left. They happened to sit together from the very first day, and they get along as well as if they had been accustomed to each other for ages. Lūcīte, too, is the only child of rich farmers. Annele thinks she looks like birch trees in spring. She is so fair and delicate, as though she had been raised in a glass case. Her skin is white, covered with freckles, her eyes bright and clear like lake water, while her strawberry blonde hair, combed smooth and braided, encircles her forehead like polished brass shaved into strips. The girls like each other. No matter what Annele is like: taciturn because of some trouble or hurt, impatient because her class work hasn't gone the way she wanted it to, or for some other reason, Lūcīte is always friendly. With her quiet way of talking, with a warm smile from the bright lakes of her eyes, she is so captivating that Annele cannot remain sullen for long. During recess Lūcīte always holds Annele's hand so some other girl won't take it; she would also love to share her lunch with Annele: every day a different delicious smell announces its presence in the desk drawer, but Annele refuses – either she's just had lunch, or she's just not hungry that day, or she had such nourishing food early in the morning that it's enough for the whole day. The truth is that there's no way she can offer Lūcīte part of her own lunch, for she never has anything but a little hunk of rye bread with a lump of butter embedded in the center, but that's nothing she can offer to Lūcīte in return.

And here's what it's like in the mornings. When all the children are already assembled, and the stragglers have run inside breathlessly, when people are still sprawling in their seats, chattering, arguing, talking, laughing, each louder than the next, they try to shout the others down, and the noise is earsplitting. And then – in the twinkling of an eye, Sludinātājs's lanky figure is the first to subside behind his desk, the reddish-brown brothers follow suit, and in no time at all everybody is in their rows, ready for class, and their mouths have fallen shut. The teacher has come in.

This is how he usually comes in, noiselessly, and without a word being said everything goes silent. Walking down the narrow aisle, he sweeps his flock with a glance: Is everybody seated? Have they all come? As he looks at them, he narrows his eyes slightly, as though he wanted to encompass them all in his glance and hold them fast.

Annele thinks the teacher sees everything and knows everything, though his eyes are shaded by thick, dark curls, which hang deep over his forehead, but they are now searching, now questioning, now smiling, now serious, never the kind of eyes that seem to be saying: I don't care about you. They're never like that.

The teacher is young, perhaps slightly older than Sludinātājs, tall, broad-shouldered, with thick, shadowy hair and gray eyes. And since with that kind of eyes he reads the students' minds, he surely knows about Annele and her craving to learn. Surely he must realize that this girl cannot stay long in the same group as Lūcīte, Elza Mazarājs, and those other boys and girls who've been assigned to a group that takes up three rows of seats, for she must learn much, much more, and she's missed so much as it is. He must soon assign her to the next group, for she is convinced that she will listen and learn so much with these full ears and eyes that she'll soon be at the top, the very top, with Sludinātājs's group.

But something that one minute seemed easy to Annele appears impossible the next. How is she to accomplish this? Should she ask the teacher to let her go to an advanced group? In her thoughts she has imagined many ways of saying it, but she knows: When these words cross her lips, they will sound childish and silly, in fact: What should she do if she gets so muddled that the whole class starts to laugh? What then? No, Annele can't rely on her words. She has already had the experience that some people had a good laugh at them, while others shrugged: Where does that girl come up with such words? No, she couldn't manage something this big by talking about it herself.

Dictation class. "How do you spell it, how do you spell it?" whispers Vilis Vīnkalns behind her back after almost every sentence. He's used to it. Annele doesn't mind telling him. Vilis passes it on. Sentences rustle, pens scratch. But just as Annele turns around to give Vilis the answer, the teacher's gray eyes flash across the desk: "Avote, is this a time for telling stories? Watch out!"

A reprimand. The only one in the whole class to be scolded. Again she's been singled out. Guilty and innocent both. Eyes lowered, she hands in her notebook, not daring to look at the teacher. It is out of the question that she should come to the teacher with a request or suggestion now.

The teacher stands at the end of a row handing back the notebooks.

"How very strange. If Avote has a mistake in her notebook, the same mistake is in the notebooks of all those who sit around her."

Is what the teacher said in Annele's favor or not?

How bitter life can be made by mere trifles. Boots, for instance. Līziņa had sent a pair, and Annele had to wear them. The boots were beautiful. High, with many buttons and high heels. Līziņa had worn them for a while, but they hadn't stretched to fit her feet and pinched in one spot. She and Mother had thought they would fit Annele to a T. When Annele put them on, anyone would have realized this was not so. Anyone would have realized it, that's true, but Mother couldn't reconcile herself to that fact. Annele had boots, and Mother could find no fault with them. Annele had boots, but no *pastalas*. The ones she had had were worn out, and they couldn't buy new ones now, for times were hard, and besides no one was planning to drive to town. If the boots were fine, the fault lay elsewhere. "What kind of feet are those,"

Mother said reproachfully, flushed with trying on the boots. "Nothing fits you – not the Laukmalises' shoes, nor these beautiful boots." What good did it do for Annele to protest and defend herself – after all, neither the Laukmalises' shoes nor these boots had been bought for her feet. Mother just answered, curtly: "Nonsense! They'd fit another child just fine. Don't you know that younger children always wear the older children's clothes and shoes? Have you ever heard of anyone altering them? No. They're worn just as they are. Where there's a will there's a way."

Much can be accomplished where there is a will. The buttons were moved so that the top of the boot fit the leg snugly. The high heel was certainly a problem, it wobbled and threatened to break, but Mother hoped that Annele would get used to it, and that in any case by the end of a couple of weeks she would have grown into a boot that was too loose. After all, it was summer. She could run to school barefoot, and at school there was no more need for running about, seeing as how the boot did not permit it.

As for balancing on the high heels, Annele did learn how to do that; she was able to walk, though there could be no question of free or uninhibited movements, but one thing that troubled her a lot was that no other girl had boots like hers. The news of the boots Avote was wearing today made the rounds of the whole school within a few minutes; everyone who passed her would stealthily or deliberately glance at Annele's feet. Some of the girls nudged each other and whispered to each other. "They're her sister's." And another: "Well, beggars can't be choosers."

The boots, Annele felt, made her at least half a head taller, and not for the world did she want to be taller than she was already. Even as it was, her slender build attracted attention. No matter how hard she tried to make herself shorter, slumping loosely at the waist, it did no good. Those nicknames from the groups of boys were often hurled like cudgels. "Slingshot!" was one such nickname. That didn't hurt as much. They were real slingshots themselves. But "tapeworm!" That was insufferable, awful. That made her ears burn.

And wasn't it odd that she again had to endure other people's wisecracks on account of her footwear?

Lūcīte's home was just as far from school as Annele's, except that it was in the opposite direction. She was given a ride to school either all the way or halfway, and in the evenings she got a ride home. And Lūcīte persistently kept inviting Annele to come and visit her.

Annele made all sorts of excuses not to go. For then she would have to invite Lūcīte to her house, but how could they receive Lūcīte on the barrens? Not far from the school, on a newly acquired piece of land, someone had built a farm. It was a pretty good-sized cluster of buildings, and looked as though it were built out of birch bark: white walls, white shingle roofs that were, however, gradually beginning to turn gray in the spring winds and rain. The owner had called this farm Haferfeld Farm, but in common parlance the name had soon changed to Aparpaltes, and now no one called it anything else.

This was a farm Annele liked very much. It seemed to be so very different from other farms, so new and promising. The people who lived there must be happy and rich. Once she had expressed her thoughts about the farm to Lūcīte, and Lūcīte exclaimed delightedly that this was her uncle's farm. He'd just built it recently. Yes, it really was big and beautiful! The living quarters of the farmer and the hired hands were finer than you could find at any other farm. Uncle also had all kinds of books, and piles and piles of colorful pictures. And he was putting in a garden with all sorts of beds, paths, and greenhouses. There was a lot to see there. Uncle himself was a great storyteller and knew about all sorts of events. And she must go and visit. Every time Uncle met her, he asked: Well, when are you coming for a visit? And since Annele was now her friend, she must definitely come with her.

The temptation to see this new farm was too great. It overcame Annele's diffidence, and one day, when, by mutual agreement, the girls had each informed her parents they would sleep over at the farm, they crossed the field with light steps after classes were over, delighted how near it was, and saying how nice it would be if they had only such a short distance to run to school every day; how they could then sleep late in the mornings, and be done with homework much earlier at night. It wasn't until they reached Aparpaltes itself that it occurred to Lūcīte that Uncle might not be home at all. She said he was a district official and often drove to town or left on some other business, and that might be the case this time as well. But if so, it would be too idiotic, for Uncle was not married, and Lūcīte had no idea who had been running the household since Saint George's Day, whether this was a nice housekeeper or not; Lūcīte hadn't liked the one he had the year before.

Filled with these apprehensions of Lūcīte's, the girls suddenly felt all their pleasure about the visit evaporating, and entered Aparpaltes quite downcast. A plump, youngish woman was crossing the yard carrying some buckets. When she caught sight of the girls, she turned and waited.

"Good afternoon!" chorused the girls. And Lūcīte at once followed this up with a question: "Is the farmer home?"

"No, he isn't."

"Where is he?"

"He left."

"Will he be back soon?"

"I don't think so."

"Oh dear!" exclaimed Lūcīte.

"Do you need anything from the farmer?"

"We came to visit."

"To visit?" the young woman drawled.

"Yes. I'm the Pirtskalnses' daughter. Lūce."

"I can see that. I recognized you. And that other girl?"

"That's my schoolmate."

"She's come to visit too?"

"Yes. I certainly wouldn't come all by myself," Lūcīte answered, much bolder now, feeling more like a relative.

"You want to stay the night?"

"Yes. You see, we told our folks. And it's too late to go home."

"It's not too late for me to go home," was on the tip of Annele's tongue, but she couldn't say that on account of Lūcīte. Lūcīte was holding her hand tight, and would never have let her go.

"Go on, go to the farmer's end of the house, in the bedroom. The door's open," said the young woman curtly, took the buckets and left.

The girls went inside.

"That's the housekeeper he had last year. Her name is Māle," Lūcīte explained. "She's as fierce as a Cossack. I don't like her."

In the farmer's bedroom there was a narrow wooden bed with a soiled blanket and a not very clean pillow. An old table, a chair. Nothing else. Clothes hung from nails along the wall. The floor hadn't been swept for a long time. The windows were flyspecked. But the room was large, with a two-leaf door and big windows. The second room was much the same, only even emptier. In the corner there was an old trunk, an empty bin. That's all. There was no sign that anyone had cleaned the room.

"Uncle is still single," said Lūcīte. "In fall he's going to get married. His wife is bringing a rich dowry. Then the house will be full of furniture."

What were the girls to do now? They took out their books and began to do the next day's homework. They were soon done, for, thinking about the visit and about spending the night, they had worked extra hard earlier so as to have free time. Annele now mentioned that it might be nice to look at the uncle's books and beautiful pictures, about which Lūcīte had been so enthusiastic. There was no sign of them anywhere.

"I guess Uncle has put them away. If he were home we'd get to see everything."

And, after vainly waiting for a snack, not saying a word about it though both of them had the same thing in mind, Lūcīte finally couldn't help murmuring plaintively:

"If Uncle were home, he'd have her make us pancakes right now."

They had already talked about the pancakes, and had crossed the field with a secret craving for pancakes in their mouths. Their disappointment was bitter.

After sitting around in the room, the girls went outside to look at Uncle's orchard. There was not much to see with the best will in the world. A few little trees had been planted, a few small beds dug, but nothing had been completed, there was nothing to show that here somebody had started implementing some kind of big project, or any project for that matter.

The only direction to walk would have been toward the school, but they could easily run into the teacher, and he might immediately ask what they were doing here, so far from their respective homes; how lengthy and clumsy would be their attempt to explain! It was much better not to go in that direction. So for a while they walked in the opposite direction along a newly dug ditch, whose edges showed no sign of green, and which had muddy water at the bottom. It was not much fun, and they soon returned to the house and began to work on the next day's assignments.

When the sun set, Māle came in with her hands full, kicking open the door with her toes. In one hand she held a plate full of fried bacon, so full that the grease came up to the edge and soaked the maid's fingers. Her other hand held a pile of thick hunks of bread. She ran her elbow over a corner of the table and put the food down, asking:

"Well, will you be wanting to eat?"

The girls said neither yes nor no, nor did the maid expect an answer. Soon afterward, she came in again with a small dirty pallet, which she tossed right in front of the two-leaf door, asking: "Well, are you going to be needing a sheet?" Immediately she answered her own question: "I don't have a sheet, though. The one that's there is on the farmer's bed, and the others are dirty."

The girls got a thin little blanket as well, and a pillow. When they lay back to back, they were able to stretch the blanket over them like a skin, but as soon as they moved, the blanket would come off. The pillow was stuffed so tight that their heads would not stay on it but rolled off. The girls let them roll off on purpose, and laughed and rollicked about for a while. When it got dark, the farmyard became silent; only from the nearby highway was there the slow rumble of wagon wheels which faded away somewhere in the fields, then suddenly began to rumble again. The distant rumble of the wheels prompted the girls to begin telling stories. About travelers, about people asleep. They repeated them as they had heard them, a bit hard to believe, a bit hair-raising. Suddenly Lūcīte sat bolt upright and tossed away the blanket:

"There's somebody walking around, oh goodness, there's somebody walking around!"

"Where, where?" Annele listened, startled.

"In the next room. Can't you hear it?"

"Those are mice. They're running around the empty room. Gnawing on our pallet."

"Mice, mice!"

Like a shot, Lūcīte made for the middle of the room.

"I'm not sleeping over there anymore."

The girls quickly dragged the pallet to the opposite corner of the room. They calmed down. Lūcīte was furious at Māle, who had so stupidly made their bed right between the doors. But had they been any less stupid themselves? Of course not. Nobody had told them to sleep just at that spot.

A little while longer, the two of them rattled on and on, then one of them suddenly fell silent. The moon had climbed into the window, and it drove a white spike of moonbeams between their two heads.

The walls revealed themselves as bare, bleak, and stained with dirt. How needlessly big and empty was this building. "My house is so very different," thought Annele and dived with her thoughts into the vast blue expanse that surrounded a small house in the middle of the barrens, which, at this moment, was bathed in the silvery light of the moon.

When the girls awoke, the same plate filled with congealed grease with white angular slices of bacon sticking out of it was still on the table. The slices of bread were thick with flies. But the girls had to hurry. Because of going to sleep late the night before, their morning sleep had turned out to be a bit longer, and now they quickly washed and got ready so as to get to school on time. Only once Lūcīte sighed: "If Uncle were home, he'd tell the housekeeper to fry us some eggs and make some tea."

But her uncle hadn't come home, and Annele never got to see him.

And it was a funny thing about Aparpaltes. As beautiful as it had seemed when Annele hadn't been there yet, it seemed all the less attractive now that she had seen it close up. Like a bunch of tumbledown shacks you'd hate to look at.

Red Sun

Annele was the very first to come out of the schoolhouse. Almost at a run she hurried to reach the footpath. Once there she looked back. Boys and girls were leaving the school building. They laughed, teased, jostled each other on the wide highway like colts let loose. She'd escaped them.

Here it was good, it was safe. Today Annele was kindly disposed toward everybody, for she had succeeded in attaining what she had so long coveted and wished for. Today, when one of the groups of older students, the one that also included Sludinātājs's three friends, the reddish-brown brothers, had come up to stand by the teacher's podium to recite German Bible stories, she had suddenly found herself among them. How had she dared? How had her legs carried her there? She wouldn't have been able to say. She'd longed to do it for such a long time, it had to be done at some point, and now it was done. There she stood. Some of the students who, huddled in their own group, were sputtering with laughter, nudged each other with their elbows. Again they exchanged glances, burst into laughter. And then the elbows pressed outwards, pointed and sharp as needles, and butted Annele out.

"Get away! Out! Back to your seat! You know where that is? In the back benches! What are you doing here? Boys, pull that girl back! By her skirt! By her braids!"

And then suddenly the teacher had stood on the podium.

"What's this noise all about?" And, to Annele: "Oh, you're here? What is it you want?"

But now fear was in her throat and her mouth was frozen shut. Only the book had lifted hesitantly in her hands. The teacher took it. He turned over the pages, kinder now, more inclined to talk.

"That's your brother's book. I know it. Well, what do you want? Want to join the older ones? Can you keep up with them? Do you know any of this?"

Annele barely managed to nod.

"You know the story of the creation? Say it!"

Her heart had sent a wave of blood into her throat, but the words came, and could not be held back.

"Am Anfange schuf Gott Himmel und Erde. Und die Erde war wüste und leer und es war finster, und der Geist Gottes schwebte über der Finsternis.

Da sprach Gott: es werde Licht! Und es ward Licht. Und Gott schied das Licht von der Finsternis und nannte das Licht Tag und die Finsternis Nacht. Und da ward vom Abend und Morgen der erste Tag."

"And do you understand what you've been reciting?"

"Yes."

"Then you can come with the older group, and we'll see how things go," the teacher had interrupted her, and not one elbow had stopped her now as she took her place in the older students' German group near the teacher's desk.

Annele sits down in the ditch and takes the German Bible stories out of her satchel. After this day's achievements in school, they are the book that interests her most.

She fondles it, smooths out the worn corners, counts the pages. Not too many more hours if she is assigned as much as today, and she'll be through the book. And by then she'll know a whole lot more German and be able to read big books. Studying German with the help of Bible stories is child's play – after all, she knows every corresponding word in Latvian already.

And as she turns over the pages of the book, she once more thinks over everything that happened by the teacher's desk. She feels as though she has been in a swing that is carrying her high, so high.

Annele was walking through a field of rye. The ears of rye were white and heavy. She passed her hand through them in a caress. Sonorous as ripples of water, they rustled through her fingers and then straightened up again, and it seemed to her as though each of them were saying: Let there be, let there be!

When she came out on the road, she heard the noise of scythes. The people of Brook Farm – the married and single men and women, wearing white shirts, flashed bright at the end of the field, the scythes came bearing down in rhythm, the ears of rye hissed as they fell.

The rye harvest! Now Father, too, would be in the rye field. In the first big rye field of the barrens.

Father! What was it that stung Annele so painfully deep inside her breast? The memory of one father who had suddenly died not so many days ago. He was someone she did not know, the father of one of her brother's schoolmates. But when she had heard of this event, she had felt a sudden deadly fear. Never had she imagined that fathers and mothers could die, too! And here one had died. Suppose her father, too – –!

As they had during the past days, thoughts came with the memory. Quick as lightning. Hateful! How they came and went and returned again! Quickly, quickly, she must run up the hill of Brook Farm, from which you could see home.

Yes! They'd started mowing the field of rye! How many shocks already? One, two, three – Annele counted eight. No more than that?

Where was Father's white figure? He must be there. Ģelžu Miķelis, too, who came and helped Father with the rye harvest. But they weren't there. They were nowhere to be seen, not bent at work, not upright whetting their scythes, nor behind the shocks, nor by the swaths of rye, nor sitting down, eating the afternoon snack.

What had happened? Why had the work been started and abandoned? Father never did a thing like that.

A man carrying a scythe with a little rake hanging from it came out of the farm-house. It was Auka. He was all by himself.

The wagon had been pulled out into the yard. Ģelžu Miķelis led a horse up to it, left it there, ran to the barnyard, then back again, clapped his hands to his sides, then to his head, hurried back to the barnyard and now, having returned with the harness, began hitching the horse to the wagon hurriedly. Miķelis was in such a hurry, so flustered.

Mother came out of the house, said something to Miķelis and then walked back to the house, as much in a hurry as Miķelis.

This running back and forth, which at any other time would have seemed funny to Annele, now felt ominous to her, for Father was nowhere in sight.

She turned off the road and ran straight across the newly cleared field that was being made ready to be the next rye field. Miķelis came driving out of the farm, urging the horse to canter.

"Where are you going, Miķel?" called the girl, and her own voice felt strangely unfamiliar to her.

Miķelis pointed ahead with his hand, and gave no further answer.

"He's hurrying to Edgefield Farm. Something's happened," Annele whispered.

Mother hurried out into the yard to meet her. As though she did not know what she was hurrying to get, as though she could not see, she looked at Annele, sank down on a stack of boards. Seeming unable to hold back the words, she responded to the girl's wide fear-filled eyes, her unspoken question.

"Yes – it's Father. We'd just barely gone out to mow... Right in the middle of the swath, too. So suddenly, so very suddenly, as though a deadly beast had attacked him. He just slumped down. Not another step – the pain was so terrible. It seems something's ruptured inside him. We had to half carry him home. It's a good thing we've got those two horses now. I sent Miķelis off to Edgefield Farm, Jānis rushed off to get the doctor, there was nothing else I could think of."

Father was lying in the narrow little room that already had a door and windows, at the other end of the new house. Annele shuddered. His dear face had changed so much. His features were drawn with pain, his forehead covered with drops of perspiration. He was tossing now to one side, now the other and moaning in a muffled voice, but when he caught sight of Annele he contained the pain by force behind a loving smile: "Look what's become of me, lass!"

Annele hurried up to him shyly, placed her hand on her father's hot, trembling knees. Father squeezed her fingers painfully, tightly: "You go outside, lass. This is not for a child." His face grew dark beyond recognition. He turned his head toward the wall.

Where was Annele to go now, what was she to do? She riffled through her books, the letters danced before her eyes, she could see nothing, understand nothing. Away, away, back to Father's door. She was not allowed inside. Mother wouldn't let her.

She flattened herself against the wall, listening. The same moans, the same tossing from side to side. In between, when it got quieter, Father kept saying something, softly, lovingly, as though talking with a friend. Annele was afraid to listen.

"Go and see if Jānītis is coming with the doctor," her mother would send her away to keep her from being underfoot.

As though she hadn't been outside dozens of times already to look in the direction of Dobele.

The doctor, the doctor! She couldn't get him out of her mind for an instant. What kind of a person was he? What could he do?

Cold shivers went through her. She remembered: Why, the doctor couldn't do a thing. They'd bring him of course, but he could never do a thing.

"They ran and got the doctor with all speed!"

She had heard this said more than once when there was talk of people falling ill, and had imagined at such times how fast this had happened. As quick as lightning. They'd run and get the doctor. But then – "He couldn't do a thing!" It was always too late. The doctor was no help.

Restlessly, she moved about from one place to another. Studying was out of the question.

⁓⫶⁓

Annele was sitting in the yard on the boards thinking. She felt as though her chest and head were being bent into a circle like a red-hot iron hoop. It stung and smarted more than words could say. If only she could close her eyes for a moment and think it away, if only it were no longer there. If only it were all gone. She bowed her head on her arms. She sat like this for a long time.

When she opened her eyes again, she was surprised to see pale stars in the sky. Time seemed to be standing still, and yet it had passed. There was the sound of murmuring voices. Miķelis was unharnessing the horse. The master and mistress of Edgefield Farm were here.

"I think we should send a message to our older girl in Jelgava. I just don't know what to do," Mother was saying.

"We already did. As soon as Miķelis arrived, I had Aldis harness the horse and go to Jelgava. She might be here by tomorrow. It's the proper thing to do. That doesn't mean he's going to die, you know, but suppose he wants to see her, what then?" –

"Mother, has the doctor come yet?" Annele came over to them.

"No, not yet, child, but I should think he'll be here soon now."

"Send the child to bed, sister-in-law! Why put her through all this anxiety?" said Laukmalis, patted the girl on the head and slowly walked into the house. Mother sent the girl to the barn, to spend the night sleeping in the hay.

"Is Father better?" the girl scarcely dared to ask.

"Yes, yes. At least he's calmer now. Maybe everything will be all right. The doctor will come and help, maybe everything will be all right."

⁓⫶⁓

The barn door is wide open, the sun is high in the sky. Mother is standing in the doorway.

"Get up, lass, put on your school clothes and put your shoes on, too."

"Is it time to go to school already?"

"Not to school. Somewhere else. You have to take a note from the doctor, and then they'll give you something."

"Was the doctor here?"

"He just left."

"What did he, what did the doctor say?"

"Don't ask so many questions. There's nothing much he can say, is there? Hurry up and take that note!"

When Annele had gotten dressed, her mother came and met her in the yard with a note written by the doctor, and a piece of bread for the road.

"Don't come inside, don't disturb him. The doctor gave him a powder. The patient seemed to become quieter. Maybe he'll get a bit of sleep. Now you run. See that big forest on the other side of the railway line? It's called Unguri Forest. Look at those rooftops in the distance: that's Unguri Farm – and they say the woman who has the stuff you're to fetch lives in that forest. There are supposed to be a lot of paths through that forest, but if you hit on the right one it's supposed to go straight to her cottage. They say it's a pretty cottage, with flowers in front. And that woman is called the midwife. If you meet anyone, just ask them where the midwife lives. Anybody will tell you. I can't describe how to get there, I've never been there myself. If you do see a lot of paths, just ask anyone you meet. And keep more in the direction of Unguri. – If there were anybody else I could send, I wouldn't make you go, but who is there that can go? Jānis took the doctor back. He's exhausted anyway, he hasn't had any sleep, and Miķelis won't do at all for an errand like this."

Annele set off at a run. Mother called after her:

"Walk more slowly! Don't get tired out! It's a long way, and you won't have enough strength on the way back. Remember everything I told you!"

Annele started off. The forest didn't look as though it was far away. Here was the railroad track already.

But she couldn't get across here. Clayey water gleamed in the wide ditches, although there hadn't been any rain for a long time. It was low-lying ground. She had to take the long way around to the railroad crossing.

The crossing guard's wife inspected her closely as she crossed the road. She had never seen such a girl hereabouts. Perhaps the woman might know where the midwife's cottage was, thought Annele, but by then she had already passed her. How could she ask the first person she met for directions as soon as she had set out? And there was the forest in plain sight. The road toward it turned right, around a few boggy spots, across quagmires that had been filled in with brushwood, and that bemired teams and wagons in wet weather. Finally the road led into a magnificent forest and became as wide as the big highway itself. It flowed among the trees like a green stream.

It seemed to Annele that she had never before seen so magnificent a forest.

Such lush, green grass, such big flowers, blooming in what seemed to be unfamiliar colors, such mighty trees grew here! Birches that rose into endless space, oaks as glossy and green as at Midsummer, elms as tall as buildings with a broad roof of branches that scattered airy, golden fleeting shadows under the sun. All heaviness dropped from her. She felt as light as a bird. There was a kind of infinite joy surrounding all the living things in this lovely forest. Her reason for being in this forest seemed to be completely forgotten like a torturous dream. As though by magic her young heart was filled with light, and all darkness was driven from it. The tops of the trees were tall, tall, swaying in the sun, with the infinite sky beyond them! There was no pain, no suffering! Smooth, velvety paths beckoned and called to her. To walk there was easy, easy! She could have walked along these paths for days on end.

But she could not see the cottage anywhere.

The road suddenly curved and divided into three. Which one should she take now? She had to make a decision and trust her luck. Her eyes, however, chose the nicest of the three.

She walked along it for a while. But then she had the feeling that the road was turning back. It certainly wasn't going toward Unguri Farm or to some inhabited place, for it showed fewer and fewer signs of being traveled.

She must return to the place where the three roads branched and take another road.

To avoid the detour she had already taken, she ran for a while straight through the forest.

She did come out on a road again soon, only now it seemed to her that it was no longer the same road.

The trees seemed to be different, and suddenly this road, too, branched in two directions. Still, she felt doubtful. Perhaps this was the same she had walked down and she had simply not noticed the side road before.

All she could think of doing was to repeat her first experiment: to walk down one and, if that did not lead to the wide road, to come back and take the other road.

But there was no longer a wide road anywhere. It seemed to have faded and disappeared. Now she ran first in one direction, then in the other. She looked around, searched. Finally she realized she was completely lost.

She stopped walking and looked at a shadow. It was just noon. All kinds of terrifying stories about evil spirits flashed into her mind. Unfamiliar places, unknown roads. Exactly noon! To think of the stories that were going round. Suppose an evil spirit were to appear!

She quickly glanced in all directions. Shook herself hard. No, she must not get frightened. Whatever happened, she must be brave. But which way should she walk now? What should she do? If only she had asked the crossing guard's wife. Who was there to ask here? There was not a living soul on any of the roads.

Nevertheless she continued walking for a while. Heaviness laid itself across her shoulders. Now she stopped. Should she go forward, turn back? Neither made sense. And then suddenly she was seized by such weariness and despair that she fell to the ground.

Her shield, the wonderful joy nature had endowed her with, which she had felt on entering the forest this morning, was suddenly shattered and fell away like kindling wood, grief was back again, dark, black, and terrible.

Father, Father! What is he doing now? How is he? – And they're waiting for her.

Mother's been looking in the direction of Unguri Farm time after time, waiting. But meanwhile Annele is lost, lost! And yet she must get help. She must get help!

Suppose she has to walk all day and doesn't find the place? Night will come and she still won't have found it. What then, what then? She no longer knows the way there or back.

"God, God, show me the cottage!"

In her despair, as if looking for help, she lets her eyes wander in all directions. Suddenly it seems to her that in one spot the veil of trees looks lighter and thinner. She walks toward that spot, straight through the forest. The trees part, recede, and there is a roof, there is a garden, there is a house. A pretty cottage with flowers in front of it. There's a whole lot of flowers blooming there, shimmering in the sun in all the colors of the rainbow. Is it possible that she is so close to the place she's been looking for? How is it that she's been walking around all this time, lost, not seeing anything? Perhaps this is all a fairy tale?

No, it isn't a fairy tale. There are hens cackling here, piglets grunting, children playing and arguing. People live here.

A kindly young woman comes to the door. "Who are you looking for, dear?"

Annele tells her her errand. The words come out easily, unraveling from inside her like a ball of yarn, but then suddenly break off right in the middle. Why did the kindly woman shake her head so sadly when Annele told her how Father had fallen ill? Did she know more than she would say? She asked no further questions, went inside and after a short time brought out a little bundle: "Carry it carefully, now!" she told her as she handed it over. And then sighed. "Tell them to try this! Maybe it will help!"

Upon hearing that Annele was lost in the forest for such a long time, the kind woman shows her the way out by a direct little path. They walk along the edge of the forest. Stately Unguri Farm is visible not far away. The farm nestles in its orchards so peaceful, so affluent. It isn't likely that they have any troubles there today.

The girl knows her way now, and hurries home at a half-run.

Mechanically, Mother takes the little bundle. "I wonder if it will do any good now?" she shakes her head sadly. She doesn't ask where the girl has been so long. It seems she doesn't even realize that the day is drawing towards evening.

Laukmalis is still there. That's not a good sign, thinks Annele. She hasn't dared to ask how Father is doing. She hasn't dared to go into the sickroom, knowing that Mother told her yesterday not to go in. She can't be of help, she can't be merry as at other times with her father; on the other hand, if she is sad – Father will see it, and it's hard enough for him as it is, so very hard. No one talks to her, or helps her bear the heavy burden that has fallen upon her shoulders so unexpectedly. She knows: they all carry the same burden, but they talk among themselves, they all seem to know more about the terrible secret that has settled over the rooftops of New Farm and that Annele is trying to solve like a difficult puzzle, yet is unable to solve. She tries to read the solution in the eyes of the grown-ups, their faces, their remarks – do they sound brighter, is there hope, perhaps? in their footsteps – are they slower, more relaxed, or hurried and excited as they bring help? will everything be all right again, will everything be all right?

In the big, half-finished room there is a bed, and when Laukmalis is not inside with Father, he lies down on the bed and dozes awhile, for he has spent the night awake. Mother goes in to see him. They talk.

"It's no use, no use! No matter what you give him, no matter what you do! None of it's any use. How long can he endure it? Even if a man is strong as a lion, he'll be broken in the end. Just a while ago I took him outside. He can't keep on his feet by himself anymore. Leaning on my arm like a baby. And then, suddenly, as though he had his old strength back, he holds me tight: Stay, stay a little longer! What do you mean, stay, what is it you need? He just looks into the distance, lets his eyes wander, all the way around."

Mother's voice fades away, becomes inaudible.

"The strongest tree will break in a storm," says Laukmalis.

Annele doesn't want to hear any more. She can't get out of her head the image of Father standing there utterly silent and letting his eyes rove over the world, as though to say goodbye.

Brother is by the well. His face is swollen, his eyes red with weeping.

"Don't stare! Why do you stand there staring?" he fends her off harshly. And he washes his face and eyes for a long time to remove all traces of tears.

"You're going to Father, then?"

He knows what will come next – Annele's request: Take me, too! And answers without having heard it: "You can't come. Father needs rest. And you can't help. Children just get underfoot and upset people. D'you understand?"

Yes, she can understand that. That's the answer they all give. How hard this is for the child. Isn't he her father? Doesn't she know how to creep into a little corner, quiet as a mouse, invisible even. Just so as to be able to be where the others are. Just to see and know what's happening at every moment.

Annele sits in the barn on her makeshift bed, rolled up in a blanket. She doesn't want to sleep, just to warm herself a bit, for sometimes her teeth start to chatter. She wants to be awake and not let her dear father out of her thoughts for a single moment.

People have been coming and going, talking and doing things, but no one has been able to help. Most likely the doctor couldn't either, or the medicine Annele brought home.

But wait a minute! That time when Līziņa had her long illness, she was seemingly without all sense and feeling for such a long time, as though sunk into oblivion, and then one day she opened her eyes and had her senses back, saw Annele, saw and recognized everyone, was back among people again and got better.

There was no longer any hope, but God saved her.

Annele herself prayed to God then, fervently prayed in the dark little corner behind Father's loom, and God heard her prayers.

Not right away, of course. It happened a long time after, softly, imperceptibly. Like when spring comes. But this was a disease where help was needed immediately. This couldn't wait.

But she was praying, with every breath she drew: "Make Father well."

Still, prayer alone was not enough. You had to have faith.

Christ said: "With faith you can move mountains."

An infinite rush of joy had overwhelmed her when she first read these words. If you had faith, you could do anything you wanted to.

She had tried to pray and to have faith at the time, but nothing had come of it, of course. It was always about the same old thing – books and school. For she'd had no other worries then.

After that she avoided such experiments. Perhaps the words were too lofty and holy, and must be interpreted differently.

Now, however, here they were again, so fresh and powerful, as though she were hearing them for the first time. Just as credible, just as convincing, they filled her whole being with the same rush of joy. Christ had not spoken of mountains only, but had said, "Whatever you ask for in prayer, you will receive, if you have faith."

To have faith, to have faith! As much as was in her power. To go beyond faith! But how? Nothing had come of the kind of faith she had had until now. What was needed here was a different sort of faith, a different strength. And perhaps it was too difficult for her on her own. If only all of them had faith! If only they would all come to her help!

But what about all the others? That was what was so terrible – none of them believed that Father would get better! No matter what their lips might say, they no longer believed it in their hearts. Not her mother, not her brother, not Uncle Laukmalis, not the doctor, nor that kind stranger who had shaken her head so sadly today. Annele was well aware what the woman had been thinking when she said, "Tell them to try this!" None of it's any use anyway – that's what she'd been thinking.

She had no other choice. She had to have faith all on her own.

But how was she to find faith? And suddenly she had the feeling that she had found the way. She suddenly remembered that bright spring morning in the meadow when, down to the tips of her toes, she was filled through and through with a kind of intense ineffable bliss, and it felt as though there was nothing in her but this bliss. Yes, that was it! Faith, too, must be pure, serene, and joyful. She would not think about her sick father at all, she'd think of him when he was well. She called up a memory she loved, when she was still quite young at Spring Farm and Father was coming back at noon from harvesting the rye, young and tall and stately, his scythe and rake hanging over his shoulder, his cap pushed back from his forehead, smiling, with shining eyes. Singing in his sonorous voice:

"Lost my horse, lost him in the clearing..."

But as she thinks these thoughts, she realizes this is not the way to go. As soon as she thinks of her father well, she cannot help thinking of him ill, and at once there is pain, such sharp pain that things are no longer the way they used to be. If she wants to have faith, she must no longer think of what is in the world at all. She must throw it out, every bit of it, so that the great strength of faith can come flooding inside.

She tries to go deep into herself and to catch hold of it, but then the scraping of a whetstone reaches her ears. There was a swish of scythes. A corncrake was chirring far away. What was that? Oh yes – that was Miķelis and Auka mowing in the rye field.

When the mowers had reached the end of the windrow, they sharpened their scythes, walked back to the beginning of the windrow and began mowing again.

Annele put her fingers in her ears. She didn't need that, she didn't want to listen to that. But it didn't do any good. Her ears seemed to be deliberately struggling to be open to all noises. These seemed even sharper, even closer. On the other side of the wall the cows were lowing softly and chewing their cud. What? Was it so late already?

Yes. A pale moon was shimmering outside. The mowers were mowing late because they had gone out late. In the heat of the day the grain would shed.

Annele recalled everything, and as she recalled it she felt that at this very moment the strength of heart she would have needed in order to have faith was oozing out slowly, as sap oozes from a tree that has been tapped. Her head leaned earthward, it was droning.

I'll lie down a bit. I'll get warm. I'll wait till everything is quiet. Then I'll have faith. Then I'll have faith.

But suddenly the noises broke off. An immense silence settled over her limbs. Annele's own voice was audible as though from far, far away: "Then I'll have faith, then I'll have faith."

A different kind of strength is needed for the great act of faith.

⌁

Annele is dreaming. A great big forest. She's walking, she's lost her way. She's supposed to go somewhere, she's got to run quickly, quickly. Robbers and werewolves are after her; green eyes jeer at her from behind one tree, then another, hide again, something won't let them come near Annele. "Go quickly, hurry, go find it, find it!" somebody urges her. "What am I supposed to look for?" Annele wonders and can't remember. Like an iron band the thing she has forgotten holds her head in its vise. "Hurry, hurry!" the somebody who is urging her seems to be treading on her heels, but she can't move a muscle.

Trees? But these aren't trees. They are men muffled in gray cloaks. They leave their places. They huddle behind her back, close, so close together. They whisper to each other, covering their mouths. Hey, that girl over there! Let's grab that one! Annele tries to scream but can't. All sound has left her lungs. Now you're finished, a remaining small voice calls in her breast, while another voice reassures her: No, you're not, you're not! –

And now here's the wide green road. Shady trees. The cottage at the end of the road. Now she knows. This is where she had to go to get Father's medicine.

She walks and walks, – but the cottage has vanished again. The forest is thick as could be – it presses so close that she can't take a single step, or move her limbs. Branches lie on her arms. No, not branches. Those are flowers, wonderful flowers. – No, they're not flowers either, but heads, living heads. And as soon as Annele makes a move, they're back on the trees as large flowers. Now it feels like home, so good and light. And there's Father, too. He seems to be coming from Brook Farm, carrying something for Annele in his cap. That must be Krančelis, thinks Annele.

Why, Father doesn't have a cap at all. He's all in white, the way he looks on Sunday mornings. And he's got one of those big forest flowers in his hand. "Look, Annele, – how do you like this one?" he says gaily. "Pet it a bit!" And now it's not a flower he has in his hand anymore, but a bird. It turns its head this way and that, and the beautiful feathers on its neck shimmer like gold.

"But Dad, don't you know you're sick, I've got to run and get you some medicine," Annele remembers.

"Oh, get away with you, silly girl!" Father laughs. And then he's gone. Besides, it wasn't Father anyway. It was only a little white cloud she was looking at, for Annele is lying on the barrens.

Annele is lying on the barrens. But why is she lying here? She must, she must get up. She's got to see that the cattle are safe. Listen! A roll of thunder! There's a storm coming.

"Get up, get up, Annele! Come this minute!"

Yes, yes, she certainly will. She'll go this minute. If only she can rub the great heaviness from one eye and find out why she had to lie on the barrens.

Yes. The storm is coming. A black, black sky. The whirlwind is already roaring through the forest. If only Father would take the horse at once, get on its back, and gallop after the cattle. The storm will carry the cattle off with it.

"Annele, get up! Can't you hear? Get up and come this minute!"

Yes, yes. She'll get up! This minute, this minute! But where are her clothes? She's got them on already. Yes, she'll go at once. Where is she supposed to go?

She has to climb a high, high wall. And then there's a wide stream, with a narrow plank footbridge across it. Annele isn't afraid. She can cross it on tiptoe. But suddenly the stream below begins to roar. Now she'll fall in for sure. She suddenly screams.

Her eyes open wide. Where is she?

She's up in the hayloft, on a narrow plank thrown across the rafters, for the barn only has a temporary ceiling. She'll never understand how on earth she managed to climb up the tall stack of hay from the barn and get to the top like a sleepwalker.

Below, the cows are snorting, lowing, and chewing their cud. The swallows under the rafters below the roof aren't awake yet. It's still quite early. She slides down the haystack, burrows under her blanket, stretches her limbs, which seem to have grown completely numb and to be tied up in knots. At once, sleep settles on her eyelids again like a leaden weight.

Here someone roughly and quickly grabs her by the hand. Pulls her to a sitting position. Shakes her hard. It's her brother.

"You just sleep and sleep and don't even hear us running to get you one after another and calling you. How can you sleep? Father's calling for you. Come on! Father's dying!"

And he's gone. The barn door is left wide open. The out-of-doors is filled with rosy light.

As though struck by a blow, Annele remains behind. By the barn door, leaning against the doorpost. Who was Brother talking to? Whom was he telling to get up? Was it her? What was it he said? What was it he said? And then, suddenly – she knows. Like a thousandfold echo the words resound from the walls, from the roof, from outside: Father's dying! Dying!

She must go, but she can't. Something terrible has shackled her feet and her hands, frozen her blood. She, too, must die now. She tries to lift a foot or a hand, but they fall back helplessly, and she leans against the doorpost for support.

But meanwhile her eyes rove about incessantly and see every detail: the swallows are darting in, out, one with a new little yellow stalk in her beak. "She must have brought it from the rye field," Annele clutches at this insignificant side thought as she might at a straw.

Suddenly the black wings and white breasts of the swallows flame red, iridescent light flows in broad streaks across the barrens, the white grains of dew in the grass light up with tiny red stars. The sun! Crowned with a garland of rays, it is rising above the earth.

Bathed in rosy light, Līziņa is running across the yard. She takes hold of Annele by the armpits, pulls her along, half carrying her.

"Sister! Little sister! Where have you been all this time? Father's waiting for you. All morning he's been calling: Where's my little girl? Where's my little girl?"

Tears choke her.

Trembling, Annele steps across the threshold. Many eyes are looking at her. Why don't you come? – they seem to reproach her. The room is full. Here are Father's closest brothers: Laukmalis, Melnzemis, and Avots. The room is filled to the ceiling with rosy light, for the sun is in the east window. All the faces are illuminated, transfused with light.

"Go on, go to Father," whispers Līziņa.

Annele sinks to her knees by the bed. As though through a mist, she sees Father sitting up, the white shirt over his chest open, his dark hair like shadows surrounding deep, unprecedented pallor.

Father's face is unutterably changed. It no longer belongs to the world.

Then she feels her father's hand on her head, and her eyes close. As though in deep, light-filled silence somewhere, a voice begins to speak. Is that Father's voice? It no longer belongs to the world. One by one, words drop over her like softly sonorous silver drops of water. "May the Lord bless you and keep you. May the Lord make his face to shine upon you and be gracious to you. May the Lord lift up his holy countenance upon you and give you his peace."

Then silence sets in, even deeper silence.

The whole window is full of the red rising sun. Father's body, bathed in light, lies on the bed at full length, but Uncle Ansis holds one hand over Father's eyes, puts his other hand to his own lips, looks at those who are present as though signaling to them: Be silent! Be silent! Hold back your voices, hold in your sobs, hold your breath!

And then he says in a solemn, unaccustomed tone:

"Sleep sweetly, sleep sweetly, dear brother, in God's peace!"

They all fall to their knees around the bed as the uncles begin to sing, with shaking voices: "Who knows how close my end is to me."

⁓⫘⫯⁓

The sun is climbing. The cattle are let out. The farmhands go off to the fields. Annele can't understand why all this is happening. How can they drive, walk, talk, do things when Father is no longer there? Haven't these people seen anything, don't they know anything? Perhaps everything that happened isn't real at all? Perhaps it's a dream, just like the one last night when everything also seemed so very vivid and close at hand, yet it was all a dream. If only she could fall asleep right now and sleep, sleep, and then, when she'd wake up, time would have moved backward and everything would again be the way it used to be. She puts her head on her knees. If only sleep would come and carry her away. But there's talking going on.

Father's brothers are sitting on a pile of boards in the yard, talking about Father. Laukmalis says: "One of us is gone. In the very summer of life, and such a strong man, too. He didn't have it easy. None of us have accomplished as much as he did. This brother of ours was faithful in all things. Faithful as gold, faithful until death. I don't know which of us was like that. And then, look at the way he thought about those children. I have neither silver nor gold, but I can give you my blessing. Those were his words. And after he had blessed the big children, he had no peace to die and pass away until he had seen the little one. You could see how he struggled with almost supernatural strength to stave off death so it would let him bequeath to the child the only possession he had."

"Things are going to be hard for the children," said Melnzemis, who was never one to say much.

"It doesn't make that much difference to the big ones, but what about the little one? It's a good thing she's too young to know the meaning of such a blow," said Laukmalis.

Annele left quietly. How little her uncles knew after all, how little people knew about other people.

The uncles drove away. Annele's brother and sister got ready to go to Jelgava, for there were lots of things that were needed. Mother had no money. Līziņa reassured her, promising to take care of everything.

"Where are you going to get it all, poor dear?" worried Mother.

"I'll scrape together every penny and borrow the rest. Later I can pay it back little by little. We're going to give Daddy a decent funeral, though."

Mother did her chores all day long. So much had been put off because of Father's illness. Every once in a while, however, she would slump down somewhere – either on a chair or even on the ground, and cry and cry.

Annele could not cry. She went around, eyes filled with despair, not knowing what to do with herself. She would walk a long, long way into the barrens and come back again seemingly without finding anything, or seeing anything. Indoors and out, every road and every footpath, clouds and winds, sky and earth – all had died when Father died.

Sweltering heat. Mowers taking their noon rest. Not a blade of grass moves on the barrens. Only above the fields of summer wheat the air, grown hot, restlessly shimmers in tiny waves.

Annele sits in the shadow of the shed, knees pulled in, her back to the wall. In her limbs she still has what feels like numbness after a blow, the selfsame thoughts lie on her eyelids like a stone, they shut out the world, make it dark and invisible.

Suddenly she gets up and goes to the threshing barn. She must see Father. The yard, the barrens are empty. Noonday peace reigns everywhere.

She opens the door to the threshing floor. It creaks barely audibly. Here, everything is still new, clean, and unused. Cemented into the foundation of the threshing barn with all the others is the big rock from the barrens that was split by Father.

The deceased has been laid out in the middle room where the oven is, for that is the coolest.

Annele enters on tiptoe, yet hearing her own footsteps, hearing her heartbeat in her throat. She feels as though the distance from one door to the other were very, very long, as though with each step she had to push back throngs of unseen sentinels that fill the room.

The walls and the drying racks gleam white and smell fresh like resin. But whitest of all is the figure on the platform of boards in the very middle. All the light in the narrow enclosed space seems to flow toward the one and only dear, motionless face.

Annele looks for a long time. It seems impossible, impossible to believe that the quickening smile has been extinguished. Extinguished, that's true, but he has left his mark, imprinted like tracks in the ground made by countless footsteps.

But now he's gone, he's gone, gone!

Grief constricts her heart like a narrow prison, presses close to her forehead like an icy wall of darkness.

But her heart does not want darkness, does not want sorrow, her heart calls its unceasing: He is here, he is, he is! Her heart calls, Let there be light.

"Let there be light! And then there was light!"

Yes, yes, yes!

Suddenly, like fiery bells, the great words of Genesis ring out in her young soul.

Somewhere, he exists. Light exists. Forever.

Daddy, too, was light.

He cannot be extinguished. Cannot vanish. Never, never!

"Dear Daddy, dear Daddy," the girl stretches out her arms toward her dead father. And, breaking forth suddenly, an intense wave of feeling passes across the dark waters of grief like a bright stream. It seems to have been released by a miracle, it is holy and resonant. It's like an incomprehensible joy that bears her soul upward like rushing winds.

He exists forever! Forever!

The following day, Miķelis brought a white, roughly hewn coffin. It had been taken down from some attic, where an old grandfather had been keeping it for his own funeral. Laukmalis knew this old man. He had personally driven over to see him and had arranged to use the coffin for his brother, promising to have another one made in its place right after the rye harvest. Now that the grain was shedding on the field, no craftsman had time to make a coffin for the deceased, who had passed away at such an inopportune time.

Līziņa brought thick purple paper back with her from Jelgava. It looked like velvet, and felt like velvet to the touch as well. She cut the paper into long strips and covered the white wood of the coffin with it. Then she and Annele went to the woods, picked armfuls of lingonberry vines, which were already covered with heavy clusters of reddish berries, made many small wreaths all the same size and nailed them to the sides of the coffin. The long garlands they made were for the funeral horses. They had no other ornaments to decorate them with.

Early on Sunday morning they left for the cemetery, for they had a long way to go. The row of wagons was not long. There were all five of Father's brothers, as well as the brothers and sisters of Annele's mother. The more distant relatives had not been invited, for there wasn't enough money.

The coffin was placed in a wagon drawn by two horses. At the foot end, on either side, sat Annele's brother Jānis and her mother's youngest brother, who was the driver. They were both skinny and slender, and there was enough room for them there on the narrow plank. Her brother had his arm around the end of the coffin. Behind the coffin, snorting and shaking his head, Father's dappled Gray, who had been worked quite hard during the summer, pulled the narrow work cart, in which had been placed a rolled wicker mat with sacks to sit on. In this cart, on the back seat, sat Mother and Līziņa, while Annele sat facing them in front. All three of them were so close together there was nowhere to put their feet. None of them spoke. Under Mother's black kerchief, which was drawn down deep over her forehead, large tears rolled slowly down her cheeks. This was so habitual a thing these last few days that she didn't even raise her hand to wipe them away. Weary with working, her hands lay in her lap with a rolled-up handkerchief clasped tight around them. Līziņa held the reins. But her eyes seemed to be riveted on the coffin under the greenery of its ornaments, making its wobbly way along the bumpy road.

The dogs of Fork Farm awaited them and accompanied them, barking fiercely and for a long time. People came out of the buildings, stood in the yard. Motionless, with grave, thoughtful faces, they watched them drive by. Then Fork Farm was behind them, with its people, buildings, garden, the woven fence of spruce branches around it. Annele thought she even knew how many branches were woven into the fence, how the women stood in the yard, what kind of kerchiefs they were wearing, how they clasped their hands. Every little detail was imprinted in her soul so clearly, so firmly, so obtrusively. Her soul eagerly seized upon every detail and threw it down to be a stopper for the great floods of grief that threatened to suffocate, to ruin, to destroy her.

The noonday sun is oppressively hot. A herd of cattle runs past seeking the coolness of the barn. The farm vanishes from sight behind white fields of rye and yellow fields of wheat. The air is still, so still. Only the ears of wheat are humming.

Left behind, too, is the field that Father had begun to mow, and now he himself is going to his eternal rest.

Father's life, what she has seen of it, flashes by in the mirror of Annele's thoughts. She cannot stop looking at it and thinking about it. She hears the sound of Father's footsteps, his voice, his merry talk, his loving encouragement, his laughter. His lovely singing long ago – so it seems to her – when she herself knew no more of the world than the hills of Spring Farm. His song could be heard from far away as he came home after a day's work, his step was light, as though he did not feel the burden

of work on his shoulders. She had to smile at herself – how she had once thought that it was to give Annele pleasure, as a game, that he lifted a load of threshed straw as big as a cartload on his shoulders and then, at a half-run, hurried up the steep ladder to put it in the hayloft. She had so loved to see her father's bare feet flashing under the golden yellow load of straw. By himself, he carried all the straw that had been threshed, day after day.

A hard worker.

That's as much as she has understood of Uncle Ansis's funeral oration this morning. Uncle is a popular speaker and funeral orator. You can hear a pin drop when he speaks, and everyone's eyes are wet, but this morning he was unable to say anything. All you could hear were the words "a hard worker," repeated several times, and then he himself had begun to sob, and then everybody else couldn't fight back the tears. They had just stood there quietly for a while without a word and without a sound. –

Just behind the cart she is in, Uncle Ansis is riding in a wagon with his brother

Dobelnieks. They are deep in conversation. The handle of Dobelnieks's whip is raised now in one direction, now in another. They are speaking about the fields, the farms they are driving past, about people, about life. Sometimes when one or the other brother turns suddenly or raises his hand, it feels like being stabbed in the chest with a knife. As though some gesture that used to belong to Father had not been laid in the coffin with him, but had been left behind to survive in his brothers' hands and bodies. It is so strange that Annele cannot comprehend it, and she has the feeling that they've appropriated something they're not entitled to. And the way they walk and point at the surroundings reminds her of that drive on Saint George's Day, when she and her parents moved to New Farm. How lovely that journey now seemed to her, how lovely that road! Father had turned toward his family that same way, looking into the distance now and then, and had told them what farms were along the road and what kind of people lived in them. And now it would never happen again – ever?

No, it must all be a dream, after all.

The funeral wagon stops, and the row of wagons behind it. Has something happened?

No one asks any questions, and no one answers. Everyone waits solemnly.

A wagon passes the funeral procession and comes to a stop in front. Ģelžu Miķelis and Auka are sitting in the wagon, and between them lies a large wooden cross. It is made out of a stately juniper tree that Father himself once found in the woods and kept like a great treasure. The two men have carved a cross out of it. The work has made them late, and they were thus not able to catch up with the funeral procession until it reached the cemetery hill.

Yes. The long road is at an end, and the funeral wagon has reached the cemetery. The traveler who is on his last journey must stop here according to ancient tradition and wait for the bells to summon him.

The sound of the bells rings out in the church tower. It leaps into the tops of the pine trees. As though tripping down four steps of a staircase, it speeds toward the funeral wagon.

"Lullaby, lullaby! Rest in peace, rest in peace!

"Sleep sweetly, sleep sweetly!"

The horses snort, stir. Begin to pull with great effort. Legend has it that the closer to the graveyard, the more heavily the horses breathe, because the spirits come to the cemetery hill to meet the new traveler, and settle like clouds on the funeral wagon, the horses, and the coffin.

The legend had come near, was close, was tangible. Annele felt that she could not raise her hands. Perhaps they were heavy with the souls that lay upon them.

The sons of the Avots family are tall of stature. The coffin rises on four shoulders and climbs the path to the top of the cemetery hill. Annele wishes she could touch the people, the crosses, the earth, to see if everything is indeed just as it is in life.

Why is the cemetery road so eroded?

Has it always been like that?

How long?

How come there are so many rocks on it?

Big ones and little ones.

Thus her thoughts roam over tiny, over the minutest, things, as though running away from what her heart is no longer able to bear.

As if from a distance she hears talking, singing, sand is falling, striking wood with a hollow sound, and near her a voice whispers, "Why, that little one isn't crying a bit." Her sister and brother bring the wreaths with which the funeral horses were decorated, and cover the fresh mound of sand with them. Then all four of them fall to their knees.

Only Avots and Laukmalis have come back to the funeral house together with a few of Mother's relatives. Annele doesn't like listening to their talk. She goes outside into the vastness of the barrens.

The sun is already lying over the treetops of the forest. Red. Radiant.

Jets of rays fly across the barrens. As if someone were running, scattering sheaves of flames at intervals. This is how it was on the morning Father died. Only then these sheaves of flames set fire to the day, and now the flames are going out. But there seems to be some kind of connection she can't figure out between sunrise that day and this day's sunset. As if in the interval between the two times when the sun seemed to flame through a kind of slit in the clouds she herself had grown older. And as though she were seeing everything differently, or does everything look different now? It probably does. Every moment offers something different, and she experiences it differently. Is this life?

The numbness she felt at the cemetery has been shattered. She is sad, there is pain, but there is also something great, something bright. Just as there was when she stood by her father's body the day he died.

Father has not vanished. There is an unknown, wonderful world somewhere.

It is there for all eternity.

The barrens have finished blazing, and so have the tops of the trees in the distant forest, and those two round linden trees standing on the horizon near the unknown farm.

Hush, hush.

Crown Farmers

Fall arrived warm, but unpleasantly damp. Līziņa wrote: at the end of October she would be at Pike Farm to make a bridal gown for Amālija Līdaka, and also to stay for the wedding. She said she couldn't come home because the roads were bad and she didn't have much time, but she hoped to meet the family at the wedding, and therefore Mother and Annele must be sure to come.

Mother understood. She had been invited to Amālija's wedding for Līziņa's sake – Līziņa was great friends with Amālija, as well as with other young female relatives her age. In the past, Annele's parents had never been invited to celebrations at Pike Farm.

Pike Farm was that fine farm with red roofs that was visible from the barrens at the very edge of the horizon. It belonged to one of Granny's younger brothers, who had married at quite an advanced age, when he had already acquired wealth and respect. Amālija was his youngest child, who was being married to a farmer who was getting on in years but rich. The whole neighborhood for miles around talked about the wedding at Pike Farm morning, noon, and night.

Taking short cuts along boundary lines, ditches, and across fields, the two wedding guests arrived at the site of the festivities around noon. A large group of kitchen maids were running back and forth setting tables and preparing the midday meal, for breakfast was already over, and the wedding party was just then on its way to the marriage ceremony in the church of Dobele. The women had all been up since cock-crow, for the wedding guests had started arriving at eight, and so they already had a stretch of hectic work behind them.

In the yard, motionless, stood a fat old man observing the comers with wide hawk eyes. Mother went right up to him. "Good day, Papa!" She reached out to kiss his hand, but he curtly said, "That's all right, that's all right," without taking his hands from his trouser pockets. So Annele, too, was lucky to avoid having to kiss his hand.

"Papa" looked at them without a sign of recognition.

"Well? Where are you from?"

Then he realized who they were.

"Ah, Krišjānis's widow?" And as though to make doubly sure: "Līze's mother?"

"That's right," Mother agreed.

"Well, how are you doing without a husband? – See what it's like now that he's gone?"

Papa gave a short laugh followed by a wink, and his expression was so cheery it looked as though he were trying to tease Mother, who had deliberately sent her husband off to the hereafter and now got to regret her action. And when instead of a reply Mother just quickly pulled out her handkerchief and pressed it to her eyes, he finally took his hand – a broad, fleshy hand – out of his trouser pocket and patted her on the shoulder soothingly: "Come, come, it'll be all right. It'll be all right. Let's go and have a bite to eat."

They walked through many rooms, and Mother expressed her amazement about them. Parlors fit for the gentry, proper parlors, she praised.

Papa proudly lifted up his shoulders.

"Oh, you haven't been here before?" And added:

"Yes, this is how we live. Crown farmers. Are the gentry better than us?"

He showed off a few more rooms.

"Once they come back from church, you won't be able to see a thing. The place will be jam-packed. Over a hundred buggies left from here, and there'll be another lot joining them in Dobele."

"Hey, bring us a bite to eat! Hurry, hurry!" Papa ordered a maid who was running past.

"What shall I bring?"

"A bit of everything, a bit of everything."

And already he was busy uncovering one corner of a long table that was set, and sitting down himself as well as inviting the guests to sit.

The maid came running, a bowl of meat in each hand. And immediately scolded:

"Goodness, Papa, you've messed up our whole table."

"I certainly didn't! I was being careful. I uncovered the table so as not to get stains on the tablecloth, but you're still not satisfied."

"This is no time to eat! What are you going to do when the wedding party gets back?"

"Don't waste my time blathering, just do what needs to be done."

After the maid left, he went on more quietly:

"She talks like a child. Here's people that have walked for miles and she expects them to go around with empty stomachs."

"You really shouldn't have done it on our account. We're not hungry," Annele's mother apologized.

"You talk like a child: not hungry!"

Placing a hefty piece of headcheese on a plate, Papa looked at his guest with a friendly smile and said, in a whisper, as though confiding a nice secret:

"Why should I lie to you? I want some myself. All day long the smell of roasting meat has been making my mouth water. But as soon as you ask for some, these women immediately go, 'You just ate, and now you want more.' I ask you, are these women completely crazy or what? Why on earth do they bake and cook for days on end if they don't want people to eat the stuff? And if I can't eat as much as I like at my own daughter's wedding, then what good is it all to me, huh? You tell me!"

Mother didn't know what to say.

"Should I bring some roast goose as well?" asked the maid, entering with a new load of dishes.

"Ask sick people, give to healthy ones," replied Papa.

"You eat too much, Papa," the maid shook her head.

"Are you sorry?"

"Why should I be sorry? It's just that you're bound to come to grief."

"That's no skin off your back."

His mouth full, Papa turned to the guests.

"Help yourselves, go on, help yourselves! Don't miss this chance. You can't get this kind of stuff every day. This has all been roasted and cooked by a head housekeeper who used to work for a count."

And he laughed heartily.

"It's certainly good," Mother agreed with approbation.

"Eat up, and you'll be all right. Later on there's going to be such a slew of people here that you won't have room to sit down, and nobody will have time to serve you besides."

Papa made the round of the tables, picked up a bottle here and there, chose one that contained a clear red liquid and, after filling a glass, moved it in Mother's direction.

"Try it!"

Mother made a face and shuddered, but did drink some.

"Must be wine, I suppose," she said, admiring it and still feeling the taste on her tongue.

"Well, what did you think?" Papa indicated the table with a sweeping wave of his hand. "Look at all this. I'm certainly not serving anything second-rate today. Who's putting on this wedding for Amāle? Not her brothers, but her father. And I don't want anybody to say her father was stingy."

"Such opulence, such opulence!" was all Mother said.

And it sounded to Annele as though she heard a sigh under these words.

"And now for the girl," Papa filled the glass a second time.

"No, no, I'm not having any!"

"None for her, none for her!" Annele and Mother exclaim almost simultaneously.

"Drink!" Papa, looking as though he wanted to swallow her with his bulging eyes, banged on the corner of the table sternly, and his hand shook.

Annele quickly looked into his reddened eyes: was he really so stern or was it just in fun? She couldn't really tell, but still she refused the glass.

"Silly girl," Papa grumbled good-naturedly, and tossed the contents of the glass into his own throat. All his sternness had been just in fun.

When he had had a drink with the guests, Papa advised them that they would be better off in the *klēts*; it would of course be a little cool but otherwise comfortable and nice there. The girl, too, would be more "out of the way" there, for now that children were no longer taken along to festive occasions, following a trend set by the gentry, it was doubtful whether there'd be anybody for her to play with.

The path to the *klēts* was decorated with little spruce trees along both sides of it.

The *klēts* itself had been cleared out, and more spruce trees had been placed along the walls. Several women were there ahead of them, each accompanied by a child. Maybe they, too, had been sent here by Papa. The children were younger than Annele. Pressed close to their mothers' knees, they all rolled their eyes at the unknown intruder, but could not be persuaded to take even one step closer to her. The mothers, on the other hand, were soon deep in conversation, looking for common family connections by long roundabout routes.

Why are these women sitting here, and why did Papa send us here also? Isn't it because we're the poor relations and he's embarrassed to admit us to his fine rooms? But Annele doesn't have time to think about this too long. Like a cloud, the wedding party arrives. Horses snort. Mud splashes in all directions. With a single tug, the bride's coachman stops the lather-covered horses right before the front door. The bride takes off the wrap that has protected her from mud and spattering roadside gravel. The yard is full of horses, head after head. Laughter, chatter, shouts, hurrahs. The cracking of whips. Young men bragging. Threatening each other, shouting at the top of their lungs. The man who is directing the traffic stands in the middle, commanding as a general. From some of the wagons, a couple of hired hands are lifting out large baskets with handles. "Where do those go?" they shout. "To the *klēts*, to the *klēts*!" a gaggle of high-pitched voices chant in reply.

"Līziņa, we're over here, over here!"

"Where?" Līziņa approaches hurriedly.

"In the *klēts*."

"Later, later! I don't have time now. The bride's headdress is crumpled, her hair is dishevelled. Just stay here and wait!"

The *klēts* is stuffed full as a sack. From overcoats, furs, woolen shawls, wraps, like white birds from black waves, young girls emerge, one more elegant than the next, one more beautiful than the next. The young women are almost all in white, while their mamas are in blue, brown, green, black silk, with long gold chains around their necks, gold pins on their bodices, gold earrings on their ears. One is more formidable than the next, one more ample than the next. Annele's eyes grow wide. What a wedding! Uncle Ansis's wedding was nothing compared to this! The women who had been sitting here earlier reverently flatten themselves against the wall, whisper to Annele's mother, mouth hidden behind a hand: Look at that one! Watch this one! The dress that one is wearing! And this one! Mother, shrugging her shoulders high, whispers back: "Crown farmers! Show-offs!"

The unknown children, too, are stiff with amazement.

In the middle of the *klēts*, a mother is helping her daughter smarten up. They're full of airs and graces. Glittering with brown silk and gold, the mama is busy with the big basket. One of the women peers inside.

"My goodness! Filled to the brim with all kinds of dresses!"

"Maybe for the meal I could keep on this one," the daughter struts about in front of her mother a bit. She looks as though she had bathed in milk, so plump and white are her bare arms and neck.

"Fat," thinks Annele.

"No, no," the mama replies firmly, lifting a rose-colored outfit, light as a poppy, from the basket. "The one you're wearing has been sat on and crumpled. You've got plenty. You can wear a new one every hour."

"The others will keep on their white ones."

"You don't have to look at the others."

Quickly, she takes the dress off her daughter, throws another one over her head, buckles her belt, rearranges her hair, replaces a golden chain with a string of white pearls. The mama adorns her daughter like a doll.

The kitchen maids are running across the courtyard looking for the guests.

Dinner is served, dinner is served!

Whether they've changed their clothes or not, the young women rush head over heels to find a seat closer to the bride: in the place of honor, not at the foot of the table.

The table of the mamas is in another room. Their places of honor are not jeopardized. It all goes according to tradition: the more distinguished a person is, the nearer to the head of the table. They're in no hurry, for Papa is going to seat them each in her proper place.

The whole length of the bride's table, candles are burning in branched candlesticks. The bride sits there hidden behind her veil. She neither speaks nor eats. She's – well, she's neither beautiful nor ugly. As soon as you've seen her, you forget what she looks like. The bridegroom is tall and stout. When he looks across the table with his chin raised you'd think he's about to issue orders to his hired hands. On the bride's side sit all those beautiful dressed-up young women, but the haughty white daughter of the rich mama sits at her right hand. Līziṇa is a lot further away. She's wearing a simple white dress with a long black ribbon around her throat.

"But supposing it was Līziṇa sitting at the head of the table in the place of the bride, what would that look like?" wonders Annele. These thoughts occur to her all of a sudden. For, if all young women get married, then surely Līziṇa will get married too one of these days. And which of the young men sitting across from her would Annele want her to marry? She scrutinizes the row of young men. There is one that might do. He is dressed in black and has a white cravat. He's handsome, and he seems stately, too. He's twirling his mustache with two fingers and keeps looking across the table. And sitting right across from him is Līziṇa.

But next to the bride sits the plump young woman, and she too does nothing but look across to the other side where the young man in the black frock coat with the white cravat has his seat. But since she is not sitting directly opposite him, she has to look at him with her neck twisted to one side.

The music makes the walls vibrate, dancing is in full swing, people are chattering.

"Who's that white plump one? It's not even dark yet, and she's already had four outfits on: all white, all pink, pink and white, and white and pink."

"Which one, which one?"

"The one over there. She sat on the right of the bride."

"You mean you don't know her?"

"No, I don't."

"Well, I never! Lilija Pabērzs! The grandest of all the young women?"

"I've heard the name, I've heard the name. Oh, so that's her? The only daughter?"

"The only daughter. And as they say: one wedding comes in the wake of another. She's as good as engaged to Sīlis. They're neighbors. They've got adjoining farms."

"Which one is Sīlis? The one with the white cravat? Looks like a city fellow."

"That's him."

"Well, well, well! Is he rich too?"

"Is he ever! A farm like a mansion. A crown farmer!"

"Crown farmers, crown farmers. It's obvious."

Something like a wave of restlessness seems to flow from the rooms into the yard, to the *klētis*, and back again. Looking for things to see, for things to hear. Everybody's got ears and eyes. Annele too. Maybe a hundred times sharper than other people's.

Here comes Lilija. And, treading on her heels, her mama. There's a lot left to do until they get through the big basket, which is still half full. The mother keeps holding up one dress after another, recommends each one. The daughter rejects them. Then both reach an agreement, and the changing begins.

"Oooh, is it ever hot!"

Lilija sprinkles flour on her neck, her face, her arms. Laughs gaily.

"I really let her have it just now, Mama. I gave it to her once and for all."

"Who, who? Oh, her?"

The mama understands.

"So what did you say? What did you say?"

They both talk in whispers. Laugh. Then the mama goes:

"Did you tell her right to her face?"

"There was no need to. I let her have it indirectly, so she could hear. And she did hear. She understood, too. Turned as red as a beet. And she was gone like that."

"What exactly did you tell her?"

"I said that the stupid daughters of hired hands shouldn't expect rich farmers to marry them. No, no! Any woman who hopes for that is a silly goose."

"Right, right!"

"I said what a certain man had told me personally. He told me: a wooden spoon is no match for a silver handle."

"Did he mean it in the same sense?"

"What's the difference? Let her figure it out. She can ask him if she likes. But she's not going to. She'll lose interest in marrying into money. The penniless hussy!"

"She looks all right to me."

"All she's got is that one rag. Not a single change of clothes. Wonder why Amāle invited somebody like her to be her bridesmaid."

"They're relatives. Her father was one of the Avots sons."

"What's past is past: nobody gives a damn who he was."

Oh, these women, these strangers! They've been talking about Līziņa. Annele understands. Understands everything.

Līziņa sits by herself in a small empty room. Riffling through a book. She turns the pages and her eyes move rapidly, but without seeing the letters.

"Līziņ!"

"Yes? Oh, it's you! We're going, we're going. Where's Mother?"

They haven't gone out the door yet when Sīlis comes in. The rich landowner. The crown farmer.

"So this is where you've been hiding? And I've been looking for you all over. Do come!"

He is merry and flushed. Just like any wedding guest.

But Līziņa is cool.

"What is it you wish?"

"I'd like to invite you to dance. They've just started."

"I'm not going to dance."

"You promised me you would."

"That is of no importance anymore."

"What? Is it just me you're no longer going to dance with?"

"Not with you or with anyone else."

"Tell me the reason!"

"No particular reason."

"No, tell me the reason!"

He seizes Līziņa's hand, but she brusquely pulls it out of his grasp.

"Leave me alone!"

The smile completely vanishes from his face.

"Well then, I need to talk to you."

"We've been talking all this time."

"That girl – "

"That's my sister."

"I'm going to read that book," Annele interjected, frightened, but Līziņa pressed her close to herself.

"You don't have to!"

"I'm not going to give up so easily, you know. You have to tell me why you don't want to

dance with me," the stranger insists harshly.

And Līziņa, just as harshly:

"Because a wooden spoon is no match for a silver handle. Now you know."

"Who said that?"

"Wasn't it you yourself?"

"It could only have been Lilija."

"Lilija was quoting you."

"But what if I explain what I meant by that?"

"Whatever you meant, it's something one remembers. Something one remembers the rest of one's life. And so it is better that we should not dance, Mr. Sīlis."

She jerked forward and went past him quickly.

Annele and her mother were walking home.

The night was not completely black, for somewhere there must be a moon.

Every time Annele looked back, the lights of the wedding house had shrunk a little smaller. But they stung her heart with an unaccustomed sharp pain.

Līziņa!

She had remained behind where the lights were glittering, but although she had smiled, laughed, and even joked as she said goodbye to her mother and sister, she couldn't have been very happy at this wedding.

Why was this, why was this?

And suddenly Annele said out loud:

"That's the same crown farmer."

"What crown farmer?" Mother asked.

"The one Līziņa said was among those people from Dobele and danced with her such a lot."

However, Mother had no idea what Annele was talking about, and Annele had to tell her as best she could what she had witnessed this night.

For a good long while, Mother walked along in silence. At last she said: "Yes, it's quite possible that it's the same crown farmer. But if it is, it's a good thing that Līziņa thought of a quick response. We want to have no truck with the likes of them! Stuck-up rich folks!"

Winter

The farmhouse at New Farm hadn't gotten finished this summer. The chores were uphill going. They were short not only one worker, but this worker's skill and advice as well. The temporary cabin had been turned into a *klēts*; at one end of the house, where they had lived in summer and where Father had died, there was no stove; so therefore, when winter came, they all moved into the big servants' room which not only had a good kitchen stove, but was dry and warm and completely finished. The Auka clan occupied the big corner by the stove. Annele and her mother, who now both slept in the wide bed, took the sunny corner by the window, while by the wall facing the window was the hired hands' long bunk where Miķelis slept when he came over from Edgefield Farm to work. This happened less frequently now, and more for appearances' sake, so that Auka would not get lazy all on his own. Besides, he lacked all competence when there was no other person to lead the way.

Miķelis was not one to lead the way, either. As he confessed, "What can I hope to do, with this rheumatithm of mine? Can I move mountainth? If only Krithjanis were thtill here!"

There was a little bitty table by the window. There Annele studied, plugging her ears with her fingers, for the Aukas' corner was constantly in an uproar. Mother looked over at her. Stared in surprise. "Does that noise bother you? What would you do in the mornings, when Aukiene teaches the boys their ABCs? Is that ever a free-for-all. And the tears! Buckets of them!"

How happy, how happy Annele would be to share with others what she knows. Every day she could then bring home her new knowledge like a fresh loaf of bread. But whom can she tell about it? Mother? Mother listens for a while, sometimes smiles: "Ah yes, if only I could have spent time in school when I was your age. Now I can't get anything into that head of mine anymore."

If Father were here now, the two of them would study together. Father wouldn't say that he can't get anything into his head anymore.

Kristapelis now – he should study. It's almost time for him to start school, and if he goes off to school without a previous store of knowledge, then it would almost be like going off herding without bread. Annele struggles with Kristapelis to the best of her ability, but he bristles like a hedgehog. He refuses to accept anything.

"He's got a hard head, a hard head! Can't drum a thing into it!" sighs Mother Auka.

"Yes, you can!"

Annele is sure of it.

The spinning wheels whirr. Kristapelis has to look after little Mārcis. He makes him cry whenever he can by choking and squeezing him. Aukiene stops the wheel so abruptly that the yarn breaks. Kristapelis gets slapped. "That's for making him cry on purpose. Give me that child."

"Come on, Kristap, you have time now, let me show you something."

Kristapelis, still blubbering, to his mother:

"Can I go?"

"Will it do any good?" his mother shrugs as though without hope.

"You'll see that it will," Annele reassures her.

Kristapelis comes over to the girl. Half defiantly:

"Well, well, well? What have you got to show me?"

"Watch carefully! I'm going to prove that the earth is round and turns around its axis."

Annele's idea is: if she drums this into Kristapelis' head, then he'll already know a lot.

"A pack of lies! I'm not going to fall for that!"

"I don't believe it either," chimes in Aukiene. But Annele's mother goes: "You'd better believe it if they teach it in school!"

She'd like to help Annele.

"I don't care what they teach in school! All this time it hasn't turned, and now all of a sudden it's supposed to turn," persists Aukiene.

"It's always turned," says Annele with the earnestness of a young scientist. And then it occurs to her that there was a time when it seemed unbelievable to her, too. You can't understand it until somebody teaches you. And, fervently:

"I'll show you everything. You'll have to learn it in school, and then you'll already have it in your head more or less."

"Who says I have to let it into my head if I don't want to let it in," says Kristapelis.

"I don't care who believes it, I certainly don't. Just teach those poor kids their ABCs."

"Maybe thith turning of the earth is jutht thomething the gentry thought up," Miķelis now joins in.

"But that stupid girl believes everything," boastfully smirks Kristapelis.

"Come now, Miķel, you're saying that to please the boy, and here he's got to go to school!"

If there's nobody but unbelievers around you, how can you make any progress?

Miķelis now refuses to take the blame and holds up both hands in protest.

"No, no, no! If they teach it in thchool, you've got to believe it!"

Kristapelis proudly pulls himself up.

"All right then, let's hear it," he says.

On a piece of paper, Annele draws a curved line, which is supposed to be the sea, and moves little crosses, which are supposed to be ships, up the curve.

"The sea with all its water is level as a board. That's the way it seems to you. But when you sail on it, it rises up toward you like a hill – "

"When do I ever sail on the sea?" Kristapelis shrugs his shoulders disdainfully.

Annele does not let it bother her, but goes on, as though down a trail blazed by her teacher:

" – it's the same way as on land when you look and first see only the tops of tall objects – when you're sailing on the sea, you first see the top of the mast, and that's why – "

"You say that's the sea, and those are ships! Don't make me spit!"

And Kristapelis does just that, pulling the piece of paper from Annele's hand and flinging it on the ground.

"Don't try to make me believe that rubbish!"

"They are so ships! They're my ships! Annele, you want me to make you hundreds just like these? And I've got seas, too. Here, I'll show you," yells Jancis, pouncing on the paper with his eyes wide as an owl's. Things that Kristapelis refuses to hear are sweet as honey to his ears. Everything that Annele tells him. Is there anything he couldn't believe? There is no such thing, for he himself lives surrounded by miracles. And his sworn fellow believers are always the two little kids, who run from Kristapelis, but stick to Jancis like burrs. So it is to the eager ears of these three that Annele now tells her stories of countries where nuts grow the size of a baby's head, birds are as fat as calves and in the forests, animals roar with voices like thunder.

Miķelis also listens, but then remarks skeptically:

"Yeth, they certainly tell you about foreign partth. But ith there a thchool anywhere that tellth you about our own land? No way! That would be the day! The gentry are againtht it. The landlordth."

"What land is that?"

"What land? The land that ought to be dithtributed. Krithjanith, if he hadn't paththed on. He often talked about it. There will be land, he thaid. They're going to dithtribute it, he thaid. Juthtice mutht come into thith world. Where ith it now?"

"He got his six feet of land," interjected Auka.

"People will be thilenced, they'll be thilenced, you'll thee. There'th no faith. And if no one talkth about it, it'll never come to pathth."

"It will come to pass. You wait and see. Was Krišjānis the only one that had faith?"

"What good ith your faith if you have no tongue. Krithjanith had thtrong wordth. He would have made it come to pathth."

⚬─≈⁓

One day when she came home from school, Annele saw a stranger on the hired hands' bunk. He had arrived in place of Miķelis to go cut firewood with Auka and help with winter chores. Miķelis's rheumatism had confined him to bed. The stranger had been hired for the whole winter and would now be a regular member of the household.

This change was not to Annele's liking. Miķelis had always been a welcome visitor. No matter how serious he was, he always made people laugh with his lisping, funny way of talking. And he was good with children. But recently he had been especially dear to Annele because he always remembered her father and lovingly mentioned the work they had done together.

"What's that stranger doing here?" she shrugged her shoulders coldly.

"He's not a stranger, he's the hired hand."

"What's his name?"

"Spricis."

She was amazed. Whoever heard of a name like Spricis for a hired hand! And if it could be said that the new member of the household was to blame for anything, then his name was something else he could be blamed for.

Spricis was tall, his shoulders hunched, his waist drawn in as though he was in pain; his face was quite young, but faded, his eyes pale blue, his thin, fair hair stuck to his forehead.

Mother was cooking when Annele came home from school. When the food was ready, she called Spricis as well. "What? That stranger?" Annele couldn't believe it.

"Of course! A person needs something hot at least once a day, you know. The rest of the time he'll eat on his own."

"Is he always going to come and eat with us now?"

"But Miķelis also ate with us, remember?"

Yes. That was true. Miķelis ate at the same table, and so substantially that he would not stop till you could see the bottom of the bowl. And still you somehow didn't notice or see Miķelis. The same way you don't see a fly buzzing on the ceiling. The same way you don't hear the wind rattling the window. He was there and yet he wasn't there. He took up space, but did not trouble one's thoughts. If you wanted to hear him, you'd listen, if not, you'd ignore his talkativeness. But it wasn't like that with the stranger. He settled into the empty place like something heavy and uncomfortable. It's true that he didn't talk a lot. He ate even less. Slowly and pickily, as it were, he ladled the food. But when he did talk, Annele felt even that was too much.

"Maybe you don't like the food?" asked Mother when the stranger soon put down his spoon.

No, the food was as fine as could be, said the stranger, only he wasn't a big eater. He couldn't take it. It was his "digestive tract."

That's what he called his stomach. Just like Annele's Rīga aunt. He had a lot of such foreign loan words, which New Farm soon adopted, while the old words were discarded. Spricis had served in the army, and had later had city jobs, but city "luft" was bad for him, and so he was now in the country.

Mother, too, soon puts down her spoon. After Father's death she has completely lost her appetite. Spricis soon notices. What's wrong, he asks, why isn't she hungry? Is it such and such, he questions her. Mother answers, seemingly reluctantly, but he's already guessed the answers with his questions, just confirms them and nods his head in agreement. It's the digestive tract, what else, he finally says decisively. He says he will give her some herbs.

Nimbly, as though he had suddenly found a pleasant and appropriate occupation, Spricis, walking with slightly wobbly knees, goes to the trunk he brought with him, where paper bags and little boxes are carefully grouped side by side. He has all sorts of teas that he has collected and dried himself. He knows the name, importance, and purpose of every one of them.

Spricis has suddenly risen by a foot in the eyes of the household. He prepares his herb teas himself. At night he comes with a little pot and pours out a cup. They make Mother feel better. Much better. She praises them and is grateful.

Aukiene also needs Spricis's tea. Her head spins, she has a stitch in her side, and her insides are bloated. She drinks, and all her ailments are gone in a twinkling.

Spricis also had good luck with the children. Little Mārcis had had the following accident: as Kristapelis was rocking and dandling him by a lighted, almost red-hot stove, he had dropped the child on his little bottom, and the bottom was now raw and covered with blisters. It didn't do any good that Kristapelis got slapped for it daily by his mother, followed by a squall of the usual dreadful threats and rebukes that Aukiene always had at hand – the blisters did not heal, and the child kept crying incessantly. Spricis looked at the sores, cleaned them, prepared an ointment, and a few days later the child was better. Aukiene now requested medicine for her other boys. It is true they had no ailments, but they were hardheaded. This was true not only of Kristapelis, but of Jancis also. The latter had the following problem: if he was not allowed to go sliding on the ice barefoot or to wade up to his knees in snowdrifts, he would scream fit to burst. When his mother insisted that he should wear something on his feet, he would almost turn blue with crying, fall down, and kick his feet. At such times Aukiene would ask everyone whether the boy was right in his head. He wasn't, was he? And she believed that Spricis's medicine would help her thickheaded boys so they'd be right in the head.

Spricis was helpful, was kind, was wise. And he did not waste his wisdom. He listened to what others said, grinned, and then said his say. And the interesting thing was that nobody raised any objections afterward. Too clever by half – thought Annele.

He made his teas, recommended them to everyone, but recognized nothing beyond them. As far as he was concerned, physicians were ridiculous, and people who cured by incantation were despicable. Bunch of witch doctors! What do they know? is what he said.

But Granny, too, healed by incantation and drew crosses on blue paper with a ring around them. And her words helped, and the crosses helped both people and animals, for otherwise people wouldn't have come in droves looking for help. And she was just as knowledgeable about herb teas as Spricis, maybe more so, for her fame was widespread. And now Spricis said: bunch of witch doctors! Was Granny one too, then? Out of the question!

No, Annele could not forgive Spricis for those words.

Spricis was praised left, right, and center. One Sunday, a neighbor woman came over who had heard about the reputation of the hired hand of New Farm for giving good medicines. She chatted with Aukiene. Annele's mother was not home. She had gone to church and to visit relatives. Spricis needed to go in the same direction, and so he had offered to drive. But since Spricis was driving, Annele did not go with them. She suddenly had so much homework that she could not go visiting.

The women's talk gushed like a waterfall. You could stick your fingers in your ears as much as you liked, you still heard them. About Spricis and his magic medicines. He was a benefactor, and he'd go on being a benefactor – if only he got a good wife, he could live in clover.

"Who'd marry him?"

Annele must have thought out loud, for the answer came at once:

"Who wouldn't? Your own mother would if he'd only ask her. Didn't they leave together today like a courting couple? They're certainly a pretty good match, and so maybe you're going to have yourself a stepfather soon."

"Oh my!" Aukiene almost exclaimed, clapping her hand over her own mouth.

The way that girl suddenly leaped bolt upright facing her, the quick hand that threw down the book, the trembling lips that made the words freeze on her lips, the eyes whose looks flung sharp blades at the speaker! And out she went, that Annele!

"Did you see that temper!" Aukiene said, as though frightened by the effect of her words.

"Well, her stepfather better stay out of her way. She'll claw his eyes out," laughed the visitor.

They both laughed, for the whole conversation was just a joke as far as they were concerned.

But for Annele, Aukiene's words were a sting that entered her heart. Her very heart. She ran outside, for she did not want to show her feelings. As though she had received a blow, she clung to the doorpost. What's this she had heard? Stepfather, stepfather, stepfather! The words thudded incessantly like stones thrown by an enemy.

Now she knew why she hadn't been able to stand Spricis right from the first time she set eyes on him. This was why! Her heart had foreseen this.

He sat in Father's seat, ate with Father's spoon from Father's plate. Mother had allowed it.

It did not occur to her that there was no other alternative. That there was no extra seat, extra spoon, or plate.

And then those teas of his. Mother had not refused them at all, but had accepted them. Had praised them. Drinking the teas, she had become healthier and more cheerful. What did this all go to show?

And people were already talking. Like the women just now. Maybe the gossip had already made the rounds and had now reached Annele. Now they were saying it to her face.

Things had come to a pretty pass, it was obvious!

When Pearl needed a rope, a strong, smooth rope was made before you knew it, when the pigsty collapsed, a new and strong one had been made by the next day, when Mother had a hard time lighting the fire with big sticks of wood, a little pile of finely split kindling soon appeared on the hearth. Every need was thought of and provided for. And what did it all suggest?

How was it she hadn't seen it before? Oh Lord!

Mother hadn't refused the stranger's services, but had accepted them. Had praised, had been grateful. She had said he was a resourceful person, and that he was good at whatever he did.

It didn't occur to the girl that it was not possible to act otherwise, that Mother had to express her gratitude if somebody did for her what she was unable to do herself. Annele's thoughts were distorted and crazy. They boiled over like a pot licked by a sudden flame. Never gave her any rest. Showed everything in a different light. Plunged heaviness like a rock in her heart.

Grief and pain about her father turned her soul topsy-turvy again. The feelings were far sharper, far more cruel, for now they were mixed with doubt and hatred. For the first time, Annele hated a person. He had come like a trickster, like a thief, and had robbed her of everything. These were terrible emotions that plunged her young soul in a loneliness and darkness she had never known before, a loneliness in which she defiantly buried herself, brooding on the imagined wrong that had been done to her.

She did not speak a word to Spricis, and only what was necessary to her mother. When the others ate, she would not come to the table. She hid behind her books as in a fortress.

She was silent, unfriendly, insufferable, completely changed. But for a long time her mother paid no attention to this. This caused the girl even more pain. "It's because Mother is thinking about something else," is how she explained it to herself.

She became pale and thin.

"What's the matter with you? Are you ill? You aren't eating anymore?" Mother finally asked.

This made Spricis sit up and take notice.

"That's not unusual with a growing child. I'll give you a tea."

Annele would not touch a drop of the tea.

They were out of sugar. Spricis brought some. Annele did not take a single grain.

She had no one to tell her troubles to. Christmas passed. Her sister did not come. There was no place for her to stay. Brother was at Spring Farm over the holidays, then he and Uncle both came, like visitors calling. They stayed for a short time and then left.

Annele had nothing to talk about, nothing to say. How could she find words for what was gnawing at her heart? It would have been like talking about ghosts in broad daylight.

⚬―※―⚬

During this time of great trouble, on a cold, dark winter's night, Mother suddenly woke Annele:

"Get up, girl, get up! It looks like the light is dawning in the window. The train just went by. We've overslept. The clock has stopped."

The train? Yes. It was thundering through the forest. Time to get up then.

The girl sits in bed for a while feeling confused. Her limbs are heavy with sleep. Is everybody sleeping? Have they all overslept? They're drawing deep, heavy breaths. Darkness sticks to the frozen windowpane like a heavy wet cloth. Oh, the urge to put her head back on the pillow!

"Get up, get up! You'll be late!"

She can't find her books. Where did she put them last night? Can't remember. Her head seems encircled by a ring of sleep. She's still struggling with a dream.

There they are, tied up in a bundle.

"Do have something to eat! A bit of bread. Milk. You won't be home till dark, you know."

"No time, no time."

Mother opens the door:

"Run along now! – But how dark it is this morning," she adds anxiously. Then the door closes. The candle goes out. All around are the cold and the dark.

The girl accustoms her eyes to it. Finds her path in the snow. Narrow and meandering, it goes through deep drifts, trodden only by her footsteps. There's so much snow this winter. Sometimes the drifts are so deep that when she wades through them her knees are scraped bloody.

The girl starts walking quickly and confidently. She grows warm. She is no longer sleepy, her head is clear. The unpleasant feeling upon getting up has been left behind in the house. She enjoys walking through the frosty morning, in the creaking snow, sharply watching the path so as not to run into a drift.

She still feels home behind her. Still feels safe. But once she is across the hill, on the other side of the frozen slough, home has already become entangled with the black shadows of the night, and seems to have vanished. But in front of her the bare branches of the birch grove of Brook Farm stand out against the glowing background of the sky: there, she thinks, day is breaking.

The birch grove is so deeply black. The jackdaws are still so fast asleep in their nests. Brook Farm itself, down by the frozen brook, doesn't show a single glimmer of light yet. Has the whole world overslept this morning then?

Annele walks quickly to the top of the rise. Stops. Overcome by a sudden fearful realization. What is that? – It can't be morning. The red stripe in the east has spread like a huge bird with a wide body, the tips of its wings long and white. This isn't dawn, but a distant fire.

The darkness, it seems, has grown even thicker. Every corner of the sky is stuffed with darkness. The snowy plain seems covered with soot, the sky has clouded over.

Midnight, it's the stroke of midnight!

The train was the last, shortly before midnight. That and the reflection of the fire is what misled Mother.

As soon as the girl realizes what time it really is, the whole world seems to change. Instead of the swelling energy of early morning, there is something indefinable. Menacing. She stops, not knowing what to do. Should she go forward or back? The birch grove is behind her shrunken and black. Go back there, have every bush rise up in front of her, and leave it in back of her with all its shadowy secrets – no, she'd rather go forward. She decides to walk slowly. Quite slowly. There is no hurry, for morning is far away. The more slowly she walks, the later she will reach the highway. The highway is the part of the walk she hates the most. She could meet somebody there. The idea of meeting somebody – an unknown stranger at night on the highway seems dreadful to her.

And yet it is pleasant to know that somewhere people are awake. The only place alive now in the whole wide world, she feels, is the site of the fire. There, people are busy saving livestock, human beings, belongings. There, their voices ring out in the night. Annele has the feeling she can hear them overhead like distant echoes or like the voices of spirits or shadows, seeming to tell of events in the distant past.

The little path goes downhill. The pale reflection on the horizon is hidden under clouds.

But there is something standing down below. Again Annele stops, rooted to the ground. What is over there?

Only her own life, beating in her veins like an inseparable friend, responds to her fearful question. Nothing else.

As she stirs again, the "something" also seems to get up and move toward her.

She has to stop again and take a careful look.

"How silly. Why, it's a stone by the roadside. A stone is not alive."

"Took-took-took!" goes her pulse. "Who says it's not alive?"

Did somebody really say that?

And suddenly the young night walker has a sense of no longer being alone, of not having been alone for some time now.

From the hollows, from barely visible forests, from the horizon, from all directions, shadows begin to stream. Silent, shapeless, immeasurable, inscrutable.

Are the shadows alive?

Like an iron ring, this shapeless void chokes her soul.

She must, she must break it! She walks as though her feet had shackles, she is a mote of dust in the face of the mystery contained in the void.

She must simply go on, go on walking. She is not frightened. No, not frightened. The heart that beats so loudly would like to face everything, see everything.

The black mobile silence walks with her. The stone, growing taller and taller, stretches toward her, alone among the dense shadows as the ruler of night and eternity.

And now she is close to it. It feels good. Yes, like being with a friend. She puts down her bundle and clasps her hands over the stone. She feels safe. A kind of sweet weariness settles in her limbs, as though the ring that compressed her brain had broken in two.

Her head sinks over the stone deeper, deeper.

But look what's happening now. What happens is that something begins to take shape out of the shapelessness. All this time she had been thinking that somebody was following her, and now here they are.

Apparitions.

Ahead of them all – Father. Like the time when he came to her in a dream, after the day when he was laid to rest in the cemetery. She and Līziņa were in that sooty little room next to the smokehouse, the one that had always felt empty and black as a grave, and then suddenly Father was there too, along with somebody else. Who is that, she asked. Pastor Zimmermann. In a dream, of course, you know everything. Father is holding a little golden wreath. He places it on Līziņa's head. Then, as though he had made a mistake, he takes it off again and puts it on Annele's head. He does not say a word… He's wearing his summer working clothes, he is luminous and weightless like the glitter of moonlight on a winter's night: she could touch him and have nothing in her hand. That's the way it is now. His dark hair is like a wreath around his neck. He does not seem sad, but neither does he smile or speak. And she can't see his eyes. Yes, the look in his eyes is gone.

And behind him are many, many. In the mist, in the shadow – many.

Is that a song? What song is that? It's the song Father sang on Sunday nights when the reflection of the sunset began to grow dim in the little window. Mother's and Father's voice, the two of them alone, for Annele does not join in this song. She feels it is as sad and eternal as a river that flows through the ages and has neither beginning nor end. When they sing this song she feels she can hear a hammer blow that marks the passing of time – time that is gone, never to return again.

> "And just as season follows season
> Or floods abate and then run dry,
> We too shall vanish from the earth
> Before our minds can comprehend it."

Are the apparitions all those who have "vanished"? Are they not stretching their hands out for Annele to draw her to them? She feels as though she were walking with her head down, quickly, quickly, while they flow behind her like a black wave, and as though her heart were beating time to their inaudible footsteps.

"Annele, don't fall asleep, don't fall asleep! You'll freeze to death if you fall asleep!"

What was that? Did somebody call her? She felt she could hear the voice clearly. No, it's just her heart beating.

Get up, get up!

Where is she? – Oh yes, she remembers everything. Was she asleep? Dreaming? Impossible, impossible! And still she must have been. Just for a short, short time.

Got to leave this place.

Her teeth are chattering. So cold, so cold.

She starts running.

From the highway she looks back. It seems as though the shadows had remained far behind her on the plain, had thickened into two black eyes, hollow, motionless, and sad, unutterably sad. And as though they were sadly gazing after her.

At school they are still asleep. She goes around from the schoolyard side and gropes for the door. It is locked. But can she call out and knock for admission? On the way there she thought she could. The closer she got to school, the happier she was that she would now soon be out of the cold. But as soon as her hand reached for the knocker, she stopped short. What would people say when she woke them up? Wouldn't they think she was weird? How would she explain that she had arrived so early, or the fact that her mother had woken her up in the night. Wouldn't it all seem unbelievable and ridiculous? Yes, ridiculous. At first the people at school would be annoyed, maybe scared as well, and then they'd laugh. At her and her mother.

No, that would be unbearable. She mustn't do that. Much better to sit down on the doorstep and wait for dawn. Opposite her is an old *klēts* with a deep black door. How strange. There are shadows flickering in this doorway! As though invisible spirits were closing and opening the door, and going in and out. Part of her mind makes her smile and say with conviction that there is nothing of the kind there, but another part nudges her and irrationally whispers in her ears that there really is something there that she must keep an eye on. This is what keeps her eyes from falling shut.

From the compressed banks of clouds, snow begins to fall. Big, soft flakes. A thick carpet descends over the yard and the rooftops. And finally in the black darkness of night the gray light of morning begins to shimmer and weave. A little light appears in the school. Voices can be heard. The teacher's maidservant is waking those students whose homes are so far away that they can't walk there and back and have to spend the night at school. There are not many of them, about five or six. Since there are no extra rooms, they sleep right on the school benches. They have to get up early in order to straighten up the classroom. This is something they have to do themselves. And so begins a scurrying, as of ants, with pallets, brooms, and rags. Even now Annele cannot go inside. Their first question would be: How come you're so early, did you get thrown out?

The highway comes back to life. Sleighs go flying past the school, on an early morning ride somewhere.

The first students arrive. Annele can go inside with them without fear. The snow in the yard has already been tramped down.

There is still a long wait until everyone arrives. Lūcīte is brought in a beautiful sleigh drawn by a fine horse. She is accompanied by her own father. She is merry. Smiling. She claps her frozen hands together. Says it was lovely riding over the newly fallen snow.

Annele had been waiting for Lūcīte. The night's experience weighed heavily on her. Now she would tell Lūcīte everything. But when she wanted to open her mouth, her tongue stopped short, like her hand at the knocker just a while ago. No! Once a word has passed your lips, it cannot be recaptured, and she'd be sorry later. How would she explain the whole thing to Lūcīte, and how would Lūcīte interpret it?

Tonight Annele had been alone, all alone in the whole wide world. But hadn't it been this way for a long time now? Whenever she wanted to say something, the word was arrested in her throat: Better not, better not! Hadn't she, as it were, grown away from her fellow students a long time ago, as though she were a stranger? Alone. But she had not felt it so deeply until this night.

She must study, study!...

She will have to walk on her own and cope by herself. Just as she did tonight on the plain. Nobody will help her. Nobody will give her anything. Only what she learned will be hers. And so she continues to take on new challenges. She learns ahead, seemingly not with her brain alone, but with every pore in her body, laboriously or easily mastering what the next highest grade is learning, and then goes and stands with them by the teacher's desk. The teacher looks at her a little surprised, smiles slightly, barely noticeably, but doesn't object. That's why her fellow students dare not say anything, as though recognizing such privileges. Only Sludinātājs, one day in early spring when Annele has already reached his group – the highest in the school – and fearlessly takes her place next to him at the teacher's desk waiting for the teacher to come out of his room, darts a sideways glance at her from his burning brown eyes: "Run, run, crazy girl, let's see how far you get," he says and is really furious.

It's no skin off Annele's back. The time is long past when she thought that Sludinātājs was such a remarkable student, that his words deserved special attention, that he was so far ahead, that he was truly awe-inspiring; now she feels he is falling behind; she does not hear, or rather listen to, what he and his clique say behind her back, their name-calling or their taunting. She no longer cares, for she has endured far worse troubles.

Easter, immediately followed by St. George's Day. One more week and the school year will be over.

Around the school the paths have been swept, in the classroom the floor has been scrubbed, and the windows washed. The teacher comes in one morning unusually solemn, sweeps the entire class with a searching glance, curtly announces:

"Today, there will be a visit by the pastor."

The students are surprised and amazed. Hardly any of them realized that the pastor is also the inspector of this school.

Sludinātājs shrugs his shoulders disdainfully.

"What's he going to do here?"

Sludinātājs is so big and bold that he has the nerve to do this. But the teacher answers reprovingly:

"The pastor is going to examine you. He has a right to."

The pastor is a fine figure of a man, stout, middle-aged. His large white hand with its shining gold ring lies on the teacher's desk. The teacher stands respectfully at his side. They converse softly in German. Then the pastor asks questions, not calling anyone by name, but pointing at one or another among the students, and gets now a quick and bright, now an incoherent, hesitating answer, or no answer at all. The children are too scared. Then he again talks to the teacher, makes notes. And now he calls a name:

"Jānis Sludinātājs."

Sludinātājs gets to his feet, but the teacher waves him over to his desk.

"Oh dear, oh dear, oh dear!" Lūcīte is in a panic, touching Annele with a trembling hand. "Now it's the girls' turn! I hope he's not going to call on me. This is what the pastor usually does. At first he examines all of us together, and after that one boy and one girl out of the whole class. The ones that are the best students. The teacher tells him."

Sludinātājs answers intelligently and without hesitation. He doesn't bat an eye. The pastor seems satisfied. His head held high, Sludinātājs returns to his seat.

"It's the girls' turn, it's the girls' turn," a whisper goes through the rows of benches.

The pastor is in no hurry. Again he is deep in conversation with the teacher. And upon some remark by the teacher, he responds with a satisfied, "Ah!"

"Anna Avots!"

Annele jumps to her feet. Surprised. At a loss what to do. Then she goes to the teacher's desk under the teacher's kindly, inviting eyes.

"Well, my child, your teacher has been telling me about you. Then tell me –"

The pastor asks Annele questions of every description. She knows all the answers.

"Well done, my child!"

And his large, manicured hand comes to rest on Annele's head.

"Whose daughter are you? Are you from Spring Farm? No, that can't be. From Edgefield Farm? I know your father well. A man of honor."

"My father is dead."

"What?" The pastor has forgotten. Annele has to tell him which of the Avots sons this was. Finally he makes the connection. "Ah yes, Krišjānis! The one who worked as a hired hand!" he drawls.

And Annele feels as though the pastor's hand, which slips off her head, had suddenly turned cold and his voice chilly. The daughter of Krišjānis. The one who worked as a hired hand.

"He would have liked me to be from Spring Farm or Edgefield Farm, while there was no need for Krišjānis's girl to do so well in school." These were her thoughts.

"You may go now," she heard the teacher's voice, but as she left he told the pastor as though by way of apology: "Very gifted children."

"My father's children," Annele thought with defiance in her heart, for the same teacher had already prepared her brother for school in town.

The two older cows and several sheep have been sold in Dobele. A few of the younger ones will stay here, to be part of Krists's livestock. As of St. George's Day, Krists is coming to live at New Farm. No doubt they'll come to some arrangement about the animals. With the rest of the belongings – there is not much left over – Mother will go to Spring Farm, where Uncle Ansis is giving her a small room in his new house. Mother is an excellent spinner and is quick at other household chores, she'll manage somehow.

What about Annele? – For the time being, she will stay with Mother until Līziņa writes to them. Then they'll see. She'll have to go to Jelgava and learn her sister's trade. What else?

This is what Mother has talked over with Annele, and the two of them have counted the money that was received for the livestock.

Most of it has to pay for Brother's school and room and board in town. "This will be the last of Father's hard-earned money. There's no more to be had or to give away," Mother says. And now we must also put aside some money for your school. We haven't paid any all this time."

A weight lifts off Annele's mind. That's just what she's been waiting for. Finally she can pay. She will no longer have to quake under the teacher's casual glance and think: I wonder if he'll say: "Avote, you haven't fulfilled your responsibility yet."

"Lots of money for my teacher. Lots and lots of money."

The teacher did not set a fixed amount. When Father took Annele to school that first day, he said they should pay according to their ability. Mother now slides silver coins across the table as she counts: how much would be left over if she gave this much, and how much if she gave that much.

No matter how much she puts down for the teacher's share, Annele is still not satisfied.

"More, more for my teacher."

No matter how well-intentioned they are, they cannot give away all of it.

Finally they agree to bring him three rubles.

Annele had not realized that a person who goes to settle his debts could walk with his head held so high. She is happy but nervous. This is the first time she has ever had to deal with money. What's the best way to go about it?

The three rubles lie in her palm as in a cage. She has been clutching them tight the whole time. They are hot, stuck together.

"Well, Avote, what have you got to say?"

She is still confused. How can she start talking about money all of a sudden?

"Did you have anything special on your mind?"

The three rubles drop on the table, still stuck together, with a hollow sound.

"My mother sends her greetings and says she hopes you won't mind that it isn't more than this and that you had to wait so long, sir."

She's added the last part herself. She has come to the conclusion that the rubles should be covered over with good words. Still, they're not good enough, and she blushes at her awkwardness.

The teacher sits quietly, his hands on the table. He has no intention of touching this money, neither with one hand, nor with the other.

"Why are you bringing me this?"

"For your trouble, sir."

"I had no trouble with you. I had only pleasure in teaching you. I don't need money for that. Take it back."

"Sir!"

"Take it! You can make better use of it. I know that right now your mother has to count every kopeck."

"Sir!"

Annele stands there, her hands clasped. Her eye sockets sting. Is it possible that people like this exist?

She stands there and has no idea what to do.

The teacher takes the money, opens her palm, puts in the money, which is still warm with her own warmth, closes her palm with her own fingers, turns her toward the door.

"And now go!"

She ought to have said thank you, kissed the teacher's hand, somehow expressed her great happiness that someone like him did exist.

She hadn't had a chance to do any of these things.

How could she help walking on air? Whatever she did, a sweet song rang in her ears: "I had no trouble with you. It was a pleasure. A pleasure teaching you."

A harsh wind was blowing, stinging her eyes and burning her cheeks. Sharp as only the wind of the barrens can be. Annele ran in the teeth of it so the mud splashed every which way on the narrow footpath by the side of the road. She had to stay close to the highway, for the boundary paths and banks of the ditches were knee-deep in mud. New shoots were sprouting. The marsh marigolds were in bloom. The larks sang exultantly. Spring.

Her heart was light, luminous, free. How had this suddenly happened? How had her burden lifted? Not all at once. Now and again, in the recent past, a sudden rush of joy and recklessness had passed across her heart like a swift ray of sunshine, and she felt as if someone were saying: It's time! Get well again! But soon her sky clouded over again, for she was still not able to have faith. How could she get well, when everything was still the same and nothing had changed?

A horse and cart were coming toward her. It was not a big load, but the driver was walking next to the cart. Narrow, hunched shoulders, his waist drawn in. As soon as he got level with her, he stopped the horse.

"Good day, Annele! And goodbye!"

"Good day, Sprici! Why aren't you sitting in the cart?"

"The road is bad. It's hard on the horse."

"That's exactly what Father would have said," a quiet thought flashes across Annele's mind.

"I'm leaving now," Spricis says.

"Where are you going?"

"To Edgefield Farm and then on to another place. A relative sent for me. He's got a big farm, and I'll be in the garden a lot more."

Annele is surprised. She has known nothing of all this.

"I didn't decide till last night. I said to myself: I better go. Can't be helped. And since I have to take one of the horses to Edgefield Farm, I'm taking my stuff at the same time. Once I'm there, I'm sure I'll get a ride somehow."

There is no more to talk about. "Giddyup!" Spricis urges the horse. As it begins to pull the wagon, he looks her straight in the eye and shakes his head as if in affirmation: "Yes, Annele, that's the way of the world."

Annele walks deep in thought. "That's the way of the world!" With these words, Spricis has meant to say something different than he actually said. Maybe that she was so mean to him all this time. He looked at her so strangely. And what had he done that was so terrible? On second thought, he did nothing but good. And look at the way things have turned out for him. Here he is, roaming through the world with no place to call his own.

Maybe Mother was sorry for him? Speaking of Mother – didn't she have troubles? And it had been a good thing that somebody had lent her a helping hand now and then. He was not a bad person. He was good. Should Mother have hated him for that, as Annele had?

Strange. If you look at things from another perspective, everything appears in a different light. And she feels shame, as it were, regret at some wrong she has done. She shouldn't have acted that way.

And still – what about Mother? – Suppose she is in tears now? – Suppose she is sorry to see Spricis go? – No, no! That's unthinkable.

Mother is friendly and loving. So pleasantly surprised.

"Are you home so soon?"

"Yes. It's our last day, you know."

The food is ready. Mother brings it in and serves it. But Annele has no appetite, no peace until she has said the thing that makes her heart beat so fast.

"Did Spricis leave too?"

"Ah! So you met him?"

"Yes."

And now Annele's voice sounds quite unlike itself, but this is something that must be said.

"Weren't you sorry?"

"People come, people go. You can't be sorry every time somebody goes."

Annele struggles on.

"You were sorry when Father died."

"Father? There's no comparison. There was only one like him in the world."

Yes – now the bond that had been strangling her heart is completely gone. Oh, glory be!

Does she have anything good to tell Mother?

The three rubles.

Suddenly turned reckless, mischievous as if by magic, she throws them on the table.

"Look, money!"

"Where did that come from?"

"From the teacher."

"You didn't give it to him? Why didn't you give it to him?"

"I did, but he gave it back."

And now she tells Mother. She's embarrassed to tell her, but her happiness outweighs the embarrassment.

Mother listens.

Oh, so that's the kind of student you were!"

She thinks for a while, shakes her head, and says:

"Well, may God provide for you!"

But why the heavy sigh?

⸺∦⸺

Tomorrow they must leave New Farm.

Annele visits the pastures. The more the fields have expanded, the narrower the pastures have become.

Before her very eyes, a human habitation has grown up. The buildings are new, the fields lush. Oh, how well everything grows there! A gold mine, as Father used to say. And he mined it, putting the strength of his healthy limbs into the work. For what? For whom? He never asked those questions.

"And just as season follows season..."

Vanished, gone, like yarn that has been unwound from a shuttle, is the time he spent on earth. Gone is the singer who sang this song at night after work with the sunset in the little window, gone is the place, for the little house languishes sadly, its window nailed shut, filled with old junk, littered, unswept. What's left is only a memory, a shadow, an image. She'll carry those with her in her soul, while the place itself will remain alien to her heart, as it always has been.

Suddenly the girl becomes almost entranced as she looks into the distance, and loses track of the passing of time. Is she thinking of the future? The future is dark, unknown. Nothing has changed, and yet she is aware of a wide-open space, the floodwaters of her heart overflow their banks. What makes them rise so high? It is not the prospect of good days ahead. It is something else. For there again is the unknown, the inconceivable, a something that is forever close to her, the reason, so it seems to her, for all life, for all that is and will be. And from that world which she cannot grasp, an invisible hand reaches out to her, holding her and guiding her. And she follows. Follows.

PART III

IN A STONE CAGE

Under Aunt Meire's Wing

Flinging itself from side to side and writhing like a snake, the train rattled over the railroad siding: clackety clack, clackety clack! Rat-tat-tat, rat-tat-tat! It howled like a mortally enraged beast, poured out hissing clouds of steam with its last snort, and then stubbornly stood still as though riveted to the ground. Now all those who for some time had been standing between the seats of the carriages and the emptied luggage racks could tumble outside, carrying their bundles on their shoulders and under their arms, teetering at each unexpected jolt of the wheels, blocking the aisles, jostling the unprotesting country girl from her place in line, so that she was the last of the passengers to get off.

Twice already Līziņa had searched for her along the row of carriages. She quickly shook hands and at once scolded:

"What on earth took you so long? I was beginning to think you hadn't come. Now it'll be too late to get a cab."

Of course there are no more cabs. It can't be helped. There isn't a lot of luggage. They'll walk.

Annele's head is spinning. The whole journey hasn't stopped reverberating in her mind yet. Her first journey by train.

Clackety-clack–rat-tat-tat! Clackety-clack–rat-tat-tat!

She still sees fields, houses, forests, roads rushing past. Fields: there were plowmen, and herds of cattle. A little herd boy followed the train with eyes full of longing. Houses: what kind of rooms would there be inside and what kind of people? She barely had a chance to think about it when they had already raced past, been left behind. Rat-tat-tat, rat-tat-tat! Now they were in a forest. But the woods were thick and deep, with shadows scalloped by sunlight, and mysterious winding roads. Where did those go? She hardly had a chance to think about them when they were already past.

Clackety, rat-tat-tat!

Flights of dragonflies pelted the carriage windows. All the time. That signaled a long spell of sweltering heat.

The forests, the fields hummed with bees, but she was town-bound.

"Let's go, let's go," Līziņa urges.

How those people run. What's their hurry?

The sisters, too, are hurrying so fast they're beginning to drip with perspiration. The bundles are heavy, they slide out from under their arms and out of their hands.

You'd never have imagined they were so heavy. Just there, in the middle of the street, a cabman's horse clops along lifting its shod hoofs, and the cabby's insistent eyes invite them: "Hey, how about it? I'll take you wherever you like."

But Līziņa shakes her head in refusal:

"It doesn't pay to ride after walking all that way. We're pretty close to home."

These people in Jelgava have a strange idea of what "pretty close" is. Pretty close turns out to be very far. At last they're on Skrīveri Street.

A big yard. Gray wooden stairs weathered by rain and sun; upstairs, an open porch all along the second floor. Opening onto this porch a window, then a door, a window, and a door.

The stairs creak. At every creak, a head is stuck out of one, then a second, then a third window. An inquisitive nose, grayish hair, eyes quick as lightning.

Who are they? Annele answers her own question: the ladies of Jelgava.

"Moyn, Fräulein, moyn, Fräulein!"

"Moyn, moyn!" Līziņa walks past them quickly.

"Here, this is it, come in!"

This is where Aunt Meire and Līziņa are living for the duration of the summer. This will be the little country girl's home, too. The room is rather dark, cool. Annele looks around her. There is a dresser with brass fittings, a wide two-door wardrobe, a table with strong oak legs, twelve straight-backed chairs with bulging upholstered seats. The furniture is yellow and gleams like butter. It is Aunt Meire's dowry from the *klēts* at Hook Farm. It moved to Jelgava with her and was crammed into the narrow little city rooms. Not that these objects are happy about it! Few of them have a chance to stretch to their full width. Some stand a little askew, some turned completely sideways, and the chairs are even stacked in piles of three in a pyramid over in one corner.

"Hello there, hello!"

A big, tall woman comes and stands in the small space in the middle of the room. All in black. Wide blue eyes look for the new arrival.

"So this is your little sister?"

With a quick movement, her hand turns the girl around.

"Let's see, let's see, what do you look like?"

Mercilessly she criticizes Annele:

"The skirt's too long! Why? She hasn't been confirmed yet, has she?" And, to Līziņa: "Fix it."

"Yes, of course!"

She's not finished yet.

Dissatisfied, she shakes her head: "Skinny as a rail. Freckles. Her nose is too short. Her eyes are too narrow. Where did you get those from? In our family, everybody's got eyes as big as windows."

Now Annele knows what it is about Aunt Meire that is so dear and familiar. It's Granny's eyes. For they're both from the same side of the family.

She looks into her aunt's "windows" and laughs heartily. She's glad to have such an aunt.

Aunt Meire responds.

"Aha! You know how to laugh, too? Well, may God be with you, then! The rest doesn't matter. What counts is a good heart. And an obedient spirit!"

In back of the wardrobe there is a recess, almost like another little room. Here, there's a trestle made of boards, two little white cots. Those will be for the two sisters.

In the roof, a little skylight. And beyond it – more rooftops. Steep, flat, red, greenish, with patches and without. It all feels as though she had seen it before. When? The first time Annele was in Jelgava. And yet now it seems quite different.

"Lunch time, lunch time!"

One corner of the big table has been spread with a yellowish-white linen cloth. There are many more like it in Aunt's dowry.

A little saucepan has been placed on a tray in the middle of the table. It is still boiling hot, with beads of fiery soot on it. Each of them pours straight from it into her plate to save ladling and needless dishwashing.

The three of them eat quickly and in silence.

The sisters put down their spoons, but the bottom of the saucepan is not in sight yet.

Aunt Meire takes a look, shakes her head.

"Līziņa, take another spoonful!"

"Thank you, I can't any more!"

"How about the little one?"

"I can't."

"What do you mean you can't? What shall I do with this gift of God? The pan should be clean."

"Maybe one of your Malchens or Dorchens will drop in."

"Don't invent excuses! Neither Malchen nor Dorchen is coming today. Come on, girls, take one more spoonful apiece!"

They had to take one more.

But Līziņa began to tease.

"Auntie's hand must have been overly generous today."

"How was I to know that squirt would eat so little?"

That squirt was their new companion.

When the table had been cleared, work began.

"But the girl can go and take a look at Jelgava now," decided Aunt.

"By herself?"

"I shouldn't think she'll get lost. A big girl like her!"

Annele was given detailed instructions.

"Turn right, go straight, then left as far as the church. That's Grand Street. There you can take whichever street you like, just don't lose sight of the church. That way I'm sure you'll find your way home again."

Annele couldn't admit that she would not know how to get back, so she left.

In the heat of the day, the street lay as though dozing. Boring, monotonous. The houses looked as though they had been stuck into uniforms: a khaki one, a greenish one, another khaki one, then a greenish one. There was only one nice spot on that street: Aunt Meire's window in the triangle of the gable. Snowy white curtains, pots of blooming geraniums.

The wooden turnpike gave a startled moan, turned reluctantly, let Annele into a small enclosure. This was called the church garden. Little dusty broken-off acacia shrubs. And here is where Grand Street stretched out and contracted again. There were few pedestrians, for market hours were long since over. By the arcade right at the street corner, a shopkeeper was turning this way and that, so broad that one had to make a detour around him. Without taking his hands out of his trouser pockets, he swiveled about on his feet like the turnpike by the church, swiveled and revealed himself in all his grandeur. Over his white waistcoat he wore a shiny fat gold watch chain. A wide strand of hair had been combed across his bald head from one ear to the other. Golden spectacles perched on his beak of a nose. Fiercely and malevolently, he examined the country girl from head to toe: "Hey, you! Why have you come to town, huh? Isn't there room for you in the country anymore?"

Fragrance rose from the river. The shady paths of the residence park began here. The silver ribbon of the Lielupe River shimmered. With a hundred windows, the white ducal palace looked out at the expanse of the countryside, at green meadows and birch groves. Its white façade was cooled by country winds. Over there was the big highway to Rīga. Many horse-drawn wagons were on their way out of town. Country folks on their way home, having concluded their business in town. They were disappearing, dwindling in the distance, light as dragonflies looking for a place to settle at night. By evening, they'd be back at their own farms.

Annele, too, had returned home like that from her Jelgava visit that first time, had gone back into the vast expanse of fields, back to the flowers and the sun. But now it would not happen again. Never again, never. The sharp pain of homesickness suddenly stung her breast and choked her breath. She must stay here. Must live here. These narrow streets would now be her home. She was locked inside a stone cage. For a long time she sat there, and her thoughts sang a song of farewell to the country, while an occasional tear rolled down on her folded hands.

Two machines were humming. Each did a different kind of work. Līziņa sewed fine fabrics. Even during this comparatively slack summer period she had more offers of work than she could handle. Aunt Meire worked on much simpler things. Her customers did not make great demands. Whether it was for Sunday or day-to-day wear, they wanted a simple cut, a durable fabric. These clothes would be worn by members of that vast army of Malchens, Julchens, and Dorchens who had been raised on a farm, and living with their German mistresses in the houses of Jelgava had lost the Latvian endings of their names and would never find them again. These Malchens did not act confident, like employers with a purse full of money; quite the contrary: it looked as though Aunt was working for them free of charge. "Just make whatever comes out best. You're the expert!" they would say, easily satisfied and humble.

They cared not so much about how the work turned out than about talking. Whispering mysteriously, bending close to Aunt Meire, they could go on and on with their stories. Sometimes these would be interrupted by brief sobs or quick, delighted laughter, and would then resume again. Aunt never stopped work for an instant. After all, her ears were free. But her large face with its broad white forehead shaded by tightly smoothed-down hair was attention itself. The network of tiny wrinkles around her mouth and eyes was constantly in motion. When she spoke, she never raised her voice, her answers were soft-spoken and restrained, like water murmuring in an unvaried rhythm, except that they were by no means monotonous. Oh no! The words seemed so close to her lips that they leapt out like little ripples from behind a dam of pebbles. Laughing words, around which sparkled the merry little flames in her eyes. It was obvious that she liked to laugh, liked to talk – words for her were like the flourishes of a baton that put order in the log jams of her visitors' great floods of talk and showed them in which direction to go.

Līziņa's machine, too, never stopped for a moment. You couldn't hear much in the constant hum.

"What do they talk about all that time?" Annele asks her sister in a low voice.

"Affairs of the heart," retorts Līziņa curtly.

"Affairs of the heart? What a long time they take!" Annele shrugs. What a puzzling answer!

It often happened that one of these Malchens or Dorchens had no job. Then she brought Aunt not work but hunger. She was given the little two-handled pot to hold in her lap, and was told to eat the contents. No excuses were accepted. Then she was supposed to wash the pot and put it back in its place. Those were the rules.

Goodness only knows how many extra mouths Aunt Meire fed during her lifetime! It was as though she had a secret storehouse to grab handfuls from. Her right hand did not know what the left hand was doing. Just as it said in the Gospel.

Who said Aunt Meire was an impoverished workingwoman? Nonsense! She was a Zemgale patrician, untiringly looking after her retainers who, like herself, had been thrown out of the nest.

Aunt's younger brother Ansis also lived in Jelgava, while the two older sisters, Līzīte and Līnīte, still lived on the farm with the brother who ran it. This brother, the oldest of them all and also the least good-looking, had gone and gotten married one fine day, causing no small surprise to his other brothers and sisters, who had long since given up all thoughts of marriage. In no time, the rich farmer had been bewitched by a nimble young Lithuanian woman who worked as his housekeeper. The first to leave the old nest as a result of these changed circumstances were Aunt Meire and Ansis.

Farm families had a wealth of children for whom there was no longer any room on the farm.

The city took many fine, strapping farmers' sons and daughters of good family, and turned a lot of them into laborers and hired hands.

Ansis was a real giant of a man, straight and erect, broad-shouldered, with a bushy mustache, who cut an imposing figure. He worked in Vale Street as the coachman of a baron. He would come over once a week when his sister had cooked

him some special dish that he loved to eat in happy remembrance of his childhood. In return he brought his sister the week's laundry to wash and mend.

Ansis was the opposite of his sister. He had the same Meire bones, the same stately figure, but under his bushy mustache there was not a spark of laughter, and in his broad chest he did not have a heart that felt compassion for everyone. He moaned and sighed a lot. What kind of life was this? Unjust, preposterous! The baron had more crazy notions than you could shake a stick at. Ansis had to put up with it all. He had to obey him to the letter. Had to go where he was told. Had to take his scoldings. What for, what for? – And then those servant girls! Hovering around him constantly like crazy women! They'd eat him alive if they could. No place was safe from them!

"You've got to get married, Ansi, then they'll leave you alone," Līziņa advised.

Ansis's blue eyes glinted angrily.

"What kind of foolish talk is that! Who can support a wife in these hard times?"

"Ask that girl if she herself would have you," interjected Aunt.

"Yes, Ansi, would you take me if I was willing to marry you?" Līziņa tosses her curly head at him provocatively and mischievously.

Such a question is a hard nut for Ansis.

He sighs.

"The times are too hard."

"What are you sighing about? You think an old bachelor like you will catch this little golden cuckoo? Why would a girl like her marry the likes of you?"

"And you think she wouldn't? What about the princesses that have climbed off their thrones when a good man came along and asked for their hand?"

"You don't say!" Līziņa slowly shakes her head in disbelief.

"But can you guarantee that I'll be better off when I get married than I am now? No, you can't guarantee that. And if you can't guarantee that, then I'm certainly not going to throw every penny I've earned by the sweat of my brow out the window. I'd have to be crazy."

"There, you see! There's no hope for me!" Līziņa threw up her hands with a great show of disappointment.

"What's he always sighing about, that great big giant?" Līziņa said when Ansis had closed the door behind him.

"Heaven only knows. It seems he's having a hard time of it."

"The reason he's having a hard time of it is because he has no sense of humor, and because he's so stingy. He could at least have brought you a pretzel once in a while in return for all the favors you've done him. You shouldn't let him get away with it. You should have taught him better."

"Oh, what's the use! You can never reeducate somebody once they've become obsessed with saving money. And we're the kind of people who aren't used to haggling over money."

"And so he saves. He just makes money and saves it. What for, though? It won't do him any good, or to anybody else. No, no. A man like Ansis is unfit for life."

Annele sews. Places one stitch next to another. Aunt takes a look. "Why do it that way? You won't earn your bread with such tiny stitches. A piece of plain sewing isn't like embroidery."

"I don't know any other way."

Aunt Meire gives it some thought and says:

"If she can do such fine stitching, then give her some buttonholes to make."

Līziņa looks at her sister's work. She herself is tired to death of making buttonholes.

"Could you do this?"

And she shows her a shirtfront made of fine fabric.

"I'll try."

And so she is given that job, and she makes buttonholes by the tens and hundreds in both smooth and fuzzy materials, in silk and velvet and in snow-white men's shirts as thin as paper. Nothing but buttonholes for hours and days at a time.

Her thoughts are somewhere else. Of course. By all kinds of paths they force their way out of the cramped cage she herself is in. First of all: How could she change her fate? How could she force it to treat her more kindly? How enter the world for which her whole self yearned, but from which she was separated by an abyss? It was quite clear to her that buttonholes were no help in bridging this abyss. She needed money. In town this question was all the more urgent.

The kind of money that could abruptly change circumstances could only be obtained through a miracle. For example: if she were suddenly to find a fat wallet on the street, stuffed almost to bursting with banknotes. Such a wallet could easily drop out of one of the coaches that sped along the streets of Jelgava drawn by teams of two or even three pairs of long-reined horses. Now, if she were to pick up such a fat sack of a wallet and hand it in at the appropriate place, and if it had thousands or even millions of rubles in it, then something special was certainly bound to happen afterward.

Another way of earning her good fortune would be, for example, if she were to save someone from mortal danger, especially the child of some rich man: either by carrying it out of a burning building, after running inside with a wet sheet – as she had read in books – or by pulling it out of the Driksna or Lielupe rivers as it was drowning, or else by snatching it up from under the hoofs of galloping, frenzied horses. Oh, there was no end to the situations and complications whose final outcome might be crowned with brilliant success! There were all sorts of ways that a kind fate could benefit those it smiled upon.

But was she favored by fate? That was the question. Up to this point, she hadn't seen any sign of it. Perhaps she, too, was one of the people who, like Ansis, were unfit for life. For life? Then what sort of people were fit for life? People like Līziņa and Aunt Meire? Especially Aunt. It seemed she began each day with a kind of new freshness and that even her everyday words, interspersed with soft laughter, sounded special and new.

So many women come and tell her their "affairs of the heart." But what about Aunt herself? "Līziņa, ask Aunt if she ever had 'affairs of the heart,' and how come she never got married!" Aunt overhears this through the hum of her machine and answers at once merrily, glad to tell her story.

"I see! Is that what you'd like to hear about? Well, the pain of love never gnawed my heart the way I see it happening in other people. Fall in love? I wouldn't know what that is. There were certainly lots of men who wanted to marry me. There was no end to them when I was young. But after I had taken a closer look, there was always something there I couldn't abide, try as I would. Often it was something funny. And as soon as you feel like laughing at someone who's proposing to you, there's an end to love. Goodness knows why my youth passed without it. It was probably meant to be. It was that way for me, and for my other sisters as well. Maybe the schooling we got was bad for us. You see, now I had different expectations. There wasn't a single man I liked. Once, though, I got to the point where an engagement had been decided upon. My mother wanted it, my father wanted it. My fiancé, though an older man, had had a certain amount of education and was quite wealthy. But then I suddenly felt such sorrow at leaving the family farm and the lovely meandering river that I cried my eyes out. So that was that. He was probably not the right man, was he, if my parents' home seemed dearer to me."

"Now and then," continued Aunt, "it did occur to me that I had missed something in life. Thus when I was little I once spent a whole spring struggling with a boring childhood illness. And out of my whole youth, I regret this one spring I wasn't able to spend in the meadows, birch groves, and on the banks of the river. So perhaps in some little corner of my heart I regret the love I never experienced. Who knows! Still, nothing comes of marriage without love, either. I've had no lack of opportunities to this day. This very spring a country schoolteacher, a widower with

grown-up children, sent word to me. A good job, has his own farm, too; life would be carefree if that was all I wanted, but I can't, you see. My heart isn't willing."

"This very spring," Līziņa exclaimed in surprise. "Why didn't you say anything about it?"

"Why should I tell you every little thing? – And it wouldn't have hurt me at all to get all that outdoor exercise. This darned sitting around is no good for my bones."

"So it goes," continues Aunt. "I haven't lost any sleepless nights over my own troubles, but I have over other folks'. Take these country girls that come here. They're as naive and credulous as children. Sometimes they've gotten themselves into a tight spot, and they don't know which way to turn. And so you think about them. There's times when it makes you laugh, and times when you have to suffer as grievously with them as though it was your own trouble. But when you've helped a poor creature out of her predicament, there's joy, too. And it's not just the young ones that have troubles. No matter how old a person is, a heart is a heart. What a runaround I had with a woman close to my age. She'd stumbled and fallen, and now all she did was repeat over and over that she'd drown herself in the river. There wasn't much I could accomplish by talking to her. I had to go find the man. And it isn't as though it was hard to talk sense into him. You just had to know how to handle him a bit, and he became gentle and docile as a lamb. And so they're together now. I've got a fine godson. A joy to behold."

"For you, everything is a joy."

"Life is a joy to me. You're right about that. Large or small, our allotted share is given to each of us. And so, when I wake up in the morning, my first thought after saying the Lord's Prayer is, "Ah, here it is again, here's my day! What'll happen today? What shall I hear and see and experience?"

Toward evening the sun climbed in the window. Aunt Meire interrupted her stories:

"Why don't you sing a bit, girls?"

Līziņa began. She knew by heart several stirring pieces she had heard at the theater, where singers from Rīga gave guest recitals every spring. She remembered everything easily, and as her fingers nimbly continued working she sang the songs with all their unfamiliar words and sounds in her clear young voice.

"That certainly sounds nice," said Aunt, "but I'd rather hear our own country songs, where the two of you make such rich and beautiful harmony together." And when the girls were right in the middle of the best singing, she got up, noiselessly opened the window and, hidden behind the curtain, looked down to see if anyone was listening below, neck craned. If there was, she smiled, not begrudging them the pleasure.

"That's how it is with country songs. You think you've been in your father's apple orchard, and they're just harvesting the first honey of summer, and the smell stays in your clothes, and the taste stays in your mouth for goodness knows how long," said Aunt, daydreaming in the silence, for the songs, too, had died away.

"Moyn, moyn!"

"Moyn, moyn!"

That's how it goes morning or evening along the porch, around Aunt's front door, into her flat with winds of laughter and talk.

"Madame Zirniņ, Madame Kociņ."

"Fräulein Meire!"

Especially at dusk, when it is no longer possible to see by daylight but still too early to light the lamp, these neighbor ladies come one after another to pay hasty flying visits, buzzing like flies around Aunt's worktable. Their heads with bonnets tied under their chins sway like ears of wheat in the reflected light from the window, their talk rustles like leaves, stirred up every once in a while by spirited interjections from their interlocutor. They are living newspapers of Jelgava, pouring the day's latest news and events higgledy-piggledy on Aunt's quiet worktable, while Aunt, like a true editor-in-chief, orders, evaluates, and places them in their true and definitive perspective. And she does all this because of her joy in life.

Sunday. A white cloth on the table, coffee, brown, crunchy croissants from Süsslack's in a little basket, sweet cream in a little jug. Nice!

Līziņa is unhappy. Again she has overslept, and all this Sunday morning work of tidying up and preparing breakfast has been done by Aunt alone.

"Don't worry! You won't always be able to sleep so sweetly on Sunday mornings."

The croissants disappear crackling between their teeth. Working folks eat greedily, not with relish. And besides, even on Sundays their time is accounted for.

Līziņa clears the table, goes and gets ink and paper. She is a great letter writer. She is on friendly terms with all the young women her age. She even corresponds with the legendary Lithuanian relatives who have been much talked about to be sure, but have never been seen in Zemgale. While she worked at the house of Pastor Tiedemann's widow, she finally met one of these cousins of her mother's. The cousin was still unmarried and, on her rare visits to Jelgava, would always stay with the aforementioned lady, with whose family she had boarded while going to school in Jelgava. The two relatives, who had met so fortuitously, liked each other, and had become friends. And at Easter, Līziņa had visited old Uncle Vanags's family in Lithuania. They were wealthy and proud people. The older daughters, who had been married off to Latvian estate managers, lived like real patricians; the oldest son had bought property further inland on the Polish border and married a Polish woman, and had become quite a stranger to his family; the younger son, the family's "pride and joy," was serving in the Petersburg Guards, where he had allegedly gone "riding his own horse." Līziņa corresponded with the younger relative, who was her friend. However, this correspondence was not as easy as writing to her own brother or to some childhood friend. Her young relative was educated. The correspondence was conducted in German. And no matter how fluently Līziņa could speak this foreign tongue, writing it was a different matter. So many words that had to be capitalized. How was she to figure out which ones? Often the letter writer bit down on the penholder, thought for a while, shook her head. Glanced over at Aunt: maybe she knew what to do?

What is it, tell me!

Punctuation marks! The big stumbling block! The period, question mark, and exclamation mark – these came where they had to come, and positioned themselves in their proper places with assurance, but those commas and semicolons! Where should she put them, how should she deal with them? She couldn't decide.

"What shall I put now?" Līziņa read a sentence and, nibbling on the end of her penholder, questioningly looked at Aunt.

Aunt Meire thought it over and came to a decision.

"What punctuation mark did you have before that?"

"A comma."

"Then you just put a semicolon now. Just do it, and it will be fine."

⟶∗⟵

In the nearby Church of Saint Anne, the organ began to hum. A hundred-voiced choir made the old walls thunder. "Come, O Heavenly Father!" The country congregation was singing the final hymn. In a few minutes, they had to make room for the city congregation.

Aunt already stood waiting, resplendent and wide in her churchgoing outfit. Her hat, which left bare half her head of glossy hair, was held under her chin by profusely knotted loops of ribbon. A black silk shawl ornamented with pleats and lace covered the black skirt that spread like a crinoline over a whole mound of starched petticoats. Black mesh gloves. In her hands a book with a golden chalice on one side and a cross on the other.

"Come on, stop that writing now."

"I'm just finishing," Līziņa answered, signing the letter with a strong but somewhat crooked stroke of the pen.

She read it through and sighed. It hadn't come out the way she had wanted.

"This will have to do."

"It'll be fine. After all, nobody's going to print it."

Bells were ringing in all the spires. Time for the townspeople to go to church. Moyn, moyn! To and fro.

With muffled steps, wearing light cloth shoes with thin soles, the people of Jelgava hurried to their churches, the Latvians in one direction, the Germans in the other, while the large majority of half-Germans milled between them. They all held black books with gilded pages, with a chalice on one side and a cross on the other.

In the afternoon Līziņa was going to visit her friends. These were two sisters called Gūze. They had been the subject of many conversations. To Annele in the solitude of the barrens, they had seemed like princesses who live in glass castles on inaccessible mountain peaks. And they had caused unaccustomed excitement in her life that spring before Father died, for they had promised Līziņa to come visit her in the country. Mother had been terribly anxious: she did so hope things would be elegant enough for them. So Līziņa had brought back with her not only white porcelain plates, but also a glass sugarbowl and painted cups. From the big bolt of linen cloth, they had cut and hemmed big tablecloths and little napkins. And even after all this they had been so full of worry! How very refined those Gūze sisters must be!

Annele never got to see them. Father died, and all their plans came to nothing.

And now Aunt said:

"Listen, can't you take your little sister along to visit the Gūzes? They've got a big garden, lots of room, she'll have a chance to run around all she wants to."

The Gūze sisters lived on the outskirts of town, in a beautiful house with a garden. Their parents were well-to-do.

Lines of worry etched themselves in Līziņa's face.

"They didn't invite her."

"They know your sister is here, but they haven't invited her?"

"That's right."

"Then, of course, it isn't possible."

"And I wouldn't go, no matter how much they invite me. Even if they came to get me with a team of four horses, I wouldn't go!"

Annele said this with excessive and needless energy.

"Come, come, come!"

That was all.

After that, more mildly now:

"All right. Then the two of us will go to the Residence park."

With Sunday slowness, Aunt rummaged for a long time in the drawers of the dresser and chest, now rearranging old-fashioned scarves and rereading faded let-

ters, now showing the girl portraits from which people looked out, eyes popping, faces pinched tight as though with a pair of tongs, deadly serious, both hands convulsively clutching their knees. They were so quaint and wooden. But with her smiles and talk Aunt loosened their wooden limbs and showed them as they lived and breathed, and now they moved freely in their various roles, and were entirely different from the people the photographer had captured in his iron stranglehold.

It was already late when they left the house. But the townspeople were still streaming to the Residence park like crowds of pilgrims – to breathe a little of the beauty of summer, to be refreshed for the whole week to come. The heat of the day was vanishing across rivers and meadows. In the rows of windows of the white palace, rubies were already beginning to sparkle. The river glittered in the light of the setting sun. Insignificant, the size of a flatiron, a motorboat chugged in the middle of the river. There was the splash of oars. Faraway voices. Laughter. A song broken off halfway. A small fire began to crackle, then went out.

But why is all this so far away? Why are the breezes from the big river so chilly, why do these unfamiliar bridges cast such gloomy shadows? Why is there nothing to warm one, to bring ease, only things that darken the heart with sadness? Why is that?

The walk under the linden trees is filled with thick, soft twilight. There are still rare passersby walking in couples, gliding past murmuring softly, gliding past, then returning in the opposite direction. Like the two of them, strolling from one end to the other and back again.

At last Aunt tugs at the girl's elbow. Time to go home! And she says:

"What a shame, what a shame! If a person had leisure, they could spend the whole night walking here. There'd be time to finish thinking all those big thoughts – how a day like this passes, and how time has passed, and all of life."

After a while, she stops the girl.

"Notice the sweet smell? The waters, the meadows, the gardens of Jelgava. Roses, gillyflowers, nicotiana, mignonettes. It's the very middle of summer, you know."

Footsteps echo through the streets.

Suddenly, long drawn-out sounds like white blades split the summer dusk.

What's that? Trumpets?

Trumpets and a whole lot of other things, fiddling, whistling, storming, effervescing, rippling along with the trumpets there.

"Why, that's music, isn't it?" Annele exclaimed in ecstasy. "I've never heard anything like it before."

"It's a concert in Schirkenhöfer Park. Musicians from Rīga. The evening is calm. You can hear the sound from far away."

"It's lovely, lovely!"

"You see? There's something lovely even about a town."

"Town!" Annele whispered as though the word was totally new, as though she had just heard it, suddenly shivering happily under the many-colored showers of sound that rang out across the labyrinth of black rooftops, rustled away into the sky, where pale stars were beginning to glimmer. Town? Was it something that could be taken lightly? No, no! It would be a fascinating puzzle, hard to solve. It would be a book that would be difficult to read and would take a long time. Would her life be long enough to finish reading it?

Under the Highway Willow Trees

The newcomer soon acquired all sorts of duties, the way a plant grows leaves. Women are usually good at sending people on errands, and once Aunt had satisfied herself that she could put the girl to good use, she was only too willing to take advantage of the young girl's nimble feet, sending her running off here and there. Water, wood, milk, sugar, bread came home faster when Annele brought them. Later Annele was also entrusted with the task of shopping for all kinds of sewing notions in haberdashery shops, including trifles where colors had to be closely matched, something about which Līziṇa was especially particular. Sometimes Līziṇa received the purchases with praise, but sometimes she criticized them severely, and Annele had to go exchange them. Since she responded easily to kindness, Annele had not learned to tell a false face from a true one, and only became aware of the deception when she came home and got a scolding for letting the salesclerk palm something off on her with glib words.

One day, Jelgava was so strangely full. Filled with a blast of rich country winds, as it were. The gates of the inn yards were open. The yards swarmed with people. The wagons of country folk rumbled down Grand Street one after another. Other wagons stopped at the doors of general stores, with lines of customers inside. The store clerks worked so hard that sweat was pouring down their faces. Herrings, salt, soap, candles were being weighed out in large quantities. There were loud greetings, old acquaintances smoked a pipe together, exchanged pleasantries. Now and then a customer, whip in hand, planted himself legs apart in a store entrance and, in a stern trumpeting voice that almost made the townspeople's eardrums burst, yelled at his horse, which was trying every way it could to move out of its place – such a long-drawn-out "Whoooa there!" that a Jelgava lady started as though stung by a wasp, stopped, clapped her hand over her heart, spat superstitiously, and exclaimed in annoyance, "Oh, you loudmouthed hayseed, you!"

The collective of Jelgava ladies, dressed in black alpaca and silk, who were, so to speak, the bedrock of the street public, had somehow vanished from the face of the earth today, and had been replaced by an element unusual for town: gray homespun, voluminous skirts, waterproof boots walking up and down the sidewalks and, along with them, huge bundles inside white sacks or wrapped in checkered blankets. Well-to-do farmers and their wives, farmhands. Girls – girls with long and short, fair and dark braids; boys with white bandannas, sunburned as brown as pinecones.

They walked around and gathered in groups, greeted each other, called to each other across the street. Chatter, laughter, flashing, happy eyes. Yes, the rich country winds had blown them together here. It was they who would fill the schools of Jelgava tomorrow, for tomorrow school would begin.

Had the time really come, and was summer over? Annele walked among these crowds of students silent and mute, walked feeling as though her limbs had gone numb. She could not share their joy. There was no school awaiting her.

But at home a new surprise and new troubles awaited her. In the corners of Aunt's flat were piled the same kinds of sacks as those that had been walking up and down the streets today: there were apples, potatoes, pork loins, wooden tubs of butter, bedding. Aunt's boarders, the daughters of wealthy farmers from a nearby Zemgale district, had arrived, and they must be given space, the space that the sisters had occupied until now. Thus the short weeks of summer they had spent in pleasant harmony in their aunt's home came to a sudden end.

That same night, the sisters moved to a flat they had rented. At a run with their bundles, exactly the same way as a few weeks earlier going from the station to Aunt's place. And again a cabby was ambling down the middle of the street, his cab empty. Clop-clop! And looked down from his perch mockingly: "Well, how about it, young ladies, let's go for a ride!"

Yes, it was easy for him to look at them mockingly. He was a Jelgava cabby, while they were mere pedestrians.

They walked a long way. The streets ended, and the highway began. The houses lay far apart, as though deliberately dispersed, one here, one there. Clumps of dust-covered trees, tiny green garden plots; here and there, like a lonely beauty, a tall apple or pear tree, full of coral-pink fruit. Finally they reached a heavy gate that opened by lifting a crossbar. They were engulfed by a large, bare courtyard; a squat little building sat all the way in the back of the yard. Their small flat was in there. Two little white rooms with an unpainted floor.

Outside the window, squatting in a row, cabbage heads gleamed white, like buttons strung on a thread. Here and there, a shallow ditch or boundary divided them like a yardstick. Then more cabbages, plump and thriving, pressed close together so as not to leave one empty space as far as the eye could see.

Would there be sun in any of the windows?

No! The windows faced north.

"A gloomy place!" sighed Annele.

Mother arrived bringing a spinning wheel, a hackle, and a couple of bags of flax and wool. These she would spin and give to the mistresses of Edgefield and Black Earth farms in autumn in exchange for potatoes, grits, flour, which would be her pay. That was the agreement.

It is dark in the hallway between the flats. Annele often meets a dense shadow there – it darts toward her and bumps into her shoulder as though with a deliberate blow. Annele can't figure out who this is.

On the south side, there are two rooms exactly like theirs partitioned from theirs by a thin plank wall. In the tiny kitchen shared by both flats, Mother has met their neighbor.

"She's a widow like me," Mother tells them. "Her husband didn't leave her anything when he died, either, so now she lives from hand to mouth. She says her older son has a good job, so he contributes a bit, and she herself doesn't stay idle, of course. She did say her younger son isn't making any money yet, he goes and prints books at Stesenagen's or some such."

"It's Steffenhagen, not Stesenagen. With two efs and an h."

"Stop correcting me! I just listen to what people tell me."

"Then the boy who bumps me on the shoulder sometimes must be the widow's son. Does he do it on purpose?"

"I'm sure that can't be so. The hallway is dark, it can happen sometimes, I'm sure."

Another time Annele, running off on an errand, suddenly dashes back inside, grabs the little mirror, carefully inspects every part of her face: maybe the tip of her nose is dirty, maybe her hair is too disheveled? Why does that person, that adolescent boy, stare and stand there like he was glued to the wall whenever she runs past?

No. There is nothing sloppy about the way she looks.

But now things get really crazy! One time, they almost get stuck as they collide right in the front door – she has a strong suspicion that the boy did it on purpose – and then he grabs her hand quick as a flash and gives it a good squeeze. She pulls it away furiously. Well! He can't even say hello, but he has the nerve to touch her!

What does this city kid think he's doing? Guess the fashion here is to ogle people and let your hands stray where they shouldn't. A while back, Milda had told her quite a bit about this bad habit townspeople have. Well, just let him try!

The willows along the highway turned gray, then yellow, the mud got deep as a pit. In the cabbage fields, cabbage stumps poked sadly out of the ground amid large pyramids of harvested cabbages. Then these, too, were taken away in tall handcarts to factories where chopping knives and pickling barrels awaited them.

"Come on, girl, run, get the numbness out of your feet!"

Away down the highway, down that big road crowded with people!

The rows of willows on both sides stretch, stretch like caravans of dwarves with backs stooped under heavy burdens; into the distance as far as the eye can see, narrowing gradually, as though longing to reach a place where they can fraternally lean against each other. In vain! A blue ribbon of mist flows through them all like a stream of water, separating them, running on into infinity.

Loaded wagons, empty wagons going back and forth. Grain, hay, apples travel in heavy, rumbling carts sluggishly drawn by tired horses. Journeymen butchers with long whips incessantly pursue and lash a flock of hungry, bleating sheep, driving them to town from distant markets. A Gypsy, harness bells jangling, gallops past with a covered wagon full of dark heads, in the midst of which a mongrel dog, up on his front feet, furiously spits ferocious barks in all directions. A dozing Jew, teetering in his empty cart, does not realize that his scrawny horse, suddenly frightened, has jumped out almost straight across the road. A gruff shout, the sudden flick of a whip wakes the two and instructs them in the order of the road. A coach drawn by four horses driven by a red-belted, white-gloved coachman claims the entire width of the road for itself.

A tired, sleepy traveler with a long trip behind him blinks at the sight of the gray houses that line the highway: Why the devil do they stand here forever and a day, so uninteresting and monotonous?

But the houses along the highway are gray and ill-tempered: nothing but noise all the time, nothing but dust and people forever driving by. Damn it, they've no business here!

A ray of sunshine has dropped from a chink in the clouds, and suddenly a burning island is created in the gray, dense expanse: a quaking aspen at the corner of the woods, a red roof, the slowly moving sail of a windmill. D'you like it? "I do, oh I do!" And the roving play of the sun's rays has already moved off in a different direction: a tall, turreted house, flashing windows. And somewhere else: a low, gray little cottage. A well-sweep. A corner of the forest protected from the winds. – What do you think of this place? "Lovely, lovely! I'm sure the people who live here are happy."

That's what her runs down the highway are like, until late in fall, when sharp winds begin to buffet the countryside.

The horizon is covered with thick sheets of fog. Scourging rain begins to fall. Hail. You can feel that winter is near.

"Annele, run to the grocery, will you?"

The little bell over the door jangles sharply. Startled, the fat tomcat leaps up on the counter, arches his back a bit, yawns. Protecting her hips, the shopkeeper sidles out of the dark corner, filling the gap between the shelves and the counter with her body. As her hands wrap and weigh, she scrutinizes her customer, eyes half-closed: who, what, and how? who, what, and how? She knows everybody, but this girl is unfamiliar. Where is she from? From the country, huh? When? Is she alone? Oh, her mother and sister live with her, too? Well, how do they live? What do they live on? Who are they kin to? Oh, her father is dead? How did he die? Had he saved anything or did he just live from hand to mouth? How old is she? How old is her sister? Is she pretty? Is she getting married soon?

Who, what, and how, who, what, and how? Ten questions all in one breath. The girl clenches her teeth, closes her lips tight, but she is not armed against this sort of onslaught. Whatever her customer doesn't say, the loquacious shopkeeper infers as she responds to her own questions: thus and so, thus and so. After all, it's not the first time she's come across this type of girl. She knows people, she knows what category to put this new customer in, so as to have all the facts about her at her fingertips next time they meet.

But a few days later the shopkeeper suddenly remembers: Well, isn't it strange! Wonder where that country girl does her shopping? Here one day, gone the next. She hasn't laid eyes on her once.

Well!! Interrogators like her can wait for Annele till they're blue in the face.

Līziņa spends as much time in town as at home, for the women who employ her don't want to walk the long distance to the outskirts of town, and so she has to go to their homes for fittings or to get new work. When she goes away, she gives Annele work, just as the stepmother did with Cinderella, the only difference being that Līziņa is a kind and loving stepmother.

Mother's spinning wheel turns and hums regularly and rapidly. The spinner's fingers play over the yarn as over a flowing harp string, spinning it as fine as silk; fleece after fleece melts into finely carded wool light as thistledown in this spinner's fingers. Only occasionally does she stop the wheel for a moment to attach the yarn to the notch in the next spool. Then her work continues. She doesn't say a single word.

"Being without work is more bitter than being without bread," are her thoughts.

"But why do you hurry so, Mommy? You'll soon run out of work if you don't watch out."

"I'm used to it. That's the way it's been all my life."

Annele knows that Līziņa will be satisfied with her work. The tiny seam will be rolled under so daintily your fingers will barely feel it's there, the stitches will be so fine and small you'll have to look hard to see them, and she'll have finished everything she was told to do; but as for her thoughts, she can't and won't answer for them to anyone.

Thoughts. Life and thoughts. That's what she needed to deal with. Life stood all around her as close and dark as a wall; she could batter her head against it, but couldn't break through. How could she find her way in this darkness? It must be spun with threads of thought, the way Mother spun her fleece; it must be hollowed out with burrows of thought, as one who digs a tunnel pierces a mountain range he must get through. And she had no help but her own strength, no light but one small heart glowing with fervor. The darkness of night must be melted by this fervor. Just as her hand fought the little hobgoblin who would let her work peacefully for a while, and would then suddenly twist, tangle, knot the thread, and drive the needle deep into her bleeding finger, so her thoughts struggled with life's events and tasks in order to grasp the evil and good in them, to glimpse a "beginning and an end" to them. This struggle was ceaseless and began when she first opened her eyes in the morning, ending when she closed them at night. No, it did not end even then, but continued in her dreams. Her insight had to be obtained by long detours, for there was no one to show her the direct way there. And there were so many questions that could not be resolved, no matter how hard she forced herself to think. But could she remain in the dark? No. When her thoughts could go no further, her obliging imagination came along, raised them on its wings, and carried them through those tunnels of uncrossed void whose exits were always bathed in sunlight, now red, now white, now golden.

School was the ardent dream of her longings. That would be the place where all problems could be solved and all the difficulties of her thoughts could be overcome. Fortunate were the children who attended school, and blessed by God the teachers who taught them there. But those roads were barred to her, those doors were locked, and they could not be broken open no matter how much she racked her brains. What was the use of talking? It wasn't as though she hadn't badgered her mother about it. The answer she received was always the same:

"Do you think you're the only one? There are so many children in this world whose life is even harder. Look around you and study the world."

"But do those children yearn to go to school as much as I do?"

"Well, that's something I wouldn't know about."

It was also hard to appease her hunger for books in Jelgava. After a long time, Līziņa had brought one volume from the Gūzes' house: *Illustrierte Welt.*

"Can't we get more than that from them?"

"Hardly. A couple of old calendars and a cookbook. That's their whole collection."

Annele was very surprised that the Gūzes, too, those elegant Gūzes, had no books.

But once in a while Līziņa did succeed in finding something good if the Lady Luck of books truly smiled upon her. To think where such books had sometimes come from, wandering from hand to hand, some picked off the shelf of a second-hand bookstore for a few kopecks! A book like that was always instructive, telling you either about foreign countries, about events in distant periods of world history, or myths about the gods of ancient peoples, which were especially fascinating. Wonderful things were told in old pages that were yellowed and stuck together, that smelled of dust and decay.

Both sisters used to read a lovely book like that with equal craving. When Mother disappeared in the kitchen, Līziņa might suddenly stop her machine, throw down the book among clouds of flounces she had just hemmed, and with feverish eyes skim through one page, a second, a third, until the sudden opening of the door startled her as if from a dream, and the book disappeared under the folds of her sewing.

Why did this grown-up young woman who earned her own living, who took care not only of herself but of her mother and sister as well, become nervous and avoid Mother's reproach over a few minutes of lost time?

"Why do you do that, Līziņa?"

"Oh – I don't like to make Mother sad. She was young in a different time, with a different way of looking at things. All she can think of is work, work, work. Everything else is a sin. Let her think that way if she likes."

It was Sunday morning.

Annele opened her eyes. The whole room was veiled in a bluish twilight, but outside the window it was all one foaming confusion, in which sky and earth melted away. The first snow. A blizzard of snowflakes filled the world to overflowing.

But what was so unusually quiet and festive in here? Was it the fact that it was Sunday? Yes, it was Sunday morning, but there was something else besides. As though some noble, unknown guest had just been here and left.

That's still part of my dream, she thinks.

What kind of a dream had it been, though?

She had been walking through lonely, stony fields. There was not a blade of grass there, nor trees, nor living creatures. Eerie and terrifying. How would she get to her goal and what was this goal? She did not know. The horizon narrowed. The fields

ended. And then she had to climb mountains, just as deserted and stony. "Where is
the end?" she asked anxiously. "Where is
the end? When shall I reach the goal?"

"Wait! Look what's behind you!" said
an invisible voice.

She looked back and saw two ghostly
apparitions. Their mouths were wide
open, jeering, their faces distorted. You
scarecrows, you! What were they? Sneaks,
who would stab you in the back. When she
stopped walking, they would stop too and
stand there like thick dwarfed shadows, cemented together. Scoffing. Menacing.

"They're certainly not good spirits,"
she thought, "but what can they do to me?
After all, I'm not afraid."

"You certainly are," said the invisible
voice.

And at that same moment, the fear was there. At first it seemed it was in her little
toe, and only in one drop of blood, but then it rose higher like a vapor and pervaded
her whole body. And now Annele had to run, run forward with such incredible
speed that she did not feel her feet touch the ground. So great was her fear.

Where is the goal, where? If I reach it, everything will be all right!

"You've reached the goal, can't you see?" said the voice again.

Now she saw that she was in a great hall whose walls, floor, ceiling were made of
white shining marble. And those weren't walls at all, but the jagged edges of the
rocky mountains which she had crossed, and which had turned into shelves. But the
shelves were full of many books. Spine by spine they lay there in strange antiquated
bindings. As though they were alive, as though, continuing to grow in number, they
grew out of the walls, lined up like armies drawn up for battle.

"All the books in the world must be collected here!" thought Annele. "There's
enough to read for a lifetime."

"But which one shall I take now?"

"The one at the very top, that's the best one."

The book at the very top lay on its shelf by itself. It seemed to have been much
read, heavy, with gray, plain covers and the same kind of fittings at the corners as
Granny's old hymnbook at Spring Farm.

"All right, I'll take it if that's the best one."

Now she reached for the book, but it eluded her grasp. Like the apple tree in the
fairy tale that would not give up its golden apples, it seemed to be rising higher and
higher. But at the moment when, after ceaseless effort, she finally touched the book,
the ceiling fell open like the two sides of a scallop shell, and a tall, exquisitely beautiful figure, larger than life, stood on the edge of the cover in a halo of white clouds.
Beyond it, infinitely deep, she saw the blue expanse of the sky.

Annele quickly drew back her hands.

Surely she wouldn't be allowed simply to take this book?

"Take it!" said the figure. "This is the book of life and truth."

What? So this is the book of life and truth! Why, that's what I've been searching for all this time!

The book has now easily slipped into her hands. She presses it to her heart.

But the figure has raised its hand imperiously and points somewhere beyond Annele. There, by the marble wall, seemingly glued to it, stand her hideous persecutors, dwarfed, scared, shrunk like shadows.

But the figure tells them:

"Away with you, spirits of darkness! You may not enter this heavenly realm."

"Heavenly realm!" Annele marvels in awed ecstasy.

And wakes up. And everything has vanished. Her hands, crossed on her chest, guard the book that isn't there, the one she just this moment felt in her fingers.

Outside the window, white snowflakes are dancing.

In the next room the lamp was still lit. The door was ajar. The voices of her mother and sister were murmuring in there. It was Līziņa's custom on Sunday mornings to work on some beautiful small piece of fancywork with pearls and silk embroidery floss, modeled after things she had seen at the places where she worked.

Annele did not hear what her mother had said. But now Līziņa replied:

"Don't you worry, Mother, and don't get alarmed for no reason! Don't ever think that Annele will be doomed to earn her living the way I do."

"Well, how else, then?"

"I don't know that now, but I do know that her fate will be different. After all, she is a hundred times more talented than I."

Annele suddenly raised her head.

What had her sister said? A hundred times more talented than she, her big sister! Līziņa, whom she idolized and admired? And a hundred times more? True, she mustn't interpret that too literally; after all, both of them loved such strong figures of speech, and yet, and yet: the way Līziņa had said that, how resonant, how full of faith her voice had been! Dear sister, dear, kind sister!

"What do you mean, talented? And how? I don't see it."

"But I do. And have done right from the time when she was little. I've never had any doubt that she has a different career ahead of her in life."

Dear, kind sister!

"Well, all right, all right, let's assume that this is so. Still, what good does it do the poor child? You do see, don't you, that we can't provide either schooling or books for her, and even if she begins to break through those thorns by herself, why, she'll need a hundred times more strength than the others. Will that happen? Who listens to the voice of a poor person? Wasn't Father smarter than a lot of other fellows? Sometimes you'd be amazed at the things he would say. But what authority did he have among his own brothers? – 'You're just a hired hand, go to those that are paupers like you. Let them listen to you.' That's what they used to say."

"Those were the old days, Mother. A new age is coming, people will be valued differently."

"Well, I'm not sure people's views will be different even in that new age."

Yes. Mother was right. Annele's thoughts too had often, so often, come to a sudden halt, pricked by those thorny bushes. She had as much of her father in her as of her mother. What heights her thoughts could soar to along with the jubilant trills of the lark: it will, it will happen! and what sloughs of grief and despair they could creep through accompanied by the owl's doleful complaint: no, no. What you hope for can never be.

She hugged her knees with her arms, lost in thought. What her sister, her mother had said – she was at the center of it all. And she didn't like herself. She lacked something that a person needed for life. She did not have Līziņa's skill for quickly organizing and getting the knack of everything. Nor did she know how to express her thoughts appropriately. Sometimes when she said something, nobody listened to her, and at other times the others would quickly look at her as though in surprise and not say a word in reply. As for being talented... Could she carry out what she wanted, for example? True, she could think up things. Several times, working on a piece of sewing, she had tried to use a decorative design she had invented that seemed truly splendid to her, but later she had had to unravel it again quickly so Līziņa would not see her blunder. That's how little her hand obeyed what her thoughts had wanted. – But what about the dream? And that conversation afterward? Was that without significance? No matter what else was true – the book of life had remained in her hands. Wasn't that a good omen? Didn't that mean: it will, it will happen?

The boy who had been looking at her so persistently from behind every door and had tried to call attention to himself in every way he could was called Konrāds. "My little Kundrāts, my little Kundrāts!" That's what his mother called him. One morning both adolescents ran right into each other in the yard. Konrāds quickly touched his hand to the peak of his cap.

"Moyn!"

"Good morning!"

Each of them went in a different direction.

The next morning, however, Konrāds stopped. After the usual "moyn!" and after putting his cap back on, he said in a swaggering tone:

"I can bring you books. Want some?"

"Books!"

"Yes!"

"Rea-lly?"

"Yes!"

This was certainly a surprise! Who had given him that idea! Who had been telling him about books?

Annele raced back to her mother like a shot.

"Mother, did you tell the neighbor how much I keep hankering after books?"

"No, why should I talk about that?"

"Well, how come that boy knows?"

"What boy? That Kunrāds?"

"Yes, that Konrāds!"

"Well, what's he been saying?"

"He promised to bring me books."

"Well, nothing wrong with that, is there? They do say he goes to that Stesenagen's."

No, Mother hadn't said anything. Besides, it was not in her nature. But Konrāds had specifically stressed: I can *bring* you books, implying: I know you long for books, and I can bring some.

How does he know?

She thinks and thinks, and finally flushes with mortification. He knows it from her. She has told him herself through the thin partition. She has told him, talking to herself. It probably went like this: "Oh, I wish I had some books! I wish I could somehow get hold of some books!" That's probably how she talked to herself. After all, she hadn't kept silent during the long days herding cattle out on the barrens. There, she talked to the sun, the winds, the grass and with her own thoughts, so as to hear what they sounded like. In town, of course, she has had to keep such talk in check. She's been afraid someone would hear. And now, sure enough, that boy has heard. What a snoop!

Sunday. Annele is reading *Illustrierte Welt*, which she has already turned inside out. Only one more story, studded with French phrases, still remains to be conquered. "The minute I get a good textbook, I'm going to learn French," she decides.

There's a knock at the door.

Company? Mother's in church, and Līziņa is visiting the Gūzes. Who could be coming here?

Let's just hope it isn't Konrāds!

Another knock.

"Come in!"

Yes. It really *is* Konrāds, planting himself in the doorway.

"'n Abend!"

Him and his idiotic 'n Abend!

What is she to do with him? Ask him to come closer?

Her visitor isn't the type to need a special invitation. Unabashed, he comes up to her, holds out his hand. Floods her with a cloud of pungent perfume.

"Where did you get that soap?"

"From the best supplier. Here!"

He is about to raise his hand to Annele's nose, but she quickly recoils. The idea! Konrāds tosses three volumes with thin cardboard covers on the table.

"Here you are!"

He has come with good rights and as though by previous agreement.

She'd better ask him to sit down. He's company.

"Take a seat!" Annele points to a chair.

"Don't mind if I do," Konrāds chimes in. He sits down, stretches his legs, and now, praising his own offering, asks:

"Well, how d' you like them? I can bring you tons of stuff like that. Doesn't cost me a thing!"

Annele glances through them: *Rose of Pine Hill. General Eustachius.* She's read every one of them. Thanks!

"Well, if you've read these, I'll supply you with others. Doesn't cost me a thing!"

"No, no! Don't bother. I'll manage without them."

"Why manage if I can get them? I get all that stuff for nothing."

Annele is curt and blunt: "I have no time to read at all now." Why can't he take a hint?

"I'll supply you with them. If you have no time to read, let them lie there. After all, they don't have to be fed. And you don't have to pay for them, either."

There he goes again. Why the blazes does he keep on blathering? Is he never going to leave?

No! Konrāds just sat there. They had said all there was to say about the books, and there was nothing else to talk about. To fill the time, the girl busied herself as though she had work to do now in one room, now in the other.

The visitor was obviously bored. Leaning over, he pulled up another chair to the table.

"Sit down a bit. The time will pass more quickly."

As though he was in charge here!

She really ought to say something, though. After all, the fellow had come with good intentions.

"Are you from the country, too?" Annele asked now, happy to have found a topic of conversation.

"No-o-o! What would I do there? Bunch of hicks!"

What more can she say in answer to such a reply? He has come in here as an uninvited guest, and he talks like one, too. Oh, how she wishes he would leave!

She rises to her feet.

"It's getting dark. I'll have to light the lamp."

"It's up to you. You can light it or not light it."

Konrāds doesn't have the slightest intention of leaving.

Who asked his opinion? Annele restrains her anger. She hopes he won't add: Doesn't cost me a thing!

Lighting the lamp takes time. She won't have to say anything till that is done. The top has to be cleaned, the cylinder wiped out. Everything needs to be done thoroughly. A match sputters, and the tips of two noses suddenly close in on the little flame from opposite sides. This is so funny that Annele can't help laughing.

The guest has interpreted this as the beginning of good mutual understanding. When the girl tries to move away, she realizes she is pinned down. Her fingers are held by what feels like the paw of a bear.

"What do you think you're doing? Let go!"

"Let's thumb-wrestle!"

Maybe Konrāds just blurted this out unexpectedly, or maybe he intentionally wanted to say something witty so as to make her laugh. And she did feel like laughing, even if it was only rageful laughter, but of course she didn't want to give the fellow that satisfaction. And so, her eyes flashing lightnings, she disappeared in the next room.

Behind her, a chair fell over, an elbow was suddenly stuck in the door, and there was Konrāds.

The stranger's hands were suddenly flung around her waist, wound around her shoulders, her neck. The brilliantined parting of his hair touched her cheek.

She couldn't find any words. Didn't even try to. Mute, her breath choked with rage that this fellow had touched her – how dare he! With a strength that suddenly surged within her, a strength she had never known, she erupted like a volcano, struggled, struck, shoved, her elbows like awls, her fists like hammers, all but ripping that boy apart.

He leapt aside, stood there apparently scared, and looked at this girl who was shaking with anger.

"Go away! Out!"

Konrāds awkwardly grinned.

"Hey, hey, hey. It was just a joke."

And then, bolder now, his hands in his pants pockets:

"Thinks she's the lady of the manor! As soon as you touch her, she stings."

"Go! And take your books with you. I don't need them."

Annele stands there, a deep scowl on her forehead. Konrāds goes past her. The door is left open. She slams it right behind him.

There he is, pacing on the other side like a wild beast in its cage. Annele, on the other hand, is silent. She's not going to let on to that fellow that she, too, is so full of rage and agitation she could just about knock down the walls.

What had happened that was so unusual? What strange storm had swept over her? And what strength was this that had protected her? Should she tell her sister, her mother? No! They wouldn't understand. Mother would listen, then say: what do you expect from a city-bred child! Who'd teach him what is right and proper?

Who'd teach him? He should learn it by himself!

Such great, proud strength had come to her assistance in her struggle against Konrāds. It had taught her, had told her what to do. It was still sparking in her fingertips at this moment. Yes, if she had this strength no one could hurt her at all.

As for that stupid Konrāds, she'd know how to deal with him now!

Līziņa came home with good news.

"Guess what! In two weeks from now, we're moving to a new flat."

"What street is it on?"

"Green Street!"

"Green Street!" echoed Annele as though she had been given a present. Green Street sounded pleasant and full of hope.

Līziņa Goes to the Ball

Mother and Līziņa were scrubbing and cleaning the rooms. Two lovely small rooms, full of sun and fragrant as a forest, for they had been built only recently, on the second floor, above the former horse stable and coach-house, and now received their first tenants. The first floor had been made into a workshop, but the tenant had changed his mind, and the workshop stood empty. The other flat faced that of the Avots family. Both were joined together by the usual entryway, with a little kitchen in the flue of the fireplace. Outside there was a back porch with an open stairway leading down into the yard. Everything was clean and new.

Annele had to light a fire in the hearth. The flue had gotten cold and was spewing back soot. It was blowing the ashes into her eyes. With half an ear she heard someone coming, stamping down on each stair, like pounding in fence posts.

"Clump, clump!" – on the stairs, "Clump, clump!" – at the door.

"Good day, Miss," a friendly voice greeted her.

Here was the person who had come stomping down the stairs. The opening of the flue threw a gray light on a pair of black eyes smiling below thick eyebrows, rosy round cheeks, a cherry-red mouth with a row of pearly white teeth. It was a girl, not much older than Annele but shorter by a whole head. Stocky and strong.

"Good day!" replied Annele and, allowing her eyes to slide down to the stranger's feet, barely managed to pull her voice back into her chest to keep from exclaiming "Oh dear!" For she saw that what had come clump-clumping along was not two feet but straight little posts with foot-shaped protuberances at the sides. Now she quickly flung her head in the other direction so the stranger would not notice that Annele had seen anything.

"You must be our neighbors. Right?" continued the stranger with a happy smile. And went on at once, without interrupting herself: "I know, I know. Oh, how glad I am that there are good people moving in next door! I am perfectly happy. I told Madam: the new neighbors will be nice. I dreamed they would be. She laughed. – You and your dreams, you silly goose! That's what she calls me. And she doesn't believe. I don't care if she doesn't. My dreams all come true. The same thing will happen in your case. And we're the first tenants in a new house. The first tenants are lucky. We will be, too. Is that tall young lady that's washing the windows your sister?"

"Yes."

"A beautiful young lady! Oh, I like beautiful people. If only you knew how much!"

The flue spewed out another whiff of black soot. It spattered in their faces.

"Phew, phew, phew!" sputtered the stranger. Then quickly reprimanded herself.

"And meanwhile here I stand not helping you at all! That makes me a bad girl, right? And I don't want to be bad. Wait. I've got some dry kindling. Everything will be all right in a minute. You have to know that fireplace. It's got tricks like an old horse. Don't I know it?"

Chatting in this fashion and – clump, clump! – stomping around the kitchen on her little posts, the stranger rolled through the kitchen like a spinning top. Her movements were awkward, angular, but productive: soon the fire was crackling and joyously shooting up into the flue.

"Thank you, Miss," said Annele.

Startled, the stranger clapped her outspread sooty hands behind her ears.

"Oh, don't talk that way! If Madam hears you, I'll be in trouble. She doesn't like people who are not of her station being called Mrs. or Miss. She really hates it. Call me by my name. Sarah. I'm from the flat next door. I'm the maid."

"The flat next door? Are there…"

"No, no!" Sarah hurriedly interrupted. "There are no Jews living there, but Christians. German gentry. The Feldeisens. A young couple. They got married in fall. It was the deaconesses that got me a job there. I got taken on out of charity, even though I'm Jewish. Oh, they're good employers. All people are good, don't you think? Of course, I don't get any pay, and the rooms are so small I have to sleep on the floor, right by the door. But I manage. I'm so healthy, you see, and the deaconess sisters take care of me when I need clothes. I earn my bread, and what more do I need? What more can a poor orphan expect of God's mercy? You tell me. The deaconess sisters are like angels. Every day, whenever Madam lets me, I'm allowed to go to them and learn."

"What are you learning?" Annele pricked up her ears.

"About Christ Jesus," replied Sarah, reverently folding her big reddish blackened hands. "How he was born in a manger in Bethlehem, how he lived and taught, how he was crucified and rose again. Do you know that?"

"Of course. I know all of that."

"How lucky you are! You're allowed to sit at Jesus' feet, but I'm not allowed to yet. My people nailed Christ to the cross, and that's why I have to help carry their great sins. But soon my Savior will redeem me too. He'll take me by the hand and lead me like a lamb into the heavenly pastures. He's the good shepherd. When I've learned everything from the deaconess sisters and have been obedient in my job, I'm going to be baptized. The deaconess sisters are going to sew me a black camlet dress, shiny like silk. And at the same time I'm going to be confirmed as well. So it can all be done in one go and there's no need to sew another dress. Yes, and then I'll live as a Christian among Christians, and I won't be called Sarah anymore, but Mary. Oh, how I look forward to that time, that happy time! Then I'll be like you."

"Sarah?" Annele looked at her new acquaintance as though wondering and questioning.

"Yes, that's my name. Oh, I'm so happy you came to live in this flat and that I'm allowed to talk to you. I do so love to talk, and you are so good. All people are good. My master and mistress, too. After all, they took me in even though I'm just a poor orphan, just a crippled Jewish girl. I know that what they're doing is no small thing. True, I don't get any pay, but what more can I ask if they take care of me, if they feed me, and if it all happens through God's great mercy."

"Sarah, Sarah!" called an impatient voice from the flat opposite Annele's.

"Yes, yes, yes! Right away, right away, Madam! Dear Madam," called Sarah in reply, and tripping and stumbling on her little posts she disappeared through the door opposite.

The bustle of work on Green Street seemed to be even fuller and richer than it had been on Long Dam. Beside her previous employers, Līziņa had added young and elegant Mrs. Rank to her list of customers. Rank, who was foreign-born, had showed up in Jelgava a few years ago and had opened a factory where, with the help of machines, meat products were processed into sausages, jellied meats, and pâtés. Within a comparatively short time he had managed to draw almost the entire town's demand for this type of merchandise to his elegant store on Grand Street by the arcade, and had completely outrivaled his competitors, the small-scale producers who, working in their butcher shops with hand-held chopping knives, had satisfied the town's daily consumption until now. Who would now want to go shopping at the butcher shop or in some small meat store if the same merchandise – oh, and even better merchandise than that – could be had amid shiny mirrors, attractively packaged, handed to the customers by dexterous shop assistants, looking as though they'd just been hatched, stiffly pomaded, clad in white like the acolytes of priests? The shopper could follow every bite as it was processed from its original state and made its way through various machines, and could see that not a single speck of dust, not a single germ or other harmful substance adhered to it. This product could be enjoyed without any doubts, with confidence, worth more to a store than huge assets, for like a magic wand confidence drew to it all the tiny rivulets of small change that until then had flowed where they pleased, to all sorts of little shops, while now they collected in the deep riverbed of Rank's big cash register. Rank's business flourished, to the delight of the people of Jelgava. The salesclerks, initially only one, then two, three, and finally four of them, could barely handle the work, particularly at night, when the customers who bought an eighth, a quarter, and half a pound came flooding into the store, for it was only in the evening that a large part of the population – workingmen, office clerks, artisans, schoolboys, farmers, who lived on dry food all day long – would treat themselves to a glass of tea and a snack bought at Rank's store.

Rank was said to be rich. The word "factory owner" had magic power. Think of all the things a factory owner like him could afford! According to Rank, the town was too cramped for a team of horses and a carriage. As for his wife, he brought her straight from abroad. Of course, people did say she didn't have a penny to her name, but she really knew how to spend money. What else would you expect of a rich factory owner's wife? No reason for her to be stingy, was there?

Līziņa had many stories to tell about Mrs. Rank, but Aunt Meire also knew a lot, all of them in the version she had heard from her neighbors with those wide ribbons on their caps, and they in turn knew them as they had heard them from their acquaintances. Everything that had to do with Mrs. Rank was discussed through and through, for everything that was associated with her was so fresh and delightful. She wore her hat differently than the women of Jelgava, tossed her shawl across her shoulder differently, said hello, talked, laughed, sat down differently – flinging one leg so freely across the other – treated her household help differently, had them cook the food differently – why, the women of Jelgava wouldn't even take such stuff in their mouths! But all these things notwithstanding, everyone thought this beautiful and graceful foreigner was a feast for the eyes.

Annele was interested in one thing.

"What about books, does Mrs. Rank have any books?"

"Books?"

Līziņa shrugged.

"Not a one. I've never seen anything resembling a book at her house."

"A foreigner living without books! What does she do all day, then?"

"My dear child, you want to know what she does? There aren't enough hours in the day for her. She goes through the house like a whirlwind. Mornings, she's off to the market. I have to go with her. She talks to all the market women, she's learning Latvian, I have to be the interpreter. Then back to the house, into the kitchen. Either there's a cake or some such to be baked, or some other "extra" to be prepared. Or the jars of preserves in the pantry need to be rearranged. Then back to me to help me sew. That's no end of a nuisance. Rip, alter, rearrange interminably. Whatever she liked yesterday no longer appeals to her today, while tomorrow she's sure to like the things she liked the day before yesterday. Then off to the shops. That's her work for the afternoon. Again I have to go with her. And once there we turn every shelf upside down. And at night Madam sits with her legs stretched in front of her: "Oh dear, what a lot of running about! So much work! I'm dog tired.""

One morning someone came running up the outside stairs. Līziņa pricked up her ears.

"That's Mrs. Rank."

And that very moment she was inside. The door flew out of her hand and banged into the wall. She laughed. "Forgive me, forgive me! I'm in such a hurry." Brown-eyed, bright and lively like a little spark, she shook hands with them all.

"Good morning, good morning! Ah, your mother? Well, how is your health?"

"Mother's German is poor."

"So's my Latvian. It's a nuisance, a real nuisance!"

Mrs. Rank sighed regretfully and tipped her little feather-trimmed hat to one side. The next moment she turned to Līziņa with a reproach.

"And why don't you come, huh? I've been waiting for you for ages and ages."

It was only a few days since Līziņa had been at the Ranks'.

"I thought all our work was finished."

"Finished! But we forgot that I have to go to the ball, don't you know!"

"What ball? There was no mention of a ball!"

"Well, there is now. The big ball, the one the trade unions are having. My husband says: even though we're factory owners, we can't be different and not go. Solidarity demands it. And I don't mind going. But now – off to the shops. I need dresses, dresses! We're going to have to move full speed ahead. And I'm taking you with me without delay."

Līziņa folded the work she was currently doing. Mrs. Rank would brook no hesitation.

Humming softly under her breath and pulling her gloves on and off, Mrs. Rank waited impatiently for Līziņa to change in the room next door. Then suddenly something occurred to her.

"Listen, listen, this is urgent! You have to come to this ball, too, you know. No doubt about it, you've simply got to come!"

Līziņa came out and stood in the doorway.

"Me? No, that's impossible. What would I do there?"

"Listen to her: what would I do there? You'll dance! What else do people do at a ball! Yes indeed! No sooner said than done. I'm taking you with me. No ifs, ands, or buts."

"I don't know anybody there."

"You will. I can guarantee that you'll have the greatest success." And, half-whispering: "There's a certain person who's got his eye on you. I'll tell you his name, shall I?"

"Nonsense! There's no such person!"

Līziņa protested, blushing.

And hurriedly added:

"Now we can leave."

Mrs. Rank took a sidelong glance at her with a playful grin. She shook her finger at her.

"Tut, tut, tut, Miss Līziņa!"

They both left.

Annele remained deep in thought.

What had that Mrs. Rank been saying? What did it mean? There's a certain person who's got his eye on Līziņa? Who could that be?

A few days later Līziņa came home from the Ranks' and tossed a light little parcel on the table. Laughing:

"That's going to be my ball gown."

"Oh dear, daughter, how could you!" Mother was shocked. In her opinion a ball, like a book read at the wrong time, was for gentlefolk only.

"Don't be shocked, Mother dear. I didn't buy it. Mrs. Rank is determined that I should go to the ball, and she'll make sure I do. At the store she kept questioning me which fabric I liked the best. I liked this one, and so she bought it for me and gave it to me as a present to pay me back for the rush of getting everything ready in time."

"Is it expensive?"

"Not at all. I had already suspected what she had in mind, and I didn't even look at the expensive ones. This one is a nice summer fabric. Nothing pretentious. I'll have it done in two days. And this ball isn't going to cost me a penny. I've got shoes. I've got some white net gloves I wove myself. As for the dress, I'm going to make it very simple, full and gathered, with short sleeves, and a kerchief tied across the bodice, knotted in big loops in the back. I've planned it all, and it will be very becoming. That fashion is called à la Marie Antoinette, and it's all the rage now."

"What's à la Marie Antoinette? Is it named after that French queen who was beheaded on a scaffold?" Annele wanted to know. "I've read about her."

"That could be."

"Goodness! You'd better not do it that way, then!" exclaimed Mother with a shudder.

"Oh, Mommy, that happened so very long ago!" Līziņa easily dispelled her idle fears.

This marked the beginning of a tempestuous rush of activity, like getting ready for a festival. Mother washed, starched, ironed petticoats, while the two sisters fell to work with a vengeance. Since Līziņa enjoyed the work, it grew and blossomed under her fingers. By evening the body of the dress was done, and only the trimming still needed to be added, all those delicate flounces, ruches, loops, and knots that give a dress that unique, inimitable beauty. Evening came all too soon.

"Why don't you stop now? After all, tomorrow will be another sleepless day," urged Mother.

"In a minute, in a minute! Just a little while longer."

"I can't understand how you can spend your time thinking about such frippery. After all, when you're a working person, sleep is precious."

Mother shook her head dubiously. She could understand anything that had to do with work, but the word joy was absent from the dictionary of her life.

Līziņa looked up with shining, joyful eyes.

"Didn't you ever dance, Mommy?"

"How could I have? I was never one to go to taverns, I married young, and in my day a married woman would never have gone whirling about on the dance floor, you know. That would have been a scandal."

"Those days must have been something! At our ball, Mrs. Rank is going to be the leading dancer. I'd be willing to bet on it."

"But what about you? Will you know how to dance the way the townspeople do?"

"You want to see?" exclaimed Līziņa and jumped to her feet. She had already taken off her shoes, and now she quickly threw the dress she was making over her head, stood in the middle of the room, began to turn, humming softly, in a kind of swaying motion. Left, then right, faster and faster, more and more lithely, she twirled about with rippling movements, flourishes, sudden turns, obeying her own voice like some magic flute.

Mother was filled with amazement.

"Well, I never! Your limbs are as loose as a puppet's. Where did you learn those trills?"

"There, you see, I'm not going to tread on anyone's toes at the ball. But here comes a new figure."

Again she took wing, radiant, smiling. This was not the everyday Līziņa, but someone altogether different. Annele was reminded suddenly of the winter night at Spring Farm when she was very young. Windows green with ice. The house flooded with moonlight. And Līziņa dancing there with Karlīne, Luze, and the herd girls, all of them shimmering green in the greenish light, like moon maidens.

"Oh, oh, oh!"

A loud sob that seemed to come from a choking throat suddenly startled everybody and caused the dancer to stop as well.

What was that?

There, leaning against the doorjamb, hugging it tight, stood Sarah. She swallowed, trying to restrain her sobs, and could not control them.

"Sarah, Sarah! What's wrong? What's happened?"

"Nothing, nothing! Oh, nothing!" She hurriedly wiped the tears from her cheeks, laughing with her eyes, begging with her lips.

"Forgive me, forgive me! I didn't mean to. But it just slipped out. It's so incredible! Oh, I am so thrilled. Do dance, Miss! Please, oh please! It's so heavenly to see. Please, oh please!"

"Enough, enough!" Līziņa laughed and dropped on a chair.

"What happened to you, Sarah?" For tears were still pouring down her cheeks.

"Oh, nothing! It's nothing, I tell you. Don't listen. Just a stupid girl bawling. I was in the kitchen and heard the sound of dancing, and I took the liberty of coming in. And then suddenly it just grabbed me. I was so thrilled. When I was little and played in the yard with the children of your people, they told me a story: once upon a time, there was a poor girl who turned into a princess and drove to the ball at the royal palace. And I suddenly remembered, I remembered – oh – oh – – "

So as not to have to show her eyes anymore, she turned suddenly and disappeared through the door.

"Sarah sees me as a princess. That's nice!"

"Sarah thinks that she herself can never be such a princess. She's chained to the ground. That's why she's crying."

⸻ ❦ ⸻

The evening of the ball had arrived.

Līziņa stood there all dressed up. The happier and the more excited she was, the more her hair curled around her head like a garland. She looked majestic and inviolate in her flounces and ruches. Sarah, who this time had asked for special permission to come over, walked around her again and again, picked up now one end of a loop of ribbon, now another, always excusing herself first: "I won't get it dirty, I promise! I rubbed my fingernails with soap." She looked her fill: "Oh, oh, oh!" – shook her head in admiration, and without much more talk left quietly.

Līziņa was still lingering, waiting for something.

"Don't you have to go now?"

"Yes, yes, Mommy!"

There was an unexpected knock. A gentleman they did not know, wearing a shiny top hat, a coat over his shoulders, came in. Under the coat gleamed the broad front of a white waistcoat and a white tie. Brown, glittering eyes saw nothing but Līziņa. The ends of his mustache, twirled into pointed handlebars, trembled slightly.

"Good evening, Ma'am! Shall I have the honor of accompanying you to the ball?"

"Very kind of you. Thank you so much."

The two of them left.

Annele kept looking at the door for a long time.

Wasn't that the gentleman who "had his eye" on Līziņa, as Mrs. Rank had said? There was no doubt about it. It was him, none other.

⸻ ❦ ⸻

Līziņa lay in bed, and next to her on a chair like a cloud of wrinkles was the dress with its frills and flounces. Her eyes were open, sparkling with the same little flames of pleasure as last night when she had left for the ball.

"Have you had enough sleep?"

"Definitely. If it were only possible, I could start all over again."

"Then you had a good time!"

"Take a look at my shoes! Just don't let Mother see them," she laughed gaily. The shoes were ruined.

"There, you see. Now I'll have to earn myself a new pair."

And she said this with such satisfaction – as though it was a piece of great good luck to earn money for a new pair of dancing shoes.

"Did you dance just with the one that came to take you to the ball?"

"No-o-o!" drawled Līziņa. "He didn't even get close to me. At a ball it's like this: once they start pestering one dancer, there's no end to it."

"Fancy that!" said Annele.

Spring in Town

Saturday night, and work was over. Līziņa hurriedly ironed one more time the black silk skirt that must be delivered to Mrs. Tiedemann, the pastor's widow, by this evening, for tomorrow one of her many sons was being confirmed. Annele stood waiting while her sister was still carefully folding and arranging pleat after pleat so that when it was taken from its wrapping, the rustling silk would look as though it had just come from the needle.

"Run along, Annele, take it over! But not under your arm. Carry it lightly on your arm."

"All right, all right!"

"You know the address?"

"I do!"

The girl grabs the parcel and is out the door. Out in the open!

A wave of warm air caresses her. The streets were clean, washed by the rain last night and that noon. Barely audible, a distant murmur as from many beehives hummed in her ears. It was the big rivers carrying away the winter's ice. There was something unaccustomed in the air. Alertness, attentiveness, expectation. A sense as of sleepers waiting for morning, their blankets still over their eyes, but their eyelids already half open. And who were these sleepers? The buds of the earth, the shoots of the earth! Tomorrow was Palm Sunday.

Broken in the middle, a greenish-red ring embraced the gray rooftops, but toward the south black and red piles of clouds rose layer by layer, while above them grew foam-white walls like blossoms with their petals ready to drop. Annele had never before seen such a beautiful sky in town. That scene up there was a town too, a town of clouds whose builders and painters were hard at work splashing about, their brushes dripping with light from a distant, invisible sun. As long as towers and domes were growing and taking shape up there, Annele couldn't leave without watching, but walked up the quiet street and returned the same way, grateful and happy. Finally, just as it seemed that the cloud city was completed, a broad, bloated hand crept out from below and swept away walls, columns, towers; a black finger poked into the most beautiful of the minarets that had been about to climb into the very glory of heaven. And now it was all over.

But something still shone iridescent in her breast. Something like the bliss of dreams, a sharp pain of longing, farewell greetings from the cloud city. She walked as though in a dream and, the cloud farewells still in her heart, climbed a narrow brown staircase that had recently been scrubbed till it shone, lit by a pale gaslight. A black tomcat humped his back against the locked door. He purred.

"Wait, I'll let you in. I don't have to say anything but 'Good evening!' and 'Here you are.' Then I'm free to go."

She pulled the bell cord. Stretched out her hand. But what was this? She stopped as if petrified.

If lightning had suddenly struck the staircase, she couldn't have been more terrified.

Her arm was empty.

Where was the parcel with the expensive silk dress? Where?

She can't say how she slid down the stairs, was it with both heels together? – Perhaps that's how it happened, because much later she often sees herself in dreams sliding down a long flight of stairs, and with both heels at once.

Where? Where? Where? Oh God! Suppose I don't find the parcel anymore? Suppose some uninvited hand has grabbed it?

It's already dark. But the street is deserted. Her eyes dart in one direction, then in the other. Over there? No! There? Yes, yes! As though placed there by an angel's hand, the little parcel lies peacefully by the porch of a somnolent house.

What luck, what wonderful luck!

At the top of the staircase under the little yellow flame of the gaslight stands Grietiņa, Mrs. Tiedemann's housekeeper.

"Good evening!" Annele greets her cheerfully while still at the bottom of the stairs.

"Who rang the bell here?"

It's got nothing to do with Annele. She hands over her parcel.

"Please give this to Madam."

But Grietiņa can't get over her amazement.

"Yes, but what I'd like to know is, who rang this bell? Because your arm isn't long enough to reach all the way to the top. Surely it can't have been the black tomcat that rang the bell?"

"I don't know, I'm sure! Good night, Miss Grietiņa!"

And off goes the bearer of the parcel. Grietiņa shrugs her shoulders.

"Well, bless my heart! Was it some kind of ghost that rang then? I ought to tell Madam. But why tell her? If we both don't understand something, all she says is 'dumme Gans'! That's what she says to me, but what am I supposed to answer?"

On the street, Annele stops. She can't go on. She recovers her breath, tells her heart to stop racing. She must relive it all one more time. What would have happened if she hadn't found the parcel? What would Mrs. Tiedemann have said, what about poor Līziņa – for the loss would certainly have had to be made good – what about Aunt Meire and her boarders? It would have gone from mouth to mouth the very next day. Who could have kept it quiet? And what would Annele have done herself? How could she have endured the shame and mockery that would have been directed at her? What could she have said in reply to all their questions? What excuse could she have found for what had happened? That she had been watching the clouds! Hadn't she heard, ever since she was little, the mockery that usually greeted "cloud-gazers" like her? And how could she have faced Līziņa? Could Līziņa still look at her with the same affection, would she still think Annele was a "talented" girl?

She did not spare herself. She lived through to their very depths all the troubles that might have befallen her, and finished by enjoying, equally deeply, the pleasure that had come in actuality when the parcel was luckily found, grateful that she had not been punished – that would really have been too cruel a fate – but had only been taught an easily remembered lesson.

On Easter Saturday Mother came home in high spirits, flushed. In her hands she held a little covered basket that gave off the kind of tantalizing fragrance you only smell when there's a holiday.

"What have you got there? Fresh flatcakes?"

They drew aside the cloth.

"Here, you can grab one apiece!"

"Where did you get them?"

"I baked them."

"Where?"

Mother laughed, so impishly young.

"If I tell you, you won't eat them."

"Then you've been at the Jews' house," exclaimed Līziņa, not knowing whether to continue eating the cake she had been nibbling on or to refuse it at once.

"Well, and doesn't it taste good? Where else could I have baked them? After all, there's neither a stove nor an oven in our kitchen. And when that Jewish lady kept begging me and begging me yesterday to come and light their fire and make some tea for Shabbes, because the old man was dying for something hot, I said: if you let me bake a bit of bread for the holidays, I'll come. And she was glad to. Just as long as she could get a pair of hands to do a bit of work, for they're not allowed to move as much as a finger on Shabbes, of course. And so we got to have some rolls. It wouldn't be the same without them, would it? Besides, Jānītis is coming."

Mother loved her son and was waiting for him eagerly.

The Rīga train didn't arrive until about ten, but the sisters had run to meet it a good hour earlier. Many footsteps crunched along the sidewalks going in the same direction. Some people had someone they were waiting for, others had nobody, but they, too, wanted their share of the general pleasure and excitement of anticipation. After all, you had to get more out of a night before a holiday than out of an ordinary one.

In the cemetery grounds, the graves were already green, the willow trees gleamed with a honeyed warmth, but from the station platform you could see nothing but an expanse of water rarely interrupted by narrow ribbons of raised dry land to which clung low brown shrubs swollen with sap.

Those who were waiting were in a pre-holiday mood. They chatted, exchanged witticisms, showered caustic remarks on any unfamiliar physiognomy they saw – for example, a good-looking young man in checkered bell-bottom trousers and a coat buttoned tight at the waist like a lady's, who was scurrying to and fro, haughtily pouting, and seemingly looking for something through his pince-nez. One wise guy thought this fine young gentleman had put on his mother's skirt by mistake as he ran to meet his date, another recommended that he put double windows in front of his eyes, for if he didn't he wouldn't catch sight of his intended through a single pane alone. And so their tongues wagged as they killed time; only the policeman, rattling his sword, walked about like a wound-up automaton, ill-tempered and aware of the authority vested in him, but otherwise impassive.

Emitting sparks and howls, the train finally came rushing into the station like a charger that refuses to be reined in. How lovely it must be to ride through the Easter night in such a fiery chariot! But it was also lovely to stand here and wait for its arrival. Līziņa was the first to catch sight of their brother. She ran up to him. Hugged him. Hugged him after giving him a kiss inspected him from head to foot. "It's obvious you come from Rīga!" she then said with pleasure, for the new arrival was attractively dressed. His broad-brimmed hat, his overcoat were new. Unfamiliar. He tossed a little bundle to his younger sister: "Here, you can carry this."

"What've you got inside?"

"A present for each of you. You'll see soon enough."

The older sister caressed his elbow, to which she was clinging and which she would no longer let go of.

"You're a dear."

"I've got a bit of money, too, for Mother. Whatever I managed to save. First I needed to get something to wear myself."

There was no room on the sidewalk for three people walking abreast. Annele had to walk by herself. When her brother and sister were together, she always felt a little bit like a fifth wheel. They were closer in age, and from early childhood they had held similar views about everything, as true friends and companions do, while she had always been more of a loner.

"Come on, tell me everything!" the sister urged the brother.

And he certainly had a lot to tell. Since leaving for Rīga, he hadn't been back to see the family, and he was also not much of a correspondent, so now his sister wanted to know every last detail about things he had described only in general terms: all the places he had gone to until he found a job, how he had looked both in Rīga itself and on the outskirts of town wherever he heard of anything, or wherever they needed a secretary, teacher, or office worker. How many tens of kilometers he had walked with his feet rubbed raw because there was no money for a cab. His pockets were empty. But since he hadn't given in to despair, he had finally succeeded in finding work quite unexpectedly. During the first months, when he was on his noon break, he had wandered around Bastejkalns chewing on a pretzel, for a hot lunch was out of the question. And then at his job he'd had to establish his position through a struggle with the "old man," who had wanted to test his new assistant's trustworthiness with all kinds of methods, temptations, and other German tricks, so that the devil himself could not have thought up anything more cunning; finally, taken to task and after a long talk with the new assistant, his superior had come to see what kind of a person he was dealing with, and had at last realized that it is possible to work successfully only where there is mutual respect.

"He wanted to teach me, but I taught him a lesson," their brother concluded with a laugh.

"And that was as it should be. You've got to show them that you're human too, and from then on it's plain sailing. If only you weather the hard part and get to catch your breath again, what more is there to worry about?"

But the store and the job are not all there is to life. And Rīga is full of traps and temptations. Līziņa wants to know how this young fellow is coping with those.

"But how are things otherwise? How do you spend your free time?"

"Mostly at the Society. Where else?"

"The Latvian Society?"

"That's our home. That's the gathering place for all those who have a Latvian's heart in their breast."

"At the Latvian Society! How strange and lovely that sounds! But still! What can you be doing there all the time?"

"All sorts of jobs! If only I had that much time!"

"What jobs? For you? Why, you're just a young whippersnapper!"

"And you think there are all that many people to do the work? It's true that there are a lot of members. We get not only gentlemen but also hired hands who consider themselves to be Latvians, but do you think they all want to get involved in the work? That's a different matter. Now, the ones that have a skill and are also willing to work don't have a moment's peace. For them there's no end of offices and responsibilities. And after all, who's to do the work if not the young folks?"

"True, true! But – hey, girl, where have you brought us?"

They were by the bridges.

"I wanted to look at the night," Annele explained apologetically.

"Yes, the night is beautiful."

They stopped and pensively gazed at the dark expanse overarched by the stars. Near the horizon, in gentle relief, faint dimming streaks gladdened their eyes. Those might be farms, orchards, or birch groves. The slow-flowing Driksa River was scattered full to the brim with the dissolving reflections of stars. The waters and the earth were fragrant, for there had been no frost all of Holy Week.

"How wonderful such a night is. When does a person ever get to see it, though?" said the older sister.

"And this is the way it was maybe a thousand years ago, when there was no Jelgava or anything. But the Lielupe and the Driksa flowed even then," said Annele.

And they stood silently for a while looking into the darkness, each perhaps thinking of a night like this as it had existed a thousand years ago. Then they turned back.

In the streets there were many people hurrying in the direction of the Russian church. There was a lot to see there on this night. The church was aglow with candles, and the door was open, but uninvited people were not allowed in. However, the outside was surrounded by the same restless spirits who earlier on had run to meet the train and did not know what to do with the night now that they had broken off a few crumbs. And what do you know? The dandy in checkered trousers, accompanied by a lady, also hurriedly emerged from the obscurity of the streets and disappeared in the church without any hindrance. And again sarcastic witticisms by the dozens were dropped at his heels.

"Those people in there have something holy, while out here you do nothing but snigger," someone reproved the scoffers.

"Just wait. You'll see their holy stuff. All we want is to see the holy stuff," was the reply.

"What's going to happen?"

"A whole lot of kissing, that's what," another laughed.

"When?" Līziņa unwisely asked.

"When! Oh boy, is she naive! Soon enough. When the bell starts – "

That very moment, the first stroke of the bell rang out, people shrank back, but immediately scattered in all directions screaming, for at that moment a man wearing a long robe had come running out of the church and rushed in among the crowd, shouting: "Hats off, hats off!" Those who did not manage or want to take off their hats fast enough had their hats knocked off their heads. There were shouts and screams on all sides, people were cursing, but the bells thundered in the midst of it all. Something alien and cold choked Annele's heart. Avots hurriedly dragged the sisters away.

"Let's go! What brutality!"

"Yes, let's! We shouldn't have gone and joined the crowd!"

"The Russian shows his bear's paw in more nasty ways than the German. But he'd never dare do that in Rīga. Oh, whatever people may say, there's a different spirit in our city."

On Easter Sunday, when the midday soup was already steaming in the bowl, Brother came in from a walk and immediately walked around the table inspecting it.

"What's the lunch situation? Can I invite one more person?"

"Who is this person?"

"An old classmate of mine. Kaparsons. Ever since I happened to run into him, he's been sticking to me like a bur, and I can't get rid of him. What am I supposed to do with him?"

"Where is he?"

"He stayed down in the yard. I had to find out first what you had for lunch, don't you see."

"Go ahead, bring him upstairs! I'm sure he's not the type that wants roast meat or is hard to please. He'll have to make do with what's here."

Līziņa hadn't had time to put out an extra plate when the guest already stood in the doorway. "Goodness! It's the fellow with the checkered trousers!" Annele almost blurted out. He bowed repeatedly, clicking his heels: "Prost Fest! Prost Fest! Ah!" he exclaimed in surprise as he caught sight of Līziņa.

"How do you do? We know each other, don't we? Well, how is your health?" Without waiting for a reply, he looked around him with darting eyes: where should he put his coat, and his hat? He kept on his gloves – light yellow with long cuffs – for a while, gracefully and slowly peeling one finger after another out of them; when he felt he had showed off the gloves long enough, he tossed them on the little table in

the corner. He pulled out a small handkerchief, holding it elegantly with his fingertips, flicked a bit of fluff from his trousers, wafted the handkerchief over his boots,
which shone like glass: "Patent leather!" he threw a whisper toward Mother, who
had glanced his way as she passed by to see what it was that was so shiny there. He
turned on his heel, eyes searching for something.

"You must be looking for a wall mirror? We haven't got one."

"That's all right!" the guest took a little mirror and a brush from his waistcoat
pocket, brushed his tuft of hair from one side, tossed it over to the other side, shook
his cuffs down toward his fingertips: did they notice the gold-chased green-eyed cat
heads on the cufflinks, did they see the huge signet ring on his index finger? Only
after thoroughly putting things in order did he raise his head above the horns of his
white collar, which stabbed into his chin, and address a question to Līziņa. Still in
German, though:

"Well, Ma'am, how is Her Grace, Baroness Hamann?"

"I don't know, I'm sure. Training her greyhounds at her estates, no doubt."

"Where do you know each other from?" asked Avots.

"I worked for Baroness Hamann, and Mr. Kaparsons came to the house from
the Estate Owners' Building with messages from his employers. Every once in a

while I happened to show him in. Isn't that right? You work in the Estate Owners' Building as a butler, don't you?"

Kaparsons winced as if stung by a wasp, and rose almost on tiptoe:

"Oh no, Ma'am. You're quite uninformed regarding my duties. Not a butler, no. My occupation is – in a nutshell: I am not a butler, I am a factotum. That is what I am called. It is a foreign word, and you may not be familiar with it. Fac-to-tum. Baron and Baroness Korff said to Baron and Baroness Hahn only yesterday: that Kaparsons is our factotum."

Jānis was biting his lips, while Līziņa asked:

"And what is that – a factotum? What sort of things does he have to do?"

"That's somebody who can do everything and knows how to do anything. And what does he have to do? I am just about the steward of the household. When Baron and Baroness Korff go away, all the affairs are handed over to me."

"Come on, let's sit down and eat," invited Avots. "And you'd better give your German tongue a rest now. So you don't swallow it with the Latvian broth."

"My brother Jānis is an ardent Latvian. He's joined the Latvian Society of Rīga. And he's already been elected to many offices," boasted Līziņa.

"Bah! What good are those?" Kaparsons retorted haughtily.

"No, seriously! Brother's been telling me all morning, and I can't hear enough. Our nation, our nation, that's all we hear. And just the fact that the Latvians have the kind of men he's been telling us about makes my heart leap with joy."

"I wouldn't give five kopecks for the whole lot. What men? *I* don't know them," Kaparsons said, leaning back in his chair.

"You haven't heard anything, not even about Krišjānis Kalniņš, or our great poet Auseklis? Where on earth have you been all this time?"

"I don't have the time to spend on that kind of claptrap. I pay attention to my job."

"And remain a slave and a servant."

"There have always been masters, and there always will be."

"If so, it's going to be us, the Latvians themselves."

"Well, if we're going to argue about the Latvians being the masters, you can bet your life I'll be the first. I'd love that. I'd crawl through the eye of a needle if I have to. I intend to join the upper class."

"Last night you sneaked into the Russian church, while the Russians wouldn't let the others in," Annele interrupted.

"Ah, you saw me? Too bad I didn't recognize you yesterday, I could have gotten you admission tickets. As many as you like! I'm on very good terms with those people. Ask me who I'm not on good terms with!" Kaparsons gave a self-satisfied laugh.

"You ought to come to Rīga and go to the discussion evenings," Avots fervently tried to persuade his companion. "Then you'd see Kalniņš and hear how that man can talk. He'll take the most insignificant question and analyze it so thoroughly that a new world will open before your eyes. In everything he has only one goal before his eyes: to awaken, to teach, and enlighten the people."

"That's just it – Latvians always have to be taught. Your typical Latvian is still a child and a country bumpkin."

"Don't talk so foolishly!" Avots was beginning to get excited. "You have no idea at all what it means to work for our nation. There is nothing more wonderful!"

"Nation, nation! I don't give a hoot about all that stuff!" Kaparsons, too, was getting excited.

For some time now, Mother had been signaling to her son not to annoy their visitor – how would it look? – and to come to the table. Now Līziņa, too, clapped her hands: "Enough, enough! The food's getting cold!"

Now they all sat down and began to eat with relish. That created harmony. The guest, too, when he saw that the elegant way he raised his spoon and stabbed the bone with his fork did not impress the others, gave up all elegance and concentrated only on getting more food inside him. Quite thawed out, he praised the *pīrāgi* and flatcakes, said they tasted just like country cooking, finally begged for one more plateful, adding that at home the servants' food always tasted the same whether it was a holiday or a workday, correcting himself that of course he himself pretty much got everything from the baron's own table.

"As a factotum should," agreed Līziņa. Looking at him sideways and mockingly winking, she went on:

"You know, Mr. Kaparsons, it's the greatest surprise to me that you've turned out to be Latvian. I could have sworn you were a German."

"What? Is that a fact?" Kaparsons almost jumped with joy and added, beaming at the whole table:

"That's what other people have told me, too. Well, I try. I have great success. I've already given several speeches in German."

"Speeches? Where did you give them?"

"Just recently, at my cousin's funeral in the country."

"Good gracious! Why did you speak German at this funeral?"

"Well, I had to do something, don't you see. They were so sad. Their only son!"

"But was there anybody there that understood you and your German speech?"

"I don't know. They did cry buckets, though. I don't want to boast, but that's the way it was."

"Come on, you're making it up!" laughed Jānis. "And you want me to believe you?"

"I swear to God. I can bring you witnesses. Besides, I've got the speech written down in black and white."

"It's too much trouble to figure out what it says," Jānis shrugged.

"I believe you, I believe you without witnesses," declared Līziņa, biting her lips.

"Thank you, Ma'am," Kaparsons raised his chin above the corners of his collar with a bow in Līziņa's direction. And suddenly, as if this movement had reminded him of something, he asked matter-of-factly: "Please, ladies, could you perhaps recommend a washerwoman to me? I am not satisfied with the one I've had until now, and my position demands that I change my linen frequently."

Mother, who as soon as there was a mention of work pricked up her ears as though at some joyful news, at once responded:

"I could wash your clothes for you if my daughter would agree to iron them."

"I'd be very happy," Kaparsons, hands folded, bowed to Līziņa.

And so one thing led to another talking about practical matters like these. They came to an agreement on the washing and ironing of the laundry. Annele, who had looked on the guest's dandified behavior as an amusing show, was somehow dissatisfied with this outcome. Fine, she thought. They'll wash and iron the laundry. But who's going to carry it over to Kaparsons's place? Why, who else but I myself – after all, I'm the messenger girl.

Sighing softly, she shrugged her shoulders:

"The things I have to do!"

Kaparsons was walking about with his hands in his trouser pockets and amicably admonishing Jānis:

"If I were you I wouldn't go messing about with that national stuff. What good does it do you? A man should toe the line, stand at attention, and make his way up in the world," he said, giving his own shoulders a shake and lifting his head.

"What's the use of talking to you," Jānis answered calmly, "it's a waste of time showing the sun to someone who's blind!"

"Oh, so I'm the one who's blind!" Kaparsons replied, stung. "Well, we'll see, my friend, we'll see which of us will be the first to see the sun."

"We'll see, we'll see!"

Līziņa clapped her hands abruptly.

"Enough, enough! We don't need an argument on a holiday. Why don't we sing instead?"

"Excuse me, but I still have important business to attend to today," said Kaparsons, preparing to leave.

"Thank God!" Annele watched him leave with a sigh of relief.

"But now, let's get going! What have you brought us from Rīga? You did say you sing in the chorus of the Latvian Society, didn't you? You're going to have to teach us all the songs they sing there."

"Good, I can do that," Jānis responded joyfully. Standing before them like a conductor, he threw back his curly head.

And now they began singing fervently, as they had at New Farm when Brother came home for the holidays and brought the songs he had learned in school. By now there were a good many that they were familiar with already: "Among My Brothers," "I Planted a Birdcherry Tree," "What the Crested Titmouse Sings," and others. However, there were new ones to learn as well. Annele liked to sing, and to become intoxicated with the sound of their voices, with the way they all harmonized so wonderfully! To think of all the songs she'd already sung in her lifetime! And at that moment she felt that songs were the loveliest thing there was.

When a pause set in, Aunt Meire appeared in the door.

"I've been listening and thinking all this time: those girls certainly sound good, but add a man's voice, and you've really got something. Where'd you get that voice? From your father, huh? It's turned out so velvety," she praised Brother.

"Yes, I love his voice, too," said Līziņa, hugging Brother's curly head affectionately and pressing her cheek against it. They both looked very much alike, and their younger sister couldn't stop admiring them. Līziņa was so uninhibited, and not at all afraid to plunge both hands into Brother's curly hair and to rumple it thoroughly. Now, would Annele ever have dared to do that? Never!

Day by day the weather grew warmer. The sisters worked with the windows open. The quiet and clean backyard ended in a garden hidden from prying eyes by a double fence: one a rail fence, one made of boards cut in a zigzag pattern at the top. Day by day the foliage of the trees and shrubs in the garden swelled fuller of buds and greener. One day, sudden gusts of sound suddenly burst forth from the open windows of the house on the street side.

"What's that?" Annele exclaimed in surprise.

"A piano. Somebody's playing. And we get a free concert."

"A piano! I've never heard one before."

For a long time she listened, fascinated.

"A piano, a piano! How wonderful it sounds! As soon as I can, I'm going to learn to play the piano like that, too."

Meanwhile, Sarah told her that the person playing the piano was the landlady's daughter. The landlady had recently acquired the house from a landowner who had formerly owned large estates and had squandered all his property playing cards. The house, said Sarah, did not provide a large income, but the landlady wasn't exactly poverty-stricken. Her husband, a miller, had left her a heavy purse. The daughter had had a lot of schooling and was a real restless spirit. Now at the relatives', now some place else, now back home again. That's because she had had an unhappy love affair, Sarah whispered, her hand over her mouth so the words wouldn't carry too far. No peace anywhere. She wouldn't even sit at the piano very long. She'd play for a bit, then run through the house, race around with the dog and the cat or off to the garden. The daughter was her mother's spoilt darling, but not so the son. The son was the household drudge. He hadn't been able to finish school, and now he hung around the house, did all household chores, even swept the yard and the street at night, when no one was watching. But he spent most of his time in the garden. Looked after it like it was a baby.

With the breezes of spring, the inhabitants of this big house finally surfaced. When the pearl strings of sound suddenly broke off indoors, Miss Lonija, the one who had been unhappy in love, soon appeared in the yard. Her throat swathed in a shawl, her face pale under a shock of bushy hair, without raising her eyes, she clattered in her high heels across the smooth cobblestones of the pavement over to the garden, to return a short while later with an armful of flowering branches, whatever happened to be in bloom at the time: bird cherry, acacia, or spirea. And indoors, the rhythms of sound once more began surging up, down. After this, the landlady herself went to the garden – a stout woman, always dressed in her Sunday best, a long gold chain wrapped twice around her neck, shiny earrings in her ears, always dignified and stern, as though to remind everyone constantly: I am in charge here. Mind your manners! Young Uldis would slide across the yard like a shadow. With his homespun suit closely buttoned, his cap pulled down low over his forehead, he seemed to have no eyes or ears for the world.

What Annele had imagined really did come to pass. Every Sunday she had to go to Kaparsons's place with a bundle of ironed laundry.

"Do I really have to do it?"

"Yes, you have to taste the bitterness of life. It can't be helped."

She did not like this errand, or the house to which she had to go. Quickly she slipped in through the door, as though afraid that somebody would see her enter. A vast vestibule with dark oak paneling engulfed her. The stairs as she ran up seemed to groan. At the top there were many doors on each side. The last door at the end of the corridor led into Kaparsons's room. Behind the door, no matter when she knocked, the same voice would always answer, "Herein!"

The room was large. Quite dark. The paneling of the walls was dark, the windows recessed. In one of these recesses, behind a table covered with piles of books, stood Rimeiks, Kaparsons's roommate. Perhaps he was a relative of Kaparsons's, or perhaps he merely shared his quarters. As soon as he saw who had arrived, he disappeared through a side door to call Kaparsons, but he would not come back in with him. Kaparsons, as always, was supple, lithe, affable, and inviting.

"Come in, come in, young lady! Closer! Take a seat! Do take a seat, please!"

No matter how much he insisted, Annele ignored him, remaining where she stood. After a while Rimeiks came in and stayed by the table, stiff as a ramrod, his hair sticking up like bristles. Meanwhile Kaparsons darted about the room, looking in the dresser, counted money, and kept repeating at odd moments:

"You could sit down, you know!"

"That's all right! I'll stand."

Nothing came of Kaparsons's search. He had no intention of finding anything, of course.

"Tell you what, I'd better come over myself and bring everything that's necessary."

"All right. Goodbye!"

And the girl was already out the door.

Kaparsons began to come over more and more often. And every time it seemed as though he had brought about some sort of transformation in his person. At times some particular movement would stand out with special emphasis. Either he would drum on the tabletop in a peculiar way with his fingers, where another giant-size signet ring shone on his index, or he would stick out his chest garbed in a silk waistcoat they hadn't seen before, or he would gesture with his hand, in which fluttered a kerchief with polka-dotted borders – all of these movements came off not as something belonging to him, but as though they had the things stuck to them with which he had decked himself out. And Annele who, though she looked at the visitor only briefly and intermittently, never lost sight of him, thought: "That must be the way his barons act."

"Well, what's your Rimeiks up to?" inquired Līziņa, for Kaparsons enjoyed talking about Rimeiks.

Rimeiks was a former schoolmate and distant relative of his. So Kaparsons was boarding him half for free, he said. He said he not only gave Rimeiks a place to sleep, but Rimeiks even got to eat there, for as everyone knows, there's no cheeseparing in the kitchen of the gentry. Obviously, there's plenty of everything, and of course there are no dogs and cats in town to take care of the leftovers. So there's enough for every Tom, Dick, and Harry.

"You wait! Rimeiks will be a great man one of these days, and then he'll repay you for everything."

"What, him?"

Kaparsons gave a loud laugh and could not find the words to reply immediately. He paced back and forth through the room a few times jingling his little gilded watch chain. Then, stretching his right hip across the table and putting his weight on it, he asked benevolently:

"So you think Rimeiks is going to do better than me?"

Līziņa shrugged.

"How should I know? He does study so terribly hard."

"He studies like an idiot. This year, he's planning to take his teacher's exams, a couple of years later it's going to be the private tutor exam, and after that I'm sure he'll be clambering higher to be a senior teacher. That young fellow won't rest till he gets there."

"Well, there you are!"

"What's so bad about studying?" Annele interjected, for her most fervent interests were being touched upon here.

"Bad? Who says studying is bad? But this guy's turning into a block of wood, you know. Blind and stupid. All the stuff he crams into his head lies there like iron fetters. He can't even budge it himself."

"So you're saying he doesn't have much sense himself."

"Exactly."

"Then you must be a lot smarter."

"And how! Without that whole pile of book learning, you'll see where I'm going to be and where 'certain other people' are going to be."

Kaparsons pronounced this "certain other people" so meaningfully that it could be interpreted as referring to someone quite different from Rimeiks – for example, to Jānis Avots in Rīga, for he did not have a good opinion of young men who had a better education than he did himself.

This annoyed Līziņa. And she retorted:

"Some great man you're going to be! Still the baron's errand boy."

"What makes you think I'll stay with the baron? If you're quick-witted and bold, you can get wherever you like. When I've had enough, I'll leave. I'm keeping my eyes open. You'll see, I may very well have something of my own in no time at all."

"Such as, for example?"

"Well, let's say a hotel."

"Why not say a pub?"

"A pub brings in money."

"There, you see!" said Līziņa in a tone that implied: "There, you see how far your aspirations will get you!"

But Kaparsons was unabashed. He bent very low over the table, so low that the tip of his nose almost touched the curls on Līziņa's temple. And he was as sweet and sugary as syrup.

"And maybe you could come, too, and be the innkeeper's wife."

Līziņa looked at him sitting there. A handsome young fellow, with brazenly glittering brown eyes and red cheeks. A really handsome young fellow. His shiny watch chain gleamed, draped on both sides across his baronial silk waistcoat, and so did his long, crescent-shaped, trimmed fingernails, which he kept flashing past her eyes.

And what did she say?

"Listen! Why don't you trim those spades of yours in a civilized fashion? You're not going to go and dig ditches with them, are you?"

Kaparsons straightened up with a jerk. Stiff and speechless. Completely stiff and speechless. "Kh, kh, kh!" he finally managed to utter.

"You jolted me out of my mood."

"How so, how so?" Līziņa refused to understand.

"What a way to talk! When it's quite obvious to you that I – why I keep coming here. Yes, here you've got a person talking seriously, and look at the way you react! A person talking completely seriously, I assure you. Quite seriously."

"That person is talking drivel," said Līziņa and pushed him and his hip off the table so forcefully that he barely managed to balance himself on his feet.

Kaparsons remained silent for a while, walking back and forth, sticking out his chest, and expelling his breath violently through his nostrils.

"All right, have it your way! If it won't be you, it'll be somebody else," he finally said spitefully. "Goodbye then!"

"Now that factotum will stop coming over," Līziņa thought after Kaparsons left in none too rosy a mood.

But he did come.

One evening he came running in hurriedly with little slips of red paper in his hands. Without even saying hello, he urged the sisters:

"Quick, quick! To the theater! Here are some tickets for you."

"Tickets? Where did you get them? Did you buy them?"

"Why should I buy them! The baron and baroness had handfuls of them. Said I could have as many as I wanted. The baron and baroness buy up tickets and let people in for free. Just so there's a full house. Imagine: musicians and singers from Rīga. Magnificent, magnificent!"

"Then I suppose we must go."

"And also I want you to see I don't hold a grudge."

"No, no, no! I see that now, of course."

Without saying another word, Līziņa threw down her work. It took the sisters only a few minutes to change. It was high time if they wanted to get to the theater by the time the performance started. Out of breath they ran, out of breath they arrived at the gloomy building that stood on the other side of the market square. Cheerless and dark all year round, it had now opened its doors, through which people flowed from all directions. The damp basement air felt rather stuffy. The throng of people was sweeping up the steep staircase.

Halfway up the stairs, Kaparsons turned to go in another direction, urging the sisters:

"Go on, go on! Your seats are up at the top. In the gallery. I exchanged mine for a different one. My position demands it."

"What a clown!" Līziņa gave a laugh, and they went upstairs.

Their seats were at the very edge of a horseshoe-shaped semicircle. Above their heads was the ceiling, below their feet an abyss. Behind them, rising like steps, were a few more rows of seats, and those who sat in the last one almost touched the ceiling with their heads. There were many different kinds of people. Like the giant's daughter in the story who scooped the plowman and his field into her apron, Annele with a quick glance scooped into herself everything she saw, so that later, at her leisure, she could go over each impression again. Below, various kinds of musical instruments were humming, squeaking, whistling, fiddling, as though arguing among themselves, and then suddenly shouted out to each other in what seemed like one voice, and let fly so noisily that not only the naive country girl but even the worldly-wise townspeople who surrounded her gave a jump in their seats. A brightly colored wall burst open at the sides, and people disguised in all sorts of costumes began to twirl on what looked like a huge tabletop, twisting their bodies every which way, dancing, singing, and talking strange talk. It was an overpowering impression that attacked her with such force and chaos that her senses had to struggle to keep from being overcome with confusion as well. Of course she could see *what* was happening, but it wasn't easy to figure out *why* it happened just that way. Her sister, however, replied:

"You and your questions! What's the sense of trying to figure out why those comedians do things? Just watch and that's that!"

And she did watch. When the curtain fell, Līziņa had to recall her from what seemed like a dream.

But why, why, Annele kept asking for a long time to come, living with these first impressions of the theater as with a lovely, extraordinary dream.

⸙

Next time she went to Kaparsons's house with her bundle of laundry, no one replied when she knocked, and so she finally opened the door without waiting to be asked inside. Rimeiks's place was empty. She was used to seeing him standing there with his hair sticking up, like a motionless watchman, and she was somewhat surprised that he was no longer there in his usual place. But here came Kaparsons himself, dashing into the room. And his first words were:

"Well, how did you like the theater?"

Annele answered that she had liked it very much. Kaparsons, smiling slyly, nodded his head.

"And who deserves gratitude for that?"

The girl was a little surprised.

Gratitude? Hadn't there been gratitude? She thought she and Līziņa had both expressed their thanks several times. But, if it was necessary, it was not hard to say it one more time:

"Well then, thank you again!"

"That's not enough!"

"What? Not enough?"

Kaparsons turned this way and that, dissatisfied, and went on flashing his bright eyes before her, shiny as the buttons on a policeman's uniform. His hands in his trouser pockets, he approached so close to her he was almost stepping on her feet. The girl looked at him blankly: well, what more was she expected to do? What exactly did he want?

"Gratitude must be shown in a real way."

"In a real way? What do you mean: in a real way?"

He must be thinking that now he ought no longer to pay for the laundry. Well, let him go without paying!

"You don't know? And it's so easy!"

He must be trying to teach her. His breath blew all around her like a summer wind. And why does he sidle closer and closer to her? And why does he suddenly grab her forearm like that?

"Let me go!"

But now she sees that she can't escape. Now both of Kaparsons's arms block her way. And then they're around her waist. Honestly, he's as stupid as Konrāds. What does he want? A kiss? What next! What next! Like an eel she suddenly contracts, slides, and slithers out from under his arms. Her eyes flash lightnings. A hail of incoherent words explodes all over Kaparsons.

"I! You! I! You're crazy! Crrrazy!"

This "crrrazy" must have shaken Kaparsons into the bowels of the earth, for she can no longer see him. She doesn't know what is happening to her, for she has tossed her bundle down haphazardly and is outside again. Never again is she going to set foot in that Kaparsons's house. He'd better get that into his head!

The Whitsunday Picnic

"If the weather is good on Whitsunday, we're going to have a picnic."
This was the piece of news Līziņa brought from Aunt Meire's house. That's what they'd both arranged. The boarders are going to the country, and Aunt is free.

"Were you thinking of going as far as Baloži Cemetery?" asked Mother. Baloži Cemetery was the furthest she had walked outside Jelgava.

"No, not Baloži Cemetery, but to a real green forest. A spring forest."

The days before Whitsunday were windy and overcast. However many times their glances flew out the window like Noah's doves seeking land, they returned downcast. There was nothing good to see. So their plans for Whitsunday might easily go up in smoke.

"Don't worry! No matter what the weather is like, we're going. Just so long as it doesn't rain. After all, Whitsunday comes but once a year."

Annele thought so too. And she believed the weather would be good, that it had to be good when they were going on their first picnic.

Whitsunday did not deceive their hopes. When the picnickers rose early, the morning and its bright sun already lay in the spacious courtyard, making the freshly painted garden fence sweat so that it looked as if it had wept greasy tears. Mother had already made sandwiches. The girls got dressed. What should they wear? Līziņa had sewn a little green belt for her much-washed, much-altered simple white dress, and Annele, too, had a light-colored dress, a gift from their Lithuanian relative, altered to fit her. It did seem as though Mother didn't want to let her wear it. Just to go out in the woods and fields?

"But Whitsuntide is nicest out in the woods and fields, and that's why you need festive clothes there as well."

And Aunt Meire, who was not long in arriving, agreed. She came in, tall and stately, and her wide eyes smiled like the Whitsunday morning itself when she scrutinized the girls with pleasure.

"Nice. That's the way it ought to be. A holiday should be a holiday, and not remind you of workaday dust."

But then she urged them to hurry. She had left some people waiting downstairs. She didn't want them to get bored.

"What people?"

"Mrs. Emke and her son. A fine woman. You already know her, Līziņa."

"I do, from when she came to you with her troubles. But I don't know a thing about her son. Is he grown-up?"

"He was just confirmed. He's getting ready to go to Rīga to start at some sort of job. I'm very happy about it. He'll survive anywhere. Takes after his mother."

"Then I'm sure he's a decent person. But why are they coming with us?"

"I invited them myself. When I told her we were going on a picnic, she looked at me with such excitement and longing in her eyes that I couldn't help asking her too. Imagine! Born and raised in the country, and here it's been years since she last dipped her feet in dewy grass. She's got no family in the country, and after all a working person can't take extra time off to go and walk in the country. When it's an occasion like this one, it's like a great gift."

Mrs. Emke and her son were waiting by the gate. A tall, thin woman, a little hunched over. Maybe that was from carrying laundry baskets or other heavy loads. She wore a black alpaca jacket, and a silk kerchief on her head. These were her churchgoing clothes, without signs of wear and tear, while her son wore his confirmation outfit. So new and clean, without a speck of dust, down to the black peaked cap on his head. Their clothes had been tended and maintained by careful hands.

"My Andris," Mrs. Emke humbly pointed at her son, and her gaze slid over him from head to foot with hidden pride and yet anxiously, as though wondering whether everything about him was in order. Were the others, too, happy to see him? Would he know how to behave?

He does. He raises his cap, bows to each of them in turn as he shakes hands. Still like a boy who learned to do this in school.

Aunt now links arms with Mother Avots, Līziņa walks with Mrs. Emke, while Andris is left for Annele. Turns out they're all in couples. Their footsteps resound rhythmically in the early morning street.

Annele is tormented by one thought: she's going to have to have some kind of conversation with the unknown boy. But how should she begin?

"Lovely weather we're having today."

"Yes."

"Yesterday it certainly looked as though there'd be rain."

"Yes."

"The days were so windy and cool."

"Yes."

How long would they keep turning around the weather, like the sails of a windmill? Līziņa would often say that if a person didn't know how to start a conversation with a stranger, they immediately clutched at the weather, like a drowning person clutching at a straw. As though there was nothing else to talk about.

"The streets are so quiet, as though nobody lived here anymore."

"Yes."

"Probably the people of Jelgava are all still in bed."

"Yes."

"It's a wonder that they're not getting ready to go on a picnic like us."

That topic, too, was exhausted, and again they walked along as though struck dumb.

Līziņa looked back. Why were they so quiet back there? She came to their rescue.

"Can you see that tiny white cloud in the clear blue sky above the tower of St. John's Church?"

Where? Where? Not one of them could.

"But I can. Sure, it's no bigger than the head of a pin. But it means a lot. It means we'll have fine weather clouds all day today. I know the sky from back when I was a herder."

St. John's was left behind them. Now came houses with little gardens. Here, acacia bushes were already in bloom, lilacs scented the air. Annele directed Andris's eyes now right, now left, and he gratefully replied and no longer made her wait for his answers. Thus their mouths had been unsealed and their talk began to blossom. Their walk now became rich, for they included every detail in their morning's delight: a canary loudly whistling in a cage by an open window, children in blue pinafores staring sullenly at the passersby as they took bites out of their holiday sweet rolls, a cat which, frightened for some unknown reason, arched its back, shot out between the quick feet of the walkers, and vanished in a willow by the roadside. Each impression went from one of them to the other and thus became their common property, but many impressions were such that the two of them received them merely by communicating with brief glances or smiles. And it was all delightful, as is every experience that is novel, fresh, and unique, as though newly emerged from nonbeing.

Across the fields they went, towards the woods. The dirt path was easier on their feet. A grove of young trees rose up from the plain and concealed what was behind them.

"Jelgava's gone!" exclaimed Līziņa.

"So what!" said Annele as though burying something, and they all laughed at this happily.

The order of the procession had long since fallen apart. The young people were in front. Aunt, who had untied the ribbons of the bonnet from her perspiring face, was already beginning to cast questioning looks at the others from time to time: how about sitting down for a while?

"Keep walking, keep walking! Not till we get to the edge of the big woods – there we can have a rest," Līziņa urged them on.

But look how far the big woods were! Quite a distance away. Over there, a farm lay in Sunday peace. Someone was moving about in a field at a snail's pace, stopped, looked at the townsfolk suspiciously from afar, kept moving. He had set his mind at rest. Apparently these would be neither the kind of people that would trample his meadows nor company come to call.

A couple of horses were grazing tethered close to the farm buildings. There were no other farm animals in sight. Here were meadows that cattle must be kept out of. As far as the eye could see, brightly speckled with shimmering flowers, the meadows lay before them like an exhibition of richly woven woolen shawls.

Andris picked a flower here, a flower there along the roadside. He tied them into a posy.

"For you!" he presented it to Līziņa.

And soon he had another one ready. This one was for Annele: "For you!"

"What? Me, too?" she was surprised. "I can pick my – " Then she broke off and flushed. She mustn't reject his kindness like this. "Thank you very much!" she curtsied. Flushed even more deeply. A curtsy? Surely that wasn't necessary? Andris wasn't a grown-up, was he? Someone who had to be respected? She glanced at him stealthily. How was she to know? After all, he had been confirmed.

"Don't you think the woods might be too far for us?" Aunt Meire piped up in back of them, somewhat out of breath.

"No, no! We'll run and pick a spot! Meanwhile you can follow slowly. We'll wait till noon," answered one of these cruel young folks.

And the light-colored dresses of the girls went flashing across the flowering meadow, dwindling till they looked like a patch of blossoms.

"Just try and catch those rabbits!" sighed Aunt a bit crossly. And they had no choice but to go on, for the big meadow was generally spongy and damp. It was unthinkable that they should sit down here!

The edge of the woods rose out of the marshy meadow with a dry knoll, overgrown like a pillow with rosy pussytoes. Annele bent down and lightly passed her hand over the velvety little heads. So dear, so familiar to her from the edge of the woods at Spring Farm.

"Well, isn't this like the land of Canaan? This is where we'll pitch our tents," called Līziņa, encouraging the older women who were following behind, and glanced at her sister who stood there, her arms opened wide.

"What are you waiting for? Somebody to hug you?"

"The wind!" was Annele's whispered mysterious reply. The fragrance-laden wind of the woods and meadows murmured in her hair.

"Yes, it's a gentle, gentle breeze!" agreed Līziņa, and she, too, threw down her bonnet.

"Well, you've certainly brought us to the end of the world. Let's see how you're going to get us back," Aunt wagged her finger at Līziņa, then spread her black skirts around her like a giant umbrella, and sank down on her starched petticoats.

"I'm not budging another inch."

"Who says you have to? We couldn't find a nicer spot," said Mother Avots.

The forest spread its fragrance in back of them, the meadow at their feet; in the distance were farms and birch groves. But the horizon, incredibly vast, herded pure white clouds like huge flocks of sheep.

"Didn't I say there'd be fine weather clouds? There, you see?"

Now it was time to have breakfast. The little bundles they had brought with them tickled their nostrils so tantalizingly. Each of the women opened hers. They offered each other food. With the wind blowing on them and the meadow flowers scenting them with their fragrance, the sandwiches tasted like spring and reminded Annele of her morning meals as a herd girl by which, eating with her eyes closed, she had always been able to tell the season. How delicious this meal was, on the forest carpet with its pattern of pussytoes! You'd never find a meal like this in town!

After they finished their meal, they were thirsty. They had brought cups, but where would they find water? Andris got to his feet and scrutinized the surround-

ings. Not far from them, on the left, where the meadow sank into an even deeper slough, they could see a wide ditch whose end disappeared behind a spur of forest. There must be some kind of spring there. He said he would go and take a look.

"Who's coming with me?"

"I will!" called Annele.

They ran off, waving the cups in their hands.

The end of the ditch was stuck to the foot of the hill like a slice of black bread. Water came seeping from countless tiny veins. But as soon as it flowed into the ditch, it turned muddy. How could they collect it while it was still clear? Andris knew how. He cut a switch from a nearby osier bush, carved a trough-shaped spigot, made a fairly deep cavity at the end of the ditch and drove the little trough into it. The water collected and began to drip with clear drops. When a good mouthful had collected, the boy tasted it.

"Delicious."

He handed some to Annele.

Their hands touched gently and lightly.

"Oh!" Annele blurted out.

"I'm sorry!"

Andris immediately drew back his hands.

"Well, how does it taste?"

"Good," praised Annele, glancing at Andris. The way he stood there with such a kind, questioning look. The water was good, and so was the one who had given her the water. "A nice-looking boy!" she had to admit, and it occurred to her how strange it was that just yesterday she had known nothing about him, while here they were today scooping up water together, almost friends. Funny how things went sometimes.

"But now let's bring the others something to drink."

"Yes, yes, of course!"

And now began a joyous running back and forth.

Andris collected the flow of water while Annele went to the thirsty waiting women with a full cup, then back again with an empty one, until they had all had enough to drink and, with grateful hearts, had praised the tasty mouthfuls that had been received straight from depths of the earth.

Refreshed and rested, the picnickers began planning what to do next. But Aunt was resolutely opposed to moving on. She wanted to save her strength for the walk back.

Mrs. Emke had seen some marsh tea blooming at the edge of the woods. She must pick some to make tea with. Annele's mother, too, knew a lot of spring-blooming plants that were useful against all types of ailments. She definitely couldn't pass up this chance to gather them. There were heaps of them growing here.

"As for us, we could play 'last couple out' if only there were more of us," suggested Andris.

"Why not? After all, we've got one couple and one caller. – One, two, three! Last couple out!" Līziņa immediately clapped her hands and braced herself in readiness for running.

The wind just whistled past Annele's ears. She ran, ran out of pure joy at being able to fly like a bird – the lighter she ran, the deeper into this flower-strewn, sun-baked open space. It wasn't till some time later that she looked around: where were those two? Far off in the other direction Līziņa was chasing Andris. Limber though she was, he was even more limber. With unexpected twists and turns, with sudden backward turns, with zigzag runs, he tired out his pursuer. One moment she almost had him, while the next he slipped from her grasp and shot past her like a pike in the brook, heading straight as an arrow for his partner. Holding hands, they came back as winners.

And that's the way it was every time the two sisters were together: Andris would always do his best to catch up with Annele, but when he was together with her, he would not allow himself to be caught at all, and Līziņa never succeeded in separating them.

"You planned this, you rascals!"

"What? Does he really manage to do this on purpose?" Annele asked herself. And immediately began to have doubts. "No, no, how could it be on purpose? It's just a coincidence."

Līziņa was soon tired of chasing those "rascals."

"You like to run? Run all you want! My feet are not expendable," she laughed and sank down in the grass next to Aunt.

"Can't you all be still for a change and just use your eyes to look at God's world? Where are you going to get an opportunity like this again?" Aunt scolded them. She had no need of anything. She sat there, hands folded, softly and sincerely reciting something to herself. Perhaps the verses of some song.

But who could sit still out here in the country! Annele reminded Andris that she had noticed a beautiful road winding into the forest from the place where they had collected water. She was curious to know where it might lead to.

"Let's go and have a look," offered Andris.

And they ran off, happy to have found a reason.

The road was shady and green. The forest reminded her of the forest back at Spring Farm with its pine trees and hazelnut bushes; deeper in the woods, there were fewer pines, while in turn there were more deciduous trees – aspens, birches, lindens, even oaks.

Now there was no longer any need for them to rack their brains:

"What are we going to talk about?"

Their talk came as though of its own accord. Annele began to talk about Spring Farm, about the barrens, and her father. She was not really good at telling stories, but now, suddenly, on this lovely day in the shady forest, her tongue loosened. Her companion listened as attentively and eagerly as if he were hearing some spellbinding fairy tale, and so of course she enjoyed the telling. Then Andris, too, told her about himself. He had grown up in town. His father, a carpenter, was a good worker and made good money, too, but his lungs were "not too strong." Andris's younger sister had also been in poor health. She had spent the entire last year of her life in bed. On Sundays he and his father used to walk a short distance out of town, though never as far as today, for Andris's sick sister would stare her eyes out watching for Andris's return. That's how close they were. When his sister died, he had mourned her deeply.

"That's why he wanted to be partners with me all the time. Thinking about his sister, no doubt," speculated Annele.

Soon, however, Andris had had even greater grief, for his father, too, had died. A good thing that he'd been able to finish school, for his father had had a bit laid by. Now he was off to Rīga. He had found a position as an apprentice office clerk through the recommendation of a kind relative, and once he was set on his course he was sure he'd get ahead.

And so they spoke about how they had both already had their share of grief. True, Annele's sister had not died, while Andris, on the other hand, had been able to go to school much longer and thus to stand on his own two feet sooner.

Thus, immersed in their talk, they had walked quite a distance. Andris stopped.

"Isn't it time to go back?"

"Oh dear, yes," Annele suddenly realized, "the shadows are already starting to lengthen. And they'll be expecting us."

"What a shame, what a shame!"

"I could have walked like this I don't know how far!"

"Me too!"

"How far, though? To the end of the world?" she asked provocatively.

"Why not? I'd have loved to!"

"But look – what have we got here?" she interrupted herself with a joyful exclamation, and was already in the forest where, a few dozen paces deeper, seemingly puffed up with pride, stood a white flowering shrub bedecked with flat grapes of blossoms like little gleaming china plates.

"A bird cherry?" Andris ventured a guess.

"A bird cherry! Just what you'd expect from a townie! Where would you find a bird cherry in bloom as late as Whitsunday? This is a guelder rose, the loveliest shrub in the forest. Look how perfectly it's formed! Stately as a king! No hand has ever broken a branch from it yet."

"We'll break off a branch or two though, shall we?"

"If we can do it in such a way as not to hurt anything. – Take a look from underneath!"

Andris crawled under the branches. The trunk was so thick it would have held him if he had climbed it. But Annele would not allow it.

"A guelder rose breaks easily. If a branch were to break off, it would be a shame and disgrace to leave this nice shrub in the woods in such a condition."

She walked around the shrub giving instructions where to break off branches so as not to tear out too big a gap. Andris cut off the branches according to her directions. Two pairs of eyes thus met again and again. One blue, one brown. Question and answer, question and answer. There was so much to think about, to discuss, and point out! If only it didn't end up being too hard on the shrub!

Involuntarily, Annele remembered another such exchange of looks that other time, with that boy, that Konrāds! There was just no comparison between him and Andris, though! The difference was so enormous! They had enough branches. And they must hurry. By now they were most certainly being expected, and would be received with a scolding. They joined hands and set off at a run. The first to be startled was Annele. What was this? They weren't playing "last couple out" now, were they? And she pulled away so quickly that their hands came apart at once.

But she was anxious that Andris should not realize it was on purpose and take it amiss.

She took a guelder rose branch from the bouquet and hit him lightly on the arm with it. "Bird cherry!" she laughed.

Andris laughed, too.

And then he got to keep the branch.

They weren't late at all. The herb pickers had also just arrived that moment. Aunt urged them to eat up the leftover sandwiches and then start walking back.

The wind had dropped completely. The air resonated like a giant lyre. It was sultry and warm. Streaks of vapor were beginning to thicken below the sun.

"Let's go, let's go, we don't want to get caught in the rain."

"It would come just right for the grass and the new shoots. Look how parched every-

thing is. Before Midsummer Day the growing things are always thirsty," said Mother.

At the edge of the forest, quite near them, a cuckoo began to call. All day they hadn't heard one, so that the picnickers had started wondering at this and yearning for it.

"Quiet, quiet, everybody! Let it finish calling!" Līziņa exclaimed as she eagerly listened to its call.

Meanwhile, not far away, a second one began to sing, then a third one deeper in the woods.

"Count the years, now! How long will it be? We may never return to this spot again, you know."

On the way back, they walked in the reverse order from the one they'd had when they came. The older ladies walked ahead, while the young people were far behind, lingering among the meadow flowers and still listening to the calls of the cuckoo.

Around the towers of Jelgava, the clouds spiraled thicker and thicker. The sun had already vanished among them.

Andris had brought so many flowers that their hands could not hold them all, and he had to carry them himself.

In silence the picnickers reentered the grey streets. It was time to say goodbye.

"No, we'll walk you to the gate. Where we first waited for you," insisted Andris.

"What, you still haven't had enough?" wondered his mother, but raised no further objections.

And here was the gate, much too soon.

"Stay well, Andri! Good luck to you in Rīga!"

"Goodbye, goodbye, and thank you for this day!"

Annele looked back one more time. Andris was still standing in the same spot, as though waiting for her to look back. Again he raised his cap. His mother was already a long way away. They needed to hurry. Already there were black clouds above the rooftops.

Andris, Andris, Andris!

As mother and daughters were going upstairs, lightning flashed through the black clouds.

"I do hope they get home dry," worried Annele.

"Yes, Aunt is afraid of thunder."

Oh yes, Aunt. But what about Andris, Annele wondered.

Wearily, Mother sank into a chair and untied her shawls, but said with satisfaction:

"How lovely and rich this day has been! It's as though we'd lived a small lifetime from morning till night. And yet it's not as though anything special had happened today. We didn't go to church either, as would have been proper on a holiday like this. Still and all, we did honor God in our hearts all the more."

Annele, meanwhile, was thinking:

"Andris is a nice boy! Wonder if I'll ever meet him again in my lifetime?"

No, she never did meet this one-day companion again as long as she lived.

Ulis, Bearer of Roses

In the mornings, the cobblestones in the yard emerged from the shadows and steamed dry, giving off a sweltering warmth that came flooding down from the sun whose bow of rays was raised higher every day. Spring with its troops of flowers passed the town by; only a few remained in captivity among its walls, in the wretched parks and cramped gardens. With pain and yearning, Annele's thoughts accompanied summer as it grew, and dwelt on the Whitsuntide woods and meadows. How they were growing more magnificent day by day now! How they rang with the songs of birds and gave off wonderful scents. It seemed to her that never before probably had there been as much beauty as this summer! The world seemed like a giant bell becoming more splendid with each day, beckoning ever more melodiously. Where should she go? In town there are stones, but in town there are also beautiful gardens that anyone may enter – its cemeteries. And wherever beauty was to be found, Annele went in search of it. On Sunday mornings, early, before services began, it felt good to be there. The churchyard gates were quiet, oiled at the hinges. It seemed that not even a human shadow could be seen on the paths, which were overarched with blossoming shrubs. Those who had come there seemed to glide past on tiptoe. Birds were singing undisturbed. Each grave mound had been cared for meticulously, fenced in with greenery and flowers like a separate little house. Acacia bushes, lilacs, mock orange, meadowsweet stood peacefully side by side. Here were the graves of privileged citizens who "rest from their labors, and their good works accompany them." But there were also long-forgotten graves, whose memory had vanished from the face of the earth like smoke – untended, their gravestones overgrown with moss, their inscriptions faded.

Annele read: "Love is stronger than death." "Love never ends." "Plant ye hope upon these graves." "Death, where is thy sting?" These and similar words were engraved in stone in memory of an "ardently loved bride," an "eternally unforgettable husband," "dearly beloved parents." The inscriptions said where and when people had been born, how long they had lived. – She deciphered them letter by letter and tried to guess the deceased person's relationship with the world and with those who were left behind. She shared unknown, far-away destinies, as though she had to give her due, as it were, to the great sorrow of the universe that murmured around the stones like the song of eternity. It was as though her heart had been caught up in a current that flowed from many springs and washed away all silt and obstructions with its new flood. Look, you too are part of the whole. You are like a wave surging back and forth in the great waters of the world. Everything passes through your heart, and that is why the sorrows of all people are your sorrows, and the joy of them all is your joy.

Annele and Sarah were sitting on the open porch one night. All day long not a sound had come out of Lonija's piano. What had happened? Did Sarah know?

Sarah did know. Miss Lonija had come out of her house this morning with her mama and with big suitcases, and they had left for the seaside.

"The seaside? What are they going to do there?"

"Have a rest."

"A rest from what?"

"I really don't know, but that's what fashionable people do."

"I've never seen the sea," Annele said pensively.

"Ah yes! Neither have I," sighed Sarah.

"The sea can't be as beautiful as a forest. Just now the forest is as green as could be. The wood hyacinths are coming into bloom, and then the strawberries start getting ripe. Wood hyacinths and strawberries always come at the same time."

"Ah yes, I've never seen the forest, either. Where could I run with my feet!"

"And in the water meadows, the nightingales are still singing. Yes – it's still their peak season for singing."

"I've never ever heard a nightingale sing," coos Sarah even more sadly.

Annele thinks for a while. As a matter of fact she, too, had never heard a nightingale sing, she really hadn't. But she *knew* what it sings like, she knew it unmistakably, and when she now closed her eyes and listened, she could hear it, yes, she couldn't have heard it more clearly with her actual ears than she heard it now.

"All I know is what the garden is like, and the garden is wonderful," said Sarah rapturously.

And she began telling Annele about the garden.

"In the garden there are trees so tall that they tower above the houses at twice the height, and they're as dense and wide as the thickest umbrellas, and in the garden there are little paths that zigzag and twist and turn, for there is one place that's called a Maze, so that after walking there for hours you no longer know where you are, and then there are also summerhouses in the garden that are so deep under the branches they seem to be under a roof, and those who don't know can't tell that two people have gone inside one and are so quiet that there isn't even the rustle of a breeze. And in that garden are creepers called "sweet love," and wherever there's an open space in the garden, there are roses, real, full, fragrant roses."

"Where is this garden, tell me!"

"Where the trees are dense as houses and their tops are like spires, over there, the direction we're looking in right now."

She stretched out her arm and pointed.

"Our landlady's garden?"

"Yes, that's the one."

"Have you ever been inside?"

"No, I've peeked at the gate, and then I saw it in a dream."

"But that garden can't possibly be as large as you describe."

"Well, it's got a certain size," Sarah explained vaguely.

"And there are roses blooming in it? Roses?"

"They're as wondrously fair as the valley of Sharon."

"But you've never been in the valley of Sharon either."

"In a dream," breathed Sarah, gazing into a distance that was not there, her eyes fixed, glowing with rapture.

⁓⁓

Early one morning Mother came in, hiding some sort of surprise under her apron.

"Look what I've got!" And, raising her apron, she showed them a small bunch of briar roses, cut off evenly, flower heads aligned next to each other, carefully tied with a string. The way children usually tie flowers they have picked.

"Where did you get that?"

"They were on our doorstep."

"On our doorstep?"

"Put there just a short time ago."

"Well, wonder of wonders! Who could have done that?" Līziņa clapped her hands in surprise, while Annele thought, "I'm sure these roses are from the landlady's marvelous garden."

Līziņa cut the string and placed the flowers in water. Reminiscing, she exclaimed with delight, "Oh roses, dear little roses, the joy you brought me when I was a herd girl! The edge of the woods at Chisel Farm was red with your blooms, and by Midsummer Day every ditch was full of them." And sitting down to work again, she hummed, "Rosebud, rosebud, rosebud red, in the hedgerow blooming!"

Another morning, and there were a different kind of roses on the doorstep. Rosy white, fragrant little Whitsuntide roses.

Wonder who put them there?

Annele put her thoughts into words:

"It's Ulis, the landlady's son, and he's been bringing the roses for Līziņa."

"Me? Why should they be for me?"

"Who else?"

"I simply don't believe it. He can't even look a person in the eye."

"That may be so, but I'm sure what I said is true."

"So let him bring them. We never asked for his roses, and what he does is no business of ours."

"We ought to say thank you."

"To whom? If you don't know who gave the gift, there's nobody to thank. Suspicions aren't enough."

The roses came, roses of every description, filling their hearts with delight. Tiny hedge roses, white, rosy, saffron yellow; tree roses, the kind that grow in young girls' gardens in the country, making their heads spin all through the night with their sweet scent; moss roses, lying like drops of blood on unusual elongated moss pillows. Cut at an early hour, they were full of dew, cool dampness, and untouched beauty.

Every morning there was a new and wonderful surprise.

In the mornings, Annele hurried to be the first to go look what the doorstep with its roses looked like, for there were always not only a different kind of roses, but differently arranged as well, speaking their own special code as it were. One morning, however, the doorstep was empty. She came in with a long face, but her sister laughed.

"Look, look, our roses have taken a different route." And, holding the heavy sunset-red blooms with their glossy reddish leaves by their long stems, she wafted their fragrance into her sister's face. Annele was enraptured.

"I've never seen roses like that before!"

"Yes, those are something quite different. They're from a grafted, expensive variety, the kind that are just coming into flower now, when the season for all the others that bloom only once is over. And that kindhearted boy wanted to let us know, 'These are a different kind of roses, and they need a different place, be sure you keep that in mind.'"

"Where had they been placed, then?"

"Outside the window, on the brick wall of the lintel. Put right up to the windowpanes, looking at me as though begging to be let in. He'd scrambled up the wall like a cat and put them there, that rose-bearer of yours."

Annele didn't quite hear the words, "that rose-bearer of yours," for Mother had come in so she too could enjoy the roses.

"Oh, I know that kind very well," she said, "Vārens used to grow those." Vārens was Mother's foster father at Bisteri Estate, where she had lived during the short period of her engagement.

She always had something good to say about this Vārens, or Vārns, as she abbreviated his name. He was thoughtful and gentle. Kind to the peasants. And good to all living creatures. And he, too, had grown this kind of roses. He had looked after them and watched over them like children. And just like human beings, each one of them had had its own name.

"This one has a name, too," exclaimed Annele as she unwrapped the little piece of paper she had suddenly seen wrapped around the stem of one of the roses, like something around a little bird's foot.

"Love's Miracle," she read, marveling. "What a name! I wonder – did he make it up himself?"

"No, no! Vārens said the name was always given by the person who was a rose's first father and grower. That person would be the one to baptize it, too," explained Mother.

Just as the roses had once been found on the doorstep, they were now found on the lintel wall every morning.

And this is what they were called:

"Love's Miracle."

"Golden Dream."

"Glory of Dijon."

"Prince Camille de Rohan."

"Princess Margarita."

And there were many others with fabulously beautiful names, and fabulously beautiful themselves. As though they had descended straight from paradise. Placed in a glass, they stood on the girls' table and perfumed the air. Silent and aristocratic, they brought all of summer into the little room. Through the scent of the roses, they heard the songs of birds. In their imagination they ran through the woods filled with green shadows, the fields and meadows where flowers were rocked by summer winds. And they were constantly reminded of the mysterious garden in whose bosom these children of the sun had basked.

However, the flowers did not come by themselves like birds that knock against a windowpane with their wings. Thinking of them, one had to think of the person who had brought them – Ulis, the landlady's son. How could they repay him? What should they give him in return for so much goodness? Annele spoke of this very often.

Līziņa didn't let it worry her.

"I'll tell you how I see it. If a person does something and is good at what he does, he wants others to see it and praise it a little or at least acknowledge it. Well now, Ulis is a sort of household drudge in his mother's house, everybody knows that. But here he's been growing these roses, and he wants to show people what he's capable of. Why should they wither there without anyone seeing them? His mother and sister aren't home, and maybe he hasn't got any friends or relatives. He lives in the house like a monk, you know, and does nothing but lie around in that garden all day. Who knows? Maybe this is his only pleasure – to creep up to the door and window secretly every morning and leave his roses there."

"If only we could at least tell him thank you, though!"

"Well then, tell him if you see him."

"Oh dear! Tell him? Do you think it's so easy?"

"Of course it's not easy."

"How can I tell him when he does it all on the sly?"

"And suppose you do thank him? – That could be the beginning of all kinds of problems. We might say, 'Thank you, sir, what do we owe you?' Or maybe, 'Thank you, but we never asked you to do us those kinds of favors.' Or something similar. And that's what he's afraid of. He thinks we might spoil his pleasure. After all, he doesn't know what sort of people we are. No, no! If he starts showing up here expecting gratitude, it won't be the same anymore. We could, after all, throw his roses out the window. Thanks, but no thanks! But we don't do that. Every morning, when he brings a new lot, he can see them in a row here through the window. Isn't that gratitude?"

"I ought to talk it over with Sarah," thought Annele, but immediately abandoned the idea. Sarah! What would be her views on the subject? One thing was sure, this news about the roses would be a surprise to her, like a bolt from the blue. Perhaps she would loudly rejoice when she heard, perhaps start crying uncontrollably like the day when she saw Līziņa getting dressed for the ball. You had to be very careful with Sarah. Why tell her everything anyway?

One night Annele caught sight of Ulis. He stood pressed to the banisters just where she had to walk past to go upstairs. Ulis. The rose-bearer. Now she was in a tight spot. There he stood, and now she had to make a decision. She had no choice. She could go neither forward nor backward.

"I knew the time would come when I'd have to confront him face to face. What shall I do now? How shall I behave? What shall I say?"

The best thing would be to make herself invisible. But how should she go about it? He's standing right there. Waiting. He *is* waiting, isn't he? Yes, but now she must say something. What should she say? What should she say?

"Thank you so much for the roses."

"You gave us such pleasure."

"How can we ever repay you?"

"We were so delighted – so happy."

Yes, but – yes, but – does she *have* to say anything at all? How about this – I don't know a thing, and this person standing here is no concern of mine. I'm simply going about my business.

"You know there are two alternatives, and then again you don't. It's a sin to pretend!"

So now two pairs of eyes look at each other. Strange eyes – looking at her timidly somehow, yet boldly too, without turning away. Quite pleasant, warm. His face smooth and young. He looks a bit like Andris. – Yes, and here's what happened: two faces suddenly turned toward each other. The one asks no questions. The other can't say a single word. And then they've passed each other already. In an instant Annele is at the top of the stairs. From behind the door, she stealthily looks back: the figure has vanished.

Well, this was her chance. Who could call it back now? Who could change it for the better? But the thing she had neglected to do gnawed at her.

Another time, Annele consoled herself.

And here is what this other time was like. They both met at the gate. But Ulis, although he had seen her, having darted a quick look at her, pulled away his eyes so quickly she would have had to yell at him as if he were deaf, "Thanks for the roses!" How could she do that? And so she didn't.

The roses now came at longer intervals. One morning they were huge, white as snow, half-open, with a thin pink edge.

Līziņa sewed and sang:

> "White rose, white rose,
> Blooming amid green leaves,

You are like hopeless love,
Bitter renunciation!"

The white roses were the last.

On the evening of that same day, the landlady and her daughter returned from their rest at the seaside. Ulis, his cap pushed deep over his forehead, raced across the yard like the wind, defiantly, it seemed, looking neither left nor right. The torrents of sound from the keys of the piano began to flow again in the house that faced the street, and when they stopped, the musician herself, picking the smoothest cobblestones to step on with her little spike heels, tripped over to the garden and soon returned with her arms full of flowers. She never stayed in the garden for any length of time.

"Our landlady is home again," announced Sarah to Annele as though it was joyful tidings. And added with satisfaction:

"The ladies had a good rest."

"So when is Ulis going away for a rest?"

"Oh, Ulis! He's got his garden, you know!"

And, leaning close to Annele's ear as though confiding a secret:

"Let me tell you something: Ulis can't ever go out in fine society. He's tongue-tied."

"What do you mean, tongue-tied?"

"Well, no matter what he tries to say, it all stays inside him. That's why he never talks to anybody, you see."

Aunt Meire had come over to see them. She looked at Annele searchingly and shook her head. Arms akimbo, stern as a judge, she enquired:

"My, my! What's this I hear? Is it true that young gentlemen have been bringing you roses?"

"Me?" Annele flushed with embarrassment. How mortifying! Who says so? Who could have said a thing like that?

"There was no need to say anything! Every time I'd come over, I would see those roses."

"There's no way they could have been for me."

"Sure, sure – no way at all! Tsk, tsk, tsk! It's too soon, much too soon!"

"You can say what you like, but this is quite preposterous. It's too funny for words!"

"Then tell me, who else were they for?"

"For Līziņa!"

Līziņa warded off the idea with both hands.

"You see: Līziņa will have none of them."

"And I – – and I – – "

Yes, but now that she thinks about it a bit, perhaps it really is true. She herself had had a faint, a very faint suspicion, after all. And who was it that waited for them most and was most delighted about them? – – But now she – no, no. "Then it must have been for both of us."

Annele got no further. Seeing the sparks of mockery around her aunt's lips and Līziņa's head bowed with laughter, she realized what it all meant and ran outside.

The way they talked! Who needed it? It didn't matter who Ulis had brought the flowers for – it had been his language, the most beautiful language a human being could have invented; she just hadn't known how to respond, she didn't know how to express her gratitude. And that was the end of it. She never *was* able to repay that debt.

By Starlight

Dusk came warm and quiet on this July Sunday evening. The windows of the house that faced the street were dark, the piano silent. The ladies were probably away on a visit somewhere, the young gardener was nowhere to be seen. Undisturbed, Annele walked through the large courtyard, which was like a tent roofed with stars, its ends secured to black stacks of buildings.

Stars, stars!

There was the Big Dipper, and there the Little Dipper. There were the Pleiades. Across the zenith, the broad, unraveled ribbon of the Milky Way shone silvery white. There were all the countless constellations in zigzags, triangles, and rectangles, so familiar and dear to Annele from early childhood even though she did not know all their names. That didn't really matter. What did matter was that you could commune with the stars as though they were living creatures. That they spoke to the heart. That they elevated and bore your thoughts with them on their boundless path. Was there anything greater than the wisdom of the stars? For thousands of years, they had been watching human lives. They knew everything that happened. Not even one's most secret thought was hidden from them. It felt good to talk with the stars.

The gate banged. There came Sarah, back from the deaconesses' house, her regular Sunday visit. It was difficult to hide from her – she had eyes like a hawk.

"Come on, let's go," she summoned Annele rapturously, "I've got something nice."

The "something nice" was a new song she had learned at the deaconesses' house today during evening meditation. She knew a lot of them. Her voice was a little hoarse and not sonorous, but she had a good ear for music.

The girls went up on the porch, past which whirled the stars. Sarah sang her song. At first, making friends with the song, fumblingly, they explored the words and the melody, then gave free vent to the song. There were still a few snags, but neither of them minded much. At the same time, their rapture knew no bounds.

> Where shall the soul find peace in its pain,
> Whose pinions shall shield it in storm and rain?
> Will worldly pleasures bring it relief,
> Or fame and possessions save it from grief?
> Oh no, oh no, these are but toys,
> Beyond the stars dwell the soul's true joys.

"Beyond the stars dwell the soul's true joys," said Sarah, nodding her head in agreement, and tears burned in her eyes like black diamonds.

"There, there, beyond the stars," she pointed at the glittering heavens.

"But beyond which stars? After all, the ones we can see aren't all there are."

"What do you mean, all there are?"

"The multitudes of stars are boundless and infinite."

"Who says so?" sternly asked Sarah.

"That's the way it is. If the two of us could rise up to the tiniest little star right now, we would see that before us is a sky even larger than the one we see presently, with totally different stars."

"That would really be something, us being able to rise to such a tiny speck," Sarah smiled incredulously.

"Every one of those specks up there is a whole world."

"What do you mean, a world? Like this?" Sarah hit the porch railing with her fist.

"Yes, like this and like the earth that you see, and the sky and everything, all this vastness put together."

"And here I thought that the stars were just tiny little lights."

"Haven't you ever heard about the earth and the sky and the heavenly bodies?"

"No, who would tell me things like that? The deaconesses teach me reading and writing and stories about Jesus. They don't teach me anything else."

"Well then, listen!"

And now Annele tells her about fixed stars and planets, about suns, comets, and the Milky Way, about the motion of the stars, and how fast it is: "How can I even give you an example of how fast they move?"

"As fast as a train?"

"Much faster."

"As a bird?"

"Much faster."

"As the wind?"

"Even faster. As fast as thoughts."

"As thoughts!"

That is something Sarah cannot grasp. She is crushed.

But now Annele made the heavenly bodies revolve around her, then all whirl together around the sun, and finally shoot at lightning speed together with the sun off into unknown expanses of space. And so on, second by second, moment by moment, for hundreds, thousands, millions of years. Toward unknown destinations.

As Sarah listened, her face began to crumple more and more painfully, as though she were in great danger. Finally she could no longer control herself. She cupped her cheeks in the palms of her hands and trembled.

"I'm scared, I'm scared!"

"Scared? What for? Why, the heavenly bodies are the most beautiful thing that can be imagined under the sun!"

And Annele herself became absorbed in looking at the abysses of stars where they shone in their countless multitudes so calmly, seemingly motionless. Didn't she herself find it difficult to believe in their mad race through space? No, no! It was a proven fact, it said so in all the books, and she had read it, it was not proper for her to doubt it like Sarah, who knew nothing about it.

"So big, so big!" Sarah spread her arms as wide as she could and drew an arc in the air with them. "And I always thought they were tiny little lights. Whenever I lit a fire in the kitchen stove, I used to think: Oh little fire, you've dropped from heaven."

"And that's quite true. Fire did come from heaven. Listen, let me tell you something else: once upon a time there was a very wise nation that had many gods. Some were low, while others were high, and the lower gods had to serve the higher ones and obey their commands. Now, all the gods together ruled over the world and over the human race. At that time, people had no fire. It was guarded by the gods, while human beings lived in darkness and cold. Then one of the lower gods, whose name was Prometheus, felt pity for the human race. He stole the fire from the dwelling places of the gods and brought it down to earth to human beings. From that time on people had light and warmth. But the big gods punished Prometheus severely for this. They had him carried up to the high mountains and chained to a rock with unbreakable fetters. Then they sent an eagle to peck out his liver. During the night, his liver would grow back again, but the next day the eagle would peck it out again. And since Prometheus is a god, he can never die and his torment is eternal."

"Oh, oh! What are you telling me, what are you telling me! It's so terrible," Sarah whispered.

"Yes," said Annele in a dark voice blurred by ecstasy, "Prometheus suffers horribly, but he has done the most beautiful deed you could imagine."

"He felt pity for the human race."

And suddenly Sarah drew a deep breath. Her shoulders shook.

"What is it, Sarah? Why? Don't you believe it? Can't you understand?"

"I don't care if I don't believe it, I don't care if I can't understand – I'm crying for joy because you're talking to me like this. To a poor Jewish girl. Look at the way you tell me all these things. I'm glad there are those who feel pity for the human race!"

"But now *you* tell me something! Tell me your whole story!"

"Oh, Sarah is a poor creature!"

"So what if you're poor! Every person has a story."

Sarah's story is short but grim. She was born in Žagare. Her father was a shoemaker. He hammered nails into soles from morning till night, she says, but was unable to provide enough food for eight mouths. Five brothers, all born healthy, but she, the youngest, was born a cripple. The cholera came and carried away her brothers one by one. Then her mother. Her father had wept, torn his hair, scattered ashes on his head, but had found a new wife half a year later. After that, one windy night, the town of Žagare caught fire. Half of the town's little wooden shacks burned down, and her father's with them. Trying to save his house, her father got burned himself, suffered excruciating pain for a while, then died. That's when an old uncle had taken her in. Leading Sarah by the hand, he had gone the rounds of all the relatives to get somebody, anybody, to give her a home. But who'd do a thing like that? Every one of them had had an excuse. Some gave one reason, some another. So Sarah had been left with that same uncle. He had been good to her, he really had – oh, Sarah felt all people were good – but still she had had more scoldings than kind words. And not only scoldings, hunger, too. Because after all, how much money could an old ragpicker like him earn? Not much, not much at all. Bread was a rare thing. And when you get up in the morning but you don't get a bite to eat, you learn to fight for it. And Sarah had learned. God knows how long ago she'd started working as a servant. When she was just a tiny little girl! For a piece of bread, for the clothes she wore on her back. To begin with she'd always worked for Jews, but then had come heaven-sent good fortune and she had met the "kind lady." The kind lady had found her a job with Christians. This one, with the newlyweds, was her second one. At her first job, what with the overly heavy workload, she had broken a lot of dishes and had been so clumsy she had soon been fired. Here, too, she wasn't getting any money, but that didn't matter. Her life was on its way up, in the direction of paradise. The kind lady had sent her to the deaconesses, and they were now taking care of her. Once she had had enough preparation, she together with many other poor Jews would be admitted through holy baptism to the congregation of Jesus. It would be the happiest day of her life.

Annele shook her head.

"If I were you, I wouldn't get baptized. Once it's done, it can't be undone again. You'll leave your people and your family, but what will you be among the Christians? You'll always be alone and a stranger."

"Oh, and aren't I a stranger among my own people? Do they want me? Who should I go to?"

Annele thought it over. What advice should she give Sarah? She suddenly thought of the Jewish couple to whose house Mother went on Saturdays to light the fire. She'd often told Annele what fine old-fashioned things they had, what heavy silver dishes and pitchers. Though they themselves seemed poor, kept only a tiny store on the street side of the house and served their customers without outside help, their household proved the opposite. They showed special attention to Annele. When she came in to shop and the wife was in the little store alone, she would quickly run over to the back door of the apartment and call, "Come, Leiba, the little one is here!" When Leiba was in the shop and the girl happened to come in, he would do the same. "Come, Rachel, here's the little one." And Rachel would come out, sometimes with a basket of cookies she had hurriedly grabbed, from which she'd take and place before the girl now a star, now a little cookie pretzel, and Annele would have to take it, they wouldn't take no for an answer; or else Leiba would lift the glass jar of brown sugar candy off the shelf, and she would have to taste it. And once, when Annele stretched out her hands, Rachel seized them, clasped them in hers as though in a bird's claws, pressed them, and stroked them: "Take a look, Leiba, aren't they just the way Miriam's were? The fingers thin as kindling wood and the skin like porcelain." – "Quite right," said Leiba, bringing his reddened eyes close to the girl's hands, "quite right, Rachel."

"What do they want from me?" the girl pulled away, looking quickly at her hands. "Why, my hands are just like anybody else's."

But Rachel went on:

"I'll tell you the way it is: I had a little granddaughter, sweet and beautiful like the morning star."

"Like the morning star," echoed Leiba.

"Her cheeks were like little roses and her little hands were like porcelain. Exactly like yours they were, I said to Leiba."

"That's what you said, Rachel."

"And there was something about her that you remind me of, when she'd turn her head to the right and look out of her eyes, even though her eyes were black and yours are blue. The first time I saw you, I said to Leiba: 'That's the way Miriam looked at us, and her hands were the same.'"

"Yes, Rachel, that's what you said."

"And her father had a little property, and she would have gotten our property, too, she could have lived like a countess, but she didn't live. She got a sickness that choked her throat, and then she died."

"Five doctors I called from all over town, and I would have called another five, but it was no use, and she died," echoed Leiba, and his voice fell and rose monotonously as though he was walking around with his prayer shawl, murmuring prayers.

"And by now she would have been your age."

"Yes, she would be exactly your age and she would be the apple of our eye in the morning and our delight in the evening, but now she's gone."

"And when I take your hands in mine and caress them a bit you mustn't mind," Rachel went on, but Annele pulled away and vanished out the door as soon as good manners would permit.

It was these people Annele was thinking of now. They no longer had a child. Couldn't they help Sarah?

"Who should I go to?" Sarah repeated thoughtfully. "Who'll have me? The Jews curse me with terrible curses. I'm to be cast out and spit upon for leaving Moses and his commandments."

"But have you tried talking with the Veinshteins? They seem to be good people."

"Leiba Veinshtein and Rachel? Ohh! Leiba Veinshtein is the worst of the lot. He'd kick me, he'd stone me if he could. He'd have me buried alive. He has piled curses like mountains over all the Jews who have reneged."

"But that makes hardly any difference."

"Yes it does. He's a big man in the community. And he has a family tree."

"What's a family tree?"

"He knows who his ancestors were. My *tateh* didn't. We're descended from obscure people."

"Ah, I understand!" responded Annele. "Just as it says in the Bible: Melchidesek begat Abigail. And Abigail begat Joel. And Joel begat Isaac. And Isaac begat Issachar. And on and on. Right from the beginning of the world."

"I guess so. You understand everything better than an ignorant girl like me."

"Don't talk nonsense! You know all sorts of things in life a lot better than I do. You have a story to tell about everybody. When I want to know about someone, I immediately think: I must ask Sarah."

"Well, I can't get too far with my legs, you see, but I do have eyes and ears, and I let them roam around and take in whatever my mind can grasp. It's no big thing."

"And you're full of courage. In defiance of your whole people and in defiance of Leiba Veinshtein you want to be baptized."

"Oh dear no! I have neither defiance nor courage – he's the one that does. He gives me strength and faith," Sarah said with reverent humility.

"Who is this he?"

"Pastor Gurland."

"The one that turned from a Jewish rabbi into a Christian pastor and is now at Trinity Church? I've heard of him."

"He is our protector and shepherd. He prepares us so we'll be worthy to receive manna from heaven."

"He baptizes other Jews as well?"

"The number of our faithful is growing day by day."

"But don't his fellow Jews curse him?"

"Oy, and how they curse him! If their curses could turn into fog or mud, the whole town would be engulfed to the tops of the towers. He was the wisest rabbi, they say, the likes of whom you'd find only once every century, and people used to come to him from near and far to ask his advice on the teachings of the law. And it's a shame and disgrace for the whole Jewish community that he's gone and joined the goyim. But he doesn't care in the least. He walks like a hero and like a young lion at break of day, even though his enemies number more than the sand at the seashore. What am I compared to him? A tiny speck of dust that he carries on his shoe. What do the rabbis and the elders of the community care about me? My name will be Mary, I won't be Jewish anymore, and no one will recognize me."

"But that's quite impossible, don't you see? You're – "

Annele stopped abruptly. For of course she couldn't say to Sarah what she had been on the verge of saying: "You're Jewish, and you always will be till the end of your life." Yet she couldn't tell Sarah. That would make her too unhappy. She wanted to crawl out of her skin. And so Annele just said:

"It's up to everybody to do as they like. As for me, I don't think I'd do that."

Sarah smiled a little slyly.

"But supposing some kind lady were to come, a rich baroness or countess maybe, and say to you: 'I like your voice. I'm going to give you money and you can get some training.' I bet I know what would happen then. You'd jump with joy and say: why not? Yes indeed! And once you were a great lady and sang for the public and for people of quality, and you had fame and honor, would you still be a Latvian? Can a Latvian attain such high honor and fame?"

Eyes wide, Annele stared at her interlocutor. Some rich lady might come, give her money and say: Get some training! This was something new! She'd never encountered this possibility in her flights of fantasy. Quickly she explored this path in her mind. The path of fame and honor that Sarah was showing her. She'd study and study, and then she'd be good at what she did! She'd stand in front of lots of people and she could sing all those inexpressible things that were tangled and twisted in her thoughts like a knot that can't be untied. There was power in knowing how to do something worthwhile. Wasn't that what she told herself a hundred times a day?

But wait, wait! Could she really stand there like that and say this to strangers?

Could she sing like that and turn this way and that, as she had seen the singers from Rīga do last year on the stage? No, she wasn't sure, not sure at all whether she'd be capable of it!

And there was something else: wait! About being Latvian. What was it Sarah had said: if fame and honor came to her, then she, Annele, would no longer be a Latvian? Why, that was nonsense. For she still felt so closely connected to the people whose lives she had shared in her childhood. There were Granny, old Anyus, Jurītis, Ingus, Karlīne, and all the others. That's where she belonged, just as she belonged among the hills, wheat fields, meadows, and woods in her dear Latvian countryside. What else could she be if not a Latvian? How absurd it was, what rot Sarah talked! And she firmly replied: "No matter what happens to me, I'll still be who I am."

Sarah felt small and insignificant. Since she was bound and determined to leave her people, she felt she had to appear more worthy in Annele's eyes. And so she realized she still hadn't said all that had to be said in that respect.

"Even if I'm committing a sin in leaving my people, Christ will forgive me, for I am going to him. I shall be a worker in his vineyard."

"Where is it you're going to work?" Annele did not understand.

"Well, all right, I'll tell you what I haven't told a single soul. I'm going to be a nurse!"

"What? A nurse?" Why, this was something magnificent! A higher goal in life could hardly be imagined! Sarah, Sarah! What was she saying?

"You're going to be a nurse?"

"Ye-e-e-s!" Sarah drawled an affirmative answer. "That's right."

"You mean at the deaconesses' house?"

"Right, and I'll tell you about the house."

And here's what the deaconesses' house was like. The finest in the whole town, thought Sarah. It was nestled deep in a garden. Tall trees cast their shadows over it.

Could this garden really be lovelier than the one here, their own landlady's garden, which they had so often admired? – Annele doubted it.

Of course it was lovelier. The deaconesses' garden was something entirely different. It had hundred-year-old linden trees and elms, weeping birches and willows whose branches jutted out over the lawns, there were all kinds of flowering shrubs and endlessly long flowerbeds, there were roses, whole fields of them.

"But there are fields of roses in 'our' garden, too!"

Annele was surprised that Sarah could have forgotten what she'd been saying about 'our' garden all morning long.

"No, no, no, this one is nothing!"

In the deaconesses' garden, there were zigzagging paths along which recovering patients walked alone or accompanied by the sisters. And the sisters themselves! They were scarcely human. They were kindness, humility, love, and compassion itself! The way they walked, inaudible in their light slippers, the way they silently bent over the patients, handing them medicines or food, arranging the pillows, wiping their perspiration, always comforting and reassuring them, promising happiness, joy, and health to those who were seriously ill! They were all dressed alike, and they themselves were alike in their humility and mercy. No matter how noble her birth, each sister was the equal of the humblest among them. And how they were loved and respected! And there were even cases where some aristocratic patient, maybe a count even, fell in love with a sister and married her. Then she would live in a magnificent palace, drive around in a fine coach and have everything her heart desired. There had been a case like that at the deaconesses' house. That was the great event that was often talked about, but there were quite a few lesser events when the sisters became the wives of rich merchants or well-to-do master craftsmen. But it was even lovelier to remain faithful and spend all one's life in this palace of selfless love and peace! That's what beautiful and wise Sister Beatrice, who was teaching Sarah how to read and write, had done. People said she had had a great unrequited love and had not been able to find peace anywhere until she entered the deaconesses' house.

"Beatrice?" exclaimed Annele, and her thoughts immediately leapt one level higher in the direction of her rising thoughts. And she began to tell Sarah about a great poet who had loved a certain Beatrice. But Beatrice had died early, and the poet, in search of her, had walked through hell and the fires of purgatory, and had reached heaven, where he had found her at last. He had described this journey in a wonderful poem that had become famous all over the world.

Sarah listened and nodded assent. And, assenting, she declared:

"Oh yes. Sister Beatrice could be like that. Although all the sisters are the same, she surpasses them all."

And she began to describe this sister so enthusiastically that Annele exclaimed:

"How I wish I could get to see her, this Beatrice!"

"But you can! Yes, yes! God himself put the idea in my heart!" exulted Sarah. "You must become a sister, too, and enter the deaconesses' house!"

"Me?"

"Yes! And then we'll both be together. Wherever Sister Beatrice is, we will be too. Sister Mary. Sister Anna. What bliss! What heavenly bliss that would be!"

This idea surprised Annele like a blow on her forehead. She was still incapable of answering. But Sarah was jubilant.

"And every Sunday, Pastor Gurland comes and gives a Bible class. It's heavenly! The sisters look forward to it as though to a festival, and if it's summer, the chapel is full of flowers. And then we all sing the beautiful hymns. I'd stand next to you, and your voice would sound so lovely among the others. Listen, this is how it would sound!" And she began to sing:

> "When Salem receives us
> What joy there will be!
> The city will open
> Its gates of gold.
> What joy there will be,
> What bliss untold!"

There was a murmur of voices in the yard. People were approaching from the courtyard gate. Startled, Sarah jumped up as though waking from a dream.

"My master and mistress! And I've got the front door key!"

And she was gone in a flash.

The Deaconess

For a long time Annele stood there by the light of the stars thinking, thinking, then she rubbed her hand across her forehead and went inside.

Mother was already asleep, but Līziņa was still sitting by the lamp working hard. When she worked on Sundays, she would always sew something for herself. What was it this time? Annele took a look. A very elaborately worked shirtwaist with tiny pleats and tucks like a finely embroidered armor.

"What's that you're sewing?"

Līziņa cast a glance at her sister. A strange smile briefly appeared on her lips.

"Dowry shirts."

"Dowry shirts?"

"Yes. Don't you think it's about time?"

Whether her words were a joke or in earnest, they slammed into Annele's chest with a hollow, sharp pain. What should she say in response?

"Aren't you coming to bed?"

"No, I'm going to finish this first."

Annele couldn't fall asleep. The conversation with Sarah and the words her sister had just casually uttered were the winds that ruffled the waters of her soul. Especially the latter. "Dowry shirts" and "It's about time." Was that really so? She herself was fourteen now, and Līziņa was more than nine years older. Some of their female relatives who were her sister's age were already married, but nothing in that regard had been heard or said about Līziņa. Līziņa herself, no doubt, was the kind of person that didn't talk about the "affairs of her heart" the way Aunt Meire's visitors did. That must be it. Annele wouldn't either. But supposing, quite without her knowing it, something menacing were to approach, the way a thunderstorm approaches when you're driving at night? And supposing it suddenly swept away her sister, changed life completely, then she too would have the ground pulled away from under her feet, the roof that now arched over her head dismantled. This terrifying prospect now faced her for the first time in all its seriousness. She was well aware that she was not yet capable of earning her living on her own and of helping her mother as well. She was not making any progress in learning how to sew. Whatever her sister told her to do, she did well, but she herself lacked initiative. Maybe she'd never have any. That skill seemed to her like a locked gate that it would be futile to try to break open.

But suppose there was a way out? Suppose Sarah's advice, of all things, was like a pointer from fate which way to go? A deaconess! Yes, that was a lofty and worthy goal in life. If she could achieve it, she would also have averted those minor worries that preyed upon her so relentlessly. Yes, that was surely so. These thoughts were good and came at the right time. She mustn't be a burden to Līziņa if her sister was getting ready to try her wings as she looked for a new nest. If there was ever talk of her, Annele, and worry about what to do with her now, she'd be able to answer confidently, "I already have something in mind."

And the girl's thoughts began to form more and more concretely the image of a deaconess, which took on Annele's own features. That was how she fell asleep.

And that was how she awoke. Her eyes were turned towards a new goal, and she must now move forward in that direction. She imagined herself in the deaconesses' house, walked along the shady paths of the garden and the quiet hospital wards. And when a kind, compassionate face bent over a patient, it was her face, and where the eyes of a suffering woman gleamed with sudden gratitude, they were turned toward her, Annele. At night she and Sarah spoke of nothing but the life of the sisters of mercy, which Sarah, as usual, praised in the most fervent terms, persistently urging Annele, while the latter, though she always listened attentively, was reticent in her answers, implying that this kind of thing must be thought through very seriously.

Where could she thoroughly think over this important life step? She'd need a place of silence and peace to do so. Again, she must go to the cemetery. The departed and their destinies seemed to her like hieroglyphs locked into caskets. If she deciphered and unriddled them, she would receive advice as to what path she must follow. Bowed low to the ground, the weeping willows, weeping birches, weeping roses, no less than the hedged and fenced-off graves, which in their insignificance perpetually proclaimed, "Look, here is all that is left of a once mighty human being,"– permeated this abode of peace with a strange sorrow. And of course the life of a deaconess would also be tinged with sorrow, no matter what anybody said. A deaconess, as far as the girl was concerned, was no different than a cloistered nun who has completely renounced the joys of this world. And that is why Annele must acquaint herself in good time with the woes of the world and of all human beings. The pain they caused her was sometimes particularly sharp. All the sharper since she herself was in the middle of them all, indeed, in the very forefront. What a shame that now she too, young as she was, never having seen or enjoyed anything, must renounce everything.

Potential joys and pleasures to which she had paid little attention or of which she had hitherto even been completely unaware suddenly came and barred her way, showing themselves in the most attractive light: – Do you really want to turn your back on us, to ignore us? How seldom, how very seldom she had hitherto thought about dances and dancing, but now suddenly a ball seemed like the pinnacle of delight. Wasn't it possible that there would come a time when she, just like Līziņa, would put on a gown à la Marie Antoinette and be a great success in the ballroom? Be a success? Yes, yes, she was sure she could! She would never have believed it before, but now she selfishly believed it. From the time she was little she had loved wearing new clothes. They gave her a festive feeling, so light and clean. Like her sister, she liked specially selected color combinations and harmonies. Not what everybody wore, but what nobody else had. A deaconess's dress, on the other hand, striped white and gray or blue-gray, which she would now have to wear day in and day out, was not at all to her taste. Her fantasy began showing her other images that also had her own facial features but that were so very different from a deaconess. She must struggle against all such temptations and conquer them so as to stay on the right path, for of course it was too late now to change anything.

At Trinity Church they were expecting an important day. Senior Pastor Gurland had announced the baptism of ten Jews, which gladdened all the believers, while all the nonbelievers awaited it like some great sensation.

Sarah was in ecstasy.

"Oy, how our minister is going to speak, how he will speak! You've got to hear him and see him. You've got to go."

Annele realized she must go. After all, it fit in so well with her future life work. She must hear this man.

She went at the appointed time, but it was already too late to get a seat. The church was jammed to the doors. Candles fluttered in the heavy candelabras. The altar was decorated. The hum of the organ rose and fell tempestuously.

And far above this sea of heads, by the altar, she saw coal-black hair and a beard which, narrowing like a wedge, surrounded a shiny white forehead and cheeks. The organ stopped thundering, and a solemn silence fell. And then, from that stiffly extended wedge of a beard, arrows of words shot as from a taut bow and flew across the crowded room. The voice that was heard here was a scorching voice, destroying the silence, it made the churchgoers, quietly frozen in their pews, rise to their feet and made those who were already standing and waiting in awe tremble. It was not like a single voice, but seemed like a whole multitude, lamenting, weeping, accusing, judging, warning.

"What did I do to you, what did I do to you, my people, that you scourged me with scourges and stoned me, that you drove me out through the temple gates and spat at my feet? That you placed your foot on the nape of my neck and kicked me like the ground? That you destroyed all memory of me with my ancestors and blotted out my name in the house of my father? I came to you with light and truth, my countenance shone like the sun, and my words rained upon you like fertile rain, but you turned from me and closed your ears; thus your eyes became blind and your soul as empty as a field parched in the summer heat. Woe unto you who did not recognize the chosen of the Lord and who paid no heed to the signs and portents that the Lord's anointed showed before you! Woe unto you, for your day of retribution is close at hand, your day of retribution, which will come upon you like a thief in the night – "

Higher and higher into a treble rose this voice, so high that one must fear that it would suddenly dwindle away and break. Annele's attention really did suddenly break like a worn thread. The words from the altar rushed past her like an icy wind. They had nothing to do with her. An alien spirit, unacceptable to her, emanated from the man who stood up there. She understood that he was lamenting his own woes, but this did not move her. The shriller, the more devastating, the more agitating the voice that breathed its flames from the altar, the chillier became her heart.

She turned sideways and began to move toward the exit. She no longer liked it. Her heart would not accept it. And here is what her rebellious heart was saying:

"What do I care about this Gurland? I'm never going to his sermons at the deaconesses' house."

"Then you can't become a deaconess either."

"I'm never going to be a deaconess, so there!"

It was out! As a fire that suddenly flicks at a straw puppet turns it into ashes in the wink of an eye, so Annele's thoughts in the wink of an eye tore down the edifice she herself had carefully cherished for days on end: I'm never going to be a deaconess. Whoever heard of such fickleness! She raced home. Past the window of the little shop. Rachel ran out the door, waved, and called:

"Miss, little miss, come up and visit me today! I'll show you Miriam's little pictures, I'll show you her little toys, I'll show you, and we'll talk."

"I'm not coming, I'm not!"

"Oh? Why aren't you coming? And what if I beg you with all my heart, what if I have something nice for you?"

"Thank you, but I'm not coming."

Rachel's lips drew together with sadness, but Annele ran off. In conflict with herself.

She was torn by thoughts. What kind of a sister of mercy was she? A sister would need meekness, patience, love, kindness. She had imagined that she, too, had these noble qualities, but it was a delusion. At this moment obstinacy and disapproval were within her like sharp thistles. She had expected Gurland to fill her with ecstasy, but here was disappointment, which meant that her heart was cold, for the others had been moved, hadn't they? Going to Rachel's house and listening to her talk about Miriam was repugnant, even impossible for her, so she couldn't make even that small a sacrifice. What was left, then? As though it had raced down the wrong path, her heart now galloped back the other way. She must put an end to all delusions.

Sarah was making a racket in the kitchen. What? Hadn't she gone to church? Then Annele must tell her at once how things stood.

And she did with her very first words.

"Sarah, I just wanted to tell you I'm through with being a deaconess. I'm giving it up. I can't be as good as a deaconess is supposed to be."

Sarah threw up her hands in despair and looked up with eyes red from weeping that immediately filled with new tears.

"Oh, that's just what I had been thinking. I saw a dream that means delusions and disappointment. Oy, what troubles! So many troubles all at once!"

"What other troubles, Sarah?"

"Well, that nothing came of our plan and that my master and mistress are moving away from here."

"To another apartment?"

"That's their way: one month they get everything settled and arranged and are very happy, the second month they're only half happy, while the third month they run all over Jelgava searching and searching till they find an apartment they haven't lived in yet. Then we move to that apartment. We've got everything packed in baskets and bundles, and tomorrow I'm going to start carrying it all away. Oy, it'll be hard for me!"

"Then you can come and visit us."

"How should I come and visit you, a meshuggene girl like me?"

"But you're going to be a deaconess, aren't you?"

Sarah suddenly drew in her breath and sank down on the edge of the fireplace. When the first eruption of tears had abated, she managed to say between sobs:

"I'm not going to be a deaconess. Never, never!"

"Who told you that?"

"Sister Beatrice."

"How did she tell you?"

"'Sarah,' she said, 'you see how lightly deaconesses walk. On thin soles, they must glide inaudibly like lizards and fly as swiftly as birds. You do understand, don't you, Sarah?'

"'I understand. I'm a meshuggene girl. My feet bang away like stone mallets on the highway.' That's how I answered her.

"And then she said:

"'When you've been baptized and confirmed, we'll hire you in the kitchen, and you can wash the dishes. There, nobody can hear you.'"

"Well, did you tell Sister Beatrice you'd like to be a deaconess?"

"Come on, how could I tell her such a foolish thing? I know all that, don't you see. I understand and know – but – but – I would so have liked, I would so have wanted... And then I told you, too – and then Sister Beatrice also understood."

"Sarah!" Annele said softly, stroking the girl's thick hair.

This provoked another shuddering wave of sobs.

"Oy, I had it good here! It'll never be this good again. Who will talk to me now, the way you accepted me and talked to me? And then, the way Ulis sent you those roses. That was so heavenly!"

"So you know? About the roses, I mean?"

"Why shouldn't I know? I told him what a nice girl you were and what we talked about together. Maybe he liked that, and then he thought about it and figured out what to do. So what? Why not let him have his pleasure?"

"Sarah! And you never told me?"

"I swore to him that I'd never tell a soul, with three fingers raised. Then he believed me."

"And now you broke your vow."

"How can I go away and stay mute as a fish? You've got to know, right? And it was such a pleasure for that Ulis. He can't say much with his tongue. So he said it with those flowers, see?"

Hard at Work

Reaching out her hands like a dancer in a circle dance, summer changed places with autumn. Pupils from the farms of sunny Zemgale flooded the streets of Jelgava once more. More piercing than ever was the pain in Annele's heart at the word inscribed over each of her days: renunciation. She no longer spoke of it, for it was no use. The path she had tried to crawl along on her own through life's thicket had turned out to be the wrong one, unacceptable to her. Now she must put her whole mind to the work fate had pushed into her hands: maybe she would finally manage to learn it properly after all.

Bright and early one morning, Melnzemis and his oldest son Kristaps drove into town. From the inn where they had left the horse, they arrived, each carrying a full sack. In one of the sacks were Kristaps's bedclothes and other clothing, the other contained provisions. This caused a certain amount of consternation in Green Street, for not a word had been said about Kristaps. Melnzemis said that he and the wife had decided it could all be discussed once they got there themselves. One thing they knew for sure – there was plenty of room with the relatives and Kristaps could live there quite well the one year he would hang around the city school and improve his figuring and his German, which he couldn't quite get the hang of. It didn't pay, said Melnzemis, to send him to school any longer than that, for he'd be a farmer in any case. They'd bring in food for Kristaps. When the Avots family were cooking their own meals, they should throw in Kristaps's share as well, then there wouldn't be the waste of lighting an extra fire. And surely they wouldn't deny him a little corner for his bed and a table to study on, would they? After the rye had been threshed, Melnzemis said, he'd send a kopeck or two as well, by way of remuneration.

Kristaps got the little table by the window in Mother's room and a bed frame on sawhorses concealed by a plaid blanket behind the wardrobe. On the first day, he went around dressed to the nines with a black cravat and starched collar that was hard as a board and yellow as a shelf fungus, having lain in his mother's trunk for a couple of summers. That evening, he removed this trashy piece of non-clothing from a neck that was rubbed raw and red. He said there was no way he would put on such a horse collar again tomorrow; the other boys were wearing colored bandannas dotted with white, as was the fashion in the country. And besides, his school was not a proper *gymnasium*, but just a public high school.

As fall approached, the amount of work grew by leaps and bounds. Mrs. Rank,

Līziņa's favorite employer, was abroad just now and had sworn she would bring back at least half a railroad car full of nice things. It was for her that they now had to free their hands, but first they must satisfy previous employers who insisted on their rights and prerogatives. These were Baroness Heimann and Mrs. Tiedemann, the pastor's widow. The Baroness had announced her return one day earlier than Mrs. Tiedemann, and that is why they had to go to her house first.

"I told those ladies of mine that I have a little sister who is my apprentice, and that I have to bring her along. Only on that condition will I go work for them in their homes."

"What? You want to bring me along? Am I some kind of bundle?"

"Get along with you, child," Līziņa stroked her shoulder. "How else are we to arrange things?"

"Well, did they agree to what you said?"

"Why on earth shouldn't they? They're getting two pairs of working hands for the price of one."

"But isn't that terribly unfair?"

"You go and tell them that!"

Annele tried to sweeten the bitter pill with a jesting tongue.

"So we're going to be running through the streets of Jelgava with a yardstick and an iron like that Jewish tailor Joske and his son, or slow Jaņķelis followed by Fast Jaņķelis."

"Got to do whatever works best," responded Līziņa without a grin.

Their working day when they sewed away from home was from eight till eight, without a break. On their morning walk, the sisters met little groups of students hurrying to school with their briefcases and satchels. Annele tried not to look at them, to walk past them with her head proudly raised. But no matter how she walked, they – the elect – paid little attention to a working girl, though they themselves remained before her eyes and in her thoughts all day long.

The Heimanns lived in their own house by the Driksa River. In back of the house was a garden full of trees and bushes, without bright sunlight. The sisters worked in a room whose window was shaded by the dense foliage of horse chestnut trees. The rooms exuded a strange smell. What did it remind one of? Wilted flowers, fragrant herbs, a bit of mold. In summer the house was uninhabited, the windows for the most part closed. The air was cool, it even made one shiver. The sun never entered here.

Silently Līziņa disappeared somewhere inside the rooms and returned with an armful of clothes.

"Here, rip the seams on this one!" she tossed a piece of clothing to Annele. She did not speak. Did not laugh. Seemed like a different person. You could see that something weighed on her here.

Are we going to live here as though we were in a graveyard, then? Annele sighed softly.

They had worked in silence for a while when an octave of trills rushed past the door, then the door burst open – and the warbler herself came flying into the room. White apron. White cambric cap perched like a crest on the bushy pinned-up hair. Carelessly shook hands with Līziṇa, so hasty and loud.

"Hello, hello! Back in our neck of the woods again, are you? Well, well, well!" She was almost bellowing now.

"Are you out of your mind, Jetiṇa?" Līziṇa shushed her.

"Not a living soul in the house. Can't you hear what a ruckus we're making in the kitchen? Dūdiṇa's stopped being a dove, she's turned into a magpie. Bring a little life back to this mausoleum! No sooner had the master and Alphonse gone out one door than the mistress with both her little goats was off to the shops. Right now those three are in clover, because yesterday he loosened the purse strings. And then, you may be sure, there'll be no coming home before lunch. Maybe they'll even order that lunch should be brought over to the shops, to the Jews."

"The baron is away again, is he? I thought he just came home last night?"

"That was enough! One night of being raked over the coals was plenty for the man," laughed Jetiņa. "My dears, he's not used to that dragon. And who can deny him the pleasure? He'd rather be off hunting."

"What do you mean? That's all you hear the whole time: Baron Heimann has gone hunting. Where does he do all this hunting?"

"I'll show you."

Jetiņa ran over to the table and rapped it smartly with her knuckles:

"Slap, slap, slap! That's how he hunts."

"Cards?"

"Well, what else do you think? He drinks and gambles like there was no to-morrow!"

"How about the young baron?"

"Little Alphonse – a greedyguts. Short on brains. Learning from his father's ex-

ample. Soon as he wins anything, he blows it all. Like last night. Then we get our
share. We stick around like flies around a honey pot only because of His Lordship's
kind heart."

"So you must be on the baron's side?"

"Where else? He shows up at the house like a visitor, and it's partying time
again. The kitchen is full, the tables are full. But before you know it – war again. The
son sides with the father, the daughters with the mother. She's like a dragon. And
when she starts in on him – hey, not even the devil could stand it! So why shouldn't
he run away, when he's called by angel voices."

"Cards, you mean?"

"Cards are cards! That's not what – – ! There's also this and that, this and that,
that's the world for you!"

Jetiņa blinked her eyes vaguely.

"Hm, hm, hm," she bent down to Līziņa secretively: "I'll tell you…" But then
caught sight of the girl. The storyteller broke off. And now changed the subject completely, drawling out the words: "So this is your kid sister, eh? Learning the job?
That's right, you go ahead and learn! What else can a person do? The needle, why,
that's a poor girl's bread. Say, maybe I should call her 'Miss,' hey? What a laugh! A
spook like her! Hasn't been to confirmation class yet, has she? Heavens no!"

Now Jetiņa seemed quite nonchalant. She went over and rummaged around in
the pile of clothes.

"Here, what's she going to do with these old rags? Go to an amusement park?
Keeps having them sewed and altered. Two more trunks full of stuff like this. A
dozen for her, a dozen for one little goat, a dozen for the other. You've got work here
to last you till three weeks after doomsday."

"I told the baroness she should bring some fabric for new dresses. That's what
we agreed on. One outfit for each and no more this time. My time is limited. I'm not
going to mend that old trash."

"Good, you show that dragon what's what! Does she have to scrimp and save,
huh? And it's not as though there won't be anyone to wear these old rags. There'll be
plenty. Let her throw them our way."

"The baroness is thrifty."

"Thrifty? Stuff and nonsense! But listen: I'm going to tell you something that'll
make you laugh."

Instead Jetiņa's tongue suddenly stopped short and a smell of something
burning reached their nostrils.

"Oooh, my tongs are burning!" she exclaimed, yelling over her shoulder even as
she went out the door: "I'll come and work in here with you!"

She was back shortly with the ironing board. She propped one end on the
windowsill, the other on one end of the worktable. Then she brought in an armload
of cambric, and finally a little perforated coal stove that had iron tongs stuck in it on
all sides. With nimble fingers, Jetiņa used the hot tongs to pinch little starched blisters that circled the Baroness's gown from top to bottom in row after row like endless chains of piano keys.

"Siberia!" sighed Jetiņa. "How many are there in all? Seven, eight rows of such ruffles! You pinch, pinch, pinch, feeling like an idiot."

"The new outfit that we're going to sew now will have twelve rows."

"Come on, aren't you afraid of committing a sin?" Jetiņa stopped and shook her head reproachfully. But as she tested her tongs with a moistened finger, she looked at Annele repeatedly, and her look clearly said that the girl was not wanted here. Finally she couldn't stand it anymore.

"Listen, love, how would you like to take a look at the barons' rooms? Pass through two rooms, and the third is the drawing room. Plenty for you to see!"

And when Annele still wouldn't budge, Jetiņa came up to her during a pause in her work, took the article she was ripping out of her hands and gave her a push toward the door that led inside.

"Don't you need to stretch your legs? That dragon isn't going to pay you anyhow."

There was no help for it. She had to go so Jetiņa could have a good long talk with Līziņa.

Annele stood in the drawing room and allowed her eyes to wander from the polished parquet floor over the glittering bronze-colored wallpaper and fragile tables and chairs, light as reeds, ornamented with gold decorations. Mirrors stood along the walls wreathed with clusters of golden grapes. The mirrors pulled your whole body into them, from head to foot. So many mirrors!

They drew her closer. She wanted to have a look, to examine herself as though she were a stranger. It was so odd. What did she actually look like? Much too slender, much too thin. And she wasn't making much headway as far as being pretty was concerned. If she took a good look at herself, there was a lot left to be desired.

Further back in the depths of the mirror, she caught sight of a painting in a gilded frame. She turned around to face it.

My, how beautiful it was!

Four stallions harnessed to an unusual two-wheeled chariot were rushing at a gallop into bluish-red piles of clouds. Chains of winged boys, holding hands, hovered around them. Beautiful youths, standing upright, drove the chariot. Others caught at the reins as though, in their daring, they were trying to stop the horses, but were themselves so full of joy, so overwhelmed by the swiftness of the race that they surrendered and flung themselves into the tumult with apparent exultation. The light beyond the rim of the clouds boiled up as if from bottomless wells, the flesh of the little cupids was transfused with light down to the very dimples in their ruddy cheeks. The stallions' flaming eyes were dizzy with light, their knees, gracefully bent in mid-race, glittered with light, the radiant faces of the youths exulted in the light. And they were all united in one single pulse, in an endless surge, endless bliss and joy. Where, where were they bound for? For the world, the great wide world as messengers of light! Toward the sun! No, for it was they who brought the sun itself!

Annele's heart was thrilled as if by a fiery arrow. She exulted with them. Never before had she seen such a beautiful painting. In one corner of it were the words "Guido Reni." That must be the painter who had painted it. What a magician! So great and magnificent, to be able to fascinate and thrill you this way! For a long time she stood there unable to tear herself away, as though trying to absorb all this beauty and take it with her for all time.

"Well, see anything you liked?" asked Jetiņa absently, having satisfied her great craving for talking.

"The painting."

"The painting? What painting?"

"The one in there."

"Will you listen to her!" Jetiņa shrugged. "So you still like little pictures? What a child you are!"

"But listen!!" she interrupted herself, one ear cocked toward the drawing room. Her face stiffened in anxious expectation, and her upraised finger froze. "Frau Baronin!" she blurted out quickly. And then, menacingly to some person unknown:

"This is Dūdiņa's doing. She's jealous that I come here to have a chat with you. Now she must have heard the bell first and secretly shown the baroness in without breathing a word to me. But I'll get even with her for this! She better watch out!"

Dūdiņa was the cook.

In the distance they heard the noise of something trailing across the floor. Jetiņa, who wanted to vanish without delay head over heels with all her equipment, remained where she was as though rooted to the spot and said:

"Here she is, hay wagon and all. We're in for it now."

The baroness came in, a long train of black silk trailing behind her. Eyebrows raised, lips pinched together, eyes sharp and stern, and the first person her eyes saw was Jetiņa.

"You're introducing a new order here, Jete," said the mistress, barely moving her lips.

"It's too hot in my room," Jetiņa, totally cut down in size, tried to come up with an excuse.

"I am speaking, Jete, you are wasting your breath."

The baroness took her eyes off her.

"Guten Morgen, Frau Baronin!" Līziņa greeted her. Annele stood up and curt-sied. The baroness did not so much as bat an eye in her direction. "She didn't see me. I'll have to curtsy one more time." And, not wanting to seem impolite, she did so, catching a moment when it was completely impossible for the baroness to look past her. But the baroness's eyes slid over her with such skill that it seemed there was nothing but air where Annele stood. "What? She doesn't want to see me! Aren't I a human being at all?" A lump of bitterness collected in Annele's throat, and now she stared at the woman, examined from head to foot this baroness who no longer seemed like a living human being to her.

Eyebrows raised and lips barely moving, the mistress continued her instructions and discussion of the work. Her monotonous speech was interrupted by Līziņa's prompt and quick "Ja, Frau Baronin. Nein, Frau Baronin." Not much more. But these interjections were nevertheless proof of her businesslike manner and her refusal to compromise in the face of her employer's capricious remarks.

Jetiņa did not move her things elsewhere. She picked up her little coal stove as though intending to go and replenish the coal, but as soon as the baroness's train was out the door, she was back once more. With her big mouth.

"Well, so that dragon finally cleared out? Now she'll leave us in peace till tonight."

"Jetiņ, Jetiņ!"

"Dearie, one of these days all of them are going to clear out. How much d'you want to bet?"

"What do you mean, all of them?"

"The landowners!"

"When will that be?"

"I don't know just when, but it's going to happen one day. Haven't you heard anything, how things are seething and boiling down below?"

"Not a whole lot, though I *have* heard something. I was told that on the first of May they arrested some young girl. She hung a red flag somewhere. My aunt heard it from the milkwoman, who had been out driving at daybreak. A beautiful young girl apparently. It seems the police walked on either side of her with bayonets, but she walked arms akimbo and held her head high."

"I know about that, and I know the girl, too, but I daren't say anything."

"What happened to her?"

"They let her go. It turned out that it was better for them to keep the whole thing quiet, so people would think there was nothing the matter. Let them think that. But how are you going to hide the smell of burning? Once one person has smelled it, he'll tell another. Things are seething and boiling down below, but who knows? One day, the fortresses of the tyrants will collapse!"

Jetiņa concluded her speech with pathos.

"Will we live to see that day?"

"If we don't, our children will."

And, again cocking an ear in the direction of the door that led inside, she announced:

"The little goats are on their way. Nosy as magpies. Their mother's told them that there's a strange new mug here, so they have to come and have a sniff."

"A strange new mug? Could that be me?" wondered Annele, for the remark couldn't possibly refer to Līziņa. They certainly had a funny way of talking in this place.

The "little goats" were Baronesses Kitty and Daisy. Girls in their teens. They said hello of their own accord, and Annele realized there was no need to curtsy this time. Unlike their mother, they talked a lot, especially with Jetiņa, and asked her questions whose purpose was to demonstrate their own precociousness and the ignorance and obtuseness of their interlocutor, and – wonder of wonders! – Jetiņa was indeed so slow-witted now that she gave the most stupid answers, or else she herself with the most serious face asked questions that caused the baronesses to exchange secret glances and to go into fits of giggling, whereupon they would proffer their explanations, which they must "hammer" into Jetiņa's head, and which she couldn't understand for love or money.

"There. Now they can laugh at those 'stupid peasant wenches' again for the rest of the day," said Jetiņa after the baronesses had run outside.

"Do you always pretend like that?"

"Always, always, Miss Līziņa."

"But do they actually believe you're that stupid?"

"Oh, you'd be surprised at the things they believe! See, they've been raised to think we're not part of the human race. That's the trouble with all of them, you see. But our advantage is that we know them through and through, while they hardly know us at all."

That night, Līziņa dropped on the chair exhausted.

"I don't know what it is, but when I work for that Heimann woman, the work seems twice as hard. The baroness is so arrogant that she crushes a person. You have to struggle against it with all your strength. And maybe she doesn't have an easy time of it, either."

Annele, too, felt that this day in a strange house was different. She had sat still for twelve hours almost without interruption, for even their food had been brought in to them and placed on a small separate table. This was a grueling test for her young limbs. And yet it was not the difficulty she remembered but the day's impressions: Jetiņa, the two "little goats," Frau Baronin. Then they scattered like sand from the palm of one's hand. Had there been anything else?

The very nicest thing of all. The painting!

Four stallions raced out, their knees gracefully bent, sped into ravines of clouds cleft by light. The light urged them to a gallop, lashed at their hooves with fiery whips. And the winged boys shouted with joy, the beautiful youths who raced alongside the chariot shouted with joy, the earth and heaven shouted with joy.

"Light, light! There's just nothing more powerful and more beautiful in the whole wide world!"

"What's that you're saying?"

Oh dear, she had been talking out loud to her thoughts again. Now she said to her sister:

"You know, when you walk through the Heimanns' drawing room, have a look at that painting."

"What painting?"

"It's there on the wall."

"What is it a painting of?"

"You'll see."

"All right, if I remember, I'll take a look," Līziņa said, and her head sank wearily on her pillow.

But Annele kept smiling for a long time in happy remembrance.

"Isn't it lovely that I got to see that painting, and now I'll never forget it. How nice to be rich so you can get something like that and hang it in your rooms."

⌒⫘⌒

One night, when they came home from work, the sisters found Grietiņa, Mrs. Tiedemann's cook, waiting for them. Ruddy-faced, short, stout, she sat fanning herself with the headscarf she had taken off, and wiped perspiration from her face. She waved it at the sisters and said reproachfully:

"Lordy, how we've been waiting for you. Like waiting for the sun to rise. The black one has to be altered, and we don't know what to do."

"The black one was altered just this spring."

That was the same black silk dress that Annele had once lost as she looked up at the clouds.

"And so it was, but now it's no longer the right size. What do you expect: the mistress spent the whole summer at her sister's estate, her that's the provost's wife. You wouldn't believe the ducks, the chickens, the butter and cream there! She's swelled up like an ear of wheat."

"What are her plans?"

"Two weddings, my dear. That's why she has to have both the black and the gray. The provost's two oldest girls are getting married."

"So things are finally starting to move there?"

"Thank God, thank God!" Grietiņa beamed with happiness. "Of course, there are still Theachen, Luischen, Mariechen, and Walfridchen left, but once one end of a string of beads has come untied, the rest will get scattered, too."

"And who is it that's marrying them?"

"Candidates, nothing but candidates," Grietiņa opened wide a pair of stern and proud eyes. "The two of them, while they were with the provost one after the other, took a fancy to the two girls." And, bending closer to Līziņa, lowering her voice: "They do say that it wasn't Luidorchen and Friedachen they wanted, but Theachen and Mariechen, but the old man – that is, God forgive my sins! – the reverend took a firm stand: no picking and choosing! If you're going to take one, then start from the end. And how could they not take one when along with a wife there'd be an estate and a position, as easy as falling off a log? After all, the provost's name is like oil – it greases every wheel.

"One's off to Kurzeme, the other to Vidzeme. Good positions, big estates." Grietiņa told them all about it, but then suddenly jumped to her feet as though startled.

"Oh dear, I've forgotten how late it is! The stack of dirty dishes is still in the kitchen where I flung it down after supper. She told me to leave the lot and run over here, because this is so very urgent."

"We'll manage, you wait and see. Tell me, how many heads are there now at your house?"

"A whole dozen, counting our sons. Madam says: like the apostles of the Lord. She's a holy person, you know, she can quote the Bible. And counting the two of us, and then you – "

"There'll be two of us as well. My sister's coming with me."

"Is that so? Well, let her come and welcome!" Grietiņa invited Annele as though she were company. "Madam isn't one to complain. What's one stomach more or less?"

"I believe my sister will earn her keep."

"Is that right! Well sure, sure! – Me and my big mouth." Grietiņa stopped in embarrassment. But immediately began to impress upon Līziņa: "Now you *must* come, you hear? Come soon. If you don't, we'll get too upset."

The black dress of the reverend's widow was bursting at the seams. There were only two alternatives. Either they could insert pieces at the sides or else wait till it fit again. That would be in spring, when – as the wearer said herself – she had worn out nine skins with work and worry and become "as thin as a rail." It was difficult to imagine this plump, rosy matron with the tightly stretched skirt that strained at its buttons and with a waist encircled by a wide gathered apron "as thin as a rail."

Mrs. Tiedemann flaunted the splendors of her flesh and pondered. Should she insert pieces at the sides? This suggestion was unacceptable. How could she go to a wedding with a dress that was patched? The bride's honor demanded that her relatives' outfits should be brand spanking new. There were great faultfinders on the groom's side of the family. Should she buy a new one? But what would her Kuno, Herbert, Gottlieb, and Helmut say? She'd be robbing them, wouldn't she? No, no! – And yet, come to think of it, she needed a new outfit in any case. Would those be all the weddings there'd be? Among her relatives alone there were four pastors who had nests full of grown-up sons and daughters, not to mention among her friends and acquaintances. Yes, yes!

All things considered, it almost, almost seemed as though she needed a new one! What did Līziņa suggest?

Līziņa said that a new one was urgently needed.

But what kind? Black rep or taffeta?

That didn't much matter, but why black? Wasn't Madam tired of black? There were other suitable colors, weren't there?

"Oh goodness, goodness!" She was too old for a bright-colored dress, she said.

"Not in the least," Līziņa dispelled her doubts.

Well, all right, she would do it on her seamstress's responsibility. She'd tell everybody so. Miss Avots, she would say, had not permitted her to keep on having black dresses made for her, five whole years after her husband's death.

Cheerful and plump, the mistress now got to her feet and left.

And soon afterward, Grietiņa poked her head, flushed from the steam in the kitchen, through the door.

"Well, are we going to have new dresses?"

"Yes indeed!"

"Well, thank God, thank God! That's good. We certainly can't have that Mrs. Katerfeld going around telling people that the widow Tiedemann has no taste at all. That's a lie. We do what we can. It's just that we sometimes try to make a lot out of a little. And that doesn't work."

Next door, in the kitchen, a kettle began to hiss with great fierceness, and Grietiņa's head vanished again.

To make a lot out of a little. Apparently the pastor's widow had to practice that skill quite frequently. Even her flat was too small to allow sufficient freedom for the twelve future "apostles of the Lord," four of her own and eight of the sons of her relatives and friends who had been boarded with her. The relatives and friends did it out of class consciousness, in order to let her earn an extra penny for the education of her four sons, acting all the while as though it were a terrible sacrifice, and often shaking their heads at the widow's skills as an educator. The young people, on the other hand, were perfectly satisfied, even the spoilt ones among them were glad to put up with all the discomforts of the small apartment and the somewhat scanty fare, assuring their parents that nowhere in the world was it as nice as at Aunt Tiedemann's. She too, of course, never said one unkind word about "her boys." A silent unwritten contract kept both sides at an equilibrium. If their foster mother, with characteristic indulgence or, to put it bluntly, cowardice, turned a blind eye to many of the boys' liberties, her twelve-man guard, on the other hand, were careful not to overstep certain boundaries, which would have meant risking the loss of a highly regarded boardinghouse.

Once a week one of the fathers took his turn to come to town in order to discuss the boys' behavior and to instill them with the necessary respect for authority. For what it was worth.

That very first morning, the sisters had met the "flock of apostles" at the front door. They came like a roll of thunder, some tearing down the stairs, some sliding down the banisters. With a rumbling noise they disappeared down the streets, each off to his own school. What would it be like when they all came back to the narrow confines of the flat?

Mrs. Tiedemann stayed away a long time, but not too long for such an important matter. For this purchase involved not only the respective sales clerk, but also the owner himself, who had been especially summoned for this transaction, and who had to inform her of the provenance of the fabric, whether it came from a reputable factory, whether there was no cotton mixed in with the warp, or wool with the weft, whether the shopkeeper could guarantee that it would neither get wrinkled, nor fade, nor wear out, nor show any other sly hidden defects that would shorten its life and prevent it from being passed down to her children's children. And the purchase could not be made until the owner of the shop had taken it upon his conscience like a vow: I pledge my word of honor.

The bell jingled. Grietiņa tripped to the door at a run. But it wasn't the mistress that came.

"Is Mama home?" shouted a voice.

"No, she's not!" Grietiņa shouted back and returned tripping to the kitchen.

"Hurrah, she isn't home!" shouted one and – "Hurrah, she isn't home!" shouted a second, a third, and a fourth.

For a while, doors slammed, footsteps pounded, tables and chairs rattled. There was warbling, whistling, roaring, yelling. Suddenly the door of the workroom burst open, one teenager, armed with a chair, stumbled in backwards, warding off the four legs of another chair, which stabbed him like pikestaffs. Protecting his sides, protecting his back, the fugitive hurled himself under the table, under the girls' feet, which they barely managed to pull out of his way. His pursuer caught up with him. Snorting, they threw themselves on each other and scuffled until finally, in the fist-

fight, the fugitive was bent over like a pocketknife and, surrendering and seeking a reprieve, plaintively moaned, "Mama, Mama!"

At once the pursuer stopped tormenting the little guy, took his hands off him, stood over him arms akimbo, screwed up his face scornfully, spat in an arc: "Coward! Mommy's little darling! Shame on you!" – and was gone.

The pastor's widow came in, throwing up her hands helplessly.

"Children! Children! What kind of devilry are you up to now? What's going on here? Who called out: Mama?"

The fugitive quickly crawled out from under the table, straightened his shoulders, shook himself.

"Nothing at all, Mama! We're being perfectly well behaved. Why do you always attack us for no reason at all?"

The meal was ready. The sisters came in last of all as Grietiņa was lugging in a huge bowl full of meat which she placed before her mistress. The boys sat six on each side. Mrs. Tiedemann at the head of the table. Facing her at the other end of the table, the sisters squeezed into two narrow seats.

Mrs. Tiedemann dished out the food. Each person sat in front of the piece of meat and pile of potatoes he had received until they all had food in front of them and the lady of the house, after helping herself, took up her knife and fork, when all at once all the other knives and forks began to clink and there was no sound but the hurried work of teeth.

Only a few pieces were left in the bowl. Big but bony. These were the ones the lady of the house would offer the second time around. And that's what she did, starting with the oldest:

"Ferdinand, one more little piece?"

"Thank you, no!"

"How about you, Kuno?"

"Thank you, no!"

"But surely Franz is going to have some?"

"No, no, Aunt. I'm full."

If one of the boys and particularly big Ferdinand has said no, they'll all say no, Mrs. Tiedemann can be sure of that.

And they were right. They'd be charged for it, but what was there to gnaw on, on that leftover bone?

Now, however, the widow also notices Annele's quick eyes, following everything. She misunderstands.

Not yet knowing the girl's name, she hospitably offers:

"Well, little one, how about you? One more little piece? Here you are! The bowl is looking at you."

Annele is overcome by embarrassment. At this moment she feels she is the focus of everybody's attention. What should she do now? How should she behave? And then she shoots up straight as a rocket. She makes a deep curtsy:

"No, thank you, Frau Pastorin!"

"Cra-cra-cra-cra!"

As though a chair had suddenly cracked somewhere next to her.

No, it's only Herbert, who has jumped involuntarily, choking back a titter that has involuntarily escaped onto his lips. But the titter is already out. It has run across twelve faces, now as a grin, now as a smirk, now as a weirdly grimacing mouth or mockingly turned-up nose.

"They're laughing at me," there is a burst of heat through Annele's head. "But what'd I do? Oh, the curtsy! I guess it's out of place here. In fact, it's out of place, period. Everybody here behaves like a grown-up, while I'm acting like a little girl."

There was a rumble of chairs. The widow had pushed back hers, and this was a signal for everyone to disappear in a hurry, like partridge chicks from their nest.

In the little room next to the kitchen there was room for only one extra chair.

This was for Mrs. Tiedemann when, from time to time, she would come in to see what progress the construction work on her new heather-colored gown was making.

After the noon meal, silence set in briefly in this noisy house. The young folks were sitting over their books, Madam was taking a nap, and the rattling of dishes next door and the tripping of Grietiņa's footsteps had sunk into oblivion somewhere. But it, too, stopped, and Grietiņa herself, plump and shiny as though she had been oiled, slid into the room and sank down on the mistress's chair. Her limbs were heavy with the day's work and her heart was heavy with the complaints of which she wished to unburden herself. At moments like this she was no longer some "we" who, feeling solidarity with Mrs. Tiedemann, proud in her heather-colored silk dress, went to annoy the Katerfeld woman, who was descended from "the gentry," – now she was only a little "me," alone with her worries, the hardships of her job, and the bitterness that could barely be expressed in a brief interval of leisure by a tear stealthily dropped on her greasy hands.

And this was her song of lamentation:

"Can you imagine it, can you imagine it? Up at four and to bed at eleven. No less than twelve pairs of boots lined up like soldiers every morning. Couldn't she have arranged things so each of them would polish his own? It wouldn't have made the rings drop off their fingers. But no! 'They're not used to doing it at their own house, how can I make them do it now?' says Madam. And if she doesn't make the strangers do it, her own children are hardly going to do it, are they? And so it's all up to me. Not to mention the rooms, the baker, the dishes! And the market! My arms get strained with the stuff I have to carry by the time I bring home supplies for that army! But d'you think they're grateful? 'Dumme Gans!' is all I hear out of this one's mouth, out of that one's mouth. Madam wouldn't do that, I'd be a liar if I said so, but it's no picnic for her, either. And believe me, she's often scared of those rapscallions. What can you do? Twice Madam and I wanted to go our separate ways, but then there was an ocean of tears. We both cried. And that was that. She's got to live, I've got to live. Where can you go? How long can I live on those few pennies I've earned during this life of hardship? You think I won't eat my bread with tears at my relatives' house? It would be just the same. If you have no roof of your own, you're buffeted by every wind that comes."

"Gretchen!" the widow's voice was heard calling somewhere. And Grietiņa sprang to her feet as though stung, responding with the words she always had ready: "Yes, Madam!" She tripped off in a hurry.

Supper was at eight. They all sat in the same order. Each of the people at the table received a sausage and potatoes. The sausages had been counted, and there were none left to offer a second time around. Later, Grietiņa brought in a bowl full of cream of wheat pudding. There was quite a lot of it left over.

"Ferdinand, have another spoonful! Please do! You can see there's plenty in the bowl!"

As if he had been waiting for just such an offer, Ferdinand, like someone pricked by a needle, shot to his feet, pulled a silly face, made a deep curtsy, and breathed as though embarrassed: "No, thank you, no, thank you!"

Mrs. Tiedemann gave him a funny sort of look, but said nothing. Then she turned to the next one:

"Well, how about you, Kuno, another spoonful?"

Kuno jumped to his feet and mimicked what Ferdinand had done to a T.

So did Herbert. After this, all three sat down again in their places.

All this was so conspicuous and so funny that Mrs. Tiedemann gave a loud laugh.

"Children, children! What's the meaning of all this, eh? I do believe you're making fun of somebody, aren't you?"

She didn't have an inkling who it was, for she had not even noticed Annele's thank-you at lunchtime.

Annele, however, knew who it was they were making fun of. She saw herself mimicked and ridiculed. It wasn't enough that at lunch the boys had exchanged looks, made signs to each other, and mocked at her gauche behavior with suppressed laughter; no, even now they had to go out of their way to draw attention to it in this distorted form and embarrass and ridicule her for a second time. Līziņa, too, realized that it was her little sister who was the butt of the boys' tomfoolery; she quickly thanked the lady of the house and rose to her feet, anxious to leave and take her sister with her.

But Annele wasn't about to leave yet. Red as a beet, her hands clenched around the back of the chair, she did not avoid their glances or hang her head, although standing there like that was as hard as carrying a load of rocks. But her eyes were trying to provoke a fight: Look at me, you boys! And they did look at her. For one moment, the blade of her eyes was crossed with twelve others, and if it had been able to, it would have spoken as follows: "Don't think I don't realize what you're trying to do. You're trying to hurt me and treat me with contempt, but you yourselves are contemptible for acting this way. There are twelve of you while I'm all alone, you live in abundance, while I live in poverty, but I shall persevere and strive for higher things, and I shall be where you are; who knows, perhaps I'll even surpass you. You wait and see."

Her eyes had no more to say.

"You mustn't take it to heart. Stupid boys," Līziņa soothed her.

"What makes you think I do?" retorted the girl, but felt the sting of tears in the back of her eyes.

"That's good! No sense letting it get you down!"

Artistic Aspirations

The graveled paths of Schirkenhöfer Park were densely packed and washed clean by the many showers of July. Though it was no longer raining, you could feel the fragrance of the surrounding gardens and distant fields in the air: new-mown wheat, ripening apples. In the thick velvety foliage of the park's linden trees – who knows when – long golden curls had secretly appeared here and there.

The little white tables, with chairs neatly arranged around them, were empty and waiting, while a few scattered people sat on the long benches by the platform. There was no one on the platform itself, and the door at the back was locked.

And people began to arrive in larger groups. Among them were Līziņa, Aunt Meire, and Annele. The latter a few steps ahead of the others: mustn't be late! Flushed and a little out of breath under the thick ruffles of her black silk bonnet, Aunt begged them, "Don't run, don't run! We'll get there, don't you worry!"

In the middle of the park, they suddenly stopped short. There was a quick consultation: where should they sit? Aunt's eyes slid toward the side. At one of the little tables would be nice. There they could hear and have a good view as well, which was important, wasn't it? But suppose they were expected to eat and drink something there? And of course they'd be expected to do just that. Not for nothing was there a battle line of waiters, the tops of their heads glossy smooth, shirtfronts white, drawn up by the restaurant building. Distrustfully and watchfully they observed the crowd that was gathering here. An unaccustomed one in this park.

In the meantime the first three rows of benches had already become dotted with people. They must hurry. Annele ran into the fourth one from the left end, while floating toward her from the right came a burgher with a bowler hat, his coat pushed untidily back over his shoulders. Together, they reached the middle of the bench, together they sat down. The burgher sighed:

"Made it at last! Almost too late. Wouldn't want to be jostled by all sorts of riff-raff in the back rows. It's all because they've got no numbered seats. No order. Typically Latvian."

"What's he scolding for?" Annele drew away from him. When he scolded about the Latvians, she, too, felt offended.

From the bench in front of them, a lady turned the veiled tip of her nose in their direction.

"Ah, so you're here too, Mr. Wachtel!"

"Certainly, certainly," responded the man she had called Wachtel, bowing courteously and benevolently. "I had to bring Mamma, you see. The Latvians are singing. Childhood memories. And seeing as how I was bringing Mamma, I brought the children as well."

With his elbow, he nudged a boy in short pants who jumped up and clicked his heels as he bowed to the lady; behind the boy, a slightly smaller girl curtsied, and finally Mamma bowed her head covered with a gray checkered silk babushka.

"Same here. I also only came because of Mamma. I've certainly heard enough concerts in my life," said the lady as though apologizing, but Mamma, next to her in a heavy velvet bonnet, pretended she hadn't heard and began a rather loud conversation with her daughter in German as though to indicate that she dissociated herself from the mamma in the fourth row with her gray checkered babushka, and that she was not at all the type of person for whose sake they'd have had to come to hear the Latvians sing.

"Wonder if this is just going to be a concert for the mammas, and if these people are going to act as though they were only sitting here out of pity?" Annele thought to herself, and felt a sort of shadow pass over the great enthusiasm that had filled her from the moment Līziņa came home with the happy news that on Sunday Latvian choirs from Rīga would be singing in Schirkenhöfer Gardens, and that they must go no matter what, for the two of them, working so hard these last weeks, had earned it, so even Mother could raise no objections that this was an extravagance. She didn't object, but she herself could not be talked into coming and thus spending additional "bitterly hard-earned" pennies.

Annele turned her back on her right-hand neighbors. She felt they'd have a hard time thawing out in her presence, and she preferred not to listen to their talk.

"They're coming, they're coming! Gathering! The place is going to be full. Well, I think they deserve it," rejoiced Aunt Meire. "But isn't your Kaparsons here?"

"Since when is he 'our' Kaparsons?" retorted Līziņa. "Why, he keeps climbing higher and higher. I hear he can't stand the smell of Latvians anymore. They say it makes him sick."

"Just like my godson Glomis. You know what he calls himself now? – Gianno Glomé. Supposedly that's what it will say on the new signboard he's having painted for his shop."

"Well, you see, he married that Germanized hairdresser's widow, shop and all. She probably wants it that way."

"Ah yes. Our lost sons and daughters. Our nation certainly has enough of them!" sighed Aunt.

In the park, there was a sudden upsurge of murmuring, and then it stopped. The singers, who had appeared noiselessly, already stood on the platform. The conductor waited a moment and raised his baton. Holding back and summoning, subduing and reassuring, he drew forth sounds from the singers' breasts, in turn tossed them up to serene heights, plunged them in deep gloom, made them thunder and warble, hum and jubilate. Oh, how rich it sounded!

Annele had been a child of song from the time she was little. The sound of songs had accompanied her short life like a river rushing past its banks. There were the early evenings in spring when women and young girls had welcomed the new season

with their songs on the hills of
Spring Farm. There was Midsummer night, full of holy mystery with its fires and endless Līgo
songs. There was the work of the
harvesters, with Father at their
head, and the endless skeins of song unwound by the light of kindling wood in
winter. And there was Annele herself, knee-deep in song, herding the cattle on the
barrens! She had acquitted herself creditably in the little choir of her summer school,
too. One holiday, her teacher had even taken this choir of his to church to "enrich
the divine service." But this was the first time she had ever heard singing like this.
Shivers ran through her limbs. As though a curtain had opened, and her soul was
able to fly into another world where a vaster space, a different freedom, awaited it. As
though some puzzle had been solved, as though scattered fragments of memory had
been reassembled and become clear to her. But where did these memory fragments
come from? What were they connected with? The ancient past of her people, or-
phans singing at night with the sun gone, an orphan girl running to catch up with the
setting sun, a gray horse wading through a marsh. How was it possible to feel this
and love this with such fervor? How was it possible to be so fearful and downcast and
at the same time to soar with such joy into distant times and futures! Songs raised
you from the grave, songs were the guiding star. Dark pinewoods, treetops from
which sunlight had fled, faces of sufferers overcome by tears. How dear the songs
were. And near. Undying was the longing for the sun, undying the hatred for foreign
tyrants and abusers. Undying as the life of her people. The songs expressed it, the
heart felt it.

When the singers had finished, everyone clapped, and floods of suppressed
chatter burst forth.

"They can sure belt it out!" Annele's neighbor nodded his approval.

"Yes, I guess they can sing," added the lady with the veil over her nose, as though to intimate that she, of course, would not allow herself to be taken in and moved by singers like these.

"Well, what more can you expect of these people?" said Mr. Wachtel, so that she would not think he, too, hadn't heard anything "better" or that he was about to praise the performers.

"And always the same old songs!" the lady went on. "Why, in the country all the herd girls sing those."

The conductor tapped his baton, and everyone grew silent. The sounds of music began to rustle like breezes in a forest.

> "How dear you are, my Latvia,
> My precious native land,
> With birch groves cool and green,
> With bounteous fields of grain;
> Unless our love for you is fervent,
> We are not fit to dwell upon your shores!"

What a song! Who had made it? After singing of the hardships of the past, of a people who longed for the sun, the singers now told of Latvia itself, their "dearly be-

loved" country. Here was everything that was so precious and familiar: the woods of
Spring Farm, the hills, the fields, the little house on the barrens where she had spent
the years with her father and mother, green birch groves, bountiful fields of grain,
visible far off in the distance from Shepherd Hill. All this was contained in the singers' song and shimmered brightly as though under a summer sun. And the sun's
circle spread further, much, much further, and comprised as yet unknown distances, fused them together into one word: Latvia, overspread them with an all-em-
bracing feeling: how dear, how dear!

> "Born from your womb,
> I grew up in your bosom,
> Cradle of my destiny,
> You made me what I am;
> I am your child, sent forth
> With all your blessings."

Cradle of my destiny! Oh, what lovely words, so rich with promise! Her soul
folded its wings, small and quiet it lay down in the cradle of its destiny and returned a
promise for a promise: "From you, I shall receive my destiny, I shall raise it until it is
full-grown and return it to your bosom again."

> "Your blessings will go with me
> Wherever I will roam,
> And I will love you constantly
> Till I am laid to rest;
> Then in your bosom oh how gently,
> How sweetly shall I sleep!"

"Ah yes! In our native soil," whispered Aunt Meire, wiping her eyes. The
mamma with the gray checkered babushka, too, suddenly had a handkerchief in her
hands, while the lady and her mother sat motionless and apparently did not want to
show their tears.

"That's a song I'm not familiar with at all. It's the first time I've heard it," the
lady expressed her surprise.

"Then it must have been made up by one of those Young Latvians," conjectured
Mr. Wachtel.

"You're probably right," agreed the lady.

"Lately the Young Latvians have been blathering about nothing but Latvia and
the nation and such."

Not until the singers disappeared from the platform did they turn back into
flesh and blood human beings in Annele's eyes. They were men and women of various ages dressed in dark clothes, wearing black boots and shoes.

The lady with the veil had a program. She announced:

"Now come the students from the teachers' college."

"Student teachers, eh? Wonder what they're up to?"

"Wait and see, wait and see!"

The intermission was over. Helter-skelter, people ran back to their seats. A
group of young men wearing college uniforms were already standing on the plat-

form. Their conductor was young, too. Looking back over his shoulder, he looked at the audience proudly and sternly, back to the farthest corner, as though to tell them: Hey, quiet down, will you! As soon as there was silence, he turned to his group and nodded at them encouragingly. Maybe he was saying: Do a good job, boys! That's what it looked like. And the boys did do a good job. While the preceding singers had been lovely, this was something different again. This was youth, this was Annele's own heart ringing with song as though in joyous battle, singing against the winds. It felt as if they were not just singing with their voices, but with every minute fiber of their bodies, every pulse throb, though they themselves stood there motionless as if carved from stone. One in particular seemed to surpass all the others not only because of the sonorousness and richness of his voice, which like a river pulled the brooks of the other voices into itself, but also because of his stateliness and proud bearing. Taller than the rest, he had fairly long blond hair that curled around his forehead like a garland. And when the clouds suddenly parted and the sun shot a golden arrow exactly over the spot where the young men were standing, one might have thought it wanted to point out that one special singer in all his strength and pride.

No matter what the students sang, the songs all bubbled forth from their breasts like rippling springs. Much too quickly they passed over the listeners' heads like birds with golden-tipped wings.

Already the veiled lady who had the program was turning toward Mr. Wachtel: the last piece. And it seemed that the singers were making extra-special preparations for this last piece. The conductor stood there for quite a while communicating with his group, particularly with the fair-haired man who stood facing him right in front. Only then did he tap his stand, giving the signal, and raise his baton.

"Rīga dimd, Rīga dimd!" Rīga reverberates with a sound like thunder! – like a thunderclap the song resounded in the listeners' breasts, made them tremble, jarred them so that to the farthest corner of the park none could fail to be attentive or remain indifferent to the question that followed, sharply and distinctly posed by the singers:

"What makes it reverberate like that?"

The song gave the answer: "Thrice nine brothers, forging a hope chest for their sister, fill Rīga with the sound of thunder."

And the song provided an explanation. Who was the sister? It was Latvia herself. That was clear. The thrice nine brothers were the sons of the people, makers of a magnificent hope chest in honor of their sister. Rīga rings out, rings out with the sound of thunder. This was a cry of warning directed at foreign tyrants, at those who sought to stifle the light, at those who oppressed their brothers in servitude. Oh, how liberating it was, how releasing, how it drew forth joy from your breast, so that you had to push it back with both hands to keep it from breaking forth as loudly as from those singers, those jubilant young men on the stage. How she wished she could tell them that now she, too, knew what they knew, that in this hour of song the word "Latvia" had emerged from the darkness for her as a shining star emerges from the black mists of an autumn night. If they are young men, strapping young fellows, forgers of Latvia's hope chest, and if that young lad is the one who cast the golden lid, no doubt the bravest, the proudest, the noblest of them all, they mustn't disparage her, Annele, either. She too would be capable of something, she too would be something one day in the distant future…

"It's over. Finished."

The veiled lady rose to her feet.

"Bravo, bravo! Encore! Great voices!"

Annele's neighbor was enthusiastic.

"Yes, I liked them too," the lady nodded her approval. "The songs may be old, but when they sing them like that they're all right. And the fellow with the bushy hair was especially good."

"Yes, he could really belt it out."

Annele clapped her hands. Her aunt nudged her: "Girls don't do that." She didn't care. When the others waved their handkerchiefs, she did the same. How was she to show her enthusiasm, her joy and gratitude? Nothing seemed enough. They should have showered them with all the flowers in this park and in the other gardens, especially that one singer.

The young men stood motionless for a moment while the conductor bowed to thank the audience, then he left the platform and behind him one after another the singers slid out the narrow door at the back. The shining bond that had linked them in one breath had been loosened. And look where they passed, one with his overcoat flung over his shoulders, another with a cigarette in his mouth, chatting merrily, hurrying to catch the train. Proudly and gaily they walked, like heroes.

Mother had given them strict instructions to be sure and ask Aunt home to tea after the concert. Kristaps's father had brought bread made from newly threshed rye that must be sampled.

The sisters set the table and waved songs at each other like flowering branches. As soon as one would finish, the other would begin. Aunt listened.

"I wish you could remember that beautiful one, the one about Latvia. That would be worth something."

"Yes, yes, let's. Before we forget."

Līziņa propped her elbow on her knee, tucked her chin in the palm of her hand and began "chasing" the song through the chambers of her mind. Soon she had it. She was better at remembering tunes, while Annele was better at the words.

Kristaps came in. He too had been at the concert, but only just by the gate.

"Go ahead, sing! I'll add the bass."

"D'you know it?"

"Wait and hear."

The song turned out all right and delighted both listeners. Mother was amazed.

"My, how beautiful!"

"I still can't do it properly," said Līziņa.

"It'll get smoothed out, you'll see. Why, who ever heard of anybody joining choirs and such in the old days? People used to learn from each other and just start singing. I can't tell you how many songs I learned from others that way, and how many I passed on myself. Now my well of songs is all choked up," Mother said, shaking her head.

"But how come Kristaps can do the bottom part? It's a wonder to me. I could see how a person could remember the top part fairly easily, but I'd never get the bottom part into my head even if you paid me," mused Aunt. "How can you remember it?"

Kristaps pulled his left eyelid down, thus managing to make the right side of his face look swollen, too funny for words.

"How could I not remember it when all I listen to is the bottom part? I don't even hear the top part."

While they talked over the day's impressions, they were all still together. Only Kristaps had disappeared. But then they were all startled by a voice behind them.

"Habe Se net was zu verhandele?"

Mother jumped to her feet.

"Crazy Jew! Can't leave people alone even on Sunday!" She expected to see the Jew Shmuel – as he was called – who, like the wandering Jew Ahasuerus, roamed the streets day in, day out with this question, climbed every flight of stairs, shuffled through all the hallways, looked behind every door and gate.

"Crazy Jew! Can't leave people alone even on Sunday!" her own voice echoed back at her.

"Kristaps! You clown," they all laughed.

Wearing Mother's old coat, he had tied on a beard made of shredded silk and wool rags, drawn lines on his face with charcoal, which suddenly made it screwed up and old like a turtle's, had powdered his hair with flour, and stood there hunched over, shoulders pulled in, with an old umbrella that he had opened and was wildly brandishing this way and that. The umbrella was one over which Mother and Shmuel had already bargained more than once. The way Mother stated her price and Shmuel made his bid, the way Mother chased him away and he kept sticking his head with its long peyes in the door again and again and would not take no for an answer, the way in spite of all the haggling nothing ever came of the bargain – Kristaps played it all, doing both voices in turn, so true to life that the spectators couldn't stop laughing and Mother, too, had to laugh so hard that she neglected to scold the boy for all his tricks, though she did admonish him never ever to play such a practical joke again or to make fun of grown-ups like that.

"Just look at the way that boy was playacting, you'd think you were at the theater," Aunt praised Kristaps after he had disappeared with the torn-off shreds of beard, muttering even as he went out the door, in the old Jew's voice, "Habe Se net was zu verhandele? Habe Se net was zu verhandele?"

"Well, he certainly has the gift of the gab," laughed Mother.

It wasn't customary for Kristaps to offer people anything from his sack of apples. He kept it secret, munched the apples on the sly, throwing the cores under the table. And now, for the second time, he came up to Annele with his hands full.

"They're kind of wormy, but not bad to munch on."

The girl looked at him mistrustfully. How come he was so generous? And, sinking her white teeth into the delicious fruit, she gave vent to her suspicions:

"You've got something up your sleeve. What do you want from me?"

"You guessed it," said Kristaps, gratified. "All right, here's the deal: we're going to put on a play."

"A play?"

"Sure!"

"Who's we?"

"Me. And you, too, of course."

"Me? That'll never happen."

"It will, too! I'll bring a nice play, and we'll put it on."

"Who's going to teach us?"

"I will!"

"You?"

"Sure!"

Annele looked at her cousin as though trying to figure out if Kristaps had suddenly lost his mind. But then shook her head:

"I just don't believe that. You think that just because you can mimic the Jew, you're some big shot and can play God knows what. No, no, it's not that easy."

"You'll see, you'll see," Kristaps said with great self-confidence. "You're going to have a big surprise one of these days."

The very next day, when he came home from school, he tossed a skimpy little book to his cousin.

"Here you go."

"What is it?"

"A play."

"Are you still seriously thinking of putting one on?"

"Quite seriously. Here, read it!"

"Deaf Daniel," Annele read the title.

"What kind of a play is that?"

"Start from the beginning, come on! Read it! Then you'll see."

She read a scene or two. Kristaps kept his eyes glued on her, listening with his mouth open.

"You're good at reading, so you'll be good at acting, too. If you say it exactly that way, then it'll be right," he gave his opinion with the certainty of an expert.

The unexpected praise gratified the girl, of course, and made her more accommodating.

"But there are several characters playing in it, aren't there? Where are we going to get them?"

"We'll get them. Zete and Marija Kauliņš, who live with Aunt Meire, can take the women's parts."

"Will they want to?"

"Why shouldn't they?"

"And the men's parts?"

"I'll get a hold of a few boys from my school."

"You keep saying 'get a hold of': as though you had a warehouse somewhere. What makes you think they'll come running?"

"Well, what do you think? Why shouldn't they? They'll come with bells on. In other schools there are Latvian clubs, but we don't have any in our school because we're all Latvians there, so why have clubs? But lots of fellows would like to do something, they just don't know what. They'll be glad when I tell them."

Annele tossed the book back to him. She had a low opinion of the play. Kristaps defended it.

"A good play. I've seen Alunāns act in it. You could split your sides laughing. Of course, we've got to sing comic songs. They're a must. Comic songs are the most important thing in any play."

"Are you going to sing them?"

"Of course. I'm going to be "Deaf Daniel," you see. His part is made up of nothing but comic songs. And you have to write your own comic songs. That's the trick. Alunāns does, too. And I've got one in mind already. Listen to this!"

He struck a pose, stretched out his arm and bellowed out in his deep voice:

"Through the city streets they go,
Scaring dogs and cats and sparrows..."

"So that's a comic song. Pretty crude, if you ask me. One word is short, the other one is long," Annele interrupted.

"Which one is short?"

"Go and sparrows! That doesn't rhyme."

"A fat lot you know. A comic song is not a couplet, don't you see. You don't measure it with a ruler. If you could only hear all the stuff that Alunāns makes up! Just as long as it comes out funny and that people laugh. The rest doesn't matter. Listen, here's how it goes on:

"Farm boys with their muddy boots on,
Lasses dressed in country fashion!"

"Boots on and fashion. Worse and worse! Well, and how does it go then?"

"That's all I've thought of so far. But later there'll be a dig at some boy or girl that everybody knows. That's the most important thing. You must always pick a target that everybody knows, then everybody gets to laugh. And that's the joke. Everybody gets hauled over the coals. Nobody is spared."

"Find me one person who'll laugh at your comic songs."

"We'll see, we'll see. When people write something good, they show their wit. These things aren't easy to write, but I'm going to do it," Kristaps vowed, waving his arms about and acting quite intimidating.

"We can learn our parts in advance, and when the others come, we'll be ahead of them and we'll have it easy. I'll talk to the boys, and it won't take long to convince the girls at Aunt Meire's. Then we can start on Sunday."

"What part am I going to have?"

"The more stage business there is, the better the part, and that's the sort of part you'll have. There's this genteel lady that writes plays, she's afraid of her own shadow, screams, has fainting fits, and generally acts like a crazy woman. You take that part. There's something to sink your teeth into. Alunāns also takes only those parts where you can act wild and crazy."

Annele read the play and shrugged her shoulders. Where did things like this happen in real life? Nowhere. But of course the theater was not real life. After all, that's how it had been in the big building by the market square where the German actors from Rīga had shown their skills in spring. On that stage, one piece of foolishness had followed another in such quick succession that Annele had not felt like laughing at all. She had merely wondered why on earth it was all happening that way. Meanwhile other people, including people who were quite old, had roared with laughter. Some even laughed so hard they had tears running down their cheeks.

If Kristaps liked, she could act the part of the genteel lady who wrote and had fainting fits. Simple as ABC! She could already visualize her from top to toe. How she minced and flounced, how she ran and stumbled over the train of her dress when she was scared, uttered a shriek, swooned, and lay dead as a fly till somebody poured water on her face. A scarecrow, not a human being.

Sunday morning she and Kristaps had a rehearsal. Mother was in church, and Līziņa was in the back room. She was not in sight.

First Kristaps went over his scenes. Annele had to read whoever his partner happened to be.

"I've got a new gimmick," Kristaps said with a wink.

"What sort of gimmick?"

"You'll see!"

The whole action and complications of the play were based on the fact that Daniel was deaf. This gave rise to endless misunderstandings.

Daniel was a footman. People called him. They gave him orders. They pushed and shoved him. He shouted back, ran, stumbled, did things. But of course his answers were completely off, and everything he did was inappropriate. And then he resorted to the comic songs.

Kristaps's trick was this: At the start and finish of every sentence, he would cause a thundering Wha-a-t! to explode like the cork from a seltzer bottle.

This is what Zemgale farmhands would shout to each other when they came to Jelgava and communicated with each other across two city blocks.

"Wha-a-t!"

It wasn't in the book.

"Wha-a-t!"

The walls reverberated. Līziņa flung open the door.

"Have you got cannons mounted here?"

"Wha-a-a-t?" Kristaps retorted as she stood in the doorway, for after all he was acting in character.

"What are you two doing here?"

"Studying."

"Studying? Good God! You people take the cake! What are you studying?"

"Studying our parts in the play!"

Līziņa, of course, thought Kristaps was pulling her leg.

In her raised hand, her penholder stabbed the air like a pikestaff. She was writing a letter to the Lithuanian relatives. And after watching a while she quickly closed the door so as not to lose the sentence that had just occurred to her.

Kristaps lowered his voice.

"That'll do for me. I'll sing the comic songs later, when Līziņa goes to mail her letter. I'll perform my part all right, you'll see. But now you practice yours."

"Me?"

"Yes. I'll read the other part."

Annele gave him a puzzled look. Was he serious? Oh, that's right, she really had volunteered to play a part.

But how was she to do it? Why, just a while ago it had seemed easy to her. But suddenly it was as though a door had slammed shut. No, I won't do it. What will it be like if I act like that? I can't jump out of my skin and jump into another, can I? And such a silly creature, too. No, no! What'll I look like? My arms and legs will stick out of that other skin and my head too, and meanwhile Kristaps's boys and Aunt's girls will sit here laughing at me, laughing because it will turn out to be neither fish nor fowl, and I'll be embarrassed.

Embarrassment! There was the big obstacle. If she had been able to pull the unfamiliar skin of her role over her head, over her eyes, then she would have tried to cope with her role as brazenly and boldly as Kristaps did with his. At least that's how she imagined it. But if she herself was visible in the role – no, then she just couldn't.

"Well, why don't you start!" Kristaps was impatient.

"I won't. I'm not going to play."

"What *is* this? You most certainly are!"

"Leave me alone! I'm not going to make a fool of myself."

"Are you saying that I'm making a fool of myself?"

"Well, what do you think?"

"Then actors make fools of themselves, too."

"Actors are trained, they're good at it, but how do you think our play will turn out? A disgrace!"

"Well, if *you* can't do it, then don't assume others can't either. The others will be able to do it all right, only you can't."

"I don't want to."

"You can't. Not everybody is talented, you know."

There, he had said it. Annele was so surprised that she didn't know how to respond.

There you are! Kristaps is talented, but she isn't.

She tried to change the subject.

"Besides, where are you going to put on the play in this house? In a mitten? And who's going to come and listen to you?"

"That's no way to talk," said Kristaps with restrained superiority. "Where there's a will there's a way. But what's the sense of talking about it? I don't have to beg you. There are more educated people in the world who know something about art."

He'd said it again: there are more educated people who know something.

After this stinging remark, Kristaps folded the little book and left. This artistic aspiration had gone up in smoke. And it wasn't as though Annele weren't sorry.

"I really could have played if I had made up my mind to and if Kristaps wasn't like that," she thought.

"You couldn't do it because you're not talented," an inner voice answered her from Kristaps's mouth.

"It's not as though I've ever wanted to be an actress."

"That's what you think now. You'd like it all right if you could do it, but you can't. You simply don't know how to, so there!"

This was a heavy load on Annele's mind. She couldn't be an actress. It weighed on her all day long. She couldn't be a sister of charity, she couldn't be an actress, so where was the talent Līziņa had had in mind? She didn't see it.

Annele never found out if Kristaps got to play Deaf Daniel anywhere. For a while he closed himself off from her, and closed his sack of apples as well.

Is This Happiness?

What had happened to Līziņa? The young woman who had been so talkative, who loved to laugh, who so courageously leapt over all hurdles, who had all this time been able to keep the impudent nose of Mother Care away from the door of her heart – Come, come, love, you'd better stay outside – that young woman had completely changed. She would run somewhere, turn back again: I forgot something. She'd give Annele work to do, explain it, but a minute later she'd say, "Did I tell you how to do it? It's slipped my mind." – "You did, you did." Annele would ask her something, two, three minutes would go by, five minutes, Annele would repeat her question. Her sister would give a start as though waking from sleep: "Oh yes. Was there something you wanted to know?" And again she'd forget to answer. That was the way it was. She would look without seeing, speak without waiting for an answer, go somewhere, but her feet would forget their destination and return to the same place. A long interval while she was lost in thought, a sigh, an even longer interval – a tear swiftly and stealthily brushed away by her slender fingers, which like cogs in a machine did not interrupt the rhythm of the work for a single instant.

Mother did not notice much of this. She looked after the little household, and her spinning wheel hummed in the next room whenever she had free time. The mistress of Black Earth Farm, when she sent an extra little sack of groats and a cut of bacon along with Kristaps's provisions, had not forgotten to tie on a sack of wool and flax, asking the diligent spinner to hurry before the autumn mud came. She badly needed to pay the men and women hired hands, to make sheets for the beds, trousers for her husband, jackets for the children. At Black Earth Farm, there were many bellies to be fed, many bodies to be clothed.

Mother was submerged in her work like a diver under water. Prrr, prrr! The purring waves of the spinning wheel, now rising, now falling, filled the room. The purring waves brought the life that was gone flooding back. The spinner, her head bent slightly to one side, rocked gently in a rhythm produced by her own magic. Her lips moved almost imperceptibly, as though she were in secret conversation with someone. To Annele it seemed as though she were not speaking but singing. Singing, singing with inaudible, unending words intelligible only to herself.

When the work filled her whole day, Mother felt content. No, she had observed no change in her older daughter.

But Annele had. The antennae of her soul were constantly alert, extended in all directions: what is it? What's going on? A premonition of the change that was now becoming visible had dawned in her consciousness long ago. But she could not see anything clearly. The horizon was dark. Nebulous. Her sister was suffering and bearing a burden. There was something difficult she had to do. Something she had to decide. Some journey she had to take whose end she could not discern. Dear sister! If it were only possible to help her somehow!

Līziṇa worked alternately at home and at the Ranks' house. Sometimes she was occupied there for several days, even as much as a week, but she would not take her sister with her. Her excuse was that it was a sort of interim period, and that sewing was of secondary importance. Mrs. Rank was putting up large stores of fruit and berry preserves for the winter, and Līziṇa had to help as much as she could. Mrs. Rank knew how her mother had done it, but Līziṇa had gathered all kinds of knowledge and instructions during her working life, as a bee sucks honey from many kinds of flowers. She had notebooks filled with recipes. There were household hints not only from the fancy cook at the Heimann house, but also from Mrs. Tiedemann and from Aunt Meire, whose beehive of knowledge and experience was the joint property of all her Jelgava-born and -bred neighbor ladies who came to visit her.

Līziṇa's characterization of Mrs. Rank was brief: she was a "human being." She did not try to squeeze, as though from a lemon, the last drops from the young woman who worked for her. Perhaps she hadn't learned how to do it yet. But this benefited Līziṇa, always busy as a beaver. Mrs. Rank did not count the hours or even minutes, did not listen to the stroke of the clock to calculate if a stitch had been left out of her property – the time she had paid for; often she would impetuously rush into the room in the middle of an afternoon's work, throw the cover over the sewing machine and say: "Enough stitching, enough pricking. Spread your wings a bit!" Oh, she did not have to repeat it twice to Līziṇa, who longed for wings, whose feet were light, who regarded all work that contrasted with her daily tasks as a pleasant relaxation and diversion.

One day, night had already fallen. The usual hour at which Līziṇa would ordinarily return from the Ranks' was past, but still she did not come.

"What's keeping her?" Annele was getting impatient.

"She's probably dropped in to see Aunt."

"No, she was there yesterday."

"Maybe she's spending the night at the Ranks'."

That, too, could not be the case, for the Ranks' spare room was now occupied by Mrs. Rank's brother, who had arrived two weeks ago from Germany to take a job at Rank's store. The girl was well aware of this.

"Why doesn't she come home, why?" she paced restlessly from one room into the other.

"She'll come by and by, you'll see," her mother reassured her, though she, too, had begun listening for the sound of the door more often.

Kristaps had already clambered into bed.

Time was passing.

"You go to bed, too. I'll hear the door," Mother told Annele. "I'm sure something's kept her late."

"She never, never stays out without telling us first. No, no, she never does that," the girl said anxiously.

"She never does, but there's always a first time. Now you go to sleep."

Her mother put out the light, and Annele lay down on her bed. But sleep was unthinkable. She was listening, her ears absorbing the least little noise. Somewhere, the clattering of horses' hooves. Perhaps Līziņa was coming home by cab? The noise clopped closer, receded into the distance. Silence returned again. Such unaccustomed silence, in which nothing could be heard anymore. It was probably very late now. There was no clock in the little flat. The nearby church served their use with its timepiece. But ever since eight o'clock – and this seemed an infinitely long time ago – she hadn't heard the clock strike. This, too, seemed so strange.

Kristaps was breathing heavily in the next room. Then Mother's deep breathing joined the sound of his. So she, too, had already fallen asleep. Annele's heart was suddenly filled with terrifying loneliness. Now it was up to her alone to be with her sister in thought, up to her alone to pray for all good spirits to protect Līziņa. Her anxiety waxed and waned. One moment it seemed that something terrible had happened, the next such a fear seemed unfounded.

After all, nothing dangerous had been happening in Jelgava. There had been no reports of robberies or burglaries. The streets were peaceful. The Ranks' house was right in the center of town, and their own flat was not in some out-of-the-way place. How could anything bad happen here?

The sound of the clock striking floated over from the belfry. Annele raised her head and listened. The wind was carrying the sound in the opposite direction, that's why it had been impossible to hear it before. Perhaps it wasn't so late after all. When you are waiting for someone anxiously, even minutes seem like hours. She counted.

...nine, ten, eleven, twelve!

Twelve! Midnight already! Twelve!

Like a wild beast that has broken out of its cage, her vivid imagination, freed from all restraint, hurled itself upon her and began to maul her.

Twelve o'clock, twelve o'clock!

Now it was all over! Something terrible had happened to Līziņa. She was no longer among the living.

A silent scream was choking her breast.

"I'm going to lose Līziņa! I'm going to lose Līziņa!"

But what should she do? What should she do now?

Get up. Wake up Kristaps, wake Mother, and go search. Go to the Ranks', to Aunt Meire, from street to street, to the Gūze sisters... To the Gūze sisters? A ray of hope! That idea had not occurred to her. But as soon as it did, she rejected it at once.

No, no, what would she be doing so far away on the outskirts of town in the middle of the night? Besides: ever since these two friends had begun planning marriage, their old warmth toward Līziņa had died down.

Sitting up in her little bed, Annele in turn rocked her knees, wrung her hands, whispered all kinds of advice to herself and rejected it again. She was ashamed to upset the others with her fears and to ask their advice, knowing full well that they would not be able to come up with any solutions, either.

There was a faint scratching noise at the door. Faint, like a little mouse scrabbling around. And at once the girl was on her feet, but she hadn't managed to take one step before Mother's bare feet preceded her. So she, too, had been tossing sleeplessly.

Annele quickly stretched out on her bed. Calm. Completely calm. The noose across her chest had snapped, like heavy fetters her senseless fears dropped from her hands and feet. What a relief, what a relief! With a deep breath, she expelled the deadly toxin of fear. Senseless, foolish fear! How it had tortured them! After all, what could happen to Līziņa, young, strong, healthy, and self-assured as she was, in this peaceful town?

Mother unlocked the door with whispered words of reproach.

"Daughter, daughter!"

"Oh dear, it's probably very late, isn't it?"

"Past midnight."

"Is it really? Don't be angry, please! We simply didn't notice we had walked so far."

Didn't Mother hear that she was speaking in the plural? She asked another question:

"Weren't you afraid so late at night?"

"But I wasn't walking alone."

Annele listened. Dear, lovely voice! She heard nothing else. How terrifying it had been without it! But now it was here again. Belonged to her sister, her mother. The rooms were full. Filled with sound, they felt like home. Her heart was at peace.

Līziņa lit the lamp.

"You're not asleep yet?"

But she was in no hurry to get undressed. She was still holding her coat, her hat, and gloves. She started taking them off, but never finished. She stopped, touching her cheek with the palm of her hand, gazed somewhere into the distance with unseeing eyes, then carelessly pulled off her hat, again gazed within herself, smiled a little, sighed, took a few steps in the direction of Annele's bed: "You're not asleep yet?" The coat, the gloves slid to the floor. And again, for the third time, without waiting for an answer, she asked, "You're not asleep yet?" She half-opened the door to Mother's room.

"What is it?" Mother asked.

"Come into our room for a while."

Wearing only her nightgown, Mother came in and scolded:

"You've got to go to bed. It's late as it is."

"I won't be able to sleep anyway."

Līziņa took the checkered blanket from her bed and wrapped it around Mother's shoulders. Mother looked up in surprise:

"Well, is there something you want to tell us?"

"When I tell you, you won't believe me."

Again she sighed, again gazed into the distance, and then, plucking up her courage, said it:

"I just got engaged."

"Daughter, daughter!"

Mother clasped her hands with shock. Silence fell. Engaged! Heavens! What did that mean? There were so many questions that every question got in the others' way. What had been said was so unaccustomed, so unheard-of! Annele exclaimed:

"To the one that took you to the ball!"

"How did you know?"

"I've known for a long time," was on the tip of Annele's tongue, but she broke off in mid-sentence. That wouldn't be quite accurate. It was true that something in her had been secretly checking on the threads that had been weaving through Līziņa's life ever since that night in spring, but all that time she had paid no attention to it, and only now, when the ends of the threads were tied together, did it feel as though she had followed it all with this secret eye of hers: it proved to be true after all. I saw it coming even then.

"He's one of the Ranks?"

"He has a job there. He's the chief manager at the factory."

Her mother looked up, her eyes serious.

"Then he's not one of our people?"

"Edgar Reikschat. That's his name."

"A Lithuanian name, by the sound of it?"

"No, he's German. A Prussian from Königsberg. He says his mother still lives there."

"Child, I just wonder if this will be for the best? Are you like-minded?"

"Just what are you afraid of?"

"His being a foreigner. From a different country, from a different world. That changes people."

"Well, as for me – I'm certainly not going to change."

"Why should you change! But with him – won't it be hard for you, won't it be hard?"

All three of them fell silent. Then Līziņa said, quickly:

"Come on, let's go to bed. I'm sure there's nothing more we can solve by talking tonight."

Had she expected greater surprise, more impetuous enthusiasm from her family? Who knows, who knows!

And suddenly, taking the blanket from her mother's shoulders, she sank to her knees, over her mother's hands. Began to sob.

Now all three of them burst into tears.

"May God help you, may God bless you! You've found your own way, and you'll go your own way!" Mother caressed her.

Then Annele felt her sister's burning lips on her own.

After that, none of them spoke anymore. To bed, to bed!

They went to bed, but sleep would not come to settle in the three pairs of eyes. Each of them was pursuing her own thoughts in the dark.

Mother:

"My dear, dear daughter! Don't I wish you every happiness? I pray day and night that God should protect you all. And I've been waiting and waiting for this day. Your life isn't easy, I know, dear. I can already see your dear cheeks turning paler, your sweet eyes getting sadder. What's to be done? Life runs over us like a river, furiously tearing everything with it. Don't you think we would have sent you to school, seen to it that your life was easier? But how could we? A good thing that you yourself were able to help us, support us, and provide for us.

"Still, I only hope happiness is where you think it is. He's a foreigner. Who knows who his relatives, his family are? If you're compatible, it'll be fine, if not – a life full of tears..."

She had imagined a different sort of happiness for her daughter. Her eyes had always been turned toward the country. Even though a farmhand's child without dowry horses and cows, without a penny of her own, could not hope for a farmer, at least it was possible that someone else might come along, someone who valued decency, virtue of the heart, good bearing, and common sense, perhaps some teacher, or a clerk – one couldn't dictate to fate what sort of person this would turn out to be – he had been longed for and awaited full of hope, but he had not come. Instead, a stranger had come, had taken a look at her, and she had taken his fancy. Taken his fancy? Why even talk about it! Couldn't this pretty face have taken anyone's fancy? But no! Others had passed her by. What could one do, what could one do! Now she must turn her back on that cherished, hoped-for life which she would have had among wheat fields and forests.

Līziņa:

Her thoughts were tossed about like the leaves of a tree in a storm. Questions, questions:

"How could it happen? I don't know it myself. If anyone had told me yesterday, I wouldn't have believed it. I couldn't have imagined it. He had hinted at it, long, so long ago: in one way or another. I sensed it, but didn't say one syllable to meet him halfway. What did I care? Just let him go his way! And then that Mrs. Rank. The things she said! All about him. Now I know: it was the trap to catch the mouse. Maybe I did say a word or two. Why was he suddenly so sure of himself tonight? He just happens to be on the street ahead of me. Waiting for me. A shiver runs down my spine. What now? – May I walk you home, ma'am? – Thank you, I don't have far to walk. He won't take no for an answer. Comes with me. – I must talk to you. Let's take a stroll. We keep walking. Ever so long! One word follows another. I already know, I know everything. Why did I stay, then? Why didn't I run away? "No" – short and sweet: "no!" And that would have been that. I can't. My tongue won't obey. The way that man talks: – I like you. It's either you or nobody. I feel bewitched. All right, so be it. So be it! After all, it had to happen some time...

"Me, a bride? I should laugh, but, but – what will happen now, what will it be like?..."

A lump sticks in her throat. Tears squeeze between her lids, but she is too tired to wipe them away. Let sleep dry them.

Annele:

"Līziņa is engaged. What's that? What does it mean? The bond is cut, it's the parting of the ways." For a long, long time, Annele has feared: it will come some day. Now it has come. She had this fear even long ago at Spring Farm. At Easter by the swing, when the fellow with the red cap revolved about Līziņa alone. At the time her sister wasn't much older than Annele is now. – And that crown farmer at Amāle's wedding, at Pike Farm! The pain of that hour, that time, still stung deeply. It stung for Līziņa's sake. Why did fate have to decree that nothing would come of it? That crown farmer had been a handsome man. He and Līziņa made a fine couple. Whereas now – this – Reikschat, his name was – who'd taken Līziņa to the ball. What could she say? Search as she might – there was not a trace of surprise there. No, no! And if she did have to part from Līziņa some day, then the man who married Līziņa would have to be like, like – that Indian prince with twelve gardens, twelve palaces, and twelve playfellows. Annele couldn't finish imagining what he would have to be like, for sleep overtook her.

On Sunday, Reikschat was supposed to come over. As she cleaned and tidied up, Līziņa turned the little flat upside down. She thought its usual cleanliness was not enough. She rearranged the furniture, taking a few steps back and scrutinizing: wondering which way would be more homey and prettier, asking her mother's and sister's advice as well. Try as they might, there was no way their simple belongings could look more luxurious, though they did the best they could. Līziņa opened her "hope chest," which contained all kinds of little doilies and runners made during breaks at work, on Sunday mornings and evenings to satisfy her taste and her delight in color. Now they came in handy, now they helped embellish this all-important day. There were flowers, too, brought from the market yesterday: asters, sunflowers,

calendulas, mignonettes. What unprecedented extravagance! Out in the kitchen, a
duck was braising in the oven, filling the apartment with unaccustomed aromas.

Aunt Meire came up to see them. She already knew. The first place Mother had
gone to with the news was to her house. Now she came to congratulate everyone. She
was beaming with joy. Beaming, she looked into Līziņa's face as Līziņa flushed under
the gaze of those bright eyes. As usual, the words that accompanied her smiles sparkled with wit.

"Oh, so that's what a bride looks like? The happy bride! What joy, what joy!"

Then, to Mother: "Well, what have you got to say about that girl? It was worthwhile raising her, wasn't it? She waited and waited till she found the man she was
waiting for. She certainly deserves him. May the Lord grant her an easier life from
now on."

"I hope you're right."

"Of course, how could it be otherwise? In years to come he can expand his business just as Rank is doing now. Goodness, he's certainly got what it takes! He's hardworking, he's capable. That's what they've been telling me at my employer's house.
Mrs. Zirniņš's brother also works at the Rank store, you know."

"What? Have all of *them* got wind of it, too? Who told them?"

"I did, dear. You don't want me to be happy all by myself, do you? Līziņa Avots a
bride. Everybody in my building is just so excited! They're all awfully fond of you,
you know."

After chatting a while, Aunt could not be talked into staying any longer to meet
the future son-in-law.

"Another time! We mustn't scare the young man so soon with such a lot of relatives."

Now everything was ready. There had been many unnecessary trips running in
and out. They had counted on their fingers: such and such is on the table already, we
still need such and such. Finally Līziņa shot outside and told Mother: "I knew we'd
forget something. We haven't got any beer!"

"Beer? Won't tea be enough?"

"No, it won't. They always have beer at the Ranks'. That's what he's used to."

"But not at our house. Let him get used to our ways," Annele tossed her head.

Līziņa looked at her sister disapprovingly.

"We must do what pleases our guest. I thought you'd know that."

"But I'm not going to the pub for beer."

"Nobody's going to send you. Kristaps will go."

"Kristap dear, do me a favor."

Kristaps struck an attitude and rolled his eyes.

"How many shall I get? A dozen?"

"What, are you crazy?"

Mother and her older daughter looked at each other. They had never bought
such things.

"Yes, but how many? Surely one bottle will be enough, won't it?"

"Let him bring two," Līziņa counted coins into Kristaps's hand.

As soon as Kristaps had left, footsteps were heard on the stairs.

"What? Here already?" Līziņa exclaimed, threw down her apron and ran to meet the guest.

"And here we hadn't even thought of fixing a snack, just supper," Mother anxiously hurried into the kitchen.

Annele did not want to be in the way and disappeared behind Kristaps's curtains. The young people walked past without seeing her. But her sister came back at once, called her.

"Hey, what happened to you? And where's Mother? Don't you know that Edgar wants to meet you?"

The Edgar she was talking about stood in the middle of the room waiting. He had memorized a speech; true, it was all twisted and garbled, with German words mixed in, but he said everything that was necessary. He introduced himself and asked Mother for her daughter's hand.

Mother wanted to say something, maybe the sort of kind words she had said to Līziņa the other night, but nothing came of it. She shrank into herself and began to sob.

Edgar patted her shoulder to comfort her.

"Mustn't cry, mustn't cry. You'll have a good son-in-law and Līziņa will have a good husband, I'll guarantee you that."

With such self-assurance did he recommend himself.

"And this little gal must be Anna, right? I know, I know. Well, girl, do I get a kiss?"

"No!" Annele retorted, blushing to the roots of her hair at the suggestion.

Edgar laughed.

"Come, come, come! We Prussians aren't such terrible monsters!"

He stroked the little bushy whisks of his mustache that stuck out so proudly in the somewhat chubby face with the small brown eyes and narrow arching forehead and, feeling not the slightest bit offended, smiled at Annele as though to encourage her: "Hey, why don't you give us a smile, too!"

The little bundle he had brought contained a cake and wine.

"But where are we going to get wineglasses? We're hardly used to such things," worried Līziņa.

And Edgar replied as though he intended to bring this kind of present every day:

"Then you'd better get used to them now."

Mother hurried off to get some wineglasses. Meanwhile the guest had another surprise in store for everyone.

"What do you think? D'you think that's all I brought?" he looked at his fiancée with a mischievous grin.

"How should I know?" she shrugged her shoulders diffidently.

"Funny kind of fiancé I'd be if that was so!"

A little box appeared from his breast pocket. There was a gleam of gold. Inside were a ring, a brooch, and earrings.

Līziņa clasped her hands with surprise.

"They're beautiful! And they're for me?"

"Who else? And I think my taste is nothing to complain of. Isn't that right? Like them?"

"Very much! It's really lovely jewelry. Look, Annele!"

Annele, too, saw that it was lovely. Especially the brooch and the earrings. A little polished gold flower on a matte background. Oval in shape. But she did not let one word of praise pass her lips. She did not like the giver's self-assurance.

Līziņa held the jewelry as though she did not know what to do with it.

"Well, why don't you put it on?"

No, first she had to say thank you. He was waiting. And with a blush she clung to her fiancé.

"There he stands waiting to be thanked. Just like Kaparsons," Annele thought contemptuously, and slipped out the door.

When Mother came in with the wineglasses, the girl was no longer there. Līziņa looked for her.

"Did you send her on an errand?"

"No, I thought you had. She went running past me quick as a flash."

So they told the guest Annele had been sent somewhere. The toasts were drunk without her.

Though the day was sunny, a real sun was no longer visible in the streets. Here it was late afternoon, and already shadows were rising from the rooftops. An autumn dusk.

Where was it Annele felt the urge to run like that, with her rush of rebellious feelings? Her feet knew without being told, and took the road to the cemetery. That felt like the right place to her – here the trees and shrubs were already turning yellow. Amidst many overgrown graves, she found her favorite mossy gravestone with faded lettering, shaded by dark, pyramid-shaped oaks. The stone and a little bench, half-sunk in the ground, were scattered with yellow leaves. No flower had ever been placed on this stone, no caretaker's hand had ever touched it.

Here she sat down. Here she lamented her grief. Here she gave vent to the questions that broke forth out of stubbornness, hurt feelings, bitterness, and something else, she did not know what: why, why did it all have to happen this way?

But as soon as this question had erupted, its contentious opposites were there with their replies, explanations, and attempts to put things in order.

They had an answer to everything.

"So what's wrong? What are you complaining about? What is it that shouldn't have happened?"

"This thing with Līziņa. The life we had was so good."

"Has anybody caused you pain?"

"Oh, so much, so much pain! How can she forget me?"

"Is that what she's done?"

"She needs that Edgar!"

"Are you still such a little girl that you can't understand that your sister is your sister, while Edgar is Edgar?"

"No Edgar will ever love her the way I love her!"

"Oh, speaking of love, I wonder if what you say is really so! Remember what happened at New Farm when you imagined that Spricis might marry Mother, and how you raged in anger, grief, and anguish then?"

"But I do feel love. How can I bear it?"

"You love only yourself. You're afraid: what's going to happen? What will happen to me?"

"No, no! It's not just that."

"That's a big part of it. Under your sister's wing you were like a fledgling in its nest. Now you don't know what will happen!"

"True, true!"

"And that's how you repay her. What is she to think? You repay good with evil."

"Oh no! I didn't intend to. Not that."

"Love? That's something you should have shown her on this, her happiest day. She didn't see it. You left her, ran away, you traitor!"

Sudden sobs.

"Oh God, oh God!"

Long, long sobs.

"I feel so troubled, so troubled."

"You must overcome yourself. You must overcome all this."

"Cry. Have a good cry. It will be all right."

Gently, gently her tears release the heavy burden. So there she sits comforting herself. Who else is there to comfort her?

Huge crimson clouds come floating out over the trees and cover the blue chasm of the sky. The walls of the white church, the crosses, the autumn wreath of treetops suddenly gleam in golden splendor. But only for a moment, when it is all changed again. What a shame! But isn't it this changeability that constitutes the greater part of beauty? What would happen if it stood there motionless and you could watch it for an hour or even two, or even a whole day? Lifeless, frozen? No, only in transformation is there life, and in life there is beauty.

A cheerful mood is sure to follow the tears.

Sunset. They were already ringing the closing bell. Annele hurried out among the first people to leave, for her cheerful mood had returned. In the crowd walking in front of her a lady was walking with strangely wobbly movements. She wore a long black dress, a black cape and hat.

Sarah? Could it be? "Sarah!"

The woman she had addressed turned her head and flushed all over her broad face, which seemed even broader than before, for her thick curly hair had been brushed back tightly and twisted into a bun on the nape of her neck. Her hat, whose brim was much too narrow, would not stay on but slipped now over one ear, now over the other. It seemed as though Sarah was unhappy with her hat, and the hat with her. She took hold of Annele's hands.

"Oh, how happy I am to have run into you! I've been meaning to visit you. But I get out so rarely! So much to do! And now I'm not Sarah anymore. Don't call me that anymore."

"Marija! Miss Marija?"

"That's what you can call me," she was radiant with joy. "I'm a Christian."

"And you're with the deaconesses now? And you're doing well?"

Sarah understood.

"Oh, you mean because I'm dressed up like this? This is my christening and confirmation dress. I have to pay back what it cost. They take something off my pay every month. What can you do? Each must take care of his own. And even so God's mercy toward me has been great. What more can I want? If I behave well, they may increase my wages some day, and then I can finish paying for it sooner."

Sarah was reticent, but from what she said one could infer that life with the deaconesses was not really – not really all that nice. Quickly she changed the subject, waxing really enthusiastic about the cemetery, which she was visiting for the first time.

"I came to see the place where I, too, will now be allowed to lie one day. Oh, how nice it is here, how nice! There are flowers and crosses everywhere, holy crosses! A Christian cemetery, I'll lie among Christians."

"You mustn't think about it too much. We're still so young. We have such long, long lives ahead of us," said Annele and was amazed to hear her own voice so sonorous and joyful. The heavy cloud of sadness had lifted. And, without herself understanding why she now felt compelled to say something that half an hour earlier no one could have forced from her lips, she fired off her news, though only to cheer up Sarah, of course.

"Have you heard the news? My sister is engaged."

"O-o-oh!"

Sarah uttered a long exclamation of amazement and surprise and stood transfixed like a pillar of salt. For a while she was speechless, she looked past Annele and a strange glow appeared in her brown eyes, she did not ask who the fiancé was and where he was from, her face contracted in an agonizing smile, she whispered as though in ecstasy:

"Oh, a bride! Your beautiful sister is a bride. She'll stand at the altar in a white gown, and she'll have myrtle leaves in her hair and a veil over her shoulders. – A bride – oh – what happiness! What happiness!"

Suddenly she buried her face in her hands and began to sob.

Oh no! Sarah was at it as usual, crying again!

"Sarah! Marija dear!"

Sarah was laughing again.

"Oh no, no! It's nothing, really. Don't look at me. I'm a meshuggene girl. Those tears just rushed out. That's from joy at your sister's happiness, don't you see."

But Annele was thinking:

"No, Sarah, that's not true. You're crying about yourself. You're sorry for your-self because you think you may never be able to stand at the altar in a bridal gown."

She suddenly felt terribly sorry for Sarah. Such a strong, healthy young girl, and fate had bound her in fetters.

She struggled, grew weary, and renewed her struggle with even greater courage. How favorable was Annele's own situation when compared to Sarah's.

Healthy limbs. What a great, great good fortune that was!

At home no one reproached her for her impolite behavior. They didn't even mention it. Līziņa – as though she had been expecting her – warmly invited her into the back room where she and Edgar were sitting together.

"Come, Annele, listen to the interesting things Edgar has been telling me about his family."

True, what Edgar said was interesting, for it was all new, but he didn't know how to tell it in an interesting way. He allowed Līziņa to repeat what he had already told her, filling in and correcting a detail here and there. His news was short. His fa-ther, now dead, had been a small tradesman in Königsberg. His income had been good, so that Edgar's mother's old age was adequately provided for. Of five children, only the youngest daughter was still at home, the rest had scattered in all directions. One brother was in Saint Petersburg, one beyond the Urals, the older sister had mar-ried an Italian and lived in Lombardy.

This thrilled the listeners.

"Italy, listen to that! And has she been there long?"

"Since she got married. Now she has grown-up children."

"And so you haven't seen each other at all?"

"No. At first you think: we'll meet at such and such a time, but later that be-comes unimportant. Out of sight, out of mind."

"But what about her native land and her relatives? Doesn't she long to see them?"

"Her native land and relatives are wherever her daily bread is. We're made of different stuff. Not like you Latvians."

The thread of conversation was thin and fragile. It would break constantly, and the pause would be filled by the exchange of caresses, which Annele tried hard not to see. She was embarrassed.

How horribly boring! As soon as she could disappear inconspicuously, she did so.

At supper Edgar ate meat, and in between he drank beer. He pushed away the dessert, with which Līziņa had taken special pains and which was called "nectar and ambrosia," claiming it was gruel for women and children.

This was unheard-of! At least he could have tasted it, since Līziņa had prepared it. Tasted it and praised it.

"And I suppose men's gruel is nothing but beer," the girl couldn't help saying.

Edgar shook his bushy mustache.

"Yes, beer and tobacco. That's men's consecrated wafer. You remember that, my girl, if you want to get a husband."

"Think I need that kind of husband? I wouldn't take a smokestack like, like – – "

"Like you, you were going to say," calmly interrupted Edgar, lighting a cigarette. "I'm glad you've noticed that a brother-in-law should be addressed by the familiar thou. Let's drink to that. Besides, you still owe me that kiss."

The girl quickly pulled her shoulders away.

What was the use of talking to him. He probably imagined she was still a little kid who would dance to his tune!

Since she still owed her new brother-in-law a response to his challenge, she challenged him in turn:

"Will you be wanting more beer?"

"Have you got any more on hand?"

"There's one bottle."

"Bring it here!"

And Edgar stayed there with his bottle of beer after supper had been cleared away, sat drinking and blowing clouds of smoke.

What a ridiculous man! How could Līziņa stand him?

Silvery Moon

There was not one pedestrian on the street. Down the bumpy middle of the road rumbled a long line of carts loaded with wood, next to which walked the drivers dressed in short sheepskin coats and sheepskin caps whose flaps hung over their ears.

Annele hurried along, keeping step with the drivers. The rattling of the carts was so loud it covered any other noise, and it was safe to toss into it a song that seemed to demand such a loud accompaniment. The song was one that her brother had brought back from Rīga that Easter:

> "When courage springs within a free man's breast
> Whose strength life's struggle has not broken yet,
> Then let us all united strive together,
> Let songs ring out, proclaim our sacred faith:
> Though rock and stone should burst asunder,
> We shall arise and boldly we'll go forth.
> Young man, o haste on wings of storm,
> Your country calls – do battle unto death!"

O glorious song! What words, what images! What overwhelming rapture! Battle unto death! The enemy is attacking, trying to conquer the native land. On wings of storm the young men speed toward them. There they go galloping off with a clatter of hooves, flags fluttering, spears uplifted, like a rush of clouds. Behind them an ocean of tears. Mothers, sisters, brides. Farewell, farewell! Forever! They do not hear, do not listen. Do not look back. Only the winds rage about them. Onward, with the recklessness of heroes! There are special lines she cannot help singing over and over again:

> "Though rock and stone should burst asunder,
> We shall arise and boldly we'll go forth..."

But suddenly, right in front of that race on wings of storm, a heavy black bedraggled obstacle comes down like a gate at a railroad crossing. It looks exactly like Aunt Meire's old umbrella.

And here is her own big, bright face.

"Don't trample on people, don't trample on people!" she scolds sternly.

Stopped in her tracks, the girl catches her breath.

"Oh dear, I didn't see you!"

Aunt is still standing there like a barrister.

"Listen, who was that bawling? Sure it wasn't you? If my ears don't deceive me, you were singing, weren't you?"

"I was," the girl answers with laughing eyes still misty with rapture. And, after casting a look up and down the street:

"Nobody heard me, you know."

"It's unheard of, simply unheard of!"

Aunt can't throw up her hands with amazement or for the purpose of scolding, for in one hand she has the umbrella, while in the other is her inseparable companion – the black leather handbag; thus she is forced to confine herself to shaking her head in condemnation, so energetically in fact that both her shoulders shake too. Then she puts the strap of her leather bag in the girl's palm and, with her free hand, takes her by the elbow.

"Come walk with me for a while."

"I suppose I'm in for a big scolding now."

"Scolding? What's the sense of scolding you? But I must say one thing: you don't know how to live in town. You walk as though you were in the fields and woods. You're too wrapped in thought. The country is the country, while town is – town. There, people have to rub elbows with each other and learn a different sort of slickness. You don't have that. And I'm sure you don't have a girlfriend either, do you?"

"I have Līziņa, don't I?"

"Līziņa! It's not the same thing. You need somebody your own age. I see that in my girls. All that giggling and whispering and secrets! Like seeks like, don't you see, and like understands like. And wouldn't it be nice for you to get to know my Lizete or Marija a bit better? Why don't you come over more often, make friends! They're not that proud."

"But maybe I am," was on the tip of Annele's tongue, but she preferred not to say so. She didn't want to annoy her godmother with arrogance. So she thanked her for the invitation and promised to come and visit very soon.

After doing a few errands in the shops on Grand Street, Annele came outside as dusk had already fallen. Clear and cool. In the red blaze of sunset everything had become fluid and alive. Into the stream of shadows would drift now a tree stuck between the houses, the fleece of its foliage lit up in seeming haste, now a projecting rooftop with a window that burned with red sparks, while over there – – there stood the strangest apparition of this strange evening.

Across the street someone stood at the top of three semicircular steps in front of the door of an elegant store, and shimmered from head to toe in the reflection of the red sunset. So shimmering, different, unprecedented. He surprised, he dazzled her so much that she couldn't help stopping in her tracks. He was quite young, wore black patent leather boots, a dark suit. One hand on his hip, his shoulder limply pressed against the doorjamb, he was dreamily gazing off into the distance. His face was pink and white. The whiteness of his face was interrupted only by the narrow, dark, straight lines of his mustache and eyebrows. But across his forehead hung a dark curl.

A dark curl across a white forehead! Where had she seen that before? Where had she heard of that? Annele quickly ran through every chamber of her memory in search of it. Across one threshold, a figure leapt out to meet her, a figure that had dwelt there since the days at Spring Farm. That is where it had come from, from that book about the unhappy youth, how he had lived and suffered, how he had looked at the world with pensive, mournful eyes, had often grieved, leaning against something, deep in dreams, bending down his white forehead across which hung a dark curl.

And here he stood, a creature of flesh and blood. Mournful and silent, in the mournful light of sunset. The dark curl was just heartrending.

Annele could not stand there lost in contemplation of the unknown youth as though he were an apparition. Good manners required that she should pass by quickly. This she did, and she walked a good distance. But by the bridge she remembered that she had no business on that side of town, and turned back just as quickly.

The figure who had stood in the doorway was no longer there. The lights had come on in the store.

What was the store, though? None other than Rank's big delicatessen. And, that being so, the curly-headed youth could be none other than Mrs. Rank's younger brother Adalbert Verein, who had arrived to take a job in his brother-in-law's big store. Līziņa had already told Annele how tall and handsome he was, and how happy Mrs. Rank was that now she would have one of her own family to pamper a bit.

Yes, that was it. She no longer needed to search for him in a book, but in real life, here on earth, in the town of Jelgava.

And the town with its houses around her seemed to be asking her:

"He certainly is handsome, isn't he?"

And she was forced to answer:

"Yes, very handsome."

So she passed by the door of the store once, then a second time. It would be nice to be able to take another look at the young stranger. And to do so she would need to go into the store and buy something.

But what about money? How much was left over from her shopping? There was probably enough for a quarter pound of bologna. A ridiculous purchase. Could she show her face in Rank's store on such an errand?

But why not, why not? Her devouring interest was stronger than all objections. She'd walk in quite proud and cold. She'd walk in and take a look. If "he" was behind the counter, she would get a glimpse of him, and nothing more. Quite unnoticed, she would slip outside again. There were so many shoppers that no one would notice her at all.

He's not behind the counter. He stands to one side, his shoulders propped against the cashier's cage, legs crossed, one hand in his trouser pocket. This did not look as good as the way he had stood in the doorway just a few minutes ago, but the man was still handsome, no doubt about it.

Now it was all clear to her.

For a month, they were letting him visit and rest awhile before he began work at the store, and that was why he was leading an idle life as he got accustomed to being here.

Now it was her turn at the cash register. How mortifying! Where was her pride now? The stranger would not move from the spot. His eyes seemed to register every detail. And her purchase was so insignificant, the payment so small. What did he think of her now? She flushed and turned red as she counted her kopecks. And because mishaps have a way of arriving out of the blue when they're not wanted, Annele's hand suddenly falters, instead of the money she hands over the little parcel, snatches it back, it leaps over her hand, and now the stranger, too, springs between her and the cashier so that their two foreheads almost collide. Thank you, thank you! the girl whispers, embarrassed. And the stranger looks at her with dark, velvety eyes that are even more beautiful than she'd thought.

Outside there is a joyous, greenish translucent sky with a crescent moon whose pointed horns slowly drip mysterious brightness over rooftops and streets.

She walks along and thinks: how beautiful the world is tonight! And his eyes were so dark and velvety! And how he stood there, surrounded by light like a cherub, and even the stairs under his feet shone with gleaming metal fittings such as she'd never noticed before. It was simply wonderful. Such a strange evening, such a coincidence! To be sure, she didn't really like the fact that he was called Adalbert. She would have preferred Victor or Florentin. The velvet-eyed protagonist in the book had been called by one of these names, though she no longer remembered which one.

It wasn't until she was close to home that she remembered the little parcel that she had exchanged at Rank's store for the pennies left over from her purchases. What about that? What would she tell them at home when the cross-examination began? What's this? How come? It was an unauthorized action that she would have to justify, and how would she manage that? No, she wasn't the kind of person who could somehow prevaricate and conceal things that were unpleasant for her. As a result she would always tell the unadulterated truth. But what about now, in this case? It was completely impossible. How could she say all this in clear, direct words? Oh dear – here it was, life's reality falling heavily on her heart.

But everything turned out well and pleasantly. Mother received her with a smile of relief: "Why, you've brought supper as if you'd known!" For they had to provide a special treat for Uncle Ansis Avots, who occasionally, when business detained him in town, came to spend the night with his brother's family. There he sat now like the king in legend, his bushy beard propped on the table, snorting through wide nostrils. The flimsy rush chair was not enough to hold his broad hips, and every once in a while he would get up to look for a more comfortable seat to place them on, but there was none, and he sank back on his rushes again like a heavy wind.

When Uncle spent the night, everyone had to move. The best and widest bed was occupied by the guest. The sisters slept together. And there their talk easily shifted to the Ranks, and Annele was able to ask quite unobtrusively whether the young stranger she had seen in the store was Mrs. Rank's brother and would now be working in the store?

Līziņa gave a laugh.

"Him and work? He's quite a windbag. All he has is that handsome mug of his. He's been spoiled quite a bit by his mother, and now by his sister as well. You should see the black looks his brother-in-law gives him sometimes! Well, he'll certainly teach Adalbert how to stir his stumps. There's no loafing at Rank's delicatessen!"

Her sister's words were a rude shock for Annele, and she felt as though she herself had been rebuked. What a way to talk! Her sister, who was usually so kind, had no understanding at all how things stood with Adalbert.

Annele understood him, though.

What pleasure could there be for him in standing behind a counter day in, day out, selling sausages and delicatessen? What sort of prospects for the future were there in a job like that? It was unattractive work, just as unattractive as Annele's was to her. And he was so dreamy-eyed and sad only because he had maybe already buried many of his hopes. Just as she had. Perhaps he had wanted to be a famous musician like that Victor in the book. But what was the use! His brother-in-law, who was so wealthy, had tightened the purse strings and refused to part with so much as a penny! And he himself had nothing.

And maybe he was grieving for a loving heart left behind in his native land, and for his native land itself, there by the beautiful Rhine River, and doubtless a hundred times nicer than Jelgava and its gray streets.

She would have loved to talk with her sister and find out more about this whole fascinating subject, for who would be better informed than Līziņa? But Annele did it in a roundabout way.

"Do you remember that book?" she tried to remind her sister of what they had read long ago, and described the youth whose name had been Victor or Florentin.

"Was that was he was called?" interrupted her sister. "It seems to me that fellow's name was Peter or Mick."

Her sister was fond of a joke. At the moment she felt anything but romantic. But Annele persisted.

"But do you still remember that lovely story about the Indian prince?"

"Yes, I do. That was something quite different, though."

"I've been thinking about him all evening. I wonder what he looked like. He must have had black eyes, too."

"Most likely. People over there in India are as dark as blackamoors, and so their eyes are probably black, too. But who *else* has such black eyes?"

Annele remained silent. Scared.

All she needed was for her sister to ask:

"Doesn't Adalbert Verein have black eyes like that? Did you really look so deeply into them?"

No, no, no! This kind of questioning and roundabout way of talking was a very dangerous thing. Far better to stop the conversation.

After a few dark, cloudy days, the first snow fell. The weather cleared up. That night the sky burst into bloom – a big, white moon, the rim that had not yet filled with light held together at the top by a barely visible tiny line.

Saturday night and white light tugged on her to leave the house. But where should she go? She was all by herself, always by herself. Would today be the day to go visit Aunt Meire? She could meet the two girls and have a talk. It was about time she obeyed, since Aunt was always inviting her so warmly.

The streets rang with the sound of footsteps. Many footsteps.

Heels clattered in Aunt's backyard, on the creaking wooden stairs. There came Lizete and Marija. Their faces were bathed in white moonlight, they looked strangely restless.

Lizete said hello and stopped, while Marija slipped past in a hurry.

"I wasn't expecting you."

"Do you both have to go somewhere?" asked their visitor.

"No. Just out. For a walk. Such a nice night."

"Very nice."

"You're here to see Aunt?"

"Yes, I thought I'd – "

What should she say? There really wasn't anything she needed at Aunt's house. Lizete seemed to realize this, too, and after a short hesitation invited her:

"Want to come with us?"

"Yes, I'd love to."

"Then please do."

She urged her to hurry and hurried herself.

Within this short time, the sky had been transformed. The moon had crept under a large cloud whose crusty edges it transfused with clear silvery light. Meanwhile the entire dark blue firmament had filled with a scattering of such silvery clouds. As though behind every stack of clouds there sat yet another moon, tracing the clouds' delicate outline in shiny silver with a glittering brush. A dreamy shadowy brightness enveloped the houses and streets. The whole zenith was spun full of twists of silver, and seemed to burn with tiny white flames.

Lizete was excited, distracted, and gave inappropriate answers.

"Could it be she finds me an inconvenience?" wondered Annele. But when she tried to disengage herself, her companion nevertheless held her arm tight under her own elbow.

"Let's go, let's go!"

The quieter and emptier the side streets were, the busier was Grand Street itself. Pedestrians came and went incessantly. The storefronts were washed in an uninterrupted flood of footsteps, especially on the moonlit side. They walked arm in arm, in twos, in threes. Boys with boys. Girls with girls. When two longer chains of walkers ran into each other, they did not fall apart but slid past each other sideways. These were the students of Jelgava's secondary schools, promenading here by moonlight.

Lizete started forward. Her eyes darted about continually, searching. Suddenly, appearing like a bolt from the blue, a tallish girl linked arms with her in the free elbow on the other side. They began a whispered conversation.

"Did you see him?"

"Is he here?"

"Behind us."

"Alone?"

"With Tall Bear."

"Shush!"

Two voices were muttering behind them, two slender young men passed close by them. One, turning his head toward the girls as though taking note of something agreeable, grinned without a word of greeting. And this person was Sludinātājs from Annele's summer school.

This was a surprise.

What was he doing here? Was he still at some school? And which one? Presumably at the most advanced of all? The *gymnasium*. He'd boasted about it back in summer school.

And the unknown girl said so. Nudging Lizete, she went:

"Will you look at that! *Gymnasium* boys!"

"Conceited as devils," retorted Lizete.

"They've got good reason to be conceited. A cut above all the rest, don't you think?"

"In height!"

"In every way. Whichever way you look at it!"

"I wouldn't say that."

"You wouldn't say it, but you think so."

"Oh, go on with you!"

Lizete pushed the elbow her companion was on, but did not push her away. Nor did she want to. And her companion stuck to her like a leech. On the other hand, Lizete's elbow on Annele's side became limp and slack.

Annele would have liked to join in the conversation and say a word or two. After all, she knew Sludinātājs. And the other one, what was his name again? Tall Bear? Was this his real name or was it just a nickname? Be that as it may, she had often seen him on her street, where he always disappeared through the gate of a certain courtyard. Presumably he lived there. Hm, and so he was a *gymnasium* student? That must be why he walked aloof like that, so slow, proud, never turning his head, merely glancing sidelong with laughing eyes at girls as they passed. Not at her though, she wouldn't say that.

Still, she herself would have loved to throw in a few words about those two, but Lizete did not even turn in her direction. She exchanged whispers, signals, short, pleasurable bursts of laughter only with her companion on the right side, as each of them pushed her face now into the other's neck, now into her fur muff; they were so close not even a drop of water could have squeezed between them.

"Let's walk more slowly. Otherwise we'll meet them much too soon," Lizete's companion urged her.

And they were almost marking time.

Now the other girl nudged Lizete.

"They're coming. Deer Eyes is trying to get a look at you."

Deer Eyes? She must mean Sludinātājs with his brown eyes, for Tall Bear's eyes were blue. And if Sludinātājs was nicknamed Deer Eyes here, then Tall Bear must also have a completely different name. The girls were using their own special secret names and codes. That was obvious.

The moon now stood between two clouds and threw its brightness directly into the faces of the approaching boys. Two shiny cigarette ends came glowing toward the girls.

"They're smoking, look! Those boys are really something! Not afraid of the devil himself. After all, there could very well be a teacher among the passersby."

"No teacher is going to walk here before nine. This is the students' hour. And even if one did happen to come by, what could he possibly say to the smokers? They're just about grown-up, really. They have to be treated differently, don't they?"

Just then their paths crossed. The girls stopped talking, only their elbows were busy.

"I do hope Sludinātājs doesn't notice me!" worried Annele, pressing closer to Lizete's shoulder. But she need not have worried. Sludinātājs did not even look in her direction.

"He had eyes only for you! He would have devoured you with them if he could!" The classmate pinched Lizete's forearm.

The latter proudly shrugged.

"He needn't think I want him to look at me!"

"Oh, fiddle-faddle! You say one thing, but you mean just the opposite. There's not a single girl that wouldn't want one or the other of those two to look at her. All the girls are in love with them, because they're so superior to the others. But the boys are jealous of them."

"How do you know all this?"

"'Cause I couldn't care less about them."

"Oh, come on!"

The classmate pressed even closer to Lizete and spoke even more softly.

"Listen, I'm going to tell you something. I know where you can meet them."

"Well?"

"Our neighbor's boy is a good friend of mine. They go to his house. They're all at the same school. Sunday, they'll all be together. Let's go over there."

"Lordy! How can we?"

"We can! We can do anything. Don't worry, I'll arrange it."

"Crazy girl!"

"Later you'll say: not so crazy after all."

Now the two of them put their heads together. Short bursts of pleased laughter, a long whispered conversation. Then the classmate again:

"Nothing's for free, though. You've got to do something in return."

"What?"

"Introduce me to your cousin."

"To Dave?"

"Shush!"

Now it was her classmate's turn to grab Lizete's arm in warning. And, clapping her hand to her mouth, she said:

"What's that bur you have clinging to you on the other side? Who is that? She talk or what?"

Lizete mumbled something. Apparently her classmate hadn't understood.

"Is she in school? What school's she from?"

Annele's sharp ears had heard everything. Including the words Lizete had snorted through her nostrils. She'd had enough.

The other girl didn't wait for an answer, merely urged her hastily:

"Let's turn back! We'll run into them one more time. But this time don't be a fool. Make eyes at him."

When the friends quickly turned around, the "bur" had dropped off.

Is she in school? What school's she from? If the other girl repeats her questions, Annele does not want to hear Lizete's reply.

"In school? Her?"

That's what Lizete will say with a laugh.

Oh no! Annele is not one of them, this swarm like moths gliding through the moonlit night, chattering, murmuring, gossiping, laughing, full of something joyful, mysteriously exciting, the agitation of bravado; she does not know herself what it is, but she understands it as well as if she could physically hear all that teeming and hubbub that murmurs and rustles around and past her, as though she heard it expressed in conversations just like the one Lizete had with her friend, though she herself had no part in it at all. Her? Who cares about her?

She is excluded. These here are all in perfect harmony, schoolboys and schoolgirls, they have their own world, their own adventures, all kinds of relationships among themselves, while she is outside. So she leaves by herself, too.

Behind her there is the clatter of an iron-tipped cane, and a moonlit shoulder glides past. A velvety broad-brimmed hat, and under it, dark curls. Casting sharp shadows on the walls of the white buildings, a figure glides by.

Who's that? Wasn't that – ?

Yes, it was. The man walking over there, weaving his way between strings of pedestrians in a leisurely way, is Adalbert Verein. None of the schoolboys have a hat like that, or a cane. And even if one of them did, he wouldn't have the nerve to bring it down so loudly and with such devil-may-care abandon on the time-ravaged pavement. Only a foreigner like him could do that. How good that it was him. And look at the way he walked there alone. A stranger, proud, without ties, just like herself. Silent, melancholy, serious, unapproachable – that was the way he was, she would not have wanted him any different.

What satisfaction that there were two of them like this in the world. What did it matter that she was alone now? She could walk without fear. And so they both walked with long strides, Adalbert in front, and she behind him. She scarcely noticed that they were now almost alone on the sidewalk, for other promenaders had turned back at a certain curve in the street past which the evening walk usually never continued. From this point people would stroll back to the corner of the marketplace, the more enterprising under the colonnades to the Driksa bridge, then back.

But what did this young stranger, what did she herself care for the customs of Jelgava!

Adalbert's slim cane clicked faintly against the bumpy pavement. Shadows glided past the walls of the white buildings. The one in front was slim, handsome, encircled by the broad brim of the hat as if by a black halo. But, oh Lord, the other one! If one suddenly caught sight of it, it was enough to paralyze a person! The other figure was downright ludicrous! She looked like a heifer without horns, her sloping head stuffed, ears and all, into a black silk hood that ended in a wide lined collar that covered her shoulders. Such hoods were worn only by very small girls or old crones, but certainly not by schoolgirls like Lizete, Marija, and their friend. They all had hats. Whereas she did not have one. Līziņa had made her this head covering last winter, and after her country babushka she had been delighted with it. But now it suddenly underscored the difference between herself and the other girls. That stung deeply and painfully. She now understood, thought she understood, why Lizete and her girlfriend had quite deliberately tried to shake off the "bur." They were ashamed of her and her ridiculous hood.

Should Adalbert, then, see her like this when he turned around? No, never! After all, she wasn't one of these darlings of fortune walking here by moonlight, was she? She wasn't even wearing a decent hat.

As though the ground were burning under her feet she crossed the street, hurried into the next side street and made for home. Everything seemed to have turned dark. Bitterness swelled in her throat. Tears began to fill her eye sockets. Words whispered on her lips: "Oh, I am profoundly unhappy!" And her heart, as though dropped to the bottom of a deep, deep well, answered, "Yes, you really are profoundly unhappy!" And what had made her so unhappy? Such a tiny trifle. A shadow! After she entered the courtyard, she heaved a sigh of relief, as though she had left pursuers beyond the gate. It was silent and bright here. The moon, which had fled into the yard with her, shone peacefully in the blue firmament. In the shadow of the house that faced the street, a faint scratching noise was barely audible. There, someone was sweeping the snow. In the yard, paths had been cleared to the gate, to the garden, and as far as the stairs that led to the upstairs flat. Shuffling along slowly, an old man with an apron came from the back of the yard carrying a basket and a broom, walked past without a look or a word. Annele heard him lock the gate and then vanish as though he had crept under one of the corners of the street-facing house. This was the caretaker who had been taking Ulis's place for several weeks now. But where was Ulis, that silent, swift lad who had kept house and yard in order, nimble as a pixie and as inaudible? Ulis, who'd brought the roses, where was he? Annele did not know, but there was one thing she did know – that he was a loner, wherever he might be. To be a loner was his fate.

She began walking along the newly cleared paths, which creaked underfoot. Creaking snow. Silence. White moonlight. What could be lovelier? By the garden fence she stopped. Deep in light, fluffy snow, the garden sparkled in the moonlight, mysterious, inaccessible. In the silence and whiteness, this paradise of Ulis lay there as though under a spell. Perhaps he was longing for it. Who knows! The town was out there. Somewhere in the distance a little sleigh bell began to jingle, jingled on until it died away. The windows of the big house on the courtyard side were dark, shuttered. All alone with her shadow she could glide through the yard here as if across a lonely plain. And above were the stars. The eternal expanse of stars, so accustomed and familiar, a promise of clarity and peace ever since she was a little girl. – You are grieving and weeping? Your heart is heavy? Throw away your burden. Make your way upward, come join us, take the celestial staircase. Leave all that has only a moment's duration.

Thus she walked and forgot the world. Did she forget the lonely passerby on Grand Street? Not quite. Once in a while her thoughts fluttered down to him as well, perched on his shoulder, watched the thin, sharp-tipped foreign-made cane striking the cobblestones, and the shadow of the soft hat gliding along the walls of the buildings, but then they left him again. The power of the stars was a hundred times greater. Where they reigned there was no longer room for Grand Street and those who walked there.

A half-hour or an hour in such celestial dreams could pass like a single moment. Her feet were frozen. She ought to go upstairs.

But it felt so good to stand at the foot of the stairs, letting myriads of stars shine down upon her face. To stand there enraptured. When would there be another such night when myriads of stars would join in celebration?

"But am I really unhappy if I can feel such joy about the stars?" she wondered. "No, I'm not unhappy at all. Though just now I could have died of grief. Isn't it strange how your heart swings between grief and joy as if in a swing, and how it sheds tears, now of grief, now of bliss?"

By the light of a little kerosene lamp, Mother sat reading. Annele sat down on the other rush chair and stamped the toes of her frozen feet. Behind his curtain, Kristaps was already breathing heavily. He liked to crawl into bed early.

"Hasn't Edgar left yet?" asked the girl, nodding in the direction of the other room.

"Still muttering away."

"What on earth do they find to talk about?"

"What do they talk about, you ask? Why, they've got a long life ahead of them."

"Well, did you and Father chat like that for hours on end?"

"Me and Father? Why, when would we ever have had the chance? There's just one single time I remember: I'd had a message that my mother had fallen ill and I was to go see her. When could I go? The whole day long it was one chore after another. There was only the evening left. So I screwed up my courage and ran, for I had to go through a forest. The moon is out just like tonight, shining over the forest. And when I look down the path – guess who's there ahead of me?"

"Father!"

"Who else? You know, I hadn't told a soul, but he had this special knack – he could read people's minds. And so here he was on the path. How can I let you go by yourself at night, why even a falling pinecone could give you a fright? And so we left together and came back together. No more worries, with such safety by my side! And the road so nice. The moon and the stars shining. Everything shone like pure silver."

"And then you did talk a lot, didn't you?"

"Did we talk? I really can't remember. We hadn't had any talks together at that time, you see. We just walked along hand in hand, so we could stay on the path more safely."

"I can understand that," Annele nods in agreement. And, looking at the green and red checks of Kristaps's blanket, she sees the valleys of Tauragi, which she has never seen in reality, but which seem to her as deep as wonderful ravines, and at the very deepest part is the forester's cottage with a glittering wolf's eye of a light, but the path to it zigzags along the slope amid the blue shadows of pines and spruces shining like pure silver, and there she is walking along it holding hands. – No, it isn't her, of course; those who walk there are her father and mother, both young and beautiful. Father, they say, was the stateliest son of the Avots family, while Mother –

"Were you beautiful, too?" asks Annele.

Mother gives a short laugh.

"I wouldn't exactly say beautiful! But people certainly found me attractive. Even though I was so short and all. Your father used to have a song:

> "Small is my bride
> Like a wagtail in the fields,
> I'll wrap her in a silk kerchief
> And stick her in my pocket."

The smile takes a long time to fade from Mother's face, but in the girl's eyes a shadow soon appears:

"How good it is to have beauty. I haven't got it."

But then she, too, gives a laugh.

"I don't care! It's the least of my worries."

A Number of Important Events

The holidays were drawing near. The days were short, but there was so much work that they had to begin early, when the stars, large and surrounded by haloes of rays, were still glittering in the cold light of early dawn. Their heads bent close to the little kerosene lamp, the sisters worked in silence, shrunk back into themselves, for their limbs were stiff from lack of sleep and the coolness of the morning.

Submerged in their work and each in her own thoughts, they did not notice that the white light of morning was already making the small flame in their room invisible. Then Mother came in. She did not scold at all that they had not put out the lamp in time, took it, blew it out, put it away, then approached the girls again solemnly, smiling the merry mischievous smile with which she always introduced a pleasant surprise.

"Guess what I have!"

The busy hands stopped working, and the heads suddenly looked up.

"A letter!" Līziņa exclaimed, snatching for Mother's joyfully raised hand and deftly peeling the letter from it.

"It's from the Lithuanian relatives."

"That's what I thought. Who else could be writing to us?"

Smiling, Līziņa caressed the letter as though it were a flower whose fragrance and color she was scrutinizing, turned it over and over, looked at the seal and the stamps, and only then tore it open and became immersed in it as though in deep water. She did not notice that her needle dropped on the floor and her sewing slid from her knees, did not hear her sister's and her mother's questions – blissful, now bringing the letter closer to her eyes, now holding it further away, she deciphered and read word for word, line after line, scribbled in each other's laps as it were, crisscrossing, filling every last little gleaming spot of blank paper that had remained empty. When she reached the last word, she started all over again, maybe there was something especially nice that had to be reread or that she had not quite understood. Then she stopped, lost in thought, radiant, as though looking forward to some joyful event.

"Well?" Mother asked, and her sister looked at her full of curiosity. They too wanted their share of the letter.

"Oh yes!" Līziņa exclaimed as though awakened from sleep. "Līna writes. And she says hello to everybody."

"Is that all she says, just hello?"

"A lot of things. She writes a lot of other things. And over the holidays they want me to go and stay with them. She says it's no good making excuses. A promise is a promise. And we had planned this. They're waiting for me, all of them, she says. Last time, I met such a lot of people. – Yes, and she's written me every last detail – when I must leave and where the horses will be sent to meet me, everything. And it's about time, too, for the holidays are near."

"So everything's arranged and the horses are being sent to meet you? I find that hard to believe. Can you really go off like this, the way they think?"

"I can. It was just as if I'd known – no, the truth is, I thought this might happen, and arranged my work in such a way that I'll be finished with it in time; of course, I'll have to stay up an extra night or two, no doubt."

Mother shook her head dubiously.

"And the most important thing of all doesn't occur to you?"

"You mean clothes? I've figured it all out," Līziņa answered gaily. "Even though my clothes aren't as expensive, they're all so well made that none of the other women will have anything like them, and I'll look elegant in my new outfit, the one Father wove himself. If everybody here in Jelgava likes it, people will like it even more out there, where they don't know the latest fashions yet. All I need to worry about is an evening gown, because they're always having dances, which is when the young women change into light colors. But I can make do quite well with my old ball gown, I'll spruce it up so you won't even recognize it. And I'll wear it as though it were goodness knows what kind of fancy silk or velvet, then everybody else will believe it, too," she concluded with a laugh.

"That's all well and good, but hasn't it occurred to you to wonder what Edgar will say? Will he even let you go?"

The smile was extinguished. As though frightened, Līziņa abruptly turned her head.

"Edgar? Why shouldn't he let me go? What objections can he possibly have!"

"I don't know, I'm sure," Mother vaguely shrugged her shoulders.

"What right has he not to let me go?" as though looking for justice, she stared now at her mother, now at her sister.

"Maybe he'll want to go with you," suggested the younger sister.

"With me? No! Why should he want to go with me? None of them know anything about him there."

The conversation came to a stop. A shadow had passed over Līziņa's joy. She felt that her mother and sister were also on Edgar's side, defending some kind of rights he had.

For a while she worked so energetically that the wreath of curls around her forehead trembled. But then, as though her mind was firmly made up, she said:

"I must go, no matter what Edgar says. After all, it will be the last time. When will I ever get to go again in my lifetime? That's why I must use this one last chance."

"Do as you think is right!" said Mother.

Edgar was indeed unwilling to let Līziņa go so easily. The two of them discussed the subject at great length, and it almost seemed as though the trip would come to nothing, for at the end they no longer mentioned it at all. But then one day their talks had taken a favorable turn, for Līziņa had become radiant as the rising sun. All obstacles had been cleared away. There was so much work at Rank's factory during the holiday season that Edgar, who was in charge of everybody there, wouldn't have the time to drop in even for the briefest of visits in the Avots' tiny flat; but as soon as work eased off, he had decided once for all to "dash over" to Königsberg, where his aging mother had persistently been inviting him to go, claiming she was close to the grave and hadn't seen her son, her oldest, since he went off to the vast land of Russia to seek employment. That had been more than ten years ago. Now he must go and see his mother, tell her about the coming changes in his life and thus cheer her up in her old age. And so they could go off each in their own direction toward destinations they would never again have a chance to visit later.

Mother Avots very much liked this decision of Edgar's.

"It really does seem as though he's got a good character if he thinks of his mother with such affection. A man who's a decent son may be a good husband some day."

Now there was such a hustle and bustle that their heads were in a whirl. The work that was on order had to be finished and delivered, it was necessary to plan what sort of presents to bring everyone that would not make too big a hole in the pocketbook, yet still surprise and please the recipients. Līziņa was never at a loss about such things. Why, she had seen such and such a nice little trinket here, and such an other somewhere else. All she had to do was go and gather them. What a joyful race it was through all sorts of stores! Her eyes shone as she placed her purchases in her traveling bag. This one was for Uncle, this one for Aunt, that one for Līna. And so on. How happy they would be! The value of a gift consisted not in how expensive, but in how special it was.

"Ideally a present should make everyone clap their hands in surprise when they receive it!" said Līziņa.

The day before she left, Edgar came to say goodbye for a brief moment. After he had left, a wide gold bracelet shone on Līziņa's arm.

"Why's he always giving you all that gold?" wondered her sister.

"It's what fiancés do."

"Do you like it?"

"I would have preferred a narrow little bangle or a little chain. But this one's all right, too. I wear them so rarely!"

She took off the bracelet and pressed it into its case.

"Are you going to take your gold jewelry with you?"

"No, what do I need it for! I never used to have such things before, you see, and nobody knows I've become engaged in the meantime."

"You are going to tell them though, aren't you?"

Līziņa hesitated before answering.

"I don't know. Maybe Līna, maybe not. There's plenty of time to tell them, after all."

Her sister, absorbed in thought, remained silent. There was something about this that she didn't quite understand.

The sisters paced up and down the platform waiting for the train, which was supposed to come at any moment. They'd been pacing like this for a good half-hour, shivering with cold. A sharp wind was blowing, shaking their clothes, whirling white columns of snow above the railroad tracks. The sky looked gray and heavy, no doubt it would start snowing soon.

"I do hope you don't get cold, traveling such a long distance."

"I shan't be cold in the carriage, and when I arrive, they'll have sent fur coats for me. Don't you worry!"

"I keep feeling that all you can think of now is: I wish I could get away faster."

"It's true, it's true," she laughed and, placing her arm around her sister's shoulders, pulled her close.

"The only thing I'm sorry about is that you can't come with me. What fun it would be!"

Annele kept silent, but her thoughts once more ran through all those "can't, can't, can't"! All those obstacles that kept her from attaining the external and – most important – the inner brilliance that would have enabled her to go visit the rich Lithuanian relatives.

"You know quite well that I'm deficient in all sorts of things."

"And I'll tell you something else: your character is much more splendid than mine."

"No, I'm sure you're wrong. On the other hand, why is everyone delighted and expectant at your coming? Because they take your laughter and your words, and they feel so good, and they think they're the ones who are so merry and cheerful. There's no need at all for you to bring gifts, you yourself are a gift. But it's not like that with me. I'd always feel that I couldn't ever give anyone anything, and that all I need is to receive. And nobody needs people like me."

"Don't be ridiculous! That's no way to talk!"

Her sister, pretending to scold her, gave the girl's shoulder a push and looked into her earnest eyes as if unable to understand.

"You mustn't take life too seriously."

Annele smiled.

"I won't have such a bad time of it at home, either, you know. Kristaps has left all his books, and I'll learn whatever I can from them."

The train arrived. In the carriage window Līziņa's smiling eyes flashed through a tiny patch thawed in the ice, a hand waved, then a boy's chubby cheek appeared in the patch, followed by a red mustachioed face. Between them they kept the window occupied the whole time until the train began to move and rolled away, whirling clouds of smoke. Līziņa now belonged to the world to which she was on her way. Annele did not know that world.

"And maybe I, too, will leave one day, off into my own world, of which Līziņa will no longer have any knowledge."

Snow began to fall slowly, swirling around the drifts that had accumulated in the middle of the road. It was good to turn into the wind with the pleasant knowledge that the afternoon before her was fairly long and completely free. She could take a leisurely detour to Grand Street. This had always been and still was one of the streets she found most interesting, and she had not seen it for such a long time.

But was this Grand Street really just like other streets? Full of snowdrifts, the sidewalks slippery, the shop windows covered with ice where they had not been thawed open with the aid of kerosene lamps or by some other artificial means. In Rank's large display windows, behind snowy, iced-over glass panes, all you could see were the shapes of chunks and links of sausage and pork loins. On the other hand, the door of Goldstein's big dry goods store was clean and shiny, and behind it, as though in the embrace of a mirror, filling it without leaving a gap, stood Goldstein himself awaiting the shoppers, for the holidays were just around the corner, but people did not even want to realize that and hurry up and do their shopping. And, as though calling and beckoning to them, he impatiently jiggled his gold watch chain, which curved in two arcs over a black velvet waistcoat. In summer he used to wear a white one. This was the shopkeeper Annele had noticed on the first day of her life in Jelgava. And he had noticed her. It seemed to her that as she went by, his eyes always followed her reproachfully and with surprise: "What? You're still here in Jelgava? Oy, oy, oy! Then who will see to it that we have butter and eggs and bread, when all these hayseeds like you come and live in the towns?"

She walked down the street for a stretch and then turned back. If she wanted a good walk, she needed to go further down under the arcades. And she did. Always with a secret hope. Maybe, maybe something would happen.

But nothing did happen. And after all, what could happen if everything was behind iced-over panes, as though behind prison walls? The only thing that happened was that she had to pass Goldstein for the third time. She couldn't risk doing so more often than that.

And then came the miracle.

As she reached the door of Rank's store, it burst open almost in her face, and down the slippery curving staircase with its brass mountings a young German shepherd dog came sliding down on all fours and shot off like an arrow, incessantly egged on by a voice: "Apporte, Caesar, apporte, apporte!" And there in front of Annele, taking up the whole narrow sidewalk, stood Adalbert Verein.

Caesar, believing that some tasty morsel had been thrown in the snow for him, searched through and dug up the drifts, barking impatiently in between: "None, none, none!"

Not finding anything, he shot back, sniffed for and located Adalbert's hand, which the latter, smiling mischievously, held concealed behind his back. In his hand there was sausage wrapped in paper, which the dog had rushed off to retrieve. For the second time, Adalbert made as if to throw the sausage. Once again the dog shot off and, after searching in vain, ran back to the trickster, whining and eager. The third time, the sausage really did go flying, and Caesar found it and brought it back to his master triumphantly, placing it at his feet. But such self-control was beyond his power. The dog would not touch the sausage, but neither would he take his nose away from it as he growled fiercely.

Is there anything a dog loves more than sausage? And yet he was not allowed to touch it. He had to obey his master's commands, which he had to figure out from the latter's warnings, threats, and coaxing. Here is what Caesar had to do: he had to remove the sausage from the paper himself with his teeth, whereupon Adalbert would place it on the dog's nose. When Adalbert exclaimed, "One, two!" Caesar tossed the sausage in the air, at the word, "Three!" he caught it and gulped it down. The trick came out so exactly and perfectly that Goldstein – who, the better to see what was going on in the street, had thrown his door wide open and stuck his head out in the cold air – couldn't help shouting, "Bravo!" and clapped his hands. Adalbert, himself delighted by his success, gave Caesar a shake. "Just don't shake him by the ears!" Annele was already about to intervene, but he didn't do so after all. He petted the dog's back and then waved a greeting to Goldstein, who was still applauding, wanting to show the trained dog the attention that the pet of wealthy and fine folks deserved.

"Smart, isn't he?" Adalbert flashed a smile at Goldstein and turned to Annele with the same smile:

"Smart, isn't he?"

"Yes," she answered, radiant.

She ran home. She neither expected nor wanted more. The cup of her experiences was running over. How had it all happened? As though it had been planned. Just at the moment when she was near the door, Caesar had to run outside. And she couldn't take one step to move away, for after all Adalbert had stood in the way, on the sidewalk. What was she supposed to do, wade through the snowdrifts? And wouldn't that have looked as if she were running away? And that business with Caesar had been so interesting that even Goldstein had thrown open his door to get a better view. And so it had finally come about that the two of them were looking in the same direction. And they had both liked him. And then they had both looked and smiled at each other – true, only after Adalbert and Goldstein had first exchanged smiles. But that didn't make it any the less exciting. He was a splendid fellow, this Adalbert Verein, and this event involving him had truly been a remarkable event on this remarkable day!

On Christmas Eve, Annele accompanied her mother to church. This happened rarely, for the precious free time she had on Sundays was spent reading or studying. But Christmas Eve in town, with those pealing, beckoning bells, was special, unlike any other evening during the whole year.

The church was packed. Mother slid into a pew close to the door, but Annele was drawn further, where an enormous fir tree scattered the sparkling light of its little candles in the soft twilight of the altar. From the vapors off the frost-covered walls, from the undulation of the breath and movement of hundreds of people, a thin bluish mist formed around the dull little yellow stars of the great candelabra. Coughing, so typical of churchgoers, constantly hacked at the silence; it would end in one place only to begin in another, but could not destroy the solemnity of the long wait.

An old woman, squeezing herself quite thin, made room for Annele at the end of a pew. The organ began to rumble slowly and soon to drone and roar so tempestuously that its storm filled the large space full, so full from floor to arched ceiling, until suddenly from this saturated bonfire of sound a sparkling flame shot up with a hundred tongues:

"From heaven above to earth I come."

With the first verse, Annele's voice flew up in jubilation together with the others, but then she was submerged in the billowing ocean of sound and let it rock her.

The little flames on the tree crackle, and she sees the woods at Spring Farm. They're taking her to church, for there is to be an unprecedented miracle, a dream all children long for: the church in a blaze of light. But an unexpected obstacle rises before the churchgoers: the road that leads up the slope from Spring Farm is glazed with ice from top to bottom. A veritable glass mountain. The churchgoers crawl and slip, crawl and slip down again with such momentum that they slide into snowdrifts, turning somersaults. At first there is laughter, shouting, and delight, but soon they are filled with worry because time is passing in futile efforts, for the hill does not capitulate to any of their repeated assaults, and in the end they might even have to go back, eyes full of embarrassment. Among the churchgoers is almost the entire household of Spring Farm, and each of them sees the mishaps of their journey differently. Luze, who is always closer to tears than to laughter, is already beginning to weep softly, hiding her face in her kerchief. She is afraid of Ingus's teasing. But there's not a sound from Ingus, nor Karlīne either. And suddenly their two voices and halloos are already at the top of the hill. They've blazed a roundabout trail through deep snowdrifts. Now all the others cotton on too. To be sure, they have to wade in snow up to their knees, but who cares? Annele, of course, cannot follow them, but Father and her mother's youngest brother, who has come to visit at Spring Farm and pampers her in every way, take turns lifting her on their shoulders. The pines are covered with snow, but their burden of flakes is so airy and light that at the slightest touch they dust the passersby with snow from head to foot. And Annele loves to knock against a branch here and there so that the white foamy cloud of snow comes down into their eyes and behind their collars, for on the shoulders of those who carry her she is nearer to the trees and nearer to the sky, which with its multitudes of stars thrusts itself through the empty spaces between the treetops. The stars do not get tired; no matter how far you go they always follow.

Did they reach the church that night and what did it look like inside? – Annele does not know. There's a gap there, an emptiness that her memory is unable to fill. All she remembers is the shiny glass mountain and the snowy forest by the glow of the stars. And now it's her first Christmas Eve in the brightly lit city church, where everything is still new and unfamiliar.

In the pulpit stands the pastor. He begins to speak, and so gains her attention with his very first words that it is a joy to listen. It seems to her as if all the words were coming to her, and as if she alone was meant to listen to them. Her hands in her little muff, her shoulders hunched, motionless, she looks at the speaker. What does he have to say? A great deal. His words are unvarnished, he does not even raise his voice; in his simple way, coming close, he shows you the way as it were, with a light raised in his hand. The way to where? Through life to the human heart. She feels as though she were in conversation with a wise companion who interprets her own thoughts in good, simple words. How good it would be to talk to him and to order the paths of thought together with him!

When the sermon is over, she is amazed: why is it so short? With other sermons, she's had a hard time waiting till the end, but this one has fascinated her from the first word to the last. It has given her elation and holiday joy.

The houses of the town shine with the glow of candles. In many families Christmas trees are lit as soon as darkness falls. Through the windows you can see children's heads moving and hear Christmas carols. Every house sparkles and glitters.

But the street is still full of pedestrians, and the stores are open. There are no shoppers to be seen in them, however, except for Rank's delicatessen store, which is crammed full. Facing the row of shoppers is a row of salespeople, all so hard at work that their foreheads are wet with perspiration. Even the windows of the store have thawed from the heat. The usual staff has been increased by people who work in the factory. Reikschat is there, too. He is everywhere at once, and he is quick at his job. In his fingers, the knife slashes almost playfully, plunging into dark brown sausage links and into the soft flesh of rosy pork loins. He is attentive toward the shoppers, but serious, as though he were a bit irritated. And there, too – a white apron around his waist – is Adalbert Verein. He is not having too easy a time of it. The shop assistants, brushing past, bump into his hips with their elbows. His dark curl is combed back smooth. No, he doesn't look half as good as he did the time he romped with Caesar. And anyway – so what if he is there! Her heart feels no pang, does not even give the least little quiver. Like a bird on a branch full of blossoms, she remains up there in the lofty heights of her serene holiday joy. That is quite sufficient for her. And this place here, outside the shop window, can no longer hold any charm for her. She hurries home.

On the table, stuck in a bottle, is a fir branch with three little burning candles.

⁕

Epiphany was already drawing near, but Līziņa had not returned yet. One evening Reikschat came up to visit. Waited around for a while. Not home yet? And nothing else to say. He seemed dissatisfied and ill-tempered. They did not know what to do with him. The sooner he left the better.

The same thing another night. Epiphany is already past.

"What's keeping Līza so long?" Edgar, who hasn't taken off his coat, paces restlessly and smokes a cigarette.

"Why don't you take off your coat? And come on in. Sit down! No sense getting upset about Līziņa. She'll be back, you'll see."

"Me, get upset? I'm not upset at all. But it *is* strange if a person goes away for barely two weeks and stays going on three."

Finally he does take off his coat and sinks into a wicker chair right there in Mother's room. Seeing that the visitor is planning to stay after all, Mother goes for the door, but he, as though guessing her intention, quickly forestalls her:

"You're going out to get supper? No need, no need."

Annele shrugs her shoulders.

"Maybe he doesn't like our supper at all."

"True, I'm not one to slurp down that Latvian gruel."

Insulted, Annele opens her eyes wide. Some guest!

"Nobody's forcing you."

"Easy, easy there! Don't get so bristly!"

In an attempt to mollify her, Edgar grabbed hold of the girl's braids. She whirled around and struck them out of his hands.

"You've come in a bristly mood yourself."

The visitor waved her away.

"No offence meant. I may have all kinds of other problems. When you get bitten, you snap at others."

"Do you really think you'll always keep Līziņa on a leash?"

"It's not just that!"

Finally she began to suspect that Edgar wanted to discuss something that was preying on his mind. And so Annele asked him:

"Weren't you planning to go to Königsberg? Why didn't you go?"

Edgar did not answer until a good bit later, after blowing a lot of smoke rings.

To Königsberg? No, he hadn't gone anywhere because his good mood had been completely ruined. Who was to blame? A conceited, arrogant person, a person ridden by the demon money, dancing to its tune. For what had this very same Rank been only five years ago? A mere boy, poor as a church mouse, who had started in business with borrowed money. Sure, he had had guts, but very little business know-how. Now that he was rich, he knew it all. But would all this have been possible if five years ago he hadn't found a manager like Edgar Reikschat, who knew what kind of merchandise to carry in order to attract customers so the store would prosper? And if he imagined that Edgar could be replaced by that young whippersnapper, that Adalbert, whom Edgar himself would have to train in, then he was barking up the wrong tree. It wasn't something you could train anyone to do. Each job had its secret that came with the person who did the job. And where was the secret of his – Reikschat's – job? It was hidden here – he put out his tongue and tapped it with his finger – here, in this tongue, in his palate, in his unerring sense of taste. What sort of spices should be added to a meat mixture? – You could write it down in recipes, but only the knowledge gained by experience could tell you how much to add and when, in order to obtain the refined, delicate flavor that made Rank's products famous; and this knowledge must be observed like a law. And that's what this great "manufacturer" had forgotten or perhaps never understood. How else would he dare to make foolish remarks to a man who had never digressed from the performance of his duty by as much as an inch? Remarks on the quality of the merchandise to him, who was in charge of all the work! He had always been so obliging, too, he had been so willing to go out of his way to help! Why, on Christmas Eve he and all the people working with him had come and helped the salespeople in the store. He'd wanted to show those monkeys that the people in the factory could be useful everywhere, both at the machines and behind the counter, not like them, who knew only how to clink their knives, bow to customers, and roll their pretty eyes. Shouldn't a real employer value all this gratefully? Oh no! Well, to hell with all of that! As far as he was concerned, they could do what they liked. Let them stick that kid in the factory – a kid from the Rhine that they couldn't find a position for! Him in the factory? Oh? What would he do there? Learn? What a laugh! He wouldn't learn fiddlesticks from him, Reikschat! Maybe the kid would be the foreman? Prying everywhere? Well, let them do what they liked. He would not put up with a supervisor over him. The door wasn't locked, and the gate wasn't locked, and he wasn't tied down, either. He had come as a free man and was free to leave, too. Any time he felt like it.

And so Edgar got things off his chest, lighting many cigarettes in between, throwing them down half-smoked. It was as though he were talking to himself, without listening to interjected questions, nor answering, either. When he had finished what he had to say, he rose to leave.

"Ah yes! That's the way it goes in the world. – Well, and how are you? When's Līza coming home?"

To Annele these questions seem so absentminded, so detached. Silently, she holds out her hand.

"I'll be here tomorrow," says Edgar as he leaves.

"It looks as though he's had some very serious troubles," says Mother, shaking her head sadly. "What will Līziņa say, and how will their lives turn out if he wants to leave Rank's?"

What was going on? – thought Annele. Here came worries from the outside, trying to take up residence in their home. They came with a person who only recently had been a complete stranger and now came to hand his troubles to Līziņa as their joint property. To unburden himself. To make her face sad and bow her shoulders? Now they would walk life's path together. All right. But would Līziņa, too, always be able to come to him with her cares? With every single one of her cares? Somewhere inside her, she heard the soft whisper of doubt. Why did he ask so coolly, "When's Līza coming home?" And it was always "Līza," not "Līziņa," the dear name of her childhood. And then that "Latvian gruel." Wasn't there something alien about this Edgar? About the gruel, it is true, he had later said, "No offence meant!" But those words, which had escaped involuntarily, had surely been on his mind before, and had now been said and were there to stay.

And why did he have to get so mad at that "kid from the Rhine"? After all, what harm had he done Edgar? None so far. Did he even know him? What did Edgar know of Adalbert's grieving for his home and loved ones, of his pride and silent suffering? After all, the boy did not show his deepest heart to anyone.

That same night, Līziņa came home at an unusual time. What train had she come on? For Annele had gone to meet every one of them. – On the same one she would normally have come on, but it had lain in the Lithuanian forests for three hours, buried in snowdrifts. Līziņa merrily recounted the adventure, interspersing her story with greetings from Uncle, Aunt, and all the relatives, and unpacking and distributing the presents she had brought with her. There was something for each of them: for Mother, a few of the delicacies produced on the estate, for Annele, a warm shawl from the large store of things Aunt had knitted since her legs had begun to ail and she could no longer move about very much.

"And for yourself?" Annele asked.

"Don't you see my present?"

Yes. She had caught sight of it at once. It was a beautiful little gray fur hat with a matching collar and muff. It suited Līziņa very well.

"I was half hoping they'd cut me off a piece of one of those big bolts of cloth that Aunt and Līna had been showing me in the *klēts*. It would have come in useful just now, but do you think they gave me any?"

"The rich don't understand the poor, don't you know," said Mother.

"We'll manage, we'll manage even without it. Things were good and pleasant just the way they were," Līziņa quickly interrupted her narration.

But that wasn't the end of it, of course. Annele waited impatiently to be alone with her sister. She had come home so strangely joyful. Rosy, full of bliss.

"It's as though you had come to life again, as though you were a different person from the one that left. You had become pretty pale. Mother says so, too."

"How could I not be rosy and happy when I've come from the fields and the forests, forests so deep that there are even bears and wolves in them?"

"You don't say!"

"I'm serious."

"Then you certainly do have a lot to tell."

Līziņa smiles. She hardly knows where to begin her tale of things that are fairly burning to be said. What sort of adventures would they be if their memory could not be evoked and thawed out over and over again? If the holidays she had spent had been lovely, she could make many gray days beautiful by remembering them. And here was another person who was willing to listen with both ears. Who wanted her to start right from the beginning. And, as her sister was still hesitating, Annele was the first to invade this fortress of silence.

"Come on, get started! Was it a long drive from the station?"

"I'd say maybe fifteen, twenty versts. I don't really know. It seemed quick as a flash to me. Two horses pulling the sleigh, I tell you – stallions as strong as bears! Flying from one drift into the next with a roar. All you could see was a white cloud of snow. I covered my eyes, but my heart was seized with joy. What a ride, and what a driver! Nothing to fear, not even if we went as fast as the wind."

"A driver? Who was your driver, tell me!"

"Well, it wasn't some old Lithuanian coachman! Oh no! Quite elegant. In a beaver coat."

And now the story was off to a flying start.

The name of the driver who has come to meet Līziņa at the station is Artūrs Silmežs. He is the manager of a large Polish estate adjacent to the land of the Vanags family. The owners of the estate are in St. Petersburg, while he, during the winter off-season, has the duty of taking the many horses in the count's stables out driving so that their legs won't get stiff, and he is in Varneviķi almost every other day. And he and his neighbors have long since arranged that their visitor must be driven back from the station by none other than him; that goes without saying. They can't send someone to the station who has never met Līziņa; on the other hand, she met Silmežs during her first visit. Though that was in a hurry, when Silmežs came to Varneviķi for a short time, for it was Easter, a time when the manager of such a large estate is constantly busy as the many hired hands are relocating, and when he is occupied with all kinds of summer projects. In winter it's something else again. Then it's possible to celebrate the holidays not just for days, but even for months.

And that's exactly what they do in Varneviķi. Līziņa has never in her life had such a Christmas. On the same day as she arrives, they are already celebrating and visiting with each other as though it were Christmas, while on the next day Silmežs is back again with freshly harnessed horses, and not just with one, but with no less than three sleighs. More sleighs join them in Varneviķi. In the first, there is room for the young ladies and for anyone else who wants to go along for the ride, while the others are for the hired hands with shovels and axes. Now everyone is off to the woods! To get Christmas trees. The runners cut into the soft snow like plows, the horses are steaming, clouds of snow whirl about them. The young women are wrapped in their furs to the tips of their noses, and wear snow boots up to their knees. There's no lack of such things in Varneviķi. Is there a lack of anything at all on this large estate, amid those vast fields? Forests, and what forests! Fir trees like church spires, rising into the sky taller than towers, with little titmice whistling in the branches. But who has time to look at all that! Laughter, jokes, banter, chatter everywhere. Everyone chasing each other, falling into snowdrifts. Such joy and pleasure, as though they had all become children. How long since she'd felt that way? Oh Lord! It's like something you'd dream about or read about in books!

Now they drive home with huge loads, and put up Christmas trees in every room; the stateliest of all – the one that reaches to the ceiling in the center of the largest room – is strewn all over with little candles. Silmežs is on the ladder, but Cousin Līna lavishly keeps giving him more and more. To Līziņa they say: "That's in honor of your being here."

After that comes the singing of songs. Now here's where the kind hosts do feel a lack. Līna doesn't sing, and what about the older generation? We've forgotten, we've forgotten, they shake their heads mournfully. Līziņa's treasury of songs is inexhaustible. And Silmežs joins in at once. He has a beautiful voice. Uncle says he hasn't heard such singing for a long, long time. He says it sounds as though all of Latvia had come to visit. And why shouldn't it sound wonderful, when they're feeling so good and in such a joyful mood!

On the first day of Christmas, a large number of guests assemble at Varneviķi. That's a time-honored tradition. For the most part, they are Latvians who settled in Lithuania a long time ago: tenant farmers, millers, managers of estates. Well-to-do people, all of them. Once a year and on winter roads, they come driving here even from far, far away. And how eccentric and unique each of them is! With some it seems: he's stayed exactly as he was when he went to Lithuania – with his outmoded jacket, his outmoded language, and habits that stick out like bristly hair out of a fur; meanwhile another is overgrown with a foreign skin like a tree stump with moss, and now you can't tell whether he's a Latvian or the devil himself. Līziņa presents them all and displays them like portraits in a gallery, and there is still a lot to be said about them and to discuss in detail, but now she can't take time for each of them, for she must briefly give a broad outline of all that happened.

The next day they visit the Vanagses' married daughter Marija. That's deeper into Lithuania, and there's a different type of crowd there. Among the Latvians there are many Lithuanians and Poles. Polish *pans* and *panis*. Līziņa's relationship with Marija is not as warm as with Līna who, still in the nest with her parents, felt at home in the midst of Latvian openness and cordiality. Marija, after all, is also a *pani* here, and her husband is a *pan*; here, Līziņa does not feel like a relative at all, but just like any other guest, and she receives the same amount of kindness, too. But she and Līna are always together, and then Līziņa is all right.

When the guests have spent some time feasting at the richly laden tables in the warm rooms, suddenly a crash of sound is heard through the walls. Bagpipes and trumpets begin to play in the room next door. The guests all utter cries of pleasure. They surround the hostess, showering her with compliments. She has sent for musicians, and a dance is about to begin. Wanting it to be a surprise, she's been pretending that there is nothing planned this time. But the ladies, of course, haven't believed her, for it is customary here to play this type of trick. And so the ladies have all brought light-colored evening dresses with them, and they vanish, only to reappear soon, transformed as if by magic. Līziņa's little white frock is the simplest of them all, yet many eyes follow her. She likes to mention that with pride and shining eyes.

Pani Marija's house is a real manor house with vast rooms. In the ballroom, the floor is like a mirror. You slide as though on ice. They are all whirling about, so that the musicians barely have a chance to toss down an occasional tankard of the beer that young Lithuanian maids in checkered skirts and wide aprons carry around without interruption. The guests are all great tipplers, too, even the ladies don't say no, but Līziņa becomes dizzy from the second sip, that's how strong the drink is, and Silmežs, too, whenever she steals a glance at him, refuses the tankards when they are offered to him. *Pani* Marija has a fine brewer who is famous far and wide, but he brews the Evil One himself into his beer, says Silmežs.

They dance polkas, they dance françaises and schottisches, but the Poles say: that's nothing yet. The true fires are lacking. What's needed is a mazurka.

And then comes a mazurka.

Oh, what a dance it is! All at once, at the first notes, the guests are practically swept into the ballroom from all the rooms. Drinkers throw down their tankards, cardplayers their cards. The old *pans* line up like young men, holding themselves elegantly erect, one hand raised gracefully, beating time with their feet, dance around at a gallop, then, going down on one knee, twirl their ladies around them like spinning tops, flashing lightning glances toward them, shaking their grizzled mustaches. And if the old men seem transformed, just think what happens to the young ones! You can imagine how full of joy and abandon they are.

"Did you know how to dance this mazurka, though?"

"What's there to know? Does a tree not know how to bend in a storm, or a river not know how to run when there's a flood? That's how it is with this kind of dance. The music itself, you see, beats the rhythm into your feet. And then, I had the best dancer by my side!"

"Who was that?"

"Silmežs."

Annele is puzzled.

"You keep saying Silmežs, Silmežs."

"But he's the one I knew best, don't you see. Wherever we went, he went too.

That's customary there. It's the holiday season. Whenever you say goodbye at one place, they invite you to the next. And so the days rushed by as if in dreams. And yet the last week was the most beautiful of all, though we spent it rather quietly. We did go to the woods every day. When I started getting ready to go home, no one would hear of it. Just one more day, and one more! And I almost feel as though this 'one last day' was the nicest of them all."

And suddenly her sister breaks off and there is no more. There's an end to all the storytelling. She takes her things from the little traveling bag and puts them away, humming softly.

"Trallala! La-lala-la!"

Who knows, who knows! It seems as though the long Lithuanian trumpets have blown a snatch of a mazurka into her thoughts from afar.

Now that there have been so many stories, Annele and her thoughts are also with the Lithuanian relatives, running through woods where the firs stand tall as church spires, and little titmice whistle in the branches. Annele's thoughts gallop with wild stallions to Lithuanian estates lying white in deep drifts of snow. There is the sound of fiery rhythms, and couple after couple whirls by at a gallop. *Pans* shake their grizzled mustaches – she has to laugh at the thought of those grizzled mustaches! And there is Līziņa with – with Silmežs.

Silmežs?

But meanwhile there's something she's forgotten to tell.

"Listen! Edgar was here, you know – "

"Oh yes, Edgar? How's he doing?"

Annele now tells all about Edgar and his troubles and worries.

Līziņa stares with wide-open, motionless eyes. Very astonished at the whole thing. As though, from a sunny hill, she had descended into the gray haze and worries of the valley.

"I'm sure it can't be the way Edgar tells it! No, no! I'll go and have a talk with Mrs. Rank."

The Door of the Soul

Kristaps is going to go to confirmation class. That's what he and his parents decided while he was home over the holidays. In spring he's leaving school anyway, and then it's nice if everything has been taken care of. In the country, the parsonage is far away, you have to lose weeks with confirmation instruction there, and the well-to-do whose children go to school in town no longer send them to the parsonage, preferring to have them confirmed in town. Everybody's doing that now. And starting with summer Kristaps is going to help his father with all the farm work. He has to be ready.

This is an unexpected surprise, like a bell going off in Annele's head. Kristaps has shot up quite a bit. He's planning to leave school and confirmation class behind him like a grown-up. He has to be ready.

But what about her? Doesn't she have to be ready? Yes indeed, much more so than Kristaps, who is going back to his own father's farm, a secure place, a job, and a livelihood. That's where he will live till he's old and gray – the oldest, only son and sole heir. Whereas her life hangs at the tip of a branch as it were.

Reikschat's relations with the Ranks have been patched up, it is true, but not for good. Reikschat himself no longer wants it. He has become obsessed with the idea of starting his own business. Only then will his life be truly secure and stable. Will it really be that way? He's ready to vouch for it with his energy and his abilities. He has a definite goal in mind. He feels the best thing would be to settle in one of Kurzeme's seaports, where a lot of sailors come and go constantly. There the type of good merchandise he produces can never fail to find buyers. Why, there he won't have to work for quarter-pound and three-slice customers; orders might come in large quantities when he supplies seagoing ships with food. You have to know not only how to manufacture your goods but also how to market them. And he knows how, for he is wise in the ways of the world.

Five years ago, when he first arrived in Kurzeme, before starting his job with Rank, he thoroughly explored working conditions in Liepāja and Ventspils. The latter town especially holds out the best prospects. There, all the people employed in the "meat business" are well off, even though they are somewhat slipshod at their trade, and work according to old, long-discarded methods, so that the boats of the large shipping agencies can't even get the finer kind of products here at home and have to put in supplies of them in foreign ports. All things considered, it would be

folly to go on pulling another man's chestnuts out of the fire when he could be sitting by his own fire and be a master in his own house.

And here are Reikschat's plans. In a few weeks he's going to go to the place he has in mind. If circumstances there turn out to be suitable, he'll rent a shop and begin working, but as soon as he's settled down a bit, he'll come and get his bride and then they'll have the wedding.

How will Annele's life change then? Whichever way she turns with these thoughts, for the time being she encounters darkness. And, as though by doing so she would gain greater security and independence, she suddenly clutches at the idea tossed out by Kristaps. She, too, has to be ready. It's time to end the stage of childhood. And so, having made a quick decision, she asks Kristaps:

"Which pastor did you sign up with?"

"Who else but Valdens in Saint Anne's parish."

Valdens is the pastor whom Annele heard speaking on Christmas Eve.

"With that one!" she exclaims happily. "I like him. I'll go and sign up too."

Kristaps, raising his head with a jerk, takes a sidelong glance at her, one eye screwed up with laughter:

"You? Nothing doing. You're still just a child."

She doesn't listen. It's true that she's a little afraid to take this first independent step. She hopes the others won't object as well.

What will Mother say? That's what matters most. And she immediately goes and asks her.

Mother doesn't say much. In her day everybody was confirmed young. And she, too, quickly comes to the conclusion that it is a good idea for the girl to be confirmed now. Who knows what life has in store for her later!

Kristaps is big and worldly-wise.

"You don't even realize what's involved. This confirmation is only for students from the more advanced grades. It won't be enough just to recite sections from the catechism and the Ten Commandments. Maybe the girl knows them by heart, but Valdens doesn't even require them. His classes are about entirely different matters, and people have to be able to grasp them. I was told this by boys who don't want to take Valdens's confirmation classes because he's too strict and talks above people's heads. Like a real professor. And that's why the period of instruction is longer than with any other pastor. As for me, I can't get out of it. The boys from my school are going to Valdens too, but who's forcing that girl to go? After all, she's not in school, and won't be able to cope at all. And when she can't answer and Valdens sends her about her business – and they say he shows no mercy to those who aren't capable of following his classes – what then? Then she'll be covered with shame."

"I'll deal with my own shame, you stay out of it."

She is blunt. She hasn't forgotten the affair of "Deaf Daniel."

"Well, I'm warning you seriously," Kristaps gives her a haughty look.

"Talk all you want, I'm going."

"I've already said all I'm going to say. Don't blame me later if you get into trouble."

The pastor's office hours are drawing to a close, but the waiting room is still full of people. The majority of those waiting are young, girls and boys coming to register for confirmation classes, some with their mothers and fathers or some other grown-up person accompanying them. That probably looks more proper than coming alone, – thinks Annele. She would like to leave the most favorable impression, and that is why she wishes she could have done everything correctly, but now it is too late. Today is the last day to apply.

And thus she is the last to go in to see the pastor and, so she feels, still unprepared, for she doesn't quite know what to say. Her turn has arrived much too fast, and she hasn't been able to think of anything. She stands there confused. A lot of things crowd to the fore, except for the words she ought to say. Every object seems to be shrouded in a faint mist. A large desk, two huge bookcases – so many books together in one place, turning broad, dignified backs to the room! – On the wall facing her, as though about to climb out of his gilded frame, hangs an old pastor with a gold cross on his breast and a white, ruffled wheel of a collar, his eyes grave and stern.

That one must be the father and this one, the young one, must be his son with the same grave, pensive eyes. He looks deep within, as though he wanted to bore through a person.

"Well, my child?"

Annele now quickly tells him what she needs. Not the way she should have said it, in clear, well-placed words that would satisfy her – still, the pastor has understood her.

She's not in school. An orphan. Fifteen years old.

"Too young."

"That really doesn't matter," she impulsively retorts.

"It matters inasmuch as you won't be able to keep up. My young men and young women are all older, and besides they've been trained in good schools. I adjust my teaching to their level. And I'm not easy on them, I demand a great deal."

"That's exactly what I like."

Again the deep, slightly surprised look.

"It would make me so very, very happy."

"All right, I'll register you. Let's give it a try. If you can't keep up, then that's that – you'll have to wait a few more years."

She is registered now. But she can't run home with a great feeling of triumph. The pastor has told her the same thing as Kristaps. She probably looks pretty foolish, pretty insignificant, if people have such doubts about her. Wonder if things will really be so bad that she can't keep up? And suppose they are, she wouldn't be able to show her face, she'd be so ashamed. Then Kristaps could make fun of her every day, and rightly so.

Maybe her decision and the speed with which she implemented it is just a little bit too hasty, but now she can no longer turn back.

The confirmation classes are scheduled to take place in one of the large schoolrooms belonging to the church. The confirmands sit divided into two groups just as in church, the girls on the right, the boys on the left. There's the din of voices, chatter. People sit with people they know, and students from the same school also keep together. Friends greet each other, and the friends of friends get acquainted. Annele has arrived pretty much on time, but all the benches are already full. What she does not know is that this first time they've all hurried to ensure they get the desirable seats. Wherever you sit today is where you'll sit the entire duration of the classes. It is true that one bench is completely empty, but it's all the way in front. How can she sit there, visible and observed by all? Searching the benches with her eyes, she walks down the center aisle a bit. Here and there she sees an empty seat. But as soon as she makes a move toward it, she hears, "Taken!" And there, by chance, she catches sight of Marija. She is sitting with Lizete's friend from the bright moonlit night. Annele could comfortably find a seat with them, for there is still a wide gap next to them. Marija, too, has seen her, but then, quick as a flash, she jerks her head in the other direction. Doesn't she want to recognize me, doesn't she want to show she has seen me? Definitely. That's definitely so. For a moment she remains as though turned to ice in the middle of the aisle, all eyes are turned toward her: Who's that? What's she doing here? Who knows her? A stranger. Then she slowly walks back and sits down on the front bench almost under the lectern. Where else can she go!

It is a moment full of agony. Without doubt they've all seen that there is no place for her anywhere.

"I know that now they've all looked me over from head to foot and are making remarks about me, noticing how plain my clothes are, not to mention my patched-up boots which, in the first row, are so clearly visible – how can I hide them? – I know they're shrugging their shoulders: we've never seen her before, nobody knows her. Where? What school's she from? Oh, she isn't *in* school! And if I'm not in school, then I'm not their equal at all. And what will the pastor think? Look at that! Here's this girl sitting right in front of me! Even on registration day she seemed too forward! Oh no, I'd much rather hide somewhere in the back benches, listen quietly so no one notices me or pays attention to me. Because it is possible, it is possible that I won't be able to keep up, and now they've all seen me, and they'll even whisper to each other later on the street and laugh at me."

At the very last moment a girl hurries in late, her face flushed, and without looking around at all, drops on the front bench not far from Annele. Now there are two of them.

The din suddenly dies down. The pastor has come in.

Slender and silent he stands on the speaker's podium waiting until there is dead silence. Then he bows his head. They all rise to their feet.

When the prayer is over, the pastor calls out the names to make sure that all those who registered have come. Each person whose name is called jumps to his feet and acknowledges that he is present by answering "Yes!" more or less audibly. While the boys' names are being called, all the girls' heads are turned left. Many of the boys – and the girls, too – are people Annele has often seen in the streets, and now she hears their names.

"Jēkabs Kamols!"

A rather gruff voice answers in the boys' rows, and a young giant straightens up to his full height. But that's Tall Bear, isn't it? – wonders Annele. So he, too, is a member of the confirmation class?

The first class concludes with general instructions and explanations about the course of their studies and the pastor's objectives. In this class the confirmands will not have to learn Bible stories, catechism, and verses, the pastor assumes they have already learned all this in school. While they are here, he will help them understand themselves and understand life a little, and he asks them to be watchful and attentive. When the pastor leaves, Annele quickly disappears after him. So she doesn't have to see anyone. So she doesn't have to rub shoulders with anyone. "If they don't want me, then I don't want to know anything about them either." That's how defiant she feels.

Valdens was not one of those people who captivate you at first sight. He was quite tall and slender, with rather long brownish hair that showed a white thread here and there at the temples. His face was clean-shaven, his eyes, when he looked at you, deeply and earnestly searching, stern, demanding attention. There was something familiar about the pastor's face, his gestures, or his voice. Where had she seen this before? When? Wasn't there something about him that reminded her of the friendly teacher in summer school? No! He'd been more imposing, younger. More carefree, too. He hadn't had that painful expression about his lips that would fleetingly pass across them, though only sometimes, but was there nevertheless, and when it appeared would pierce her heart so strangely and feel so strangely attractive.

The pastor stood and waited until even the slightest noise had abated, for he was used to speaking in silence so deep you could hear a pin drop; then his eyes swept across all their faces. For a moment, just the shadow of a moment, his glance fell into Annele's eyes as well, and now it felt warm, benevolent, caressing. She trembled. Father! Didn't Father look at her like that? It was like suddenly hearing a voice from eternity; just as quickly, the sound died away, vanished, but an invisible bond, a resemblance remained and drew her heart closer to the man who stood on the podium; perhaps there was also something about him of that great, benign power that had watched over and cherished her as a child. She kept her eyes riveted on him when he began to speak. She absorbed every word as a parched plant absorbs the dew. Her heart hurried to meet each word like a long-awaited guest. And rejoiced. Why, those aren't incomprehensible strangers! No! I know them. They're the companions of my own thoughts. Except that these come dressed in more resplendent garb. Their faces are much wiser, experienced, and knowing. These are the older brothers of my thoughts, who have roamed through other worlds and now spread their acquisitions before me. They knock at the coffers of my thoughts to make their home there, bringing warmth and light. And if we understand each other so well, then I'm sure the speaker on the podium won't send me home again, for I need to listen and take to heart everything he has to say.

When the class is over, Annele wakes up as though returning from a different world. She has no need to take notes as she sees others doing, all the words are in her head, filling her days with profound and great thoughts. She needs to learn whatever there is to learn, her granaries are wide and deep and crying to be filled.

⌁~⊩~⌁

When more than a week has passed, Valdens one day asks questions about the material they have covered in the classes. Not calling upon anyone in particular, he waits to see if anyone will volunteer an answer.

But nobody does. He scans first the boys' benches, then the girls', till he comes to the very first one in front. Maybe Annele has raised her hand slightly. Maybe she's dared do that, for she could answer very well, and so Valdens's gaze has finally stopped on her.

"You? Can you tell me something?"

And he waits.

She stands up and answers. At first she doesn't do too brilliantly, for her heart is beating so hard in her breast that her voice shakes. But she controls herself: for she does know the material. All he has to do is ask. And the more he asks, the more the terrible shaking abates, her voice sounds clear, and the two of them converse freely for a while exchanging questions and answers, like two acquaintances, two friends, while all eyes are on them.

"Sit down!"

The pastor now takes Annele's answers, both the ones that came in direct response to his questions and those that diverged from the topic and looked for their own path, he strings them like beads and then, using them as a gauge, once more gives a general overview of the direction his classes have been taking.

Her ears are burning. It is so strange to hear her own words coming from another's mouth. And what does the pastor think of them? Are her answers sufficiently good, clear, do they prove that she can keep up, and that she won't be turned out of the class? After all, it's the first time that she's been called upon, that he can see what she's capable of. Yes or no, she has to find out now. And when the pastor is about to leave the podium, she plucks up her courage and goes and stands in front of him: "Can I – can I keep coming to class now?"

Valdens gives her a friendly nod of affirmation: "Yes, yes, yes. Why shouldn't you come? You can come, you're perfectly welcome."

And so it now often happens that while asking review questions to find out how deeply the principles of his teachings have penetrated the minds of his listeners, Valdens, having gone the rounds of all the rows of seats, now asking questions of his listeners at large, now calling on individuals, correcting and filling in the details, finally comes to his youngest listener below the lectern, whereupon both of them together through questions and answers recapitulate the lesson and create, just like the first time, what seems like a short, friendly conversation, to which the whole class listens attentively.

Annele's status among the young people in the confirmation class has improved considerably.

When she meets Jēkabs Kamols on the street as he comes from his *gymnasium* with a group of other young men, he always takes off his cap in greeting, and the other boys walking with him follow suit.

Marija knows her again. When she passes, she not only nods, but also stops and shakes hands, and her girlfriend says: "We're old acquaintances, you know, from that moonlit night. Remember?"

One day, before the pastor's arrival, Emmija Vītole, a *gymnasium* student and the proudest girl among the confirmands, comes up to Annele: she is not sure of the meaning of something Valdens said that she copied in her notebook. What is Avote's opinion? Could she explain it to Emmija? – "Yes, certainly, I'll be glad to!" And as they both sit there leaning close to each other and absorbed in exchanging ideas, many other girls, and boys as well, have gathered around them to listen. Wherever Annele looks, she sees friendly eyes. And she feels so unbelievably good. She presses her lips together to keep sudden joy from escaping through them with a word, for she is still unwilling to show it. She has found a home in warmth. In the midst of these boys and girls who all attend secondary schools, she has now gained the rights of citizenship. An equal among equals.

⌒⚬⌒

A sunny afternoon. For some time now the days have stretched to such a length that it is no longer necessary to light the gas during class. This lesson is the last. Six weeks have passed, and tomorrow is the confirmation.

Is it possible, is it possible that this happy time is over already? Something fills her with such deep sorrow. Do the others feel it, too? There is a kind of deep emotion, the chatter has a different sound to it, but isn't that more likely to be happiness that they'll be rid of one obligation and be able to keep up with regular schoolwork more easily?

Valdens speaks.

There are two kinds of lives, two kinds of paths, and two kinds of thirst. There is the thirst for the good life, for wealth, fame, and honor. And human beings are like travelers in the desert tormented by such thirst. They go into battle, often ruthlessly pushing their fellow fighters out of the way and even trampling or destroying them. And when they have reached the longed-for goal, they pitch their tents by their wells and enjoy the fruits of their efforts and struggles. They consider themselves fortunate, and others look upon them as such: the fortunate ones who have quenched their life's thirst. But soon, with amazement and terror, they notice that the wells by which they have pitched their tents are drying up and that their gardens are parched, their hearts are athirst, and in despair they say: was that all we strove for so fervently? Are we now to stand at the gate of eternity with empty hands and lackluster eyes? To stand there with the terrible realization: we have forfeited our entire lives and gained mortality in return.

But life must be lived, mustn't it? We are not given life to flee from it and to avoid it. No, it is given to us so that we should take our full share of it. If a person thirsts for wealth, then that means he is also given the capacity for increasing it, and then he should go and do that; if a person thirsts for knowledge and education, then he must seek his life's path in that direction. And all the obstacles are there only so that the weapons should be sharpened for battle, and all the wounds and injuries are there only to make the longing for a goal that must be reached deeper and harder to silence. But all the thirst of the earth is thirst for truth, eternity, and the divine. And we must not shun the illusions of this world, for only in illusions do we catch a glimpse of the path of truth, just as we sense light beyond the shadows. But woe to those who do not see and search for truth amid illusions, and light among shadows! They are left with a handful of empty husks at the very end, and their life has crumbled into ashes.

But how do you tell the true thirst from the false? How do you recognize the kernel of the seed of eternity in the disintegrating husk? How do you know where truth is, when thousands of wise and famous men have died with a cry of despair on their lips: where is this truth of yours? Is there anyone who can guess it and discover it? Is it so hard and impossible, then? No! That magic formula is simple, accessible to all and infallible, and here it is: – If you were to speak in the tongues of men and angels, and if you had prophetic powers, and understood all the mysteries and all knowledge, and if you had all faith and could move mountains, but had not love, then you would be only sounding brass or a tinkling cymbal, you would be nothing in the face of eternity.

The divine magic formula and key to all mysteries is love.

Love is the most infallible lodestar, it is like a fire that absorbs and melts earth's darkness and illusions in it and transforms them into a white flame, it comes from

God and goes to God, therefore its thirst is unceasing and cannot be quenched here on earth, for it is thirst for the highest that human beings can attain, thirst for divine perfection.

The scheduled time to end the lesson is long past, but Valdens still cannot bring himself to finish. Like a solicitous father with his children as they set off for a distant and unknown destination, he would still like to say many heartfelt words and to give helpful advice. Both speaker and listeners are moved. Parting. The last time. These words are always imbued with sorrow. They have just heard the last sentence. Then a conclusion with brief words of thanks. And silence. No one stirs. The young people sit there as though transfixed. The pastor waits. Something is still to come.

From the last bench on the boys' side, Jēkabs Kamols gets up and walks toward the pastor's desk with somewhat faltering steps. He stands in front of it, big and tall, head slightly bowed, and begins to speak. True, at first he seems to stutter, searching for words, but what he says is fine. The young people hang on his words, for he thanks the pastor in the name of all the confirmands for the beautiful classes. They have come with pleasure, have listened with enthusiasm, and will treasure the pastor's words all their lives.

With a bow, he shakes the pastor's hand and leaves the desk, but after him other young men now come from the back rows in the same order as they had been seated, and after them the girls, so that again it is Annele's turn to be the last of all.

The pastor takes the hand that Annele respectfully holds out to him, and to her sudden shock grasps it in his hand.

"Anna Avote, a few words, my child." And raising his voice, as though deliberately, so everyone can hear: "You are the last to come and shake my hand, just as you were the last to come register with me. I accepted you without really wanting to, for I doubted whether you would be capable of keeping up with the class. But things turned out differently. Not for one moment did I notice that your interest was flagging. I had the feeling you received with your mind, with your heart, with your hands. That can only be done by a person who has experienced the kind of thirst I spoke of today. Poverty, obstacles, renunciation – you know them all, but they have been a blessing for you, they have taught you how to long and how to be fervent. May your longing not be just an empty husk, may it contain the precious kernel of eternity – I wish you this with all my heart."

The pastor's hand lightly touches the girl's forehead. And very softly, audible only to her: "Blessings upon your path!"

Annele dares not raise her bowed head: she wishes everyone hadn't seen and listened! But it can't be helped. It's happened.

The narrow cloakroom is full to bursting. Soft muttering, chatter, and, over there, loud laughter. Enough, enough of being serious and solemn! Their limbs seem numb from sitting so long. Time to stretch their legs!

Annele feels a warm hand on her head. She looks back in surprise. It's Jēkabs Kamols's hand.

"Good, good, my child!" fatherly, imitating Valdens's deep voice, he nods his bushy head in front of the girl.

How dare he! She pulls away haughtily. But Jēkabs's look is a bit smiling, a bit quizzical, yet not malicious, indeed you might say it is friendly and warm. And now, she, too, cannot help laughing. But that is the best way to deal with the remarks that now come raining down on Jēkabs's head.

"Will you look at that! Kamols is practicing his new duties!"

"What duties?"

"A pastor's duties. Didn't you see how benignly he placed his paw on Avote's head? He's off to Tartu this fall."

"Well, he's definitely cut out for Tartu! But what makes you think he'll be a clergyman?"

"I'd say that your Kamols has a stuttering tongue. What kind of a clergyman is he going to be?"

"A stuttering tongue? That only happens to him in affairs of the heart. Do you have any experience with him in that direction?"

Jēkabs himself goes off tall and smiling without another word.

At the street door, Emmija Vītole is waiting for Annele.

"Who are you planning to walk with in church tomorrow? Have you made arrangements with anybody yet?"

No, Annele does not know who she is walking with. She hasn't even thought about it.

"I haven't made any arrangements with anyone either. If you like, we can walk together. We're the same height."

"I'd be glad to, very glad. Thank you."

"Goodbye, goodbye!"

Warm hands touch, friendly eyes exchange looks, they are all so warm and merry, like the children of the same father.

Now this day had dawned, as all long-awaited and important days arrive and dawn. Annele woke up early. Would the weather be nice today? The sky, as much of it as she could see from her pillow, was not cloudy, but not clear either: veils of rosy red filaments trailed here and there. These March days were faintly misty, windless. Perhaps by midday the sun, which was already noticeably warm, would be shining.

She lay in silence, not wanting to wake her sister yet. Her thoughts came and went. She did not linger on any one of them, but allowed the mood of this day, a mood she had never experienced before, wash over her like warm waves.

Mother was walking about in the next room. Now it was time. Quickly the girl jumped up and went outside, where a basin of water and a white towel were already waiting for her.

"Don't you braid your own hair, wait for me," called Līziņa through the open door.

"Wonder where Kristaps is today?" Mother said regretfully. "Now the two of you could both be getting ready, but it didn't turn out that way."

Yes, Kristaps was no longer there. One day, his mother had arrived and had had a long, whispered conversation with her son. Melnzemis had been elected head of the district council, and so now he had a lot of business away from home, while on the farm there was need for someone to replace him. And the son was already so grown-up and sensible that it would be a crime and a shame to look for someone else instead of him, though such a person could certainly have been found among the relatives. Forget about the few months of school, that did not make any difference. The same with the confirmation – it could easily be done in spring, in the local church together with the other young people of the parish. After all, he had gone to confirmation class, and could get a certificate from the Jelgava pastor to that effect. Of course, Valdens was glad to give him one.

Kristaps did not go home willingly. He resisted for a long time, trying in every possible way to bend his parents', or rather his mother's, decision in his own favor. He did not succeed. Although he took after his mother, his will was not so hardened that it could have contended with his mother's well-forged and steeled weapon, by means of which she had always won a position of supremacy for herself in the family. All things considered, there was every reason today to say regretfully, out of sympathy for her cousin: wonder where Kristaps is today?

Līziņa made the part so straight that not a single hair was allowed to cross to the side where it did not belong. She divided the hair into equal strands and braided it so carefully that the braids looked as though they had just left a hairdresser's shop window. The ends of the braids remained loose for a few handbreadths, and were tied with black, almost new velvet ribbons knotted in richly falling loops.

Everything down to her shift was new, worn for the first time. You couldn't go to Holy Communion with something that had been worn previously. Then came the white dress. A present from her brother in Rīga, though thin and cheap, it was appropriately full and long, and even touched the ground in the back. The wearer herself had bitterly opposed this fashion, she felt it would get all tangled around her feet and that it would be difficult to take a step, but her sister had the deciding vote here: the first long dress must really be long.

The white gloves had gathered lace borders through which a narrow velvet ribbon had been threaded.

"Gloves, too?" wondered the confirmand.

"Yes, everything that's proper," said her sister firmly.

What else? A little silver gilt cross with a velvet ribbon, Aunt Meire's contribution. She'd brought it last night. – Goodness gracious! Go to communion without a cross? The other girls would all have one, and she wouldn't. Dear, kind aunt!

Now they are all ready. Silence in the little flat. Annele hugs her sister first. Thank you, thank you, thank you! – she'd like to say a hundred times, but her lips are trembling. Then Mother's dear toil-worn hand! – "My baby! If only Father had lived to see you grown-up." She is unable to go on. There are many words, but they do not want cross her lips. All three of them stand and wait lovingly, for Mother is nevertheless going to say something else. And, still holding the girl's hand in her own, she quietly begins to recite one of her favorite psalms: "Praise the Lord, O my soul." After the reciting of the psalm, none of them speaks anymore. This is customary according to ancestral tradition, so that humdrum conversation will not intrude upon their walk to the sanctuary.

The place where the confirmands are to gather is in the very school where the classes were held. By the time Annele comes in, the majority have already arrived.

They are all standing. The boys in black suits, with a scattered few in new gray country homespun, the girls in white, and only a few here and there in black.

Annele now has the feeling that she is extremely dressed up, that as she passes by all eyes turn toward her, and that she would rather become invisible now. But this cloud passes quickly. In come other girls, erasing the impression of the one before. Many are expensively dressed, in low-cut dresses, wearing glittering new jewelry.

Emmija comes in and takes her place next to Annele. She is wearing white silk, and around her shoulders is a cloak edged with fur. She is the daughter of Zemgale patricians, and one of the best-dressed of them all.

But all these facts are submerged in the great solemnity like melting snowflakes in the warm light of the sun. One thing alone remains: it is good to be there together with all these young human beings, with the boys and girls, standing there in the midst of a great fraternal community as it were and waiting for one thing, thinking and feeling one thing. Every moment is precious, but every one has wings.

Valdens enters, and the young people line up in a long row, there are more than a hundred and thirty of them, and they are quite a sight this cool March morning. Many have relatives waiting outside, and other passersby stop on both sides of the street forming a lane; some are surprised: wonder what these confirmands are doing here? – for it's a weekday, when such celebrations do not usually take place. But Pastor Valdens says he cannot divide his attention between a church crowded with parishioners and the young people who are being confirmed. And so this day is dedicated to the young people alone.

Now he speaks to them for the last time. No longer as intimately as during the classes, but more as if to say farewell; even as he pauses on the threshold, he still cautions and caresses, warns and speaks words of love to guide these young souls who are still gathered together today, but who, when they leave the church, will go out into a world whose paths are so complicated, full of obstacles and stumbling blocks.

The organ rumbles softly. Around the altar, the girls kneel like a garden full of white flowers. The pastor gives each his benediction.

Annele listens expectantly. What will hers be?

"Blessed are the pure in heart: for they shall see God."

The words drop like dew on Annele's head. They fall into her heart like fire. What words are these? Heard and yet never heard before, familiar and spoken for the first time, for they have been spoken to her, spoken to her from eternity, to her alone. Today they are her great gift, the wonderful thing she has gained. Are they not prophetic, and have they not been given to her as her guiding star throughout life? The pure in heart shall see God. Of all the verses in the Sermon on the Mount, these are the most beautiful. Shall see God! What can compare to this promise? It shows the way to a mountain peak illuminated by the sun of eternity. But how is she to find the way? What does it take to find it? Purity of heart. What does that mean? Where is it to be found? Only now, in this hour?

Light, as though no longer feeling the weight of her body, Annele has returned from the altar to her seat. She has felt the waves of the communion liturgy wash over her, has heard *Holy, Holy*, that great hymn of praise. She does not join in, her heart is so full that she does not sing; when she tries to, her voice breaks and stays in her throat. She sits silently, and her thoughts caress all that is past and that is now. As if from a garland that is disintegrating, the days of her early childhood drop away – in the servants' room at Spring Farm, where during the day spinning wheels hummed amid the silence of work, and Father's harnesses rattled as he wove, and where at night songs rippled and stories were told, with little Jurītis, dashing Ingus, beautiful Karlīne, with Granny, and Father's supple figure on his weaver's bench. There is the forest at Spring Farm, and the first days of herding, life on the barrens and at school. The speckled nose of her herding companion Krančelis also appears for a moment. And there are all those who are near and dear to her heart, who have stretched their hands over her and wished her nothing but good; her dear, departed father, her mother, sister, brother, the kind teacher at summer school, Pastor Valdens, Aunt Meire. How good that she can take them all into the holiness her heart now feels, that she can give them all such a large share, and that her heart becomes all the fuller and richer from it. How good that these dear boys and girls have come close to her as well, and that she has spent such lovely hours with them and experienced this one last, forever unforgettable hour in their company. Now Emmija returns to her seat, her lips are closed tight and tears tremble in her cast-down eyelashes, there goes Jēkabs Kamols, silent, grave, and filled with rapture. A nice boy. Perhaps some day he'll be an eminent and decent man. Yes, all, all of them are there, near and dear. She'd like to take their hands, to embrace them as brothers and sisters. They are all in the light, in the wondrous light of this hour, which has melted away all shadows, troubles, poverty, all renunciation and sufferings. But isn't the light and holiness of this hour, this goodness that flows over everything caressing it like the sun, isn't that already part of the miracle, a small part of "seeing God"?

She bows her head deeply. Her inward-looking gaze beholds world upon world.

The benediction. The final hymn. Too soon, too soon!

The organ rumbles, thunders, exults, storms. The organ accompanies them on their way out. Out into the world, into life!

"Goodbye!" Emmija hastily extends her hand, smiles distractedly at this companion of an hour, while with her next smile she is already off to meet the people who are waiting for her, who wave, call out to her, and greet her joyfully. All of them are now surrounded by their own little groups. Annele too surrenders to her family's affectionate congratulations. Mother places Annele's coat around her shoulders for her. Aunt Meire says approvingly:

"That was awfully, awfully nice, I must say. When you remember your own youth on a day like today, your heart turns young with these young people." And, measuring the confirmand with her eyes, she says:

"And look, you've shot up, you're almost as tall as your sister."

"Yes, I've grown," replies Annele pensively.

The organ rumbles, thunders, storms. And when the impetuousness of its loud exultation reaches its peak, the sounds suddenly break off and vanish abruptly. The church is left silent and empty.

Outside, the March day is foggy and cool.

Oh, If Only I'd Known!

It had already been several weeks since Edgar had quit Rank's and left to explore a new place to work and live. As yet there had been no news of him, but Līziņa was not worried. They had agreed that he would write only once there was something definite, a place to hang up your hat, so to speak. He did not like purposeless letter-writing.

If an outsider had observed life in the little flat, he would have found it odd that there was so little mention of Edgar Reikschat here. Annele especially found everything that had to do with Reikschat not very real, not very believable. It was all still far off in the future. It might be months before he came back, and until then life went on as it always had.

But was this not an illusion? After all, changes are usually not announced by a bell. No matter how carefully we watch for it, we will not capture that indeterminable moment when day turns into evening, summer into fall, wakefulness sinks into sleep. Imperceptibly, Līziņa had lost much of her gaiety, though she did not want anyone to know. But her effort was transparent anyway. And often she would become lost in thought, a pained smile would flit across her face, sometimes she would even stealthily wipe away a tear. Annele saw all this. Full of anxiety she saw that her sister was hiding something, and so she, too, did not feel free to question her about it. Was Līziņa grieving for Edgar, who was alone in a strange place now? That did not seem quite plausible to Annele, but perhaps it was an appropriate thing for brides to do? But then came a letter from their Lithuanian cousin. Her sister read it once, a second time, surreptitiously as it were, did not show it to the younger girl, nor discuss it as she would have done in former times. A lot of things were no longer as they used to be.

Finally, Edgar wrote, too. These were news that could at once be announced to everyone. As he had predicted earlier, Ventspils had proved to be the most acceptable place to settle after he had convinced himself that there was "nothing much going on" in the other "dumps." Now, in Ventspils they would have food on the table. Here, there were large shipping agencies that owned a lot of ships. The butchers' guild was pretty prosperous, every master butcher had his own house; they got along well with the sailors, of whom there were naturally large numbers here. This, obviously, was one of the main prerequisites. But here, too, there was no need to go to too much trouble. You'd have to wine and dine them a couple of times, live it up a bit once in a while, since sailors are the kind of people that love to "kick over the traces" now and then when they step on dry land. And there's nothing wrong with that, is there? You join them on their night on the town, thus ensuring that you will have customers. That's what all the master butchers do here – and, generally speaking, they're all a pretty fun-loving bunch of fellows. What better way to pass the time! They're making a good living, and there's nothing pressing to do. Plenty of leisure. And so they fill up the time a bit, enjoy life, and take it easy. And, like all easy-going people, they aren't envious at all. Edgar was well received by the most prominent master butchers, and was given useful advice. – Oh, so he's been a manager at Rank's, and for such a long time! That in itself opens every door. And besides, there's nothing to be envious about. He'll take merchandise from them and process it into fine delicatessen, the kind they neither know how, nor want to produce themselves. Thus there will be no conflict of interest. If these people are at all smart, then they must realize that his arrival will be a gain not only for the townspeople, but for them as well. Anyway, it's very important for Edgar to get along with people, and he likes these "brothers." He's already rented a flat and a workshop, an entire house in one of the finest streets, and the best location on that street. But it's been standing empty for more than a year, living proof that there are very few people who have enough sense to see money lying around on the street just for the taking. – Now, this house is being fixed up, and that may take some time longer. And so forth. All kinds of observations and trivial details, and in between are lines that Līziņa reads moving her lips silently. Then the promise to write again soon and a request for an answer.

But the days pass so strangely gray, although spring is beginning to blossom outside.

And one day yet another letter arrives for Līziņa. When she receives it, she starts as though she had grabbed hold of a burning coal: oh dear, who is this writing to me?

"Who's this writing to me!" she exclaims, turning crimson as a coal herself. It is obvious that the handwriting is unfamiliar to her.

And she reads it for a long time, a long, long time, though it's only a few lines long. And then, rising to her feet abruptly, overcome with confusion and haste:

"I need to go out."

Her sister asks no questions. Is the letter so upsetting? Finally Līziņa herself can't help asking:

"Do you know who's written to me?"

"Līna?"

"No, Silmežs. He's planning to be in Jelgava in the next few days. Maybe even today. I ought to get something, because I'm sure we'll have to ask him to stay for lunch."

After putting on her hat, she changes her mind and rereads the letter.

"No, it can't be that soon. It says here: toward the end of the week."

"Well, does he say he's coming to our house?"

"Yes, definitely, definitely."

She puts her hat down again, sits down in her place and picks up her work. But her hands lie in her lap as though she had forgotten them.

"It's so strange, so strange," she whispers and smiles to herself.

Annele, too, senses that something is "so strange," but she does not understand what it could be. Something about Silmežs?

They can hear Mother next door.

"Don't you tell Mother about the letter, d'you hear?"

No, why should she tell if there's a secret involved? For her, another's secret is like one of her own, she's not going to divulge it. Although – she doesn't understand what could be so special about Silmežs coming to visit them while he is in Jelgava.

All day long, Līziņa is silent, though she works feverishly. That evening she asks Mother to go to Aunt Meire's for a pattern Līziņa has lent her. Now they are alone.

That's what she wanted.

And now, into the silence that has prevailed all day, she breathes a short, deep sigh.

"Listen, girl, what would you say if I – if I – well – if I – were to break off with that Edgar?"

This has come so suddenly, so inexorably.

"Break off with Edgar? How? But aren't you – – "

"I know, I know what you're going to say. Yes, we're engaged, but being engaged isn't like being married."

"But isn't that the same thing?"

"Oh, you don't know what you're talking about," she tosses her head impatiently.

True, Annele doesn't know. Where could she have heard about such things! She's read a lot about eternal constancy and love. She liked that. And isn't an engagement a promise, and isn't marriage a promise? And isn't that exactly the same thing? If you've given your word, it's like something engraved in stone. A promise is more binding than anything else, isn't it? That's what she thinks.

Her sister's face is so deeply moved, agitated, what should Annele say to her?

"Līziņa, is this about – about that Silmežs, is that why you're talking like this? You like him?"

"Do I like him! I don't just *like* him! – Oh, if only I'd known earlier! If only it had happened the year before! Why couldn't it have? We saw each other that first time when I was at Līna's house. A few hours together, we got to know each other, were full of high spirits, felt as though we were old acquaintances. He liked what I said, and I liked what he said; but it was just for that short time, and I didn't think much about him afterwards. Especially not that this might be at all serious. If I had, there wouldn't have been anything between me and Edgar, you see. But now, last Christmas, when he met me at the station, he immediately reminded me of that first time. And it gave me a strange sort of pang. He hadn't forgotten. And so, all that time, almost day in and day out, we were together constantly, just constantly. But even now, when I left for home, I thought: well, it's over and done with. Although I myself was so sorry, so sorry that it was over and done with, full of regret for something... And now suddenly this letter!" She opened a button in her shirtwaist – where the letter was concealed – and read: "I am not a poet, I cannot tell you in writing what I have to say, but permit me to call on you when I am in Jelgava." Well, and what does he have to say – I have a premonition it can be nothing other than – –"

"Didn't anybody in Varneviķi know you were engaged?"

Līziņa shook her head.

"Not even Līna, nobody, nobody?"

"No, in the beginning I was still debating with myself: should I tell them or not? I thought: why on earth should everybody know? When the time comes, they'll find out, too; but later, as the days passed, it got harder, you see – and the days passed before I knew it. – And so – why am I telling you this, you're still a child – "

"I'm fifteen, you know," interrupted Annele.

"And fifteen, twenty, or twenty-five amounts to almost the same thing if you've never experienced anything like this – well, I never had. – After all, what kind of a life have I had? Work and more work and maybe a little bit of fun once in a while. I hardly know anybody. But the years don't stand still, before you know it, youth will be over soon. And what's in store for me then? At best, a life like Aunt's. Not that hers is bad, that's not what I'm saying, but I doubt if I'll have as much strength and endurance left by that time! And making do with what I have, that's it. O sweet frugality! as our Granny used to say. I certainly haven't been as content with what I have as it may have seemed. But what I did have was something that gnawed and burned inside me – just as you told me your pastor had said – that thirst, I mean. I know it too; I know all that I could have been if I'd had a fortune and an education. – There's so much, so much that gnawed at me, but I hid it under laughter and smiles and cheerful talk. Why show your heart to the whole world, and what's the use? Strangers will just laugh, and you'll make your own folks sad, that's all. And so, when a serious suitor comes along and he's not exactly repulsive – no, I wouldn't say that – and there's a prospect of somehow changing my life for the better and helping Mother, helping you get ahead, get a better education – all that was a consideration – and Mrs. Rank did her bit, too, praising, extolling, and recommending him – besides, you must admit that Edgar is a good person, I can't very well disparage him, but now, but – "

"And now he has left in the firm belief – "

"He's left in the firm belief and writes exactly as if he were already married and there weren't the slightest doubt about anything. And he hasn't the least idea how I really feel. Oh, what shall I do now? Here I've been telling you and chattering away, and you almost a child, while this thing has been choking me to death. Mother? I can't tell Mother, or Aunt for that matter, for them an agreement and an engagement are the same thing as marriage. – And besides, you know how people are – they're afraid of excitement, they just want everything to go smoothly, they want there to be no snags, but the excitement comes when the snag is so serious that there's no going forward or backward."

Her sister fell silent. The hand that held the needle moved at lightning speed. And Annele had no idea how to respond, though her thoughts came and went turbulently, and she felt so terribly, terribly sorry for her sister.

And then Līziņa suddenly asked another question:

"Still, you haven't given me a straight-out answer: what would you say if I were to act the way I said?"

"Oh, Sister!" Annele exclaimed evasively. Such a distressing question. What answer should she give? What answer?

"Then there's no need for you to answer, then I know what you're thinking. You're thinking I'm wrong, while Edgar alone is right? And all of you would think so. If I weren't involved in this myself, I'd think so, too. Only a person who's wounded knows how deep is the pain from the wound."

"Sister, maybe everything we've been saying is nonsense. Maybe that Silmežs has something entirely different to say to you."

Līziņa looked at her with startled, reproachful eyes:

"Why, what else are you thinking of, what else could it be?"

And then, some time later, in a voice meant to sound nonchalant:

"Oh yes, you could be right, it's probably something entirely different."

On the third day, Silmežs arrived. The way he came in was so surprisingly quick and silent – even as he knocked, he had already opened the door – that Annele did not catch sight of him until he stood by the table. Both sisters sprang to their feet as one, and so all three of them stood there, each at a different corner of the table. Silmežs bowed. Līziņa flushed red as a beet:

"Mr. Silmežs – my sister!"

Silmežs held out his hand. The left hand? Why the left? Annele looked for the right hand; what was wrong with it? It hid very nimbly now in a pocket, now behind the buttons of the jacket, but was also very nimbly active. The visitor put down his coat, pulled over the chair he had been offered, and there was a lightning glimpse of his right hand on the back of the chair. Annele was startled: it had only three fingers. The thumb and index finger were missing.

Līziņa had not mentioned a word about it. Did she not know it, then? After all, he drove his mad stallions himself, helped cut down and saw the spruces in the woods, danced the stormy mazurka – in all the stories about him in which Līziņa showed him alive and active, his hand had played an important part, hadn't it? But she had never noticed it, or else had deliberately paid no attention to it, or else had not wanted to talk about it. This gave a new direction to Annele's thoughts. Why was this, why was this? What was it about this Silmežs that was so powerful, that so appealed to her sister that it didn't even allow her thoughts to dwell on that poor crippled hand? She must study this question with twice as much attention. And at once, unbidden, a comparison thrust itself upon her. There was Reikschat, and here was Silmežs. On the one hand, Reikschat's somewhat short, stocky figure with its round head covered with thinning hair, his plump face with its thin, drooping mustache —on the other, Silmežs, young, slender, with thick hair, his eyes alive, full of expression, to put it in a nutshell – engaging, you might even say – handsome. On the one hand, sluggishness, love of comfort, a little vulgar both in language and in gestures, on the other – impetuosity, suppleness, attentiveness, elegance. Yes indeed, Silmežs was elegant from head to foot. Edgar could never be elegant, no matter how hard he tried. Soon, Silmežs and Līziņa were both deep in conversation. Silmežs carefully guided the conversation in such a way that "Miss Anna" would not be left out. But that was not the only thing that was likable and captivating about him. It wasn't just that he was a master at the art of conversation. He had something to talk about as well. While Edgar came in full of himself and left full of himself, keeping to his own narrow sphere, Silmežs extended his sphere till it was very wide and filled it with interesting contents. He did not talk about himself, but everything around him was alive: the people, the fields, the forests. The birds in the forest, the dogs and horses. He approached them as friends. He was good at bringing in delightful reminiscences of the time of Līziņa's visit, and presented each incident as an important event. He gave excellent descriptions of people whom they had merely encountered in passing at that time, showing them in a completely new light. He saw and observed, felt and thought everything. Annele was in heartfelt sympathy with everything he said, for she understood very well how much it was possible to experience in the silence of the country. What an infinitely rich world even her bleak barrens had been. The visitor's language was rich, sometimes sparkling with wit and humor, but never hurtful or funny at another's expense. Annele listened, and liked what she heard. Yes, he was captivating, it couldn't be helped. She could understand Līziņa. If this man had a flaw, it was no more than those two missing fingers. But was that a flaw? All the more reason for him to be even more attractive.

Oh dear, how fast the time had flown talking! Startled, Silmežs pulled out his watch. He still had some business to attend to at the seed store. There was a lot still to be done within the next hour. He must, he must go. He rose to his feet.

"What? So soon? Do you have to return home already?"

"Yes, this very day. By the evening train. Now is the busiest season for us country folks."

Līziņa's lashes began to tremble a little.

"Well then, please come and have lunch with us."

"On the contrary," smiled Silmežs. "I came to invite you to lunch. I've already made reservations at Zehr's."

With a quick glance at Annele. Lowering his voice a little: "I'd like your advice on a few matters."

"At Zehr's, at the hotel?"

"May I hope that you will not refuse me? I'll wait for you there in an hour and a half, let's say – two hours. By one o'clock I'll have settled my business and I'll be there ahead of you."

Līziņa hardly knew what to say. It seemed incredible to her that she was being invited to lunch here, at Zehr's elegant hotel. That was such an unusual thing in Jelgava. It would be strange if she met an acquaintance there.

Silmežs seemed to have guessed what she was thinking.

"There's such a hustle and bustle there now, as there always is in spring, it's like a public house. People don't pay any attention to each other. You will come, won't you?"

He had grasped her hand with his left and placed the slightly trembling fingers of his right hand on it. He looked at her imploringly.

"I'll be there," promised Līziņa.

Both hands over the wardrobe door, Līziņa stood for a long time with wide, unseeing eyes, then opened the wardrobe, took out her new suit and slowly flicked off some imaginary piece of fluff here and there; her thoughts were not on what she was doing.

"Are you going, Līziņa?"

"You think I shouldn't go?"

"How could you not go? You promised, you know."

"And I'm sure it's just as you said: he probably doesn't have anything special to say. He says he needs my advice about a few things. Well, that's perfectly all right with me."

But it seemed as though she herself did not believe what she was saying.

The new suit was made out of what was left of the cloth Father had woven, which, originally white, had been dyed a grayish violet. Trimmed with black as was the fashion just now, it looked very striking. There were a little black hat and black gloves to go with it. When Līziņa stood there dressed from top to toe in an outfit she had made herself – for the hat, too, had been designed by her – she looked so lovely and elegant that her younger sister could not resist telling her so.

"Well, how could I not be elegant! I've got an aristocrat's nose, don't you know," she laughed, running her finger down the barely perceptible aquiline bridge of her nose.

"That's the least of it. But your eyes are like violets now. Such a deep blue."

"Oh, get along with you, you little fibber!"

And she passed her hand over her sister's head.

"But so sad. And your braids are as shiny and golden-brown as chestnuts in fall."

"Now you're really talking nonsense."

And yet she enjoyed her sister's heartfelt admiration all the same.

Līziņa did not walk directly along the streets she took when going to work, but made a detour to the Driksa River, and reached the Hotel Zehr from the other direction. She was afraid to get there ahead of Silmežs. What would she do then? She'd have to stroll up and down the street or wait in the lobby. She liked neither of these possibilities. But from the market square, she could see Silmežs hurrying down Grand Street in the direction of her house. "Back, back!" called her thoughts. As though they had reached him and stopped him in his tracks, he abruptly turned around and caught sight of Līziņa approaching. His face lit up as though illuminated by a sudden light, and with long strides, so as not to lose another moment of the time they were to spend together, he hurried toward her. He's happy that I'm coming, thought Līziņa and smiled. Silmežs greeted her, hiding his ardent joy under a correct smile. They had reached the entrance of the hotel, and with an inviting gesture

Silmežs showed in his companion, whom a good many eyes observed with surprise as she glided past.

The Hotel Zehr was the most elegant in the whole town; this is where the country squires of Zemgale and other wealthy people stayed when they wanted the same comforts they enjoyed in their mansions and estates. Those who stopped for the day liked to have lunch here, for the hotel kitchen was generally well-known and renowned.

They entered the large dining room with its oak furniture and carved moldings. Silmežs had already located their seats and made a sign to the waiter. The seats were in an alcove, at a separate little table from which one had a view of the room. Silmežs asked Līziņa to take the chair nearest to the wall, and himself wanted to sit with his back to the room.

"If you don't mind, I'd like to switch, please."

"With pleasure."

And they changed seats.

In the center of the room, there was an elegantly set table covered with gleaming dishes and snow-white tablecloths. In the alcove across from theirs ate a windblown head forester with tall Wellington boots, and as he chewed, his swaggering mustache, whose tips touched the green-edged collar of his jacket, moved up and down. He called out loudly to the waiters all the way across the room, driving them like slaves to do his stomach's bidding. More guests were beginning to gather, so that the side tables were soon taken. Some people who sat at separate tables knew each other and conversed freely over their roasts and bottles of wine. Finally a rather large party of gentlemen and ladies came in, obviously members of the rural landed gentry, and were seated at the center table. With this, the big dining room seemed to have been given a fitting sense of completeness. The group in the center behaved as though they owned the place, laughing and chattering among themselves with that disregard of their surroundings – in this case, of those who sat at the side tables – that is typically shown by the landed gentry when they are among themselves. They felt only they themselves were tangible and visible, everyone else simply did not exist. The waiters spent all their time hovering over them, and they kept a tight rein on the waiters as drivers do to horses. At an incredible speed everything they could possibly want materialized in front of them, as on the magic table in the fairytale, while those who sat at the side tables watched with their mouths open.

Silmežs had ordered their lunch earlier, but he did not get it. "Ober," he had impatiently called out several times as the waiter's coattails went flying past. "Yes, yes, sir!" retorted the waiter, but he was gone like the wind. Silmežs flushed and impatiently rapped on his glass, then still more impatiently when he did not get the desired result. From the center, someone cast a reproving look at him: how common! Why's he creating such a disturbance? For they, of course, had everything they needed.

At last a waiter came by with a groaning tray of food.

"I'm sorry, but you can see how many gentlefolk we have here today!"

"Keep that to yourself. All I need to know is that I am the gentleman you are supposed to wait on," Silmežs replied haughtily, and his nostrils became dilated.

"Wine!"

This time the waiter was back like a shot.

Silmežs filled the glasses and asked his companion to clink glasses with him.

Līziņa barely touched it to her lips. The wine was strong. Silmežs emptied his glass.

"Why did we have to have wine? You're not a drinker either, are you?"

"On a festive occasion you can make an exception."

Silmežs smiled and sought the young woman's eyes, but it was obvious he was trying to conceal his irritation at the waiter and was unable to do so, even the flush had not disappeared from his face, and this kept him from being free and spontaneous.

How can that upset him so? Such a trifle? A shadow! Unobtrusively yet searchingly Līziņa looked at the face across from her as one looks at a mirror against the light. It was different today, strangely agitated, and she would so have wished to see the face she was familiar with, that she had grown to like and love.

The conversations at the center table were unconstrained and loud: they were forced to listen whether they liked it or not. They destroyed any attempt at a more intimate mood that might have been made at the little side table.

They hurriedly finished their lunch. Silmežs called the waiter. He paid. The tip he tossed on the table was extremely small. Līziņa's quick glance had taken note of it, and Silmežs, too, noticed that she had seen it.

"If he had been as attentive toward us as he was toward his gentry, the tip would have been more gentry-like," he explained.

Yes, Silmežs could not bear the least little shadow on his pride.

During lunch at the hotel, Silmežs had not been able to accomplish what he had intended.

"You know, I've never seen your palace gardens," he now said as they left the hotel. "Won't you show them to me?"

Yes, she'd be glad to. They turned off in the direction of the Lielupe River.

A lovely, lovely day.

Everything was newly green. Blue sky, blue waters, and the buds were opening. The river shimmered slowly, like their talk which blazed up and went out again, never really staying on one subject, for their words did not reflect their thoughts.

Līziņa stealthily looked at her companion. The little cloud that had cast a shadow on his forehead at the hotel was gone. And now all was well. It was so good to walk, to look at the spring, and to be together for a while. This hour, she knew, would never come again. The thought ached darkly within her, and she felt that she could now see clearly, very clearly: "The thing that he is thinking about, the thing he wants to talk about, will never come either."

They had passed several benches. All of them were too much in the way of passers-by. As though by silent agreement they looked for a more secluded spot. Oh, how she wished they would have to search for it much longer and further! In a corner of the park, there was a path overgrown with bushes and an old, decayed bench.

"We could sit here for a while."

"Yes, it's nice here."

They sat down here, and suddenly their conversation ran dry and would not start again.

In the lilac bushes, which had already taken on an overall violet glow, birds were fluttering and hopping about. Further away, hidden by the tender green fringes of a birch tree, a blackbird whistled sweetly. And then the moment they had been expecting all this time arrived. Suddenly Silmežs asked:

"You got my letter?"

"Yes," Līziņa answered barely audibly.

And again both of them fell silent, each quickly clutching at their own thought.

Silmežs: "How can I tell her what I have come to say?"

And Līziņa: "But I must speak first. I can't allow him to do it before me. It could be so painful afterwards."

And then she heard her voice hurrying ahead, heard it so strangely dark.

"Wait, I have to tell you something, have to tell you first, something you don't know – that might – I – I'm already engaged."

She could hardly pronounce the word "engaged."

"What?" he stared at her blankly.

"I've given my word."

As though he had been struck a blow, Silmežs drew back suddenly against the back of the bench. As if unable to understand, he whispered: "I've given my word?" And then, with a frozen look, stared at her stiffly, questioningly, and finally with comprehension. And not another word. He sat there, lips pressed together tightly, and looked down at the sand.

Why doesn't he speak? Why doesn't he shower me with questions: Who? What? When? Then he would hear how it all happened. How she gave her word long, long ago, before she knew anything about herself, about her heart. And that now everything has changed. And she did need to tell everything exactly the way it had happened, didn't she? But now? Why doesn't he himself say: there are no obstacles that we can't overcome. I like you, you like me. Our love is great. I'll do everything in my power to make you mine. You can lean on me now, let me take care of things, and I won't desert you.

Thus went Līziņa's thoughts in feverish haste. That's what the person next to her should have said, but he sat in silence. Līziņa glanced at him quickly. This was no longer the familiar bright face – it had become transformed. Surprise, astonishment, indignation. More than that. He was insulted. Just as he had been at the hotel, when the meal wasn't served fast enough. Yes – he was probably quick to take offence, but not as quick to forget it. And by the time he was able to, it was too late to make amends. That must be his nature. In struggle with himself, he could not control himself soon enough and get things clear in his mind. But wasn't clarity the first thing expected from a man? A man was expected to ask questions, to make inquiries, to investigate, and, once he had seen what was what, to engage in battle. But if he himself did not want to know anything further, how could she force her explanations on him? She had said what she had to say. She had no choice. And he should understand. That was the bridge across it all. But he sat in silence, as though bereft of speech. Where was the youthful voice that had held her under its spell, where was the gaze that had fascinated her?

The birds were twittering. The blackbird amid the green fringes of the birch tree went on whistling. Slowly the downy seed of a dandelion floated toward them, alighted on the sleeve of Līziņa's violet suit, then rose in the air and floated off to pay a visit to Silmežs's gray hat. And then suddenly the air all around them was flooded with dandelion down. Līziņa turned her head. Not far from them on the path stood a nursemaid with a little boy about four years old who had a handful of dandelions that had finished blooming, and he would not stop until he had blown all the seeds into the world.

Again Līziņa stealthily looked at the man beside her. Did he see it, too? Wasn't he glad to see the child? Perhaps a very subtle common chord was struck here? In former times, they would both have looked together and burst out laughing.

No, he had seen nothing, would see nothing. This was no longer the Silmežs she knew, but an entirely different person.

Shadows grew between them. Huge and dark. An abyss of shadows. The longer they sat there in silence, the harder it was to leap across to the other side.

This abyss of shadows was destined to remain there – without the slightest attempt to build a bridge across it.

It became awkward, just sitting there.

Then Silmežs suddenly seemed to become alarmed, took a look at his watch and rose:

"Time for me to go!"

"And so it will all remain unsaid," said Līziņa softly, as though trying to delay this moment a while longer. But Silmežs answered:

"What's the point of talking about it? Let bygones be bygones. I am not accustomed to receiving anything from another's hand."

That was certainly clear. What else was there to say?

She stared at him, eyes wide. Shocked, deeply hurt. Could the man she had so admired be saying these things? Did he have to say them?

Walking hurriedly, they went back to town.

At the same spot near the Hotel Zehr where they had met a few hours earlier, he took leave of her.

"Goodbye!"

"Goodbye!"

Līziņa did not have the courage to say: "Give my regards to the Vanags family!" Now it had all become unnecessary.

Slowly she came home, slowly she undressed and placed the new hat and suit in the wardrobe and then began to work so fast her fingers burned. She was silent, deep in thought.

Annele watched her sister anxiously. Her heart ached, but she dared not ask. "Everything's over between them," she already knew.

After waiting for a long time to no avail, she tried anyway:

"Līziņ!"

"Yes!"

How should she begin talking about it?

And again there was the whish of the needle. Until finally this heavy silence was shattered by Līziņa's words:

"Oh yes, now you've all finally got what you wanted."

"What we wanted? Who's this we?" Annele asked in amazement, and was immediately sorry she had asked, for her sister, too, regretted having spoken as she did.

"Oh, it just slipped out. Nothing could have come of it anyway."

And then, as though she had regained the power of speech, word for word, she told her young sister this day's brief but momentous events.

"I will tell *you*, but no one else must know, not even Mother. It would upset her needlessly, and would she understand?

"Be that as it may, did we have to part like that? I wish it had remained a pleasant memory at least. Perhaps I shouldn't have begun the way I did, perhaps I should have introduced it in a roundabout way and then told him? Would that have been better? No, I needed to get straight to the point. That's the way I am. Christmas in Varneviķi always did seem just like a dream, you know, and it was destined to remain one. I wish it had been possible to know all this beforehand somehow! But who ever heard of people being able to reach out and touch their future? It never happens. Or we'd all be smart.

"And so a dream it was and a dream it shall remain. Enough said. I never want to mention Silmežs's name again as long as I live."

Storm among the Blossoms

Clouds scudded with arrow speed. The storm tore into the new verdure of the trees and tossed shreds of leaves and twigs into the streets. At times a fog would pass overhead and with its fine drizzle swathe everything in gray veils of haze that were soon swept away by a new gust of wind. The rain did not amount to much.

Līziņa was writing a letter and only slightly raised her head toward her sister, who was putting on her coat.

"Where are you off to?"

"I'm going out for a while."

"In this weather!"

"I like the storm."

And, without listening to further objections, she left in a hurry.

She wanted to go out in the storm, for her heart, too, was stormy. She was suffering along with her sister. She saw and knew that Līziņa might indeed be able to banish Silmežs's name from her lips, but was it easy to banish his person from her mind? That was the question. She read the sad smile on her sister's face beneath the laughter, the sigh hidden beneath cheerful small talk. And the thought of her sister's words kept running through her mind: "Now you've got what you wanted." It is true that she had taken back the words, but they had been said, and they gnawed at the little sister as though she really *was* partly to blame.

But even now, if her sister had asked: What would you say if I were to break off with Edgar? – she would have had to answer as she had then. True, Silmežs was superior to Edgar, she could see and feel that herself, but still, Edgar had been given a promise, and a promise was sacred. And yet some other mind told her that it is better for two to be happy and one to be unhappy than for one to be happy and two to be unhappy. And this, too, was a wise mind. And another secret presentiment told her that there is a power that shatters all promises. But could she know that? Here was the uncertainty. Her sister should not have asked others, but should have done whatever she thought best. And she had indeed done just that in the end, but, but – it was a bitter decision, whichever way you looked at it. When there are two roads before you, you can only go down one of them. You never find out what was waiting for you on the other one, the road not taken, and so you always deeply regret it.

Sorrow is a weight that pulls you down into the depths, sorrow is a magnet that attracts other sorrows. Her heart labored under its yoke, incessantly sending out antennae of sympathy in all directions, only to add new burdens to its load. Perhaps for

Līziņa her everyday work and the winds of her responsibilities had begun to fill in with drifting sand the tracks that Silmežs's brief appearance had left in her life, but on Annele's life those tracks left a deeper imprint the longer she circled them with her thoughts. Such was her nature. And the more deeply she felt her sister's sorrows, the more deeply she felt her own and the more acutely she felt the sorrows of others as well, of which of course the whole world is full. Her heart palpated this world like a doctor palpating a patient, looking for the tender spot, and allowed its troubles to rise and fall in deep waters that were no longer illuminated by the sun of the mountain peak that was her confirmation day. Everything had turned gray, where there should have been spring and sunshine. And today the storm was roaring and clouds shot across the sky like arrows seeking a target. It was a day that was so perfectly in keeping with her own life, with the burdens she had to bear.

Now she remembered the time when she had been able to spend the confirmation classes together with others her own age – something she had had to do without so long – as much nicer than it had actually been. Although no friendships had been established, and not even close ties of acquaintance, it had still felt good to be in a group sharing a journey as it were, and even though her traveling companions were strangers, they all had a common destination, she could perhaps even share their laughter and their troubles. She could think back on it all in her thoughts, those were given to her, but she was denied the chance to live it in real life.

Several times she had met Emmija on the street. Nodding slightly, Emmija had passed by without even looking back. Enough! What do I care about you. Kamols did raise his cap, and with respect, every time they met; these were the only ones with whom she still exchanged greetings, the others no longer even recognized her, or rather – pretended not to recognize her. And now summer was coming, the school year was over – these, the finest of them all, Emmija and Kamols, were graduating from their respective schools and would go their way into a shining future. Jelgava would be empty soon.

She had met Valdens once as well. His gaze slid past her as he walked by and when she had said hello, he had raised his hat as though in surprise, apologetically. He was in charge of another flock now, and his concern was for them. Meanwhile she, too, was moving on, rarely attending church, for her heart ceaselessly looked for new directions and insights. This sometimes made her uncertain and vacillating: which way shall I go? What shall I do? Today, for instance, the bells were hurling wind-tossed peals from the belfries. It was Pentecost. Should she go to church? Listen to Valdens? No doubt he wished to see the people he had confirmed, and if they did not come he might think they had forgotten everything they had been taught in the classes. But that wasn't so at all. Nothing was forgotten, but now her heart no longer yearned for peace and shelter, but for battle and storm. And there was nothing she could do about it. The call of the voices of nature was stronger. She went to the palace gardens. The storm pushed her around, tore at her clothes, snatched at her bonnet, but that was all right.

"I never felt the spring till now, when rough winds shake the flowers and tear them, for in my heart is pain, defiance, daring." – She had read the words somewhere, and now they were really appropriate.

In the rivers, the waves were black, crowned with whitecaps. The storm drove them back while they, hissing fiercely, eddied and swirled and rushed forward along the course they were destined to follow. The trees groaned. On the other side of the Lielupe, the tall, storm-tossed meadow grass now blazed silvery gray, now grew dark as though a light had gone out, and so did a row of willows further away, near a cluster of buildings that under their black roofs seemed to be sagging under a weight of despondency as they submitted to fate.

Everything suffered. Including all living things, crazed with pain and struggle. But there was such fullness about this struggle, such power and grandeur that her heart was too small and weak to be able to grasp it, and it flowed over her like the spring floods flowing over the bed of the Lielupe.

Who could express this struggle and grandeur, this sting and anguish! Who could find words for all this! Great minds could. – "A god gave me the power to tell my pain," was what the great poet Goethe had said, and Valdens had quoted those words in one of his classes. In Annele's heart they stung as though they had been branded there. To express what you suffer, what you feel! Why, there was no greater happiness and no mightier power on earth. It meant freeing oneself and freeing others who felt like you but were unable to express it.

"A god gave me the power to tell my pain."

Hands clasped, walking through the storm under the groaning and hissing linden trees by the Lielupe, she cried aloud and implored these great divine and generous powers.

"God, God, give me, too, the power to tell my pain. Let me be one of your elect. And if this is not possible and you do not wish to give it to me, then let me at least feel until the last moment of my life as fervently as I do now. Even if this should mean torment and anguish, do not extinguish in my heart the ardor with which I feel everything, with which I touch the world and comprehend it."

She walked like this a long time with her stormy thoughts and faithful heart, and wandered through the park looking for the bench on which Līziņa and Silmežs had sat. She found it by the description of its crumbling backrest and out-of-the-way location just under the lilac bushes behind which a fence marked the boundaries of an adjacent garden. Here they had sat and talked as the sun gleamed down on them and birds sang their songs above them. And she imagined her sister's feelings. Now there was a storm, and nothing was left of it all. Now and then, as though in despair, a small bird would flit out of the shrubbery, wings angled back, and surrender to the turbulent currents of air, for it had to hurry and find food for little beaks that were hungry even during a storm.

Annele took a sheet of paper from her pocket. There was something written on it. She wanted to go over it again in this place. She held the sheet in both hands, for the winds were whipping and rattling it, and read:

> J u s t o n c e
> Just once, as twilight softly draws nigh,
> To stand on that mountain peak
> And hear all around me in the sky
> The voice of nature speak!
>
> As sunset's glow begins to fade
> Over the distant trees,
> And night's black mantle is gently laid
> Over this cosmic peace,
>
> I'd fall on my knees in awe of the art
> Of nature's vast monument.
> What feelings then would flood my heart,
> By this single moment sent!

"What feelings then would flood my heart!" she exclaimed bitterly, crumpling the paper and clenching her hands around it.

"That's just it, I have no idea how to express what feelings would flood my heart at that moment. Not the slightest idea! I finished at the point where I should have started, just when all that grandeur I felt while I was writing should have come. The odd thing is, I know what it feels like then. Probably just like being a drowning person when the water reaches up to their mouth and now they'd like to shout out, to cry out, to speak out all of it, all. Where is it though? Not a sign of it."

So what had happened? While she was writing she had thought it was good, she really had. Later, too, as she was rereading it, she had liked it. And now, not a sign of it. Empty words. It was enough to make her cry.

Tears had dimmed her eyes, so that she had not seen the approaching figure and now started at the sound of footsteps, shoved the piece of paper in her pocket, drew her coat around her shoulders and was still unsure, like someone caught being naughty, whether to get up and run away or to wait quietly for the person to pass by, when he had already glided past her eyes, one hand lifted to his turned-up coat collar, the other to his hat, which he held down with the crook of his raised cane to protect it from the wind.

Wait, who was this passerby? Why, didn't she know him? Surprised, she jumped to her feet and followed him with her eyes. Yes, she recognized this passerby's figure and the movement with which he now swung the cane in his hand, having removed it from his hat, and tapped it regularly against the gravel of the footpath.

"That was Adalbert Verein."

Like a fleck of foam in the river her heart leapt up on the crest of a wave of blood. And this was a leap of joy, for lo and behold, it was no trick, no illusion. The person walking there was really and truly just as she had imagined him. Proud, reserved, alone, forever alone with his sorrowing heart. He seeks no one's company, just like herself. Where nature storms and rages is his place, that is where he thinks his thoughts and feels his feelings – he feels at home in the bosom of great, mighty nature.

> I never felt the spring till now,
> When rough winds shake the flowers and tear them,
> For in my heart is pain, defiance, daring!

Yes, that is what he thinks, for why else would he be here? But what's to be done now? Should she follow him and meet him on the path along the bank of the Lielupe? Join him in watching rebellious white-crested waves eddying and wrestling with the storm in a black rage? Know that he, too, has seen the rushing grandeur of the Lielupe amid the struggle of the forces of nature, the wind-lashed meadow grass beyond the river, the flashing mad dance of the long row of silvery willows, then carry this knowledge home like shared treasure? Should she go? Stay here? Pay no attention? Yes, surely this is the only correct thing to do. She mustn't disturb someone who perhaps on this Pentecost morning is going on some private pilgrimage. Accompanied by his thoughts, his feelings, his longings. After all, even this encounter is a great and unexpected surprise. It is good simply to know they are here alone, just the two of them amid this wind-swept grandeur and beauty! For there is not another human being in sight. That in itself is so extraordinarily unusual and unprecedented. And what a special coincidence – running into Adalbert like this! She's always running into him…

But wait, what's this? While she is still undecided what to do, it appears he is already coming back. In the gap torn by the wind amid the branches, a hat has just glided past. So he didn't go very far? So he's afraid to leave the shelter of the trees and plunge into the harsh embrace of the storm that awaits him by the river! But why? Now that he has come here, he should have gone all the way, as she did. Into the thick of the battle, the only way to know what it is you have experienced! Whereas he coddled himself. That's the way he was. Perhaps he's spoiled? What was it Līziņa had said? "Quite a windbag." No, no! Away with such thoughts! She mustn't malign him. So what if everybody else does, she never will. For even as it is he has to suffer in innocence, like all those who are lonely, proud, rejected. Who understands him?

Nearer, through the branches, glides the hat. Her heart announces its presence louder now: listen, maybe he's coming back so soon because – because – you are sitting here?

But if that's the case, she must go. Vanish. Better that the storm should blow her away like a leaf.

No, it's too late. There he is on the open path. Should she run for it now? No! She mustn't let on that she's seen him. It would look as though she were paying him special attention.

And she tries to ignore him so that he too does not see her. And her efforts are completely wasted, for he walks past her exactly as before, the crook of his cane hooked into the edge of his hat, the other hand holding his coat collar, no doubt so that the wind won't pull out his tie.

One thought stings: "What if he sees me!" The other: "Oh, it makes no difference. No difference whatsoever!"

That's all she needs, for him to sit down next to her on the bench. No sir, he better not do that!

For a long time she remains motionless. The wind shakes her and blows right through her. She isn't aware of time passing. Taking paper and a stub of pencil from her pocket, she tries to write.

> Green leaf in springtime
> Battling the April gale,
> Come November's fierce winds
> You'll be withered and pale.
>
> Young heart in love
> Battling the storms of life,
> An early grave waits
> At the end of your strife.

She reread it. Once, twice. What was this? It seemed there was something there, but then she again couldn't help laughing such a bitter laugh, and all because the thing that was supposed to be there was not there at all. The thing that would mirror all the grandeur around her. It wasn't there.

Young heart in love?

Nonsense!

Suddenly a finch alighted on the backrest of the bench as if flung down. Quite close, as if seeking help, it twitched its head chirping piteously and then suddenly flew off seeming to flee from danger. And danger was close. At that same moment, with gale force, came a gust of wind that exceeded all the others. Cracking at their very roots, the trees bent and swayed. Cleaving a wound down to the ground, a young shoot was torn from the lilac bush and fell across the path, strewing it with broken blossoming twigs and stripped-off buds.

Bringing damage and destruction, the gale swept on, leaving the roar of billowing treetops behind it. Annele watched open-mouthed. What a mighty force, and what a mighty language! Was there anyone who could drop his heaviness like a storm, rain himself empty like a cloud, shed his radiance like the sun? What does the little finch feel in the face of the thunderstorm's terror, or the lilac bush by the fence now that it is cleft in two? Oh, to know and express it all! If only God would grant one such a gift!

She went on sitting there like that for a long time deep in thought, and let the storm shake her, then with particular satisfaction tore the sheet of paper with the poems on it into tiny shreds and let the wind carry them off, sending a deep sigh with them like a heavy puff of wind, then broke a few bruised lilac blossoms from the torn-off bush and went home.

Reikschat had sent a whole "sack full" of questions that needed to be answered. This took Līziņa the greater part of this stormy, dark day. But when the letter was written and mailed, she felt relieved as at the successful conclusion of a difficult, yet somewhat necessary job.

On this day of leisure Mother had a lot of things she wanted to discuss: what would happen now? What would life turn out to be like with all the changes that faced them? But Līziņa answered curtly:

"I've made a decision about something, and I also wrote about it to Edgar. If I manage to get it arranged, then I'll tell you, but not before. So don't you start fretting yet, wait and see. I'm sure it will all turn out fine."

Again Līziņa showed herself to be a provider who thought of her family's welfare.

Only Annele was silent and passive, as though she were completely indifferent to her fate. "I don't care!" she gestured her lack of interest. Since nothing had come of all that her heart had hoped and longed for, she also did not care what road she was to follow. She'd take whatever came along and go wherever she was told to go, straight ahead, in defiance of this cold world and hostile destiny.

Late that night, sitting in the window, which was filled with the shadows of storm-tossed clouds, she again tried to write something.

> In vain you'll struggle in this hated world,
> In vain your blood will sear you to the heart.
> All is illusion! Far better then to hide
> Your passionate, true feelings deep inside.
> They are too precious for this cold and pompous throng
> That hides its nakedness beneath the intellect's rags.
> Too good to be their peer, you would be wrong
> To trust their glibness and their crocodile tears. – –

Crocodile tears! Oh Lord! Didn't those words sound funny? Why would "this cold and pompous throng" have to weep "crocodile tears"? And why did a "pompous throng" have to cover its nakedness with rags? Was that correct at all? Could you say that? Again and again, words would sneak in that she felt doubtful about and that seemed not to walk straight, but with a stagger.

And then what about those tears? Weren't there too many of them? No matter what she wrote, there they were. – "As gentle rain refreshes the earth, so tears, they say, refresh a heart; yet the more my tears flow from my eyes, the sadder of heart am I."

Like that simpleton of a youngest son in the fairytale: walking down the road, crying his eyes out. Why? Annele had wanted to know even as a little girl. Why does the simpleton always cry? And the storytellers would say: Ah, if he doesn't he won't get anything.

Say what you like: she hated these constant snivelers. Nor was she herself like that. From early childhood, she had shown her tears to no one. She'd rather clench her teeth and be sent to stand in a corner for being sulky. But unwept tears rippled in her heart. Deep down, like an underground stream. Did they serve any purpose? The simpleton always had all the luck in the world at the end. But that wasn't because of all the crying. That was because of the deep wellsprings from which the tears had sprung. Because the simpleton was always portrayed as kind and helpful, and felt other people's sorrows as though they were his own. Now in order to do that, you had to first suffer your own sorrows. – "One who has never shed hot tears for himself will not weep them for others, either." This, too, had been written with the insight born from the experience that such rippling "underground" streams always carved channels – deep, mysterious, and still unknown.

Did it have to be like that? Did everything that led into the depths have to hurt?

The clouds were flying so low they almost touched the rooftops. Now and then a squall of rain struck the window. Dusk that night fell as impenetrable as in fall.

A good thing that night and sleep came to lull to sleep all sorrow and pain about herself and others. But it was also good that there had been a day like this, which, when all was said and done, still seemed rich in experiences and feelings.

That night she had a dream.

She was in a place enveloped in a great fire, she was running and getting lost, but found no way out anywhere. The flames came directly out of the ground, they appeared to grow from it like unusually large leaves with thin stalks, they spread upward, and their tips flickered like giant tongues. Yet they did not fuse and join together as flames do, but stood out separate and alone, although they were as close together as stalks in a field of wheat. Each stood out red, glowing, and frozen as it were.

Frozen flames! What a strange idea! Were they capable of inflicting harm?

She ran through them, but none of them touched her, nothing bad happened to her. Also, she could see through them. Far, far away, to the edges of the horizon, she saw nothing but flaming earth like a red field at harvest time. There were neither houses, nor trees, nor people.

Then came a deep gap in the dream vision, like an untied string whose ends she could no longer manage to join. Then came another scene.

Again she was standing somewhere in the middle of a vast plain. Like a basin with gently sloping sides, the plain ended at the horizon with a relief of undulating hills. It was a country she had never seen. It was hard to imagine that this could be above ground. "Perhaps there was a desert here or some large body of water," she thought. But now this endless plain was covered with thick, green, velvety soft grass. "How lovely that there are no more flames, and that everything is so green," she thought, pleased. But again there were neither houses, nor trees, nor people in sight, only this grass, strangely green, flickering in a strange light that came neither from the sun nor the moon, for although the sky was clear and bright, no heavenly body was visible in it.

Solitude, green grass, and silence.

But the silence was so strangely alive, like an attentive listener.

What would happen now? And as she listened more closely, somewhere a gentle vibration began, as though the string of some musical instrument stretching from one edge of the sky to the other had been plucked. And soon it was as if several strings were being strummed together, and more and more, until finally voices emerged from the sounds, singing some song whose words were unintelligible. They sounded like communion hymns: "Holy, holy, holy" or "Oh Lamb of God," or like the singing of the teachers' college choir in Schirkenhöfer Park, or the songs of young girls welcoming the summer in the hills of Spring Farm, as though the song contained everything she had ever heard and yet at the same time none of it, but something quite unfamiliar, exceedingly lovely, a torrent of sounds that filled earth and sky, now breaking like a wave, now ebbing, subsiding into barely distinguishable humming as it were.

But where were the singers? They could only be hiding in the thick grass, for there was no other hiding place. The grass, however, stood as motionless as if all breezes had been silenced in this strange universe. She searched the grass, parting it with her eyes as it were. She herself was dubious. These were not mosquitoes or grasshoppers, which could have hidden in the grass. Nevertheless, continuing to search, she turned in the opposite direction and suddenly froze, dazzled by an extraordinary brightness. Over there appeared the one whom the silent plain and the invisible singers seemed to be expecting. The horizon was burning as though in white flames, and amid this bright light, clad in a kind of shining cloud, a rider rose from the horizon, larger than life. He sat astride a strange, unidentifiable beast that climbed, or rather slowly flew, upward, its head gracefully stretched forward, with wings on both sides of it. The beast and the rider, and his clothing as well, whose rich folds almost touched the ground, were that same white light. Behind the rider, however, like a hump attached to him, rose his own image with a great black seemingly petrified shadow whose metallic sharp rim was visible overhead. But the higher the rider rose, the more his shadow dwindled, the brighter he shone himself. She could no longer hear the song. There was no sound except for the beating of her own heart in her breast, and it was small and timid.

"Don't you see I'm only human, and these are supernatural forces. I have no right to see all this. Hide, hide!" her heart urged.

"Where shall I hide?"

"Throw yourself on the ground and cover your eyes."

Yes, she would do that. She covered her eyes with her hands and threw herself on the ground.

But nothing vanished.

She saw. Saw the shining rider as he rose higher and higher. His shadow had disappeared, his eyes blazed like suns, and she felt warm light pouring over her starting from her heels. The light emanated from him and diffused over the whole grassy plain.

"How is it I can see when my eyes are covered and I'm lying on the ground?"

"You can see because everything is light. You are light, too. And your flesh sees as well as your eyes."

Who were these, talking like this, and what was it they were saying?

"And your flesh shall be light."

Wasn't it the great bringer of light, the Savior of the world himself, who had spoken these words?

And now they had come true.

She saw with her eyes covered and answered speakers she could not see.

No – now she could see them as well.

Like the blades of grass below, all around her like shining clouds, pressed face after face, light as petals so as not to hurt each other, turned toward her as they had always been, since time immemorial, familiar and close.

"Do you know us?"

"My brothers and sisters."

"Yes, that is who we are."

Then I am finally, finally reunited with you all! How lovely, how lovely!

"Weren't you singing, though?"

"We *are* singing. Can't you hear?"

"Yes, now I can – and now I can also understand the words," she listened blissfully. And the words of the song seemed to say:

"There was no life before He came to be.

There was no light before He came to be.

There was no truth before He came to be.

There was no love before He came to be.

– And there was no beauty before He came to be!"

Now she heard her own voice amid the others, and they echoed hers:

"There was no beauty before He came to be!"

"Now you and I are united," said her thoughts, "but who is He?"

"Don't ask, you know it."

"Yes, I know it."

The song rang out free, light, but incomprehensible by now, undecipherable, fading away.

The shining rider was at the zenith, had crossed it, everything was dissolving like a shimmering mist.

"It is vanishing, vanishing, and I am left behind!"

Beauty. Holiness.

With these words on her lips she awoke. Outside, a quiet, clear morning was dawning.

As though overcome by wonderment, she lay still.

What was this? She usually slept soundly and was not given to dreaming much. Her young organism was trying its hardest to make up for the sleep she had lost during her herding days. It is true that in the mornings, when she waded out of the deep river of sleep, she often had a sense of boats full of dreams vanishing with their fantastic cargoes, but even as she turned over they had faded and been forgotten. This dream, however, remained with all the brilliance of a vision, carved in stone as it were. What kind of forces could create such unusual scenes and sweep her away in such an extraordinary whirlwind of feelings? It hadn't been like a dream at all, it seemed much, much more vivid than life itself. From what sources had it welled forth? Were they outside her? Within herself? What promises did it hold out? What mysteries for her to unriddle?

She thought about it a great deal, for her heart was responsive to the "signs and portents" of outward and inner life, just as the surface of water is responsive to breezes, to the shadows of clouds, and the changing face of the sky.

Wedding Days

Līziņa's wedding was set for after Midsummer Day, right in the middle of summer, when in the evenings the stale emanations of sweltering city streets mingled with the bittersweet scents of flowers in gardens confined between buildings, while the sky blossomed into the immeasurable shimmer of warm stars. Līziņa wanted the wedding quiet, simple, inexpensive. That is why, for a few weeks, she had rented the flat across from theirs, which had been empty since the time Sarah's employers left. It would now serve their extended needs, and so everything would be comfortable and nice. But the bridegroom's plans, which were just the opposite, forced Līziņa to give up her "comfortable and nice" and drove her into a flurry of excitement and haste as preparations for the wedding proceeded. Edgar had been making a good living, and wanted a wedding that would be "appropriate for someone in his social position." He had invited to it his relatives and a few friends of his youth, faithful "comrades" in their day who now lived somewhere in the cities of Russia. On such an important occasion, he must see them again. During the five years he had spent in Jelgava he had also acquired friends, and then there were the Ranks. For the wedding reception, Edgar had arranged for rooms in the home of an acquaintance of his, a very well-to-do master basket maker called Bender, who had a comfortable flat in a house he owned. With a yard and a garden, there would be plenty of room for the guests to circulate. The master basket maker was glad to offer his flat, wishing no other reward for his help than the knowledge that he would be able to see even the factory owner Rank and his lovely wife at his place, and the hope that they would be satisfied with his house and home, indeed more than satisfied perhaps. He had told Līziņa so when she went over to take a look at the rooms. Both he and his wife had proudly shown her that they had enough of everything: not only mirrors and sofas, but also silver and crystal in transparent glass cabinets, for they had no children, and thus had acquired only possessions and had always purchased the best that money could buy. But who could they show it to, eh? Here was their chance, though, and that was good. Now wider circles would get to see how a thrifty craftsman lived.

They even had a piano in case the wedding guests might want to play a waltz or a galop – and the lady of the house took a padded cover from a piano-shaped box – of course it hadn't been used for ten years, but she was quite sure it would sound just fine if only there was someone who could strum one of those polkas or galops.

And at night they could illuminate the garden – a "night in Italy." They would provide the Chinese lanterns themselves, and at no charge. They'd been keeping them from year to year and using them only once, in the middle of August, for Mrs. Bender's birthday celebration, when they always created a great furor and thrilled the whole neighborhood.

"You should see them lined up by the gate here, the people, I mean."

Everything else, too, such as dishes, tables, and chairs they would be glad to provide, but the bride herself could take care of anything that was still missing, while they'd be happy to assist with advice any time.

"Just ask my wife," the basket maker kept pointing to his wife with a commendatory gesture. "She planned our silver wedding and my fiftieth birthday, when the place was jam-packed with people – your fiancé was there, too – and she was so successful at it that everybody had plenty to eat and had a great time and left here singing her praises."

And the basket maker's wife had smiled a gratified smile and said that since she had so much experience and was good at it she didn't mind keeping an eye on the kitchen, to make sure that everything was going according to schedule, particularly since the Ranks had been invited and she thought that was precisely why they ought to show these factory owners that folks in the trades could and would throw a superb party. And she could also tell Līziņa how much meat, bread, and beverages they'd need per person. "There *is* going to be drinking, isn't there?" she had interjected. And the basket maker had supplemented Līziņa's hesitant answer with a loud burst of laughter: "Well, for goodness' sakes! This isn't going to be a gathering of monks! Why, these are good Christian folk, and they'll all be wanting to whet their whistle."

And thus, showing them every courtesy, the basket maker and his wife neither asked for nor expected payment or even gratitude. They were in good health, there was nothing troubling them, and a bit of a fling was just what they needed to get rid of excess fat.

And so, satisfied on that account, Līziņa sat adding up and taking notes how much food, how many plates, knives, and forks the guests would need, which guests had already been invited and which ones would still need to be invited.

And then an unexpected question for her sister:

"What would you say if you got Adalbert Verein as your groomsman?"

This was a thunderclap Annele hadn't expected, and she was unable to defend herself against it. Her sister was looking straight at her, into her hot, blushing face. And so she quickly sought refuge in a counter-question:

"What? Are you going to have groomsmen and bridesmaids, then?"

"I'd really like to. A church wedding is so much more sumptuous if you do. Everybody looks to see how many couples follow the bride and groom. I'd hoped to get together at least four couples, but now there's nobody. Oh poverty, poverty! After all, I can't ask strangers, can I? But all our women relatives my age are already married, and the others are too young. And so for the time being I've only got two ladies: you and one of the Gūze sisters, for the other is already married."

"What about Līna Vanags? She did write to you, didn't she?"

Līziņa shook her head.

"She made her excuses, said she couldn't come. By what I'm given to understand, there's something in the offing for her, too."

"Such as what?"

"The same as for me."

"A wedding?"

She nodded in the affirmative.

"Do you know the man she's – "

"Yes. There's every indication that it's Silmežs," Līziņa cut her off quickly.

Annele started. Here was the name that had not been mentioned all this time. What was her sister thinking now? How did she feel?

Her sister sat bent low over her sheet of paper so that nothing could be seen of her face. And after a while she said in her normal voice:

"Well, so what about that Adalbert?"

"It's all the same to me," answered Annele, drawling the words with as much indifference as possible. Her sister mustn't think that Adalbert mattered to her in any way.

"Good. Then I'll invite him specially to be a groomsman, because that has to be done. Then here's how it's going to be: Jānis and the Gūze girl and you and Adalbert. It's not much, but you're all young and good-looking, and that in itself will look nice."

Not until her sister had gone outside could Annele allow her surprise and delight to show openly.

"And I'm going to have Adalbert as a groomsman! Oh heavens! So now we'll really have a chance to look at each other and be together? How strange, unexpected, and wonderful! It was destined by fortune, that's all."

The day before the wedding, quite early in the morning, not having been expected so early at all and with a merry "hello!", Edgar arrived. Happy that he had surprised them when they had not expected him until later. There was a shower of eager questions and answers. Tables and chairs were covered with hampers, bundles, and traveling bags, filled for the most part with delicacies for the wedding made by Edgar himself, as well as fish, as was to be expected coming from a town by the sea. For his solicitude he received directly and indirectly asked-for gratitude and praise both from the bride and from Mother, who could best appreciate the significance of the gifts.

It was not until there was a short lull that he had a chance to say hello to his new sister-in-law.

"Well, how do you like me?"

Weather-beaten after long exposure to the sea air, and endowed with a good appetite, Edgar practically shone with good health, corpulence, and naturally also the excitement of the reunion.

Annele inclined her head with a laugh.

"You're fat!"

He didn't like that.

"Don't talk such nonsense!"

"He isn't fat, not at all," Mother hurried to his defense. "He's not a bit fatter than when he left. He does look healthier, though."

"Well, and is that bad?"

"Why ask me? Do I have to like you? Ask Līziņa!"

"You need to be taught a lesson, my girl," Edgar shook his finger at her. "You've got to keep your eyes open. Don't let yourself be carried away by some 'wasp waist.' What good are they? They're not the marrying kind. For marriage you need a man of substance. Those are the only ones in demand."

"People like you?"

Now they were in a state of war.

Līziņa, who had carried a few of the bundles into the adjacent flat and had now come back to join the others, carelessly interjected:

"What are you arguing about?"

For Edgar's voice had sounded slightly raised. He answered:

"We aren't arguing at all. I was just trying to tell that chit of a girl that a man of substance can get five gals for every finger any time he wants to."

"In Ventspils?" Annele asked sarcastically.

"You think I couldn't? The biggest master butcher kept practically forcing his daughter – and a pretty gal at that – on me. He wanted to know why I was so set on bringing in a wife from outside. Said I was one of them anyhow. And that I could get as fine a wife as I could wish for right there, with a dowry chest you could barely lift, with rich relatives, property, a house. Being a German and all, and so good at my job! He said I could go to any door I liked and he'd guarantee for certain that they'd all fly open."

Edgar smiled with pleasure, and his chest was noticeably puffed out.

But Līziņa seemed to have turned to ice, and stood there, a bundle in each hand, eyes motionless and wide, her face quite pale.

"Was that how it was?"

"Would I tell you something that wasn't true?"

"Well, so why didn't you take that pretty daughter?"

Edgar answered proudly:

"What do you take me for! I am a man of honor, you know. When I have given my word, I keep it."

"It wasn't necessary. Not necessary. I wish you *had* done it. I wish you'd taken her!" Līziņa whispered with trembling lips and quickly rushed out the door.

"Oh dear, oh dear, what have I done now!" Annele was frightened. "How careless I've been with all my talk! Just now Līziņa thought of Silmežs and how nice it would have been if Edgar had married another and she were free. Yes, I'm sure that's what she thought. Oh, how unfathomable such things are!"

But Edgar noticed none of this.

With the same smile of pleasure, having untied some bundle, he raised his finger and, pointing at the door with a meaning look, gestured to his sister-in-law.

"She's jealous! Oh, you can't fool me!"

Līziņa came back in and was friendly, as though nothing had happened, but her eyes were red and the smile around her lips seemed frozen. She helped Edgar untie the strings. He pulled her close to him and said with a smile:

"That was all nonsense. I never forgot you. As for this Trude that he tried to get me to marry, what's she to me? They're all so wild to get married that there's no knowing what kind of rumors they've spread. And I hate it when a woman chases me. No, no! A real man wants to choose for himself and marry for himself. Then he really knows what he's getting."

Līziņa did not respond, and the subject was now closed. Edgar began to talk of something else.

"What's with Heinz? He hasn't arrived, and he probably hasn't written either, eh? I gave him this address."

Heinz was Edgar's younger brother and lived in Petersburg.

No, there was no news of Heinz.

"And, what's more, he couldn't care less! You'll see. Heinz has no family feeling. I'm not saying the rest of my family are all going to come – the trip is just too long and expensive for them all. But why couldn't Heinz just scoot over from Petersburg? It's a hop, skip, and a jump! But what's a brother to a fine gentleman like him! Might as well be a total stranger! Ah, yes! And the things I've done and gone through all on account of him! A lot, quite a lot!"

Edgar sighed and fell silent.

When lunch was ready and everyone had sat down to eat, Mother suddenly pricked up her ears. The front door was not locked, and there was the clatter of unfamiliar footsteps. And now the door of the room, too, flew open, and in it appeared a stranger, tall and gaunt, his stringy flaxen hair cropped Russian style, his eyes a washed-out blue.

"Eda!" It was like the blare of a trumpet.

"Ada!" echoed Edgar, leaping to his feet, flinging up his arms as though doing gymnastics, slapping his thighs, flinging his arms up again and pulling the stringy flaxen-haired head close to his mustache.

They had all risen and were standing around them. Annele was trying to smother her laughter. Two men kissing over and over again. It looked so funny.

Edgar made the introductions.

"This is Adolf Domski, the best *kamerad* of my youth. A capital fellow. And this is my bride. And here are my mother-in-law and sister-in-law. Have you had lunch yet? Of course you haven't. Well then, come and join us!"

The guest took off his overcoat.

"Do you have anything? I mean, luggage?"

"A shirt." Domski gestured, whispering and smiling apologetically, carefully placing a little parcel wrapped in a thin sheet of newspaper on a chair.

Līziņa invited the guest to wash off the dust of the journey.

Ah, he was grateful for that. For three days and nights, he'd been traveling non-stop. Now he begged for lots of water and himself lugged the water containers out on the porch.

Edgar was beside himself with joy.

"See that? Now, there's a true friend! While my own brother can't even come from as near as Petersburg. Which would be like jumping over a ditch. Such is the youth of today."

He repeated his complaint about his younger brother to Domski as well when the latter came in, slicking back his hair after washing himself. This was somebody they both knew in common.

"Heinz must have been captivated by some petticoat. Know what I mean?" he smiled a forgiving smile.

"Yes, he's certainly the biggest ladies' man of the lot of us," agreed Edgar with visible relish. And then he again turned his undivided attention to the guest, scrutinizing him closely.

"Well, let's have a look at you now. You certainly are quite a bit older!"

The stringy flaxen hair was a bit gray behind the ears, while the top of Edgar's head of hair, though growing thinner, was dark and glossy.

"I've gotten a little Russianized," confessed Domski, capitulating to fate, as it were.

"Rubbish! You're half Polish, I'm half Lithuanian, but at least between the two of us we're one genuine and unadulterated Prussian. Am I right?"

"You certainly are!"

They laughingly confirmed the fact that they were half-Prussian.

Līziņa announced that lunch was served.

Their questions and stories continued between each spoonful. To think of all the places where their guest had been! How many cities he had visited! How many winds had hardened him, how many waves had tossed him! Yet he had always landed on all fours like the proverbial cat, hale and hearty. And of all the people in his family and back home, Edgar was the only one with whom Domski had kept in touch all these years. The postcards they exchanged had almost always had one and the same text: – Such and such a place. "Hello! How are you? I'm fine." The address. Only the last postcard, written by Edgar and containing the wedding invitation, had been a few lines longer.

From all the places, Domski had sent his comrade the address. The addresses were like the little white pebbles scattered by Hansel in the fairytale to keep from getting lost in the witch's forest. The usual couple of words and an address – who needs more? One knows where Eda is, and the other knows where Ada is.

But wait! Why had Domski been tossed like a leaf in the autumn winds?

There was a reason for it.

Domski was an inventor. Even as a little boy, he had showed up in school with new ideas every other day, and of all his schoolmates had found a sponsor for these ideas in the person of Edgar. Their friendship dated from this time. They loyally shared what one had plenty of and the other lacked: one had practical common sense, the other – imagination. True, the practical common sense had soon rejected the imagination, calling it "absolute rubbish," but this had caused no breach in the comradely mood that had been nurtured by their long-accustomed mutual goodwill and helpfulness. Domski's feelings were more of a piece: "You're the best *kamerad* I've got and that's that!" Edgar, now, was a lot more complicated. His benevolence had an admixture of a sense of superiority and admiration, a kind of fatherliness, but also a little contempt and mockery. It depended on a particular situation which of these feelings gained the upper hand at any one time.

Just now, of course, Edgar wanted to know how the inventions were going: was his *kamerad* still coming up with new ones?

Why certainly! After all, they were his whole life – a life that took its course between two extremes. He'd always had good jobs, for, as a decent and honest German, he'd never had any trouble finding them. But when he was seized by the bedevilment of genius, he would be tossed, so to speak, into fire and water. He would become restless, disorganized, shirk or disregard his duties, and would be driven to think of one thing and one thing only– how to get the "knack" of the invention that kept eluding him. And as he brooded and chased after it, he would in the long run inevitably lose the job, and neglect both body and soul, and hit rock bottom altogether.

Well, what about those results? – His friend wanted to know.

The results? Why, there certainly were some! But implementing them was a different matter. How was he to get a patent? Where should he go for patronage? Where would he find the fat purse to pave the road to success? Didn't Edgar know what you had to have in Russia? Bribes, bribes, and more bribes! But how was he to get them? That was the problem.

Edgar concealed a sarcastic grin under his mustache. Maybe he was wondering: What the devil could the inventions be good for? But of course he refrained from making such a remark. He was interested in finding out at which of the extremes of his life Ada was at the moment.

At the moment, Ada had decided to swear off all inventions for a while, to take a rest and get himself some clothes. For the last six months or so, he had been working for a large shipping agency in a town on the Volga River. As their agent, he'd been traveling the highways and waterways.

"Don't forget Ventspils, if you happen to be in the area."

"I'll be there like a shot," promised Domski, placing his hand on his heart.

"And listen, I've got something else to say to you," Edgar slapped him on the shoulder in a fatherly way. "Youth passes, and life in all its seriousness stands knocking at the door. Forget about those inventions of yours and start a respectable life. A teeny weeny cage with a nice little mouse inside! Follow my example."

"Yes, if there's another fiancée like yours in the world, I'll do it without blinking an eye and without a moment's thought," said the guest enthusiastically, and bowed to Līziņa across the table.

This came unexpectedly and apparently met with everyone's approval.

"You can rest assured you'll never find anyone like her. For that, you need a special eye," laughed the bridegroom, feeling flattered.

"But we ought to have something liquid to drink to that. Don't you have anything, Līza?"

Flushing, Līziņa shrugged her shoulders. She was sorry, she had nothing to offer the guest.

"That's all right," Edgar forgave her. "We're going to drop in somewhere anyway. I'm going to show Ada around Jelgava, and then we'll have a little something to celebrate our reunion and my leaving a bachelor's life behind me. Isn't that right, Ada?"

"I'm game," agreed his friend enthusiastically.

They got up from the table. Edgar smartened up before going out and sang as he straightened his tie:

"You have all one could wish for, my dearest,
You have pearls and diamonds so fine,
You have eyes of rarest beauty,—
What else can your heart desire?"

And, as Domski immediately joined in, both sang at the top of their lungs:

"With your eyes of rarest beauty,
Be they near me or far away,
You have tortured me nigh unto death, dear, –
What else can your heart desire?"

"Let's go, let's go, let's go!" Edgar clapped his hands enthusiastically when they had finished singing.

However, he hurriedly retraced his steps from the stairwell as though he had forgotten something.

"You know, I want to tell you something: this would be the right man for Anna."

Annele made a sudden exclamation.

"Me? That's all I need!"

"Don't say anything. He's thin as a rail, just the type you like!"

"How do you know what I like?"

Edgar continued unperturbed.

"He's a couple of years younger than me, he can wait for you."

"Leave me alone!"

"Many a girl has said that and finally fallen head over heels in love. The stuff about his abilities as an inventor is no fib, you know. He may strike it lucky some day, and then he'll be filthy rich. Imagine what a life you'd have! I'm going to talk to him. All he needs is a fine wife one of these days, and you need a fine husband."

"No, no, no! You're crazy!"

Annele stuck her fingers in her ears, but she heard Edgar saying as though to himself:

"You're rejecting your own good fortune. Ada is a capital fellow."

"Oh, Lord! The things I'm going to have to endure with that stupid Domski," Annele thought apprehensively.

Late that night, her brother Jānis arrived from Rīga, and the two friends returned as well almost at the same time as he came. They looked a bit odd, as though they'd been plucked. Wherever their eyes happened to fall, there they would remain, as though astonished or fearful that the objects they gazed on might suddenly begin to move or vanish. Another strange thing was that they had less faith in their own feet than in the tables and chairs they kept trying to touch so amicably.

Domski was extremely friendly, bowing and apologizing in all directions, even to the table leg he had bumped into, but his tongue was skipping syllables and unable to say much, except to confirm and repeat what Edgar was saying. The latter, meanwhile, seemed impossible to satisfy and unsatisfied. Tea was served, but he called for coffee: "Black as the night, hot as love, and sweet as death." He rummaged around the platter of snacks looking for what was not there; where there was meat, he wanted fish, and where there was bread, he wanted pie. There was something he felt was lacking, and that was why he was sullen. At last he remembered. It was a bottle in his coat pocket that he had forgotten to take out. The bottle was received with loud cheers. He called for glasses. He must have a drink to pledge friendship with Jānis, and then Jānis must pledge Domski, and Domski must pledge Līziņa and Annele. Jānis calmly refused. After all, he and his brother-in-law were good friends already. "Doesn't matter. Just to be on the safe side," Edgar persisted. He hugged and kissed Jānis and wouldn't let go. Even if there was no need for Jānis to pledge friendship with him, he should pledge his friend Ada's friendship. Why, they were family. And this was his *kamerad*. His capital fellow. No, Jānis did not wish to pledge friendship with Domski. He did not know him well enough yet. And Domski himself, clasping his hands like a little dachshund holding up his front paws, begged and implored Edgar not to bother people on his account.

All right. Let it be then. But they must make amends to Ada. He, Edgar Reikschat, said so. Ada had been nicer to him than his own brother, who had not come to his celebration, and that's why he must now be like his own brother and go to Edgar's wedding tomorrow as the groomsman of the bride's own sister, his future sister-in-law.

And, turning to Domski as he pointed to Annele:

"There – that's with whom you'll have the honor."

"Yes!"

Domski shot to his feet like a rocket – as straight as he was able to with his head so heavy and all. He scrambled around the table and, crossing his arms over his chest Russian style, bowed down to the ground before Annele:

"I shall be honored, Miss, I shall be honored!"

Taken aback, Annele clutched her head in both hands.

"No, no, no! That's not the way it's going to be! I really don't want your honor. No, no, no!"

And she rushed outside.

Her brother followed her:

"That wasn't polite. You shouldn't have behaved like that. After all, he *is* a guest."

"Sure: a guest. Are you going to have to walk with him tomorrow? No, sir! So it's easy for you to talk. While I get treated like a child. They do whatever they like, but never ask me. I won't have it. So what if Domski *is* his *kamerad* – that doesn't make him mine. Not ever!"

"He won't be plastered tomorrow, though."

"But did you see what he looks like? His boots down at the heels, and he hasn't brought any others with him, his jacket covered with stains, and he hasn't got another. All he's got is a shirt wrapped in paper, and so far nobody knows what that looks like. A fine groomsman he'd make!"

"It's insane!" her brother laughed as though at a good joke and went back to the guests.

But Annele felt such bitterness that she couldn't laugh, and she went away altogether, to the flat at the other end.

Some time later, her brother came in too.

"Why are you hiding like this?"

"What am I supposed to do there? Everything in there smells of liquor."

"Don't exaggerate! It's not that bad!"

"Not that bad! No, it's worse than that, it's horrible! Even that Edgar! The night before his wedding, and he goes and gets drunk."

"Then it looks like you don't know how men behave if you call that getting drunk. Here these two have met after a long time and had a drop too much in the excitement. That's nothing terrible in itself."

"I can't stand drunks!"

"And where have you seen any drunks, pray tell?"

"All I'm trying to say is: I wouldn't go and marry somebody like Edgar, not even if he was sitting on a mountain of gold!"

Abruptly, her brother caught her arm.

"Shhh! Don't say that to Līziņa whatever you do. Here she comes!"

"Oh, I know that myself!" the girl whispered back.

And to herself she concluded her train of thought:

"Would a boy like Adalbert ever do such a thing? Not in a million years!"

Līziņa came in with an armful of bedclothes.

"Well, and what have you been talking about?" she asked gently with the same frozen smile that had remained on her lips all day. She threw down her burden in one corner.

"I'm going to make them a place to sleep here. Where else am I to put them?"

"Annele is anxious about her groomsman," said Jānis, trying to catch his older sister's eye: had she heard any of the preceding conversation?

"There's no need to worry! She's already got her own groomsman. It'll be as we agreed," their sister said calmly as she left the room again.

Meanwhile, at the other end of the building, Edgar and Domski began for what seemed like the tenth time:

"You have all one could wish for, my dearest
You have pearls and diamonds so fine."

On Līziņa's worktable lay an armful of fragrant myrtle branches. Some of them had been brought by Aunt Meire. They had been cut from many little trees that stood green on the windowsills of her many acquaintances, cared for with love and hope, and affectionately donated for this occasion. Others had been brought by the

Heimanns' chambermaid Jetiņa, and she herself had come to make the bridal wreath, faithful to the promise she had once made to Līziņa in jest: "If you get married, I'll come and make your wreath. I'll make you a better one than any nursery gardener." And it was a well-known fact that whatever went through Jetiņa's nimble fingers was given its own special elegance and beauty. And besides, Adalbert Verein had been asked to be Annele's groomsman, and he had promised to come.

"So you see that, all things considered, Domski can't be a groomsman."

Edgar, who was now in half as merry a mood but all the more acquiescent than the night before, grumbled:

"If he can't, he can't. I'm not trying to insist he should be, you know: but what good is that milksop, that Adalbert, to that girl? That's where my Ada is a hundred times better than him."

Nobody disputed that.

Līziņa had found it necessary to call in a young Jewish woman that day to put up their hair for the wedding. The young woman had come bright and early and taken Annele in hand first. Annele surrendered to her hands with enthusiasm, expecting from them great success in improving her looks. But when, a few hours later, flushed and perspiring as though from an oven, Annele came in to join the wreath makers, Jetiņa threw up her hands with a laugh:

"My oh my, will you look at that girl! She looks like a scarecrow!"

This not very flattering remark was enough to shatter the girl, who had so hoped for great results.

What did she look like, then?

Part of her hair had been tousled into a huge nest on top of her head, while the rest at the back of her head had been left long and with the help of red-hot tongs had been twisted into long spiral-shaped curls that had not the least tendency to stay in the ringlets the hairdresser had intended to create, but had already stretched out until they reached past her knees.

"You can't go like that," said Līziņa firmly.

"I know I can't, but what am I to do now? I'm not going to let her work on me a second time."

"Well, what can I do with a jungle like that? It's beyond my skill," the hairdresser defended herself.

"If it's beyond your skill, then keep your hands off," Jetiņa pushed her aside and immediately began to dismantle this "stork's nest" herself.

Her mouth full of hairpins that she had been pulling out of the "stork's nest" in slews, Jetiņa offered the bride a piece of good advice:

"Let that spook go and braid your hair yourself."

After Jetiņa – not always gently – had smoothed and brushed out Annele's hair, which had been ruffled and tousled "as though with a harrow," and had put it in order once more, she said with satisfaction: "There, now you look like you have your own face back. The way you are every day."

And, lifting the heavy braids, she added: "Why go and frizz or hide a treasure like yours?"

Annele, on the other hand, would today have preferred not to look the way she did every day, but different somehow, really special.

"And what kind of flowers are you going to have? You're not going to go all in white to the wedding, are you, like at a communion?"

"No, no! She does have flowers. What kind did you buy for yourself?" asked her sister.

Annele's flowers were two clusters of artificial apple blossoms.

"Oh dear, apple blossoms!" drawled Hetty. "Why apple blossoms? They don't bring good luck."

"Why?"

"Because they mean tears. As the old folks used to sing: 'The apple tree sheds white blossoms, and I shed bitter tears.'"

"Isn't that a superstition?"

"No, love, it's no superstition. When you've lived in this world for a while, you'll see that there's a reason for everything. But if you haven't any other flowers, fate must have meant you to have these. I'll pin them on for you."

At the same spot where Līziņa had once stood all dressed for the ball and waited for the first arrival of the man who "had his eye on her," she now stood preparing to receive the same man, who was about to take her away with him on the journey through life.

Annele had already put on her clothes and could now watch Jetiņa's nimble fingers as they dressed the bride bit by bit. The hem of her white woolen gown with its short train had a border of green myrtles pinned to it, and the veil was scattered with tiny sprigs. All these had to be attached and made to look as though they were growing out of the fabric.

"You have to feel light and secure and not think about your clothes. Otherwise it's no joke," said Jetiņa.

Sarah had come, too, had invited herself over weeks ago for this day.

"I don't want to go to church. Why should I disturb the others with my clattering on such a day? But I do want to have a look, I want to so much!"

And she hung around in all four corners of the room, her hands clasped, shook her head from time to time, but not once uttered her habitual and so familiar "Oh!" Had the deaconesses broken her of the habit, or was she herself trying to transform herself completely and leave all her former habits behind her? She also did not go up to the bride to shake hands as usual, but bowed to her from a distance as she said goodbye.

"Happiness and joy, Miss Līziņa, happiness and joy!"

Annele, who all morning had been fighting excitement and the stinging pain in the sockets of her eyes, but who tried now and then to lure it away with a harsh or a joking word, said:

"Sarah was looking at my sister as though she were the picture of a saint."

"And don't you agree the bride is as pretty as a picture?" answered Jetiņa. "Yes indeed! She herself is beautiful, and it's the most beautiful day of her life!"

Yes, Annele knew it herself. That was the pain that stung in the sockets of her eyes – the strange beauty that surrounded Līziņa on this day. Which made her deli-

cately shaped face shine with such a different kind of light, and her eyes, looking so profoundly dark in the shadows of her lashes and eyebrows, shimmer with such liquid sadness.

"There now, I'm done," said Jetiņa after attaching the last myrtle sprig.

"Thank you, oh thank you! How can I ever repay you?"

"Don't mention it! It was a pleasure. When will I ever have another chance to adorn such a bride, and so gladly?"

She hastily put on her little bonnet.

"I'm leaving now. I'll go and stand by the gate for a while and see you drive away. But I'm not going to church. It would just make me cry, and a bride shouldn't have to see tears, should she?"

Edgar came in dressed in black and solemn, holding his top hat. Līziņa pinned a boutonniere of myrtle twigs to his lapel, and he kissed her hand. Then he offered his arm to his bride.

Annele had to lock the apartment, for her brother had left half an hour earlier to pick up his partner, and her mother had been at the basket maker's house since early morning helping to prepare the wedding supper.

She rode with the bride and groom, and was thus able to intercept the many glances that awaited the bride at the gate with that peculiar mixture of curiosity and

enthusiasm that people usually bestow on all occasions that are unique and are never repeated again in a human lifetime.

At the church entrance, the bride's sponsors – factory owner Rank and Mrs. Rank –, brother Jānis with his partner, and Adalbert Verein were waiting for them. Annele placed her gloved fingers on the shiny black cloth of Adalbert's elbow. This was supposed to be a great moment, for the person she had always seen as so inaccessible was now close to her, was walking beside her. Their feet kept time with each other, walked at the same pace. And yet – how strangely empty this moment seemed, as though instead of the handsome Adalbert Verein only some wooden old man, or a wound-up automaton whose task it was to keep pace with her, were walking beside her. It was quite odd. A good thing that the organ was humming and that they themselves had to move and act in a certain order.

Līziņa was now Mrs. Reikschat. Each guest hastened to call her by her new name. She sat at the head of the table next to Edgar, and had to learn the words: "My husband," words that all young wives learn with great pleasure and delight. But she said little. Only her lovely smile did not leave her lips – the same quiet, sad smile she had shown all through this day.

Toasts were drunk to the newlyweds. Rank gave a speech addressed to Edgar and praised his enterprise and skills. Every few minutes Edgar raised his glass to Domski, who was sitting further away, next to Aunt Meire: "Cheers, Ada!" Whereupon Domski responded: "Your health, Eda!"

Mrs. Rank was chatting with the newlyweds, Jānis was deep in conversation with Miss Gūze; at the other end of the table, where a few of Edgar's more prominent Jelgava acquaintances and their wives, Domski, and Aunt Meire were sitting, spirits were beginning to rise, only Annele and her partner sat mute and stiff. She was racking her brains what sort of question could guide the little boat of their conversation out from where it was stuck in the rushes into the cheery waters of small talk, but she could not think of anything. Wherever she tapped to see if there would be a clink of response, he remained as unresponsive as a wall. It was only when the glasses were filled that handsome Adalbert stirred as though activated by a spring, and responded to each "Cheers!" regular as clockwork. – Could it be that he was a fool? – No, she couldn't even admit such thoughts.

After supper the ladies went off by themselves to sit on Mrs. Bender's wide sofas, where they were given coffee, while the gentlemen took their places at the card tables with glasses of drinks. Others were invited by the host to come on into the back room, while to others – the hot-blooded ones – he recommended the arbor in the garden, where the illuminations of the "night in Italy" had just been lit.

Līziņa came and went, kept herself busy, offered food and drinks. Behind her there were exclamations of: "What a beautiful bride!" – "Yes, very beautiful." – "All brides are beautiful, of course."

Among the ladies, Mrs. Rank was the focus of conversation. The wide, shiny faces of the matrons in their black flouncy bonnets revolved around her as sunflowers revolve around the sun. Mrs. Rank was not wearing a bonnet – she had flowers stuck in the crown of her hair, like an unmarried young lady. Without the extra trappings, she had slim hips, and her train was quite long, for after all she was the bride's sponsor today. If you had an eye for comparison, you could see that both she and the bride wore gowns that came from the same workshop, from Līziņa's hands.

"Very modern, very modern," the matrons shook their heads in admiration and, like Sarah, would have loved to handle the ruffles and frills to see if there was more silk under them or a plain calico lining, and as for the silk, they would have liked to rub it between their fingers to find out how thick it was and how many rubles a yard it might have cost. This wasn't as convenient as when they were by themselves, and they confined themselves to admiring it with their eyes only. And Mrs. Rank didn't mind. Gracefully, she crackled forth her long "r," which was vibrated at the back of her throat; this in itself was sweet music to the ears of the ladies of Jelgava, who were so wild about everything foreign. Her smiling head, always in motion, bowed to acknowledge now one, now another of the ladies who "had already heard so much about beautiful Mrs. Rank, but now had the honor to see her and talk to her, and found that she by far outshone the high repute she enjoyed all over town."

Meanwhile this small talk, too, runs dry and comes to a halt, but Mrs. Rank does not lose courage. Is there somewhere they can find some cards? – she asks. Cards? What for? Can she tell fortunes? No, she's going to show them some tricks.

And when the cards are brought, the table is quickly cleared of coffee cups, and Mrs. Rank begins to play solitaire, this favorite occupation of women of leisure. It is true that the women of Jelgava know this game, too, but not as many different variations of it, so interesting and "tricky." The women's eyes are glued to Mrs. Rank's nimble fingers, as though drawn by a magnet, trying to memorize and keep track of the most interesting game, or else making fate's answer depend on the game's outcome or lack of outcome with a yes or no, yes or no. Thus the hours pass. Mrs. Rank couldn't have thought of anything more interesting.

In the adjacent room, Jānis sat with Miss Gūze. Annele could see them through the open door, especially her brother, who sat facing her directly. They seemed just as engrossed in their conversation as they had been at dinner. Annele liked to look at her brother, whom she got to see so rarely. How he laughed, tossing back his head, how with his slender hand he flung back his hair, so alive, so charming and handsome. Maybe Miss Gūze liked him too. She wanted to go and join them, but her sister called her, asking her to bring something and offer it to the guests. When she came back, Miss Gūze was saying goodbye, for she had a long way to walk. Jānis took her home. This was the first warning signal. The guests were beginning to take their leave, but so far nothing, nothing at all, had happened.

Maybe Adalbert was in the back room?

At least she could still look at him. The back room was audible even from afar. They were having a great old time of it. When Annele came and stood in the doorway, she could distinguish Rank, the basket maker, Edgar, Domski, and a few others she did not recognize among the blue clouds of smoke. They were smoking, drinking, a few were playing cards. The mustachioed faces of Domski and Edgar were close together, Edgar's arm around Domski's shoulders. He caught sight of her first and winked at her roguishly.

"Anna, my Ada would still be the best husband for you. Don't say a word!"

Like a flash, she vanished from the doorway. All the men had not gone into the back room. So there must be others in the garden. Because it was impossible that Adalbert should already have left.

A narrow door let her into the courtyard. And there was the garden with its "night in Italy." A few dozen little paper lanterns hung in a row from a thin string stretched from one acacia shrub to another. Some were lit, others had gone out.

At the end of the row of lanterns there was a largish clump of bushes like a ball of yarn rimmed with darkness but illuminated inside. That was where the arbor was. In front of the arbor, flowerbeds shone with fragrant nicotiana and stock. The arbor was overgrown with festoons of honeysuckle, which diffused a sweet scent. In the arbor was a table covered with empty or half-empty bottles and glasses. A large Japanese lantern hanging over the table cast a lifeless, lurid light on the pools of spilled drink on the table, the broken-off branches of the arbor, and the sandy floor littered with cigarette butts. Otherwise the arbor was empty.

No, not empty. Somebody was lying slumped in the corner of the wide bench. Arms across the backrest, head back, mouth open, he lay there seemingly lifeless. At first glance one thing was obvious: he had had too much to drink.

Annele was about to withdraw, but at that moment the sleeper stirred and his head rolled to one side. "Oh dear!" Annele softly exclaimed as though stung by something sharp.

Oh dear, oh dear, what was this!

The person was Adalbert Verein, the handsome youth she admired.

His dark lock of hair was damp and had stretched across his nose, his mouth was still open, and spittle drooled from one corner of his lips.

His white shirtfront was dirty, his clothes were rumpled, and one hand dangled across the back of the seat.

Such a stubby and beefy hand.

What had happened to his beauty?

Where was it? Where?

It was horrible, horrible! As long as she lived she would never be able to forget this.

Everything was shattered, destroyed. As though a precious vessel she had protected and guarded, carrying it so carefully in her hands, had been smashed, broken into fragments.

"How can this be? How can this be?" she whispered, looking into the shadows among the creepers, as though demanding an answer from someone there.

She sank onto a nearby seat, but the face of the intoxicated young man across from her, lit by the Japanese lantern, shone like a ghastly mask framed by the creepers.

Maybe this was a bad dream or a nightmare?

"How can this be? How can this be?"

She clenched her hand over her breast and accidentally touched her little bunch of apple blossoms.

Now the thing predicted by Jetiņa had happened: she had said apple blossoms meant tears.

"I'm not going to cry though, not for anything! No, no!" she almost exclaimed out loud, set her teeth, and struggled with all her might to get out of the muddy waters she had embarked on, struggled until an organizing, cooling stream of thought brought a fresh breeze to the overheated steam of her emotions. And, conciliatory, it touched even the intoxicated sleeping figure.

She smiled bitterly. Yes, there he lay! Lay there, exposed defenseless to her eyes, so crumpled, ridiculous, and pitiful!

Yes, pitiful! But it wasn't the kind of pity that elevated the object to glory and transfiguration, it was the kind of pity inspired by a dog that has been run over and left by the roadside with a broken leg.

There was no help for him. Let him lie there!

The Japanese lantern suddenly burst into flames and, its string burned through, fell on the table with a crash. Adalbert gave a sudden start, sleepily blinking his eyes, and Annele disappeared from the arbor.

The guests had left, and Līziņa had begun looking for her sister. Mother had already left with the key of the apartment so as to be there to welcome them home.

Edgar repeatedly said goodbye to the basket maker, with whom he had pledged friendship this night. Domski was nowhere in sight.

"Be sure to look after Domski," Edgar instructed the basket maker.

"Will do."

"Wake him up a couple of hours from now. He's got to take the first train."

"Will do."

"And don't forget to put some provisions for the road in his pocket!"

"Will do."

Gray light was dawning over the rooftops. How quickly the night had passed – and just yesterday it had been ahead of her full of great and rich promises.

Annele fell into a restless sleep for a short time, then woke with a start and could not fall asleep again. For a while she tossed and turned and then, right from her bed, reached for a small notebook with a blue cover and began writing.

Last look

You shook hands with them all
As you took your leave,
Then gave me a look
That was full of grief.

Your look stung my heart,
For I suddenly knew:
You were trying to bid me
A last adieu.

She had thought it up while Mrs. Rank was playing solitaire and she had been sitting there not knowing what to do with herself.

But that had all happened *before*. She *could* have written like this if things had turned out differently. – But wait – hadn't it come to the same thing in the end? They *had* parted forever. But what was the sense of what she had just written?

And she began to cross out one letter after another, as though by doing so she could undo all that had happened, return it to oblivion.

A conversation started up in the front room. Her brother was getting up, for he had to leave by the first train. Annele heard her mother say:

"Well, now that's over and done with, but there is one thing that worries me a lot."

"What's that?"

"As far as I've been able to observe in the last few days, that Edgar is quite a tippler. Līziņa is not going to have an easy time of it."

"Still, he does his work and he's made so much money in such a short time."

"That's true, but what good is that if he runs through it again frivolously? And people who tipple tend to be frivolous. Why, he wrote himself that the fellows there were 'fun-loving.'"

"That's just his way of talking. I'm sure they'll have a good life."

"With another sort of wife maybe, one that couldn't care less. But Līziņa is sensitive by nature, and you know what Father was like. Children don't forget that, and if she has to experience something different now, then God knows, God knows – –"

Her brother had dipped his head in the washbasin, and the conversation broke off.

Annele tidied the room and set the table. Unexpectedly, Līziņa came in.

"I thought you were still asleep," said Mother, for the newlyweds were in the other flat.

"How can I sleep when Jānis is leaving and we still have so much to discuss. The business of the wedding was ahead of us, so it was hard to think of other things, but now the time has come to settle everything. Have you thought what's going to happen with Mother and Annele now?" she turned to her brother.

"I thought they could come to Rīga. We could take a flat and be together. We'd find ways to make ends meet. The girl could get apprenticed with a good master seamstress for a while longer."

"I have another idea, and Mother and I have already discussed it. I could take Annele with me."

"What?" exclaimed the latter.

"Wait! My plan would be this. There's supposed to be a very highly thought-of secondary school for girls in Ventspils. It would be too late, and inconvenient besides, for Annele to enroll there. She'll achieve a good deal more if she takes private lessons with the principal of that same school. Edgar says she's thought to be the smartest woman in town. Well, and so Annele can satisfy her hunger for education with her."

"But what about – how do I pay for the lessons? Because now Edgar is going to be the only one earning money. How can I take it from him?"

"Have no fear, you're going to be earning money, too. In the house that Edgar has rented there'll be a workshop downstairs, and next to it the store, with customers to wait on. The upstairs flat will be connected with a little bell on the door of the store. As soon as it starts to tinkle, your young legs will have to race down the stairs. Maybe it'll happen a lot and sometimes you won't be able to get away for hours. Edgar hopes that that's how it will be, because he thinks prospects for the store are very good. Now, it could happen that you are so busy that you'll have only evenings, or late at night, to prepare for your lessons thoroughly."

"I don't care if I have only the nights to study – I'm going to learn whatever it is Ventspils has to teach me," Annele exclaimed, flushed with happiness.

They all burst out laughing.

"But what's Māmīte going to do?"

All three looked at their mother, who had been listening with a quiet, pensive smile, occasionally, with a characteristic gesture, smoothing back her hair that still showed not the least sign of gray and was wound around her head in a circle of braids that were no shorter than her daughters', though not as full anymore. Like the hair of her two oldest children, hers was so curly it would not submit to any force in the shape of oil and water, and to keep it from sticking out "like a bundle of tow" around her head, it had to be constantly smoothed back to lie flat and even, as befitted an older person. But Mother's delicate face, even after this sleepless and busy night, looked fresh and still so young. Looking at her now, Annele felt the sting of deep heartache as she suddenly realized how good her life had been during these years she had spent in Jelgava. Even with all the hardships and renunciation – her mother's love and care had irradiated them all like a sun. In the narrow confines of city life, where her care could not extend over fields, gardens, and animals, it was her children alone to whom, from morning till night, she had devoted the thoughts and feelings of her selfless heart.

"Māmīte, you're not going to live by yourself, are you?" Annele's voice trembled.

Her mother stroked her head.

"Don't you worry!" (That expression was from Father.) "I've decided to go to the country for a while. I still have my things there, and that little room in the addition to the sauna at Spring Farm is still vacant. And the womenfolk in our family have been keeping after me to come and help them. There'll be no lack of work, and if there's work, there'll be something to live on. Don't worry about me! How my heart longs to be back in the country! The church is close by. I'll tend the graves. Till next year. Then we'll see. Maybe Līziņa will call for me – – "

Līziņa put her arm around Annele's shoulders.

"Don't think I'll keep you with me forever. The time will soon come when I'll let you go out in the world again. Just now, though, while I'm getting used to things, it would have been so hard without you, very hard. You see, it isn't just on your account that I want to have you with me."

"Līziņa!" exclaimed Annele, and both sisters hugged each other tight. The tears they had not had time to weep came surging, but Līziņa compressed her lips tightly, shook her head, and was laughing again.

"It's going to be all right. I'm sure it's going to be all right."

"So now it's all arranged and I can go," said Jānis and began to take leave of them. "We'll meet in Rīga before you go to Ventspils."

"I'll walk you to the station," offered Annele.

"If you can keep up with me. I'm going to run now."

They ran. But Annele asked:

"Why did you spend so much time with that Miss Gūze last night? Such deep talk!"

"I was telling her about Rīga and about the Latvians. It was all a big surprise to her. And then she remembered that her parents, too, are Latvian."

"Just her parents. But what is she herself, then?"

"God only knows!" laughed her brother.

"You know, you didn't tell me anything this time. I know so little about Auseklis, Pumpurs, Kronvalds, and the others. And when am I going to hear Kalniņš and Varaidošu Zanders? I'm burning to get to know them all."

"Just be patient, wait till you come to stay in Rīga for good some day. – But now – so long, and don't come any further. I'm going to make a dash for it – mustn't miss my train."

And after quickly shaking hands with his sister, he hurried off, taking long strides.

And here the basket maker and Domski, too, came running past. Domski was carrying his shirt wrapped in paper, while the basket maker had something heavier under his arm. They didn't see her.

The sun was barely above the treetops, pinkish red and sweltering. The day promised to be hot.

As she was going past the church, it occurred to Annele to go over to the mossy gravestone. "I suppose it's the last time," she thought.

She felt grateful to this spot as well. Here, she had thought many thoughts and grieved many sorrows. And in the end the mossy stone had bestowed new hope on her.

And also she now felt like a heart that has been lost in a dark tunnel and sees the gleam of a bright way out. Her future held out promise again.

And Adalbert?

Enough about him! Let him lie where he had made his bed. Maybe till doomsday. Another word had dawned and shone like gold in the rays of the rising sun: the Latvian people! There were now men who thought only of that one thing, who considered it their life's work and happiness to work for the good of the people. Couldn't she do it, too? For she felt that the fire in her heart burned no less ardently, that from day to day her powers were growing, but that in itself was not enough. She did not know how to utilize them, as the hand of an inexpert driver does not know how to control a team of fiery stallions. It all had to be learned, and she intended to do so. She would reach out not only with her thoughts and senses, but with her hands as well, as Valdens had said.

Everything had been packed in bundles and hampers. Tomorrow the travelers would set off on their voyage across land and water. It felt rather sad and painful. Annele wearily sat on a bundle and thought of a Heine poem she had enjoyed reading and still remembered. With few words, it said a great deal. She had tried to translate it, but for a long time it would not turn out as it was supposed to. Still, she did not give up, and now she had the feeling that this time she would succeed.

She found a pencil, and now the poem effortlessly transformed itself into Latvian verse, conforming to the original as well as was possible:

"With sails of black my ship sails on
Over the wild, wild sea;
You know how sad and pale I am
And yet you torture me.

Your heart is faithless as the wind
And flutters wantonly;
With sails of black my ship sails on
Over the wild, wild sea."*

Yes, away from the malicious tormentor, with sails of black, over the foamy waves of the wide ocean – toward unknown distant shores! She understood the poet.

---

*English translation by Hal Draper, in *The Complete Poems of Heinrich Heine. A Modern English Version* by Hal Draper (Suhrkamp/Insel Publishers: Boston, 1982).

Out in the Wide World

Their life in Jelgava had now been demolished and dismantled, as a builder dismantles the scaffolding once the building is finished.

The train was running through unfamiliar fields and woods. Each copse seemed new and particularly noteworthy.

The iron wheels rumbled across a mighty stream.

The passengers stood at the windows of the carriages.

The Daugava! How wide, how wide it was!

Not only Annele alone, the others who stood there admired it too.

"It takes pedestrians three quarters of an hour to walk across," someone remarked.

Oh yes, one could certainly believe that.

Little steamers and boats darted in all directions, great ships lay at anchor by the bank, their swollen shapes rising above the waves like seals.

And there were the famous spires of Rīga. Edgar listed them: John, Peter, Jacob, the Cathedral. Black and slender, they stretched their pointed heads into the sky, holding up great roosters that watched over Rīga.

The travelers had to hurry and drive to the ship to drop off their many bundles, and to reserve seats. Their ship lay downriver, by the castle. They still had a few hours till departure.

"I'll stay here and look after the luggage. If you like, you can go look at the city," Edgar said benevolently.

"Where should we go? I don't know Rīga either, you know," said Līziņa.

"I'd like to see the Latvian Association," Annele whispered to her sister.

"Well then, let's go!"

The sisters ran, got lost in the winding streets of the inner city and asked for directions.

"Where is the Latvian Association, please?"

One man shrugged and continued walking, another silently raised his finger and pointed west, but as though he himself wasn't quite sure.

They came out into a more open space. Annele thought this must be the other side of town – that's how far it seemed they had run.

On one street corner, three workingmen stood with their tools.

"Where is the Latvian Association, please?"

They did not answer immediately. One, after a good look at them, grinned:

"Will you look at that! Wearing hats like Germans and yet they're looking for the Latvian Association. – All right, come along, I'll show you."

And there it was, facing a large park with lovely spreading trees. Unobtrusive, yet dignified and homey, like a friendly, inviting old woman. It seemed to Annele that it had been built at the pleasantest spot in Rīga.

Hand in hand, the two sisters stood there looking. Here was the door through which their brother went to do his many duties in this house where he felt at home, the door that had been opened and closed so many times by all those whose names had risen like stars in the Latvian sky, and here was the place where the summer meetings of the Science Commission took place. What a proud name! The things that went on here! The comings and goings! When would she have a chance to see it all and to experience it for herself?

A short time before the ship's departure, Jānis arrived in a great hurry. He had gotten permission to leave work for just a short time, and within that time had had to do a few errands as well. The result of these errands became apparent at once. He had brought flowers for both sisters. Handed Līziņa a good-sized little box.

"It's a wedding present for you."

Inside the box, on pale blue velvet, shone a row of neatly arranged spoons.

"Oh, brother dear, silver!" exclaimed Līziņa happily, hugging the loving giver of the gift, and then wiping her eyes for a long time.

One more little box emerged from his breast pocket. A tiny little one. This one was for Annele.

"Here's a little something for you as well."

Gold earrings! Such an unprecedented treasure!

"What'll I do with these? I don't have pierced ears, you know," was on the tip of her tongue, but then she saw her brother's warm, smiling eyes, so excited about his gift, and gratefully she flung her arms around his neck.

So much affection and love had to be packed into this brief moment, for it was time to say goodbye.

Now those who were to stay must stay, and those who were to leave must leave. The sailors nudged the people who had come to see the passengers off to go back ashore, the gangplanks were pulled in. There was hissing, shouting, motors rumbled, splashing noisily, wheels began to turn, the ship reeled like a drunkard, was shunted back and forth, and by the time all these goings-on that had engaged their attention were over, it had already left the bank. There went a straw boater, spinning up in the air, here white handkerchiefs were being waved in farewell. Goodbye! Goodbye!

The travelers remained on deck. There was so much to see, now on one side, now on the other. Annele gathered all the new impressions into herself, like reading words from a book, and insistently kept her sister's attention from flagging: look over there, look over there!

Edgar sat placidly, a cigarette in his mouth, steadily looking at the deck. He was perspiring, for he had had quite a workout, and did not wish to use up any more energy.

"And see how the Daugava River stretches wider and wider," Annele exclaimed enthusiastically.

"Stretches toward the sea."

"You're not even looking."

"Why should I? Think I didn't see my fill of water in Ventspils? Up there, you're constantly around water."

"Then there are sure to be wide open spaces there!"

"Up there, you can go for a walk right in the middle of the sea if you like, because the sea wall of the harbor is built deep into the sea."

"And you can walk there amid the crashing of waves and the tempest's roar?"

"Yes, amid the crashing of waves and the tempest's roar," answered Edgar drily. "Just look out that the tempests don't pick you up like a balloon and blow you out to sea."

Rīga had already vanished below the horizon. The river's banks receded farther and farther, making way for the imperious waters.

The afternoon sun was oppressively hot. The parting flowers their brother had brought were beginning to droop.

"See if you can get some water in the cabin, or they'll fade by the time we arrive."

Annele took the flowers and went down to the cabin. When she came out on deck again, she was dazzled by a great, completely shadeless brightness as though from an endless expanse. It took her breath away. The ship had entered the open sea and was racing away from the banks, leaving eddies behind it. The shoreline lengthened, then imperceptibly shrank until it was thin and insignificant.

Hands pressed against her breast, Annele stood there filled with something like surprise and wonder at seeing this sight for the first time. She had a tendency to push back the boundaries of her experiences as far as possible, and that is why what she had just seen seemed infinity itself to her. She wanted to deal with this impression by herself, and went over to the other end of the deck, where she found a hidden spot among bundles and boxes. There she sat down.

Sliced by the steamer's cogwheels, the waves hissed fiercely and rippled in agitation. Traces of the ship's passing were cleft like a deep trench in the wake, while in the more distant field of vision they had already been smoothed out and gleamed with a motionless, golden bluish shimmer, like the rest of the sea's surface.

Annele abandoned herself to her thoughts.

Nature. Powerful nature. It was everywhere, pervaded everything, encompassed everything. She could never stop looking at it and becoming absorbed in it, it always aroused a new sense of wonder. Was there a day in her childhood when Annele had not walked accompanied by miracles? The tiny flower that was the first to open in spring on the black dirt of the barrens; a young, still half-blind nestling lark's little yellow beak opening in a horse's hoofprint, expecting food from its mother; this earth itself, the wonderful womb that bloomed, bore fruit, became numb with cold, and bloomed again; the dewdrop sparkling like a diamond in the gray grass of the barrens; the cuckoo's call in the lovely woods of Spring Farm; the shadowy mystery of evening; the heavens with their innumerable star worlds; and finally this sea in all its overpowering might – who could count all these miracles created by nature? Each moment brought new ones. Always, only a minute part would be visible, but in this little part was infinity. Whether it was the scurrying of the tiny ant, or the blast of the gale in a thunderstorm, a raindrop trembling on a spruce twig, or the great flood waters of a river rolling at each moment into the seemingly bottomless reservoir of the sea without making it fuller – everything was endowed with the capacity to be transformed, to take hundreds of shapes and thus be new and original at any given moment.

Nature performed miracles, but nature was also a teacher. Those who did not want to learn did not see its miracles. And wasn't it true that nature's great lesson was work? It was inseparable from nature.

From her early childhood, Annele had seen people laboring hard. Sweaty shirts and sweaty faces. She had seen land that had been uncultivated, useless for decades, for centuries even, turned into good and fertile land. In her mind's eye she vividly saw Father as he studied a clod of soil he had picked up in his hand: what did it consist of, how should it be tilled, and what should be sown in it to produce a good harvest? And she had seen people settle long-neglected land and build their farm buildings simple and primitive, the way they had been built perhaps hundreds of years ago, and she had seen how they all put their heads together, and even the least little suggestion was treated with respect when those who performed the work were united by someone who had been taught the wisdom of work and of life by nature herself.

And she had listened late at night as her white-haired grandmother, bent beneath the burdens of her work, had sat on her narrow bed with folded hands speaking whispered words. Granny had never sat down to Sunday morning prayers, and had gone to church once a year mainly to visit the graveyard, but some living cord held her above those days that spread and vanish like bubbles on the water's surface. Mother, on the other hand, ever forbearing, deeply solicitous, sometimes suddenly breaking into a joke, her language crackling with quick wit, clung to the Scriptures, her mighty "staff," while the source that broke forth from the strata of rock accumulated by the experience and insights of the Latvian people flowed from an even deeper level – the wisdom of eternity gained from work and from nature.

Father had had the profoundest knowledge of it. Even as a little half-pint, Annele had looked up in surprise when, at work, he suddenly fell silent and, seemingly lost in thought, gazed into the distance as though at the vast expanses of some invisible world, and his face at such times had been bright, as if illuminated by the light of this invisible world.

"What are you looking at, Dad? What do you see?" she had wanted to ask at such moments, but a kind of reverent awe had always held her back.

She, too, had learned to look at the expanses of that invisible world with the eyes of her soul. She not only wanted to gaze at them, but to enter there and look for paths. And wasn't it the same with this invisible world as with the visible one? You were aware only of some small fraction of it, and if you wanted to push on further, you had to dig, to dig with the hard labor of thinking, sometimes through deep darkness and despair. What would show the way?

Fervor. Desire.

And she feels that those will never fade, never, for they are the antennae of eternal light, the light to which all nations since time immemorial have given a reverent name – *God*!

The Pronunciation of Latvian

1. Almost all Latvian words are stressed on the first syllable: **An**nele, **Slu**dinātājs.
2. The Latvian vowels **a, e, i, u** sound like their counterparts in Italian. But diacritic marks ("lengthening signs") indicate that certain vowels are long (e.g., ā is like the long a in father). So Sludinātājs has a short u and short i, and two long a vowels.
3. The Latvian vowel **o** is pronounced much like the English wa in walk. E.g., Dobele sounds like Dwabele.
4. The Latvian diphthong **au** sounds like the English diphthong in how.
5. The Latvian dipthong **ie** sounds like the combination of short i and short a – e.g., Lienīte sounds like Li-a-nī-te.
6. The Latvian consonants **b, d, f, k, l, m, n, p, s, t, v, z** are fairly similar to English consonants, but b, d, k, p, t are not accompanied by the explosion of air that is typical of English (their quality is more like that of Italian or French consonants).
7. The Latvian consonant **g** is pronounced like the first consonant in the English word garden.
8. The Latvian semivowel **j** is pronounced like the English semivowel **y** in year; thus Jānis is pronounced Yānis.
9. The consonants **f** and **h** occur only in foreign words. There is no q, w, or x in the Latvian alphabet.
10. The consonant **c** is pronounced like the ts in English bits.
11. Consonants can be "softened" by using diacritic marks:
12. When **c** has a diacritic, it is pronounced like the English ch in chain – e.g., Čiepiņa is pronounced Chiapinya, and Krančelis is pronounced Kranchelis.
13. When **g** has a diacritic, it is pronounced dy (e.g., Eņģele = Endyele)
14. When **k** has a diacritic, it is pronounced ty (e.g., Āķis is pronounced Ātyis).
15. When **l** has a diacritic, it is pronounced ly (as in Italian figlio) – e.g., Amaļa = Amalya.
16. When **n** has a diacritic, it is pronounced like the Spanish ñ in Español – e.g., Līziņa is pronounced Līzinya. This sound occurs in a lot of diminutives ending in –iņa and –iņš.
17. With a diacritic, **s** becomes š and is pronounced like the English sh in push.
18. With a diacritic, **z** becomes ž and is pronounced like the French j in bon jour.
19. The consonant **r** is lightly trilled with the tongue against the hard palate, like the Italian r.

In Latvian, spellings are pretty standardized: what you see is what you get. If you adhere to the rules above, you can't go wrong.